ERIC CLAPTON
DAY BY DAY

ERIC CLAPTON
DAY BY DAY

The Early Years, 1963-1982

MARC ROBERTY

An Imprint of Hal Leonard Corporation

Published in 2013 by Backbeat Books
An Imprint of Hal Leonard Corporation
7777 West Bluemound Road
Milwaukee, WI 53213

Trade Book Division Editorial Offices
33 Plymouth St., Montclair, NJ 07042

Every reasonable effort has been made to contact copyright holders
and secure permissions. Omissions can be remedied in future editions.

All images are from the author's collection unless otherwise noted.

Photo credits can be found on page 325, which constitutes an
extension of this copyright page.

Book design by Kristina Rolander

Printed in the United States of America

Library of Congress Cataloging-in-Publication Data is available
upon request.

ISBN 978-1-61713-052-6

www.backbeatbooks.com

CONTENTS

It's hard to imagine putting together a complete record of the daily activity of someone who has been so busy for an entire fifty-year career as Eric Clapton. But Marc Roberty knows more about him than most anybody on the planet, as he is the quintessential Eric Clapton authority, having written several books about him already. I've known Marc since September 2008, when he came online on a music forum to encourage me to write my autobiography. He then became my friend, editor, and writing partner. Our book took eighteen months to put together, so I know that he is a stickler for details. Every date, place, and person had to be right and backed up. He would check and double-check, then check it again to make sure that it was right.

I know firsthand that Eric stayed busy even when he wasn't doing anything. His world was always full of

activity at all times, as everyone called on him when they needed to get the job done and it be exactly what the doctor ordered. He was a very busy man.

These books cover Eric's career from his days with the Yardbirds to Cream, Blind Faith, Delaney & Bonnie and Friends, and the part of his career that I am most familiar with, the Derek and the Dominos era. Aside from the conception of Derek and the Dominos and the writing and recording of the *Layla* album, we were also the core band for George Harrison's siminal recording "All Things Must Pass."

So from day one in 1963 right up to today, Eric's life has been full of recording and live appearances, and Marc Roberty has managed to compile it all and lay it out for everyone to read, enjoy, and be enlightened.

—BOBBY WHITLOCK

Eric Clapton's name is synonymous with the guitar, and in 2013 he celebrated fifty years as a professional musician. It certainly was not an easy road for him, and these two volumes cover his entire musical history to the present day. Research for these volumes was done over several years at the National Newspaper Archive, local libraries, music newspapers and magazines from my personal collection, official itineraries from Eric Clapton's office files, and a multitude of interviews over the years.

There are many people I need to thank for their help with this massive project: Laurie Asprey; Jonathan Bacon; Mal Barker; Brian Carroll; Paul Cook; Norman Dayron; Fred Dellar; Rita DeVries; Michael Eaton; Tony Edser; Barry Fisch; Roger Forrester; Christopher Hjort for help and guidance in researching the John Mayall dates (he was the first person to uncover most of these in his wonderful Strange Brew book, and both he and I know there are more shows to find, so the quest continues); Robin Jones, who spent a lot of time with me talking about RG Jones and showed me the studio diaries from 1963; Vic King for the information on the Yardbirds' appearance at the Commodore on the Isle of Wight; Thorsten Knublauch for help in clarifying the dates and venues for the Delaney & Bonnie German and Scandinavian shows; Cecil Offley; Luke Pacholski for his help with the various mixes of the Eric Clapton solo album as well as providing the correct setlists for the Derek and the Dominos Fillmore shows; Graeme Pattingale; Roger Phillips; Pogo; Mike Sawin; Gerhard Schinzel; Jan Inge Sommerseth via Christopher Hjort, who found out the name of the venue for the show in Oxford with Traffic where Eric jammed and which had eluded me for years; Billy Stapelton; Klaus Wachtarz; Steve Weintraub; Linda Wnek; Larry Yelen; and Andy Zwick.

I would like to thank the following whom I have interviewed and spoken with for this project over the years: Howard Albert, PP Arnold, Jon Astley, John Altman, Eric Andersen, Renée Armand, John Barham, Jeff Beck, Marc Benno, Joe Boyd, Delaney Bramlett, Gary Brooker, Nigel Carroll, Eric Clapton, David Courtney, John Crome, Norman Dayron, Hughie Flint, Claire Francis, Albhy Galuten, Paul David Griggs, George Harrison, Charlie Hart, Corey Hart, Keef Hartley, Jon Hiseman, Glyn Johns, Paul Jones, Aashish Khan, Jonathan Kelly, Corky Laing, Albert Lee, Bill Levenson, Marcy Levy, Dave Mason, Eric Mercury, Chris Michie, Mike Molloy, Micky Moody, Stephen Munns, Jamie Oldaker, Tom Parkinson, Shawn Phillips, Chuck Rainey, Ken Scott, John Simon, Russ Titleman, Derek Varnals, Barrie Wentzell, Bobby Whitlock, Tony Williams, Mark Wirtz, and Steve York.

I would also like to thank the following photographers, who have been so generous in allowing me to use their amazing photos: Carl Dunn for his incredible shots of Cream and Derek and the Dominos in Dallas; Russell Schlagbaum, Ronnie Lane's tour manager, for his photos of Eric and Ronnie in the studio and at Cranleigh Village Hall; Robin Jones for his historic photos of RG Jones of Morden Studios; Laurie Asprey for his stunning shots of Delaney & Bonnie from the Fairfield Halls in Croydon; Norman Dayron for use of the Howlin' Wolf Olympic Studios photos; Roger Phillips for use of his Cream photos from the *Goodbye* Cream album shoot; David Stanford for his great shot of Eric in the studio during sessions for Fresh Cream and a live shot from the Marquee Club (these and more are available to buy from David via his website at www.davidstanford.co.uk or by emailing him at davidwstanford@btinternet.com); Peter Stringfellow for use of his photo of the Yardbirds from his King Mojo Club in Sheffield; Peter Cross for his lovely photos of Eric and his four-piece band in Newcastle in 1978; and Jyri-Hannu Erviälä for use of his Blind Faith photos in Helsinki.

All of these photos retain the copyright of all the named photographers and cannot be reproduced without permission from the individual photographers.

An extra-special thank-you to Karen Daws for her editing skills and patience over the years!

Eric Clapton was born in the front room of his grandparents' terraced house at 1 The Green in the quiet Surrey village of Ripley on 30 March 1945. His mother was sixteen-year-old Patricia Molly Clapton and his father was Edward Fryer, a Canadian soldier who was, like many other Canadian and US troops, stationed in England. The Second World War was coming to an end and the social climate was very different from today. Family decisions were made that would affect Eric's life forever.

Edward Fryer was an infantryman, but outside of the army, he had a passion for playing blues piano around pubs and local dance halls, which is where Pat had met him in the summer of 1944. As well as being an exceptional musician, he was a talented artist. They became firm friends very quickly and shared similar interests and passions, but as the relationship developed, Pat fell pregnant. Unfortunately, he was already married with a wife back in Canada, and returned home to her during Pat's pregnancy. Pat was devastated. She was an unmarried mother at sixteen, and in those days, particularly in a small village, gossip was rife and her life became pretty unbearable. People would spit at her in the street as well as shout abuse at her. She reluctantly decided that the best thing for "Rick," as she would always call him, was that he should be raised by her parents in the house in which he was born. From that moment on, in her eyes, she could never really love her son as a mother, knowing she had given the responsibility of bringing him up to her parents. It was a high price to pay, and she lived with the guilt to her dying day. As far as Eric was concerned, though, his grandparents Rose and Jack Clapp were his parents.

Pat bravely stayed in Ripley for a time and started dating another Canadian soldier, Frank McDonald, whom she was to marry. This gave the Ripley locals even more ammunition for further vicious and cruel abuse. When Eric was almost two, Pat moved to Germany with Frank, where he was to be stationed for many years. They later moved to Canada, where she had a further three children, Cheryl, Heather, and Brian. Pat had effectively moved out of Eric's life, but she had wanted to return home to Ripley to see Eric.

It was not easy; her new husband's family were devout Roman Catholic and they refused to even recognize the fact that Pat had an illegitimate child. This, coupled with the fact that travel in those times was nowhere near as cheap as it is today, made it impossible for Pat to visit her firstborn son, at least not for a while.

In the meantime, Eric was a happy if somewhat lonely child with few friends and very shy. Prior to him going to his first school (Ripley Church of England Primary School), Rose had done her best to explain to a five-year-old Eric that she and Jack were his legal guardians and not his real parents. She did this so that when other kids at school made comments he would perhaps understand, even if it was a painful experience. In 1956, two significant things happened: he transferred to St Bede's Secondary Modern school near Woking, and Pat visited him with her six-year-old son, Brian. One can only imagine the trauma Eric, who was now an eleven-year-old, would have gone through, not to mention the utter confusion and sense of loss he undoubtedly felt. To make matters even more confusing for him, Pat would be introduced to his friends as his sister who lived abroad. As her husband had now been stationed in Korea, she decided to stay for nine months. That event changed Eric. He became even more of a loner, and his withdrawn attitude at school, coupled with his skinny physical size, meant he was a prime target for bullies. He became part of a small group of school—"outcasts."

He seemed to enjoy the company of animals more than of school chums, but he also had great enthusiasm and aptitude for drawing. Although he would later join a local scout troop, he preferred solitary pursuits. These included, perhaps surprisingly, a local cycling club, the Kingston Wheelers, where he would compete against other local clubs. He spent many hours cycling alone and losing himself in a dream world. However, over and above everything else, he enjoyed drawing and found this to be the best form of escapism, along with going to see films and listening to the radio. By 1958, rock and roll had made its way over the Atlantic via films and records on the radio. It did not escape young Eric. He was immediately drawn to this new culture, which appeared to offer a different and exciting lifestyle.

Eric would listen to the radio a lot and hear the sounds of Guy Mitchell, Gene Vincent, Frankie Lane, and Buddy Holly among others. The "Uncle Mac" children's request program on Saturday mornings was a particular favorite of his. A variety of records were played, including classical, rock and roll, pop, and occasionally blues. Some of the earliest blues records he heard were by Big Bill Broonzy, Blind Willie Johnson, and Sonny Terry & Brownie McGhee. But Eric quickly fell in love with the black rock-and-roll artists such as Little Richard, Chuck Berry, and Fats Domino. These sounds fueled his desire to become a musician.

So, at the tender age of thirteen he asked his grandparents for a guitar. They could not really afford it, but they could see his enthusiasm and decided they would pay for it in installments if necessary. They took him to Bell's in Surbiton, certainly the best music shop in the local area. Eric chose a Spanish Hoya acoustic guitar. He also had a little Grundig Cub reel-to-reel recorder, which took three-and-a-quarter-inch reels. On these he would spend days and days perfecting and copying sounds he heard on the radio.

That same year, another significant event occurred in Eric's life. He moved to Hollyfield Road School in Surbiton, after doing well in his art and English exams. They had a dedicated art department and he found like-minded individuals there. Two to three days of the week were dedicated solely to art, working with clay and paint, still life and figure drawing. In the evenings, he would also learn basic design at Kingston Art School. His new mates also shared his musical tastes, and he set out on a quest for more knowledge of the blues roots of American rock and roll. In those days information was scarce—no Internet, nor even many books. It became a real labor of love that showed a determination that continues to dominate his personality to this day.

Playing guitar took a back seat for a couple of years when Rose and Jack felt he should concentrate on his studies with a view to getting into Kingston Art College full-time. However, by the time he was sixteen and accepted into Kingston Art College, he matured rapidly and found a real identity for himself. He met another blues fan there called Keith Relf, and together they would spend time talking about blues artists they admired and music in general.

Eric started hanging around the young beatniks that played the local pubs such as the Crown in Kingston and L'Auberge coffee bar in Richmond. He was impressed at their proficiency and was clearly influenced by them and their musical knowledge. He adopted their dress style and played regularly in these local venues. It was a difficult period in some respects, because he was torn between whether to pursue a life of an artist or that of a musician.

Big Bill Broonzy was Eric's first favorite bluesman. He had seen a clip of him on Cliff Michelmore's *Tonight* television program on the BBC. Broonzy was born 26 June 1903 in Jefferson County, Arkansas. His influences were the likes of Blind Lemon Jefferson and Lonnie Johnson. In the early days, his style of blues varied from ragtime and hokum blues to solo acoustic country blues and city blues backed with jazz musicians. He is, however, best remembered for his traditional folk blues, which he adopted later in his career. Perhaps his most famous song is "Key To The Highway" which has been covered many times by different bands and individuals over the years, including Eric (most notably with John Mayall on the *Blues Breakers* album and later on the *Layla And Other Assorted Love Songs* double album). Broonzy's first recording, "Big Bill's Blues" backed by "House Rent Stomp," was cut for the Paramount label under the name of Big Bill and Thomps. He was one of the first blues performers to come to England in 1951 and 1952. Incredibly, as with other blues stars in those days, he had to work outside of music to support himself. Tragically, he developed throat cancer and died on 15 August 1958.

Robert Johnson probably resonated with Eric the most. While Johnson did not particularly influence him as a guitarist, he was certainly a major inspiration, as well as someone Eric could relate to. The pain and loneliness expressed in his songs were a comfort to Eric. There was someone out there who knew about emotional torment and how to express it eloquently through music. Eric has admitted that he could never listen to Robert Johnson records in the company of others due to their intensity. Johnson became a somewhat mythical character over time, with locals believing he had made a pact with the devil at the crossroads of US 61 and US 49 in Clarksdale, Mississippi. His reward would be musical genius.

He was born in Hazlehurst, Mississippi, on 8 May 1911 and died in mysterious circumstances in August 1938. Like Eric, he was more interested in music than working, and he was also a ladies' man. It was that reputation that led to rumors of him being poisoned by a jealous lover. In fact, research has shown that a more probable cause was an aneurysm caused by his congenital syphilis coupled with heavy consumption of moonshine.

Eric would venture out into London to see what he called "the real thing," often sleeping rough on park benches before catching the morning bus back to Surrey. Some of his favorite haunts were the Marquis of Granby pub on Cambridge Circus, Ken Colyer's Studio 51 in Great Newport Street, and the Duke of York pub, just off Oxford Circus. Although Eric loved the London scene, he still felt too much like a "country boy" and would only feel comfortable playing in Kingston and Richmond, on relatively safe home ground.

Eric enjoyed his newfound bohemian lifestyle, and his passion for playing guitar returned. So much so, in fact, that his art studies suffered. He simply wasn't producing enough work for his portfolio, and ultimately he was asked to leave Kingston Art College, after repeated warnings. His grandparents had despaired of him, really, and Jack offered him an opportunity to earn some money by helping him on various building projects that he was involved with. So Eric became a bricklayer/plasterer, and a good one at that. His perfectionism and attention to detail were impressive. When he wasn't working he would practice all day, and late into the night, much to the annoyance of Rose. She could not see that it would lead to anything.

Eric left the comfort of Rose's home for a while and shared a flat in Twickenham with a fellow blues lover, which gave him more freedom to stay out late. Around this time he would occasionally team up with Dave Brock (Yes, "that" Dave Brock from Hawkwind), performing as a folk-blues duo in local pubs and clubs in Richmond and Kingston and occasionally venturing as far as the Apron Strings coffee bar in the Fulham Road in London. Some of the numbers they would perform included "San Francisco Bay Blues," "Alberta," "Hey, Hey," and "Nobody Knows You When You're Down And Out." On the same circuit was his friend

from Kingston Art College, Keith Relf, who was also playing in a folk duo with guitarist Roger Pearce. Eric was not a particularly good player yet and would often be seen practicing his guitar technique by playing along to blues records in a record shop on Richmond Hill owned by Gerry Potter. The shop stocked a fine selection of rare blues and jazz albums, and fans would travel for miles to visit this Surrey mecca. When not playing, Eric and Dave and other friends would hang out on the banks of the Thames in Richmond, just opposite L'Auberge, and get drunk on cider and play their guitars.

Eric also became a regular visitor to the Marquee Club in London because he liked Alexis Korner's Blues Incorporated. During the intervals, Mick Jagger together with Brian Jones and Keith Richards, before they became the Rolling Stones, would play Chuck Berry covers using Alexis's rhythm section, and Eric became firm friends with them. A friendship that lasts to this day. Seeing these people playing together fueled Eric's desire to be in a band.

At the beginning of the '60s, there where many blues parties, where like-minded people would get together and listen to someone's newest album acquisitions by the likes of Muddy Waters, BB King, John Lee Hooker, Jimmy Reed, and Bo Diddley, to name a few. The best parties were always at the homes of Mike Vernon and Neil Slaven, who both later became legendary figures in the British blues-boom era. After hearing the electric sounds of these artists, Eric knew that the next natural progression would be to trade in his acoustic guitar for an electric one. You can only imagine the look on his grandparents' faces when he mentioned this to them. But he had showed willingness to work on the building sites, and he was constantly practicing licks and songs, so this was not simply a passing phase. After seeing Alexis Korner endorsing a Kay "Red Devil" in *Melody Maker*, he decided that this would be his guitar of choice. Rose and Jack helped him out again by getting the guitar on hire-purchase.

Electric bluesmen such as T-Bone Walker, Albert King, Buddy Guy, Otis Rush, and Freddie King were major contributory influences that shaped Eric's style in later years. But two important early influences on him were BB King and Howlin' Wolf's guitarist, Hubert Sumlin. BB King was born in Indianola, Mississippi, on 16 September 1925. Two early classics were "Three O'Clock Blues" and "Sweet Little Angel." His live shows were legendary, and the infamous classic "Live At The Regal" stands as a testament to that. Although they have played many times together over the years, it was in 2001 that their joint album *Riding With The King* was released and won a Grammy. Hubert Sumlin was born on 16 November 1931 in Greenwood, Mississippi. He played guitar with Howlin' Wolf for over twenty-five years and occasionally with Muddy Waters, both formidable individuals. He pioneered a new sound for Howlin' Wolf and inspired a multitude of guitarists around the world who heard Howlin' Wolf records. Hubert recorded an album with Eric Clapton and Keith Richards in 2000 that was released a few years later.

Kay were an American firm that manufactured both inexpensive "department store"–style guitars, as well as some high-end, quality archtop guitars from the 1930s into the 1960s. Collectable Kay models are instantly recognizable by their plastic trademark Kelvinator headstock. This headstock was overlayed with attractive Art Deco patterns and was injection molded with clear acrylic plastic and then back-painted in either white or black, with gold highlights in the crest and gold dots outside of the crest. This design was used by Kay from 1957 to 1960, and, believe it or not, it was named after the Kelvinator fridge brand, whose design looked quite similar! In late 1960, Kay switched to a less expensive "half" Kelvinator design that used just the triangular Kay crest, which was screwed to a simple black plastic headstock veneer. This half Kelvinator dropped the black or white back-painted acrylic surround with gold dots. This design only lasted to the end of 1961, when the Kelvinator headstock was abandoned completely. Eric's "Red Devil" was based on the Kay Jazz II model, which looked a little like a Gibson ES 330 with more subtle body curves. It was two inches thick and had a double cutaway, a fully hollow maple veneer body stained red, a twenty-fret neck, a rosewood fingerboard with pearl inlays starting at the first fret, a black acrylic pickguard, Bigsby vibrato and an aluminum bridge, a half Kelvinator headstock, and two Gold K single-coil pickups which delivered a well-balanced tone. It was a 1961 model.

In early January 1963, a girl who had been in Eric's class during his period at Kingston Art College told him that her boyfriend, Tom McGuiness, was looking for a guitar player for a blues-based band. He was introduced to Tom and asked to attend an informal audition at the Crown pub in Kingston, which ended up being more like a rehearsal. Also in attendance was Ben Palmer on piano, another blues enthusiast and purist who would have a great influence on Eric, as well as become a close friend. He was impressed with Eric's playing, and Eric was in. The band called themselves the Roosters and consisted of Eric and Tom alternating on rhythm and lead guitars, Ben on piano, Robin Mason on drums, and Terry Brennan on lead vocals. They did not have a bass player. They probably played no more than fourteen gigs in all. The first was at the Oxford University Jazz Club evening at the Carfax Assembly Rooms in Oxford, where they played a short set in in the interval. They received five pounds for their appearance. Their furthest show was at Uncle Bonnie's Chinese Jazz Club in Brighton, East Sussex, which turned out to be a disastrous night when an abusive mob of French students started heckling the band to play "trad" jazz. Terry Brennan dived into the unruly bunch and a huge fight ensued. They also played a few shows in London at the Marquee and the Scene as a support act, but most of the gigs were local to home, such as a three-week Wednesday residency at the Jazz Cellar in Kingston. They also played the Ricky Tick clubs in Reading, Guildford, and Windsor. The Ricky Tick shows paid better than Oxford, and they received seventeen pounds and ten shillings.

The most exciting thing that happened to the Roosters was at a gig at the Scene in Ham Yard, Soho, London. They were on the same bill as Bo Diddley, which was a big deal for a bunch of innocent young amateurs. Bo's backing band were late, and the Roosters were asked to back the great man. This opportunity was met with fear and excitement in equal measure. Sadly, the backing band turned up in the nick of time, and that was that. In reality, The Roosters ended up rehearsing more often than they actually played gigs, as demand for blues bands in the early '60s was not as great as that for trad jazz. It would be another year or so before the R&B scene would really take off. Eric enjoyed the experience of playing to an audience with a band, but times were hard, with little or no money coming in. Their fate was sealed when Ben Palmer admitted that he did not particularly like playing to live audiences and felt it was unfair to hold back the more ambitious members in the group. Inevitably, the band broke up, albeit amicably. Ben believes their last gig was at the Ricky Tick Club in West Wickham.

Within a month of the split, Eric and Tom McGuiness heard that a guy from Liverpool, Casey Jones, was looking for a band. Jones's real name was Brian Casser, and he had been a leading light in the Merseybeat movement in the late '50s and early '60s. Jones had split for London and signed a contract with Columbia. His debut single for the label, as Casey Jones & the Engineers, was 1963's "One Way Ticket" b/w "I'm Gonna Love You" (Columbia catalog number DB 7083). Keen to support the single, Casser needed to get a band and hit the road. He already had a drummer, Ray Stock, and a bassist, Dave McCumiskey.

Ray Stock had a chance meeting with Eric one night at the Scene club in Ham Yard, Soho. Eric mentioned he was a guitarist and was looking for work. Stock told him about Casey Jones and that he was looking to recruit two guitarists to form a backing band. Eric saw this as a great opportunity to get more experience on the road and even possibly record an album. Eric said he was interested as long as he could bring along his ex-Roosters friend Tom McGuinness. After a rehearsal, Eric and Tom were offered the gig. Casser was very showbiz and believed in performing using various gimmicks, which Eric neither enjoyed nor approved of. The whole experience very quickly became a bad one, and Eric ended up playing only seven gigs with them, two of which were at the Macclesfield Civic Hall and Manchester's Oasis club, where they backed pop singer Polly Perkins on such numbers as "Who's Sorry Now" and "Ain't Misbehavin'." Polly remembers the shows fondly, but at the time, Eric and Tom were not so keen and had trouble finding the right chords for her songs. Casser was not much better, always singing sharp, which made accompanying him a chore. The final straw came at a gig at the Kings Hall, Manchester Belle Vue, where the band had to wear silly little cardboard confederate hats that Casser had bought earlier in the day. Eric, having nightmare visions of them developing into some sort of cabaret act, turned his back on it all and headed back to the safer territory of Surrey to contemplate his next move.

Eric would spend the next few weeks revisiting his old haunts in Kingston and Richmond. In particular, he would regularly check out his friends the Rolling Stones during their residency at the Crawdaddy Club in Richmond. Significantly, he met an old friend, Keith Relf, who told him he was in a band and that Eric should go and see them. They were called the Yardbirds, named by Keith after Charlie Byrd's nickname. They consisted of Keith on vocals and harmonica, Chris Dreja on guitar, Paul Sawell-Smith on bass, Jim McCarty on drums, and Anthony "Top" Topham on lead guitar. Topham was the youngest member of the band, and his parents were pressuring him to give up the music business to concentrate on something more solid, like art college. As a result, his commitment to the band was not as great as the other members'. Also, the band felt that as a guitarist, he was not competent enough for them to progress further and, in true "Pop Idol" style, he also did not project the right image. Eric was by now a well-known figure in the area, and his reputation as a guitarist of note did not escape the members in the band; he was asked if he fancied replacing Topham, who was soon to be cut loose. Eric joined them in October 1963 and immediately started living with Keith and Chris in a flat in Kew. In fact, Chris and Eric shared a room and for a while, at least, became like brothers.

Their early gigs would be at local Kingston and Richmond pubs and clubs and Ken Colyer's Studio 51 in Great Newport Street in London. Their early repertoire was pretty similar to that of the Roosters and consisted of covers by the likes of Chuck Berry, Bo Diddley, and Jimmy Reed. Giorgio Gomelsky, who promoted the Crawdaddy gigs and was a leading light of the early English R&B boom, soon saw their potential and became their manager. They took over the Rolling Stones' Crawdaddy residency and their workload increased dramatically. As well as the residencies at Giorgio's clubs, they would join several "package" tours with other artists which took in the length and breadth of England. It was also Giorgio who came up with the "Slowhand" moniker for Eric, based on a pun of his name, *SLOWHAND* CLAPton, and actually had nothing to do with the myth of audiences hand clapping while he changed strings on his guitar.

Eric bought several new guitars during his stay with the Yardbirds. Contemporaries like Brian Jones and George Harrison were playing Gretsch guitars, and Eric acquired one as well and can be seen using it while performing "I Wish You Would" on the *Ready Steady Go* television show in May 1964. It was an orange Gretsch "Nashville" (which was identical to the 6120 Chet Atkins), which was a double-cutaway, hollowbody electric archtop model, with Filter 'Tron humbuckers, "neoclassic" fingerboard inlays (or "half moon" markers as they are also known), and a V-cutout B-6 Gretsch Bigsby. There appears to be only one or two photos of him with this guitar. He also had a Fender Telecaster in a translucent red finish with a white plastic three-layer scatchplate. He used this guitar the most, and there are many photographs of him playing in the Yardbirds with it. Eric also acquired a further two guitars during his time in the Yardbirds. One, which was his favorite, was a cherry red Gibson ES 335, and the other was a Fender Jazzmaster. Eric's Kay guitar was sold to Roger Pearce, a friend of Keith Relf's who had played guitar with him on the folk circuit prior to the Yardbirds.

In early November of 1963, the Yardbirds recorded three songs at a small independent recording studio called RG Jones of Morden. Giorgio had an existing relationship with the studio, having used them with the Rolling Stones previously. The numbers recorded were basically what they were performing in their live act at the time. These were a Keith Relf original, "Honey In Your Hips," John Lee Hooker's "Boom Boom," and Jimmy Reed's "Baby What's Wrong," the first two of which were issued as a single in Germany. Later, they would record some demos at the same studios, which were then taken around various labels. A press release in January announced that Decca would be signing the band. That was a little premature, as Giorgio did not really want them to be on the same label as the Rolling Stones. They eventually signed with EMI. Their touring schedule was relentless, with very few days off. Both the band and Eric's reputation grew by word of mouth. Despite recording a handful of singles that did not do much chartwise, it was decided not to record a studio album first. Instead, they recorded a live album at one of their Marquee residencies in March 1964, which was more representative of what they sounded like. Understandable, as they were primarily a "live" band, and were very much at home in that environment, where their "rave-ups" were becoming legendary. However, by the time the *Five Live Yardbirds* album came out in late 1964, Eric was getting disillusioned with the band. They desperately needed a big hit single, and the message from Giorgio was to head in a more "pop" direction, which was the not the way Eric wanted to move forward. Eric became moody and uncooperative and generally unhappy, which made the atmosphere very tense in the band. When they recorded the overtly commercial Graham Gouldman number "For Your Love," with hardly any Eric involvement, he decided to have a meeting with Giorgio. What he did not realize was that he was going to be asked to leave, and the other members had voted on it. Eric was shocked, but relieved at the same time. He really felt that at least some of the band members would have backed him, but he felt a sense of betrayal when he realized that was not the case. When "For Your Love" was released in March 1965 and climbing the charts, Eric was by himself and deciding on his future.

As for the Yardbirds, they found themselves free of Eric's blues-purist aspirations, hired Jeff Beck as his replacement, and went on to become a successful band touring America, much to the chagrin of Eric, who had desperately wanted to visit the country of his blues heroes. There had been some enjoyable moments for Eric, though, which included a memorable tour backing Sonny Boy Williamson, doing a session with Muddy Waters for an Otis Spann recording, and playing on the same bill as the Beatles over a two-week period for their Christmas shows at the Hammersmith Odeon in December 1964 and January 1965.

ERIC CLAPTON
DAY BY DAY

1963

THE ROOSTERS
JANUARY 1963–AUGUST 1963

The band played only around thirteen or fourteen gigs, mainly in the London and Surrey area, including the Ricky Tick clubs in Windsor, Kingston, and West Wickham, the Wooden Bridge Hotel in Guildford, and the Marquee club in London. They also played in Oxford and Brighton.

CASEY JONES AND THE ENGINEERS
SEPTEMBER 1963

Eric performed at only a handful of gigs playing the Northern beat and cabaret circuit.

THE YARDBIRDS

Eric's equipment:
Guitars: Fender Telecaster, Fender Jaguar, Gibson ES 335, Gretsch "Nashville"
Amp: Vox AC-30

OCTOBER 1963

THE SETLISTS FOR THE SHOWS WERE DRAWN FROM THE FOLLOWING: Boom, Boom / Louise / Smokestack Lightning / Honey In Your Hips / Baby What's Wrong / Carol / I Wish You Would / Let It Rock / You Can't Judge A Book By The Cover / Who Do You Love / Got My Mojo Working / Little Queenie / I'm A Man / The Sky Is Crying / Too Much Monkey Business / Got Love If You Want It / Good Morning Little School Girl / Respectable / Five Long Years / Pretty Girl / I'm A Man / Here 'Tis / I Ain't Got You / Someone To Love Me

18 October 1963, Studio 51, Leicester Square, London

19 October 1963, Star Club, Star Hotel, Croydon, Surrey

20 October 1963, Studio 51, Leicester Square, London (late afternoon show)

20 October 1963, Crawdaddy Club, Richmond Athletic Association Grounds, Richmond, Surrey

Advert for the Yardbirds' Tuesday residency at the Ricky Tick in Windsor from 22 October.

22 October 1963, Ricky Tick, Star & Garter, Windsor, Berkshire (start of Tuesday residency)

27 October 1963, Crawdaddy Club, Richmond Athletic Association Grounds, Richmond, Surrey

29 October 1963, Ricky Tick, Star & Garter, Windsor, Berkshire

NOVEMBER 1963

2 November 1963, Star Hotel, Croydon, Surrey

3 November 1963, Crawdaddy Club, Richmond Athletic Association Grounds, Richmond, Surrey

5 November 1963, Ricky Tick, Star & Garter, Windsor, Berkshire

8 November 1963, Edwina's Club, Finsbury Park, London

9 November 1963, Star Hotel, Croydon, Surrey

10 November 1963, Crawdaddy Club, Richmond Athletic Association Grounds, Richmond, Surrey

12 November 1963, Ricky Tick, Star & Garter, Windsor, Berkshire

15 November 1963, Edwina's Club, Finsbury Park, London

16 November 1963, Star Hotel, Croydon, Surrey

17 November 1963, Crawdaddy Club, Richmond Athletic Association Grounds, Richmond, Surrey

20 November 1963, Ricky Tick, Star & Garter, Windsor, Berkshire

22 November 1963, Edwina's Club, Finsbury Park, London

23 November 1963, Star Hotel, Croydon, Surrey

24 November 1963, Crawdaddy Club, Richmond Athletic Association Grounds, Richmond, Surrey

29 November 1963, Edwina's Club, Finsbury Park, London

30 November 1963, Star Hotel, Croydon, Surrey

DECEMBER 1963

1 December 1963, Crawdaddy Club, Richmond Athletic Association Grounds, Richmond, Surrey

6 December 1963, Edwina's Club, Finsbury Park, London

7 December 1963, Star Hotel, Croydon, Surrey (with Sonny Boy Williamson).

8 December 1963 Crawdaddy Club, Richmond Athletic Association Grounds, Richmond, Surrey (with Sonny Boy Williamson)

SETLIST (FOR YARDBIRDS):

Smokestack Lightning (Chester Burnett) *Train Kept A Rollin'* 4CD box set Charly LIK Box 3 released 1993 / *Yardbirds Story 1963–1966* Charly Records box set SNAJ736CD released March 2002

You Can't Judge A Book By Its Cover (Willie Dixon) *Train Kept A Rollin'* 4CD box set Charly LIK Box 3 released 1993 / *Yardbirds Story 1963–1966* Charly Records box set SNAJ736CD released March 2002

Let It Rock (Chuck Berry) *Train Kept A Rollin'* 4CD box set Charly LIK Box 3 released 1993 / *Yardbirds Story 1963–1966* Charly Records box set SNAJ736CD released March 2002

I Wish You Would (Billy Boy Arnold) *Train Kept A Rollin'* 4CD box set Charly LIK Box 3 released 1993 / *Yardbirds Story 1963–1966* Charly Records box set SNAJ736CD released March 2002

Who Do You Love (Bo Diddley) *Train Kept A Rollin'* 4CD box set Charly LIK Box 3 released 1993 / *Yardbirds Story 1963–1966* Charly Records box set SNAJ736CD released March 2002

Honey In Her Hips (Keith Relf) *Train Kept A Rollin'* 4CD box set Charly LIK Box 3 released 1993 / *Yardbirds Story 1963–1966* Charly Records box set SNAJ736CD released March 2002

SETLIST FOR SONNY BOY WILLIAMSON AND THE YARDBIRDS:

Bye Bye Bird (Sonny Boy Williamson / Willie Dixon) *Train Kept A Rollin'* 4CD box set Charly LIK Box 3 released 1993 / *Yardbirds Story 1963–1966* Charly Records box set SNAJ736CD released March 2002

Mister Downchild (Sonny Boy Williamson) *Train Kept A Rollin'* 4CD box set Charly LIK Box 3 released 1993 / *Yardbirds Story 1963–1966* Charly Records box set SNAJ736CD released March 2002

The River Rhine (Sonny Boy Williamson) *Train Kept A Rollin'* 4CD box set Charly LIK Box 3 released 1993 / *Yardbirds Story 1963–1966* Charly Records box set SNAJ736CD released March 2002

23 Hours Too Long (Sonny Boy Williamson / Eddie Boyd) *Train Kept A Rollin'* 4CD box set Charly LIK Box 3 released 1993 / *Yardbirds Story 1963–1966* Charly Records box set SNAJ736CD released March 2002

A Lost Care (Sonny Boy Williamson) *Train Kept A Rollin'* 4CD box set Charly LIK Box 3 released 1993 / *Yardbirds Story 1963–1966* Charly Records box set SNAJ736CD released March 2002

Pontiac Blues (Sonny Boy Williamson) *Train Kept A Rollin'* 4CD box set Charly LIK Box 3 released 1993 / *Yardbirds Story 1963–1966* Charly Records box set SNAJ736CD released March 2002

Take It Easy Baby (Sonny Boy Williamson) *Train Kept A Rollin'* 4CD box set Charly LIK Box 3 released 1993 / *Yardbirds Story 1963–1966* Charly Records box set SNAJ736CD released March 2002

Out On The Water Coast (Sonny Boy Williamson) *Train Kept A Rollin'* 4CD box set Charly LIK Box 3 released 1993 / *Yardbirds Story 1963–1966* Charly Records box set SNAJ736CD released March 2002

Do The Weston (Sonny Boy Williamson) *Train Kept A Rollin'* 4CD box set Charly LIK Box 3 released 1993 / *Yardbirds Story 1963–1966* Charly Records box set SNAJ736CD released March 2002

Producer: Horst Lippman
Engineer: Keith Grant

Take It Easy Baby (Sonny Boy Williamson) *Train Kept A Rollin'* 4CD box set Charly LIK Box 3 released 1993 / *Yardbirds Story 1963–1966* Charly Records box set SNAJ736CD released March 2002

Do the Weston (Sonny Boy Williamson) *Train Kept A Rollin'* 4CD box set Charly LIK Box 3 released 1993 / *Yardbirds Story 1963–1966* Charly Records box set SNAJ736CD released March 2002

Producer: Horst Lippman
Engineer: Keith Grant

13 December 1963, Edwina's Club, Finsbury Park, London

14 December 1963, Star Hotel, Croydon, Surrey

15 December 1963, Civic Hall, Guildford, Surrey (advertised as "A Concert In Rhythm 'N' Blues" with the Rolling Stones, the Yardbirds, Carter-Lewis and the Southerners, Georgie Fame and the Blue Flames)

17 December 1963, Ricky Tick, Star & Garter, Windsor, Berkshire (with Sonny Boy Williamson)

RICKY TICK CLUB
STAR & GARTER HOTEL, WINDSOR
Tuesday 17th December
SONNY BOY WILLIAMSON
PLUS THE YARDBIRDS
Christmas Eve 8-11.30
THE YARDBIRDS
New Years Eve 8-11.30
GRAHAM BOND QUARTET

Advert for the Yardbirds' performance at the Ricky Tick on 24 December 1963.

20 December 1963, Plaza Ballroom, Guildford, Surrey

21 December 1963, The Club A Go Go, Newcastle-upon-Tyne, Northumbria

22 December 1963, Crawdaddy Club, Richmond Athletic Association Grounds, Richmond, Surrey (with Sonny Boy Williamson)

23 December 1963, Olympia Ballroom, Reading, Berkshire

24 December 1963, Ricky Tick, Star & Garter, Windsor, Berkshire (Roger Pearce steps in for Eric, who goes to visit his mother and her husband at a military base in Germany. Eric had to get a crew cut to enter the base)

28 December 1963, Star Hotel, Croydon, Surrey (with Roger Pearce on guitar)

29 December 1963, Crawdaddy Club, Richmond Athletic Association Grounds, Richmond, Surrey (with Roger Pearce on guitar)

> "When Sonny Boy Williamson came over we didn't know how to back him up. It was frightening, really, because this man was real and we weren't. He wasn't very tolerant either. He did take a shine to us after a while, but before that he put us through some bloody hard paces. In the first place, he expected us to know his tunes. He'd say, 'We're going to do "Don't Start Me Talkin'" or "Fattening Frogs For Snakes"' and then he'd kick it off, and of course, some of the members of this band had never heard these songs." —ERIC CLAPTON

1964

JANUARY 1964

3 January 1964, Marquee Club, Soho, London (Eric is now back from Germany and in the band)

4 January 1964, Star Hotel, Croydon, Surrey

5 January 1964, Crawdaddy Club, Richmond Athletic Association Grounds, Richmond, Surrey

7 January 1964, Ricky Tick, Star & Garter, Windsor, Berkshire

10 January 1964, Marquee Club, Soho, London

11 January 1964, Star Hotel, Croydon, Surrey

12 January 1964, Crawdaddy Club, Richmond Athletic Association Grounds, Richmond, Surrey

14 January 1964, Ricky Tick, Thames Hotel, Windsor, Berkshire

17 January 1964, Plaza Ballroom, Guildford, Surrey (with Sonny Boy Williamson)

18 January 1964, Star Hotel, Croydon, Surrey

19 January 1964, Crawdaddy Club, Richmond Athletic Association Grounds, Richmond, Surrey

20 January 1964, Toby Jug Hotel, Tolworth, Surrey

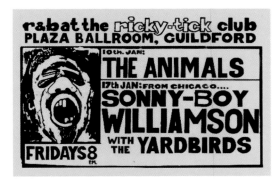

Ricky Tick advert for the Yardbirds with Sonny Boy Williamson on 17 January 1964 at the Plaza Ballroom, Guildford, Surrey.

21 January 1964, Ricky Tick, Thames Hotel, Windsor, Berkshire

22 January 1964, the Cavern, Liverpool, Merseyside (Merseyside's first genuine R&B show, Sonny Boy Williamson is backed by the Yardbirds, who also did their own set, plus the Master Sounds, the Pawns, and the Champions)

23 January 1964, Marquee Club. Soho, London (with the Allstars, Long John Baldry)

24 January 1964, St John's Ambulance Hall, Reading Berkshire

25 January 1964, Star Hotel, Croydon, Surrey

26 January 1964, Crawdaddy Club, Richmond Athletic Association Grounds, Richmond, Surrey

27 January 1964, Toby Jug Hotel, Tolworth, Surrey

28 January 1964, Ricky Tick, Thames Hotel, Windsor, Berkshire (early evening)

28 January 1964, Flamingo Club, Soho, London (benefit night for Cyril Davies with Georgie Fame, Manfred Mann, Alexis Korner, Jimmy Powell, John Mayall, Zoot Money, Long John Baldry, the Animals, and the Yardbirds)

30 January 1964, Marquee Club, Soho, London (with Long John Baldry and the Hoochie Coochie Men)

31 January 1964, Ricky Tick, St. John's Ambulance Hall, Reading, Berkshire

FEBRUARY 1964

1 February 1964, Ricky Tick, Pearce Hall, Maidenhead, Berkshire (with Sonny Boy Williamson)

2 February 1964, Crawdaddy Club, Richmond Athletic Association Grounds, Richmond, Surrey

3 February 1964, Coronation Hall, Kingston, Surrey

4 February 1964, Ricky Tick, Plaza Ballroom, Guildford, Surrey

6 February 1964, Marquee Club, Soho, London (with Long John Baldry and the Hoochie Coochie Men)

7 February 1964, Ricky Tick, St. John's Ambulance Hall, Reading, Berkshire

8 February 1964, Ricky Tick, Pearce Hall, Maidenhead, Berkshire

8 February 1964, Galaxy, Town Hall, Basingstoke, Hampshire (with The Evil Eyes)

Keith Relf and Eric Clapton in the Yardbirds, 1964.

9 February 1964, Crawdaddy Club, Richmond Athletic Association Grounds, Richmond, Surrey

11 February 1964, Coronation Hall, Kingston, Surrey

13 February 1964, Marquee Club, Soho, London

15 February 1964, Star Hotel, Croydon, Surrey

16 February 1964, Crawdaddy Club, Richmond Athletic Association Grounds, Richmond, Surrey

17 February 1964, Coronation Hall, Kingston, Surrey

18 February 1964, Plaza Ballroom, Guildford, Surrey

20 February 1964, Marquee Club, Soho, London

21 February 1964, Fairfield Hall, Croydon, Surrey (Benefit night for Cyril Davies with Sonny Boy Williamson, Ottilie Patterson, Chris Barber's Band, the Yardbirds, Alexis Korner's Blues Incorporated, Colin Kingwell's Jazz Bandits, Alex Harvey and His Soul Band)

22 February 1964, Ricky Tick, Pearce Hall, Maidenhead, Berkshire

23 February 1964, Crawdaddy Club, Richmond Athletic Association Grounds, Richmond, Surrey

24 February 1964, Coronation Hall, Kingston, Surrey

26 February 1964, the Cavern, Liverpool, Merseyside (lunchtime show featured the Yardbirds and the Undertakers)

26 February 1964, the Cavern, Liverpool, Merseyside (evening show featured Sonny Boy Williamson, the Yardbirds, Roadrunners, the Mersey Blue Beats, the Valkyries, the St. Louis Checks)

27 February 1964, Marquee Club, Soho, London (Long John Baldry and the Hoochie Coochie Men)

28 February 1964, Town Hall, Birmingham, Midlands (first British Rhythm and Blues Festival with Sonny Boy Williamson, the Yardbirds, Spencer Davis R & B Quartet, Liverpool Roadrunners, Long John Baldry and the Hoochie Coochie Men. Keith Relf was unable to attend the show as he was hospitalized for a collapsed lung. Mick O'Neil from the Authentics steps in on vocals in Keith's absence. Sonny Boy Williamson and the Yardbirds were joined for the closing jam session "Got My Mojo Working" by several artists who were also playing at the festival. A few tracks have made it to several commercial releases)

SETLIST:

Slow Walk (Sonny Boy Williamson) *Rock Generation Vol. 5* French-only album BYG 529.705 released January 1972 / *Rock Generation Vol. 5* CD French-only Spalax 14554 released January 2000 / *Train Kept A Rollin'* 4CD box set Charly LIK Box 3 released 1993 / *Yardbirds Story 1963–1966* Charly Records box set SNAJ736CD released March 2002

Sonny Boy Williamson: vocals & harmonica
Eric Clapton: guitar
Chris Dreja: rhythm guitar
Paul Samwell-Smith: bass
Jim McCarty: drums

Highway 69 (Sonny Boy Williamson) *Rock Generation Vol. 5* French-only album BYG 529.705 released January 1972 / *Rock Generation Vol. 5* CD French-only Spalax 14554 released January 2000 / *Train Kept A Rollin'* 4CD box set Charly LIK Box 3 released 1993 / *Yardbirds Story 1963–1966* Charly Records box set SNAJ736CD released March 2002

Sonny Boy Williamson: vocals & harmonica
Eric Clapton: guitar
Chris Dreja: rhythm guitar
Paul Samwell-Smith: bass
Jim McCarty: drums

My Little Cabin (Sonny Boy Williamson) *Rock Generation Vol. 5* French-only album BYG 529.705 released January 1972 / *Rock Generation Vol. 5* CD French-only Spalax 14554 released January 2000 / *Train Kept A Rollin'* 4CD box set Charly LIK Box 3 released 1993 / *Yardbirds Story 1963–1966* Charly Records box set SNAJ736CD released March 2002

Sonny Boy Williamson: vocals & harmonica
Eric Clapton: guitar
Chris Dreja: rhythm guitar
Paul Samwell-Smith: bass
Jim McCarty: drums

Got My Mojo Working (Muddy Waters / Preston Foster) *Rock Generation Vol. 5* French-only album BYG 529.705 released January 1972 / *Rock Generation Vol. 5* French-only CD Spalax 14554 released January 2000

```
Sonny Boy Williamson: vocals & harmonica
Eric Clapton: guitar
Chris Dreja: rhythm guitar
Paul Samwell-Smith: bass
Jim McCarty: drums
Steve Winwood: backing vocals
Spencer Davis: backing vocals
Long John Baldry: vocals
Art Theman: sax
Ina Armit: piano
```

Got My Mojo Working (Reprise) (Muddy Waters / Preston Foster) *Rock Generation Vol. 5* French-only album BYG 529.705 released January 1972 / *Rock Generation Vol. 5* CD Spalax 14554 released January 2000

```
Sonny Boy Williamson: vocals & harmonica
Eric Clapton: guitar
Chris Dreja: rhythm guitar
Paul Samwell-Smith: bass
Jim McCarty: drums
Steve Winwood: backing vocals
Spencer Davis: backing vocals
Long John Baldry: vocals
Art Theman: sax
Ina Armit: piano
Producer: Giorgio Gomelsky
Engineer: Philip Wood
```

The Yardbirds set was not captured due to technical difficulties

29 February 1964, Ricky Tick, Pearce Hall, Maidenhead, Berkshire

MARCH 1964

1 March 1964, Crawdaddy Club, Richmond Athletic Association Grounds, Richmond, Surrey

2 March 1964, Coronation Hall, Kingston, Surrey

3 March 1964, Town Hall, Farnborough, Hampshire

4 March 1964, Star Hotel, Croydon, Surrey

5 March 1964, Marquee Club, Soho, London (Long John Baldry and the Hoochie Coochie Men, the Yardbirds)

6 March 1964, Telephone House, Wimbledon, Surrey

7 March 1964, Ricky Tick, Pearce Hall, Maidenhead, Berkshire

8 March 1964, the Refectory, Golders Green, London

8 March 1964, Crawdaddy Club, Richmond Athletic Association Grounds, Richmond, Surrey

11 March 1964, Star Hotel, Croydon, Surrey

13 March 1964, Marquee Club, Soho, London (Sonny Boy Williamson, Long John Baldry and the Hoochie Coochie Men, the Yardbirds)

14 March 1964, Star Hotel, Croydon, Surrey

15 March 1964, Crawdaddy Club, Richmond Athletic Association Grounds, Richmond, Surrey

18 March 1964, Star Hotel, Croydon, Surrey

20 March 1964, Marquee Club, Soho, London (first headliner for the Yardbirds supported by the Impulsions. *Five Live Yardbirds* is most likely recorded tonight. The resulting live album was a good representation of how the Yardbirds sounded live in one of their favorite venues. The almost trademark rave-ups are a joy to listen to)

The Yardbirds' first album was Five Live Yardbirds, *recorded at the Marquee Club in London on 20 March 1964.*

SETLIST:

Too Much Monkey Business (Chuck Berry) *Five Live Yardbirds* album UK-only Columbia 33SX1677 released December 1964 / *Five Live Yardbirds* CD US Rhino R2 70189 released 1988, UK Repertoire 4775 released 2003

Got Love If You Want It (James Moore) *Five Live Yardbirds* album UK-only Columbia 33SX1677 released December 1964 / *Five Live Yardbirds* CD US Rhino R2 70189 released 1988, UK Repertoire 4775 released 2003

Smokestack Lightning (Chester Burnett) *Five Live Yardbirds* album UK-only Columbia 33SX1677 released December 1964 / *Five Live Yardbirds* CD US Rhino R2 70189 released 1988, UK Repertoire 4775 released 2003

Good Morning Little Schoolgirl (HG Demarais) *Five Live Yardbirds* album UK-only Columbia 33SX1677 released December 1964 / *Five Live Yardbirds* CD US Rhino R2 70189 released 1988, UK Repertoire 4775 released 2003

Respectable (O'Kelly Isley / Ronald Isley / Rudolph Isley) *Five Live Yardbirds* album UK-only Columbia 33SX1677 released December 1964 / *Five Live Yardbirds* CD US Rhino R2 70189 released 1988, UK Repertoire 4775 released 2003

Five Long Years (Eddie Boyd) *Five Live Yardbirds* album UK-only Columbia 33SX1677 released December 1964 / *Five Live Yardbirds* CD US Rhino R2 70189 released 1988, UK Repertoire 4775 released 2003

Pretty Girl (Bo Diddley) *Five Live Yardbirds* album UK-only Columbia 33SX1677 released December 1964 / *Five Live Yardbirds* CD US Rhino R2 70189 released 1988, UK Repertoire 4775 released 2003

Louise (John Lee Hooker) *Five Live Yardbirds* album UK-only Columbia 33SX1677 released December 1964 / *Five Live Yardbirds* CD US Rhino R2 70189 released 1988, UK Repertoire 4775 released 2003

I'm A Man (Bo Diddley) *Five Live Yardbirds* album UK-only Columbia 33SX1677 released December 1964 / *Five Live Yardbirds* CD US Rhino R2 70189 released 1988, UK Repertoire 4775 released 2003

Here 'Tis (Elias McDaniel) *Five Live Yardbirds* album UK-only Columbia 33SX1677 released December 1964 / *Five Live Yardbirds* CD US Rhino R2 70189 released 1988, UK Repertoire 4775 released 2003

Keith Relf: vocals, harmonica
Eric Clapton: guitar
Chris Dreja: rhythm guitar
Paul Samwell-Smith: bass
Jim McCarty: drums

Producer: Giorgio Gomelsky
Engineer: Phillip Wood

> "We were building to musical climaxes, trying to develop crowd frenzy. Paul would start it on the bass, going up the fretboard, and everyone else would go up and up and up, and then you'd get to the leading pitch, and come back down again. If you do that on just about every number, there's very little time for reflective or serious playing." —ERIC CLAPTON

21 March 1964, Star Hotel, Croydon, Surrey

22 March 1964, Crawdaddy Club, Richmond Athletic Association Grounds, Richmond, Surrey

27 March 1964, Marquee Club, Soho, London

28 March 1964, Star Hotel, Croydon, Surrey

29 March 1964, Crawdaddy Club, Richmond Athletic Association Grounds, Richmond, Surrey (Keith Relf is ill and Brian Jones from the Rolling Stones steps in tonight to play the harmonica)

APRIL 1964

3 April 1964, Marquee Club, Soho, London (the Yardbirds supported by the Impulsions)

4 April 1964, St. Peter's Hall, Kingston, Surrey

5 April 1964, Crawdaddy Club, Richmond Athletic Association Grounds, Richmond, Surrey

6 April 1964, Town Hall, High Wycombe, Hampshire

8 April 1964, Refectory, Golders Green, London

10 April 1964, Marquee Club, Soho, London (the Yardbirds supported by the Impulsions)

11 April 1964, Star Hotel, Croydon, Surrey

12 April 1964, Crawdaddy Club, Richmond Athletic Association Grounds, Richmond, Surrey

13 April 1964, the Cellar Club, Kingston, Surrey

17 April 1964, Marquee Club, Soho, London (the Yardbirds supported by the Impulsions)

18 April 1964, Star Hotel, Croydon, Surrey

19 April 1964, Crawdaddy Club, Richmond Athletic Association Grounds, Richmond, Surrey

20 April 1964, the Cellar Club, Kingston, Surrey

22 April 1964, Star Hotel, Croydon, Surrey

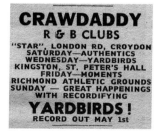

Advert for Crawdaddy Clubs and an appearance by the Yardbirds at the Star, Croydon, Surrey, on 22 April 1964.

23 April 1964, Town Hall, High Wycombe, Hampshire

24 April 1964, Bluesville!, Manor House, Harringay, London

Advert for an appearance by the Yardbirds at the Manor House, Harringay, on 24 April 1964.

25 April 1964, Town Hall Ballroom, Abergavenny, Monmouthshire, Wales

26 April 1964, Crawdaddy Club, Richmond Athletic Association Grounds, Richmond, Surrey

27 April 1964, Bromel Club, Bromley Court Hotel, Bromley, Kent

28 April 1964, Star Club, Star Hotel, Croydon, Surrey

30 April 1964, Olympia Ballroom, Reading, Berkshire

MAY 1964

1 May 1964, Marquee Club, Soho, London (the Yardbirds supported by The Authentics)

2 May 1964, Star Hotel, Croydon, Surrey

3 May 1964, Crawdaddy Club, Richmond Athletic Association Grounds, Richmond, Surrey

4 May 1964, the Cellar Club, Kingston, Surrey

6 May 1964, Refectory, Golders Green, London

8 May 1964, Marquee Club, Soho, London (the Yardbirds supported by the Authentics)

9 May 1964, Star Hotel, Croydon, Surrey

10 May 1964, Crawdaddy Club, Richmond Athletic Association Grounds, Richmond, Surrey

11 May 1964, the Cellar Club, Kingston, Surrey

13 May 1964, Ted Willis's home, Chislehurst, Kent

The Yardbirds play a short afternoon set in the garden of Labour peer Ted Willis's Chislehurst home. Earlier that month, Lord Willis had declared in a House of Lords speech that youth music was "a cheap candyfloss substitute for culture" and would not last more than five minutes. So the thought of the Yardbirds playing in his home was pretty out there and bound to attract attention. In fact, the whole event was a brilliant

The Yardbirds on Ready Steady Go *television show.*

publicity stunt arranged by Greg Tesser, their publicist. It turns out that Ted Willis was a childhood friend of Greg's father and he agreed to do Greg a favor. Greg, quite rightly, thought it would be cool if the band just turned up and demanded to play in his garden to show him that their music was not part of the so-called candy floss culture. This was to be done in front of the national press, who naturally had all been tipped off by Greg and were waiting for the band to arrive. Ted was in on it all, of course, and did not mind participating in this caper. The next morning, the press ran the story with pictures and gave the band a huge amount of publicity.

13 May 1964, Bromel Club, Bromley Court Hotel, Bromley, Kent

14 May 1964, the Yardbirds make an appearance at the Bond Street Record Centre in London to promote and sign copies of their new single, "I Wish You Would"

15 May 1964, Marquee Club, Soho, London (the Yardbirds supported by the Authentics)

16 May 1964, Star Hotel, Croydon, Surrey

17 May 1964, Crawdaddy Club, Richmond Athletic Association Grounds, Richmond, Surrey

18 May 1964, the Cellar Club, Kingston, Surrey

20 May 1964, Star Hotel, Croydon, Surrey

21 May 1964, Town Hall, High Wycombe, Buckinghamshire

22 May 1964, Marquee Club, Soho, London (the Yardbirds supported by the Authentics)

22 May 1964, Associated-Rediffusion Studios, Television House, Kingsway, London, appearance on *Ready Steady Go* playing a live version of "I Wish You Would." RSG was produced by Rediffusion and broadcast on a Friday evening with the catchphrase "The weekend starts here!"

24 May 1964, Crawdaddy Club, Richmond Athletic Association Grounds, Richmond, Surrey

25 May 1964, the Cellar Club, Kingston, Surrey

27 May 1964, Beckenham Ballroom, Beckenham, Kent

29 May 1964, Marquee Club, Soho, London (the Yardbirds supported by the Authentics)

MARQUEE
90 WARDOUR ST.
LONDON, W.1

Friday, May 29th
★ THE YARDBIRDS
★ THE AUTHENTICS

Saturday, May 30th
★THE AFRICAN MESSENGERS
★DICK MORRISSEY QUARTET

Sunday, May 31st
★ JOHNNY DANKWORTH
AND HIS ORCHESTRA
with BOBBY BREEN
and Guest Artists

Monday, June 1st
★ MARK LEEMAN FIVE
★ BLUEBIRDS

Tuesday, June 2nd
★ BLUE BEAT
★ THE BLUEBEATS
★ DUKE VIN'S SOUND SYSTEM

Wednesday, June 3rd
★ HUMPHREY LYTTELTON
AND HIS BAND
★ DENNIS REAY TRIO

Thursday, June 4th
★ LONG JOHN BALDRY
and the HOOCHIE COOCHIE MEN
with ROD STEWART
★ THE GREBBELS

Sunday, June 7th
The Great American Blues Singer
JIMMY
WITHERSPOON
Tickets in advance—Members 6/6
Guests 8/6 from 18 Carlisle St, W1

Fri, Mon, Tue, Wed: Members 5/-, Guests 6/-
Sat., Sun: Members 6/-, Guests 7/6
Thur: Members 5/-, Guests 7/6

Advert for the Yardbirds at the Marquee on 29 May 1964.

31 May 1964, Crawdaddy Club, Richmond Athletic Association Grounds, Richmond, Surrey

JUNE 1964

1 June 1964, the Cellar Club, Kingston, Surrey

3 June 1964, Twisted Wheel, Manchester, Lancashire

5 June 1964, Marquee Club, Soho, London (the Yardbirds supported by the Authentics)

6 June 1964, Trade Union Hall, Watford, Hertfordshire

7 June 1964, Crawdaddy Club, Richmond Athletic Association Grounds, Richmond, Surrey (canceled due to Royal Horse Show)

8 June 1964, the Cellar Club, Kingston, Surrey

9 June 1964, Town Hall, High Wycombe, Buckinghamshire

10 June 1964, Blue Moon, Hayes, Middlesex

11 June 1964, Brighton Dome, Brighton, East Sussex (the Animals, the Yardbirds)

12 June 1964, Marquee Club, Soho, London (the Yardbirds supported by the Authentics)

13 June 1964, Fleur De Lys, Hayes, Middlesex (maybe early evening show)

13 June 1964, Club Noreik, Tottenham, London

14 June 1964, Crawdaddy one-off at the Wimbledon Palais, Wimbledon, Surrey

15 June 1964, no Cellar Club tonight

16 June 1964, University Hall, Cambridge University, Cambridge

17 June 1964, probable filming for BBC2's new *Cool Spot* television show at the Nottingham ice rink, Nottinghamshire. Broadcast 7 July 1964)

18 June 1964, the Cavern, Liverpool, Merseyside (supported by Freddy Starr and the Flamingos, Jimmy Powell and the Five Dimensions)

19 June 1964, Marquee Club, Soho, London (supported by the Authentics)

20 June 1964, Uxbridge Showground, Uxbridge, Middlesex) first of two shows in Middlesex)

20 June 1964, West London Jazz Festival, Osterley Rugby Club Grounds, Osterley, Middlesex

Advert for the West London Jazz Festival at the Osterley Rugby Club Ground.

21 June 1964, Crawdaddy Club, Richmond Athletic Association Grounds, Richmond, Surrey

22 June 1964, the Cellar Club, Kingston, Surrey

23 June 1964, Assembly Hall, Aylesbury, Buckinghamshire

24 June 1964, film segment for *Discs A Go-Go* in Bristol (Television Wales and the West production filmed and recorded at their Bath Road television studios in Bristol. The program was set in a fictional coffee bar and hosted by Kent Walton. Due for broadcast 29 June)

25 June 1964, the Attic Club, Hounslow, Middlesex (the Yardbirds supported by the Snowballs)

Advert for one-off show at the Attic Club, 25 June 1964.

26 June 1964, Northern Jazz Festival, Redcar Racecourse, Redcar and Cleveland (Rhythm & Blues Spectacular with Manfred Mann, Long John Baldry and the Hoochie Coochie Men, the Yardbirds, the Crawdaddys)

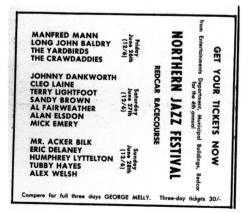

Advert for the Northern Jazz Festival at the Redcar Racecourse and an appearance by the Yardbirds on 26 June 1964.

27 June 1964, appearance on *Thank Your Lucky Stars* television show. Brian Matthew hosts with guests: the Searchers, the Mojos, Danny Williams, Jess Conrad, the Yardbirds, Debbie Lee, Troy Dante and the Infernos, Elkie Brooks, Janice Nicholls, Cathy McGowan, and Michael Aldred. Guest DJ: Pete Murray

28 June 1964, Crawdaddy Club, Richmond Athletic Association Grounds, Richmond, Surrey

29 June 1964, the Cellar Club, Kingston, Surrey

29 June 1964, appearance on *Discs A Go-Go* broadcast

30 June 1964, Casino Hotel, Taggs Island, Hampton Court, Surrey (supported by the Grebbles, the T-Bones)

JULY 1964

1 July 1964, Blu-Beat Club, Lord Wakefield Hall, Hayes, Middlesex

2 July 1964, Kimbells Ballroom, Portsmouth, Hampshire

3 July 1964, Marquee Club, Soho, London (the Yardbirds supported by the Authentics)

5 July 1964, The Cavern Club, Liverpool, Merseyside

6 July 1964, no Cellar Club tonight

7 July 1964, appearance on BBC1's *The Cool Spot*. This was the first in a series presented by David Jacobs, which mixed pop music with dancing on ice)

7 July 1964, Tuesday Blues Club, Churchill Hall, Kenton, Harrow, Middlesex

8 July 1964, Blu-Beat Club, Lord Wakefield Hall, Hayes, Middlesex

9 July 1964, Olympia Ballroom, Reading, Berkshire

10 July 1964, Marquee Club, Soho, London (the Yardbirds supported by the Authentics)

11 July 1964, Rhodes Centre, Bishop's Stortford, Hertfordshire (supported by Shane and the Shane Gang)

12 July 1964, Scala Ballroom, Dartford, Kent

13 July 1964, Monday Night Beat Club, the Sparrow Hawk, Edgware, Middlesex

14 July 1964, Tuesday Blues Club, Churchill Hall, Kenton, Harrow, Middlesex

15 July 1964, Il Rondo Ballroom, Leicester, Leicestershire

16 July 1964, Olympia Ballroom, Reading, Berkshire

17 July 1964, Marquee Club, Soho, London (the Yardbirds supported by the Authentics)

18 July 1964, second Scottish Jazz and Blues Festival, Dam Park Stadium, Ayr, South Ayrshire, Scotland

Advert for the second Scottish Jazz and Blues Festival at Dam Park in Ayr. The Yardbirds are on the bill, among several jazz and blues bands.

19 July 1964, Commodore Theatre, Ryde, Isle of Wight (two shows, 6:15 p.m. p.m. and 8:45 p.m. With Lulu and the Luvvers, Mike Sarne, Vince Eager, the Leroys, the Wild Ones, Brian Freeman)

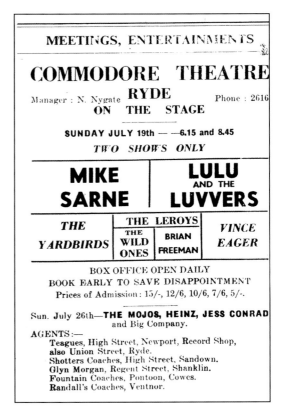

Advert for the Yardbirds' appearance at the Commodore Theatre in Ryde. Mike Sarne and Lulu and the Luvvers headline the bill.

A highly respected Isle of Wight guitar player, Brian Sharpe, went to one of the gigs. Here is what he had to say about Eric Clapton: "He was the loudest guitarist that I had ever heard. Eric had 'Slowhand' written on his guitar case. He stood in the wings watching the Luvvers' guitarist. I was stood next to him, and he turned to me and commented that the lead guitarist was good. Eric went off to the beach at Appley after the gig for a swim." Mike Sarne films some of the bands on his cine-camera.

20 July 1964, the Cellar Club, Kingston, Surrey

21 July 1964, Tuesday Blues Club, Churchill Hall, Kenton, Harrow, Middlesex

22 July 1964, Twisted Wheel, Manchester, Lancashire

22 July 1964, the Yardbirds play live versions of "Louise" and "I Wish You Would" on *Go Tell It On The Mountain* show, guesting on a Peter Paul and Mary TV special produced by Granada Television Manchester. Program featured Peter, Paul, & Mary, Johnny Duncan & Blue Glass Boys, the Yardbirds. Their performance was probably recorded earlier in the day.

23 July 1964, Queens Ballroom, Cleveleys, Lancashire (with Jimmy Powell & the Five Dimensions)

24 July 1964, Marquee Club, Soho, London

25 July 1964, King George's Hall, Esher, Surrey

26 July 1964, Crawdaddy Club, Richmond Athletic Association Grounds, Richmond, Surrey

27 July 1964, Town Hall, Clacton-On-Sea, Essex

28 July 1964, Tuesday Blues Club, Churchill Hall, Kenton, Harrow, Middlesex (Chris Dreja's Gibson ES 335 is broken in two when a monitor speaker falls on the instrument)

29 July 1964, Bromel Club, Bromley Court Hotel, Bromley, Kent

30 July 1964, the Locarno, Swindon, Wiltshire (the Yardbirds supported by Cadillac and the Playboys)

31 July 1964, Marquee Club, Soho, London (the Yardbirds supported by the Authentics. This night may have been recorded and released as "Live! Blueswailing July '64." Other sources list either 24 July or 7 August as possible dates. The clue is given when Keith Relf announces that Chris Dreja's Gibson ES 335 was broken last Tuesday at Churchill Hall. My reasoning for this date is that Chris is seen playing the 335 on the *Go Tell It On The Mountain* television show on 22 July, which is recorded the following day in Manchester, which would not have given him any time to get it repaired had it been damaged on 21 July. Also, when this tape turned up, it was labeled July 1964)

SETLIST (INCOMPLETE):

Someone To Love Me (Snooky Pryor) *Live! Blueswailing July '64* CD Castle CMQCD 793 released September 2003 / *Glimpses 1963–1968* 5CD box set Easy Action EARS035 released February 2012

Too Much Monkey Business (Chuck Berry) *Live! Blueswailing July '64* CD Castle CMQCD 793 released September 2003 / *Glimpses 1963–1968* 5CD box set Easy Action EARS035 released February 2012

Got Love If You Want It (James Moore) *Live! Blueswailing July '64* CD Castle CMQCD 793 released September 2003 / *Glimpses 1963–1968* 5CD box set Easy Action EARS035 released February 2012

Smokestack Lightning (Chester Burnett) *Live! Blueswailing July '64* CD Castle CMQCD 793 released September 2003 / *Glimpses 1963–1968* 5CD box set Easy Action EARS035 released February 2012

Good Morning Little Schoolgirl (Sonny Boy Williamson) *Live! Blueswailing July '64* CD Castle CMQCD 793 released September 2003 / *Glimpses 1963–1968* 5CD box set Easy Action EARS035 released February 2012

She Is So Respectable / Humpty Dumpty (O'Kelly Isley / Ronald Isley / Rudolph Isley) *Live! Blueswailing July '64* CD Castle CMQCD 793 released September 2003 / *Glimpses 1963–1968* 5CD box set Easy Action EARS035 released February 2012

The Sky Is Crying (Elmore James) *Live! Blueswailing July '64* CD Castle CMQCD 793 released September 2003 / *Glimpses 1963–1968* 5CD box set Easy Action EARS035 released February 2012

Keith Relf: vocals, harmonica
Eric Clapton: guitar
Chris Dreja: rhythm guitar
Paul Samwell-Smith: bass
Jim McCarty: drums

Recorded by Philip Wood

AUGUST 1964

1 August 1964, Market Hall, Redhill, Surrey

2 August 1964, Crawdaddy Club, Richmond Athletic Association Grounds, Richmond, Surrey

3 August 1964, the Cellar Club, Kingston, Surrey

4 August 1964, Fender Club, Churchill Hall, Kenton, Harrow, Middlesex

5 August 1964, Town Hall, Torquay, Devon (with Shane and the Shane Gang, Rona and the Romeos)

6 August 1964, Flamingo Club, Flamingo Ballroom, Redruth, Cornwall

6 August 1964, Queens Hall, Barnstaple, Devon

7 August 1964, Marquee Club, Soho, London (the Yardbirds supported by the Brakemen)

9 August 1964, fourth National Jazz and Blues Festival at the Richmond Athletic Association ground, Richmond, Surrey. The stage was divided in two halves so that when one band was finished the other could go on without delays for changing over equipment. There was a jam session at the end of the Yardbirds set with Georgie Fame, Jack Bruce, Graham Bond, Ginger Baker, and Mike Vernon. They all took over the two halves of the stage. BBC1 recorded several portions over the course of the three-day festival and were broadcast on the night of the shows.

SETLIST:

Boom Boom (John Lee Hooker) *Train Kept A Rollin'* 4CD box set Charly LIK Box 3 released 1993 / *Yardbirds Story 1963–1966* Charly Records box set SNAJ736CD released March 2002 / *Glimpses 1963–1968* 5CD box set Easy Action EARS035 released February 2012

I'm A Man (Bo Diddley) *Train Kept A Rollin'* 4CD box set Charly LIK Box 3 released 1993 / *Yardbirds Story 1963–1966* Charly Records box set SNAJ736CD released March 2002 / *Glimpses 1963–1968* 5CD box set Easy Action EARS035 released February 2012

Little Queenie (Chuck Berry) *Train Kept A Rollin'* 4CD box set Charly LIK Box 3 released 1993 / *Yardbirds Story 1963–1966* Charly Records box set SNAJ736CD released March 2002 / *Glimpses 1963–1968* 5CD box set Easy Action EARS035 released February 2012

Too Much Monkey Business (Chuck Berry) *Train Kept A Rollin'* 4CD box set Charly LIK Box 3 released 1993 / *Yardbirds Story 1963–1966* Charly Records box set SNAJ736CD released March 2002 / *Glimpses 1963–1968* 5CD box set Easy Action EARS035 released February 2012

Respectable (O'Kelly Isley / Ronald Isley / Rudolph Isley) *Train Kept A Rollin'* 4CD box set Charly LIK Box 3 released 1993 / *Yardbirds Story 1963–1966* Charly Records box set SNAJ736CD released March 2002 / *Glimpses 1963–1968* 5CD box set Easy Action EARS035 released February 2012

Carol (Chuck Berry) *Train Kept A Rollin'* 4CD box set Charly LIK Box 3 released 1993 / *Yardbirds Story 1963–1966* Charly Records box set SNAJ736CD released March 2002 / *Glimpses 1963–1968* 5CD box set Easy Action EARS035 released February 2012

Here 'Tis (Ellas McDaniels) *Train Kept A Rollin'* 4CD box set Charly LIK Box 3 released 1993 / *Yardbirds Story 1963–1966* Charly Records box set SNAJ736CD released March 2002 / *Glimpses 1963–1968* 5CD box set Easy Action EARS035 released February 2012

10 August 1964, no Cellar Club, Kingston, tonight as everyone departs for Switzerland. As Keith Relf was ill, Mick O'Neill filled in for him in Switzerland

10 August 1964, leave in convoy for Switzerland

14 August 1964, Lido Locarno, Switzerland

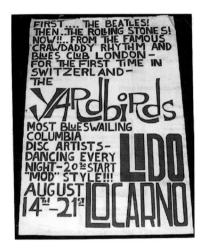

Poster advertising the Yardbirds' concerts at the Lido in Locarno, Switzerland.

15 August 1964, Lido Locarno, Switzerland

16 August 1964, Lido Locarno, Switzerland

17 August 1964, Lido Locarno, Switzerland

18 August 1964, Lido Locarno, Switzerland

19 August 1964, Lido Locarno, Switzerland

20 August 1964, Lido Locarno, Switzerland

21 August 1964, Lido Locarno, Switzerland (the band are allowed a short holiday after doing the shows before returning in convoy back to England)

SEPTEMBER 1964

4 September 1964, Marquee Club, Soho, London (the Yardbirds supported by the Dissatisfieds)

5 September 1964, appearance on BBC2's *Open House*

6 September 1964, Crawdaddy Club, Richmond Athletic Association Grounds, Richmond, Surrey

7 September 1964, Marquee Club, Soho, London (the Yardbirds supported by the Dissatisfieds)

8 September 1964, Tuesday Blues Club, Churchill Hall, Kenton, Harrow, Middlesex

Eric Clapton in the Yardbirds with his Fender Telecaster looking a little battered in 1964.

Eric Clapton in the Yardbirds with his Fender Telecaster in 1964.

9 September 1964, Il Rondo Ballroom, Leicester, Leicestershire

11 September 1964, Marquee Club, Soho, London (the Yardbirds supported by the Moody Blues)

12 September 1964, Pavilion Gardens Ballroom, Buxton, Derbyshire

13 September 1964, Crawdaddy Club, Richmond Athletic Association Grounds, Richmond, Surrey

15 September 1964, Town Hall, High Wycombe, Buckinghamshire

16 September 1964, Chinese R&B and Jazz Club, Corn Exchange, Bristol, Gloucestershire

PACKAGE TOUR

Package tour with Billy J. Kramer and the Dakotas as headliners, The Kinks or The Nashville Teens depending on the city, the Ronettes, the Yardbirds, Bill Black's Combo, Cliff Bennett and the Rebel Rousers. Compere was Tim Connor. Two shows a night.

18 September 1964, Granada Theatre, Walthamstow, Essex (canceled)

19 September 1964, Colston Hall, Bristol, Gloucestershire

20 September 1964, Odeon Theatre, Lewisham, London

21 September 1964, Granada Theatre, Maidstone, Kent

22 September 1964, Granada Theatre, Greenford, Middlesex

23 September 1964, Gaumont Theatre, Ipswich, Suffolk

24 September 1964, Odeon Cinema, Southend, Essex

25 September 1964, ABC Cinema, Northampton, Northamptonshire

26 September 1964, Granada Theatre, Mansfield, Nottinghamshire

27 September 1964, Empire Theatre, Liverpool, Merseyside

28 September 1964, Caird Hall, Dundee, Scotland

29 September 1964, ABC Cinema, Edinburgh, Scotland

30 September 1964, Odeon Cinema, Glasgow, Scotland

OCTOBER 1964

1 October 1964, Adelphi Theatre, Dublin, Ireland

2 October 1964, ABC Cinema, Belfast, Northern Ireland

3 October 1964, Savoy Theatre, Cork, Ireland

4 October 1964, ABC Globe Theatre, Stockton-on-Tees, County Durham

7 October 1964, ABC Cinema, Carlisle, Cumbria

8 October 1964, Odeon Cinema, Bolton, Greater Manchester

9 October 1964, Granada Theatre, Grantham, Lincolnshire

10 October 1964, ABC Cinema, Kingston-upon-Hull, Yorkshire

11 October 1964, Granada Theatre, East Ham, Newham

12 October 1964, Crawdaddy at the Staines Rugby Club, Feltham, Middlesex (one-off show for the Yardbirds on a day off from package tour)

13 October 1964, Granada Theatre, Bedford, Bedfordshire

14 October 1964, Granada Theatre, Brixton, London

Advert for Billy J. Kramer package tour show with the Yardbirds and the Kinks, among others.

15 October 1964, Odeon Cinema, Guildford, Surrey

16 October 1964, ABC Cinema, Southampton, Hampshire

17 October 1964, ABC Cinema, Gloucester, Gloucestershire

18 October 1964, Granada Theatre, Tooting, Wandsworth (last date of Billy J. Kramer package tour)

20 October 1964, TA Hall, School Of Art, Kingston upon Thames, Surrey

21 October 1964, Twisted Wheel, Manchester, Lancashire

22 October 1964, the Cavern, Liverpool, Merseyside (supported by the Aintree Four, the Clayton Squares, the Abstracts)

23 October 1964, Marquee Club, Soho, London (the Yardbirds supported by the Dissatisfieds)

24 October 1964, Goldhawk Social Club, Shepherds Bush, London

25 October 1964, Crawdaddy Club, Richmond Athletic Association Grounds, Richmond, Surrey (with the Grebbels)

26 October 1964, Glenlyn Club, Forest Hill, Lewisham

28 October 1964, appearance on *Three Go Round*, a Southern Television program for teenagers that was part networked

29 October 1964, BBC Maida Vale Studios, Delaware Road, Maida Vale. Radio recording for the *Rhythm & Blues* program hosted by Alexis Korner. Broadcast on 21 November 1965 ("Too Much Monkey Business" is recorded. More numbers may also have been recorded)

29 October 1964, Lakeside R&B Scene, Old Welsh Harp, Hendon, Middlesex

30 October 1964, Marquee Club, Soho, London (the Yardbirds supported by the Night Shift)

30 October 1964, Associated-Rediffusion Studios, Television House, Kingsway, London (Appearance on *Ready Steady Go* playing a live version of "Good Morning Little Schoolgirl")

NOVEMBER 1964

1 November 1964, Crawdaddy Club, Richmond Athletic Association Grounds, Richmond, Surrey (with the Grebbels)

3 November 1964, Town Hall, High Wycombe, Buckinghamshire

4 November 1964, appearance on *Discs A Go-Go* (performing "Good Morning Little Schoolgirl." Television Wales and the West production filmed and recorded at their Bath Road television studios in Bristol. The program was set in a fictional coffee bar and hosted by Kent Walton)

6 November 1964, Hippodrome, Brighton, East Sussex

"Club audiences are very possessive, and when records start selling the kids come up to you and say, 'We've lost you.' We had that feeling at the Crawdaddy. Then we left for a while to do a tour with Billy J. Kramer. When we played the Crawdaddy last Sunday (1 November 1964) it wasn't quite the same again. But at the Marquee now, it's a complete rave. But we're worried like hell that we'll lose R 'n' B fans if we get a hit record. We like pop fans, but we want both. We would look upon it as our biggest achievement if we could be the most popular band in the country without a hit record.

We're tired of the R 'n' B snobs who say they don't like an artist any more because he has a hit record. Why is it criminal to be successful?" —ERIC CLAPTON
(*Melody Maker*, 7 November 1964)

7 November 1964, Memorial Hall, Northwich, Cheshire

8 November 1964, Crawdaddy Club, Richmond Athletic Association Grounds, Richmond, Surrey (with the Grebbels)

10 November 1964, Tuesday Blues Club, Churchill Hall, Kenton, Harrow, Middlesex

11 November 1964, the Chinese R&B and Jazz Club, Corn Exchange, Bristol, Gloucestershire (supported by the Pentagons)

14 November 1964, Twisted Wheel, Manchester, Lancashire (early and late sessions supported by the Clayton Squares)

15 November 1964, Crawdaddy Club, Richmond Athletic Association Grounds, Richmond, Surrey (with the Grebbels)

19 November 1964, Pier Pavilion, Worthing, West Sussex (with the Otis Band)

21 November 1964, Ricky Tick, Plaza Ballroom, Guildford, Surrey

22 November 1964, Hippodrome, Brighton, East Sussex (running order for the Show: the Sack O'Woes, the Quiet Five, the Yardbirds, the Worryin' Kind, Twinkle, Jerry Lee Lewis)

24 November 1964, Rediffusion Television Studios, Wembley Park Drive, Wembley, Middlesex. (Appearance on Rediffusion's *The Five O'Clock Club* which was networked nationally)

27 November 1964, Town Hall, Leamington Spa, Warwickshire

29 November 1964, Sunderland Empire, Sunderland, Tyne & Wear (Jerry Lee Lewis package tour)

30 November City Hall, Newcastle, Tyne & Wear (Jerry Lee Lewis package tour)

DECEMBER 1964

1 December Golders Green Hippodrome, London (Jerry Lee Lewis package tour. Also on the bill tonight are Gene Vincent backed by the Plebs)

4 December 1964, Ricky Tick, Clewer Mead, Windsor, Berkshire

5 December 1964, St George's Ballroom, Hinckley, Leicestershire

6 December 1964, no Richmond Crawdaddy tonight

7 December 1964, BBC 2 films *Top Beat* from the Royal Albert Hall, London (with Brenda Lee, Brian Poole and the Tremoloes, the Nashville Teens, Dave Berry and the Cruisers, Sounds Incorporated, the Miracles, Wayne Fontana and the Mindbenders, the Yardbirds and compere Alan Freeman)

8 December 1964, Assembly Hall, Tunbridge Wells, Kent

9 December BBC2's *Top Beat* filmed on 7 December is broadcast. The Yardbirds play "Good Morning Little Schoolgirl"

10 December 1964, Olympia Ballroom, Reading, Berkshire

12 December 1964, Palais, Peterborough, Cambridgeshire

13 December 1964, King Mojo Club, Sheffield, South Yorkshire

A rare photo of the Yardbirds at the King Mojo Club, Sheffield, on 13 December 1964. (Photo courtesy of Peter Stringfellow)

14 December 1964, Grand Pavilion, Porthcawl, Wales

17 December 1964, Lakeside R&B Scene, Old Welsh Harp, Hendon, Middlesex

18 December 1964, Co-Op Hall, Gravesend, Kent

RICKY TICK CLUB
Barry Ave. Windsor, call Winds 60173
Every Wednesday 7.30 - 11
Ronnie Jones & the NIGHTimers   4/-
Every Sunday 4 - 10.30 p.m.
2 groups plus TV coffee lounge
29th Ink Sunday Combo
David John and the Mood   5/-
Fridays 7.30 - 11.30 p.m.
Dec. 4th The Yardbirds   6/-
Dec. 11th "do the dog" Rufus Thomas
and the Chessmen   7/6
Tues. Dec. 15th—7.30 - 11
Howling Wolf   6/-
Saturday 8 p.m. - 12
Dec. 5th John Mayall and the Blues
Breakers + supporting group 7/6
Dec. 12th Graham Bond
plus supporting band   7/6
Dec. 19th Georgie Fame   7/6
Christmas Eve 24th 8 p.m. - 12
Sonny Boy Williamson & John Mayall's
Blues Breakers   7/6
Boxing Night Saturday 26th
Zoot Money   7/6
All records played at the club available at
SURPLICES: WINDSOR & MAIDENHEAD
The Ricky Tick advertises its weekly Programme
in The New Record Mirror

Advert for upcoming groups, including the Yardbirds, for the Ricky Tick Club, Clewer Mead, Barry Avenue, Windsor.

20 December 1964, Crawdaddy Club, Richmond Athletic Association Grounds, Richmond, Surrey (with the Grebbels)

21 December 1964, Fairfield Hall, Croydon, Surrey

ANOTHER BEATLES CHRISTMAS SHOW

Two-week season on *Another Beatles Christmas Show* at the Hammersmith Odeon with the Mike Cotton Sound, Michael Haslam, the Yardbirds, Jimmy Saville, Freddie & the Dreamers, Elkie Brooks, Sounds Incorporated, Ray Fell, the Beatles

24 December 1964, Odeon, Hammersmith, London (one performance at 7:30 pm)

26 December 1964, Odeon, Hammersmith, London (two performances, 6:15 p.m. and 8:45 p.m.)

27 December 1964, Crawdaddy Club, Richmond Athletic Association Grounds, Richmond, Surrey (with the Grebbels)

28 December 1964, Odeon, Hammersmith, London (two performances, 6:15 p.m. and 8:45 p.m.)

29 December 1964, Odeon, Hammersmith, London (one performance only at 6:15 p.m. The box office proceeds from tonight's performance were donated to the Brady Clubs and Settlement Charity based in London's East End. This gala performance was called "Beatles For Brady" and alternative tickets and a different program were printed for this one-off show)

30 December 1964, Odeon, Hammersmith, London (two performances, 6:15 p.m. and 8:45 p.m.)

31 December 1964, Odeon, Hammersmith, London (two performances, 6:15 p.m. and 8:45 p.m.)

3

1965

1965

JANUARY 1965

1 January 1965, Odeon, Hammersmith, London (two performances, 6:15 p.m. and 8:45 p.m.)

2 January 1965, Odeon, Hammersmith, London (two performances, 6:15 p.m. and 8:45 p.m.)

3 January 1965, Crawdaddy Club, Richmond Athletic Association Grounds, Richmond, Surrey (with the Grebbels)

4 January 1965, Odeon, Hammersmith, London (two performances, 6:15 p.m. and 8:45 p.m.)

5 January 1965, Odeon, Hammersmith, London (two performances, 6:15 p.m. and 8:45 p.m.)

6 January 1965, Odeon, Hammersmith, London (two performances, 6:15 p.m. and 8:45 p.m.)

7 January 1965, Odeon, Hammersmith, London (two performances, 6:15 p.m. and 8:45 p.m.)

8 January 1965, Odeon, Hammersmith, London (two performances, 6:15 p.m. and 8:45 p.m.)

9 January 1965, Odeon, Hammersmith, London (two performances, 6:15 p.m. and 8:45 p.m.)

10 January 1965, Crawdaddy Club, Richmond Athletic Association Grounds, Richmond, Surrey (with the Grebbels)

11 January 1965, Odeon, Hammersmith, London (two performances, 6:15 p.m. and 8:45 p.m.)

12 January 1965, Odeon, Hammersmith, London (two performances, 6:15 p.m. and 8:45 p.m.)

13 January 1965, Odeon, Hammersmith, London (two performances, 6:15 p.m. and 8:45 p.m.)

14 January 1965, Odeon, Hammersmith, London (two performances, 6:15 p.m. and 8:45 p.m.)

15 January 1965, Odeon, Hammersmith, London (two performances, 6:15 p.m. and 8:45 p.m.)

16 January 1965, Odeon, Hammersmith, London (two performances, 6:15 p.m. and 8:45 p.m.)

17 January 1965, Crawdaddy Club, Richmond Athletic Association Grounds, Richmond, Surrey (with the Grebbels)

18 January 1965, Bath Pavilion, Bath, Somerset

20 January 1965, Bromel Club, Bromley Court Hotel, Kent

21 January 1965, Black Cat Club, Woolwich, London

22 January 1965, Marquee Club, Soho, London (pre-recording for Radio Luxembourg's *Ready Steady Radio*)

23 January 1965, Astoria Ballroom, Rawtenstall, Lancashire (with the Brystals, the Thunderbirds)

24 January 1965, Crawdaddy Club, Richmond Athletic Association Grounds, Richmond, Surrey (with the Grebbels)

25 January 1965, Majestic Ballroom, Reading, Berkshire

29 January 1965, Trentham Ballroom, Trentham Gardens, Stoke-On-Trent, Staffordshire

30 January 1965, Floral Hall, Morecambe, Lancashire

FEBRUARY 1965

1 February 1965, Marquee Club, Soho, London (the Yardbirds supported by Mark Leeman Five)

5 February 1965, Dungeon Club, Nottingham, Nottinghamshire

6 February 1965, Whiskey A Go-Go, Birmingham, West Midlands

7 February 1965, Cavern Club, Manchester, Lancashire

8 February 1965, Town Hall, Basingstoke, Hampshire

9 February 1965, Town Hall, High Wycombe, Buckinghamshire

10 February 1965, Town Hall, Farnborough, Hampshire

12 February 1965, Starlight Ballroom, Sudbury, London

13 February 1965, Railway Tavern, Catford, London

14 February 1965, Community Centre, Southall, London

15 February 1965, Marquee Club, Soho, London (the Yardbirds supported by Mark Leeman Five)

19 February 1965, Plaza Ballroom, Guildford, Surrey

20 February 1965, Il Rondo, Leicester, Leicestershire

21 February 1965, Kimbells Sunday Club, Kimbells Ballroom, Portsmouth, Hampshire (the Yardbirds supported by the J Crow Combo)

22 February 1965, Marquee Club, Soho, London (the Yardbirds supported by Mark Leeman Five)

23 February 1965, Wallington Public Hall, Wallington, Sutton

25 February 1965, Eric attends Buddy Guy show at the Marquee in London

26 February 1965, Leyton Baths, Leyton, London

27 February 1965, Blue Indigo Club, Southampton, Hampshire

28 February 1965, Crawdaddy Club, Richmond Athletic Association Grounds, Richmond, Surrey

MARCH 1965

1 March Coed Eva Youth Centre, Newport, Wales

2 March 1965, Town Hall, Lydney, Gloucestershire

3 March 1965, the Bristol Chinese R&B and Jazz Club, Corn Exchange, Bristol, Gloucestershire (Eric's last show with the Yardbirds)

RG Jones Studios control room in the early 1960s with Robin Jones at the EMI custom console.

RECORDING SESSIONS 1963-1966

The first studio recordings by the Yardbirds took place at RG Jones of Morden, Morden Park Studios, a two-track facility located in two rooms in the yard of a house located in the grounds of Morden Manor in Surrey. Dates based on Giorgio Gomelsky's bookings in Ronald Geoffrey Jones's diary entries.

RG JONES OF MORDEN, MORDEN PARK SOUND STUDIOS, LONDON ROAD, MORDEN, SURREY 6:30 p.m.

13 NOVEMBER 1963

RG Jones Studios entrance from London Road, Morden. Ronald Geoffrey Jones and his son Robin lived in the left semi-detached cottage. The studio is located in the backyard, on the left side of the house.

The RG Jones recording room, where acts such as the Rolling Stones and the Yardbirds made their first recordings.

Rare picture sleeve single for "Boom Boom," the Yardbirds' first recording.

Recording a single for the German market (original booking was for 12 November but was postponed to today)

BOOM BOOM (John Lee Hooker) single A-side Germany CBS 1433 released 1964 / *Train Kept A Rollin'* 4CD box set Charly LIK Box 3 released 1993 / *Yardbirds Story 1963–1966* Charly Records box set SNAJ736CD released March 2002

HONEY IN YOUR HIPS (Keith Relf) (Version1) single B-side Germany CBS 1433 released 1964 / *Train Kept A Rollin'* 4CD box set Charly LIK Box 3 released 1993 / *Yardbirds Story 1963–1966* Charly Records box set SNAJ736CD released March 2002

Rare color photo of the yard and studio entrance.

TALKIN' 'BOUT YOU (Chuck Berry) *Train Kept A Rollin'* 4CD box set Charly LIK Box 3 released 1993 / *Yardbirds Story 1963–1966* Charly Records box set SNAJ736CD released March 2002

Eric Clapton: guitar
Keith Relf: vocals
Chris Dreja: guitar
Paul Samwell-Smith: bass
Jim McCarty: drums

Producer: Giorgio Gomelsky
Engineer: Robin Jones

"During the late fifties and sixties I had helped the German concert agency of Lippman & Rau with their yearly American Blues Festival presentation. In 1963 I convinced them to let some artists from their show stay over with me in England. The idea was to undertake tours of small clubs backed by young English bands, so spreading the experience up and down the country. Horst Lippman, at first somewhat reluctant, soon enthused when I took him to a Yardbirds gig. On the spot he not only agreed to the plan but also offered to finance the recording of a live album with Sonny Boy Williamson at the Crawdaddy as well as a studio single (for the German market).

We had to come out with two titles that were a part of Horst Lippman's deal for a German release. Horst wanted to have an extra bit of incentive by being the publisher of at least one of the songs, which meant we had to record an original. I remember talking a reluctant Keith Relf into attempting to write some lyrics to a Bo Diddley–type beat. So 'Honey In Her Hips' was the first self-penned recording of *The Most Blueswailing*. John Lee Hooker's 'Boom Boom' was a standard tune many R&B bands were playing in those days and the band knew it well, and it took no time to tape. But apart from the 2 German titles, I wished to come out of this first session with a piece of tape as near as possible to the 'natural' sound of the band so we could get a sense of what problems we may have to face immortalizing The Yardbirds on future sessions. So we sneaked in Chuck Berry's 'Talkin' Bout You.'" **—GIORGIO GOMELSKY**
(from the liner notes in the *Train Kept A Rollin'* box set)

RG JONES OF MORDEN, MORDEN PARK SOUND STUDIOS, LONDON ROAD, MORDEN, SURREY

10 DECEMBER 1963

All-day session listed as possible in Ronald Geoffrey Jones's diary

BABY WHAT'S WRONG (Rice Miller Williamson) *Train Kept A Rollin'* 4CD box set Charly LIK Box 3 released 1993 / *Yardbirds Story 1963–1968* Charly Records box set SNAJ736CD released March 2002 / *Glimpses 1963–1968* 5CD box set Easy Action EARS035 released February 2012

HONEY IN YOUR HIPS (Keith Relf) (version 2) *Glimpses 1963–1968* 5CD box set Easy Action EARS035 released February 2012

Eric Clapton: guitar
Keith Relf: vocals
Chris Dreja: guitar
Paul Samwell-Smith: bass
Jim McCarty: drums

Producer: Giorgio Gomelsky
Engineer: Robin Jones

The band record some demos.

RG JONES OF MORDEN, MORDEN PARK SOUND STUDIOS, LONDON ROAD, MORDEN, SURREY 7:00 p.m.

16 DECEMBER 1963

I WISH YOU WOULD (Billy Boy Arnold) *Train Kept A Rollin'* 4CD box set Charly LIK Box 3 released 1993 / *Yardbirds Story 1963–1966* Charly Records box set SNAJ736CD released March 2002

A CERTAIN GIRL (Allen Toussaint under the pseudonym Naomi Neville) *Train Kept A Rollin'* 4CD box set Charly LIK Box 3 released 1993 / *Yardbirds Story 1963–1966* Charly Records box set SNAJ736CD released March 2002

YOU CAN'T JUDGE A BOOK BY THE COVER (Willie Dixon) *Glimpses 1963–1968* Easy Action EARS035 released February 2012

These demos were presented to EMI and Decca in January 1964.

Eric Clapton: guitar
Keith Relf: vocals
Chris Dreja: guitar
Paul Samwell-Smith: bass
Jim McCarty: drums

Producer: Giorgio Gomelsky
Engineer: Robin Jones

"We worked very hard on 'A Certain Girl.' Pushing the technology into the red, we recorded the songs in the old synagogue Baker Street location of Olympic Sound in a 3 hour session—the norm for a single in those days—with our old friend Keith Grant. If you listen carefully there is a lot going on. Notably a nice fat and fuzzy guitar riff, all manners of percussions and various double tracking intended to outline, illustrate, pinpoint and fill the biggest possible sound-frame known to mankind at that time. There is even a vocal punctuation performed by yours truly with impeccable sense of timing! Alas, on the whole, our ambitious sound construct turned out to be a respectable failure and the more airy and uncluttered 'I Wish You Would,' recorded in less than 20 minutes, became the choice for the A-side of the first single.**"** **—GIORGIO GOMELSKY**
(from the liner notes in the *Train Kept A Rollin'* box set)

OLYMPIC SOUND STUDIOS, STUDIO 1 Carton Hall, Carton Street, Marylebone, London W1

MARCH 1964

I WISH YOU WOULD (Billy Boy Arnold) single A-side UK Columbia DB7823 released 1 May 1964, US Epic 5-9709 released 17 August 1964 / *Train Kept A Rollin'* 4CD box set Charly LIK Box 3 released 1993 / *Yardbirds Story 1963–1966* Charly Records box set SNAJ736CD released March 2002

"I remixed a Yardbirds single for Giorgio Gomelsky, A side only in about half an hour! 'I Wish You Would,' early summer 1964.**"** **—DEREK VARNALS** (engineer)

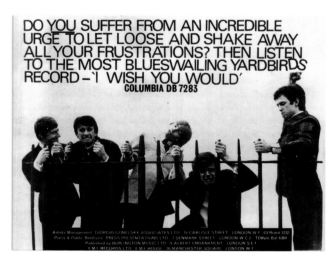

Advert for Yardbirds single "I Wish You Would."

A CERTAIN GIRL (Allen Toussaint under the pseudonym Naomi Neville) single B-side UK Columbia DB7823 released 1 May 1964, US Epic 5-9709 released 17 August 1964 / *Train Kept A Rollin'* 4CD box set Charly LIK Box 3 released 1993 / *Yardbirds Story 1963–1966* Charly Records box set SNAJ736CD released March 2002

Eric Clapton: guitar
Keith Relf: vocals
Chris Dreja: guitar
Paul Samwell-Smith: bass
Jim McCarty: drums

Producer: Giorgio Gomelsky
Engineer: Keith Grant

ERIC CLAPTON
GUEST SESSION

DECCA STUDIOS
165 Broadhurst Gardens,
West Hampstead, London NW6
Session for Otis Spann

4 MAY 1964

PRETTY GIRLS EVERYWHERE (Eugene Church) Raw Blues album Decca Ace of Clubs ACL 1220 released 1967 / *The Blues Of Otis Spann...Plus* See For Miles SEECD 389 CD released in 1993 / *The Blues Of Otis Spann and Cracked Spannerhead* Beat Goes On BGOCD668 CD released in 2005

STIRS ME UP (Otis Spann) single A-side Decca F11972 (of "Pretty Girls Everywhere") / *The Blues Of Otis Spann...Plus* See For Miles SEECD 389 CD released in 1993

Otis Spann: piano, vocals
Ransome Knowling: bass
Muddy Waters: guitar
Willie Smith: drums
Eric Clapton: guitar

Producer: Mike Vernon
Engineer: Roy Baker

> "Muddy Waters was playing rhythm guitar and I played lead, which was strange, and it was two sides we did with Mike Vernon. It was great actually—they were both really friendly, you know, very encouraging. And they had these beautiful shiny suits, with big trousers. I was knocked out by the way they looked."
>
> **—ERIC CLAPTON**

OLYMPIC SOUND STUDIOS, STUDIO 1
Carton Hall, Carton Street, Marylebone, London W1

8 AUGUST 1964

The first session for "Good Morning Little Schoolgirl" was done without lead singer Keith Relf, who had suffered a collapsed lung brought on by his ongoing problems with asthma. This was his most serious setback so far, and he would be away from the band for six weeks recuperating. The session was booked and paid for, so the remaining band members had to turn up. Several takes were attempted until they had a backing track they were happy with. Although Eric sang this number in concert, it was decided that Keith should sing it for the studio version, even though it meant waiting until he was fit enough to return. "Got To Hurry" was recorded at the same session and was originally considered for the B-side. It was a real showcase number for Eric, and it was eventually used as a B-side to "For Your Love."

GOOD MORNING LITTLE SCHOOLGIRL (H. G. Demarais) backing track Train Kept A Rollin' 4CD box set Charly LIK Box 3 released 1993 / Yardbirds Story 1963–1966 Charly Records box set SNAJ736CD released March 2002

> "'Good Morning Little Schoolgirl' was Eric Clapton's idea of subject matter, which proves that despite statements to the contrary, he was just as concerned as we all were with resolving the marketing propaganda conundrum.
>
> We were able to get a mid afternoon session, not the best of times for working bands to record."
>
> **—GIORGIO GOMELSKY**
> (from the liner notes in the *Train Kept A Rollin'* box set)

> "We remembered this 'Good Morning Little Schoolgirl' from a rather obscure R&B artist—a friend of ours had it on a long-player. So we rushed in and recorded it."
>
> **—ERIC CLAPTON**

GOT TO HURRY (Oscar Rasputin) take 1 (unreleased)
GOT TO HURRY (Oscar Rasputin) take 2 false start *Train Kept A Rollin'* 4CD box set Charly LIK Box 3 released 1993 / *Yardbirds Story 1963–1966* Charly Records box set SNAJ736CD released March 2002
GOT TO HURRY (Oscar Rasputin) take 3 *Train Kept A Rollin'* 4CD box set Charly LIK Box 3 released 1993 / *Yardbirds Story 1963–1966* Charly Records box set SNAJ736CD released March 2002
GOT TO HURRY (Oscar Rasputin) take 4 (master) single B-side to "For Your Love" UK Columbia DB7499 released 5 March 1965, US Epic 5-9790 released 12 April 1965 / *Train Kept A Rollin'* 4CD box set Charly LIK Box 3 released 1993 / *Yardbirds Story 1963–1966* Charly Records box set SNAJ736CD released March 2002

Eric Clapton: guitar
Chris Dreja: guitar
Paul Samwell-Smith: bass
Jim McCarty: drums

Producer: Giorgio Gomelsky
Engineer: Keith Grant

"In those days, production protocol allowed for a three hour session to tape a single and its B-side. We had 20 minutes left to do the B-side and I was worried we might not get to do it, which would have been a disaster. So I told the boys over the studio intercom (the control room was one floor up from the recording room) that we had little time left and we had to hurry. Eric announced he had to take a leak, put down his guitar against his amplifier and disappeared to the toilet. I was sitting in the control room with Keith Grant, the engineer, when all of a sudden this intense and high-pitched sound comes through the speakers and drives the level meter right up into the red. Keith, afraid his mixer and his speakers would blow (Olympic Studios were not exactly rich themselves in those early days!), completely freaked out. We had no idea where this sound was coming from but we soon figured out it was Eric's guitar leaning on the amp—the level was so high we could hear it through the walls!

I thought it was amazing, all guitarists were trying to get that kind of 'sustain' to hold and bend notes around, besides we were all aware that new sounds electronically produced were just around the corner, so I convinced Keith to put a limiter on the guitar channel and see if we could get the sound without blowing the equipment and, by magic, it worked. It was all very intuitive. Just about then Eric came back from the loo and he, and the other band members, freaked out in turn. But the whole thing gave me the idea of trying to record it so Keith ran a machine. We still didn't have a B-side and everybody was so stunned no-one had any ideas, so I told them again we had to hurry and couldn't have a long discussion, to just start playing a blues riff I sang them over the intercom and put a couple of guitar solos in there and never mind the vocals. (That's why, justly or not, I, or rather O. Rasputin, got the credit for the song!) Fifteen minutes later the session was over and we had 'Got To Hurry' on tape, one take! When we listened to it, improvising adding reverb and other effects on the spot, everybody's jaws dropped!" —GIORGIO GOMELSKY

The Yardbirds onstage 20 September 1964 at the Odeon Theatre, Lewisham, London.

OLYMPIC SOUND STUDIOS STUDIO 1
Carton Hall, Carton Street, Marylebone, London W1

17 SEPTEMBER 1964

Keith Relf was well again by mid-September and would rejoin the band a few days into the Billy J Kramer package tour. The likely date for this recording is 17 September, as all the band are available to enter the studio. Keith overdubs vocals and harmonica for their new single "Good Morning Little Schoolgirl" and the band record a brand-new B-side called "I Ain't Got You," which highlights a short but fiery solo by Eric.

GOOD MORNING LITTLE SCHOOLGIRL (H. G. Demarais) backing track with harmonica overdub *Train Kept A Rollin'* 4CD box set Charly LIK Box 3 released 1993 / *Yardbirds Story 1963–1966* Charly Records box set SNAJ736CD released March 2002
GOOD MORNING LITTLE SCHOOLGIRL (H. G. Demarais) vocal overdub
GOOD MORNING LITTLE SCHOOLGIRL (H. G. Demarais) (master) single A-side UK-only release Columbia DB7391 released 30 October 1964 / *Train Kept A Rollin'* 4CD box set Charly LIK Box 3 released 1993 / *Yardbirds Story 1963–1966* Charly Records box set SNAJ736CD released March 2002
I AIN'T GOT YOU (Calvin Carter) single B-side of "Good Morning Little Schoolgirl" UK-only release Columbia DB7391 released 30 October 1964 / *Train Kept A Rollin'* 4CD box set Charly LIK Box 3 released 1993 / *Yardbirds Story 1963–1966* Charly Records box set SNAJ736CD released March 2002

Eric Clapton: guitar
Keith Relf: vocals
Chris Dreja: guitar
Paul Samwell-Smith: bass
Jim McCarty: drums

Producer: Giorgio Gomelsky
Engineer: Keith Grant

IBC STUDIOS
35 Portland Place, London W1

5 NOVEMBER 1964

EMI were pressuring the band to come up with a pop single. Label mate and friend Manfred Mann suggested Major Lance's "Sweet Music" and offered his services as producer. It was never released as a single but was eventually released on the US album *For Your Love* in 1965.

SWEET MUSIC (Walter Bowie, Otis Leavill Cobb, Major Lance) take 1 unreleased

SWEET MUSIC (Walter Bowie, Otis Leavill Cobb, Major Lance) take 2 unreleased

SWEET MUSIC (Walter Bowie, Otis Leavill Cobb, Major Lance) take 3 *Train Kept A Rollin'* 4CD box set Charly LIK Box 3 released 1993 / *Yardbirds Story 1963–1966* Charly Records box set SNAJ736CD released March 2002

SWEET MUSIC (Walter Bowie, Otis Leavill Cobb, Major Lance) take 4 *Train Kept A Rollin'* 4CD box set Charly LIK Box 3 released 1993 / *Yardbirds Story 1963–1966* Charly Records box set SNAJ736CD released March 2002

Eric Clapton: guitar
Keith Relf: vocals
Chris Dreja: guitar
Paul Samwell-Smith: bass
Jim McCarty: drums
Paul Jones: backing vocals

Producer: Manfred Mann
Engineer: –

> **"**'Sweet Music' came about somewhere between 'Good Morning Little Schoolgirl' and 'For Your Love.' It was a Major Lance B-side which our friend Manfred Mann thought would make a good single for the band, and offered to produce. I didn't feel this type of production particularly suited The Yardbirds style. It's in stereo though!**"**
>
> **—GIORGIO GOMELSKY**
> (from the liner notes in the *Train Kept A Rollin'* box set)

OLYMPIC SOUND STUDIOS STUDIO 1 Carton Hall, Carton Street, Marylebone, London W1

NOVEMBER 1964

PUTTY IN YOUR HANDS (K. Rogers, J. Patton) *For Your Love* US album EPIC LN24167 mono / BN26167 stereo July 1965 / *Train Kept A Rollin'* 4CD box set Charly LIK Box 3 released 1993 / *Yardbirds Story 1963–1966* Charly Records box set SNAJ736CD released March 2002

Eric Clapton: guitar
Keith Relf: vocals

> **"**This song predated 'For Your Love.' 'Putty In Your Hands' was the typical cover-version of little known American R&B songs which were the main body of the British blues bands' stage repertoire. We were always on the lookout for this type of material.**"** **—GIORGIO GOMELSKY**
> (from the liner notes in the *Train Kept A Rollin'* box set)

Chris Dreja: guitar
Paul Samwell-Smith: bass
Jim McCarty: drums

Producer: Giorgio Gomelsky
Engineer: Keith Grant

IBC STUDIOS 35 Portland Place, London W1

2 FEBRUARY 1965

FOR YOUR LOVE (Graham Gouldman) single A-side UK Columbia DB7499 released 5 March 1965, US Epic 5-9790 released 12 April 1965 / *For Your Love* US album EPIC LN24167 mono / BN26167 stereo July 1965 / *Train Kept A Rollin'* 4CD box set Charly LIK Box 3 released 1993 / *Yardbirds Story 1963–1966* Charly Records box set SNAJ736CD released March 2002

Eric Clapton: guitar
Keith Relf: vocals
Chris Dreja: guitar
Paul Samwell-Smith: bass
Jim McCarty: drums
Brian Auger: harpsichord
Ron Prentice: bowed bass
Denny Piercy: bongos

Producer: Giorgio Gomelsky
Engineer: –

> **"**Their most commercial so far. The group that has hovered on the brink of stardom for so long ought to hit big with this one. The arrangement is good.**"** **—MELODY MAKER**

JOHN MAYALL's BLUESBREAKERS

Eric's equipment:

Guitars: Fender Telecaster, Gibson ES 335, Gibson Les Paul (from May 1965)

Amp: Vox AC-30, Marshall JTM-45 (from June 1965), Marshall 100-watt (from November 1965)

Eric was not unemployed for long. John Mayall, who was well known among fans on the British blues scene, had not previously been impressed with Eric, or the Yardbirds for that matter. So when he heard of Eric's departure he thought nothing about it until he listened to "Got To Hurry," the B-side of the Yardbirds' last single to feature Eric, "For Your Love." John was very impressed with what he heard and felt that Eric could bring a new dimension to the sound of his band. He played the track to the band members and asked for their opinion. All the band except Roger Dean, that is. He was their guitarist, who was soon to be given his marching orders. It's not that Roger was a bad player, it was just that he could not play in the style of Freddie King or Buddy Guy. Everyone was in agreement that Eric was a good player and that he should be asked to join the band. "Got To Hurry" was a fabulous guitar instrumental showcase for Eric with sustain and feedback. At the time it was a highly unusual guitar sound and rightly gained him admiration from other guitar players and fans alike.

John approached Eric in late March 1965 at Ben Palmer's flat and asked if he would be interested in joining the band. Surprisingly, Eric was uncertain, which was strange, as John Mayall had a reputation of refusing to pander to the more commercial element of rhythm and blues. After a week of to-ing and fro-ing, John, in a final attempt to secure Eric, simply told him, "What have you got to lose?" After all, it was a blues band, and Eric wanted to play blues, so he finally agreed to at least give it a try. After the audition and rehearsals in London, Eric felt that John and the band would provide a more sympathetic environment for him, as well as give him some musical freedom.

After leaving the Yardbirds, Eric had been living at his grandparents' house and then with his friend Ben Palmer in Oxford. After joining, John Mayall let Eric lodge in a small room in his family home. Actually, it was more like a large broom cupboard, but nevertheless, it suited Eric at the time and gave him a bit of stability and room to practice, while also going through John's extensive collection of blues records. In his diaries, John noted that the first show Eric played with the Bluesbreakers was on 6 April 1965. That may well have been the audition date, but as John's diaries are no longer around, we will probably never know for sure.

There was already an established circuit of clubs that the Bluesbreakers would play at, and one of the regular places was the Flamingo in London's Soho. It was a great place to play, but not so good to get the gear in and out of the basement via a crowded staircase. Once you got on the stage it was very often extremely hot and cramped. On top of that the pay was low, but the gigs there seemed to have a magical feel, and many bands loved the atmosphere.

On the whole Eric was happy with his new position, but not so happy with the group's van setup. When they were touring, the band had a large transit-style van to go from gig to gig with only one fold-down bed, which was for John's use only. The rest of the band had to sleep on the floor, as John would never pay money for hotels. John was also pretty strict and did not tolerate anyone getting drunk, especially onstage. Bassist John McVie was the worst culprit in relation to the booze and would often have arguments with John Mayall. On at least one occasion, John kicked him out of the van and told him to make his own way home. John Mayall was fond of Eric and was more tolerant of bad behavior from him, although Eric was not really much of a handful at that time. At first the band would wear cocktail-hour-style uniforms when playing onstage. Eric did not like the idea of a uniform and slowly set about starting to get the band to project a younger image by wearing more trendy clothes. Eric would visit Portabello Road and buy military jackets and anything else that looked outrageous. John got the message and also let his hair grow longer.

Eric's first recordings with the Bluesbreakers were for a BBC session on the 26 April. Although he had yet to achieve what everyone knows as the classic Bluesbreakers sound, his playing is much more confident than with the Yardbirds. Eric was starting to find his own voice and identity. Eric was still largely playing his Fender Telecaster and occasionally his Gibson ES 335 at this point. It would not be until May 1965 that he decided to buy a second hand 1959 Gibson Les Paul Standard guitar from Lew Davis's shop in London's Charing Cross Road. Eric had been inspired to buy one after seeing the cover of Freddie King's album *Let's Hide Away And Dance Away*, on which he's playing a Goldtop Les Paul. In fact, Eric had really wanted a Goldtop, but could only get the Sunburst Les Paul, which had the two chrome-plated pickup covers removed. Eric recalled that it was made in Gibson's best year, which would make it a '59 or '60. It was also the year of declining sales for them, with only a few hundred being manufactured. One can only imagine the value of an original today. It had a unique tone and would soon forge the classic sound of the Bluesbreakers when plugged into a Marshall JTM-45 amp, which he also bought around this time, replacing his 30-watt Vox amp. Another big change to the sound was Mayall changing his Farfisa organ to a Hammond M-100.

By June, Eric had moved in with poet and sometime puppeteer, Ted Milton, in 74 Long Acre, above a fruit wholesaler in London's arty Covent Garden area. Eric and Ted were friends, and the flat had been rented by Ted's girlfriend, Clarissa. Before long, several of Ted's other friends also moved into the flat, as well as an adjacent property. These were Ben Palmer, a mutual friend and pianist from the Roosters, trumpeter and soon-to-be bassist Bob Rae, a friend of Ben's, Bernie Greenwood; a medical student who played tenor sax in Chris Farlowe's Thunderbirds; musicologist and singer John Baily; and Ted's brother, student Jake Milton. They all loved their wine and would drink many bottles during the evenings, smoke pot, listen to records, and generally make a nuisance of themselves until Clarissa would have enough and would chuck everyone out. This happened on a regular basis. It was on one of these crazy evenings that this madcap group mapped out the beginnings of an idea of forming a band and traveling around the world, with Greece as the first destination. By August, the tentative plans were fast turning into a reality when Bernie bought a nine-seater 1953 Ford Fairlane station wagon, nicknamed the Glandsmobile, for this motley crew to travel in along with their gear. The band referred to themselves collectively as the Glands, although they were never officially billed under that name. Ted Milton decided not to go on the adventure and volunteered his brother, Jake, who was a bebop drummer. He was a student on holiday and thought it might be a laugh to join the party. Little did he know!

On the face of it, it would be easy to think that Eric would have been unwise to throw away his job with Mayall just as he was receiving a lot of positive attention from the public and press alike, not to mention the imminent release of his first appearance on a John Mayall single, which would more than likely be followed by an album. But as you can see from this book, Eric as a young man had worked very hard with no recreation to speak of. The thought of an exciting adventure with some friends seemed irresistible. Eric wisely talked to John about his plans before giving notice and explained in great detail why he wanted to try it. He had a close relationship with John and asked him if he would take him back if it all came to nothing.

John knew that Eric was an asset and agreed to leave his job open for him with no conditions. I am pretty sure John did not extend this courtesy to any other players.

John Baily had already traveled to Greece ahead of the rest of the band to secure some bookings that would bring money in for the next stage of the trip. The group set off in the Glandsmobile in September, making a stop at the famous yearly Oktoberfest in Munich, Germany. A beer festival, for this group, seemed like a must. Unfortunately, this is nearly where the trip ended when a very drunk Bernie lit a cigarette with a one-pound note. This act incensed Bob Rae, a fierce proletarian, who went apoplectic at the sight of such a middle-class indulgence. The arguments raged on for hours before getting physical, by which point Eric and Jake wanted to head off home. Some of the others wanted to head off by themselves, and everyone started to unload their things from the car. By morning everyone had sobered up and calmed down and the trip resumed. They finally arrived in Athens at the end of September and were reunited with John Baily. By this time drummer Jake Milton had had enough, as there had been more arguments, wind-ups, and teasing during the long road trip in the confines of the car. Furthermore, he was concerned that he would have to pay back his college grants back home if he did not attend the classes. That sealed it for him, and he waved goodbye to everyone before even playing a note.

The gig that John Baily had organized for the group was at a club called the Igloo in Athens. As they had never actually played together before, they rehearsed for a day with a stand-in Greek drummer. Wisely, Eric suggested they should be called the Faces, rather than the Glands, and play well-known covers of hits by people such as the Rolling Stones, the Kinks, Chuck Berry, the Beatles, and Ray Charles. as well as a few blues numbers. After passing the audition with the Igloo's owner, the band had a deal that gave them rooms and food at a local hotel, which was paid for by the club, but they would receive no cash at first. They played the support slot to local headliners the Juniors six nights a week, with Tuesdays off, from 7 October 1965 onward. Unfortunately, on 10 October 1965 the Juniors were involved in a serious road accident that killed organist Thanos Sogioul and manager Giannis Krasoudis. Their guitar player, Alekos Karakadas, survived but was in serious condition and would be unable to play for many months. Eric generously offered to step in on guitar and ended up playing with his own band as well as in the Juniors, which stretched his workload to something like twelve hours a night, from 7:00 p.m. to 7:00 a.m. He also played a commemorative concert with the Juniors in honor of the two members of the band that had died in the accident. It was a special Sunday-afternoon concert that took place at the Cine-Terpsithea in Piraeus.

By now the owner of the Igloo was aware that Eric had been in the Yardbirds, who had a smash hit with "For Your Love." He wanted to keep Eric playing at the club as it was good for business. But Eric wanted out until it was made clear to him that any attempt by him to leave would result in physical violence. The club owner was always surrounded by heavies and pointed out to the band that as they had no work permits, they could not go anywhere else. He also claimed to have the local police chief in his pocket. Eric realized that subterfuge was the only possible course of action in a situation that had rapidly become very sinister. A plan was quickly hatched between Gland band members. On Sunday 24 October, Eric left his Marshall amp at the club as usual to make it seem like he was coming back for his regular evening slot but took his prized Les Paul guitar with him to the afternoon concert he was playing with the Juniors at the run-down Cine-Terpsithea in Piraeus. He used their guitarist's amp. The Igloo owner had no reason to suspect Eric would not be coming back as he had organized the afternoon commemorative show. Ben knew somebody in Athens that could sell the band's instruments and amps. This was done to get enough money for Ben, Bob, and Eric to buy railway tickets back home and for Bernie and John to get out of Greece. Meanwhile, the UK band arranged to meet Eric after the show in the "Glandsmobile." Eric jumped in and together with Ben Palmer and Bob Rae made their way to Larissa rail station in Athens and headed home on a journey that would take three days. To their credit, Bernie Greenwood and John Baily stuck to the plan and continued on their journey around the world.

With Eric gone, John had auditioned several guitarists on a trial-by-night basis. These included John Weider, John Slaughter, Jeff Krivit, and Peter Green. The latter was in the band for only a few shows before John got a call from Eric at the end of October asking for his job back. Poor old Peter Green only got

to play one or two shows before being replaced. Mike Vernon was another person Eric called on his return to enquire if there were any sessions he could do, as he needed some money. Mike was only too happy to invite both Eric and John Mayall to play on a session for Champion Jack Dupree's new album, which also featured Tony McPhee and Keef Hartley.

On his return to the Bluesbreakers, Eric found that Jack Bruce was now on bass instead of John McVie, who had been fired. Eric really enjoyed having Jack in the group. The whole dynamic changed, and the songs became more experimental. Eric was very impressed with Jack's improvisational skills, and together they gave the Bluesbreakers a new dimension. To a certain extent it became the Eric and Jack show, but if John Mayall minded, he was not showing it. And why would he as the band were getting rave reviews.

As much as Jack was enjoying playing with Eric he was not happy at the poor pay and like Eric and the rest of the band, hated the fact that John Mayall had the only bed in the van. When a more lucrative offer came in from Manfred Mann at the end of November, Jack did not hesitate and accepted. As a result of his defection, John and Eric quickly set about recording "Double Crossing Man," with lyrics aimed at Jack. Although planned as a B-side to a proposed new single for Immediate Records, the song is not completed and the single never comes out. It was eventually finished during the album sessions a few months later as "Double Crossing Time."

After a few stand-in bass players, John Mayall offered John McVie his old job back by early January 1966 for what is now considered to be the classic Bluesbreakers lineup. They were offered a new deal with Decca Records after some persuasion from Mike Vernon, and the band booked into Decca Studios at the end of March to record one of the most defining blues albums of the British Blues movement of the '60s. Eric could now afford to be cocky and was fully aware of his talent. When the engineers said he could not play his guitar at full volume he explained that it was their problem to solve as that is how he played live. There was no way he was going to compromise his sound for a bunch of suits. In those days, engineers at Decca had to wear suits and ties and were pretty conservative. Pushing the volume knobs past four or five was a no-no. Gus Dudgeon was freaking out, telling anyone who would listen that Eric's guitar was impossible to record. With some advice from fellow Decca engineer Derek Varnals, they solved the problem with different mic placements and a few extra screens. Eric's determination, come stubbornness, opened up new avenues of production methods for producer Mike Vernon. The resultant album still captures the imagination of any guitar player who listens to it.

Recording an album and singing lead vocals on "Ramblin' On My Mind" gave Eric confidence, and mentally he was starting to get itchy feet. He really enjoyed being in the Bluesbreakers but was starting to feel like his musical roots were in Chicago and was getting increasingly impatient to go over there. Had John Mayall been offered an American tour in 1966, Eric's musical history could well have changed. The catalyst for Eric's departure came when Ginger Baker sat in with the Bluesbreakers at a gig in Oxford on 13 May 1966. Ginger offered to drive Eric home after the show, and on the journey he asked Eric if he would like to be in a band he was thinking of forming. When Eric realized that he was the first person asked, he suggested Jack Bruce as the bass player. Ginger was adamant that he would not consider Jack, because the two of them had fallen out very badly many times during their time together in the Graham Bond Organization. Eric had no idea about the history between the two musicians but dug his heels in, saying that after playing with Jack in the Bluesbreakers he would only consider him for the bass player in any band he would be joining. For the sake of the group, Ginger went to see Jack and his wife Janet at their Hampstead home and made a truce with Jack, and soon the three of them started rehearsing in secret. Eventually, of course, these things have a habit of coming out, especially when a band member tips the press off. Ginger knew exactly what he was doing by calling his mate at the *Melody Maker*. This time it was a rather public outing by Chris Welch on the front page of the *Melody Maker* in the 11 June edition, with the headline announcing the formation of a sensational "Groups' Group" starring Eric Clapton, Jack Bruce, and Ginger Baker. The only problem was that John Mayall, Manfred Mann, and Graham Bond had no idea they were about to lose their key players.

John was fuming and tried to get Eric to change his mind. But Eric was already too committed mentally to reverse his decision. John accepted four weeks' notice, and Eric was replaced by Peter Green on 18 July 1966.

APRIL 1965

As no tapes are available from this period, the only clue we have to the numbers played are drawn from reviews and eyewitness reports.

SETLISTS BETWEEN APRIL 1965 AND AUGUST 1965 WERE TAKEN FROM THE FOLLOWING SELECTION OF MAYALL ORIGINALS AND COVER VERSIONS: "Crawling Up A Hill," "Crocodile Walk," "Chicago Line," "Bye Bye Bird" (Sonny Boy Williamson song), "I Need Your Love," "Heartache," "Hideaway" (Freddie King number), "My Baby's Sweeter" (a Willie Dixon number made popular by Little Walter), "I Ain't Got You" (Jimmy Reed number), "Bad Boy" (Eddie Taylor number), "The Last Meal" (a Jimmy Rogers number).

9 April 1965, King Mojo Club, Sheffield, South Yorkshire

10 April 1965, The Lyric, Dinnington, South Yorkshire (with Screaming Lord Sutch)

11 April 1965, Le Metro Club, Birmingham, West Midlands

13 April 1965, Grand R&B Concert, Haymarket Theatre, Basingstoke, Hampshire (along with the Evil Eyes support to headliner Them [featuring Van Morrison])

15 April 1965, Waterfront Club, Southampton, Hampshire

16 April 1965, Ricky Tick, Plaza Ballroom, Guildford, Surrey

17 April 1965, Flamingo Club, Soho, London (with Geno Washington and the Ram Jam Band from 7:30 p.m. to 11:30 p.m. A regular haunt for John Mayall, this is Eric's first appearance at the Soho club. Owned by Jeffrey Kruger, the two clubs, Flamingo and the All Nighter, have earned a good reputation for serious music since opening its doors in 1962)

19 April 1965, King Mojo Club, Sheffield, South Yorkshire (with Tony Knight's Chessman, Rod Stuart & the Soul Agents, the Blues Herd, the Sheffields. All-night session from 7:30 until 11:00 p.m. followed by another from 11:30 p.m. until 6:00 a.m.)

22 April 1965, Flamingo Club, Soho, London (billed as "John Mayall Night")

23 April 1965, John Mayall's Bluesbreakers play live on *Ready Steady Goes Live!* from Rediffusion Television Studios, Studio 1, Wembley Park Drive, Wembley, Middlesex. They play "Crocodile Walk" and "What I'd Say." The program is hosted by Cathy McGowan. John Hammond Jr. is also on the program and tells *Record Mirror*, "The scene here is really good and the groups feel for the blues. My favourite is John Mayall. I just can't say enough good things about him."

23 April 1965, Flamingo All Nighter Club, Soho, London

24 April 1965, Rendezvous Club, Oddfellows Hall, Portsmouth, Hampshire (with Hogsnort Rupert's Good Good Band. Eric can't have been pleased to read today's *Record Mirror*, whose gossip columnist boldly states what many fans have been thinking since Eric's departure from the Yardbirds: "Eric Clapton can't seriously think John Mayall is a better prospect than The Yardbirds")

26 April 1965, pre-recording session for *Saturday Club* recorded at the BBC's Maida Vale Studios, 4 Delaware Road, London W4

Songs recorded between 4:30 p.m. and 6:30 p.m. are:

CRAWLING UP A HILL (John Mayall) *Blues Breakers* 2CD Deluxe Edition Decca 984 180-1 released November 2006 / *John Mayall and the Bluesbreakers Live* at the BBC CD Decca 984 466-5 released 2007

John Mayall: vocal, organ, harmonica
Eric Clapton: guitar
John McVie: bass
Hughie Flint: drums

CROCODILE WALK (John Mayall) Blues Breakers 2CD Deluxe Edition Decca 984 180-1 released November 2006 / John Mayall and the Bluesbreakers Live at the BBC CD Decca 984 466-5 released 2007

John Mayall: vocal, organ
Eric Clapton: guitar
John McVie: bass
Hughie Flint: drums

BYE BYE BIRD (Willie Dixon / Sonny Boy Williamson) Blues Breakers 2CD Deluxe Edition Decca 984 180-1 released November 2006 / John Mayall and the Bluesbreakers Live at the BBC CD Decca 984 466-5 released 2007

John Mayall: vocal, harmonica
Eric Clapton: guitar
John McVie: bass
Hughie Flint: drums

Other songs recorded and broadcast, but sadly lost: "Heartache," "Hideaway" (Freddy King instrumental). Show is broadcast on 1 May 1965. Eric is clearly playing his Fender Telecaster on this session.

27 April 1965, Bluesday Club, Rhodes Centre, Bishops Stortford, Hertfordshire (now the Bluesbreakers have appeared on television, they can be billed as "The Bluesday Club presents the outstanding R&B TV and Recording Stars John Mayall's Bluesbreakers")

30 April 1965, Flamingo Club, Soho, London

MAY 1965

1 May 1965, CubiKlub, Rochdale, Lancashire (with the Country Gents and five other unbilled bands. All-nighter from 7:00 p.m. to 7:00 a.m.)

4 May 1965, appearance on ITV-Rediffusion's *Ollie and Fred's Five O'Clock Club*, probably playing "Crocodile Walk." No tape has survived of this show. ITV were attempting to emulate the BBC's consistent success with children's shows by coming up with a cross between *Blue Peter* and *Crackerjack*

8 May 1965, Twisted Wheel, Manchester, Lancashire (early and late sets supported by Tea Time 4)

9 May 1965, Dungeon Club, Nottingham, Nottinghamshire

10 May 1965, Bluesville Club, Manor House Ballroom, Ipswich, Suffolk

12 May 1965, recording with Bob Dylan, CBS Studios (formerly Levy Sound Studios) in London

14 May 1965, Fender Club, Churchill Hall, Kenton, Harrow, Middlesex (early evening show)

14 May 1965, Ricky Tick, Plaza ballroom, Guildford, Surrey (late evening show. With John Lee Hooker, who is backed by Cops 'n' Robbers)

15 May 1965, Arbor Youth Club, Pyrford, Surrey

15 May 1965, Flamingo All-Nighter Club, Soho, London (from midnight until dawn with Geno Washington & the Ram Jam Band)

16 May 1965, Riverside Club, Cricketers Hotel, Chertsey, Surrey

21 May 1965, Flamingo All-Nighter Club, Soho, London (from midnight until dawn with Zoot Money's Big Roll Band)

22 May 1965, Flamingo All-Nighter Club, Soho, London (from midnight until dawn with Herbie Goins & the Night-Timers)

Advert for an appearance by John Mayall's Bluesbreakers at the Cubiklub in Rochdale on 1 May 1965.

24 May 1965, Cromwellian Club, Cromwell Road, London (the Brian Auger Trio are joined on the tiny stage by Eric Clapton, Eric Burdon, Hilton Valentine, Chas Chandler [all three from the Animals], Spencer Davis, and Zoot Money)

25 May 1965, Klooks Kleek R&B Club, Railway Hotel, West Hampstead, London (with Champion Jack Dupree)

28 May 1965, Club A Go Go, Newcastle, Tyne & Wear

29 May 1965, King Mojo Club, Sheffield, Yorkshire

30 May 1965, Kirklevington Country Club, Kirklevington, Yorkshire

JUNE 1965

3 June 1965, Cellar Club, Kingston-upon-Thames, Surrey

CELLAR CLUB
22a HIGH STREET, KINGSTON, SURREY
KIN 5856 / 6240

On WEDNESDAY, JUNE 3rd from America
THE GREAT
JOHN LEE HOOKER
with the
JOHN MAYALL BLUES BREAKERS
supported by the exciting new group
THE PLEBS
Admission: Members 7/6. Non-members 10/-
Commencing 8 p.m.

Advert for an appearance by John Mayall's Bluesbreakers at the Cellar Club in Kingston, Surrey, on 3 June 1965.

Advert for an appearance by John Mayall's Bluesbreakers at the Ricky Tick in Guildford on 4 June 1965.

4 June 1965, Ricky Tick, Plaza Ballroom, Guildford, Surrey

4 June 1965, Flamingo All-Nighter Club, Soho, London (from midnight until dawn with Herbie Goins & the Night-Timers)

5 June 1965, New Georgian Club, Uxbridge, Middlesex (early evening)

5 June 1965, Flamingo All-Nighter Club, Soho, London (from midnight until dawn with Chris Farlowe and the Thunderbirds)

6 June 1965, Flamingo All-Nighter Club, Soho, London (from midnight until dawn)

7 June 1965, Blue Moon Club, Hayes, Middlesex

9 June 1965, Orford Cellar Club, Norwich, Norfolk

10 June 1965, Klooks Kleek R&B Club, Railway Hotel, West Hampstead, London

12 June 1965, R&B-ville, Galaxy Club, Town Hall, Basingstoke, Hampshire

17 June 1965, Hull University Hullabaloo Ball, Locarno Ballroom, Hull, Humberside (with the Fourmost, Sounds Incorporated)

18 June 1965, Pontiac Club, Zeeta House, Putney, London

THE 1965 BLUES and FOLK FESTIVAL
Programme of Events
◆ ◆ ◆

Your compere for the afternoon session :
Star Radio Luxembourg D.J. and Record Mirror columnist
TONY HALL

SHOW OPENS 2.30 p.m. SHARP!
2.30 p.m.   RAY MARTIN GROUP
2.50 p.m.   JOHN MAYALLS BLUESBREAKERS
3.15 p.m.   ZOOT MONEYS BIG ROLL BAND
3.25 p.m.   SOLOMON BURKE (backed by Zoot Money)
3.45 p.m.   THE WHO
4.15 p.m.   SPENCER DAVIS GROUP
4.45 p.m.   MARIANNE FAITHFULL
5.00 p.m.   THE BIRDS
5.30 p.m.   DAVID WHITTLING - Folk Singer
5.45 p.m.   LONG JOHN BALDRY
Afternoon session finishes at 6.30 p.m. then re-opens again with the Evening Festival Dance at 7.30 p.m.

Festival Dance . . .
featuring **CLIFF BENNETT**
and the REBEL ROUSERS
LONG JOHN BALDRY
and the HOOCHIE COOCHIE MEN
plus RAY MARTIN GROUP

the whole show finishes around 11.30 p.m. by this time we sincerely trust you've had a great day with the show.
SEE YOU NEXT YEAR !!

Program of events including an appearance by John Mayall's Bluesbreakers at the Uxbridge Blues and Folk Festival on 19 June 1965.

19 June 1965, Uxbridge Blues & Folk Festival, Uxbridge Showgrounds, Uxbridge, Middlesex (they are scheduled to play at 2:50 p.m.)

19 June 1965, Ricky Tick, Clewer Mead, Windsor, Berkshire (evening show)

Rare poster advertising for an appearance by John Mayall's Bluesbreakers at the Uxbridge Blues and Folk Festival on 19 June 1965.

20 June 1965, Galaxy Club, Woburn Park Hotel, Addlestone, Surrey

26 June 1965, Rag Day Hop, Roundhay Park, Leeds, Yorkshire (with the Four Pennies. Melody Maker's "The Raver" column is suitably impressed: "Eric Clapton is a knockout with John Mayall's Bluesbreakers")

"Being 16 and playing guitar in one of the top bands in Blackpool in the early 1960's was pretty cool; the world was our oyster even though we only made £2 per night each.

Just 30 miles down the road in Preston another band David John & The Mood were also getting tremendous local and national recognition. They not only played their own brand of R&B to packed audiences they also had that icon of rock star trimmings—a van! They were really far ahead of their time—playing Stones R&B before the Stones and influencing a whole new raft of bands and artists such as The Pretty Things and even David Bowie. Despite being acclaimed as one of the best bands in the UK and recording with the legendary Joe Meek they never quite made the big time.

My band became friends with 'Miffy' (David John Smith) the lead singer and also the other members of the Mood and often we would travel to Preston to hang out together. One hot Friday night in July I caught the train to Preston with the keyboard player from my band to meet up with Miffy and the rest of the guys. When we got there we found out that we were all going to the Cubiklub in Rochdale to see Clive Kelly and also to watch John Mayall's Bluesbreakers, a band I had never heard of.

We pulled up outside and walked into the Cubiklub. Kelly was there larger than life and although the club wasn't licensed Kelly's office which was on the left hand side as you entered the club entertained a fully stocked bar. It also served as the band dressing room.

The Cubiklub had a strange stage set up. It was almost two different stages separated by a narrow wall. Mayall was already playing and had taken over the right hand side of the stage with his Hammond organ, box full of harmonicas and a Burns amp stuck on top of the Hammond that served as a PA system and also added a wonderful warm distortion to his harmonica playing. On the left hand side of the stage there was a bass player, drummer and a skinny guy with a crew cut sat on a small stool playing a blonde Fender Telecaster.

The club was empty with only a few die hards hanging around. I listened to a couple of songs from Mr. Mayall but as I couldn't make out any of the lyrics I was a little unsure just what was going on. It seemed a very strange little outfit, there was Mayall wailing away, the drummer was far too jazzy for my taste the guitarist looked bored and the bass player had a shit sound.

I was losing interest quickly when all of a sudden this skinny guitar player let rip. I was totally in shock…

Not only was he playing some really cool stuff he was bending his strings to reach notes. I had never seen or heard this kind of playing before, sure we all pushed our standard gauge strings a little, but this guy was bending like they were elastic.

My jaw must have dropped at least a foot it was like a religious experience.

I stayed to watch the whole set and followed this guitarist into the office/dressing room like a love struck idiot.

He put the Telecaster into a battered case and I just stood there looking at it as though it was the Holy Grail. Someone shoved a beer in my hand and I finally woke up. 'How the f*cking hell do you bend your strings like that' I asked the skinny one.

'Oh it's easy' he replied 'Look I'll show you. I use a banjo third instead of a standard guitar third and you can get some really terrific bends, look.'

He then spent the next 30 minutes showing me how to get some great effects, up bending and down bending and allowing me to try on his guitar in-between his tuition. He advised me to buy 'Clifford Essex' strings and also where to get them. We then sat and talked guitars for about an hour before a reprise of the guitar lesson. I thanked him, said that not only would I change my strings, I would also sell my Gretsch and buy a Fender.

When we all got back in the van to travel back to Preston I was on a high and kept telling the guys what a great guitar player Mr. Skinny was and such a really nice guy. 'Yeah,' said Miffy, 'I loved his playing. I'd like to see him again his name's…Eric Clapton.'

I have told the story over and over again and not many believed that at 17 years old I had a one-on-one guitar lesson from Eric Clapton. I have played a Fender ever since and I used Clifford Essex strings right up until they eventually invented the light gauge sets. My one-on-one with Eric changed my life. I fortunately got to tell him and thank him again several years later."

—JOHN WILLIAMS (guitarist)

JULY 1965

2 July 1965, CubiKlub, Rochdale, Lancashire

7 July 1965, Bromel Club, Bromley Court Hotel, Bromley, Kent

8 July 1965, Klooks Kleek R&B Club, Railway Hotel, West Hampstead, London

10 July 1965, Flamingo Club, Soho, London (evening set with the Stormsville Shakers)

10 July 1965, Flamingo All-Nighter Club, Soho, London (from midnight until dawn with Tony Knight's Chessmen)

Advert for an appearance by John Mayall's Bluesbreakers at the Blue Moon Club in Hayes, Middlesex, on 11 July 1965.

11 July 1965, the Blue Moon Club, Hayes, Middlesex

12 July 1965, Rhythm & Bluesville, Galaxy Club, Town Hall, Basingstoke, Hampshire

14 July 1965, Orford Cellar Club, Norwich, Norfolk

Advert for an appearance by John Mayall's Bluesbreakers at the London College of Fashion on 15 July 1965.

15 July 1965, London College of Fashion, London

16 July 1965, Ricky Tick, Plaza Ballroom, Guildford, Surrey (early evening)

16 July 1965, Flamingo All-Nighter Club, Soho, London (from midnight until dawn with Inez & Charles Foxx)

18 July 1965, Gaumont Theatre, Bournemouth, Dorset (two shows 06:30 p.m. and 08:45 p.m. as support to headliners the Rolling Stones. Also on the bill are: Tommy Quickly & the Remo 4, the Paramounts, Twinkle with Bobby Rio and the Reveilles, the Steam Packet with Long John Baldry, Brian Auger, Rod Stewart and Julie Driscoll, John Mayall's Bluesbreakers)

19 July 1965, Rhythm & Bluesville, Galaxy Club, Town Hall, Basingstoke, Hampshire

20 July 1965, Marquee Club, London (with Spencer Davis Group, Moody Blues, Chris Farlowe & the Thunderbirds, and the Mark Leeman Five. Benefit for Mark Leeman's widow. Mark was killed in a car accident in June on his return from a summer show in Blackpool with Manfred Mann. The Mark Leeman Five carry on using the name in the singer's honor)

22 July 1965, Bowes Lyon House, Stevenage, Hertfordshire

23 July 1965, Il Rondo Club, Leicester, Leicestershire

24 July 1965, Bluesday Club, Rhodes Centre, Bishop's Stortford, Hertforshire (early evening with the Sugar Beats)

24 July 1965, Flamingo All-Nighter Club, Soho, London (from midnight until dawn with Tony Knight's Chessmen)

25 July 1965, Blue Moon Club, Hayes, Middlesex

26 July 1965, Rhythm & Bluesville, Galaxy Club, Town Hall, Basingstoke, Hampshire

Adverts for an appearance by John Mayall's Bluesbreakers at the Ricky Tick in Guildford on 16 July 1965.

28 July 1965, Blue Indigo Club, Southampton, Hampshire

29 July 1965, Klooks Kleek R&B Club, Railway Hotel, West Hampstead, London

30 July 1965, Bluesville R&B Club, Manor House, Finsbury Park, London

AUGUST 1965

1 August 1965, Boat Club, Nottingham, Nottinghamshire

2 August 1965, Majestic Ballroom, Newport, Wales (with the Cellar Set)

4 August 1965, Pontiac Club, Zeeta House, Putney, London (start of two month residency at the Putney club. Jimmy Page and Jeff Beck joined John Mayall's Bluesbreakers one night at the Pontiac Club, and tonight is a likely date, as Eric and Jimmy record some informal jams in early August at Jimmy's house in Epsom)

6 August 1965, Fender Club, Churchill Hall, Kenton, Harrow, Middlesex

Advert for an appearance by John Mayall's Bluesbreakers at the Fender Club in Harrow, Middlesex, on 6 August 1965.

7 August 1965, New Georgian Club, Cowley, Uxbridge, Middlesex (early evening)

7 August 1965, Flamingo All-Nighter Club, Soho, London (from midnight until dawn with Zoot Money's Big Roll Band)

11 August 1965, Pontiac Club, Zeeta House, Putney, London (filmed by Peter Manley on behalf of Clarendon Productions as part of four twenty-minute films under the title *Romance And Courtships Throughout The World*. Manley recalled, "Pattie Boyd's sister, Jenny, is playing the part of the girl in London film. We have already shot in India, Thailand and Hong Kong." Sadly, so far I have been unable to trace the footage and it may well be lost)

15 August 1965, Cellar Club, Kingston-upon-Thames, Surrey

16 August 1965, Bluesville Club, Manor House Ballroom, Ipswich, Suffolk

Rare photo of John Mayall, John McVie, and Eric Clapton at their Pontiac Club residency in Putney in August 1965.

18 August 1965, Pontiac Club, Zeeta House, Putney, London

21 August 1965, Flamingo Club, Soho, London (evening set with Tony Cotton's Big Boss Men)

21 August 1965, Flamingo All-Nighter Club, Soho, London (from midnight until dawn with Herbie Goins & the Night-Timers)

22 August 1965, Galaxy Club, Woburn Park Hotel, Addlestone, Surrey

24 August 1965, Klooks Kleek, Railway Hotel, West Hampstead, London

Rare photo of Eric Clapton and John McVie at the Pontiac Club in Putney in August 1965.

25 August 1965, Pontiac Club, Zeeta House, Putney, London

28 August 1965, Flamingo All-Nighter Club, Soho, London (from midnight until dawn with Tony Knight's Chessmen)

30 August 1965, Black Prince, Bexley, Kent (Eric's last show before leaving with his mates in the Glands)

SEPTEMBER 1965

The Glands head off to Greece in their Ford Fairlane across mainline Europe. They wind their way through Germany until they get to Munich in time for the annual Oktoberfest, a two-week celebration of beer drinking and partying. After Germany they carry on and eventually drive through Yugoslavia and cross into Greece on the 23 September. They finally get to Athens on 29 September.

OCTOBER 1965

The Glands secure a contract to play a nightclub in Athens called the Igloo in a support slot to the local headliners, the Juniors

7 October 1965–10 October 1965, Igloo Club, Ioannou Drosopoulou, Kipseli, Athens, Greece

11 October 1965–23 October 1965, Igloo Club, Ioannou Drosopoulou, Kipseli, Athens, Greece

24 October 1965, Cine-Terpsithea, Piraeus, Greece (last gig before Eric makes his escape)

NOVEMBER 1965

SETLISTS BETWEEN NOVEMBER 1965 AND JULY 1966 WERE TAKEN FROM THE FOLLOWING SELECTION OF MAYALL ORIGINALS AND SEVERAL COVER VERSIONS: I'm Your Witchdoctor, Double Crossing Time, Maudie (John Lee Hooker), It Hurts To Be In Love (Julius Edwards Dixon / Rudy Toombs), Have You Ever Loved A Woman (Billy Myles), Bye Bye Bird (Willie Dixon / Sonny Boy Williamson), Hoochie Coochie Man (Willie Dixon), Stormy Monday (T-Bone Walker), Little Girl, Hideaway (Freddy King, Sonny Thompson), Parchman Farm (Mose Alison), Tears In My Eyes, On Top Of The World, Key To Love, Burned My Fingers, All Your Love (Otis Rush), Hi-Heel Sneakers (Robert Higginbotham), What'd I Say (Ray Charles), Steppin' Out (LC Frazier), It Ain't Right (Walter Jacobs).

4 November 1965, Decca Studios, West Hampstead (Eric and John Mayall play on a session for Champion Jack Dupree)

4 November 1965, Blue Triangle Club, Ealing, London (Eric's first gig with Mayall after his return from Greece. Jack Bruce is now on bass having replaced John McVie in October)

6 November 1965, BEA/BOAC Sports & Social function, London Airport, Heathrow, Middlesex

> **"**It was a huge hall, more like an aircraft hangar. It was probably a sports and social club for the staff.**"** —HUGHIE FLINT

7 November 1965, Flamingo Club, Soho, London (parts of the show were recorded by John Mayall on his portable Grundig recorder)

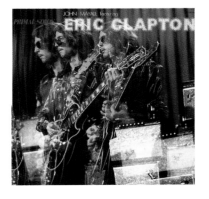

Rare Japanese album sleeve for Primal Solos *featuring live tracks recorded at the Flamingo Club on 7 November 1965.*

SETLIST (INCOMPLETE):

Maudie (John Lee Hooker) *Primal Solos* album US London Records LC 50003, UK Decca TAB66 released 1983 / *Blues Breakers* 2CD Deluxe Edition Decca 984 180-1 released November 2006

```
John Mayall: vocal, organ, harmonica
Eric Clapton: guitar
Jack Bruce: six-string bass
Hughie Flint: drums
```

It Hurts To Be In Love (Julius Edwards Dixon / Rudy Toombs) *Primal Solos* album US London Records LC 50003, UK Decca TAB66 released 1983 / *Blues Breakers* 2CD Deluxe Edition Decca 984 180-1 released November 2006

```
John Mayall: vocal, organ
Eric Clapton: guitar
Jack Bruce: six-string bass
Hughie Flint: drums
```

Have You Ever Loved A Woman (Billy Myles) *Primal Solos* album US London Records LC 50003, UK Decca TAB66 released 1983 / *Blues Breakers* 2CD Deluxe Edition Decca 984 180-1 released November 2006

John Mayall: vocal, organ
Eric Clapton: guitar
Jack Bruce: six-string bass
Hughie Flint: drums

Bye Bye Bird (Willie Dixon / Sonny Boy Williamson) *Primal Solos* album US London Records LC 50003, UK Decca TAB66 released 1983 / *Blues Breakers* 2CD Deluxe Edition Decca 984 180-1 released November 2006

John Mayall: vocal, harmonica
Eric Clapton: guitar
Jack Bruce: six-string bass
Hughie Flint: drums

Hoochie Coochie Man (Willie Dixon) *Primal Solos* album US London Records LC 50003, UK Decca TAB66 released 1983 / *Blues Breakers* 2CD Deluxe Edition Decca 984 180-1 released November 2006

John Mayall: vocal, organ, harmonica
Eric Clapton: guitar
Jack Bruce: six-string bass
Hughie Flint: drums

Stormy Monday (T-Bone Walker) *Looking Back* album US London PS662, UK Decca SKL 4804 released September 1969 / *Blues Breakers* 2CD Deluxe Edition Decca 984 180-1 released November 2006

John Mayall: vocal, organ
Eric Clapton: guitar
Jack Bruce: six-string bass
Hughie Flint: drums
Producer: John Mayall

9 November 1965, Scotch Of St James, London (Eric jams with Wilson Pickett and members of the Animals, who are backing him for this evening. Ahmet Ertegun, founder of Atlantic Records, is in the audience tonight, having flown over with Pickett. He is very impressed with Eric's playing skills and his star-quality demeanor)

Advert for an appearance by John Mayall's Bluesbreakers at Manor House in London on 12 November 1965, with Eric Clapton's name now in large letters.

11 November 1965, Klooks Kleek, Railway Hotel, West Hampstead, London

12 November 1965, Bluesville R&B Club, Manor House, Finsbury Park, London

13 November 1965, Blue Moon Club, Cheltenham, Gloucestershire

14 November 1965, Ricky Tick, Plaza Ballroom, Guildford, Surrey

16 November 1965, Marquee Club, Soho, London (on his day off, Eric jams with the Spencer Davis Group, who are headlining this night at the Marquee)

17 November 1965, Scaffold Club, Northampton, Northamptonshire

19 November 1965, Zambesi Club, Hounslow, Middlesex

20 November 1965, Leicester University, Leicester, Leicestershire

21 November 1965, Red Cross Hall, Sutton, Surrey (early evening)

21 November 1965, Blue Moon Club, Hayes, Middlesex (late evening)

22 November 1965, R&B-ville, Galaxy Club, Town Hall, Basingstoke, Hampshire

27 November 1965, Burtons Ballroom, Uxbridge, Middlesex

28 November 1965, Southall Community Centre, Southall, Middlesex (probably early evening but may have been canceled)

28 November 1965, Flamingo Club, Soho, London (evening set)

29 November 1965, Majestic Ballroom, Reading, Berkshire

30 November 1965, Bowes Lyon House, Stevenage, Hertfordshire

DECEMBER 1965

2 December 1965, Pye Studios, London (Recording session for potential second single for Immediate Records)

4 December 1965, New Barn Club, Brighton, East Sussex

6 December 1965, Bluesville Club, Baths Hall, Ipswich, Suffolk (advertised as "The Big R and B Beat Show of 1965 with THE BOSS ORGAN GRINDER John Mayall and his Bluesbreakers featuring the superb Blues Guitar of Eric Clapton")

10 December 1965, Ricky Tick, Town Hall, Staines, Surrey

11 December 1965, Chelsea College of Art, Kings Road, Chelsea, London (with Georgie Fame and the Blue Flames)

12 December 1965, Agincourt Ballroom, Camberely, Surrey (with Norman's Conquests)

16 December 1965, Mistral Club, Sidcup, Kent

17 December 1965, Il Rondo Club, Leicester, Leicestershire

18 December 1965, Twisted Wheel, Manchester, Lancashire

19 December 1965, Boat Club, Nottingham, Nottinghamshire

23 December 1965, Refectory, Golders Green, London (billed as "A Grand Xmas Party in Golders Green")

24 December 1965, Blue Moon Club, Cheltenham, Gloucestershire

26 December 1965, Eel Pie Hotel, Eel Pie Island, Twickenham, London

27 December 1965, Flamingo Club, Soho, London (evening set with Peter B's Looners with Peter Green on lead guitar)

28 December 1965, Klooks Kleek, Railway Hotel, West Hampstead, London

29 December 1965, Orford Cellar Club, Norwich, Norfolk

31 December 1965, Bluesville R&B Club, Manor House, Finsbury Park, London (billed as "New Year's Eve Great Rave")

4

1966

1966

JANUARY 1966

1 January 1966, Flamingo Club, Soho, London (evening)

1 January 1966, Flamingo All-Nighter Club, Soho, London (from midnight until dawn with Tony Knight's Chessmen)

5 January 1966, Launch of BBC Television's new youth program called *A Whole Scene Going On*, which features a few seconds of Eric playing his Les Paul in the opening credits. The footage of Eric was shot at the BBC, without sound, sadly, and without John Mayall and the Bluesbreakers)

9 January 1966, Beachcomber Club, Nottingham, Nottinghamshire

11 January 1966, Town Hall, High Wycombe, Buckinghamshire

13 January 1966, White Lion Inn, Edgware, London

16 January 1966, Bromel Club, Bromley Court Hotel, Bromley, Kent

17 January 1966, Starlite Club, Star Hotel, Croydon, Surrey

21 January 1966, Skerne Park Hotel, Darlington, Durham

22 January 1966, Liverpool University, Liverpool, Merseyside

23 January 1966, Community Centre, Southall, Middlesex

26 January 1966, Town Hall, Farnborough, Hampshire

28 January 1966, California Ballroom, Dunstable, Bedforshire (with Sons Of Fred and Peter Fenton & the Crowd)

29 January 1966, Club A Go Go, Newcastle, Tyne & Wear (with Junco Partners)

31 January 1966, Bluesville Club, St Matthews Baths Hall, Ipswich, Suffolk

FEBRUARY 1966

1 February 1966, Civic Hall, Grays, Essex (more kudos for Eric Clapton when the advert proudly says, "with wonderful Eric Clapton")

Advert for an appearance by John Mayall's Bluesbreakers at the Civic Hall in Grays on 1 February 1966.

4 February 1966, Links International Youth Centre, Borehamwood, Hertfordshire

5 February 1966, Ricky Tick, Clewer Mead, Windsor, Berkshire

6 February 1966, Woolwich R&B Club, Shakespeare Hotel, Woolwich, London

8 February 1966, Klooks Kleek, Railway Hotel, West Hampstead, London

9 February 1966, pre-recording session for the BBC Radio Light Program *Jazz Beat* recorded at the BBC Playhouse Theatre, Northumberland Avenue, London WC2

Songs recorded between 3:30 p.m. and 7:00 p.m. are:

HIDEAWAY (Freddie King / Sonny Thompson) (3:21) unreleased

John Mayall: organ
Eric Clapton: guitar
John McVie: bass
Hughie Flint: drums

LITTLE GIRL (John Mayall) (2:47) unreleased

John Mayall: vocal, organ
Eric Clapton: guitar
John McVie: bass
Hughie Flint: drums

TEARS IN MY EYES (John Mayall) (4:31) unreleased

John Mayall: vocal, organ
Eric Clapton: guitar
John McVie: bass
Hughie Flint: drums

PARCHMAN FARM (Mose Allison) (2:43) unreleased

John Mayall: vocal, harmonica
John McVie: bass
Hughie Flint: drum

All four songs are broadcast on 12 February.

11 February 1966, Combined Engineering Societies Dance, Avon Room, Birmingham University, Birmingham, Midlands (with Kris Ryan & the Questions, the George Huxley Band)

12 February 1966, Regent Street Polytechnic, London (with the Stormsville Shakers)

13 February 1966, Beachcomber Club, Nottingham, Nottinghamshire

15 February 1966, Fishmongers Arms, Wood Green, London

16 February 1966, Orford Cellar Club, Norwich, Norfolk

18 February 1966, Bluesville R&B Club, Manor House, Finsbury Park, London

Poster advertising a gig by John Mayall and His Bluesbreakers at Bluesville R&B Club, Manor House, Finsbury Park, London, 18 February 1966.

19 February 1966, Flamingo Club, Soho, London (evening)

19 February 1966, Flamingo All-Nighter Club, Soho, London (from midnight until dawn with Tony Knight's Chessmen)

20 February 1966, Cosmopolitan Club, Carlisle, Cumberland

25 February 1966, Hermitage Ballroom, Hitchin, Hertfordshire (with Fernando & the Hideaways)

26 February 1966, Twisted Wheel, Manchester, Lancashire

27 February 1966, Bromel Club, Bromley Court Hotel, Bromley, Kent

MARCH 1966

4 March 1966, Blue Friday Club, Beechwood Court Hotel, Harrogate, Yorkshire

5 March 1966, Club A Go Go, Newcastle, Tyne & Wear

6 March 1966, Kirklevington Country Club, Kirklevington, Yorkshire

9 March 1966, Eric Clapton and the Powerhouse recording session at Olympic Sound Studios

11 March 1966, Blues By Night club, Royal College Of Advanced Technology, Salford (with the Graham Bond Organisation, Paddy, Klaus & Gibson)

13 March 1966, Boat Club, Nottingham, Nottinghamshire

14 March 1966, pre-recording session for the BBC Radio *Saturday Club* recorded at the BBC Aeolian Hall, 135–137 New Bond Street, London W1, with producer Brian Willey

Songs recorded between 02:30 p.m. and 4:30 p.m. are:

ON TOP OF THE WORLD (John Mayall) *Blues Breakers* 2CD Deluxe Edition Decca 984 180-1 released November 2006 / *John Mayall and the Bluesbreakers Live* at the BBC CD Decca 984 466-5 released 2007
KEY TO LOVE (John Mayall) *Blues Breakers* 2CD Deluxe Edition Decca 984 180-1 released November 2006 / *John Mayall and the Bluesbreakers Live* at the BBC CD Decca 984 466-5 released 2007
BURNED MY FINGERS (John Mayall) unreleased
STEPPIN' OUT (Memphis Slim) unreleased
ALL YOUR LOVE (Otis Rush) unreleased

John Mayall: vocal, organ, piano, harmonica
Eric Clapton: guitar
John McVie: bass
Hughie Flint: drums

Broadcast on Saturday, 19 March. Eric now has the "classic" Bluesbreakers sound with his Les Paul. The session is a tamed-down version of what the album sessions would sound like only a few weeks later.

17 March 1966, Ricky Tick, Harvest Moon Club, Guildford, Surrey

18 March 1966, Ram Jam Club, Brixton, London

18 March 1966, Flamingo All-Nighter Club, Soho, London, from midnight until dawn with Ralph Denyer's Rockhouse Band)

19 March 1966, Spring Rites Festival, Refectory Dance, Southampton University, Southampton, Hampshire

20 March 1966, Eel Pie Hotel, Eel Pie Island, Twickenham, London

Front cover of the infamous Beano *album, which became one of the most influential British blues album of all time.*

21 March 1966, Bluesville Club, St Mathews Baths Hall, Ipswich, Suffolk

23 March 1966, Orford Cellar Club, Norwich, Norfolk

26 March 1966, Flamingo Club, Soho, London (evening with the Amboy Dukes, a Nottingham band)

26 March 1966, Flamingo All-Nighter Club, Soho, London (from midnight until dawn with the Gass)

27 March 1966–31 March 1966, Decca Studios, West Hampstead (recording the classic *Blues Breakers* album)

APRIL 1966

1 April 1966, Beaconsfield Youth Club, High Wycombe, Buckinghamshire

2 April 1966, Ricky Tick, Clewer Mead, Windsor, Berkshire

2 April 1966, Les Cousins, Greek Street, Soho, Central London (jam session with Alexis Korner, John Mayall, Eric Clapton, and Duffy Power)

3 April 1966, Blue Moon Club, Hayes, Middlesex

4 April 1966, Carousel Club, Farnborough, Hampshire (opening for Dozy, Beaky Mick, and Tich)

5 April 1966, Fishmongers Arms, Wood Green, London (confirming Eric Clapton's growth in stature, *Record Mirror*'s "The Face" column mentions: "After performing at the Fishmongers Arms, Wood Green, John Mayall finished with the words, "And that was the Eric Clapton show." And that was an accurate description of how people viewed the shows. Eric's guitar playing was so unique and powerful by this point that everybody who came to the shows was in awe of him. John acknowledged the importance of Eric by giving Eric's name equal billing on adverts for their shows)

7 April 1966, Kave Dwellers Club, Billingham, Stockton on Tees (with the Denmen)

8 April 1966, Bluesville R&B Club, Manor House, London

9 April 1966: Assembly Hall, Barking, London (with Long John Baldry & the Steam Packet, Geno Washington & the Ram Jam Band)

10 April 1966, Central R&B Club, Central Hotel, Gillingham, Kent

11 April 1966, Marquee Club, Soho, London (early and late sets with the James Royce Set)

13 April 1966, Market Hall, St Albans, Hertfordshire

15 April 1966, Zambesi Club, Hounslow, Middlesex

16 April 1966, Twisted Wheel, Manchester, Lancashire (early and late sets)

17 April 1966, Beachcomber Club, Nottingham, Nottinghamshire

18 April 1966, Woodhall Community Centre, Welwyn Garden Centre, Hertfordshire (local guitar player Mick Taylor steps in for an absent Eric, who has gone AWOL for the night seeing The Lovin' Spoonful at the Marquee in London. Mick Taylor recalled the event to *Guitar Player* magazine: "I was there with my friends to watch the show. We watched the first set, which was about an hour long, and Eric just wasn't there. With a lot of prompting from my friends, I got up onstage and played the second set. I went backstage first and asked John if I could play, and I was very nervous. I was still kind of learning how to play blues guitar—I was really not that good. I played Eric's guitar.")

22 April 1966, Refectory, Golders Green, London

24 April 1966, Bromel Club, Bromley Court Hotel, Bromley, Kent

25 April 1966, Cooks Ferry Inn, Edmonton, London (the local paper, the *Weekly Herald*, reports: "The John Mayall group packed the Cooks Ferry Inn, Edmonton, on Monday, and received one of the best receptions at the club in recent times. The four-man group includes talented ex-Yardbirds Eric Clapton, who plays lead guitar. Playing numbers like "Hi-Heel Sneakers" and "Hoochie Coochie Man" and "What'd I Say," they finished their performance with an Otis Slim number entitled "Stepping Out")

27 April 1966, Castle Club, Tooting, London (Pretty Things drummer Viv Prince, who was starting a solo career in 1966, sits in on a couple of numbers tonight)

28 April 1966, Club A Go Go, Newcastle, Tyne & Wear

29 April 1966, Il Rondo Club, Leicester, Leicestershire (evening)

29 April 1966, All-Nighter R&B, Town Hall, Birmingham, West Midlands (with Graham Bond Organisation, John Lee Hooker)

30 April 1966, Flamingo Club, Soho, London (evening)

30 April 1966, Flamingo All-Nighter Club, Soho, London (with the Train and Tony Knight's Chessmen, from midnight until dawn)

MAY 1966

1 May 1966, Orford Cellar Club, Norwich, Norfolk

3 May 1966, Eric joins his old band *the Yardbirds*, who now have Jeff Beck on guitar, for their encore at the Marquee. When interviewing Jeff in 2005, he had no recollection of Eric jamming with him in *the Yardbirds*. But it did happen as the photo proves. Not only that, a young Brian May, better known as Queen's guitarist, was in attendance tonight and remembers it well.

Eric Clapton joins his old bandmates the Yardbirds for their encore at the Marquee Club on 3 May 1966.

4 May 1966, Casino Club, Walsall, West Midlands

One of several photos taken by David Wedgbury over a two-day period with John Mayall and the Bluesbreakers on 5 and 6 May 1966.

5 May 1966–6 May 1966, Decca in-house photographer David Wedgbury spends a couple of days shooting photos for the cover of the forthcoming *Blues Breakers* album. David had already taken shots of the band recording at Decca Studios, which will be used on the rear sleeve of the album. Worth noting that the issue of *The Beano* (issue 1242) that Eric is reading on the album cover, hits the newsagents on 5 May

7 May 1966, Ram Jam Club, Brixton, London (with Shotgun Express)

8 May 1966, King Mojo Club, Sheffield, Yorkshire

9 May 1966, Starlite Club, Star Hotel, Croydon, Surrey

10 May 1966, Klooks Kleek R&B Club, Railway Hotel, West Hampstead, London

13 May 1966, Town Hall, Oxford, Oxfordshire (Ginger Baker jams with the band tonight and there is an instant musical chemistry between Eric and Ginger. After the show Ginger gives Eric a lift home. Once there, Ginger mentions the possibility of the two of them getting together in a band and discusses his vision for the future. Eric is very taken with the proposal, even though he knows it will upset John Mayall. But Eric wants to explore new avenues for his playing, feeling he has gone as far as he can with the Bluesbreakers. Eric suggests Jack Bruce should join them, completely unaware of the acrimonious history between Jack and Ginger. Eric had played with Jack for several months in the Bluesbreakers and knew what a great player he was)

14 May 1966, Tofts Club, Folkestone, Kent

15 May 1966, Beachcomber Club, Nottingham, Nottinghamshire

17 May 1966, Fishmongers Arms, Wood Green, London

19 May 1966, Mod Scene Club at the County Arms, Blaby, Leicestershire

20 May 1966, Royal College of Advanced Technology, Salford, Lancashire (support by the Big Three)

21 May 1966, Ricky Tick, Clewer Mead, Windsor, Berkshire

22 May 1966, Flamingo Club, Soho, London

23 May 1966, Atalanta Ballroom, Woking, Surrey

24 May 1966, Tooting Castle, Tooting, London

27 May 1966, Refectory, Golders Green, London

28 May 1966, Mansfield Co Op, Nottinghamshire (evening)

28 May 1966, Beachcomber Club, Nottingham, Nottinghamshire (all-nighter)

29 May 1966, Eel Pie Hotel, Eel Pie Island, Twickenham, Middlesex

30 May 1966, Marquee Club, Soho, London

31 May 1966, Odeon Ballroom, Chesterfield, Derbyshire

JUNE 1966

1 June 1966, Orford Cellar Club, Norwich, Norfolk

3 June 1966, Flamingo Club, Soho, London

4 June 1966, Floral Hall, Southport, Lancashire (with the Hideaways)

5 June 1966, Bromel Club, Bromley Court Hotel, Bromley, Kent

7 June 1966, Town Hall, High Wycombe, Buckinghamshire

8 June 1966, Town Hall, Farnborough, Hampshire

10 June 1966, Ram Jam Club, Brixton, London

12 June 1966, Blue Moon Club, Hayes, Middlesex

16 June 1966, Marquee Club, Soho, London (with the Amboy Dukes. *Melody Maker* reports: "During the wailing first half the audience would have been swinging on the rafters had there been any. Eric Clapton, on guitar, played like a maestro, weaving, bending, attacking, and soaring his way through a programme of blues classics. Mayall wasn't as overpowering as usual—a pleasant change—and indeed his own compositions like 'I'm Your Witchdoctor' provided an interlude to the more straight-forward blues. Mayall leapt and soared on a hectic version of 'Parchman Farm,' while Clapton was highlighted on such numbers as 'Stormy Monday,' 'So Many Roads' and the fiery Freddy King instrumental 'Hideaway')

17 June 1966, Corpus Ball, Oxford University, Oxford, Oxfordshire (with Georgie Fame & the Blue Flames)

18 June 1966, Rutlishian Jubilee Fair, Rutlish Grammar School, Merton Park, Merton (with the Torque)

19 June 1966, Beachcomber Club, Nottingham, Nottinghamshire

21 June 1966, Fishmongers Arms, Wood Green, London

23 June 1966, Leeds University Rag Ball, Refectory Hall, Leeds University, Leeds, Yorkshire (the Who headline today with John Mayall's Bluesbreakers, Wayne Fontana, the Alan Price Set, and the Swinging Blue Jeans)

25 June 1966, Flamingo Club, Soho, London (evening)

25 June 1966, Flamingo All-Nighter club, Soho, London (with the Shevells, from midnight until dawn)

26 June 1966, Carousel Ballroom, Farnborough, Hampshire

27 June 1966, Majestic Ballroom, Reading, Berkshire

JULY 1966

1 July 1966, Bluesville Club, Manor House, London

2 July 1966, Blue Moon Club, Cheltenham, Gloucestershire

3 July 1966, Bluesette Club, Leatherhead, Surrey

5 July 1966, Klooks Kleek R&B Club, Railway Hotel, West Hampstead, London

7 July 1966, Club A Go Go, Newcastle, Tyne & Wear

8 July 1966, Ricky Tick, Corn Exchange, Newbury, Berkshire

9 July 1966, Rhodes Centre, Bishops Stortford, Hertfordshire (with the Apex)

14 July 1966, Ricky Tick, Stoke Hotel, Guildford, Surrey

15 July 1966, Ricky Tick, Hounslow, Middlesex

16 July 1966, Cad-Lac Club, Florida Rooms, Brighton, East Sussex

17 July 1966, Black Prince, Bexley, Kent (this is probably Eric's last gig with John Mayall)

RECORDING SESSIONS MAY 1965-MARCH 1966
LEVY's SOUND STUDIOS 73 New Bond Street, London W1
John Mayall Bluesbreakers session with Bob Dylan

12 MAY 1965

The studios had been taken over by CBS Records in 1964 but were still referred to as Levy Sound Studios until later in 1965. Bob Dylan was in town as part of a UK tour and had to record a sales message for CBS records. As he was going to be in a studio, he also wanted to try out some new material. He liked John Mayall's "Crawling Up A Hill" and was interested in meeting him, as well as having John and his band back him on a session. Tom Wilson, Dylan's producer, was in the studio getting everything set up for the best sound. He told the assembled crowd that Dylan would be trying some new experimental stuff and that maybe an album would result from the session. In the studio were Bob Dylan, Albert Grossman (Dylan's manager), three female backing singers, folk singer Nadia Cattouse, songwriter Sydney Carter, Paul Jones from Manfred Mann, Bobby Neuwirth, John Mayall, Eric Clapton, Hughie Flint, and John McVie from the Bluesbreakers.

The session started at around 8:00 p.m., and Bob Dylan recorded two numbers on piano with all the backing musicians before picking up an electric guitar to play some new blues-influenced numbers. All in all, around five numbers were recorded before Dylan left the studio at around 10:30 p.m.

One of the electric numbers was supposedly "If You Gotta Go, Go Now," but the general consensus was that the evening was not productive, and none of the material has ever surfaced.

"It was just a jam session. He was interested in John Mayall. John had recorded a song called 'Life Is Like A Slow Train Going Up A Hill' and that interested Bob. Bob came in, looked for John Mayall, I was just the guitar player on the session. He had a friend called Bobby Neuwirth who was a fantastic player. Bobby Neuwirth was his kind of court jester at the time and he kept coming up to me and saying, 'You're playing too much blues, man. He needs more country!' I didn't actually speak to Bob at this time. He never actually came and spoke. I just watched him. We played for about two hours. Tom Wilson was behind the desk. The next thing I knew, he was gone. We did a lot of his blues songs which he was making up. He was sitting at the piano and we just joined in."

—ERIC CLAPTON

PYE STUDIOS
Studio 2, ATV House, Bryanston Street, London W1
Session with John Mayall Bluesbreakers

AUGUST 1965

I'M YOUR WITCHDOCTOR (John Mayall) A-side single Immediate 012 released 22 October 1965 / Blues Anytime Vol. 1 album Immediate IMLP014 released 1968 / Blues Breakers 2CD Deluxe Edition Decca 984 180-1 released November 2006

John Mayall: vocals, organ
Eric Clapton: guitar
John McVie: bass
Hughie Flint: drums

TELEPHONE BLUES (John Mayall) B-side single Immediate 012 released 22 October 1965 / Blues Anytime Vol. 1 album Immediate IMLP014 released 1968 / Blues Breakers 2CD Deluxe Edition Decca 984 180-1 released November 2006

John Mayall: vocals, organ, harmonica
Eric Clapton: guitar
John McVie: bass
Hughie Flint: drums

Producer: Jimmy Page
Engineer: –

The *John Mayall Plays John Mayall* album, which was released on 26 March 1965, did not sell many copies and a new single, "Crocodile Walk," released on 2 April 1965, suffered the same fate. As a result Decca decided to drop John Mayall from the label. In early July 1965, Immediate, Andrew Loog Oldham and Tony Calder's newly formed label, offered John and the Bluesbreakers an opportunity to record a single with their new in-house producer, Jimmy Page. Pye Studios at Marble Arch were booked, and a single was recorded featuring "I'm Your Witchdoctor" as the A-side with "Telephone Blues" as the flip-side.

Andrew Loog Oldham was the manager of the Rolling Stones at the time, and his immediate focus was initially going to be on the popular blues scene in England. Mick Jagger and Keith Richards were very involved with the label at the beginning. The label would eventually diversify into the rock, pop, and soul markets with varying degrees of success.

HOME RECORDINGS
Jimmy Page's house, Miles Road, Epsom, Surrey

AUGUST 1965

Eric and Jimmy were quite close at this time and would occasionally meet up. Jimmy also jammed a few times with Eric in John Mayall's Bluesbreakers, and at least once with Jeff Beck in tow, as well. Eric would make his way to Epsom British Rail station, where he would be met by Jimmy, and together they walked to his home in Miles Road. Jimmy had reel-to-reel tape recorders set up, and the two of them would play two-guitar blues jams. These were nothing more than informal jams recorded for the fun of it. That said, they are now of historical value.

TRIBUTE TO ELMORE (Clapton / Page) Blues Anytime Vol. 1 Immediate LP IMLP014 released October 1968

Eric Clapton: guitar
Jimmy Page: guitar

Producer: Jimmy Page

FREIGHT LOADER (Clapton / Page) Blues Anytime Vol. 2 Immediate LP IMLP015 released October 1968

Eric Clapton: guitar
Jimmy Page: guitar

Producer: Jimmy Page

MILES ROAD (Clapton / Page) *Blues Anytime Vol. 3 Immediate* LP IMLP 019 released October 1968

Eric Clapton: guitar
Jimmy Page: guitar

Producer: Jimmy Page

WEST COAST IDEA (Clapton / Page) unreleased

Eric Clapton: guitar
Jimmy Page: guitar

Producer: Jimmy Page

> **"**22 October 1965 saw the release of the single 'I'm Your Witchdoctor' and 'Telephone Blues' on Immediate Records, where I was a producer. It was recorded at Pye Studios with jazzer Hughie Flint on drums, John McVie on bass, John Mayall on keyboards and vocals and Eric Clapton on guitar. It was recorded in June of 1965. When 'Witchdoctor' came to be overdubbed, Eric had this idea to put this feedback wail over the top. I was with him in the studio as he set this up, then I got back into the control room and told the engineer to record the overdub. About two thirds of the way through, he pulled the faders down and said: 'This guitarist is impossible to record.' I guess his technical ethics were compromised by the signal that was putting the meters into the red. I suggested that he got on with his job and leave that decision to me! Eric's solo on 'Telephone Blues' was just superb. I would like to have seen Ainsley Dunbar on drums in the studio for 'Witchdoctor,' I also produced 'On Top of the World,' showing John Mayall's blues Top 20 ambitions, and 'Double Crossing Time,' an ironic title as the next time I heard of them they were in the very capable hands of Mike Vernon—famed blues producer. It was a good move: Eric left the Yardbirds because they had Top 20 aspirations!**"**
> —**JIMMY PAGE**
> (from www.jimmypage.com)

SNAKE DRIVE (Clapton / Page) unreleased

Eric Clapton: guitar
Jimmy Page: guitar

Producer: Jimmy Page

DRAGGIN' MY TAIL (Clapton / Page) unreleased

Eric Clapton: guitar
Jimmy Page: guitar

Producer: Jimmy Page

CHOKER (Clapton / Page) unreleased

Eric Clapton: guitar
Jimmy Page: guitar

Producer: Jimmy Page
Engineer: Jimmy Page

> **"**After Eric split from the Yardbirds and entered his historic partnership with John Mayall, it did not take long for him to earn the reputation of being Britain's number one exponent of the Blues guitar.
>
> These recordings were made around this time and as precious little exists of his ability on record between the Yardbirds and the first John Mayall and Eric Clapton albums, I thought it essential to make these tapes available to the serious collector to illustrate the transitional period which helped to build Eric's fantastic reputation.**"**
> —**JIMMY PAGE**
> (from the original *Blues Anytime* liner notes)

The last four numbers were put onto four-track tape and overdubbed with other musicians at Olympic Studios in Carton Hall, London. This was done without Eric's knowledge. When these tracks finally appeared, he was very angry that his work appeared without his consent. As far as he was concerned, these were informal jam sessions and not for commercial use.

OLYMPIC SOUND STUDIOS, STUDIO 1 Carton Hall, Carton Street, Marylebone, London W1

Probably early 1966

WEST COAST IDEA (Clapton / Page) *Blues Anytime Vol.1* Immediate IMLP014 released October 1968

Eric Clapton: guitar
Ian Stewart: piano
Mick Jagger: harmonica
Bill Wyman: bass

SNAKE DRIVE (Clapton / Page) *Blues Anytime Vol. 1* Immediate IMLP014 released October 1968

Eric Clapton: guitar
Jimmy Page: guitar
Bill Wyman: bass
Chris Winters: drums

DRAGGIN' MY TAIL (Clapton / Page) *Blues Anytime Vol. 2 Immediate* IMLP015 released October 1968

Eric Clapton: guitar
Jimmy Page: guitar
Ian Stewart: piano
Mick Jagger: harmonica
Bill Wyman: bass

CHOKER (Clapton / Page) *Blues Anytime Vol. 2 Immediate* IMLP015 released October 1968

Eric Clapton: guitar
Jimmy Page: guitar
Bill Wyman: bass
Chris Winters: drums

Producer: Jimmy Page
Engineer: Keith Grant (probably)

ERIC CLAPTON GUEST SESSION

DECCA STUDIOS
Studio 2, 165 Broadhurst Gardens, West Hampstead, London NW6
Session for Champion Jack Dupree

4 NOVEMBER 1965

THIRD DEGREE (Eddie Boyd) *From New Orleans To Chicago* album DECCA LP4747 released February 1966 / *From New Orleans To Chicago* CD BGOCD649 released December 2008

SHIM-SHAM-SHIMMY (Johnson / Jones) *From New Orleans To Chicago* album DECCA LP4747 released February 1966 / *From New Orleans To Chicago* CD BGOCD649 released December 2008

CALCUTTA BLUES (unknown) *Raw Blues album Ace Of Clubs* SCL1220 released January 1967 / *Raw Blues* London CD October 1990

Champion Jack Dupree: piano, vocals
Eric Clapton: guitar
Malcolm Pool: bass
Tony McPhee: guitar
John Mayall: harmonica
Keef Hartley: drums
Bill Shortt: washboard

Producer: Mike Vernon
Engineer: Vic Smith

PYE STUDIOS
Studio 2, ATV House, Bryanston Street, London W1
Session with John Mayall Bluesbreakers

2 DECEMBER 1965

ON TOP OF THE WORLD (John Mayall) Blues Anytime Vol. 2 album Immediate IMCP 015 released 1968 / *Blues Breakers* 2CD Deluxe Edition Decca 984 180-1 released November 2006 (new stereo mix version sourced from the original four-track master tape for the first time)

John Mayall: vocals, piano
Eric Clapton: guitar
John McVie: bass
Hughie Flint: drums

"We completed the album in three days and it was a great session to be involved with. Champion Jack was an amiable man and loved the fresh sound we added to his rolling barrelhouse piano. We turned up at Decca studios on the appointed morning and met Mike Vernon and Tony McPhee, guitarist from The Groundhogs. After maybe 30 minutes we were joined in the control room by Jack who immediately struck us as an easy going humorous guy. We made our way down to the smaller of the two Decca studios and set about arranging our gear while Mike and his engineer, Vic Smith, arranged the technical side, getting levels and balance right.

When it came to the third day's recording, we discovered Eric Clapton in the control room. As far as we knew Eric was still in Greece. Mike filled us in with the phone call he had received the previous night. Eric had phoned out of the blue to say he was back from Greece. Desperate to get some money he had phoned Mike to see if there was any session work available. Mike was totally in awe of Eric and happened to mention the session we were currently recording. He invited him to join in the third day, knowing his unique playing would add an extra element to the tracks.

I was thrilled at the chance to play on a record with Eric and thought we would all be of the same opinion, but when I looked at Tony McPhee, his face was long and his eyes clearly showed his unhappiness. I understood immediately. Tony had hoped this album would boost his profile, but knew Eric's presence would force him into the background. This is exactly what happened, with Tony taking a backseat leaving Eric to add typically effortless electric lead to a number of tracks. There was also a more strained atmosphere on the third day, with Eric getting a little vexed at Jack's habit of tacking on extra bars. At one point, whilst listening to a playback, I heard Eric say to Mike, 'If that cunt (meaning Jack) doesn't stick to a standard 12 bar, I'll fucking wrap this guitar round his neck.' This was said with humour but I knew Jack's laid-back approach to being in the studio irritated Eric. For him, studio time was a job and the job had to be done to the best of everyone's ability. Eric struggled with the session as he wasn't in control, but listening to the sound of his lead guitar through the cans was an incredible experience." —**KEEF HARTLEY**
(from his book *Halfbreed*)

DOUBLE CROSSING MAN (John Mayall / Eric Clapton) basic version of what later became "Double Crossing Time." It was titled that way because of Mayall's displeasure at Manfred Mann pinching Jack Bruce

John Mayall: vocals, organ
Eric Clapton: guitar
John McVie: bass
Hughie Flint: drums

Producer: Jimmy Page
Engineer: Bob Auger

WESSEX SOUND STUDIOS
Old Compton Street,
Soho, London W1

DECEMBER 1965

LONELY YEARS (John Mayall) single A-side Purdah 45-3502 released August 1966 / *Raw Blues* album SCL1220 released January 1967 / *Blues Breakers* 2CD Deluxe Edition Decca 984 180-1 released November 2006

John Mayall: vocals, harmonica
Eric Clapton: guitar

"I approached John and put my cards on the table. I said, 'How about making a real downhome blues record with just the two of you, and we'll split the profits, and we'll have some fun.' He'd already said to me he was thinking of going back to Decca, and said, 'If I go back, would you be interested in producing me?' So, of course, I said yes. So we went to the old Wessex studios in Soho and we did it straight mono: one microphone stuck up in the middle of the studio, just piano, voice and a guitar, and to this day it's the only record I've ever made that sounds as if it was made in Chicago."

—MIKE VERNON
(from John Pidgeon's book *Eric Clapton*)

BERNARD JENKINS (Eric Clapton) single B-side of "Lonely Years" Purdah 45-3502 released August 1966 / *Raw Blues* album SCL1220 released January 1967 / *Blues Breakers* 2CD Deluxe Edition Decca 984 180-1 released November 2006

John Mayall: piano
Eric Clapton: guitar

Mike Vernon had set up a mail-order-only independent label called Purdah specializing in blues material only. Each single had a very limited run.

ERIC CLAPTON
GUEST SESSION

OLYMPIC SOUND STUDIOS,
STUDIO 1
Carton Hall, Carton Street,
Marylebone, London W1
Session for Elektra
compilation *What's Shakin'*

9 MARCH 1966

I WANT TO KNOW (MacLeod) *What's Shakin'* album US Elektra EKL 4002 released June 1966, UK Elektra EUK 250 UK released July 1966 / *What's Shakin'* CD Collectors Choice Music CCM-622 released February 2006

"The better part of an electric blues compilation was already in the can in New York and as the new head of Elektra's London office, I suggested getting a British blues band to complete the project. A meeting with Paul Jones opened up the possibility of putting together an all-star group, which is what we did.

We recorded the tracks at Olympic Studios in Carton Hall, before they moved to Barnes, and Keith Grant was the engineer who handled the technical side. I worried about the music. Everybody set up in the room, there was no drum booth or anything, and we just made the tracks, but then Jac Holzman grabbed the tape and took it back to New York to mix, which was a disappointment. There was a fourth track recorded but I cannot remember what it was."

—JOE BOYD

"Joe Boyd Called me up and asked if I could put together a group of UK musicians for a forthcoming 'white boy blues' compilation. He was mainly looking for non-contractual people because of the vice-like grip record companies had on their artists in those days.

So I called Jack Bruce and asked if he would be interested. I then suggested Eric Clapton and Ginger Baker. Ginger said no because he did not want a Cream recording released before they had recorded anything themselves. At that time there were only four people who knew of Cream, and that was Jack, Ginger, Eric and Robert Stigwood. I called Steve Winwood and he brought in Pete York.

I know Eric recalls a slow blues being recorded as a fourth number, but I have no recollection of this."

—PAUL JONES

CROSSROADS (Robert Johnson) *What's Shakin'* album US Elektra EKL 4002 released June 1966, UK Elektra EUK 250 UK released July 1966 / *What's Shakin'* CD Collectors Choice Music CCM-622 released February 2006

STEPPIN' OUT (LC Frazier) *What's Shakin'* album US Elektra EKL 4002 released June 1966, UK Elektra EUK 250 UK released July 1966 / *What's Shakin'* CD Collectors Choice Music CCM-622 released February 2006

Eric Clapton: guitar
Steve Winwood (as Steve Anglo): keyboards, vocals
Paul Jones: harmonica
Pete York: drums
Jack Bruce: bass
Ben Palmer: piano

Producers: Joe Boyd / Jac Holzman
Engineer: Keith Grant

If Paul's memory is correct, it would mean that the above session took place after the recording of the Bluesbreakers with Eric Clapton album and closer to Cream getting together. At the time of putting this book together I have been unable to confirm this.

DECCA STUDIOS
Studio 2, 165 Broadhurst Gardens, West Hampstead, London NW6
Sessions for John Mayall's Bluesbreakers

27 MARCH 1966–31 MARCH 1966

ALL YOUR LOVE (Otis Rush) *Blues Breakers* album US London LL3492 (mono) released August 1966, US London PS 492 (stereo) released February 1967 / *Blues Breakers* album UK Decca LK 4808 (mono) released July 1966, UK Decca SKL 4804 (stereo) released November 1969 / *Blues Breakers* 2CD Deluxe Edition Decca 984 180-1 released November 2006

John Mayall: lead vocals, Hammond B3 organ
Eric Clapton: guitar
John McVie: bass guitar
Hughie Flint: drums

HIDEAWAY (Freddy King / Sonny Thompson) *Blues Breakers* album US London LL3492 (mono) released August 1966, US London PS 492 (stereo) released February 1967 / *Blues Breakers* album UK Decca LK 4808 (mono) released July 1966, UK Decca SKL 4804 (stereo) released November 1969 / *Blues Breakers* 2CD Deluxe Edition Decca 984 180-1 released November 2006

John Mayall: lead vocals, Hammond B3 organ
Eric Clapton: guitar
John McVie: bass guitar
Hughie Flint: drums

LITTLE GIRL (John Mayall) *Blues Breakers* album US London LL3492 (mono) released August 1966, US London PS 492 (stereo) released February 1967 / *Blues Breakers* album UK Decca LK 4808 (mono) released July 1966, UK Decca SKL 4804 (stereo) released November 1969 / *Blues Breakers* 2CD Deluxe Edition Decca 984 180-1 released November 2006

John Mayall: lead vocals, Hammond B3 organ
Eric Clapton: guitar
John McVie: bass guitar
Hughie Flint: drums

ANOTHER MAN (John Mayall) *Blues Breakers* album US London LL3492 (mono) released August 1966, US London PS 492 (stereo) released February 1967 / *Blues Breakers* album UK Decca LK 4808 (mono) released July 1966, UK Decca SKL 4804 (stereo) released November 1969 / *Blues Breakers* 2CD Deluxe Edition Decca 984 180-1 released November 2006

John Mayall: lead vocals, harmonica, handclaps

DOUBLE CROSSING TIME (John Mayall / Eric Clapton) *Blues Breakers* album US London LL3492 (mono) released August 1966, US London PS 492 (stereo) released February 1967 / *Blues Breakers* album UK Decca LK 4808 (mono) released July 1966, UK Decca SKL 4804 (stereo) released November 1969 / *Blues Breakers* 2CD Deluxe Edition Decca 984 180-1 released November 2006

John Mayall: lead vocals, piano
Eric Clapton: guitars
John McVie: bass guitar
Hughie Flint: drums
Johnny Almond: baritone sax

WHAT'D I SAY (Ray Charles) *Blues Breakers* album US London LL3492 (mono) released August 1966, US London PS 492 (stereo) released February 1967 / *Blues Breakers* album UK Decca LK 4808 (mono) released July 1966, UK Decca SKL 4804 (stereo) released November 1969 / *Blues Breakers* 2CD Deluxe Edition Decca 984 180-1 released November 2006

John Mayall: lead vocals, Hammond B3 organ
Eric Clapton: guitar
John McVie: bass guitar
Hughie Flint: drums

KEY TO LOVE (John Mayall) *Blues Breakers* album US London LL3492 (mono) released August 1966, US London PS 492 (stereo) released February 1967 / *Blues Breakers* album UK Decca LK 4808 (mono) released July 1966, UK Decca SKL 4804 (stereo) released November 1969 / *Blues Breakers* 2CD Deluxe Edition Decca 984 180-1 released November 2006

John Mayall: lead vocals, Hammond B3 organ
Eric Clapton: guitar
John McVie: bass guitar
Hughie Flint: drums
Alan Skidmore: tenor saxophone
John Almond: baritone saxophone
Dennis Healey: trumpet

PARCHMAN FARM (Mose Allison) *Blues Breakers* album US London LL3492 (mono) released August 1966, US London PS 492 (stereo) released February 1967 / *Blues Breakers* album UK Decca LK 4808 (mono) released July 1966, UK Decca SKL 4804 (stereo) released November 1969 / *Blues Breakers* 2CD Deluxe Edition Decca 984 180-1 released November 2006

John Mayall: lead vocals, Hammond B3 organ, harmonica
Eric Clapton: guitar
John McVie: bass guitar
Hughie Flint: drums

HAVE YOU HEARD (John Mayall) *Blues Breakers* album US London LL3492 (mono) released August 1966, US London PS 492 (stereo) released February 1967 / *Blues Breakers* album UK Decca LK 4808 (mono) released July 1966, UK Decca SKL 4804 (stereo) released November 1969 / *Blues Breakers* 2CD Deluxe Edition Decca 984 180-1 released November 2006

John Mayall: lead vocals, Hammond B3 organ
Eric Clapton: guitar
John McVie: bass guitar
Hughie Flint: drums

Alan Skidmore: tenor saxophone
John Almond: baritone saxophone
Dennis Healey: trumpet

RAMBLIN' ON MY MIND (Robert Johnson) *Blues Breakers* album US London LL3492 (mono) released August 1966, US London PS 492 (stereo) released February 1967 / *Blues Breakers* album UK Decca LK 4808 (mono) released July 1966, UK Decca SKL 4804 (stereo) released November 1969 / *Blues Breakers* 2CD Deluxe Edition Decca 984 180-1 released November 2006

John Mayall: piano, harmonica
Eric Clapton: guitar, lead vocals

STEPPIN' OUT (LC Frazier) *Blues Breakers* album US London LL3492 (mono) released August 1966, US London PS 492 (stereo) released February 1967 / *Blues Breakers* album UK Decca LK 4808 (mono) released July 1966, UK Decca SKL 4804 (stereo) released November 1969 / *Blues Breakers* 2CD Deluxe Edition Decca 984 180-1 released November 2006

John Mayall: Hammond B3 organ
Eric Clapton: guitar
John McVie: bass guitar

"Gus Dudgeon asked me what I would do regarding studio set up for the Bluesbreakers album. I think he knew Eric was going to be loud.

We had different ideas but in the end we came to a halfway house idea, mostly my idea of putting Eric's amp in the vocal booth, but Gus choosing which type of microphones and the rest of the set up, which was fairly normal. Just a few more screens to keep the guitar off the vocal and drum mics. I did nothing on the actual sessions."
—**DEREK VARNALS** (Decca engineer)

"We just went in there. I think it was either one day or two days. It didn't take much more than that. Basically, we were just playing the stuff we were doing in the clubs, so the material was totally familiar to us. It felt pretty natural. The only difference was we had to play a little quieter than we might have done in the clubs.

'Ramblin' On My Mind' was a song that Eric wanted to do and, as I remember it, he didn't want anybody in the room, so it was one that we did as a separate session after the others had gone home. He was a bit shy about singing for the first time on record, but it worked out after a couple of takes. He just didn't want anybody listening in case it didn't work out." —**JOHN MAYALL**

"It was just a record of what we were doing every night in the clubs, with a few contrived riffs we made up kind of afterthoughts, to fill out some of the things. It isn't any great achievement. It wasn't until I realized that the album was actually turning people on that I began to look at it differently." —**ERIC CLAPTON**

Hughie Flint: drums
Alan Skidmore: tenor saxophone
John Almond: baritone saxophone
Dennis Healey: trumpet

IT AIN'T RIGHT (Walter Jacobs) *Blues Breakers* album US London LL3492 (mono) released August 1966, US London PS 492 (stereo) released February 1967 / *Blues Breakers* album UK Decca LK 4808 (mono) released July 1966, UK Decca SKL 4804 (stereo) released November 1969 / *Blues Breakers* 2CD Deluxe Edition Decca 984 180-1 released November 2006

John Mayall: lead vocals, harmonica
Eric Clapton: guitar, lead vocals on "Ramblin' on My Mind"
John McVie: bass guitar
Hughie Flint: drums

Producer: Mike Vernon
Engineer: Gus Dudgeon

One of the finest English blues albums ever recorded. Eric's power and tone at the time were very unique, and the fact that he got his name on the front cover pretty much says it all really. His stature and reputation had steadily grown over the previous six months to such an extent that many people would come to gigs just to see and hear him play. They would certainly want to buy the album with his name so prominently displayed on the cover. The album was completed within five days at the end of March 1966 and was initially mixed to mono only on 2 April 1966. It was issued in mono only in the UK in July 1966. Many music fans insist this is the best version of the album, and they may have a point. It sounds glorious. A stereo mix was not made until 14 September 1966, and not released in the UK until November 1969.

The reason the album did not take long to record is that the band were so familiar with most of the material from performing it at gigs for several months.

CREAM

Eric's equipment:

Guitars: several Gibson Les Paul Standards, Gibson ES 335, 1960 double cutaway Les Paul Special, 1964 Gibson SG customized paint work by The Fool, Black Beauty Gibson Les Paul Custom, Gibson Reverse Firebird 1, Guild acoustic twelve-string

Amp: Marshall 1959 100-watt Plexipanelled Superlead Amplifier (three-switch), one 1960 75-watt 4x12 Angle Front Cabinet + 1 1960 75-watt 4x12 Flat Front Cabinet

Around the time Eric was leaving John Mayall and joining Cream, he had an opportunity to jam with a young John Etheridge. John remembers the event very well.

"In 1966 I had a band (kind of school band really) of guys where I was doing A levels (exams). It was the period of Bluesbreakers into Cream. I had met Eric a couple of times but our drummer (Rob Lipson—later of 'Gracious') got to know him quite well and invited him down to play with us at rehearsal. As you can imagine this was a big deal for me and I was petrified! We played a few tunes and Eric then played my SG standard, out of which he got a great sound. I was playing a kind of proto-fusion style as I was heavily into Reinhardt etc and this is what he noticed, I think, as this was quite unusual at the time. Most people were trying to do him! When Rob asked him what he thought on the journey back to London he apparently said that although he did not really think I was a blues player he thought I was a great guitar player. Of course these remarks are easily made but it really encouraged me (along with later praise from Hendrix) to take up music as my life path. So it was a major event for me!!" —JOHN MAYALL

As soon as Eric left the Bluesbreakers, things moved very quickly. Ginger Baker suggested that Robert Stigwood, who handled the Graham Bond Organisation, should act as their manager. Cream initially rehearsed at Ginger Baker's ground-floor maisonette at 154 Braemar Avenue in Neasden, North West London. More formal rehearsals took place at a local church hall before their first proper gig, a warm-up, at Manchester's Twisted Wheel on 30 July 1966. The official itineraries list that day, as do reference books on the Twisted Wheel. Several sources list 29 July, but I cannot find any definitive proof to that effect. Their first high profile show was at the sixth National Jazz & Blues Festival, Royal Windsor Racecourse, on 31 July 1966 in front of an estimated crowd of 20,000. The crowd and press loved them. The next move was to record a single to capitalize on the positive reviews of their live debut.

Studio time was booked, and several pop-tinged songs were recorded. Among them was the truly awful and unrepresentative "Wrapping Paper." Surprisingly, this would be the first choice for a single. Eric explained what fans should expect from Cream to *Record Mirror:* "I'm tired of being called a specialist musician. People thought Cream was going to be a

blues band, but it's not, it's a pop group really." The fact is Cream had no real idea of who they were in the early days. It was a case of taking each day as it came. Certainly as far as Eric was concerned he had even seen himself as the potential singer when Cream were forming, but Jack was already an established singer with a far stronger voice and the obvious choice. Eric accepted that because it made sense.

Jack and Ginger were not familiar with some of the names who were an influence on Eric, and he was equally unfamiliar with some of the influences they had. But they learned to appreciate each other's tastes and influences and merged everything together to make a unique sound. It took some time for that to come out, though. What did not help their creativity and search for an identity was the heavy workload imposed on them by management. There were highlights, especially for Eric, who remembers one show in particular from the early days of Cream. It was at the 1 October 1966 Regent Street Polytechnic in London when an unknown Jimi Hendrix jammed with Cream on a couple of blues numbers. Jimi had just arrived in England, and Eric was blown away by him. Eric had never experienced such playing before. The two of them became close friends and would spend time together whenever their schedules permitted.

Cream's touring schedule was tough, taking them all over England. Writing material for their first album was done while on the road and on the occasional days off. Recording was also fitted in between touring commitments. Not the best way to get a cohesive-sounding album. They started recording for their debut album in early August, and the sessions would drag on to November. By September, an official press release from the Robert Stigwood Organisation announced that the Cream had signed a five-year recording contract with the Reaction label. The statement also said that the first single would be either "Wrapping Paper" or "The Coffee Song." They had earlier announced the name of Cream's first album as *Fresh Cream*, even though it was only about half recorded at this stage. RSO were optimistically hoping for an October release.

Unbelievably, "Wrapping Paper" was chosen to be the first single, with "Cat's Squirrel" as the B-side, and was released on 7 October 1966. I know times were different then, but even so, to release this seven-inch piece of tripe as the first thing the general public got to hear from Cream was misguided and ill thought. Any school band could have done better. Jack Bruce and Pete Brown should have held their heads in shame. Cream were three talented individuals, but there was no evidence of that on the first single. The fact that Reaction pulled 10,000 copies from the shops says it all, really. It did manage to chart at 34 in the UK, which surely must have been done with back-handers rather than merit. While Eric and Jack were happy to justify the single in interviews, Ginger was the only member who expressed his total dissatisfaction with the release.

Luckily, playing live is where Cream's talent really shone. You had three virtuoso soloists playing complex rhythms and at high volume. Seeing and hearing Cream in the small clubs and pubs in England must have been quite an experience. One that could not be repeated on vinyl. Their first album, *Fresh Cream*, was made up mainly of covers with some original numbers. Eric was not yet writing, Ginger was contributing one or two songs, and the majority were written by Jack and Pete Brown. The next single, "I Feel Free," was released at the same time as the album on 9 December 1966 and was a far cry from "Wrapping Paper." It was a catchy pop song that deserved its chart placing at 11 in the UK. The album reached number 6 in the UK. It was not released in the United States until March 1967, where it peaked at 37 in the charts.

Although Cream had visited Europe and Scandinavia, it was the prospect of finally getting to America that excited Eric the most. For him it was the home of all his blues heroes. His wishes came true in March 1967 when Cream flew over to New York to appear on a five-shows-a-day package for Murray the K's Easter show. The Who were on the same bill, and they would share a single set of equipment with Cream, who got a slot of only a few minutes for each of the five sets daily. At the end of their run they had two spare days, which were spent at the famed Atlantic Studios, where they recorded a couple of tracks, "Hey Lawdy Mama" and "Strange Brew," with a new producer, Felix Pappalardi, and Tom Dowd doing the engineering. Felix was a classically trained musician with a good knowledge of studios and the modern music scene. The session went so well that it was decided to record their new album at Atlantic as soon as possible. Work permits were organized, and

Cream flew back to America in May to start work on their second album, *Disraeli Gears*.

Eric was in awe of the studios, because the great stars of Atlantic were in and out of there all the time. In fact, Ray Charles had just finished a session in the same studio that Cream would use for the new album. It was an album that was done in a record four days. Unlike *Fresh Cream*, which had to be slotted in spare time with songs written on the road, *Disraeli Gears* was a much better prepared album with specific time given to writing as well as recording demos before road testing the material. By the time they reached the studio, they were ready to lay down all the tracks. It is a much more assured album for those reasons, with quality material and potential for several singles to be taken from it. Although Eric had contributed to some of the writing for *Disraeli Gears*, such as a third of "Sunshine Of Your Love," he was still more into arranging old blues numbers at this point. The first single, "Strange Brew," was a reworking, by Felix Pappalardi and his wife Gail Collins, of "Hey Lawdy Mama" with new lyrics. It did well in the UK but did not even chart in the United States. Cream had not toured in the States yet and were relatively unknown at this stage, so it is perhaps no surprise that there was no chart placing. By the time the album came out later in the year, though, Cream would be superstars. It was not an easy road to get there.

When Cream returned to England, they were collectively on a real high about having completed their new album as well as having recorded it at Atlantic in New York. Unfortunately, their euphoria was short-lived, as they found the whole of England raving about Jimi Hendrix and his just-released *Are You Experienced* album. The whole scene was buzzing about him, and Cream seemed to get lost in a sea of indifference back home. To compound matters for them, an opportunity to play at the Monterey Pop Festival was declined by Robert Stigwood. Eric recalled, "Robert felt we would derive greater benefit from going later, on our own, and playing hip venues like the Fillmore in San Francisco." I believe Stigwood was correct in his thinking. Jimi Hendrix and the Who did very well at Monterey, and those performances put them on the map in the United States and elsewhere when the film came out. But in 1967, these two bands had a big gimmick, with the Who smashing their equipment up at the end of their performance, and Jimi burning his guitar. That is what people were talking about at the time, these wild cats doing weird stuff on stage. It got people's attention. Cream, on the other hand, had no gimmick. They probably would just have been seen as one of the many bands that appeared there. It would not have done them any harm, but equally, they would not have received the publicity Jimi and the Who got.

Finally in August 1967 Cream started their first US tour in San Francisco at the Fillmore Auditorium, where they played a hugely successful two-week run. This was where Cream found the live sound that would soon make them a huge draw in America. They started expanding the solos in their songs to make up for lack of material, and the crowds loved it. "Spoonful," a particular crowd favorite, would sometimes stretch out to twenty minutes. Other numbers would get the same treatment. Cream's first US tour created quite a storm among the hip groovers as well as the more conservative media journals, such as the respected *Time* magazine, who stated in their 27 October 1967 issue that America "was still vibrating from what may be the biggest musical jolt out of England since the Beatles and the Rolling Stones."

Almost overnight, Cream had become part of the whole "Flower Power" scene that was starting to flourish on the West Coast and gradually all over America. Cream embraced it all, including the hallucinatory drugs like LSD and pot; the fashion, including wearing many beads and peace symbols; as well as attending love-ins and be-ins. Cream returned to England to massive acclaim, and the swinging-'60s London was taking off with them. They played some high-profile gigs, including a couple of headline shows at the Saville Theatre in London. They also ventured out to Ireland and Scandinavia to rave reviews. Cream had made it big and could do no wrong. Before long they were back in the studio preparing their next album. This time it would be a double set, which included a live album for the first time. The fans wanted a live souvenir, and the *Live at the Fillmore* set did not disappoint. For years, the live version of "Crossroads" baffled fans, who believed that Eric's solo had been sped up! It had not. That is the way Eric played it on the night. The studio set on *Wheels Of Fire* was no less enthralling, with very inventive songs such as "White Room," "Passing The Time," and "Politician." Eric, once again, let his

fingers do the talking rather than write any original songs for the album. By the time the album was released, Cream were the biggest-selling band on the planet.

Financially, it was a struggle touring in England and Europe. America was where the money was, and this was where the problems started. The lucrative deals being offered were incredible but came with a price: immense pressure. The US tours were lengthy and tiring. By the time they were halfway through the 1968 tour, the band had had enough. Their sense of humor, which had gotten them through many previous pressures, finally disappeared, and the band started to become very edgy with each other. They traveled to gigs in separate limousines and would stagger their arrival times so that they would not run into each other before being onstage. Eric was at a real low ebb.

A personal attack on Eric and his playing in *Rolling Stone* did not help his depression surrounding Cream. Shortly afterward, he heard the Band's *Music From Big Pink* album. Their music opened his ears and mind to new possibilities for the future. Their versatility blew him away and clearly helped him choose a path to a new style of playing for him. The only other band he had liked at the time were Moby Grape. He felt they were far more original than many of the other San Francisco bands.

Through a contact in Los Angeles, Eric met Robbie Robertson, and that was followed by a trip to Woodstock to see them at the Big Pink house. Eric remembers, "Dylan was there too, and I hung out with them for a few days and did a little jamming. I got on best with Richard Manuel, who was a bit of a loony and a hard drinker; I wasn't drinking much myself in those days, but in later years we frequently got legless together." After Cream split, it is easy to hear how Eric followed a very different musical path. The loud power playing was replaced with a more passionate and subtle style. And if that was down to the Band, that was not a bad thing.

In a break on the US tour it was officially announced that Cream would be breaking up after a farewell tour. Naturally, that lucrative tour took place only in the United States. England had to make do with two shows at the Royal Albert Hall. The rest of the world had to make do with the records.

CREAM
JULY 1966

18–29 July 1966, St Anne's Brondesbury Church Hall, 125 Salusbury Road, West Kilburn, London NW6 (Cream rehearsals. Chris Welch from *Melody Maker* interviews the band in a café near the hall. Eric explains to him that "Most people have formed the impression of us as three solo musicians clashing with each other. We want to cancel that idea and be a group that plays together")

30 July 1966, Twisted Wheel, Manchester, Lancashire (band to arrive by 6:45 p.m. and play 2 x 30-minute sessions between 9:30 p.m. and 2:00 a.m. Exact playing times are 9:30 p.m. to 10:00 p.m. and 1:00 a.m. to 1:30 a.m. Fee: £75 cash given to band on the night)

31 July 1966 6th National Jazz and Blues Festival, Royal Windsor Racecourse, Windsor, Berkshire (playing one set on the main stage between 9:00 p.m. and 9:40 p.m. Artists must arrive at least one hour before appearing, and electrical equipment must arrive before 6:00 p.m. Band is allowed to bring wife or girlfriend as guest. Fee: £65 check given to band on night)

SETLIST: Spoonful / Sleepy Time Time / Traintime / Steppin' Out / Toad

AUGUST 1966

1 August 1966, Cooks Ferry Inn, Edmonton, London (band to arrive by 7:00 p.m. They play 2 x 45-minute sessions between 8:00 and 11:00 p.m. Fee: £65 cash given to band on night)

2 August 1966, Klooks Keek, West Hampstead, London (band to arrive by 7:00 p.m. They play 2 x 60-minute sessions. Fee: £50 cash given to band on night)

3 August 1966, recording session at Rayrik Studios

4 August 1966, recording session at Rayrik Studios

5 August 1966, recording session at Rayrik Studios

6 August 1966, Beat 'n' Blues Festival, Town Hall, Torquay, Devon (band to arrive by 7:00 p.m. They play 2 x 45-minute sessions between 8:00 and 11:45 p.m. Fee: £75 cash given to band on night)

7 August 1966–8 August 1966, Pete Brown and Jack Bruce attempt to write material for Cream's first album

9 August 1966, Fishmongers Arms, Wood Green, London (band to arrive by 7:00 p.m. They play 2 x 45-minute sessions between 8:00 and 10:30 p.m. Fee: £50 cash given to band on night)

10 August 1966–11 August 1966, more writing sessions

12 August 1966, Peyton Place Club, Bromley, Kent (band to arrive by 7:00 p.m. They play 2 x 45-minute sessions between 8:00 and 11:00 p.m. Fee: £65 cash given to band on night. Comment from DJ at the club: "The Cream played at Peyton Place on 12 August 1966, about 6 weeks before they broke into the charts. I was the dj that evening. As we primarily only played soul and ska music, the Cream's music sounded very alien to the regulars")

13 August 1966, Blue Moon Club, Cheltenham, Gloucestershire (band to arrive by 7:00 p.m. They play 2 x 45-minute sessions between 8:00 and 11:30 p.m. Fee: £60 cash given to band on night)

14 August 1966, Central R&B Club, Central Hotel, Gillingham, Kent (unconfirmed)

15 August 1966, day off

16 August 1966, Marquee Club, Soho, London (with the Clayton Squares. Band to arrive by 6:30 p.m. They play 2 x 45-minute sessions between 7:30 and 11:00 p.m. Fee: £40 cash given to band on night)

Cream at the Marquee Club, London, on 16 August 1966.

17 August 1966, Orford Cellar, Orford Arms, Norwich, Norfolk (band to arrive by 7:00 p.m. They play 2 x 45-minute sessions between 8:00 and 11:00 p.m. Fee: £50 cash given to band on night)

18 August 1966, day off

19 August 1966, Cellar Club, Kingston-upon-Thames, Surrey (band to arrive by 7:00 p.m. They play 2 x 45-minute sessions between 8:00 and 11:30 p.m. Fee: £65 cash given to band on night)

20 August 1966, Lion Hotel, Warrington, Lancashire (band to arrive by 7:00 p.m. They play 2 x 45-minute sessions between 8:00 and 11:00 p.m. Fee: £40 cash given to band on night)

21 August 1966, King Mojo Club, Sheffield, Yorkshire (all-nighter. Band to arrive by 1:30 a.m. sharp. They play 2 x 45-minute sessions between 2:00 and 4:00 a.m. Fee: £50 cash given to band on night)

21 August 1966, King Mojo Club, Sheffield, Yorkshire (band to arrive by 7:00 p.m. They play 2 x 45 minute sessions between 8:00 and 11:00 p.m. Fee: £40 cash given to band on night)

22 August 1966–23 August 1966, days off

24 August 1966, Eel Pie Hotel, Eel Pie Island, Twickenham, London (band to arrive by 7:00 p.m. They play 2 x 1-hour sessions between 8:00 and 11:30 p.m. Fee: £60 cash given to band on night)

25 August 1966, day off

26 August 1966, Il Rondo, Leicester, Leicestershire (band to arrive by 7:00 p.m. They play 2 x 45-minute sessions between 8:00 and 11:00 p.m. Fee: £40 cash given to band on night)

27 August 1966, Ram Jam Club, Brixton, London (band to arrive by 6:30 p.m. They play 2 x 45-minute sessions between 7:30 and 11:00 p.m. Fee: £40 cash given to band on night)

27 August 1966, Flamingo All-Nighter Club, Soho, London (from midnight until dawn)

28 August 1966, Beachcomber, Nottingham, Nottinghamshire (band to arrive by 7:00 p.m. They play 2 x 45-minute sessions between 8:00 p.m. and 11:00 p.m. Fee: £65 check given to band on night)

29 August 1966, Community Centre, Welwyn Garden City, Hertfordshire

30 August 1966–31 August 1966, Cream recording at Ryemuse Studios, 64 South Molton Street, London at 7:00 p.m. onward

SEPTEMBER 1966

1 September 1966, Concorde Club, Bassett Hotel, Southampton, Hampshire (band to arrive by 7:00 p.m. They play 2 x 1-hour sessions between 8:00 and 11:00 p.m. Fee: £50 cash given to band on night)

2 September 1966, Bluesville '66 Club, Manor House, London (band to arrive by 7:00 p.m. They play 2 x 45-minute sessions between 8:00 and 11:00 p.m. Fee: £65 cash given to band on night)

3 September 1966, Cream were due to play an evening session in Portsmouth, Hampshire, followed by an all-nighter in Brighton, East Sussex. However, a memo from Cream's management tells the band: "Do not worry about having no engagement for the 3rd September. We originally had an evening session at Portsmouth followed by an all-nighter at Brighton. We discovered the Portsmouth promoter was insolvent and that the audiences at the Brighton venue were not good; therefore, both engagements were cancelled. Ricky Tick Club are interested in the act for Hounslow

but the date will not be booked unless we receive the right money"

4 September 1966, Ricky Tick, Clewer Mead, Windsor, Berkshire (band to arrive by 7:00 p.m. They play 2 x 45-minute sessions between 8:00 and 11:30 p.m. Fee: £70 cash given to band on night)

5 September 1966, Woodside Community Centre, Garston, Watford, Hertfordshire (band to arrive by 7:00 p.m. They play 2 x 45-minute sessions between 8:00 and 11:00 p.m. Fee: £60 cash given to band on night)

6 September 1966, day off

7 September 1966, Town Hall, Farnborough, Hampshire (band to arrive by 7:00 p.m. They play 2 x 45-minute sessions between 8:00 and 11:00 p.m. Fee: £50 cash given to band on night)

8 September 1966, day off

9 September 1966, Flamenco, Folkstone, Kent (band to arrive by 7:00 p.m. They play 2 x 1-hour sessions between 8:00 and 11:00 p.m. Fee: £75 cash given to band on night)

10 September 1966, Marquee Dance Club, Birmingham, Midlands (band to arrive by 12:00 midnight. The band play 2 x 45-minute sessions between 1:00 and 4:00 a.m. Fee: £125 cash given to band on night)

11 September 1966, Manor Lounge, Stockport, Cheshire (band to arrive by 7:00 p.m. They play 2 x 45-minute sessions between 8:00 and 11:00 p.m. Fee: £75 cash given to band on night)

12 September 1966, Manor House Ballroom, Ipswich, Suffolk (band to arrive by 7:00 p.m. They play 2 x 45-minute sessions between 8:00 and 11:00 p.m. Fee: £75 cash given to band on night)

13 September 1966, day off

14 September 1966, day off

15 September 1966, Gaumont, Hanley, Staffordshire (Robert Stigwood promoted show with the Who as headliners. This was to have been the first date of a Reaction label package tour with the Who, Cream, Oscar, the MI5, the Merseys, and comedian Max Wall. In the end, this was the only date that went ahead after Cream doubted that this sort of tour would be beneficial for them. At the same time, the Who had also been offered a short promotional visit in the United States and saw more potential there. The rest of the dates were canceled and refunds given. Cream went off to headline their own tour)

16 September 1966, Hitchin Technical College, Hitchin, Hertfordshire (with the Farinas. Band to arrive by 7:00 p.m. They play 2 x 45-minute sessions between 8:00 and 11:00 p.m. Fee: £70 cash given to band on night)

17 September 1966, Drill Hall, Grantham, Lincolnshire (band to arrive by 7:00 p.m. They play 2 x 45-minute sessions between 8:00 and 11:30 p.m. Fee: £75 cash given to band on night)

18 September 1966, Blue Moon Club, Hayes, Middlesex (band to arrive by 7:00 p.m. They play 2 x 45-minute sessions between 8:00 and 11:00 p.m. Fee: £100 cash given to band on night)

19 September1966, Atalanta Ballroom, Woking, Surrey (band to arrive by 7:00 p.m. They play 2 x 45-minute sessions between 8:00 and 11:00 p.m. Fee: £50 cash given to band on night)

20 September 1966, Ricky Tick Club, Corn Exchange, Bedford, Bedfordshire (band to arrive by 7:00 p.m. They play 2 x 45-minute sessions between 8:00 and 11:00 p.m. Fee: £100 cash given to band on night)

21 September 1966, day off

22 September 1966, day off

23 September 1966, Ricky Tick Club, Corn Exchange, Newbury, Berkshire (band to arrive by 7:00 p.m. They play 2 x 45-minute sessions between 8:00 and 11:00 p.m. Fee: £100 cash given to band on night)

24 September 1966, Technical College, Kingston-upon-Thames, Surrey (band to arrive by 7:30 p.m. They play 2 x 45-minute sessions between 8:00 and 11.45p.m. Fee: £125 check given to band on night)

25 September 1966, day off

26 September 1966, Star Hotel, Croydon, Surrey (band to arrive by 7:00 p.m. They play 2 x 45-minute sessions between 8:00 and 11:00 p.m. Fee: £50 cash given to band on night)

27 September 1966, Marquee Club, Soho, London (with the Herd. Band to arrive by 7:00 p.m. They play 2 x 45-minute sessions between 8:00 and 11:00 p.m. Fee: £100 cash given to band on night)

28 September 1966, Ricky Tick Club, Harpenden Public Hall, Harpenden, Bedfordshire (band to arrive by 7:00 p.m. They play 2 x 45-minute sessions between 8:00 and 11:00 p.m. Fee: £50 cash given to band on night)

Cream at the Marquee Club, London, on 27 September 1966.

Cream at the Marquee Club, London, on 27 September 1966.

Cream at the Marquee Club, London, on 27 September 1966.

Cream at the Marquee Club, London, on 27 September 1966.

29 September 1966, day off

30 September 1966, Ricky Tick Club, Hounslow, Middlesex (band to arrive by 7:00 p.m. They play 2 x 45-minute sessions between 8:00 and 11:30 p.m. Fee: £125 cash given to band on night)

OCTOBER 1966

1 October 1966, Regent Street Polytechnic, London (band to arrive by 7:00 p.m. They play 2 x 45-minute sessions between 8:00 p.m. and 12:00 midnight. Fee: £150 check given to band on night. Jimi Hendrix jams on Howlin' Wolf's "Killing Floor" and another blues number with Cream tonight. Hendrix blows both Cream and the audience away that night)

2 October 1966, Kirklevington Country Club, Kirklevington, Yorkshire (canceled due to Jack Bruce having throat problems)

3 October 1966, Quaintways Restaurant, Quaintways, Chester, Chestershire (cancelled due to Jack Bruce having throat problems)

4 October 1966, Fishmonger Arms, Wood Green, London (canceled due to Jack Bruce having throat problems)

5 October 1966, Reading University, Reading, Berkshire (canceled due to Jack Bruce having throat problems)

6 October 1966, York University, York, Yorkshire (canceled due to Jack Bruce having throat problems)

7 October 1966, Union Society, Kings College, London (band to arrive by 7:00 p.m. They play 2 x 45-minute sessions between 7:30 p.m. and 12midnight. Fee: £125 check given to band on night)

8 October 1966, Sixth Session, Falmer House, Sussex University, Brighton, East Sussex (with Tony Jackson and the Vibrators, Paul Stewart, Russell's Clump. Band to arrive by 7:30 p.m. They play 2 x 45-minute sessions between 8:00 p.m. and 2:00 a.m. Fee: £125 check given to band on night. Ginger Baker collapses during his drum solo on "Toad" and is diagnosed as suffering with acute exhaustion due to overwork. He also has the flu, which does not help matters. Interestingly, management were aware that the band were working hard and stated in a message to band members: "In view of the lack of days off, 9th October, which is a Sunday, will deliberately not be filled, unless anyone violently objects." It is doubtful that Ginger would have been fit enough to play a gig the next day anyway. Management carry on to state: "At present, November is very healthy and we are not currently trying to fill the eleven dates not booked. The intention for future work is to book four or five consecutive dates with two or three vacant days between")

9 October 1966, day off

10 October 1966, Ricky Tick Club, Harpenden Public Hall, Harpenden, Bedfordshire (band to arrive by 7:00 p.m. They play 2 x 45-minute sessions between 8:00 and 11:00 p.m. Fee: £100 cash given to band on night)

11 October 1966, day off

12 October 1966, Orford Cellar, Orford Arms, Norwich, Norfolk (band to arrive by 7:00 p.m. They play 2 x 45-minute sessions between 8:00 and 11:00 p.m. Fee: £75 cash given to band on night)

13 October 1966, Club A Go Go, Newcastle, Tyne & Wear (band to arrive by 7:00 p.m. They play 2 x 45-minute sessions, one session in each of the two halls, between 8:00 p.m. and 12:00 midnight. Fee: £65 check given to band on night)

14 October 1966, day off

15 October 1966, Sheffield University, Sheffield, Yorkshire (band to arrive by 7:00 p.m. They play 2 x 45-minute sessions between 8:00 p.m. and 11:00 p.m. Fee: £100 check given to band on night. As soon as they finish, the band drive to Manchester for an all-nighter at the Jigsaw Club)

16 October 1966, Jigsaw Club, Manchester, Lancashire (band to arrive by 1:30 a.m. They play 2 x 30-minute sessions between 2:00 a.m. and 4:00 a.m. Fee: £200 cash given to band on night)

16 October 1966, Hotel Leofric, Coventry, Warickshire (band to arrive by 6:30 p.m. They play 2 x 45-minute sessions between 7:00 p.m. and 10:30 p.m. Fee: £65 cash given to band on night)

17 October 1966, Majestic Ballroom, Reading, Berkshire (band to arrive by 6:30 p.m. They play 2 x 45-minute sessions between 8:00 p.m. and 11:00 p.m. Fee: £100 check given to band on night)

18 October 1966, day off

19 October 1966, recording at Ryemuse Studios

20 October 1966, Carnival Dance, Willenhall Baths Assembly Hall, Wolverhampton, Midlands (with the "N" Betweens, Listen, the Factotums. Band to arrive by 7:00 p.m. They play 2 x 30-minute sessions between 8:00 p.m. and midnight. Fee: £150 check given to band on night)

21 October 1966, BBC *Bandbeat*. Recorded at the BBC's Maida Vale Studios, 4 Delaware Road, London W4. Recording between 2:30 p.m. and 6:00 p.m. Producer: Jeff Griffin. This is the band's first recording session for the BBC, and they are paid twenty-nine pounds three shillings and sixpence, which is the BBC rate for a three-piece band. Numbers recorded are: "Spoonful," "Sleepy Time Time," "Rollin' And Tumblin'." Broadcast on 21 November.

21 October 1966, Bluesville 66, Manor House, London (band to arrive by 7:00 p.m. They play 2 x 45-minute sessions between 8:00 p.m. and 11:00 p.m. Fee: £75 cash given to band on night)

22 October 1966, Union Hop, Leeds University, Leeds, Yorkshire (band to arrive by 6:30 p.m. They play 2 x 45-minute sessions between 7:30 p.m. and 11:00 p.m. Fee: £125 check given to band on night. The Paul Butterfield Blues Band are also playing in Leeds this evening, and their guitarist, Michael Bloomfield, manages to catch Cream's second set)

23 October 1966, Beachcomber Club, Nottingham, Nottinghamshire (band to arrive by 7:00 p.m. They play 2 x 45-minute sessions between 8:00 p.m. and 11:00 p.m. Fee: £65 check given to band on night)

24 October 1966, St Matthews Baths Hall, Ipswich, Suffolk (band to arrive by 7:00 p.m. They play 2 x 45-minute sessions between 8:00 p.m. and 11:00 p.m. Fee: £75 cash given to band on night)

25 October 1966, day off

26 October 1966, day off

27 October 1966, New Yorker Discotheque, Swindon, Wiltshire

28 October 1966, Il Rondo Club, Leicester, Leicestershire

29 October 1966, Union Dance, Bristol University, Bristol, Somerset (evening show)

30 October 1966, Midnight City Club, Birmingham, Midlands (all-nighter from 1:00 a.m. to 4:00 am)

30 October 1966, Agincourt Ballroom, Camberely, Surrey (band to arrive by 7:00 p.m. They play 2 x 45-minute sessions between 8:00 p.m. and midnight. Fee: £75 cash given to band on night)

31 October 1966, Atalanta Ballroom, Woking, Surrey (band to arrive by 7:00 p.m. They play 2 x 45-minute sessions between 8:00 p.m. and 11:00 p.m. Fee: £50 cash given to band on night)

NOVEMBER 1966

1 November 1966, *Ready Steady Go*, Rediffusion Television Studios, Wembley Park Drive, Wembley, Middlesex (band have to be there from 10:00 a.m. onward. Cream play "NSU" and "Wrapping Paper." The show was broadcast on 4 November)

2 November 1966, the Pavilion, Hemel Hempstead, Hertfordshire (the Cortinas supported Cream this evening)

3 November 1966, Ram Jam Club, Brixton, London (band to arrive by 7:00 p.m. They play 2 x 45-minute sessions between 7:30 and 11:00 p.m. Fee: £100 check given to band on night)

Cream play "Wrapping Paper" on Ready Steady Go *television show on 1 November 1966.*

Cream play "N.S.U." on Ready Steady Go *television show on 1 November 1966.*

"On 2nd November 1966 we were booked to support 'CREAM' (Eric Clapton, Jack Bruce and Ginger Baker) at Hemel Hempstead Pavillion which we were quite excited about but it turned out to be the gig from hell. The audience had obviously come to see 'CREAM,' so we played our hour set to calls of 'get off' and 'we want Cream' (and they were the polite ones). Eventually we finished and walked off the stage only to be met by the manager saying, 'Sorry boys Ginger Baker is in no fit state to play at the moment, so you'll have to go back and play another half an hour.' It was terrible to have to go back and explain to the audience and it was the longest half hour of our lives. Eventually we saw the manager saying they were ready so we finished. As we walked down stairs to the dressing room we passed Eric Clapton and Jack Bruce walking up followed by two guys virtually carrying Ginger Baker who was mumbling 'Where's the fucking stage man.' They sat him on his drum stool and they were off and I have to say they were brilliant."

—**PAUL DAVID GRIGGS** (The Cortinas)

4 November 1966, Warwick University, Coventry (band to arrive by 7:00 p.m. They play 2 x 45-minute sessions. They play between 08:00 p.m. and midnight. Fee: £100 check given to band on night)

5 November 1966, Town Hall, East Ham, London (with the Farm. Band to arrive by 7:00 p.m. They play 2 x 45-minute sessions between 8:00 p.m. and midnight. Fee: £125 check given to band on night)

6 November 1966, Jack Bruce and Pete Brown spend the day writing together

7 November 1966, New Spot Club, Thorngate Ballroom, Gosport, Hampshire (band to arrive by 7:00 p.m. They play 2 x 45-minute sessions between 8:00 p.m. and 11:00 p.m. Fee: £100 cash given to band on night)

8 November 1966, BBC Saturday Club. Recorded at the Playhouse Theatre, Northumberland Avenue, London WC2. Recording between 2:00 p.m. to 4:30 p.m. Producer Bill Bebb. Numbers recorded are: "Sweet Wine," "Steppin' Out," "Wrapping Paper," "Rollin' And Tumblin'," "I'm So Glad," "Sleepy Time Time." Broadcast on 12 November

8 November 1966, Marquee Club, Soho, London (band to arrive by 7:00 p.m. They play 2 x 45-minute sessions between 7:30 p.m. and 11:00 p.m. Fee: £100 cash given to band on night)

9 November 1966, day off

10 November 1966, day off

11 November 1966, Public Baths, Sutton-in-Ashfield, Nottinghamshire (band to arrive by 7:00 p.m. They play 2 x 45-minute sessions between 8:00 p.m. and 11:30 p.m. Fee: £75 cash given to band on night)

12 November 1966, Students Union, Liverpool University, Liverpool, Merseyside (band to arrive by 7:30 p.m. They play 2 x 45-minute sessions between 8:00 p.m. and midnight. Fee: £150 check given to band on night)

13 November 1966, Coatham Hotel, Redcar, Redcar and Cleveland (band to arrive by 6:30 p.m. They play 2 x 45-minute sessions between 7:00 p.m. and 11:00 p.m. Fee: £75 check given to band on night)

14 November 1966, day off

15 November 1966, Klooks Kleek Club, Railway Hotel, West Hampstead, London (band to arrive by 6:30 p.m. They play 2 x 45-minute sessions between 7:00 p.m. and 11:00 p.m. Fee: £75 cash given to band on night)

16 November 1966, day off

17 November 1966, Norwich University, Norwich, Norfolk

18 November 1966, Hoveton Village Hall, Wroxham, Norfolk

19 November 1966, Blue Moon Club, Cheltenham, Gloucestershire

20 November 1966, day off

21 November 1966, BBC Monday, Monday. Recorded at the Playhouse Theatre, Northumberland Avenue, London WC2. Recording between 09:30 a.m. to 11:30 a.m. Producer Keith Bateson. Numbers recorded are: "Spoonful," "Steppin' Out," "I'm So Glad." Broadcast same day between 1:00 p.m. and 2:00 p.m.

21 November 1966, The Pavilion, Bath, Somerset

22 November 1966, Chinese R&B Jazz Club, Corn Exchange, Bristol, Gloucestershire

23 November 1966, day off

24 November 1966, day off

25 November 1966, California Ballroom, Dunstable, Bedfordshire (band to arrive by 6:30 p.m. They play 2 x 45-minute sessions between 7:00 p.m. and 11:00 p.m. Fee: £150 check given to band on night)

26 November 1966, Corn Exchange, Chelmsford, Essex (band to arrive by 6:30 p.m. They play 2 x 45-minute sessions between 7:00 p.m. and 11:00 p.m. Fee: £150 cash given to band on night)

27 November 1966, Agincourt Ballroom, Camberely, Surrey (band to arrive by 7:00 p.m. They play 2 x 45-minute sessions between 8:00 p.m. and midnight. Fee: £75 cash given to band on night)

28 November 1966, BBC Home Service's Guitar Club. Recorded at BBC's Studio 2, Aeolian Hall, 135–137 New Bond Street, London W1. Recording between 02:30 p.m. to 4:30 p.m. Producer Bernie Andrews. Numbers recorded are: "Crossroads," "Sitting On Top Of The World," "Steppin' Out." Broadcast on 30 December.

28 November 1966, Atalanta Ballroom, Woking, Surrey (band to arrive by 7:00 p.m. They play 2 x 45-minute sessions between 8:00 p.m. and midnight. Fee: £50 cash given to band on night)

29 November 1966, day off

30 November 1966, day off

DECEMBER 1966

1 December 1966, day off

2 December 1966, the New Cellar Club, South Shields, Co. Durham (the band are notified by management on 29 November that they will be playing at the opening of a new club in South Shields. Band to arrive by 7:30 p.m. They play 2 x 45-minute sessions between 8:30 p.m. and 11:00 p.m. Fee: £250 cash given to band on night)

3 December 1966, Birdcage Club Portsmouth, Hampshire (Ginger Baker collapses at the end of the first set and is taken to the hospital. As a result, the second set is canceled. Eric Clapton tells the press, "Ginger had been taking pain-killing tablets for sinus trouble which developed last year. He had a couple of drinks tonight and the two reacted")

4 December 1966, Starlite Ballroom, Greenford, London (canceled due to Ginger's illness)

5 December 1966, Baths Hall, Ipswich, Suffolk (canceled due to Ginger's illness)

6 December 1966, day off

7 December 1966, Hull University, Hull, Yorkshire (canceled due to Ginger's illness)

8 December 1966, Hornsey College of Art, Hornsey, London (band to arrive by 8:45 p.m.. They play 2 x 45-minute sessions between 10:00 p.m. and 1:00 a.m. Fee: £250 check given to band on night)

9 December 1966, BBC Rhythm & Blues. Recorded at BBC Maida Vale Studio 4, Delaware Road, London W9. Recording between 3:00 p.m. to 6:30 p.m. Producer Jeff Griffin. Numbers recorded are: "Cat's Squirrel," "Traintime," "Hey Lawdy Mama," "I'm So Glad." Broadcast 9 January 1967

9 December 1966, Bluesville 66, Manor House, London (band to arrive by 7:00 p.m. They play 2 x 45-minute sessions between 8:00 p.m. and 11:00 p.m. Fee: £75 cash given to band on night)

10 December 1966, Isleworth Polytechnic, Isleworth, Middlesex (band to arrive by 7:00 p.m. They play 2 x 45-minute sessions between 8:00 p.m. and 11:00 p.m. Fee: £100 cash given to band on night)

11 December 1966, day off

12 December 1966, Cooks Ferry Inn, Edmonton, London (band to arrive by 7:00 p.m. They play 2 x 45-minute sessions between 8:00 p.m. and 11:30 p.m. Fee: £75 cash given to band on night)

13 December 1966, Exeter University, Exeter, Devon (band to arrive by 7:00 p.m. They play 2 x 45-minute sessions between 8:00 p.m. and 2:00 a.m. Fee: £100 check given to band on night)

14 December 1966, Bromel Club, Bromley Court Hotel, Bromley, Kent (band to arrive by 7:30 p.m. They play 2 x 45-minute sessions between 8:00 p.m. and 11:00 p.m. Fee: £200 cash given to band on night)

15 December 1966, University of Sussex, Brighton, East Sussex (band to arrive by 7:30 p.m. They play 2 x 45-minute sessions between 8:00 p.m. and 2:00 a.m. Fee: £125 check given to band on night)

16 December 1966, Cream fly out to Paris, France, for press interviews, a television appearance on the popular Vient De Paraître show, and a special club show. Polydor, their French record label, has just released an EP with "Wrapping Paper," "Sweet Wine," "I'm So Glad" and "Cat's Squirrel." The latter track is sought after by collectors, as it contains an alternate guitar solo to the one found on the Fresh Cream album. They mime to two numbers from that EP today, "Wrapping Paper" and "Sweet Wine," on the Vient De Paraître television show on the ORTF channel

17 December 1966, La Locomotive Club, Paris, France

18 December 1966, Cream fly back to the UK

18 December 1966, Agincourt Ballroom, Camberley, Surrey (band to arrive by 7:00 p.m. They play 2 x 45-minute sessions between 8:00 p.m. and midnight. Fee: £75 cash given to band on night)

19 December 1966, Atalanta Ballroom, Woking, Surrey (band to arrive by 7:00 p.m. They play 2 x 45-minute sessions between 8:00 p.m. and midnight. Fee: £50 cash given to band on night)

20 December 1966, Winter Gardens, Malvern, Worcestershire (band to arrive by 7:00 p.m. They play 2 x 45-minute sessions between 8:00 p.m. and midnight. Fee: £175 cash given to band on night)

21 December 1966, BBC Television Top Of The Pops. Recorded at the BBC's Lime Grove Studios, London W12. Producer Johnnie Stewart. Cream mime to their new single "I Feel Free" and to "Wrapping Paper." Fee paid by the BBC is £42. Broadcast 29 December.

21 December 1966, Bromel Club, Bromley Court Hotel, Bromley, Kent (band to arrive by 7:30 p.m. They play 2 x 45-minute sessions between 8:00 p.m. and 11:00 p.m. Fee: £200 cash given to band on night)

22 December 1966, The Pavilion, Worthing, West Sussex

23 December 1966, 36 Hour Rave, Midnight City Club, Birmingham, Midlands (Cream headlines on the 23 December, which gives time for the band to head home for the Christmas break)

24 December 1966–29 December 1966, days off

30 December 1966, Double Giant Freak Out Ball "Psychedelicamania" at the Roundhouse, Chalk Farm Road, London (with Geno Washington and the Ram Jam Band, Cream, and the Alan Bown Set. 10:00 p.m. till dawn)

31 December 1966, day off

1967

JANUARY 1967

1 January 1967–6 January 1967, days off

7 January 1967, Ricky Tick Club, Thames Hotel, Windsor, Berkshire (band to arrive by 7:00 p.m. They play 3 x 45-minute sessions between 8:00 p.m. and 11:30 p.m. Fee: £230 cash given to band on night)

8 January 1967–9 January 1967, days off

10 January 1967, BBC *Saturday Club*. Recorded at the Playhouse Theatre, Northumberland Avenue, London WC2. Recording between 4:30 p.m. to 7:00 p.m. Producer Bill Bebb. Numbers recorded are: "Four Until Late," "I Feel Free," "Traintime," "NSU," "Toad." Broadcast 14 January 1967

10 January 1967, Marquee Club, Soho, London (band to arrive by 7:00 p.m. They play 2 x 45-minute sessions between 7:30 p.m. and 11:00 p.m. Fee: cash given to band on night)

11 January 1967, BBC Television *Top Of The Pops*. Recorded at the BBC's Lime Grove Studios, London W12. Producer Stanley Dorfman. Cream mime to "I Feel Free." Broadcast 12 January

12 January 1967, day off

13 January 1967, Ricky Tick Club, Guildhall, Southampton, Hampshire (band to arrive by 7:30 p.m. They play 2 x 45-minute sessions between 8:00 p.m. and 11:30 p.m. Fee: £200 cash given to band on night)

14 January 1967, Lanchester College, Coventry, Midlands (band to arrive by 7:00 p.m. They play 2 x 30-minute sessions between 7:30 p.m. and 11:00 p.m. Fee: £250 check sent to office)

15 January 1967, Ricky Tick Club, Hounslow, Middlesex (band to arrive by 8:00 p.m. They play 2 x 45-minute sessions between 8:00 p.m. and 11:00 p.m. Fee: £200 cash given to band on night)

16 January 1967, BBC *Monday, Monday*. Recorded at the Playhouse Theatre, Northumberland Avenue, London WC2. Recording between 9:30 a.m. to 11:30 a.m. Producer Keith Bateson. Numbers recorded are: "NSU," "Rollin' And Tumblin'," "I Feel Free." Broadcast same day between 1:00 p.m. and 2:00 p.m.

17 January 1967, day off

18 January 1967, Town Hall, Stourbridge, Worcestershire (band to arrive by 7:00 p.m. They play 1 x 60-minute session between 8:00 p.m. and 11:30 p.m. Fee: £200 cash given to band on night)

19 January 1967, Leicester College of Art "Arts Ball," Granby Halls, Leicester, Leicestershire (band to arrive by 7:00 p.m. They play 2 x 30-minute sessions between 8:00 p.m. and 3:00 a.m. Fee: £200 check given to band on night)

20 January 1967, Club A Go Go, Newcastle, Tyne & Wear (band to arrive by 8:00 p.m. They play 2 x 45-minute sessions, 1 in each hall, between 9:30 p.m. and 1:30 a.m. Fee: £250 check sent to office)

21 January 1967, Floral Hall Southport, Lancashire (band to arrive by 7:30 p.m. They play 2 x 45-minute sessions between 8:00 p.m. and 11:00 p.m. Fee: £250 check given to band on night)

22 January 1967, day off

23 January 1967, Cream go to Richmond Park in Surrey to film a zany promo for "I Feel Free," which sees them dressed as monks running and jumping around the park. The playground location is Old Deer Park near the Thames. You can spot Richmond Lock in the background. At the end of the film, you can see the lads run towards Richmond Baths.

24 January 1967, Chinese R&B Jazz Club, Corn Exchange, Bristol, Gloucestershire (band to arrive by 7:00 p.m. They play 2 x 45-minute sessions between 8:00 p.m. and 11:00 p.m. Fee: £100 cash given to band on night)

"'I Feel Free' was, apart from one early Beatles, the very first promo made for worldwide TV showing. It took the music industry a long while to realise the potential of these short promos. That one was commissioned by Robert Stigwood and from it I went on to make a number of similar films for other bands. At that time I was in my final year at the Royal College of Art and had been doing a quite a lot of music photography. I was constantly encouraging various bands to do some movie film but few saw the potential, but I gradually won through in the end and the genre was born. The best that I did were for bands like the Troggs, the Bonzos, Kinks etc. As you probably know the boys in Cream did not always get along too well and although I got to know them very well, working with them could often be difficult. To this day I still do not know why they chose to be dressed as monks but they insisted. They were still unsure what look they wanted the band to project, so I took them along to a theatrical costumers and strangely, of all the outfits, that was what they chose (after a lot of argument between them). I still have the fireman's helmet Eric is wearing. The film has been digitised and still regularly appears on TV programmes all over the world."

—**DAVID STANFORD** (director of "I Feel Free" promo film)

25 January 1967, BBC *Parade Of The Pops*. Cream need to be at the Playhouse Theatre, Northumberland Avenue, London WC2, by 11:00 a.m. They play "I Feel Free" in front of a live audience. Producer Ian Scott. Broadcast same day between 1:00 p.m. and 2:00 p.m.

26 January 1967, BBC Television *Top Of The Pops*. Recorded at the BBC's Lime Grove Studios, London W12. Cream need to be at the studio by 2:00 p.m. Producer Stanley Dorfman. Cream mime to "I Feel Free." Broadcast same day on BBC1 between 7:30 p.m. and 8:00 p.m.

27 January 1967, Adelphi Ballroom, West Bromwhich, Staffordshire (band to arrive by 9:00 p.m. They play 2 x 45-minute sessions between 11:00 p.m. and 6:00 a.m. Fee: £225 cash given to band on night)

28 January 1967, Ram Jam Club, Brixton, London (band to arrive by 7:00 p.m. They play 2 x 45-minute sessions between 7:30 and 11:00 p.m. Fee: £100 check given to band on night)

29 January 1967–31 January 1967, days off

FEBRUARY 1967

1 February 1967, day off

3 February 1967, Queens Hall, Leeds, Yorkshire (band to arrive by 8:00 p.m. They play 1 x 60-minute session between 8:00 p.m. and midnight. Fee: £250 cash given to band on night)

4 February 1967, Wallington Public Hall, Wallington, Surrey (band to arrive by 7:00 p.m. They play 2 x 45-minute sessions between 8:00 p.m. and midnight. Fee: £250 check given to band on night)

5 February 1967, Saville Theatre, London (2 headline shows with the Sands, Edwin Starr. Band to arrive by 2:30 p.m. They play 1 x 45-minute session at each show between 5:30 p.m. and 8:00 p.m. and 8:30 p.m. and midnight. Fee: £225 check sent to office)

6 February 1967, day off

7 February 1967, the University of Manchester, Manchester, Lancashire (band to arrive by 8:00 p.m. They play 2 x 30-minute sessions between 9:00 p.m. and 1:00 a.m. Fee: £250 check given to band on night)

8 February 1967, day off

9 February 1967, City Hall, Salisbury, Wiltshire (band to arrive by 8:00 p.m. They play 2 x 45-minute sessions between 8:00 p.m. and 11:00 p.m. Fee: £200 cash given to band on night)

10 February 1967, Bluesville 66, Manor House, London (band to arrive by 7:00 p.m. They play 2 x 45-minute sessions between 8:00 p.m. and 11:00 p.m. Fee: £75 cash given to band on night)

11 February 1967, The Pavilion, Matlock Bath, Derbyshire (band to arrive by 8:00 p.m. They play 2 x 30-minute sessions between 8:00 p.m. and 11:45 p.m. Fee: £250 check given to band on night)

12 February 1967–14 February 1967, days off

15 February 1967, Ricky Tick Club, Assembly Hall, Aylesbury, Buckinghamshire (band to arrive by 8:00 p.m. They play 2 x 45-minute sessions between 8:00 p.m. and 11:00 p.m. Fee: £240 cash given to band on night)

16 February 1967, day off

17 February 1967, Woodlands Youth Centre, Basildon, Essex (with the Riot Squad. Band to arrive by 7:30 p.m. They play 2 x 45-minute sessions between 8:00 p.m. and midnight. Fee: £250 check given to band on night)

18 February 1967, Tofts Club, Folkestone, Kent (band to arrive by 8:00 p.m. They play 2 x 45-minute sessions between 8:00 p.m. and 11:30 p.m. Fee: £250 cash given to band on night)

19 February 1967, Starlite Ballroom, Greenford, Middlesex (with the Gods. Band to arrive by 8:00 p.m. They play 2 x 30-minute sessions between 8:00 p.m. and 11:00 p.m. Fee: £200 cash given to band on night)

20 February 1967, day off

21 February 1967, Town Hall, High Wycombe, Buckinghamshire (band to arrive by 8:00 p.m. They play 2 x 35-minute sessions between 8:00 p.m. and 10:30 p.m. Fee: £200 cash given to band on night)

22 February 1967, Bromel Club, Bromley Court Hotel, Bromley, Kent (band to arrive by 7:30 p.m. They play 2 x 45-minute sessions between 8:00 p.m. and 11:00 p.m. Fee: £250 cash given to band on night)

23 February 1967, day off

24 February 1967, *Beat Club* television show, Radio Bremen Studios, Bremen, Germany (Band catch Lufthtansa flight LH237 at 11:05 a.m. from London Airport to Bremen. Radio Bremen arrange hotel accommodation for the band. Cream mime to "I Feel Free" and it is transmitted the following day in Germany)

25 February 1967, Star Club, Hamburg, Germany (band play 2 x 45-minute sessions. Fee: £200 cash given to band on night)

26 February 1967, Stadhalle, Bremen, Germany (band play 2 x 45-minute sessions. Fee: £200 cash given to band on night)

27 February 1967, band fly home from Bremen on LH236, which arrives at London Airport at 4:05 p.m. They head off to Manchester to headline the Manchester and Salford Students Rag Ball

27 February 1967, Manchester and Salford Students Rag Ball '67, Main Debating Hall, Manchester University, Manchester, Lancashire (with the Graham Bond Organisation, Brian Poole and the Tremeloes, Jimmy James and the Vagabonds, the Nashville Teens, the Bonzo Dog Doo-Dah Band, Tubby Hayes Quartet, the Ian Campbell Group. Cream headline and do not get to play until the early hours of 28 February)

28 February 1967, day off

MARCH 1967

 1 March 1967, Ulster Hall, Belfast, Northern Ireland (with the Interns, the Group, The Few, the Styx. The band leave London Airport on British European Airways flight BE6542, which departs at 2:40 p.m. and arrives at Belfast airport at 4:00 p.m. Band to arrive by 8:00 p.m. They play 2 x 45-minute sessions between 8:00 p.m. and midnight. Fee: £200 cash given to band on night)

 2 March 1967, Rag Pop Festival, Queens University, Belfast, Northern Ireland (with the Interns, the Green Angels, the Faculty. The band to arrive by 8:00 p.m. They play 2 x 45-minute sessions between 8:00 p.m. and 2:00 a.m. Fee: £200 check given to band on night)

 3 March 1967, Band leave Belfast airport on British European Airways flight BE6527 at 11:10 a.m. and arrive at London Airport at 12:25 a.m.

 4 March 1967, Memorial Hall, Barry, Glamorgan, Wales (band to arrive by 8:00 p.m. They play 2 x 30-minute sessions between 8:00 p.m. and 11:30 p.m. Fee: £250 check given to band on night)

 5 March 1967, band fly out from London Airport to Kastrup Airport, Copenhagen. A planned thirty-minute press conference this afternoon has to be canceled when the band are detained for three hours at the airport because they have no money

 6 March 1967, Falkoner Centret, Copenhagen, Denmark (band play a 30-minute session. Fee: £280 cash paid on night)

 7 March 1967, *Onkel Thores Stuga* television show (Cream mime to N.S.U. Broadcast 19 March)

 7 March 1967, Konserthuset, Stockholm, Sweden (band play a 30-minute session. Fee: £280 cash paid on night. 5 songs are broadcast on Swedish Radio's *Konsert Med Cream*)

SETLIST (PARTIAL):

N.S.U. (Jack Bruce) available on bonus CD with *Cream: Their Fully Authorised Story* DVD Pinnacle Vision released September 2008

Steppin' Out (James Bracken) available on bonus CD with *Cream: Their Fully Authorised Story* DVD Pinnacle Vision released September 2008

Traintime (Jack Bruce) available on bonus CD with *Cream: Their Fully Authorised Story* DVD Pinnacle Vision released September 2008

Toad (Ginger Baker) available on bonus CD with *Cream: Their Fully Authorised Story* DVD Pinnacle Vision released September 2008

I'm So Glad (Skip James) available on bonus CD with *Cream: Their Fully Authorised Story* DVD Pinnacle Vision released September 2008

 8 March 1967, Cue Club, Liseberg Cirkus, Gothenburg, Sweden (band play a 30-minute session. Fee: £280 cash paid on night)

 9 March 1967, band fly back from Scandinavia to England

10 March 1967, day off

11 March 1967, St Georges Ballroom, Hinckley, Leicestershire (band to arrive by 8:00 p.m. They play 2 x 30-minute sessions between 8:00 p.m. and 11:30 p.m. Fee: £275 cash given to band on night)

12 March 1967, Tavern Club, East Dereham, Norfolk (band to arrive by 8:00 p.m. They play 2 x 45-minute sessions between 8:00 p.m. and 11:00 p.m. Fee: £240 cash given to band on night)

13 March 1967, day off

14 March 1967, Kings Hall, Aberystwyth, Ceredigion, Wales (band to arrive by 7:00 p.m. They play 2 x 45-minute sessions between 8:00 p.m. and midnight. Fee: £300 check sent to office)

15 March 1967, Demo Session at Rymuse Studios, South Molton Street, London W1

16 March 1967, day off

17 March 1967, Woodlands Youth Centre, Basildon, Essex (band to arrive by 7:30 p.m. They play 2 x 45-minute sessions between 8:00 p.m. and midnight. Fee: £250 check given to band on night)

18 March 1967, Bristol University, Bristol, Gloucestershire (band to arrive by 8:00 p.m. They play 2 x 30-minute sessions between 8:00 p.m. and midnight. Fee: £300 check sent to office)

19 March 1967, day off

20 March 1967, BBC radio *Monday, Monday*. Recorded at the Playhouse Theatre, Northumberland Avenue, London WC2. Recording between 4:00 p.m. to 9:00 p.m. Producer Keith Bateson. Numbers recorded are: "I'm So Glad," "Take It Back." Broadcast Monday 27 March between 1:00 p.m. and 2:00 pm

21 March 1967, Marquee Club, Soho, London (band to arrive by 7:00 p.m. They play 2 x 45-minute sessions between 7:30 p.m. and 11:30 p.m. Fee: cash given to band on night)

22 March 1967, Locarno, Stevenage, Hertfordshire (band to arrive by 7:00 p.m. They play 2 x 45-minute sessions between 8:00 p.m. and 11:00 p.m. Fee: cash given to band on night)

23 March 1967, day off

24 March 1967, day off

25 March 1967, Depart London Airport at 11:45 a.m. for New York on TW705. Hotel accommodation is at the Gorham Hotel. (Cream were due to leave a couple of days earlier but were delayed due to some work visa problems. As a result they missed the first day of the Murray the K shows)

26 March 1967, Murray the K's *Music in the Fifth Dimension* Show, RKO 58th Street Theater, New York City, United States (five shows per day commencing at 10:15 a.m. followed by performances at lunchtime, afternoon, evening, and supper, finally finishing at 11:30 p.m. They initially played two songs, "I Feel Free" and "I'm So Glad," before being told to reduce the length of their songs; they ended up playing only "I'm So Glad" at each show

27 March 1967, Murray the K's *Music in the Fifth Dimension* Show, RKO 58th Street Theater, New York City, United States

28 March 1967, Murray the K's *Music in the Fifth Dimension* Show, RKO 58th Street Theater, New York City, United States

29 March 1967, Murray the K's *Music in the Fifth Dimension* Show, RKO 58th Street Theater, New York City, United States

30 March 1967, Murray the K's *Music in the Fifth Dimension* Show, RKO 58th Street Theater, New York City, United States

31 March 1967, Murray the K's *Music in the Fifth Dimension* Show, RKO 58th Street Theater, New York City, United States

APRIL 1967

1 April 1967, Murray the K's *Music in the Fifth Dimension* Show, RKO 58th Street Theater, New York City, United States

2 April 1967, Murray the K's *Music in the Fifth Dimension* Show, RKO 58th Street Theater, New York City, United States

"It was great—too much. We played the Murray the K show for a week and the audiences were mostly 13- to 14-year old teeny boppers. Everybody went down well, and we only had one or two numbers each, everybody pulled the stops out. The Who stole the show. They only had to smash everything up and everybody was on their feet. We did 'I'm So Glad' and 'I Feel Free,' but the whole thing had nothing to do with music—nothing whatsoever. The kids in the audience were all very beat, and wore jeans and had long hair. They are not like our mods at all. They don't want to be smart.

We took the actual show as a joke. There was no chance for Ginger to play his solo and we had to use the Who's equipment because we couldn't take any with us and there was none provided—as usual. Wilson Pickett and Mitch Ryder were topping the bill. Smokey Robinson dropped out of the show. He refused to do it because it wasn't his scene.

The best musical times we had were in the Greenwich Village where it was more like the English Musical Appreciation Society. I sat in with a couple of The Mothers Of Invention and Mitch Ryder at the Cafe Au Go Go where Jimi Hendrix used to play. I made a lot of friends there including Al Kooper who used to be the organist on a lot of the Dylan tracks."

—ERIC CLAPTON (*Melody Maker*, 22 April 1967)

3 April 1967, Atlantic Studios, West 60th Street, New York

3 April 1967, Café Au Go Go, New York (Eric turns up to for the Monday-night jam session and plays with the Butterfield Blues Band. Mitch Ryder also joins in at some point, as do a couple of members of the Mothers Of Invention. Michael Bloomfield is also rumored to have turned up. The jams were advertised as starting at 8:00 p.m. and finishing at 4:00 am)

4 April 1967, Atlantic Studios, West 60th Street, New York

7 April 1967, Cream fly back from New York to London. A planned show at the Municipal Hall in Pontypridd is canceled and rescheduled for 5 May

8 April 1967, Imperial Ballroom, Nelson, Lancashire (band to arrive by 8:00 p.m. They play 2 x 30-minute sessions between 8:00 p.m. and 11:30 p.m. Fee: £300 check given to band on night)

9 April 1967, Redcar Jazz Club, Coatham Hotel, Redcar, Yorkshire (band to arrive by 6:30 p.m. They play 2 x 45-minute sessions between 7:15 p.m. and 11:00 p.m. Fee: £285 check sent to office)

10 April 1967, day off

11 April 1967, day off

12 April 1967, day off

13 April 1967, Matrix Hall, Coventry, Midlands (band to arrive by 9:00 p.m. They play 2 x 30-minute sessions between 8:00 p.m. and 2:00 a.m. Fee: £300 check sent to office)

14 April 1967, Ricky Tick Club, Plaza Ballroom, Newbury, Berkshire (band to arrive by 8:00 p.m. They play 2 x 45-minute sessions between 8:00 p.m. and 11:30 p.m. Fee: £275 cash given to band on night)

15 April 1967, Rhodes Centre, Bishop's Stortford, Hertfordshire (band to arrive by 8:00 p.m. They play 2 x 30-minute sessions between 8:00 p.m. and 11:30 p.m. Fee: £300 cash given to band on night)

Advert for Cream's concert at the Rhodes Centre, Bishop's Stortford, Hertfordshire, on 15 April 1967.

16 April 1967, Daily Express Record Star Show, Wembley Empire Pool, Wembley, Middlesex (band to arrive by 11:50 a.m. They play 2 x 8-minute spots at 2:00 p.m. and 6:30 p.m.)

17 April 1967, recording

18 April 1967, Chinese R&B Jazz Club, Corn Exchange, Bristol, Gloucestershire (band to arrive by 8:00 p.m. They play 2 x 45-minute sessions between 8:00 p.m. and 11:00 p.m. Fee: £250 cash given to band on night)

19 April 1967, Beachcomber Club, Nottingham, Nottinghamshire (band to arrive by 8:00 p.m. They play 2 x 45-minute sessions between 8:00 p.m. and 11:00 p.m. Fee: £200 check given to band on night)

20 April 1967, day off

21 April 1967, Brighton Dome, Brighton, East Sussex (band to arrive by 6:30 p.m. They play 1 x 30-minute session between 8:00 p.m. and 11:00 p.m. Fee: £300 check given to band on night)

22 April 1967, Ricky Tick Club, Hounslow, Middlesex (band to arrive by 7:30 p.m. They play 2 x 45-minute sessions between 8:00 p.m. and 11:30 p.m. Fee: £300 cash given to band on night)

23 April 1967, day off

24 April 1967, day off

25 April 1967, Pavilion Ballroom, Bournemouth, Dorset (band to arrive by 7:00 p.m. They play 2 x 45-minute sessions between 7:30 p.m. and midnight. Fee: £250 check given to band on night)

26 April 1967, day off

27 April 1967, day off

28 April 1967, the Students Union, Birmingham University, Edgbaston, Midlands (band to arrive by 8:00 p.m. They play 2 x 30-minute sessions between 8:00 p.m. and 1:00 a.m. Fee: £300 cash given to band on night)

29 April 1967, Leeds University Students Union, Leeds, Yorkshire (band to arrive by 8:00 p.m. They play 2 x 30-minute sessions between 8:00 p.m. and 11:30. Fee: £300 check given to band on night)

30 April 1967, day off

MAY 1967

1 May 1967, Starpalast, Kiel, Germany (band to arrive by 8:00 p.m. They were scheduled to play 2 x 45-minute sessions between 8:00 p.m. and 11:30. Fee would have been £250 in Deutsche Marks given to band on night), canceled

2 May 1967, *Hör Hin, Schau Zu!* TV show, Berlin, Germany, canceled

3 May 1967, *Hör Hin, Schau Zu!* TV show, Berlin, Germany (fee for the 2 days is DM2500), canceled

4 May 1967, day off

5 May 1967, Municipal Hall, Pontypridd, Wales (band to arrive by 8:00 p.m. They play 2 x 30-minute sessions between 8:00 p.m. and 10:00 p.m. Fee: £220 check given to band on night)

6 May 1967, BBC Television *Sound And Picture City*. New pilot episode devised by Jonathan King as a satirical pop psychedelic freakout magazine program for the younger generation. Recorded in Studio 4, BBC Television Centre, Wood Lane, Shepherds Bush, London W12. Cream need to be at the studio by 3:30 p.m. and be ready and set up by 4:00 p.m. Borrowed amps and speakers are delivered to the studios along with Ginger's kit. Producer is Tony Palmer. Three numbers are recorded, but sadly, the program never airs. However, a small part of Cream's performance is later shown on a program titled *Watch It* on 22 September. The Cream were paid £52 and 10 shillings for their original appearance and a further £15 and 15 shillings for the *Watch It* segment.

6 May 1967, RAF Station, Hullavington, Chippenham, Wiltshire (the band leave Television Centre with road manager Ben Palmer in two cars, including drum kit and head, to the venue in Chippenham. Band to arrive by 7:30 p.m. They play 2 x 45-minute sessions between 8:00 p.m. and 11:30 p.m. Fee: £350 check given to band on night)

7 May 1967, 15th Annual NME Poll Winners Concert, Empire Pool, Wembley, Middlesex (artists appearing are: the Beach Boys, the Move, Jeff Beck, Spencer Davis Group, the Dubliners, Cliff Richard, the Troggs, Georgie Fame, Paul Jones, Geno Washington and the Ram Jam Band, the Small Faces, Lulu, Stevie Winwood. Concert starts at 2:00 p.m., and Cream are required to go on at 3:24 p.m. for a maximum of 5 minutes. They play "I Feel Free" and "Wrapping Paper."

7 May 1967, The Swan, Yardley, Birmingham, Midlands (band to arrive by 7:00 p.m. They play 2 x 45-minute sessions between 8:00 p.m. and 11:00 p.m. Fee: £275 cash given to band on night)

8 May 1967, day off

9 May 1967, band fly to New York for recording sessions for new album

12 May–15 May 1967, Atlantic Studios, New York

16 May 1967, band fly back to UK

17 May 1967, day off

18 May 1967, day off

19 May 1967, *Beat Club* television show, Radio Bremen Studios, Bremen, Germany (the band fly to Germany for a short 3-day engagement. Cream mime to "Strange Brew," and the performance is transmitted the following day in Germany)

20 May 1967, Berlin Stadium, Berlin, Germany

21 May 1967, Jaguar Club, Herford, Germany (with the Tonics)

22 May 1967, band fly back to England

23 May 1967, Marquee Club, Soho, London (band to arrive by 7:00 p.m. They play 2 x 45-minute sessions between 8:00 p.m. and 11:00 p.m. Fee: 60 percent cash given to band on night)

SETLIST: Tales Of Brave Ulysses / World Of Pain / Outside Woman Blues / Dance The Night Away / Sleepy Time Time / Sweet Wine / Rollin' And Tumblin' / NSU

24 May 1967, day off

25 May 1967, day off

26 May 1967, Goldsmiths College Summer Ball, New Cross, Lewisham, London (band to arrive by 7:00 p.m. They play 2 x 45-minute sessions between 8:00 p.m. and midnight. Fee: £300 cash given to band on night)

27 May 1967, Brasnose College, Oxford, Oxfordshire (Eric turns up to see his old boss, John Mayall, before heading off to play with Cream at another May ball in Oxford. Peter Green hands him his guitar, and Eric plays a few numbers. Alan Edwards was in the audience that night and recalls: "At the time Peter Green was the guitarist and Mayall still had the huge Hammond organ. Meanwhile at another college Cream were playing. During the course of the evening I noticed a tall guy with shoulder length hair wearing an ostentatious long pale yellow coat. He walked confidently along the front of the standing/dancing audience and just stood there. I wondered who this dandy was! At the end of the song, Peter handed over his guitar to none other than Eric, who then played a few numbers with the Bluesbreakers")

27 May 1967, Exeter College, Oxford, Oxfordshire (band to arrive by 10:00 p.m. They play 2 x 45-minute sessions between 10:00 p.m. and 4:00 p.m. Fee: £300 check given to band on night)

29 May 1967, Barbeque '67, Spalding Tulip Bulb Auction Hall, Spalding, Lincolnshire (band to arrive by 3:00 p.m.)

SETLIST: N.S.U. / Sunshine Of Your Love / We're Going Wrong / Steppin' Out / Rollin' And Tumblin' / Toad / I'm So Glad

30 May 1967, BBC *Saturday Club*. Recorded at the Playhouse Theatre, Northumberland Avenue, London WC2. Recording between 4:30 p.m. to 7:00 p.m. Producer Bill Bebb. Numbers recorded are: "Strange Brew," "Tales Of Brave Ulysses," "We're Going Wrong." Broadcast 03 June 1967

31 May 1967, band leave for Paris, France. Depart London Airport at 12:30 and arrive Paris Orly airport at 13.25

JUNE 1967

1 June 1967, Palais des Sports, Paris, France (1st International Festival Of Pop Music. Other bands appearing are: Herbert Leonard, Baschung, the V.I.P.s, the Pretty Things, Ronnie Bird, Jimmy Cliff, John Walker, Dave Dee, Dozy, Beaky, Mick & Tich, and the Troggs. The Who were top of the bill, but they had to cancel their performance because Keith Moon was in the hospital for a hernia operation. There were two shows, one at 3:00 p.m. and another at 8:30 p.m. The show was taped for future transmission on French television and finally screened in April 1969. Cream probably played four numbers over two shows, but only "I Feel Free" and "We're Going Wrong" have so far surfaced)

Eric in Cream at the Palais des Sports, Paris, on 1 June 1967.

2 June 1967, band leave Paris, France. Depart Paris Orly at 12:55 and arrive London Airport at 13:50

2 June 1967, Speakeasy, 48 Margaret Street, London (Eric and Jack jam on the small Speakeasy stage with Jimi Hendrix, Jose Feliciano, and Graeme Edge)

3 June 1967, Ram Jam Club, Brixton, London (band to arrive by 7:00 p.m. They play 2 x 45-minute sessions between 7:30 and 11:00 p.m. Fee: £300 check given to band on night)

8 June 1967, Locarno Ballroom, Bristol, Gloucestershire (band to arrive by 7:00 p.m. They play 2 x 30-minute sessions between 8:00 p.m. and 11:00 p.m. Fee: £300 cash given to band on night)

9 June 1967, Civic Hall, Wolverhampton, Midlands (band to arrive by 7:00 p.m. They play 2 x 30-minute sessions between 8:00 p.m. and 11:00 p.m. Fee: £350 cash given to band on night)

10 June 1967, Wellington Club, East Dereham, Yorkshire (band to arrive by 7:00 p.m. They play 2 x 30-minute sessions between 8:00 p.m. and 11:00 p.m. Fee: £300 cash given to band on night)

11 June 1967, Starlite Ballroom, Greenford, Middlesex (band to arrive by 7:00 p.m. They play 2 x 30-minute sessions between 8:00 p.m. and 11:00 p.m. Fee: £300 cash given to band on night)

12 June 1967, day off

13 June 1967, Trinity Hall, Cambridge, Cambridgeshire (band to arrive by 7:00 p.m. They play 2 x 45-minute sessions between 9:30 p.m. and midnight. Fee: £300 check given to band on night)

14 June 1967, day off

15 June 1967, BBC Television *Top Of The Pops*. Recorded at the BBC's Lime Grove Studios, London W12. Cream need to be at the studio by 2:00 p.m. Producer Johnnie Stewart. Cream mime to "Strange Brew." Broadcast same day on BBC1 between 7:30 p.m. and 8:00 pm

15 June 1967, Pavilion Ballroom, Worthing, West Sussex (band to arrive by 7:00 p.m. They play 2 x 30-minute sessions between 8:00 p.m. and 11:00 p.m. Fee: £225 cash given to band on night)

16 June 1967, University of Sussex, Brighton, East Sussex (band to arrive by 10:30 p.m. They play 2 x 45-minute sessions, one spot between 11:30 p.m. and 12:15 a.m. and the second between 1:00 a.m. and 1:45 a.m. Fee: £350 check given to band on night)

17 June 1967, day off

18 June 1967, day off

19 June 1967, Wheels, Reading, Berkshire (band to arrive by 7:00 p.m. They play 2 x 45-minute sessions

between 8:00 p.m. and 11:00 p.m. Fee: £275 check given to band on night)

20 June 1967, day off

21 June 1967, BBC Television *Top Of The Pops*. Recorded at the BBC's Lime Grove Studios, London W12. Cream need to be at the studio by 5:00 p.m. for a 5.45p.m. recording start time. Producer Johnnie Stewart. Cream mime to "Strange Brew." Due to be broadcast 22 June on BBC1 between 7:30 p.m. and 8:00 pm, but the segment is dropped at the last moment. This was probably because the band would be playing "Strange Brew" at almost the same time on tomorrow's *Dee Time* show.

22 June 1967, BBC television *Dee Time*. Recorded at BBC's Dickinson Road Studios, Rusholme, Manchester. Band to be there by 12:30 p.m. for a 1:00 p.m. start. "Strange Brew" is played with live voices over studio backing track.

23 June 1967, Durham University, Durham, County Durham (band to arrive by 9:30 p.m. They play 2 x 45-minute sessions between 9:30 p.m. and midnight. Fee: £335 check given to band on night)

24 June 1967, Carlton Ballroom, Erdington, Birmingham, Midlands (band to arrive by 7:00 p.m. They play 2 x 45-minute sessions between 8:00 p.m. and 11:00 p.m. Fee: £300 cash given to band on night)

25 June 1967, Abbey Road Studios, St Johns Wood, London. Eric is one of many guests of the Beatles and joins in the chorus for the live worldwide telecast of "All You Need Is Love"

26 June 1967, Keele University Students Union, Keele, Staffordshire (band to arrive by 11:00 p.m. They play 2 x 45-minute sessions. They play one spot between midnight and 12:45 a.m. and the second spot between 2:15 a.m. and 3:00 a.m. Fee: £300 check given to band on night)

27 June 1967, Winter Gardens, Malvern, Worcestershire (band to arrive by 7:00 p.m. They play 2 x 30-minute sessions between 8:00 p.m. and 11:00 p.m. Fee: £250 cash given to band on night)

28 June 1967, Floral Hall, Gorleston, Great Yarmouth, Norfolk (the equipment van arrives very late due to mechanical problems and Cream perform only two songs on borrowed equipment. A replacement show is scheduled for 12 August)

29 June 1967, BBC Television *Top Of The Pops*. Recorded at the BBC's Lime Grove Studios, London W12. Producer Johnnie Stewart. Cream mime to "Strange Brew." Due to be broadcast 29 June on BBC1 between 7:30 p.m. and 8:00 p.m. This could well have been the segment that was filmed on 22 June and dropped.

30 June 1967, Bluesville 66, Manor House, London (band to arrive by 7:30 p.m. They play 2 x 45-minute sessions between 8:00 p.m. and 11:00 p.m. Fee: £200 cash given to band on night)

JULY 1967

1 July 1967, The Upper Cut, Forest Gate, London (band to arrive by 8:00 p.m. They play 2 x 30-minute sessions between 8:00 p.m. and 11:00 p.m. Fee: £350 check given to band on night)

2 July 1967, Saville Theatre, London (Cream play two shows, one in the afternoon and one in the evening. With the Jeff Beck Group, John Mayall's Bluesbreakers, Jimmy Powell & the Dimensions)

EVENING SETLIST: N.S.U. / Tales Of Brave Ulysses / We're Going Wrong / Sunshine Of Your Love / Steppin' Out / Rollin' And Tumblin' / Toad / I'm So Glad

> "From the first quiver of 'N.S.U.' The Cream obliterated what had gone before (and) it was Cream all the way. Their presence, power and command. Ginger's hunched figure throwing deformed images onto the backdrop, Jack Bruce working with the expertise of a clumsy clown and Clapton a sequined Sherwood loon standing with all the majesty of a Sherwood oak and playing with his mind."
>
> —*MELODY MAKER*

3 July 1967, day off

4 July 1967, day off

5 July 1967, day off

6 July 1967, Cream head off to Scotland for a short tour. Robert Whitaker, a photographer friend of Martin Sharpe, is along to take pictures for potential use as artwork on Cream's next album, *Disraeli Gears*. Martin Sharpe has been given the job of designing the artwork.

7 July 1967, Ballerina Ballroom, Nairn, Scotland (although the band are there, the show is postponed to July 10, as their equipment van broke down again)

8 July 1967, on the way from Nairn to Aberdeen, photographer Robert Whitaker and Cream climb Ben Nevis mountain for a photo shoot

8 July 1967, Beach Ballroom, Aberdeen, Scotland

9 July 1967, Kinema Ballroom, Dunfermline, Scotland

10 July 1967, Ballerina Ballroom Nairn, Scotland (rescheduled from July 7)

11 July 1967, day off

12 July 1967–14 July 1967, IBC Studios, 25 Portland Street, London W1. Cream start initial sessions for "White Room," "Sitting On Top Of The World," and "Born Under A Bad Sign"

14 July 1967, BBC *Joe Loss Show*. Recorded at the Playhouse Theatre, Northumberland Avenue, London WC2. Recording between 10:30 a.m. and 11:45 p.m. Producer Ian Grant. Numbers recorded are: "Strange Brew," "Tales Of Brave Ulysses." Broadcast same day between 1:00 p.m. and 2:00 p.m.

15 July 1967, Supreme Ballroom, Ramsgate, Kent (last show for a few weeks as Cream members take their summer break)

AUGUST 1967

4 August 1967, City Hall Perth, Scotland

5 August 1967, Market Hall, Carlisle, Cumberland

6 August 1967, McGoos, Edinburgh, Scotland (with the Jury)

SETLIST: NSU / Tales Of Brave Ulysses / Sweet Wine, Steppin' Out / Rollin' And Tumblin; / Toad / I'm So Glad

7 August 1967, Locarno Ballroom, Glasgow, Scotland

8 August 1967, Palace Ballroom, Douglas, Isle of Man

9 August 1967–11 August 1967, IBC Studios, 25 Portland Street, London W1. Further sessions for "White Room" and "Born Under A Bad Sign"

12 August 1967, Floral Hall, Gorleston, Great Yarmouth, Norfolk (band to arrive by 8:00 p.m. They play 2 x 30-minute sessions between 8:00 p.m. and 11:00 p.m. Fee: £300 cash given to band on night)

13 August 1967, 7th National Jazz and Blues Festival, Royal Windsor Race Course, Berkshire

14 August 1967, day off

15 August 1967, Explosion '67, Town Hall, Torquay, Devon

16 August 1967, day off

17 August 1967, Speakeasy, London (Frank Zappa is in town and is at the Speakeasy. He introduces Cream as a "dandy little combo")

18–19 August 1967, days off

20 August 1967, Cream fly out to Los Angeles for a West Coast tour

SETLIST FOR THIS TOUR WAS TAKEN FROM THE FOLLOWING NUMBERS: NSU / Sweet Wine / Cat's Squirrel / Tales Of Brave Ulysses / Sunshine of Your Love / N.S.U. / Lawdy Mama / Spoonful / Sleepy Time Time / Steppin' Out / Rollin' And Tumblin' / Sitting On Top Of The World / Traintime / Toad / I'm So Glad

22 August 1967, Fillmore Auditorium, San Francisco, California (2 sets. With the Paul Butterfield Blues Band and South Side Sound System)

23 August 1967, Fillmore Auditorium, San Francisco, California (2 sets. With the Paul Butterfield Blues Band and South Side Sound System)

24 August 1967, Fillmore Auditorium, San Francisco, California (2 sets. With the Paul Butterfield Blues Band and South Side Sound System)

25 August 1967, Fillmore Auditorium, San Francisco, California (2 sets. With the Paul Butterfield Blues Band and South Side Sound System)

Cream playing the Windsor Racecourse on 13 August 1967.

Ticket for Cream at the Fillmore in San Francisco for 25 August 1967.

Ticket for Cream at the Fillmore in San Francisco, 22, 23, 24, and 27 August 1967.

Poster for Cream at the Fillmore in San Francisco between 22 and 27 August 1967.

26 August 1967, Fillmore Auditorium, San Francisco, California (2 sets. With the Paul Butterfield Blues Band and South Side Sound System)

27 August 1967, Fillmore Auditorium, San Francisco, California (2 sets. With the Paul Butterfield Blues Band and South Side Sound System)

28 August 1967, day off

29 August 1967, Fillmore Auditorium. San Francisco, California (2 sets. With Gary Burton and the Electric Flag)

30 August 1967, Fillmore Auditorium. San Francisco, California (2 sets. With Gary Burton and the Electric Flag)

31 August 1967, Fillmore Auditorium. San Francisco, California (2 sets. With Gary Burton and the Electric Flag)

SEPTEMBER 1967

1 September 1967, Fillmore Auditorium. San Francisco, California (2 sets. With Gary Burton and the Electric Flag)

2 September 1967, Fillmore Auditorium. San Francisco, California (2 sets. With Gary Burton and the Electric Flag)

3 September 1967, Fillmore Auditorium. San Francisco, California (2 sets. With Gary Burton and the Electric Flag)

4 September 1967, Whisky A Go-Go, Los Angeles, California (with the Rich Kids)

SETLIST: NSU / Tales Of Brave Ulysses / Sitting On Top Of The World / Sweet Wine / Rollin' And Tumblin' / Spoonful / Sunshine Of Your Love / Sleepy Time Time / Stepping Out / Traintime / Toad / I'm So Glad

5 September 1967, Whisky A Go-Go, Los Angeles, California (with the Rich Kids)

6 September 1967, Whisky A Go-Go, Los Angeles, California (with the Rich Kids)

7 September 1967, travel from Los Angeles to Boston

8 September 1967, Cross Town Bus Club, Boston, Massachusetts (canceled and shows moved to the Psychedelic Supermarket)

8 September 1967, Psychedelic Supermarket, Kenmore Square, Boston, Massachusetts (2 sets. With Catharsis)

9 September 1967, Psychedelic Supermarket, Kenmore Square, Boston, Massachusetts (2 sets. With Catharsis)

10 September 1967, Psychedelic Supermarket, Kenmore Square, Boston, Massachusetts (2 sets. With Catharsis)

11 September 1967, Psychedelic Supermarket, Kenmore Square, Boston, Massachusetts (2 sets. With Catharsis)

12 September 1967, Psychedelic Supermarket, Kenmore Square, Boston, Massachusetts (2 sets. With Catharsis)

13 September 1967, Psychedelic Supermarket, Kenmore Square, Boston, Massachusetts (2 sets. With Catharsis)

14 September 1967, Psychedelic Supermarket, Kenmore Square, Boston, Massachusetts (2 sets. With Catharsis)

15 September 1967, Psychedelic Supermarket, Kenmore Square, Boston, Massachusetts (2 sets. With Catharsis)

16 September 1967, Psychedelic Supermarket, Kenmore Square, Boston, Massachusetts (2 sets. With Catharsis)

17 September 1967–21 September 1967, Atlantic Studios, New York (final sessions for "Sitting On Top Of The World" and "Born Under A Bad Sign" as well as some more work on "White Room")

22 September 1967, Action House, Long Island, New York (with the Neons, Canned Heat who replaced Moby Grape)

23 September 1967, Village Theater, New York, New York (with Canned Heat, who again replaced Moby Grape. Two shows, one at 8:00 p.m. and the other at 10:30 p.m.)

24 September 1967, Action House, Long Island, New York (with the Neons)

25 September 1967, day off

26 September 1967, Cafe Au Go Go, New York, New York (with the Paupers)

27 September 1967, Cafe Au Go Go, New York, New York (with the Paupers)

28 September 1967, Cafe Au Go Go, New York, New York (with the Paupers)

29 September 1967, Cafe Au Go Go, New York, New York (with the Paupers)

30 September 1967, Village Theater, New York, New York (early show with the Soul Survivors and Richie Havens)

30 September 1967, Cafe Au Go Go, New York, New York (late show with the Paupers)

OCTOBER 1967

1 October 1967, Cafe Au Go Go, New York, New York (with the Paupers)

2 October 1967, day off

3 October 1967, Cafe Au Go Go, New York, New York (with Richie Havens)

4 October 1967, Cafe Au Go Go, New York, New York (with Richie Havens)

5 October 1967, Cafe Au Go Go, New York, New York (with Richie Havens)

6 October 1967, Cafe Au Go Go, New York, New York (with Richie Havens)

7 October 1967, Cafe Au Go Go, New York, New York (with Richie Havens)

Advert for Cream at the Cafe Au Go Go, New York, from 26 September 1967 to 8 October 1967.

8 October 1967, Cafe Au Go Go, New York, New York (with Richie Havens)

9 October–10 October 1967, Atlantic Studios, New York, New York. Initial sessions for "Pressed Rat And Warthog" and "Anyone For Tennis" as well as further sessions for "White Room"

11 October 1967, 5th Dimension Club, Ann Arbor, Michigan

12 October 1967, 5th Dimension Club, Ann Arbor, Michigan

13 October 1967, Grande Ballroom, Detroit, Michigan (with MC5 and the Thyme)

Poster advertising Cream's concert in Detroit, 13 October 1967 at the Grande Ballroom.

"Last weekend about 4,500 kids proved that Detroit knows good contemporary music.

That was the number who packed into the Grande Ballroom, breaking all previous attendance records to hear England's super group, The Cream.

The crowd was so hip to what the Cream were playing, that their bass and harmonica player, Jack Bruce, said that there were times Saturday night at the Grande that surpassed anything they had previously done in this country—including at the Fillmore in San Francisco. There were magic moments when the musicians and crowd merged into one—each side bringing the other further into the music.

The Cream consider themselves a live band rather than a recording band since they didn't spend that much time in the studio. 'Even if we could spend a lot of time in the studio,' Eric explained, 'there still would be a difference. There's nothing about a studio that vaguely resembles a live sound. In a recording studio the sound is compact, flat and very loud. You can't always hear the other two musicians very well.' Jack added, 'It would be nice if we had a different thing going in the recording studio than on stage. This is what we're getting at.'

Neither Eric or Jack dig the stress the recording industry puts on having a hit single. Since singles have to be short to get airplay, Eric believes that singles will become an anachronism if they don't change with the times. 'It would be good if you could achieve something really good within two and a half-minutes,' Jack said. He singled out the Beatles as being able to do this on a record like 'Strawberry Fields.'

Eric said that the Cream could come up with something but it would be a 'construction' job. In other words, he said he'd have to spend hours preparing the guitar part perfectly so that each note said something.

As Eric sees it, 'The American pop music machine is so absurdly more extreme. People with a slight bit of intelligence here can turn it off. England is behind America and people don't see the nonsensical side of the scene. Pop musicians in England think it's a good thing to have a top 40 record.'"

—LORRAINE ALTERMAN
(Detroit Press)

14 October 1967, Grande Ballroom, Detroit, Michigan (with the Rationals)

15 October 1967, Grande Ballroom, Detroit, Michigan (with the Apostles)

SETLIST: Tales Of Brave Ulysses / NSU / Sitting On Top Of The World / Sweet Wine / Rollin' And Tumblin' / Spoonful / Stepping Out / Traintime / Toad / I'm So Glad

16 October 1967, Cream leave on overnight flight back to the UK

17 October 1967–18 October 1967, days off

19 October 1967, Romanos Ballroom, Belfast, Northern Ireland (postponed until 2 November)

20 October 1967–23 October 1967, days off

"Everywhere we played we broke the records. We drew a record 4,500 to the Village Theater. The only place that wasn't outstanding was in Boston where we played the opening of a brand new club.

I haven't recovered from San Francisco yet, we really had a ball. We are getting further out in playing things differently every night. We even did the same number twice some nights and the versions were so different we got away with it."

—GINGER BAKER
(Melody Maker, 20 October 1967)

24 October 1967, BBC Radio *Top Gear*. Recorded at BBC's Studio 2, Aeolian Hall, 135–137 New Bond Street, London. Recording between 2:30 p.m. to 4:30 p.m. Producer Bernie Andrews. Numbers recorded are: "Take It Back," "Outside Woman Blues," "Tales Of Brave Ulysses," "Sunshine Of Your Love," "Born Under A Bad Sign." Broadcast on 29 October

25 October 1967, day off

26 October 1967, Magoos, Glasgow, Scotland

27 October 1967, Capitol, Edinburgh, Scotland

28 October 1967, Union Dance, Southampton University, Hampshire (with Nelson's Column and the Quik)

"Jack, Ginger and Eric's cups brimmed with sweet wine, fermenting throughout marathon versions of 'Spoonful,' 'Steppin' Out,' 'I'm So Glad'...it doesn't matter what they were called because this was The Cream taking the trans-love airways and they'll get you there on time."
—MELODY MAKER

29 October 1967, Sundays At The Saville, Saville Theatre, London (2 shows, one at 6:00 p.m. and the other at 8:30 p.m. With the Bonzo Dog Doo Dah Band and the Action. Compered by John Peel)

30 October 1967–31 October 1967, days off

NOVEMBER 1967

1 November 1967, Bal Tabarin, Bromley, Kent

2 November 1967, Romano's Ballroom, Belfast, Northern Ireland (with Taste)

3 November 1967, Strand Ballroom, Portstewart, Northern Ireland (with the Playboys Showband)

4 November 1967–9 November 1967, days off

10 November 1967, Top Pot record shop, Ny Adelgade, Copenhagen, Denmark (press conference)

11 November 1967, TV-Byen, Studio A, Gladsaxe, Denmark (Cream play live versions of "NSU" and "Strange Brew" for *Toppop* television show, which is broadcast same day between 5:30 p.m. and 5:55 p.m.)

Advert for Cream, 11 November 1967, Hit Club, Vejgaard Hallen, Aalborg, Denmark.

11 November 1967, Hit Club, Vejgaard Hallen, Aalborg, Denmark (with the Defenders, the Parrots)

12 November 1967, Falkoner Centret, Copenhagen, Denmark (2 shows tonight. One at 4:00 p.m. and the other at 7:00 p.m. With Steppeulvene, the Defenders)

Advert for Cream's concert in Copenhagen on 12 November 1967.

13 November 1967, Pasila TV Studios, Helsinki, Finland (Cream mime to four songs for the Finnish pop television show *Tunnussävel* from the newly released *Disraeli Gears* album. Songs are "Sunshine Of Your Love," World Of Pain," "Tales Of Brave Ulysses," "Outside Woman Blues")

13 November 1967, Kulttuuritalo, Helsinki, Finland

14 November 1967, Konserthuset, Stockholm, Sweden (2 shows tonight. With Hansson & Karlsson, the Young Flowers)

SETLIST: Tales Of Brave Ulysses / Sunshine Of Your Love / Sleepy Time Time / Stepping Out / Traintime / Toad / I'm So Glad

15 November 1967, Cirkus, Liseberg, Gothenburg, Sweden (with the Young Flowers, Clem Dalton, the Red Squares, the Fabulous Four)

16 November 1967, day off

17 November 1967, Rigoletto, Jönköping, Sweden (with the Ramblers, the Piccadillys)

18 November 1967, Idrottshuset, Örebro, Sweden (with King George & the Harlem Kiddies)

19 November 1967, band fly back to UK

20 November 1967–22 November 1967, days off

23 November 1967, Club A Go Go, Newcastle, Tyne & Wear

24 November 1967, Marine Ballroom, Central Pier, Morecambe, Lancashire (with the Doodlebugs, Top Katz)

25 November 1967, day off

26 November 1967, BBC Television *Twice A Fortnight*. Recorded at the BBC's Lime Grove Studios, London W12. Cream need to be at the studio by 2:00 p.m. Producer Tony Palmer. Cream play "We're Going Wrong." Broadcast 2 December. Ginger falls ill after the taping and is rushed to hospital with suspected ulcer problems. The next few shows are canceled as a result

27 November 1967, day off

28 November 1967, Marquee Club, Soho, London (canceled due to Ginger being ill)

29 November 1967, day off

DECEMBER 1967

1 December 1967, Top Rank Suite, Brighton, East Sussex (canceled due to Ginger being ill)

2 December 1967, Owens Union Building, Manchester University, Lancashire, London (canceled due to Ginger being ill)

3 December–9 December 1967, Felix Pappalardi has flown over from the United States to prepare for upcoming recording sessions in New York with the members of Cream

9 December 1967, Union Dance, Bristol University, Bristol, Gloucestershire

10 December 1967, day off

11 December 1967, Cream fly to New York

12 December 1967–15 December 1967, Atlantic Studios, New York. More recording sessions for "Pressed Rat and Warthog," "Anyone For Tennis," and "White Room"

16 December–17 December 1967, Eric plays on a session for Aretha Franklin at Atlantic Studios, New York

18 December 1967, day off

19 December 1967, day off

20 December 1967, private coming out party for daughter of wealthy industrialist in Lake Shore, Chicago, Illinois

21 December 1967, day off

22 December 1967, Grande Ballroom, Detroit, Michigan

23 December 1967, Grande Ballroom, Detroit, Michigan

24 December 1967, Grande Ballroom, Detroit, Michigan

25 December 1967, band fly back to the UK

1968

JANUARY 1968

1 January 1968–4 January 1968, days off

5 January 1968, the Norwich Industrial Club, Norwich, Norfolk (with the Healers. Band to arrive by 8:30 p.m. They play 1 x 60-minute session between 8:30 p.m. and 10:30 p.m. Fee: £300 cash given to band on night)

6 January 1968–8 January 1968, days off

9 January 1968, BBC Radio *Top Gear*. Recorded at BBC's Studio 2, Aeolian Hall, 135–137 New Bond Street, London. Recording between 2:30 p.m. and 6:00 p.m. Producer Bernie Andrews. Numbers recorded are: "SWLABR," "We're Going Wrong," "Blue Condition," "Stepping Out," "Politician." Broadcast on 14 January

10 January 1968, Revolution Club, Bruton Street, Mayfair, London (filming for French television. Cream have to be at the club for 11:45 a.m. and have been allocated a recording time between 12:00 noon and 7:00 p.m. The contract states that they will probably need to mime to two songs, "SWLABR" and "Sunshine Of Your Love." Luckily, they are not required to mime and three numbers are captured live on film, "Tales Of Brave Ulysses," "Sunshine Of Your Love," "Spoonful." It is likely that several takes were done as well as a few more numbers. The three numbers were made available on the *Fresh Live Cream* VHS video)

11 January 1968–12 January 1968, days off

13 January 1968, band fly out from London Airport to Amsterdam on British European Airways flight BE426 departing at 8:25 a.m. and arriving at 10:20 a.m. They are driven to Hilversum Television Studios in Amsterdam, where they mime to "SWLABR" and "Sunshine Of Your Love" with live vocals. Their contract requires them to play two numbers, one fast and one slow. Cream will headline unless French sensation Claude François turns up, in which case

they would be the penultimate act. The show is called *Fenklup* and is produced by Ralph Inbar. The show is transmitted on 19 January. Their fee is £150 plus all travel expenses

14 January 1968, band due to fly out of Amsterdam on BE425 departing at 11:00 a.m. and arriving at London Airport at 10:55 a.m. They would have been driven to Kings Cross Station, where they would have headed to Redcar for their evening show. Unfortunately, the plane is delayed by several hours due to bad weather and they miss the train and have to cancel tonight's show

14 January 1968, Redcar Jazz Club, Coatham Hotel, Redcar, Redcar and Cleveland (canceled due to late arrival of flight from Holland due to bad weather)

15 January 1968, Locarno Ballroom, Glasgow, Scotland (band to arrive by 9:00 p.m. They play 1 x 60-minute session between 9:00 p.m. and 11:00 p.m. Fee: £400 cash given to band on night)

16 January 1968–18 January 1968, days off

19 January 1968, Top Rank Suite, Brighton, East Sussex (with the Span. Band to arrive by 9:00 p.m. They play 1 x 60-minute session between 9:00 p.m. and midnight. Fee: £350 cash given to band on night)

20 January 1968, Leeds University Union, Leeds, Yorkshire (band to arrive by 8:30 p.m. They play 1 x 60-minute session between 9:30 p.m. and 10:30 p.m. Fee: £400 check sent to office)

21 January 1968–22 January 1968, days off

23 January 1968, interview and photo shoot for *OZ* magazine at David Stanford's studio, 48 Glebe Place, Chelsea, London

24 January 1968–26 January 1968, days off

27 January 1968, St. Mary's College, Twickenham, Middlesex (with Alan Bown, the Chris Ian Dreamboat Show. Band to arrive by 8:30 p.m. They play 1 x 60-minute session between 9:30 p.m. and 10:30 p.m. Fee: £400 check sent to office)

28 January 1968–31 January 1968, days off

FEBRUARY 1968

1 February 1968, day off

2 February 1968, Student Union, Technical College, Nottingham (with Thatch. Band to arrive by 8:30 p.m. They play 1 x 60-minute session between 9:30 p.m. and 10:30 p.m. Fee: £200 cash given to band on night. The band have reduced their fee as compensation for bringing the date forward from 13 February due to other commitments)

3 February 1968, Carnival '68, University College, London (with Two Of Each, the Soundtrekkers, the Millionaires. Band to arrive by 8:30 p.m. They play 1 x 60-minute session between 9:30 p.m. and 11:30 p.m. Fee: £300 cash on night. Once again, Cream lower their fee as compensation for canceling a previous engagement at the university due to last US tour)

4 February 1968, Cream together with Felix Pappalardi leave London Airport for Copenhagen on Scandinavian Airlines flight SK504 departing at 6:20 p.m. and arriving at 9:05 p.m. The crew, Bob Adcock and Pete Jolliffe, bring the van with equipment on the Harwich-to-Esjberg ferry leaving at 6:00 p.m. and arriving the following day at midday. They then drive ninety miles to Knudshoved to pick up another ferry departing at 5:45 pm, which arrives in Halsskov at 7:15 p.m. They then drive seventy miles to Copenhagen!

5 February 1968—6 February 1968, Cream take part in a film production of *Det Var En Lordag Aften*, which translates into "On A Saturday Night." The band are informed that they will be miming two songs; one will be set on a stage ("We're Going Wrong") and the second will be on a flatbed lorry that is part of a parade ("World Of Pain"). After filming in Copenhagen, the band earn a £1000 fee along with their return air fares and hotel costs plus £5 per person for food. A VHS video of the film was released in Denmark.

7 February 1968, Tivolis Koncertsal, Copenhagen, Denmark (2 shows with Hansson & Karlsson, the Young Flowers. Fee was £600)

8 February 1968, Cream and Felix Pappalardi head back to London, leaving Copenhagen on British European Airways flight BE743 departing at 2:25 p.m. and arriving at London Airport at 3:25 p.m. The crew head back with the van and equipment and catch the ferry in Halsskov at 10:15 a.m., arriving in Knudshoved at 11:45 a.m. They then drive to Esjberb to catch a ferry departing at 6:00 p.m., which arrives back in Harwich at midday on 9 February

9 February 1968, Leicester University Arts Ball, Granby Halls, Leicester, Midlands (with the Crazy World of Arthur Brown, Family, Wynder K. Frogg and the Freddie Mack Show. Band to arrive by 10:00 p.m. They play 1 x 60-minute session between midnight and 1:00 a.m. Fee: £400 check given to band on night)

10 February 1968, Owens Union Building, Manchester University, Manchester, Lancashire (band to arrive by 8:45 p.m. They play 1 x 60-minute session between 9:30 p.m. and 10:30 p.m. Fee: £300 check given to band on night. Once again, Cream lower their fee as compensation for canceling a previous engagement at the university due to last US tour)

11 February 1968, Cream depart for New York today for more recording at Atlantic Studios before starting a massive tour. Band depart London Airport on Pan American flight PA1 at 5:30 p.m. and arrive New York JFK at 8:10 p.m. Felix Pappalardi is handling all day-to-day recording arrangements for the band. Cream will be staying at the Gorham Hotel until 23 February, when they depart for Santa Monica, California

12 February 1968–22 February 1968, recording at Atlantic Studios, New York

20 February 1968, Whitey's Loft, New York (jam session with David Crosby, Eric Clapton, Michael Bloomfield, Jack Bruce, Mitch Mitchell)

23 February 1968, Civic Auditorium, Santa Monica, California (with Penny Nichols, the Electric Prunes, Steppenwolf. Fee: $3,000 flat)

24 February 1968, Earl Warren Showgrounds, Santa Barbara, California (with Taj Mahal, the James Cotton Blues Band. Fee: $3,000 flat)

25 February 1968, Swing Auditorium, San Bernardino, California (with the Hunger, the Caretakers. Fee: $2,500/50%)

26 February 1968–28 February 1968, days off

Local KFXF radio newspaper headline for Cream at the Swing Auditorium on 25 February 1968.

Poster for Cream at the Fillmore and Winterland in San Francisco, February/ March 1968.

29 February 1968, Winterland, San Francisco, California (with Big Black, Loading Zone, Holy See)

MARCH 1968

Tickets for Cream at Winterland and the Fillmore in March 1968.

1 March 1968, Winterland, San Francisco, California (with Big Black, Loading Zone, Holy See)

2 March 1968, Winterland, San Francisco, California (with Big Black, Loading Zone, Holy See)

3 March 1968, Fillmore Auditorium, San Francisco, California (with Big Black, Loading Zone, Holy See. Fee for shows between 29 February and 3 March: $7,500 flat)

4 March 1968–6 March 1968, days off

7 March 1968, Fillmore Auditorium, San Francisco, California (with the James Cotton Blues Band, Jeremy & the Satyrs)

SETLIST (FIRST SHOW):

Tales Of Brave Ulysses (Eric Clapton / Martin Sharpe) unreleased

N.S.U. (Jack Bruce) unreleased

Politician (Jack Bruce / Pete Brown) unreleased

Crossroads (Robert Johnson) unreleased

Rollin' And Tumblin' (Muddy Waters) *Live Cream* album US ATCO SD 33-328, UK Polydor 2383 016 released June 1970 / *Live Cream* CD Polydor 31453 1816-2 released 1998 / *Those Were The Days* box set Polydor 539 000-2 released September 1997

Sweet Wine (Ginger Baker / Janet Godfrey) unreleased

```
Recorded on eight-track reels
Producer: Felix Pappalardi
Engineers: Tom Dowd, Bill Halverson
```

SETLIST (SECOND SHOW):

Spoonful (Willie Dixon) unreleased

Sunshine Of Your Love (Jack Bruce / Pete Brown / Eric Clapton) *After Midnight* (extended version) EP CD UK Polydor PZCD8 released 1988

Sitting On Top Of The World (Chester Burnett) unreleased

Stepping Out (James Bracken) unreleased

Traintime (Jack Bruce) unreleased

Toad (Ginger Baker) *Wheels Of Fire* double album US ATCO SD 2-700 released July 1968 / UK Polydor mono 582 031/2, stereo 583 031/2 released August 1968 / *Wheels Of Fire Live At The Fillmore* single album UK Polydor mono

Poster for Cream at the Fillmore and Winterland in San Francisco in March 1968.

582 040, stereo 583040 / *Those Were The Days* box set (with added edit from 8 March) Polydor 539 000-2 released 1997

I'm So Glad (Skip James) unreleased

```
Recorded on eight-track reels
Producer: Felix Pappalardi
Engineers: Tom Dowd, Bill Halverson
```

8 March 1968, Winterland, San Francisco, California (2 shows. With the James Cotton Blues Band, Jeremy & the Satyrs, Blood Sweat And Tears)

SETLIST (FIRST SHOW):

Unknown due to tape being lost

SETLIST (SECOND SHOW):

Cat's Squirrel (Traditional; arranged by S. Splurge) unreleased

Sunshine Of Your Love (Jack Bruce / Pete Brown / Eric Clapton) unreleased

Spoonful (Willie Dixon) unreleased

Stepping Out (James Bracken) unreleased

Traintime (Jack Bruce) *Wheels Of Fire* double album US ATCO SD 2-700 released July 1968 / UK Polydor mono 582 031/2, stereo 583 031/2 released August 1968 / *Wheels Of Fire Live At The Fillmore* single album UK Polydor mono 582 040, stereo 583040 / *Those Were The Days* box set (with added edit from 8th March) Polydor 539 000-2 released 1997

Toad (Ginger Baker) guitar/bass/drums instrumental edit into 7 March version on *Those Were The Days* 4CD box set

```
Recorded on eight-track reels
Producer: Felix Pappalardi
Engineers: Tom Dowd, Bill Halverson
```

9 March 1968, Winterland, San Francisco, California (2 shows. With the James Cotton Blues Band, Jeremy & the Satyrs, Blood Sweat And Tears)

SETLIST:

Setlist (first show)

Tales Of Brave Ulysses (Eric Clapton / Martin Sharpe) unreleased

N.S.U. (Jack Bruce) unreleased

Sitting On Top Of The World (Chester Burnett) unreleased

Crossroads (Robert Johnson) unreleased

Sweet Wine (Ginger Baker / Janet Godfrey) unreleased

```
Recorded on eight-track reels
Producer: Felix Pappalardi
Engineers: Tom Dowd, Bill Halverson
```

SETLIST (SECOND SHOW):

Sunshine of Your Love (Jack Bruce / Pete Brown / Eric Clapton) *Live Cream* Vol II album US ATCO SD 7005, UK Polydor 2383-119 released July 1972 / *Live Cream* Vol II CD Polydor 31453 1817-2 released 1998 / *Those Were The Days* box set Polydor 539 000-2 released September 1997

Spoonful (Willie Dixon) unreleased

Sleepy Time Time (Jack Bruce / Janet Godfrey) *Live Cream* album US ATCO SD 33-328, UK Polydor 2383 016 released June 1970 / *Live Cream* CD Polydor 31453 1816-2 released 1998 / *Those Were The Days* box set Polydor 539 000-2 released September 1997

Steppin' Out (Memphis Slim) *Live Cream* Vol II album US ATCO SD 7005 released July 1972, UK Polydor 2383-119 / *Live Cream* Vol II CD Polydor 31453 1817-2 released 1998 / *Those Were The Days* box set Polydor 539 000-2 released September 1997 (not March 10 as officially stated)

Traintime (Jack Bruce) unreleased

Toad (Ginger Baker) unreleased

I'm So Glad (Skip James) unreleased

```
Recorded on eight-track reels
Producer: Felix Pappalardi
Engineers: Tom Dowd, Bill Halverson
```

10 March 1968, Winterland, San Francisco, California (2 shows. With the James Cotton Blues Band, Jeremy & the Satyrs, Blood Sweat And Tears. Fee for shows between 7 March and 10 March: $7,500 flat)

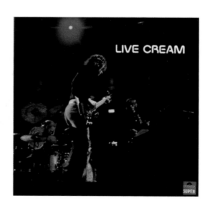

Cover for Cream's live album, Live Cream, *partially recorded at this show.*

SETLIST (FIRST SHOW):

Tales Of Brave Ulysses (Eric Clapton / Martin Sharpe) *Live Cream* Vol II album US ATCO SD 7005, UK Polydor 2383-119 released July 1972 / *Live Cream* Vol II CD Polydor 31453 1817-2 released 1998 / *Those Were The Days* box set Polydor 539 000-2 released September 1997

Spoonful (Willie Dixon) *Wheels Of Fire* double album US ATCO SD 2-700 released July 1968 / UK Polydor mono 582 031/2, stereo 583 031/2 released August 1968 / *Wheels Of Fire Live At The Fillmore* single album UK Polydor mono 582 040, stereo 583040 / *Those Were The Days* box set Polydor 539 000-2 released 1997

Crossroads (Robert Johnson) A-side / B-side was "Passing the Time." Single released in US on Atco in February 1969 (reaching no. 28) *Wheels Of Fire* double album US ATCO SD 2-700 released July 1968 / UK Polydor mono 582 031/2, stereo 583 031/2 released August 1968 / *Wheels Of Fire Live At The Fillmore* single album UK Polydor mono 582 040, stereo 583040 / *Those Were The Days* box set Polydor 539 000-2 released 1997

We're Going Wrong (Jack Bruce) unreleased

Sweet Wine (Ginger Baker / Janet Godfrey) *Live Cream* album US ATCO SD 33-328, UK Polydor 2383 016 released June 1970 / *Live Cream* CD Polydor 31453 1816-2 released 1998 / *Those Were The Days* box set Polydor 539 000-2 released September 1997

Recorded on eight-track reels
Producer: Felix Pappalardi
Engineers: Tom Dowd, Bill Halverson

SETLIST (SECOND SHOW):

Sunshine of Your Love (Jack Bruce / Pete Brown / Eric Clapton) unreleased

N.S.U. (Jack Bruce) edited on *Live Cream* album US ATCO SD 33-328, UK Polydor 2383 016 released June 1970 / *Live Cream* CD Polydor 31453 1816-2 released 1998 / unedited on *Those Were The Days* box set Polydor 539 000-2 released September 1997

Steppin' Out (Memphis Slim) (incorrectly credited on *Live Cream* Vol II / *Those Were The Days* box set) unreleased

Traintime (Jack Bruce) unreleased

Toad (Ginger Baker) unreleased

I'm So Glad (Skip James) unreleased

Recorded on eight-track reels
Producer: Felix Pappalardi
Engineers: Tom Dowd, Bill Halverson

11 March 1968, Memorial Auditorium, Sacramento, California (with the Grateful Dead. Fee: $5000/50%)

12 March 1968, ABC Televison Center (West), 4151 Prospect Avenue, Los Angeles. Cream mime to a version of "Sunshine Of Your Love" for ABC television's *Romp!!!* show. Described as a lighthearted romp through the "where it's at" world of the young, their current fads and favorites, and a look at tomorrow's fun. The show will be broadcast on 21 April. The band could not look less interested if they tried!

13 March 1968, Selland Arena, Fresno, California (with Blue Cheer. Fee: $5000/50%)

14 March 1968, day off

15 March 1968, San Fernando Valley State College, Northridge, California (afternoon show with Canned Heat)

Poster for Cream at the Shrine on 15 March 1968.

15 March 1968, Shrine Auditorium, Los Angeles, California (With the James Cotton Blues Band, the Mint Tattoo. The Buffalo Springfield is an unbilled opening act)

16 March 1968, Shrine Auditorium, Los Angeles, California (2 shows. With the James Cotton Blues Band, the Mint Tattoo. The Buffalo Springfield is an unbilled opening act. Fee for both nights $8000/50%)

17 March 1968, Star Theatre, Phoenix, Arizona (Fee: $3500 flat)

18 March 1968, Convention Center, Anaheim, California (with Spirit)

19 March 1968, the Family Dog, Denver, Colorado (postponed to 6 May)

20 March 1968, day off

21 March1968, Beloit College, Beloit, Wisconsin (Fee: $3000/60%)

22 March 1968, Clowes Memorial Auditorium, Butler University, Indianapolis, Indiana (2 shows tonight, 7:00 p.m. and 9:30 p.m. With American Breed. Fee: $5000 plus 50% over $12,500)

23 March 1968, Shapiro Athletic Center, Brandeis University, Waltham, Massachusetts (with Orpheus. The show actually started at 2:15 a.m. the next morning due to a late arrival. Fee: $3500 flat)

SETLIST: Tales Of Brave Ulysses / Sunshine Of Your Love / NSU / Sitting On Top Of The World / Stepping Out / Traintime / Toad

24 March 1968, Gymnasium, State University of New York at Stony Brook, New York (canceled due to Jack Bruce being ill. Show is rescheduled for 2 April)

25 March 1968, day off

26 March 1968, Union Catholic Regional High School, Scotch Plains, New Jersey

27 March 1968, Staples High School Auditorium, Westport, Connecticut (Fee: $2250 flat)

28 March 1968, day off

29 March 1968, Hunter College Auditorium, New York City (2 shows at 8:00 p.m. and 10:30 p.m. With the Apostles. Fee: $7500 plus 60% over $15,000 less $1,500 for support group)

30 March 1968, Music Hall, Fair Park, Dallas, Texas (with Vanilla Fudge)

31 March 1968, Music Hall, Houston, Texas (with Vanilla Fudge. Fee for the 2 Texas shows: $8000/25% plus one-way air fares for band from New York)

APRIL 1968

2 April 1968, State University of New York at Stony Brook, New York

3 April 1968, Morris Civic Auditorium, South Bend, Indiana (Fee: $3000 flat)

4 April 1968, day off

5 April 1968, Back Bay Theatre, Boston, Massachusetts (Fee: $3000/50%)

SETLIST: Sunshine Of Your Love / Spoonful / Sleepy Time Time / Stepping Out / Traintime / Toad

6 April 1968, Commodore Ballroom, Lowell, Massachusetts (Fee: $2500/50%)

7 April 1968, Eastman College Theatre, Rochester, New York (Cream do not play, as their equipment fails to turn up)

8 April 1968, Capitol Theatre, Ottawa, Ontario (with Olivus and the Heart. Fee: $2500 plus 50% over $5500)

9 April 1968, day off

10 April 1968, Woolsey Hall, Yale University, New Haven, Connecticut (with Randy Burns)

11 April 1968, The Image Club, Miami, Florida (with Blues Image. This booking was kept secret from the public by the promoters but hinted at heavily during the Country Joe and Yardbirds shows earlier that week as a "spring break special")

12 April 1968, Electric Factory Theatre, Philadelphia, Pennsylvania (with Woody's Truck Stop)

Advert for Cream at the Electric Factory, 12 April 1968.

13 April 1968, Electric Factory Theatre, Philadelphia, Pennsylvania (with the Nazz)

14 April 1968, Electric Factory Theatre, Philadelphia, Pennsylvania (with Friends Of the Family. Fee for the 3 shows: $6000 plus 50% over $1200)

15 April 1968, Cream returned to UK for a ten-day break before resuming the tour

16 April–25 April 1968, days off

21 April 1968, *Romp!!!* television show broadcast in the US featuring Cream miming to "Sunshine Of Your Love"

26 April 1968, The Cellar, Arlington Heights, Illinois (Fee: $3000 flat)

27 April 1968, Coliseum, Chicago, Illinois (with Frank Zappa and the Mothers Of Invention. Fee: $5000 flat)

28 April 1968, Kiel Opera House, St Louis, Missouri (with Spur)

MAY 1968

1 May 1968, day off

2 May 1968, Wisconsin State University Fieldhouse, Madison, Wisconsin

3 May 1968, The Scene, Milwaukee, Wisconsin (2 sets. With the Invasion, the Corporation)

4 May 1968, The Scene, Milwaukee, Wisconsin (2 sets. With the Invasion, the Corporation)

5 May 1968, New City Opera House, St. Paul, Minnesota (with the Litter. According to the Twin Cities Music Highlights web page: "The show was fraught with problems—the band was late, the equipment didn't work, the show was less than an hour, and one report was that the musicians made out like they were doing the audience a big favor—but the music was superb. Our reviewer said the show was "worth the agony: the ecstasy was delicious." It was rumored that Cream had played so loud that a structural beam in the floor had cracked and split." Interestingly, an eyewitness states that after the show, Cream went next door to an empty Magoo's club for a jam and rehearsal)

6 May 1968, The Family Dog, Denver, Colorado

7 May 1968–9 May 1968, days off

10 May 1968, Shrine Auditorium, Los Angeles (Eric joins Frank Zappa And The Mothers Of Invention on stage. He is not introduced and stays in the background near the amps. It takes the crowd some time to recognize him. A recording of this show was made by Frank Zappa and is hopefully still in his archives)

Producer John Simon and Mama Cass went to the show. John told me: "Zappa kept going over to turn Eric's amp down while he was playing, which I thought peculiar."

> **"**He played with the Mothers once at the Shrine in Los Angeles and came over to my house. He wasn't the jamming type. When I used to live in a log cabin I had some amps set up in my basement, and he came over one day and played during one of our rehearsals. But he didn't like the amp; we were using Acoustics then, and he didn't like them. And when he came onstage at the Shrine, nobody knew who he was. He came out and played the set, and nobody paid any attention to him at all, until he walked off, and I told the audience that was Eric Clapton.**"**   —**FRANK ZAPPA**
> (*Guitar Player* magazine)

11 May 1968, Akron Civic Theatre, Akron, Ohio (with the James Gang, the Poor Girls, the Brambles, and Penny Arcade)

12 May 1968, Music Hall, Cleveland, Ohio (with Canned Heat)

13 May 1968, day off

14 May 1968, Veterans Memorial Auditorium, Columbus, Ohio

15 May 1968, Memorial Field House, Huntington, West Virginia (with the Grass Roots, Kickin' Mustangs, Purple Reign)

16 May 1968, day off

17 May 1968, Convention Center, Anaheim, California (with Spirit)

18 May 1968, Convention Center, Anaheim, California (with Spirit)

19 May 1968, Community Concourse Exhibit Hall, San Diego, California (with the Brain Police)

20 May 1968, CBS Television City, Stage 43, 7800 Beverly Boulevard, Los Angeles, Los Angeles, California (Cream play a live version of "Sunshine Of Your Love" and mime to "Anyone for Tennis" on the *Summer Brothers Smothers Show*. "Sunshine Of Your Love" is available on the *Those Were the Days* box set Polydor 539 000-2 released September 1997)

21 May 1968–23 May 1968, days off

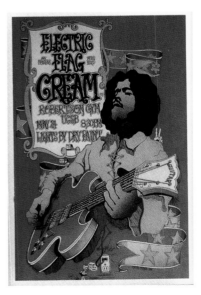

Poster for Cream at Robertson Gym on 24 May 1968.

24 May 1968, University of California, Robertson Gymnasium, Santa Barbara, California (with the Electric Flag)

25 May 1968, Civic Auditorium, San Jose, California (with Orphan Egg)

26 May 1968, day off

27 May 1968, Swing Auditorium, San Bernardino, California

28 May 1968, Pacific Center, Long Beach, California

29 May 1968, Eagles Auditorium, Seattle, Washington (with Easy Chair, Time Machine)

30 May 1968, Eagles Auditorium, Seattle, Washington (with Easy Chair, Time Machine. This was a second show added after the first night sold out so quickly. It took place at 2:30 in the afternoon)

31 May 1968, Stampede Corral, Stampede Park, Calgary, Alberta, Canada

JUNE 1968

1 June 1968, Sales Pavilion Annex, Edmonton, Alberta, Canada (with the Grass Roots)

2 June 1968, Pacific Coliseum, Vancouver, British Columbia, Canada

3 June 1968–4 June 1968, days off

5 June 1968, Massey Hall, Toronto, Ontario (with Duke Edwards & the Young Ones. The band are annoyed that they have to play though a 50-watt public address system that is normally used to talk to the audience. Jack Bruce is particularly dismayed, as this happens a few times on the tour)

6 June 1968, day off

7 June 1968, Grande Ballroom, Detroit, Michigan (with the MC5, the Carousel)

8 June 1968, Grande Ballroom, Detroit, Michigan (with Nickel Plate Express, St. Louis Union)

9 June 1968, Grande Ballroom, Detroit, Michigan (with the James Gang, Thyme. Fee for the 3 shows: $10,500/60%)

10 June 1968, day off

11 June 1968, Paul Sauvé Arena, Montreal, Quebec, Canada (with Duke Edwards & the Young Ones)

SETLIST: Tales Of Brave Ulysses / Sunshine Of Your Love / Sitting On Top Of The World / N.S.U. / Traintime / Stepping Out / Toad

12 June 1968–13 June 1968, Atlantic Studios, New York (final session for *Wheels Of Fire*)

14 June 1968, Island Garden, West Hempstead, Long Island, New York (band arrived late and played a reduced set as a result)

15 June 1968, Oakdale Music Centre, Wallingford, Connecticut (2 shows)

SETLIST: (late show): White Room / Politician / I'm So Glad / Sitting On Top Of the World / Crossroads / Sunshine Of Your Love / Traintime / Spoonful

16 June 1968, Camden County Music Fair, Cherry Hill, New Jersey (last date for this part of the tour. A well-deserved break is taken until the farewell tour starts in October)

18 June 1968, The Scene, New York (Eric and Jimi Hendrix join Jeff Beck on stage, who is there with his Jeff Beck Group)

25 June 1968, Studio 3, EMI Studios, St Johns Wood, London. Session for Jackie Lomax

AUGUST 1968

Eric jamming with Ginger Baker at the eighth National Jazz and Blues Festival in Sunbury, 10 August 1968.

10 August 1968, National Jazz & Blues Festival, Kempton Park Racecourse, Sunbury (Eric joins Ginger Baker and Phil Seamen for a hair-raising thirty-minute performance of instrumental virtuosity. The audience had no idea who the unannounced guitarist was but went wild as soon as compere John Gee shouted out, "And who's this?…Eric Clapton!"

Poster for eighth National Jazz and Blues Festival in Sunbury, August 1968.

"I went to the Festival and saw the Ginger Baker/Phil Seamen drum event. I've never been a big fan of Ginger's and have little or no appreciation of jazz drumming, so it was a predictable bore. But after a couple of numbers a long-haired guitarist in a green velvet jacket appeared on stage, plugged into a Marshall stack, and began playing a funny-shaped guitar (a Gibson Firebird) with his back to the audience. After a-minute or two I had convinced myself that the unknown player was Clapton; no-one else I could think of played with such confidence and originality. After a number or two Eric was introduced and the crowd went potty. I, of course, patted myself on the back for being such a discerning music nerd though, of course, it was not a difficult guess."

—CHRIS MICHIE

"I remember the gig quite well: it was announced as Baker/Seaman drum battle and I think it was rumoured that a surprise guest will join later. So the set started with an endless drum battle and after maybe 30 minutes a guitar player standing in the dark joined for a long improvisation, for maybe another 30 minutes. The crowd got excited because the word spread that it's Eric Clapton. The music was a mixture of jazz & blues, I don't recall any Cream riffs."

—KLAUS WACHTARZ

Cover for Cream's second live album, Live Cream Volume II, *partially recorded at the show on 10 August.*

OCTOBER 1968

4 October 1968, Alameda County Coliseum, Oakland, California (with It's A Beautiful Day. Fee: $20,000/60% with a potential gross of $70,000)

SETLIST:

White Room (Jack Bruce / Pete Brown) *Live Cream* Vol II album US ATCO SD 7005, UK Polydor 2383-119 released July 1972 / *Live Cream* Vol II CD Polydor 31453 1817-2 released 1998 / *Those Were The Days* box set Polydor 539 000-2 released September 1997

Politician (Jack Bruce / Pete Brown) *Live Cream* Vol II album US ATCO SD 700, UK Polydor 2383-119 released July 1972 / *Live Cream* Vol II CD Polydor 31453 1817-2 released 1998 / *Those Were The Days* box set Polydor 539 000-2 released September 1997

Crossroads (Robert Johnson) unreleased

Sunshine of Your Love (Jack Bruce / Pete Brown / Eric Clapton) unreleased

Spoonful (Willie Dixon) unreleased

Deserted Cities Of The Heart (Jack Bruce / Pete Brown) *Live Cream* Vol II album US ATCO SD 7005, UK Polydor 2383-119 released July 1972 / *Live Cream* Vol II CD Polydor 31453 1817-2 released 1998 / *Those Were The Days* box set Polydor 539 000-2 released September 1997

Passing the Time/Drum Solo (Ginger Baker / Mike Taylor) unreleased

I'm So Glad (Skip James) unreleased

Recorded on eight-track reels
Producer: Felix Pappalardi
Engineers: Tom Dowd, Bill Halverson

5 October 1968, University of New Mexico, Albuquerque (Fee: $20,000/60% with a potential gross of $75,000)

SETLIST: White Room / Politician / I'm So Glad / Sitting On Top Of The World / Sunshine Of Your Love / Deserted Cities Of The Heart / Toad / Spoonful

6 October 1968, City Auditorium, Denver, Colorado (Fee: $20,000/60% with a potential gross of $73,000)

7 October 1968–10 October 1968, days off

11 October 1968, New Haven Arena, New Haven, Connecticut (2 shows. Fee: $20,000 plus 60% over $40,000 with a potential gross of $84,000)

12 October 1968, Olympia Stadium, Detroit, Michigan (with Friend & Lover, the Siegel-Schwall Blues Band. Fee: $20,000 plus 60% over $40,000 with a potential gross of $80,000)

12 October 1968, Grande Ballroom, Detroit (after the Olympia Stadium show, Eric goes to the Grande and jams with John Mayall and the Bluesbreakers, who have Mick Taylor as their guitarist now)

13 October 1968, Coliseum, Chicago, Illinois (with Conqueror Worm. 3:30 p.m. show. Fee is $20,000/60% with a potential gross of $42,000)

14 October 1968, Veterans Memorial Auditorium, Des Moines, Iowa (with Conqueror Worm. Fee is $20,000 against 60% with a potential gross of $65,000)

15 October 1968–17 October 1968, days off

18 October 1968, the Forum, Los Angeles, California (with Deep Purple)

SETLIST: White Room / Politician / I'm So Glad / Sitting On Top Of The World / Sunshine Of Your Love / Crossroads / Traintime / Toad / Spoonful

The concert is recorded but nothing from this first night at the LA Forum is released

19 October 1968, the Forum, Los Angeles, California (with Deep Purple. Fee for both nights is $40,000 against 60% with a potential gross of $200,000)

SETLIST:

Introduction by Buddy Miles unreleased

White Room (Jack Bruce / Pete Brown) unreleased

Politician (Jack Bruce / Pete Brown) *Goodbye Cream* album ATCO SD 7001, Polydor 583053 released March 1969 / *Goodbye* CD Polydor 531815 released April 1998 / *Those Were The Days* box set Polydor 539 000-2 released September 1997

I'm So Glad (Skip James) *Goodbye Cream* album ATCO SD 7001, Polydor 583053 released March 1969 / Goodbye CD Polydor 531815 released April 1998 / *Those Were The Days* box set Polydor 539 000-2 released September 1997

Sitting On Top Of The World (Chester Burnett) *Goodbye Cream* album ATCO SD 7001, Polydor 583053 released March 1969 / *Goodbye* CD Polydor 531815 released April 1998 / *Those Were The Days* box set Polydor 539 000-2 released September 1997

Crossroads (Robert Johnson) unreleased

Sunshine Of Your Love (Jack Bruce / Pete Brown / Eric Clapton) unreleased

Traintime (Jack Bruce) unreleased

Toad (Ginger Baker) unreleased

Spoonful (Willie Dixon) unreleased

Recorded on eight-track reels
Producer: Felix Pappalardi
Engineers: Tom Dowd, Bill Halverson

20 October 1968, Sports Arena, San Diego, California (with Buddy Miles Express, Deep Purple. Fee is $20,000 against 60% with a potential gross of $65,000)

White Room (Jack Bruce / Pete Brown) unreleased

Politician (Jack Bruce / Pete Brown) unreleased

I'm So Glad (Skip James) unreleased

Sitting On Top Of The World (Chester Burnett) unreleased

Sunshine Of Your Love (Jack Bruce / Pete Brown / Eric Clapton) unreleased

Crossroads (Robert Johnson) unreleased

Traintime (Jack Bruce) unreleased

Toad (Ginger Baker) unreleased

Spoonful (Willie Dixon) unreleased

Recorded on eight-track reels
Producer: Felix Pappalardi
Engineers: Tom Dowd, Bill Halverson

21 October 1968–23 October 1968, days off

24 October 1968, Sam Houston Coliseum, Houston, Texas (Fee is $20,000 plus 60% over $40,000 with a potential gross of $60,000)

Eric Clapton playing a Gibson Firebird 1 with Cream in Dallas, 25 October 1968.

Eric Clapton playing a Gibson Firebird 1 with Cream in Dallas, 25 October 1968.

Cream in Dallas, 25 October 1968.

SETLIST: White Room / Sunshine Of Your Love / I'm So Glad / Sitting On Top Of The World / Crossroads / Traintime / Toad / Spoonful

25 October 1968, Memorial Auditorium, Dallas, Texas (with Terry Reid, Vanilla Fudge. Fee is $20,000 plus 60% over $40,000 with a potential gross of $60,000)

Cream at Madison Square Garden, New York, 2 November 1968.

26 October 1968, Miami Stadium, Miami, Florida (2 shows. With Terry Reid. Fee: $20,000 plus 60% over $40,000 with a potential gross of $44,000)

27 October 1968, Chastain Park Amphitheater, Atlanta, Georgia (with Terry Reid)

SETLIST: White Room / Politician / I'm So Glad / Traintime / Sunshine Of Your Love / Crossroads / Toad

28 October 1968–30 October 1968, days off

31 October 1968, Boston Garden, Boston, Massachusetts (canceled)

NOVEMBER 1968

1 November 1968, Spectrum, Philadelphia, Pennsylvania (with Terry Reid, Sweet Stavin Chain. Fee: $20,000 plus 60% over $45,000 with a potential gross of $80,000)

2 November 1968, Madison Square Garden, New York City (Fee: $20,000 plus 60% over $40,000 with a potential gross of $106,000)

SETLIST: White Room / Politician / I'm So Glad / Sunshine Of Your Love / Crossroads / Traintime / Toad / Spoonful

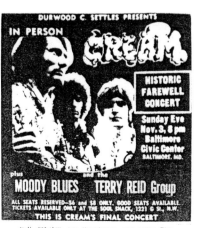

Advert for Cream at the Civic Center, Baltimore, on 3 November 1968.

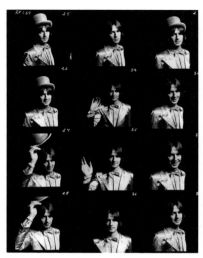

Eric Clapton during photo shoot for Goodbye *album cover November 1968.*

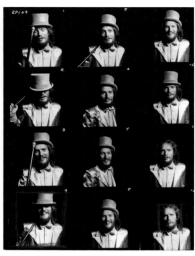

Ginger Baker during photo shoot for Goodbye *album cover.*

Jack Bruce during photo shoot for Goodbye *album cover.*

Eric Clapton playing a Gibson Firebird 1 with Cream at the early show at the Royal Albert Hall in London on 26 November 1968.

3 November 1968, Civic Center Arena, Baltimore, Maryland (with Terry Reid, the Moody Blues. Fee: $20,000 plus 60% over $40,000 with a potential gross of $60,000)

4 November 1968, Rhode Island Auditorium, Providence, Rhode Island (2 shows. With Terry Reid. The second show was cut short due to a noise curfew. Fee: $20,000 plus 60% over $40,000 with a potential gross of $76,000)

SETLIST (SECOND SHOW): White Room / Politician / I'm So Glad / Crossroads / Toad

26 November 1968, Royal Albert Hall, Kensington, London (With Taste and Yes as support. 2 shows)

FIRST SHOW: Setlist is said to be similar to the late show, but not as long due to late running

SECOND SHOW: White Room / Politician / I'm So Glad / Sitting On Top Of The World / Crossroads / Toad / Spoonful / Sunshine Of Your Love / Steppin' Out

Both Royal Albert shows were filmed in their entirety in color for the BBC by director Tony Palmer and later edited for an arts show called *Omnibus*. Tony Palmer had already filmed Cream once before in San Francisco at the Fillmore as part of a groundbreaking documentary on popular music called *All My Loving*. Filming at the Royal Albert Hall presented several problems, but the quality of the picture and sound were quite amazing, especially for a concert in 1968.

Eric Clapton playing a Gibson ES 335 with Cream at the late show at the Royal Albert Hall in London on 26 November 1968.

More footage was later reedited to make a feature-length film called *Farewell Cream*, which was not as good in quality as the *Omnibus* program.

The shows were filmed using two-color TV cameras that were so heavy that part of the stage on the right-hand side had to be reinforced where one would be positioned. The other one was based on the floor, stage left. Those two cameras had to remain static, which meant that Jack and Eric would have to stand in a particular position onstage so that the cameras could capture them. Ginger, of course, was fine, as his drums were fixed. During the first show, Eric had his back to the cameras for most of the set, which explains why only "White Room" has been used. There was also a single mobile video camera that could move around the stage when needed. Then there was a single film camera at the front of the stage as a backup. Both shows were videoed on two-inch tape, which in 1968 was incredibly difficult to edit, which explains why a lot of the footage is out of sync. There is no such problem on the original unedited footage.

Eric Clapton playing a Gibson ES 335 with Cream at the late show at the Royal Albert Hall in London on 26 November 1968.

I was very fortunate in my research to locate a complete and unedited kinescope copy of Cream's last-ever show at the Royal Albert Hall on 26 November 1968. So far there is no sign of the first show, but clearly there is a possibility that a kinescope copy for it is still around.

The footage starts with John Peel stepping slowly to the mic. He announces, "Hmmm…tomorrow they're going to be Ginger Baker, Jack Bruce, and Eric Clapton, but tonight they are still CREAM!" Eric and Jack come onstage from the left, looking

surprisingly upbeat and smiling. Ginger goes behind the amps and sits down behind his kit.

Eric politely asks the crowd to keep their cool, and Jack Bruce inquires if he needs to move his microphone stand back, presumably for filming purposes and camera obstructions. After some tuning, the band are straight into "White Room." They follow with "Politician." At the conclusion of the number,

Cream photo shoot for Goodbye *album cover, November 1968.*

Ginger announces, "And now we're going to do 'I'm So Glad.' Thank you." Eric is really playing well, as are Jack and Ginger. Eric thanks the crowd, and Ginger says, "We're going to do a slow one now…it's called 'Sitting On Top Of The World'…thank you." Eric's lead cuts through the Royal Albert Hall, and Jack's voice has never sounded so good. Ginger seems to have taken over as emcee for the evening and announces the next song: "We'd like to do a number featuring Eric singing, and it's called 'Crossroads.'" Eric says something, but the crowd are too noisy shouting and screaming to make out what he says. While not quite the famous "Wheels Of Fire" version, this evening's version is a close second.

Ginger thanks Eric, who steps up to the mic and announces, "We'd like to feature Ginger, our drummer, for the next number. This one you've all heard before, and it's one of our most popular numbers, and it's called 'The Toad.'" Ginger gives it his all, maybe because he realizes this is the last one. The crowd go apoplectic at the end, and Ginger looks exhausted after the marathon workout. Eric shouts out to the crowd, "Ginger Baker…drums!" The crowd are still going wild when Ginger thanks them several times and they drown out his announcement of "Spoonful." This has to be THE song of the evening. This is one of the best versions I have heard, with Eric leading strongly and Jack and Ginger following his intricate patterns and all three hitting a great groove before coming back to the main theme. After "Spoonful," the band thank the crowd before heading backstage, leaving the crowd shouting for more. When they come back, the band are clearly blown away by the fans' reaction. "We don't know what do to," says Eric. "We have no idea what we're going to do." Ginger tells the crowd to be quiet before Eric announces, "What if we did 'Sunshine,' would that satisfy you?" Eric quickly rushes behind his amps to talk to one of the road crew, as clearly something is wrong with one of his Marshall amps. He is getting no sound as he strums his guitar. Eric tells the crowd something but is inaudible among the shouting. After a-minute or so, the problem is fixed and the place erupts as the band play "Sunshine Of Your Love." At the end, some fans climb onto the stage and shower Eric with confetti petals. Eric thanks the crowd and waves goodbye before leaving the stage. The crowd are on their feet and demand more. After a few-minutes, Cream come back to the stage and Ginger tells the crowd, "We're going to do 'Steppin' Out'…all right?" A shortish version is played, and after the song ends Eric says, "Sorry about my amp, but [inaudible] collapsed. Thank you very much for asking us back." And that is it. John Peel announces to the crowd that there will be no more, and people start to make their way out of the hall, somewhat dazed and confused. Eric would have liked to play more: "I'd like to have done a couple more numbers, but our equipment was giving us trouble before we finished the first time. It was really a fine evening for me, and I felt very excited."

This is a concert that really should have been sound-recorded professionally on multitrack tape. RSO, who were never shy about making money, must have thought about it. Surely the farewell Cream show would have been a massive money spinner?

Cream photo shoot for Goodbye *album cover, November 1968.*

GUEST RECORDING SESSIONS DURING THE CREAM YEARS; 1966–1968 RECORDING SESSIONS

GUEST RECORDING SESSIONS DURING THE CREAM YEARS

1966 RECORDING SESSIONS

ERIC CLAPTON GUEST SESSION

PHILIPS RECORDING STUDIOS
Stanhope House, 2-4
Stanhope Place, London W2
Session for Claire Francis

1966

I'VE GOT MY OWN THING GOING (Eddie Reeves) single A-side US United Artists 50132, UK Polydor 56079 released 1966
HERE I GO AGAIN (Tony May) single B-side US United Artists 50132, UK Polydor 56079 released 1966

Producer: Claire Francis
Engineer: unknown

"When I was working for Polydor in London, I would fly in to New York with a stack of records and bring them to various record companies to sub-license them. I took 'I've Got My Own Thing Going' to United Artists because Murray Deutche, who was head of Publishing, was also a mentor to me. The writer of the song, Eddie Reeves, was signed to U.A. during the sixties. When Eddie played me 'I've Got My Own Thing Going,' he sang it with a twang and kind of country. I really liked the tune, and when I was producing my own records at Polydor, I decided to record it. Nicky Welsh, the musical director, asked Eric, Jimmy and Bill to be on the session. He had worked with them, I guess, before. I agreed. I remember him introducing me briefly to the musicians, and I was very impressed. It was one of my favorite productions. I sang my heart out on that gig, and we all had a great time. It was the first time those musicians played on my sessions I remember it was a jumpin' session. Eric was on 12 string and Jimmy was on electric. Bill Wyman is on electric bass, Coleridge Good is on stand-up bass. The background vocal is also me. I triple tracked vocals. I made sure there was plenty of food and beer—most of the musicians opted not to drink on the session, but afterwards we enjoyed the catering. I was well known for always doing stuff like that. Every time I said the word 'coffee' with my heavy Brooklyn accent, everyone used to imitate me and laugh their heads off." **—CLAIRE FRANCIS**

"On 'Here I Go Again,' Eric played my own 12 string." **—CLAIRE FRANCIS**

ERIC CLAPTON
GUEST SESSION

PHILIPS RECORDING STUDIOS
Stanhope House, 2-4
Stanhope Place, London W2
Session for Dave Rich

1966

I JUST WANNA DANCE (Claire Francis / Dave Rich) single A-side Polydor 56113 released 1966

Producer: Claire Francis
Musical direction by Nicky Welsh
Engineer: unknown

> "On 'I Just Wanna Dance' I think Jimmy Page was on the electric guitar and Eric Clapton was on rhythm. Bill Wyman played his bass on these records as well, and sometimes I had both electric and stand up bass. Coleridge Good played standup and on several of my records I had Bill and Coleridge playing together. That is probably when I was going for the heavy Spector sound." —CLAIRE FRANCIS

ERIC CLAPTON
GUEST SESSION

EMI STUDIOS
Studio Three, 3 Abbey
Road, London NW8
Session for Jackie Lynton

1966

SPORTING LIFE BLUES single B-side Columbia DB 8180 released March 1967

Jackie Lynton: vocals
Eric Clapton: guitar
Mitch Mitchell: drums
John Paul Jones: bass

Producer: Mark Wirtz
Engineer: unknown

ERIC CLAPTON
GUEST SESSION

EMI STUDIOS
Studio Three, 3 Abbey
Road, London NW8
Session for
Caroline Munroe

1966

THE SPORTING LIFE (Sonny Terry / Brownie McGhee) single B-side to "Tar and Cement" COLUMBIA, DB 8189 UK-only released April 1967 / *Dream Babes Vol. 2 Reflections* CD RPM 224 released 2001

Caroline Munro: vocals
Eric Clapton: guitar
Steve Howe: guitar
Mitch Mitchell: drums
John Paul Jones: bass

Producer: Mark Wirtz
Engineer: unknown

The record has always wrongly been attributed to Peter Eden and Mark Wirtz, when in reality this is "Sporting Life Blues" by Sonny Terry and Brownie McGhee. I have spoken with Mark Wirtz as well as researched many interviews with him over the years about this single, and the story changes several times. The one constant is that Eric plays on it, although I have seen one interview in which he claimed Jimmy Page played on it also. Eric would eventually record his own version with JJ Cale in 2006 for their *Road To Escondido* album. Caroline often refers to the Cream guys backing her, but as far as I know no musicians were in the studio with her. She was just singing her vocals to a prerecorded track. And Mark has said that Jack and Ginger had no involvement on the single.

> "Both versions (the other one being by Jackie Lynton) were recorded at Abbey Road #3. To the best of my recollection, Eric may have played on both of the versions. To be sure, he played on the Jackie Lynton version, as did John Paul Jones and Mitch Mitchell. Eric and I, in fact, were living at the same 'Rock 'n' Roll Hotel' at the time." —MARK WIRTZ

ERIC CLAPTON
GUEST SESSION

APOSTOLIC STUDIOS
53 East 10th Street,
New York City
Session for Frank Zappa,
We're Only In It
For The Money

OCTOBER 1967

ARE YOU HUNG UP (Frank Zappa) *We're Only In It For The Money* album US Verve V6-5045 released January 1968 / UK Verve VLP 9199 released October 1968

Eric Clapton stutters like a stoner.

NASAL-RETENTIVE CALLIOPE MUSIC (Frank Zappa) *We're Only In It For The Money* album US Verve V6-5045 released January 1968 / UK Verve VLP 9199 released October 1968

Eric Clapton says, "God! It's God! I see God!"

Producer: Frank Zappa
Engineer: Gary Kellgren

> "He was just in New York one day hanging out, so I invited him over to the studio to do the rap that's on 'We're Only In It For The Money.' People think he's playing on it, but he's not; the only thing he's doing on there is talking." —**FRANK ZAPPA**
> (*Guitar Player* magazine)

ERIC CLAPTON
GUEST SESSION

EMI STUDIOS
Studio Three, 3 Abbey
Road, London NW8
Session for George
Harrison, *Wonderwall*

22 NOVEMBER 1967–23 NOVEMBER 1967

SKI-ING (George Harrison) *Wonderwall* album US Apple ST-3350 released December 1968, UK Apple SAPCOR 1 (stereo), APCOR 1 (mono) released November 1968 / *Wonderwall* CD Apple CDP 7 98706 2 released 1992

Eric Clapton: guitar
Roy Dyke: drums

Phillip Rogers: bass
Shambu-Das: sitar
Indril Bhattacharya: sitar
Shankar Ghosh: sitar
Rij Ram Desad: tabla-tarang, harmonium

Producer: George Harrison
Engineer: Ken Scott

ERIC CLAPTON
GUEST SESSION

ATLANTIC STUDIOS
11 West 60th Street,
New York
Sessions for Aretha
Franklin, *Lady Soul*

16 DECEMBER 1967–17 DECEMBER 1967

GOOD TO ME AS I AM TO YOU (Aretha Franklin / Ted White) *Lady Soul* album US Atlantic SD 8176, UK Atlantic 588 099 released 1968 / *Lady Soul* CD Rhino 8122-71933-2 released 1995

Aretha Franklin: vocals
Eric Clapton: guitar
Spooner Oldham: electric piano
Bobby Womack: guitar
Joe South: guitar
Jimmy Johnson: guitar
Roger Hawkins: drums
King Curtis: sax
Selden Power: sax
Frank Wess: sax
Mel Lastie: trumpet
Joe Newman: trumpet
Bernie Glow: trumpet
Haywood Henry: baritone sax
Tony Studd: bass trombone
Tom Cogbill: bass

Producer: Jerry Wexler
Engineer: Tom Dowd

> "When I arrived at the studio she wasn't there. The place was full of musicians, including Joe South and Bobby Womack, and Tom told me, 'Go in there and show them what it's all about.' He kicked out all the guitarists and put me in there, right in front of them. It was pretty nerve-wracking but I had one pass at it and they gave me a standing ovation, which really amazed me. I was over the moon that they liked it; but I couldn't believe they hadn't heard guitar playing like that before. I mean, I'd just gone in and done it the way I normally would." —**ERIC CLAPTON**

> "Eric was in town and I asked him to come down and play. He was ashamed to walk in the studio in the face of Joe South, Cornell Dupree and Jimmy Johnson. He belonged there but didn't have the confidence to realize that." —TOM DOWD

ERIC CLAPTON GUEST SESSION

EMI STUDIOS
Studio Three, 3 Abbey Road, London NW8
Session for Jackie Lomax

25 JUNE 1968

SOUR MILK SEA (George Harrison) single A-side US Apple 1802 released August 1968 / UK Apple 3 released August 1968 / *Is This What You Want* album US Apple ST-3354 released May 1969, UK Apple SAPCOR 6 released May 1969 / *Is This What You Want* CD Apple 5099990825521 released October 2010

Jackie Lomax: guitar, vocals
Eric Clapton: guitar
George Harrison: acoustic guitar
Paul McCartney: bass
Nicky Hopkins: piano
Ringo Starr: drums

> "There was nothing else like that song at the time. It came on like gangbusters on anybody's radio. With Eric Clapton playing on it, it was on fire. When the backing tape was played back, I thought it worked as an instrumental. 'You want me to sing on top of that?!' There I am in the studio and there are three Beatles in the control room watching me. That choked up my throat a bit. Then George said, 'Are you sure you can sing it that high, Jackie?' I guess I was nervous at first, but after a couple of takes I was into it." —JACKIE LOMAX

THE EAGLE LAUGHS AT YOU (Jackie Lomax) single B-side US Apple 1802 released August 1968 / UK Apple 3 released August 1968 / *Is This What You Want* album US Apple ST-3354 released March 1969, UK Apple SAPCOR 6 released May 1969 / *Is This What You Want* CD Apple 5099990825521 released October 2010

Jackie Lomax: bass, vocals
Eric Clapton: guitar
George Harrison: guitar
Tony Newman: drums
John Barham: horn arrangements
Madelaine Bell: backing vocals
Lesley Duncan: backing vocals

> "'You've Got Me Thinking' has got a good arrangement to it that was built in by the writer. That pleased me. I proved myself, right? Eric Clapton's lead guitar sells it for me. This gets back to R&B, with the girl singers and the horns." —JACKIE LOMAX

YOU GOT ME THINKING (Jackie Lomax) *Is This What You Want* album US Apple ST-3354 released March 1969, UK Apple SAPCOR 6 released May 1969 / *Is This What You Want* CD Apple 5099990825521 released October 2010

Jackie Lomax: guitar, vocals
Eric Clapton: guitar
George Harrison: guitar
Klaus Voormann: bass
Bishop O'Brien: drums
John Barham: horn arrangements
Madelaine Bell: backing vocals
Lesley Duncan: backing vocals

Recorded at EMI Studios over three days, on 24–26 June 1968, as well as another Jackie Lomax song, "The Eagle Laughs At You." George Harrison produced the songs and played acoustic guitar, with Paul McCartney on bass, Ringo Starr on drums, Eric Clapton on guitar, and Nicky Hopkins on piano. "The Eagle Laughs At You" featured George Harrison and Eric Clapton playing rhythm and lead guitar alongside Jackie Lomax, but no other Beatles were on this session.

Paul McCartney was out of the country for the first two days and added his bass part to "Sour Milk Sea" on 26 June. "You've Got Me Thinking" was also recorded during these sessions.

ERIC CLAPTON GUEST SESSION

EMI STUDIOS
Studio 2, 3 Abbey Road, London NW8
Session for the Beatles, *White Album*

6 SEPTEMBER 1968

WHILE MY GUITAR GENTLY WEEPS (George Harrison) *White Album* US Apple SWBO 101, UK Apple PCS 7067/8 released November 1968 / *White Album* CD Apple 0946 3 82466 2 6 released September 2009

George Harrison: vocals, acoustic guitar
John Lennon: guitar
Paul McCartney: bass, piano, backing vocals
Ringo Starr: drums
Eric Clapton: guitar

Producer: George Martin
Engineer: Ken Scott

> "I worked on that song with John, Paul and Ringo one day, and they were not interested in it at all. And I knew inside of me that it was a nice song. The next day I was with Eric, and I was going into the session, and I said, 'We're going to do this song. Come on and play on it.' He said, 'Oh no. I can't do that. Nobody ever plays on the Beatles records.' I said, 'Look, it's my song, and I want you to play on it.' So Eric came in, and the other guys were good as gold, because he was there. Also, it left me to do the vocal and play rhythm. Then we listened to it back, and he said, 'Ah, there's a problem, though; it's not Beatley enough.' So we put it through the ADT (automatic double-tracker), to wobble it a bit. The drums would be all on one track, bass on another, the acoustic on another, piano on another, Eric on another, and then whatever else. I sang it with acoustic guitar with Paul on piano, and Eric and Ringo. Later Paul overdubbed bass on it." —**GEORGE HARRISON**
> (*Guitar* magazine, 1987)

ERIC CLAPTON GUEST SESSION

THE HIT FACTORY
701, Seventh Avenue, New York City
Session for Eric Andersen

NOVEMBER 1968

IT'S COMING AND IT WON'T BE LONG (Eric Andersen) unreleased
LOUISE (Eric Andersen) unreleased

Producer: Bill Szymczyk
Engineer: Bill Szymczyk

After Cream's last date in the US, Eric stayed on in New York to play on sessions for Eric Andersen's second album for Warner Brothers, *Avalanche*. The sessions took place at the Hit Factory under the supervision of Bill Szymczyk. Other musicians on the session are Herb Lovelle on drums and Chuck Rainey on bass. He also jammed with Chuck Rainey at Whitey's during his stay in New York.

> "We had done a session together at Bill Szymczyk's studio in New York. Songs as I recall were 'It's Coming and It Won't Be Long,' 'Louise' and one or two others. Eric (Clapton) had asked me to wait so he could record the whole album. But his tour was taking too long and we went ahead and recorded 'Avalanche' without him in LA. The tapes at one point had been moved to Levon Helm's garage by Andy Robinson and then Levon had a fire and unfortunately they were lost (unless Bill might still have the multitracks)." —**ERIC ANDERSEN**

> "I worked with a couple of American musicians in New York, bassist Chuck Rainey and Herb Lovelle on drums, who I'd love to bring here to record." —**ERIC CLAPTON**
> (*Melody Maker*, November 1968)

> "I remember jamming with Eric at Whitey's loft in the Village during 1968. Whitey was a cartage carrier who delivered music equipment to live gigs and recording studios for musicians. He kept everyone's equipment in a loft in Manhattan that also doubled as a rehearsal studio. My equipment and Cream's equipment was among the stuff stored and delivered there, and that is where I first met and jammed with Eric." —**CHUCK RAINEY**

8

CREAM RECORDING SESSIONS

CREAM RECORDING SESSIONS

The Cream's debut album, *Fresh Cream*, was recorded with very little studio time, but over a long period of months fitted in between touring commitments. They did not have the luxury of recording many takes and had to pretty much get it right within one or two takes. On top of that, they did not have a professional producer at the sessions, so they and sound engineer John Timperley did the best they could on the production front. Robert Stigwood's main contribution was choosing the studios, despite having his name down as producer. In reality, he had very little involvement in producing.

Eric in the studio recording Fresh Cream.

RAYRIK SOUND STUDIOS
1a Belmont Street, Chalk Farm, London NW1
Sessions for *Fresh Cream*

3 AUGUST 1966–5 AUGUST 1966

COFFEE SONG (Tony Colton / Ray Smith) rehearsals and several takes made

COFFEE SONG (Tony Colton / Ray Smith) master / bonus track on *Fresh Cream* CD Polydor / *Those Were The Days* box set Polydor 539 000-2 released September 1997

BEAUTY QUEEN (Jack Bruce / Pete Brown) rehearsals and several takes made

YOU MAKE ME FEEL (Jack Bruce / Pete Brown) rehearsals and several takes made

WRAPPING PAPER (Jack Bruce / Pete Brown) rehearsals and several takes made

WRAPPING PAPER (Jack Bruce / Pete Brown) master / single A-side UK Reaction 591007 released October 1966 *Fresh Cream* CD Polydor / *Those Were The Days* box set Polydor 539 000-2 released September 1997

Producer: Robert Stigwood
Engineer: John Timperley

RYEMUSE STUDIOS / SPOT PRODUCTIONS
64 South Molton Street, Mayfair, London W1
Sessions for *Fresh Cream*

30 AUGUST 1966, 31 AUGUST 1966, 13 SEPTEMBER 1966, 14 SEPTEMBER 1966, 21 SEPTEMBER 1966, 22 SEPTEMBER 1966

CAT'S SQUIRREL (Traditional; arranged by S. Splurge) rehearsals and several takes

Cream's first album, Fresh Cream, *UK cover.*

CAT'S SQUIRREL (Traditional; arranged by S. Splurge) master / single B-side of "Wrapping Paper" UK Reaction 591007 released October 1966 / *Fresh Cream* album UK Reaction mono 593 001, Reaction stereo 594 001 released December 1966 / US ATCO 33-206 mono, ATCO SD 33-206 stereo released March 1967 / *Fresh Cream* CD Polydor

(S. Splurge was a group pseudonym invented to spread song royalties to everyone except to Dr. Ross)

CAT'S SQUIRREL (Traditional; arranged by S. Splurge) alternate take with different guitar solo available only on French EP Polydor 27 791 released December 1966 (other numbers on the ep are Wrapping Paper / Sweet Wine / I'm So Glad)

I FEEL FREE (Jack Bruce / Pete Brown)) rehearsals and several takes

I FEEL FREE (Jack Bruce / Pete Brown) master / single A-side UK Reaction 591011 released December 1966 / US ATCO 6462 released January 1967 / *Fresh Cream* album US only ATCO 33-206 mono, ATCO SD 33-206, stereo released March 1967

N.S.U. (Jack Bruce) master / single B-side of "I Feel Free" UK Reaction 591007 released October 1966 / *Fresh Cream* album UK Reaction mono 593 001, Reaction stereo 594 001 released December 1966 / US ATCO 33-206 mono, ATCO SD 33-206 stereo released March 1967 / *Fresh Cream* CD Polydor

Producer: Cream
Engineer: John Timperley

"Rymuse Studios was quite a home-made set up with a four-track recorder. We recorded the backing track on all four tracks, then mixed that down to a Phillips mono tape machine, because we didn't own a second four-track tape machine. We then recorded that track onto another four-track and filled up the other three tracks with overdubs. You couldn't copy tapes very well in those days and if we used this process too often the bass and drums would often start to sound mushy. There was no producer per se, but there was a lot of discussion and heated arguments between the three of them. When Stigwood did come along they tended to misbehave somewhat. On one occasion, I vividly recall them forcing Stigwood into a drum case and rolling him down the stairs!" —JOHN TIMPERLEY
(from *Those Were The Days* liner notes)

RYEMUSE STUDIOS / SPOT PRODUCTIONS 64 South Molton Street, Mayfair, London W1

19 OCTOBER 1966

SLEEPY TIME TIME (Jack Bruce / Janet Godfrey) rehearsals and several takes

SLEEPY TIME TIME (Jack Bruce / Janet Godfrey) master / *Fresh Cream* album UK Reaction mono 593 001, Reaction stereo 594 001 released December 1966 / US ATCO 33-206 mono, ATCO SD 33-206 stereo released March 1967 / *Fresh Cream* CD Polydor

DREAMING (Jack Bruce) master / *Fresh Cream* album UK Reaction mono 593 001, Reaction stereo 594 001 released December 1966 / US ATCO 33-206 mono, ATCO SD 33-206 stereo released March 1967 / *Fresh Cream* CD Polydor

SWEET WINE (Ginger Baker / Janet Godfrey) rehearsals and several takes

SWEET WINE (Ginger Baker / Janet Godfrey) master / *Fresh Cream* album UK Reaction mono 593 001, Reaction stereo 594 001 released December 1966 / US ATCO 33-206 mono, ATCO SD 33-206 stereo released March 1967 / *Fresh Cream* CD Polydor

Producer: Cream
Engineer: John Timperley

RYEMUSE STUDIOS / SPOT PRODUCTIONS 64 South Molton Street, Mayfair, London W1

9 NOVEMBER 1966–10 NOVEMBER 1966

FOUR UNTIL LATE (Robert Johnson) master / *Fresh Cream* album UK Reaction mono 593 001, Reaction stereo 594 001 released December 1966 / US ATCO 33-206 mono, ATCO SD 33-206 stereo released March 1967 / *Fresh Cream* CD Polydor

ROLLIN' AND TUMBLIN' (Muddy Waters) rehearsals and several takes

ROLLIN' AND TUMBLIN' (Muddy Waters) master / *Fresh Cream* album UK Reaction mono 593 001, Reaction stereo 594 001 released December 1966 / US ATCO 33-206 mono, ATCO SD 33-206 stereo released March 1967 / *Fresh Cream* CD Polydor

TOAD (Ginger Baker) rehearsals and several takes

TOAD (Ginger Baker) master / *Fresh Cream* album UK Reaction mono 593 001, Reaction stereo 594 001 released December 1966 / US ATCO 33-206 mono, ATCO SD 33-206 stereo released March 1967 / *Fresh Cream* CD Polydor

I'M SO GLAD (Skip James) rehearsals and several takes

I'M SO GLAD (Skip James) master / *Fresh Cream* album UK Reaction mono 593 001, Reaction stereo 594 001 released December 1966 / US ATCO 33-206 mono, ATCO SD 33-206 stereo released March 1967 / *Fresh Cream* CD Polydor

SPOONFUL (Willie Dixon) rehearsals and several takes

SPOONFUL (Willie Dixon) master / *Fresh Cream* album UK-only Reaction mono 593 001, Reaction stereo 594 001 released December 1966 / *Fresh Cream* CD Polydor

Producer: Cream
Engineer: John Timperley

RYEMUSE STUDIOS / SPOT PRODUCTIONS 64 South Molton Street, Mayfair, London W1 Rehearsals and Demo sessions for next album

15 MARCH 1967

TAKE IT BACK (Jack Bruce / Pete Brown) rehearsal takes

TAKE IT BACK (Jack Bruce / Pete Brown) demo master

The first rehearsal take starts with Eric working out the intro with Jack. They then launch into a full instrumental rehearsal with Eric playing a very tentative solo. In between takes Eric can be heard saying, "It sounds like it needs some shouting in the background…like 'Everyone Must Get Stoned.'"There is clearly some influence here from Bob Dylan's 'Rainy Day Women12 & 35,' which is based on a blues shuffle chord progression. The finished demo includes various band members adding some shouts and screams.

THE CLEAROUT (Jack Bruce / Pete Brown) rehearsal takes
THE CLEAROUT (Jack Bruce / Pete Brown) demo with vocals
THE CLEAROUT (Jack Bruce / Pete Brown) demo without vocals *Those Were The Days* box set Polydor 539 000-2 released September 1997

Another whimsical ditty that might have developed into something worthwhile had time permitted. The best thing here is the Who-like ending drenched in guitar feedback.

WEIRD OF HERMISTON (Jack Bruce / Pete Brown) rehearsal takes
WEIRD OF HERMISTON (Jack Bruce / Pete Brown) demo master *Those Were The Days* box set Polydor 539 000-2 released September 1997

The rehearsal opens with the band working out the complex beat structure. Eric follows Ginger closely while Jack plays contrapuntally emphasizing the melody on lead bass. Once the initial instrumental rehearsal is finished they spend some time retuning before doing a final take. This song showed tremendous potential but sadly never progressed past the demo stage for Cream.

WE'RE GOING WRONG (Jack Bruce / Pete Brown) rehearsal takes
WE'RE GOING WRONG (Jack Bruce / Pete Brown) demo master *Those Were The Days* box set Polydor 539 000-2 released September 1997

The bare bones of this number are here, but it will develop into a dark, brooding song when re-recorded in New York and will become one of Cream's best-loved numbers.

BLUE CONDITION (Ginger Baker) rehearsal takes
BLUE CONDITION (Ginger Baker) demo master

Eric is working out the song with Jack, who is on harp. Ginger hums the melody, and Jack plays bass and harmonica. Eric will sing vocals on one of the takes to be recorded at Atlantic Studios in May (available on the Deluxe Edition of *Disraeli Gears*)

HEY NOW PRINCESS (Jack Bruce / Pete Brown) rehearsal takes
HEY NOW PRINCESS (Jack Bruce / Pete Brown) demo master *Those Were The Days* box set Polydor 539 000-2 released September 1997

Cream delve into Jimi Hendrix territory. Reminiscent of "Stone Free," Clapton soared on these takes. What possessed them to record the truly dreadful throwaway "Mothers Lament" when they could have worked on polishing this gem on the final album?

SWLABR (Jack Bruce / Pete Brown) rehearsal takes
SWLABR (Jack Bruce / Pete Brown) demo master *Those Were The Days* box set Polydor 539 000-2 released September 1997

The song will not significantly change from the demo version in terms of arrangement. Eric is displaying some fine guitar work yet again.

ATLANTIC STUDIOS
11 West 60th Street,
New York
Sessions for
Disraeli Gears

3 APRIL 1967–4 APRIL 1967

After Cream finish their run of shows for the Murray the K's *Music In The Fifth Dimension* at the RKO Theater, they make their first recordings in America. They have studio time booked at Atlantic, a much better studio than they had been using back home in London. Tom Dowd is the man behind the board, and both Robert Stigwood and Ahmet Ertegun, president of Atlantic Records, are in attendance, which shows not only commitment, but also how important they feel Cream could become.

Although Robert Stigwood is technically there to supervise the sessions, both he and Ahmet Ertegun end up sharing the producer's credit and role. With several demos done back in March at Spot Productions in London, the idea is now to start recording their new album in New York and complete it in England.

Ahmet did not particularly like the demos he heard, feeling they were too mundane and not commercial enough for Cream's obvious musical talent. He came from a serious jazz and blues background, and it is easy to see why he would have had reservations about the direction they wanted to go in. It must also be noted that Robert Stigwood had sold Cream to Atlantic as a blues trio. The demos showed little, if any, blues influences. To Jack's annoyance, Ahmet also felt strongly that Eric should be the star and frontman of the band. It would be far easier to sell Cream with him in that role. As Eric had nothing prepared, the band record the traditional blues number "Lawdy Mama," which they had been playing already in their live set back home. In fact, they record two very different arrangements. One uses the Junior Wells and Buddy Guy interpretation from 1965. The other is still bluesy, but with a very different arrangement and melody. It now has an obvious commercial appeal with a psychedelic slant. Eric has kept the original lyrics, though, and that would have to change. Compounding Jack's annoyance, Eric is doing the lead vocal, a job Jack felt he was better qualified to do.

One Toad Two Frogs, a production and publishing company formed by Felix Pappalardi and Bud Prager, are brought in to produce Cream's US sessions, as Ahmet realizes that Cream's fan base will be the young generation, and a hip producer with a good understanding of "now" sounds would make more sense. In fact, Felix is so much more than a producer—he is also a classically trained musician who will contribute a great deal to all future Cream albums. Felix is at the first session as an observer, really. He is there to give feedback to Ahmet. At the end of the session he asks to take a tape copy of "Lawdy Mama" (version 2) home, where he works on it with his wife Gail Collins. Together they transform it into "Strange Brew," with a new set of lyrics. Everyone is happy with the end result, and the song has obvious appeal for a single. At first they want to rush-release it with "Lawdy Mama" as the B-side.

In fact, the sessions go so well that it is decided to record the rest of the album at Atlantic Studios in May once new visas have been organized. They delay plans for a single release until the second sessions. As the band have two days left on their current visas, Cream enjoy a break in New York before heading home to England.

3 APRIL 1967

LAWDY MAMA (Traditional; arranged by Eric Clapton) version 1; Multiple takes are done before a basic track is completed
LAWDY MAMA (Traditional; arranged by Eric Clapton) version 1; guitar and vocal overdubs
LAWDY MAMA (Traditional; arranged by Eric Clapton) version 1 master version / *Those Were The Days* box set Polydor 539 000-2 released September 1997
LAWDY MAMA (Traditional; arranged by Eric Clapton) version 2; Multiple takes are done before a basic track is completed
LAWDY MAMA (Traditional; arranged by Eric Clapton) version 2; guitar overdubs

LAWDY MAMA (Traditional; arranged by Eric Clapton) version 2; master version / *Live Cream* album UK Polydor 2383016 / US ATCO SD 33-328 released April 1970 / *Those Were The Days* box set Polydor 539 000-2 released September 1997

Producers: Ahmet Ertegun and Robert Stigwood
Engineer: Tom Dowd

4 APRIL 1967

STRANGE BREW (Eric Clapton / Gail Collins / Felix Pappalardi) rehearsals and multiple takes are done before a basic track is completed
STRANGE BREW (Eric Clapton / Gail Collins / Felix Pappalardi) overdubs
STRANGE BREW (Eric Clapton / Gail Collins / Felix Pappalardi) master / single A-side UK Reaction 591015 released May 1967 / US ATCO 6488 released July 1967 / *Disraeli Gears* album UK mono Reaction 593003 / stereo Reaction 593003 / US mono ATCO 33-232 / stereo ATCO SD 33-232 released November 1967 / *Disraeli Gears* Deluxe Edition 2CD Polydor B0003331-2 released September 2004

Producer: Felix Pappalardi
Engineer: Tom Dowd

> "The first time with Cream, because of the political and social climate of the time, the United States and Great Britain were not in love with each other exchanging musicians. There were strict rules that you had to go by, you could not do this or you could not do that. Visas were necessary for the bands to play. It was tacky, it was sticky, and it was stinky. The English were in distress, when I say that they were in distress, they did not have that much national product going for them. So they had their hands full just trying to stay even and the greatest export that they had was the Beatles. This led to a very strange situation, where if a five man English group came over here they had a 20–28 day visa and they would work so many days, but only if America could send a five man group over to England to work for the same amount of time." **—TOM DOWD**
> (interview by Michael Buffalo Smith)

RYEMUSE STUDIOS / SPOT PRODUCTIONS
64 South Molton Street, Mayfair, London W1
Demos session for *Disraeli Gears*

17 APRIL 1967

A demo recording session takes place today based on the group's official itineraries. Sadly, no records of what demos were recorded exists, but presumably they record "Sunshine Of Your Love" and "Dance The Night Away." Jack Bruce and Pete Brown would get together after shows to work on new songs in readiness for the New York sessions. As soon as a new number was written, it was instantly road-tested in concert. That way the band would be ready to record the material they were already familiar with.

ATLANTIC STUDIOS 11 West 60th Street, New York Sessions for *Disraeli Gears*

11 MAY 1967–15 MAY 1967

SUNSHINE OF YOUR LOVE (Jack Bruce / Pete Brown / Eric Clapton) master / *Disraeli Gears* album UK mono Reaction 593003 / stereo Reaction 593003 / US mono ATCO 33-232 / stereo ATCO SD 33-232 released November 1967 / single A-side US ATCO 6544 released February 1968 / UK Polydor 56 286 released September 1968 / *Disraeli Gears* Deluxe Edition 2CD Polydor B0003331-2 released September 2004

When "Sunshine Of Your Love" was released as a single, it rapidly became the biggest-selling single in Atlantic's history.

WORLD OF PAIN (Gail Collins / Felix Pappalardi) master / *Disraeli Gears* album UK mono Reaction 593003 / stereo Reaction 593003 / US mono ATCO 33-232 / stereo ATCO SD 33-232 released November 1967 / *Disraeli Gears* Deluxe Edition 2CD Polydor B0003331-02 released September 2004

DANCE THE NIGHT AWAY (Jack Bruce / Pete Brown) master / *Disraeli Gears* album UK mono Reaction 593003 / stereo Reaction 593003 / US mono ATCO 33-232 / stereo ATCO SD 33-232 released November 1967 / *Disraeli Gears* Deluxe Edition 2CD Polydor B0003331-02 released September 2004

Cream's Disraeli Gears *album cover.*

> "'Tales of Brave Ulysses' from Disraeli Gears, Eric had the words written on a piece of paper, and what I would consider an excellent idea of the tune and the track roughed out, and everything got built from that point on. In fact, we didn't even have a wah-wah pedal in the studio when we started doing it. That afternoon, we went out and bought one, over at Manny's, and then decided well, let's try it there.
> —FELIX PAPPALARDI
> (*Crawdaddy* magazine, September 1968)

BLUE CONDITION (Ginger Baker) master / *Disraeli Gears* album UK mono Reaction 593003 / stereo Reaction 593003 / US mono ATCO 33-232 / stereo ATCO SD 33-232 released November 1967 / *Disraeli Gears* Deluxe Edition 2CD Polydor B0003331-02 released September 2004

BLUE CONDITION (Ginger Baker) (alternate version with Eric Clapton on lead vocals) master / *Disraeli Gears* Deluxe Edition 2CD Polydor B0003331-02 released September 2004

TALES OF BRAVE ULYSSES (Eric Clapton / Martin Sharp) master / single B-side UK Reaction 591015 released May 1967/ US ATCO 6488 released July 1967 / *Disraeli Gears* album UK mono Reaction 593003 / stereo Reaction 593003 / US mono ATCO 33-232 / stereo ATCO SD 33-232 released November 1967 / *Disraeli Gears* Deluxe Edition 2CD Polydor B0003331-2 released September 2004

> "When I went into the studio at ten in the morning and there were some roadies setting up double stacks of Marshalls. I was thinking 'what the hell am I walking into?' So I say okay, I had to put earphones on to protect my ears when I walked into the studio, they were loud and ferocious. I went in and moved a couple of mikes and talked to them and we did this and that and it was a long day, and they came back on Friday and we did some more songs and I said that we should do this one again and I think that we could do it better. Generally, we made acquaintances and became friendly and then on Saturday we changed some solos, and horsed around with that and I am trying to think what else we did. We overdubbed some vocals and changed some vocals.
>
> Then the next afternoon on Sunday, we came in to listen to what we had done and redo some stuff and then at about 5 p.m. a chauffeur came into the control room and said he was there to pick up three guys to take to the airport and they looked at each other and said oh, that's us. They just got up and said their goodbyes and went out to the airport. They left me with all the tape. The following week I mixed it down and sent a copy of the tape to England and like one week later the album was out on the street and was tearing everyone's head off. We did the whole album in about three and a half days. That was Disraeli Gears." —TOM DOWD
> (interviewed by Michael Buffalo Smith)

SWLABR (Jack Bruce / Pete Brown) master / *Disraeli Gears* album UK mono Reaction 593003 / stereo Reaction 593003 / US mono ATCO 33-232 / stereo ATCO SD 33-232 released November 1967 / single B-side of "Sunshine Of Your Love" US ATCO 6544 released February 1968 / UK Polydor 56 286 released September 1968 / *Disraeli Gears* Deluxe Edition 2CD Polydor B0003331-02 released September 2004

Advert for Cream's Disraeli Gears *album.*

WE'RE GOING WRONG (Jack Bruce) master / *Disraeli Gears* album UK mono Reaction 593003 / stereo Reaction 593003 / US mono ATCO 33-232 / stereo ATCO SD 33-232 released November 1967 / *Disraeli Gears* Deluxe Edition 2CD Polydor B0003331-02 released September 2004

OUTSIDE WOMAN BLUES (Arthur Reynolds, arranged by Eric Clapton) master / *Disraeli Gears* album UK mono Reaction 593003 / stereo Reaction 593003 / US mono ATCO 33-232 / stereo ATCO SD 33-232 released November 1967 / *Disraeli Gears* Deluxe Edition 2CD Polydor B0003331-02 released September 2004

TAKE IT BACK (Jack Bruce / Pete Brown) master / *Disraeli Gears* album UK mono Reaction 593003 / stereo Reaction 593003 / US mono ATCO 33-232 / stereo ATCO SD 33-232 released November 1967 / *Disraeli Gears* Deluxe Edition 2CD Polydor B0003331-02 released September 2004

MOTHER'S LAMENT (Traditional; arranged by Ginger Baker / Jack Bruce / Eric Clapton) master / *Disraeli Gears* album UK mono Reaction 593003 / stereo Reaction 593003 / US mono ATCO 33-232 / stereo ATCO SD 33-232 released November 1967 / *Disraeli Gears* Deluxe Edition 2CD Polydor B0003331-02 released September 2004

Producer: Felix Pappalardi
Engineer: Tom Dowd

IBC SOUND RECORDING STUDIOS Studio A, 35 Portland Place, London W1 Sessions for *Wheels Of Fire*

12 JULY 1967–14 JULY 1967

WHITE ROOM (Jack Bruce / Pete Brown) rehearsing and multiple takes made until a basic track is viewed as done. No vocals

SITTING ON TOP OF THE WORLD (Chester Burnett) several takes and basic track recorded

BORN UNDER A BAD SIGN (Booker T. Jones / William Bell) rehearsing

Producer: Felix Pappalardi
Engineer: Adrian Barber

A lot of time and work was spent on "White Room" with its intricate rhythm pattern and unique 5/4 time signature. It was a number that would develop significantly over the coming months. The lyrics had started out as an eight-page Pete Brown poem, which he eventually pared down to a single lyric sheet and blended with Jack's set of lyrics.

IBC SOUND RECORDING STUDIOS
Studio A, 35 Portland Place, London W1
Sessions for
Wheels Of Fire

9 AUGUST 1967–11 AUGUST 1967

WHITE ROOM (Jack Bruce / Pete Brown) overdubbing session. At this stage there is no wah-wah guitar and is effectively an alternate version to the finished one, which would have new overdubs recorded later at Atlantic Studios. Still instrumental at this stage
BORN UNDER A BAD SIGN (Booker T. Jones / William Bell) several takes and a basic track recorded
FALSTAFF (THE THIRST SLAKER) (Jack Bruce / Eric Clapton / Ginger Baker) two takes made after a few rehearsals. One version can be found on the *Those Were The Days* box set Polydor 539 000-2 released September 1997

Producer: Felix Pappalardi
Engineer: Adrian Barber

Cream record a one-minute radio spot for Falstaff beer, who are launching their "Thirst Slaker" campaign in America, which would also feature ads in Playboy magazine

ATLANTIC STUDIOS
11 West 60th Street, New York
Sessions for
Wheels Of Fire

12 SEPTEMBER 1967–17 SEPTEMBER 1967

SITTING ON TOP OF THE WORLD (Chester Burnett) master, *Wheels Of Fire* double album US ATCO SD 2-700 released July 1968 / UK Polydor mono 582 031/2, stereo 583 031/2 released August 1968 / UK *Wheels Of Fire In The Studio* Polydor / *Wheels Of Fire* Polydor CD

> **"**We were thinking of putting brass on 'Born Under A Bad Sign' but decided against it. Somebody at Atlantic took the Cream track when I wasn't there and overdubbed some King Curtis horns. I didn't like it, but I let Cream hear it and they didn't like it either. I'm glad it didn't work out, because there are no studio musicians at all on this album.**"** **—FELIX PAPPALARDI**

BORN UNDER A BAD SIGN (Booker T. Jones / William Bell) master, *Wheels Of Fire* double album US ATCO SD 2-700 released July 1968 / UK Polydor mono 582 031/2, stereo 583 031/2 released August 1968 / UK *Wheels Of Fire In The Studio* Polydor / *Wheels Of Fire* Polydor CD
WHITE ROOM (Jack Bruce / Pete Brown) re-recording work

Producer: Felix Pappalardi
Engineer: Tom Dowd

ATLANTIC STUDIOS
11 West 60th Street, New York
Sessions for
Wheels Of Fire

9 OCTOBER 1967–10 OCTOBER 1967

PRESSED RAT AND WARTHOG (Ginger Baker / Mike Taylor) initial session
ANYONE FOR TENNIS (Eric Clapton / Martin Sharp) initial session
POLITICIAN (Jack Bruce / Pete Brown) initial session

Producer: Felix Pappalardi
Engineer: Tom Dowd

ATLANTIC STUDIOS
11 West 60th Street, New York
Sessions for
Wheels Of Fire

12 DECEMBER 1967–15 DECEMBER 1967

PRESSED RAT AND WARTHOG (Ginger Baker / Mike Taylor) overdubs
ANYONE FOR TENNIS (Eric Clapton / Martin Sharp) overdubs and first master made
WHITE ROOM (Jack Bruce / Pete Brown) more work carried out with vocals being added, but still not completed

> **"**We liked the track 'White Room' but Jack didn't like the vocal and Eric didn't like his guitar playing. I did a rough mix and brought it over to England for them to hear.**"** **—FELIX PAPPALARDI**

Producer: Felix Pappalardi
Engineer: Tom Dowd

ATLANTIC STUDIOS
11 West 60th Street,
New York
Sessions for
Wheels Of Fire

13 FEBRUARY 1968–22 FEBRUARY 1968

PRESSED RAT AND WARTHOG (Ginger Baker / Mike Taylor) master, single B-side of "Anyone For Tennis" UK Polydor 56 258, US ATCO 6575 released May 1968 Wheels Of Fire double album US ATCO SD 2-700 released July 1968 / UK Polydor mono 582 031/2, stereo 583 031/2 released August 1968 / UK Wheels Of Fire In The Studio Polydor / Wheels Of Fire Polydor CD

> **"**On 'Pressed Rat And Warthog' Jack plays two basses. The second bass comes in at the end and it's a six string. Eric's on three times. I'm on twice with trumpet and tonette. When I played tonette, Jack played recorder.**"**   —FELIX PAPPALARDI

ANYONE FOR TENNIS (Eric Clapton / Martin Sharp) new overdubs and final master completed single A-side UK Polydor 56 258, US ATCO 6575 released May 1968 / The Savage Seven soundtrack album ATCO SD 33-245 released 1968

> **"**Cream told me that the only time they ever get together for rehearsal is when I'm around, which is another strange thing. Anyway, while I was in England we met at Jack's house every night at seven o'clock. One night I was playing bass, Jack played a baritone horn, Ginger was playing these giant maracas and Eric was playing acoustic guitar. Eric was showing us a new tune he'd just written called 'Anyone For Tennis.' What happened that night went into the 'Tennis' single and the *Savage Seven* album. It was a new thing for Cream and it just happened.**"**   —FELIX PAPPALARDI

WHITE ROOM (Jack Bruce / Pete Brown) new wah-wah overdubs

> **"**'Politician' has a rhythm guitar and two overdubbed floating guitars. They crisscross from right to left in stereo. Eric wanted that and it worked. He wanted it on 'Sitting On Top Of The World,' too, but it didn't work there, so I changed it. I found it was very annoying.**"**   —FELIX PAPPALARDI

POLITICIAN (Jack Bruce / Pete Brown) master completed Wheels Of Fire double album US ATCO SD 2-700 released July 1968 / UK Polydor mono 582 031/2, stereo 583 031/2 released August 1968 / UK Wheels Of Fire In The Studio single album Polydor 582 033 released December 1968 / Wheels Of Fire Polydor CD
PASSING THE TIME (Ginger Baker / Mike Taylor) initial session
AS YOU SAID (Jack Bruce / Pete Brown) basic track
DESERTED CITIES OF THE HEART (Jack Bruce / Pete Brown) basic track
THOSE WERE THE DAYS (Ginger Baker / Mike Taylor) basic track

Producer: Felix Pappalardi
Engineer: Tom Dowd

Cream's Wheels Of Fire *album cover.*

Back cover of Cream's Wheels Of Fire *double set.*

ATLANTIC STUDIOS
11 West 60th Street,
New York
Final sessions for
Wheels Of Fire

12 JUNE 1968–13 JUNE 1968

PASSING THE TIME (Ginger Baker / Mike Taylor) final overdubs and master completed. Wheels Of Fire album US ATCO / UK Polydor released
AS YOU SAID (Jack Bruce / Pete Brown) final overdubs and master completed, Wheels Of Fire double album US ATCO SD 2-700 released July 1968 / UK Polydor mono 582 031/2, stereo 583 031/2 released August 1968 / UK Wheels Of Fire In The Studio Polydor / Wheels Of Fire Polydor CD

"There are a lot of guys that work with Cream. Like Pete Brown collaborates on almost all of Jack Bruce's songs. Mike Taylor is an ex-British jazz pianist with a strong classical background. Cream had done a lot of work on songs among themselves, but we made some changes in the studio too. Like on 'Passing The Time,' nobody knew what instrumentation to use and it got bogged down. One night Ginger got me out of bed with a long distance phone call from England and played me the melody on an organ. That sound stayed in my head so when I finally saw him in the studio I called up a music shop and ordered a calliope. Jack, who is a fantastic keyboard player, did the song on calliope and I played organ pedals.

We got very excited over 'Passing The Time' and finally completed it. It was beautiful. We had the freedom to do what we wanted without any planning. With incredible Tom Dowd running the tape, we could completely forget about the engineering and just concentrate on the music. The album got bogged down in a lot of places because Cream was working very hard on tour. They were tired and they just wanted to get away."

—FELIX PAPPALARDI

"On 'As You Said,' Jack is recorded five times."

—FELIX PAPPALARDI

"The only one who's into composition per se is Jack, as what I would call a composer, someone who would score things as he hears them. Jack's deeply into that. I think the first example of it in some total form is found on Wheels Of Fire; he wrote this thing called 'As You Said.' To me it's totally original. It's scored for two acoustic guitars, two cellos, voice and just hi-hat. And it's Jack, except for the hi-hat, playing both acoustic guitars, both cellos, and the vocal. So I know he's into composition, 'cause I know what his background is, his background is very much like mine. I mean he's trained, in the elements and in the literature. In other words, he's not a rock 'n' roll musician; he's just a musician, generically. His tastes and his understanding are very catholic."

—FELIX PAPPALARDI
(*Crawdaddy* magazine, September 1968)

DESERTED CITIES OF THE HEART (Jack Bruce / Pete Brown) final overdubs and master completed, Wheels Of Fire double album US ATCO SD 2-700 released July 1968 / UK Polydor mono 582 031/2, stereo 583 031/2 released August 1968 / UK Wheels Of Fire In The Studio Polydor / Wheels Of Fire Polydor CD
WHITE ROOM (Jack Bruce / Pete Brown) final overdubs and master completed

"I'd say we worked for a good two weeks on the studio album. Sometimes we'd work till four in the morning if It was cooking. Maybe only one guy was cooking, so I'd send Jack and Eric home and just work with Ginger or percussion things. On 'Deserted Cities Of The Heart' nobody was in the studio except Jack, his wife Janet, Tommy Dowd, myself and my wife, Gail.

It was Jack's tune and he knew what he wanted. We just played cello and viola that night. We did lots of overdubbing which is one of the things that makes a great deal of difference between the art of recording and the art of a live performance. They are two separate things. This is why we wanted the two album set." —FELIX PAPPALARDI

"The last day of this album I just had to shove a lot. I don't think that was terribly pleasant for anyone, but it had to be done, that's all there was to it. We pushed, everybody pushed, and we got it done." —FELIX PAPPALARDI
(*Crawdaddy* magazine, September 1968)

"The last thing we did on the studio album was the vocal track for 'Those Were The Days.' Jack heard the tune six weeks later and he said, 'Wow, what a groovy tune. I don't think I know that one.' That's how tired they were, we used every single track we made. We didn't throw anything away. We approach tunes with a great deal of enthusiasm and thought so there isn't any waste. There's a lot of thought behind the tunes but very little chatter." —FELIX PAPPALARDI

THOSE WERE THE DAYS (Ginger Baker / Mike Taylor) final overdubs and master completed, *Wheels Of Fire* double album US ATCO SD 2-700 released July 1968 / UK Polydor mono 582 031/2, stereo 583 031/2 released August 1968 / UK *Wheels Of Fire In The Studio* Polydor / *Wheels Of Fire* Polydor CD

Producer: Felix Pappalardi
Engineer: Tom Dowd

The *Wheels Of Fire* album and CD releases have never sounded particularly good. Nobody doubts the quality of the playing, but the audio quality leaves a lot to be desired. Many people believe that the best version was mastered by Steve Hoffman on gold discs for DCC. Here are some fascinating memories of Steve's adventures with the mastering of Cream's *Wheels Of Fire* Gold DCC CD:

"Wheels Of Fire was the first DCC gold disc I worked on. I picked the title myself and there was a lot of pressure to get it to sound good. Also, it had to be a double disc and was going to cost $50.00 right out of the gate. Ouch.

I'll skip over the artwork adventures, how we found the original foil vendor and day-glow ink vendors so we could exactly duplicate the first Atco LP pressing. That took months. We were sent 'extras' to use on the disc like the edit outtake pieces of 'Passing The Time' and 'Anyone For Tennis.' When I first got the tapes, I was not thrilled. We got many reels including the master mixes. They sounded ok, but muddy and the safety reels and the overseas copies sounded shrill and thin. Someone tried to compensate for the muddiness by just jacking up the upper midrange and top end. Urrgh.

I listened to all copies of the original LP, the original ATCO, the recut ATCO, the Record Club versions, the Polydor UK versions, etc. Also the current PolyGram CD version. I sure didn't like the way ANY of them sounded. I guess I had forgotten how much I wasn't thrilled about Tom Dowd's mixes and how there seemed to be no bass but just mud down there. Some of the mixes were the dreaded CSG [Compatible Stereo Generator] and some were plain stereo. But, it was too late to turn back so I went into the studio (Location Recording Service in Burbank) and started listening to the tapes on the big ol' vintage studio monitors they had in Studio B. I guess I wanted to hear what Tom Dowd heard when he mixed everything and why he did what he did After a week of scratching my head, I realized that my best chance to get this to sound improved over other versions was to NOT try and fix the top end and NOT try to 'mask' everything (like console noise, pops and pot crackle) and just concentrate on the midrange and the bass. I needed a LOT of extra EQ to make my ideas about how to fix the bass work, so we patched in three Sontec Parametrics in a row and I set to work. I tried a lot of stuff and finally got the low end the way I liked it; you could hear Ginger's bass drum now and less mud in Jack's six string bass. I lived with this a month and then tried to do something (anything) to fix the 'practice pad' of Ginger Baker's snare drum sound. I wasted a week on this before I decided to SCREW IT and just focus in on the vocal sound. If I could get that to sound 'lifelike,' I could live with the crappy snare sound. So, I discovered some of my (soon to be used all of the time) tricks to enhance the vocals so they would at least sound like real people. Tubes came in to play here for the first time on one of my projects. Kevin Gray turned me on to the use of tubes and I always try and thank him for that, even though it raises the temperature by at least 10 degrees in the room.

When I got everything fixed to my satisfaction, I scheduled a real MASTERING date and we lined up all of the gear and I gave it a shot in real time using the actual master tapes instead of the tape copy I made to save wear and tear. Too many mastering moves for one pair of hands so I drafted Kevin Gray and even my ex-girlfriend Robin to 'do stuff' during the songs. Six hands working the mastering console was pretty trippy. Too bad I didn't take any photos. At any rate, I was finally happy with everything and even though it's not a great recording to begin with, I think the DCC version sounds the best that it can. I love the album so I forgive the sonic weaknesses.

When the DCC version was issued, both Ginger Baker and Jack Bruce loved it (phew!). I was worried that I would get a lot of letters complaining about the noisy Atlantic mixing console and hissy mic pre's because I left all of the non-musical sounds of the recordings intact, but I was mistaken. No one complained."

—STEVE HOFFMAN

"I really like to put down a basic track that knocks everybody out, and go from there. And go after the record from that point. Especially when it's a tune that one guy in the band wrote and the rest of the cats in the room have never heard because he's never played it for them. So you look to that cat for the feeling of the track. Like one on the last album, we did a basic track that was incredible, it ['Those Were The Days'] was really beautiful. The next day, when we played it back, everybody thought it was an unbelievable track, but Ginger said, 'Wait a-minute, man, it's too fast for the tune.' So in that case you have to go back into the studio and do it over again."

—FELIX PAPPALARDI
(*Crawdaddy* magazine, September 1968)

WALLY HEIDER STUDIO 3
Los Angeles, California
15 OCTOBER 1968–23 OCTOBER 1968

Tentative plans to record a final album were made back in October in Los Angeles. Several days were spent at Wally Heider recording demos with Bill Halverson engineering. SIR Entertainment Services brought along a prototype Leslie foot pedal for Eric to try out at the studio. This eventually led to Eric writing "Badge." Mal Evans brought George Harrison down to the studio, and he played rhythm guitar against Eric's flanged bridge figure, which was fed through the Leslie. No vocals were attempted at this stage, and as relations were so frosty between members of Cream it was decided to abandon the session and revisit the tracks in London at a later date.

According to the logs at Atlantic Records, the three basic tracks were at this stage simply called "Eric's Number," "Jack's Number," and "Ginger's Number."

IBC SOUND RECORDING STUDIOS
Studio A, 35 Portland Place, London W1
Sessions for *Goodbye Cream*

18 NOVEMBER 1968–21 NOVEMBER 1968

BADGE (Eric Clapton / George Harrison) basic track
WHAT A BRINGDOWN (Ginger Baker) basic track
DOING THAT SCRAPYARD THING (Jack Bruce / Pete Brown) basic track<

IBC SOUND RECORDING STUDIOS
Studio B, 35 Portland Place, London W1
Sessions for *Goodbye Cream*

2 DECEMBER 1968–6 DECEMBER 1968

"I only met this guitar great once and only for one-minute. The Cream were at IBC in November 1968 to record 'Badge' (with George Harrison on rhythm guitar), 'What A Bringdown,' 'Doing That Scrapyard Thing' for the 'Goodbye' album. He was walking around near the front of the building with a guitar in one hand and a small amplifier in the other. 'Do you know where Studio A is?' he asked. 'Up the stairs' I replied, and off he went without even offering me a pint for my trouble!! Cream also recorded the basic tracks for 'White Room,' 'Born Under A Bad Sign' and 'Sitting On Top Of The World' for the Wheels Of Fire album at IBC in 1967, but it was that brief meeting with another of my heroes that sticks in the mind as one of my memories. I like to think I helped on that album by sending him in the right direction!

Damon Lyon Shaw was the engineer on the 'Goodbye' sessions, and he was becoming one of the most sought after engineers around." —**BRIAN CARROLL** (IBC engineer)

BADGE (Eric Clapton) (overdubs and master completed) *Goodbye Cream* album US ATCO SD 7001, UK Polydor 583053 released March 1969 / *Goodbye Cream* CD Polydor 531815 released April 1998

Eric Clapton: guitar, vocals
Jack Bruce: bass
Ginger Baker: drums
George Harrison: rhythm guitar
Felix Pappalardi: piano, mellotron

DOING THAT SCRAPYARD THING (Jack Bruce / Pete Brown) (overdubs and master completed) *Goodbye Cream* album US ATCO SD 7001, UK Polydor 583053 released March 1969 / *Goodbye Cream* CD Polydor 531815 released April 1998

Eric Clapton: guitar
Jack Bruce: bass, piano, vocals
Ginger Baker: drums
Felix Pappalardi: mellotron

WHAT A BRINGDOWN (Ginger Baker) (overdubs and master completed) *Goodbye Cream* album US ATCO SD 7001, UK Polydor 583053 released March 1969 / *Goodbye Cream* CD Polydor 531815 released April 1998

Eric Clapton: guitar
Jack Bruce: organ, piano, vocals
Ginger Baker: drums, percussion, vocals
Felix Pappalardi: bass

Producer: Felix Pappalardi
Engineer: Damon Lyon Shaw

"On 'Badge,' Eric doesn't play guitar up until the bridge. He sat through it with his guitar in the Leslie (rotating speaker), and Felix Pappalardi was the piano player. So there was Felix, Jack Bruce, Ginger Baker and me. I played the rhythm chops right up to the bridge, at which point Eric came in on the guitar with the Leslie. And he overdubbed the solo later. I wrote most of the words, Eric had the bridge and he had the first couple of chord changes. I was writing the words down, and when we came to the middle bit I wrote 'Bridge.' And from where he was sitting, opposite me, he looked and said, 'What's that—Badge?' So he called it 'Badge' because it made him laugh." —**GEORGE HARRISON**

The photo shoot for the *Goodbye* Cream cover was as dramatic as the recording sessions, as photographer Roger Phillips recalls.

"Getting a shot like that off the ground in the '60s was a nightmare. They had all started to fall out by then and did not want to appear together. So for the first effort they failed to arrive. Finally at the third booking they turned up. Ginger had a sword stick for the photo shoot and proceeded to throw it at my wooden walls, where it pierced and stayed juddering. The question came up: 'Where is the H'? But I was not into it so I couldn't help.

Alan Aldridge the designer saw Lionel Blair in the street (Shaftesbury Avenue) and ran out and got him up to the studio to give them lessons in synchronized dancing; they jeered at Lionel's effeminate mannerisms. Jack Bruce spent most of the afternoon playing my jazz discs: Fats Waller, Armstrong, Billy and Ellington.

Word got out that they were in the studio, so the doorbell kept going and friends just happened to drop in, by the time I took the shots there was a big crowd.**"**

—ROGER PHILLIPS (photographer)

Cream's Goodbye *album cover.*

9

THE ROLLING STONES' *ROCK AND ROLL CIRCUS* (1968) AND *SUPERSHOW* (1969)

THE ROLLING STONES' *ROCK AND ROLL CIRCUS*

10 DECEMBER 1968– 11 DECEMBER 1968

10 December 1968–11 December 1968 Intertel Television Studios, Wycombe Road, Stonebridge Park, Wembley, London NW10 (recording for the Rolling Stones' *Rock And Roll Circus*, featuring the Rolling Stones as the headliners, with Jethro Tull, the Who, Taj Mahal, Marianne Faithfull, Winston Legthigh (John Lennon) and the Dirty Mac, Yoko Ono, Ivry Gitlis, Nicky Hopkins, Rocky Dijon, and the Robert Fosset Circus. Filmed December 11, 1968.

This was to be an entertainment extravaganza directed under the watchful eye of Ready Steady Go's Michael Lindsay-Hogg and was intended to be shown to worldwide television audiences. The sound was handled by regular Stones producer Jimmy Miller.

Although preparations had been taking place throughout the early part of December, the main activity centered on two days at Intertel Studios. The first day, 10 December, was basically for rehearsals and camera run-throughs. The second day, 11 December, was for the actual filming. Intertel television studios had been transformed into a real live circus with clowns, trapeze artists, horseback riders, fire eaters, and Mick Jagger himself as ringmaster. It was actually a pretty innovative idea, which was also very much of its time.

On the day of filming, everything should have gone pretty smoothly and run more or less to a schedule. However, the cameras used for the filming were not the usual Intertel ones. Instead they were an unusual hybrid of 16mm film camera and black and white video camera that were operated in a TV style, using electronic viewfinders and mounted on Vinten peds and a Mole crane. They were brought in from an outside company specifically for this show. Unfortunately, they were highly prone to breaking down, which they did many times during the filming, causing the show to overrun until 5:30 a.m. of 12 December. The constant delays and frustrations meant that everybody was too tired to perform well. Added to that, the Rolling Stones had problems keeping Brian Jones straight enough to perform in tune. Not surprisingly, they felt that their performance was not as good as it should have been.

As a result, nobody bothered to process the film rushes, and the Rolling Stones looked into the possibility of doing a remake of it at the Colosseum in Rome. In the end it proved impossible to get permission to film there. That, coupled with the fact that Brian Jones was fired and died a few months later, meant that the original film rushes were left in their cans at the Rolling Stones' office. When they moved offices a few years later, the film cans were moved to a barn owned by their road manager and forgotten about. After his death some years later, his wife rediscovered them. They were finally edited and turned into the extraordinary film it was always going to be and today provides a unique snapshot of the cream of the rock world in 1968.

Eric's participation was as part of a one-off group with John Lennon on guitar and vocals, Mitch Mitchell on drums, Keith Richards on bass. Winston

Legthigh and the Dirty Mac, as they were called, played "Yer Blues" from The Beatles' then recently released *White Album*, followed by "Whole Lotta Yoko," which featured some wailing from Yoko and tasteful violin from Ivry Gitlis. Both of these can be found on the soundtrack CD and DVD via ABCKO.

During the course of the two days, Eric found time to have a jam with Taj Mahal and his guitarist Jesse Ed Davis. Eric struck up a friendship with Jesse and would play on his first solo album, which would be recorded at Olympic Studios in 1970. The Dirty Mac rehearsals on 10 December saw the group joined by Mick Jagger for some rock 'n' roll covers, but nothing has ever surfaced. The Dirty Mac performed several takes of "Yer Blues," as well as a few instrumental jams, which are still in the vaults.

YER BLUES (John Lennon / Paul McCartney) *Rolling Stones Rock And Roll Circus* CD ABKO 1268-2 released 1996 / *Rolling Stones Rock And Roll Circus* DVD ABKO 0602 4982 48997 released 2004

John Lennon: vocals, guitar
Eric Clapton: guitar
Keith Richards: bass
Mitch Mitchell: drums

WHOLE LOTTA YOKO (Yoko Ono) *Rolling Stones Rock And Roll Circus* CD ABKO 1268-2 released 1996 / *Rolling Stones Rock And Roll Circus* DVD ABKO 0602 4982 48997 released 2004

Yoko Ono: vocals
John Lennon: vocals, guitar
Eric Clapton: guitar
Keith Richards: bass
Mitch Mitchell: drums
Ivry Gitlis: violin

Producer: Jimmy Miller
Engineer: Glyn Johns

SUPERSHOW

MARCH 1969

19 March 1969, Staines Linoleum Factory, Norris Road, Staines, Middlesex (the Linoleum Factory ceased manufacturing in Staines in early 1969 and the premises were converted into warehouses. Colourtel transformed one of the spaces into a television studio, and *Supershow* was filmed there over two days. The whole show was filmed and audio was recorded on the Pye Mobile Studio on eight-track tape machines. As well as producing a film, the plan was to release a double album of the event subject to the various clearances.

The numbers that made the film with Eric are:

SLATE 27

Eric Clapton: guitar
Jack Bruce: bass
Upright bass: Vernon Martin
Organ: Ron Burton
Sax: Roland Kirke
Sax: Dick Heckstall-Smith
Drums: Jon Hiseman

EVERYTHING'S GONNA BE ALRIGHT

Eric Clapton: guitar
Buddy Guy: guitar, vocals
Bass: Stephen Stills
Drums: Buddy Miles
Drums: Dallas Taylor
Harp: Duster Bennett
Sax: Chris Mercer
Organ: Jack Bruce

CLOSING JAM

Eric Clapton: guitar
Buddy Guy: guitar

Director: John Crome
Producer: Tom Parkinson
Eight-track recording engineer: Brian Stott

The idea behind this project was to assemble the best musicians from the world of pop, rock, jazz, and blues and let them jam together over two days in a large studio located near the banks of the River Thames in Staines, Surrey. The main room had a small stage surrounded by tables to give the impression this was being filmed in a small club. The first day of filming and recording took place on Tuesday, 18 March 1969, and featured Steve Stills, Buddy Miles, Dallas Taylor, Jack Bruce, Buddy Guy, Chris Mercer, Dick Heckstall-Smith, and Led Zeppelin. Led Zeppelin did not partake in any jamming other than their own in an intensely powerful version of "Dazed And Confused" from their debut album. Jimi Hendrix, who was recording in New York, was also due to come but missed his flight.

Wednesday-morning sessions featured the MJQ (Modern Jazz Quartet), Jon Hiseman's Colosseum, Buddy Guy, and the Roland Kirk Quartet. There would be a rehearsal, and then the cameras would roll for a "take." By late afternoon on that second day, things were getting interesting. At 5:15 p.m. Roland Kirk, Buddy Guy, Jack Bruce, and Jimmy Hopps took to the stage for a couple of inspiring blues jams, including a version of "Stormy Monday." On one of these, Roland Kirk used a stylophone, an instrument that was played using an electric pencil, which was a pretty novel thing back in 1969. Buddy Guy then led the small eclectic ensemble with a rousing version of "Kansas City." In the bar afterward, Buddy commented to the *Melody Maker*, "It was great playing with Roland. Any bunch of musicians can get together—if it's on a blues. There are bound to be a few mistakes of course, but you shouldn't notice them too much—unless you know a lot about music!"

By 7:15 p.m. Steve Stills and Buddy Miles are playing some blues, but not very well according to an onlooker. That all changed by 7:30 p.m., when they drove the crowd wild with a fast-paced version of Robert Johnson's "Crossroads."

At 8:15 p.m. Chris Mercer and Glenn Ross Campbell, both from the newly formed Juicy Lucy, together with Buddy Miles and Buddy Guy, have a blow. The crowd are amazed at the virtuosity of Glen Ross Campbell on steel guitar. The musicians are joined at 8:30 p.m. by Steve Ward on harp and vocals. They end their set with "Texas Blues."

A rather nervous-looking Eric Clapton, accompanied by a friend, arrives at 8:50 p.m. At 9:10 p.m., Roland Kirk, Jack Bruce, Ron Burton, Vernon Martin, Dick Heckstall-Smith, Jon Hiseman, and Eric Clapton take to the stage. Various improvisational jams keep everyone on their toes. Some of the musicians change, and Steve Stills, Buddy Miles, Dallas Taylor, Chris Mercer, and Duster Bennett jam with Eric and Buddy Guy, with jams lasting way past midnight.

"At the time we were playing together we were just riffing, and so therefore most of it was on the same level, and as far as I'm concerned, if a jazz man can't play a twelve bar blues, then he really isn't qualified to play jazz either, and Roland Kirk can play funk better than anybody, and he can play Tamla-Motown better than even Tamla-Motown people. He's just a very versatile musician, more so than a jazz man. I was on the loose at the time, and I was just keen to go and play anybody.

He threw me off for a few moments with the tempo. He counted it in so fast, I'd never played a number as fast as that. It was the fastest I'd ever played, so it took me a few-minutes to get used to it and catch up to him." —ERIC CLAPTON
(*NME*)

"As far as I know all the unused footage was dumped way back in 1969 or thereabouts. The company that made the film Colourtel went into liquidation. I personally gave the audio masters to Shel Talmy in 1970 to see what he could do with them. I have contacted Shel via his ex-wife Jenny, who lives in the US He can't remember anything about them.

There was also a mono mix made at EMI, I think, and a rough audio/visual version put together as we shot by the PA, which might still exist. I think the film was processed at Humphries labs, which no longer exists, but all their material must have been moved to somewhere. Nick Hague, the line producer, and I bought the material from the liquidator and subsequently licensed to Virgin and then Eagle Rock.

There was no significance in the 'lino factory'; it was just a studio which had in the past been a lino factory. I don't think we were the only people to use it. The *Rolling Stones R&R Circus*, the Colourtel film shot just before *Supershow*, was shot at Wembley. Vic Gardner, managing director of Colourtel (he went on to be MD of LWT), had been a senior executive at Rediffusion TV, so he knew the independent TV scene very well. I remember that the deal at West London Studios was the best available.

Both the Stones film and Supershow were shot on 16mm film using a unique French system which we imported for the purpose. The cameras were mounted on typical peds. (Vintens) and transmitted images to a scanner as in OB shoots. The cameras simultaneously photographed on film. There were 3–4 cameras shooting film which were turned on and off from the scanner. Some were left to run. I communicated with the cameras via headsets from the scanner. At the same time the PA made an edited version. Ted Hooker was the film editor. Brian Stott recorded on 8-track using the mobile unit from Pye Studios. He also made a mono back-up.

As for Eric, I hardly knew him. I first met him when he did the titles for 'A Whole Scene Going.'

On *Supershow* he met Buddy Guy for the first time. Buddy came without an acoustic guitar so Eric lent him his for 'Stormy Monday.' I had wanted Otis Rush to be the Chicago Blues element of the show, but he was not free, so his manager suggested Buddy and gave me his phone number. I called him only to find that he was working at a gas station filling cars so he jumped at the opportunity of coming to London." —JOHN CROME
(director of *Supershow*)

"There were a few songs that were not used, and I know Eric and Buddy Guy jammed on a couple numbers that didn't make the final cut." —TOM PARKINSON (producer)

"As I remember it was in Staines at a film studio, though I don't remember what it was called. I remember that Chris Welch and I went a couple of days later to interview Clapton and he said it was Steve Stills who persuaded him to come along to the session as Eric thought it was a joke phone call he got from the producers, who and whomever they were. It was strange to see Eric and the others trying to 'jam' along with Roland Kirk!

I have to confess that most of the audience, including me were rather stoned and drinking copious amounts of Southern Comfort which was in plentiful supply."

—**BARRIE WENTZELL** (*Melody Maker* photographer)

"All I can remember is that I am pretty sure it was in a warehouse space and as I recall it was all put together very quickly. I remember talking to a slide guitar player from the south saying that two days ago he had been washing dishes in a diner. Funny how some things stay with you. Alas I am afraid I can't recall anything else."

—**MIKE MOLLOY** (cinematographer)

BLIND FAITH

BLIND FAITH

After Cream's two farewell shows at London's Royal Albert Hall in November, Eric decided to retreat to his rural home deep in the Surrey countryside to consider his future, and hopefully rest. To Eric, Cream had been a wonderful as well as a painful experience. He had a close bond with Jack and Ginger, a kinship that he has never found since, but it did not help that over the course of their two years together he was also badly hurt emotionally. So much so that he has never allowed himself to be as close to any band member since.

He had bought Hurtwood Edge, a rambling Italian-style mansion with spectacular views over the countryside, with royalties earned during his Cream days. Lengthy touring and recording schedules meant he had been unable to do much with it. This was now an ideal time to settle in and make a home, something he hadn't had before and craved. This precious time gave him scope to consider his next move with relative leisure. He also had a supportive manager in Robert Stigwood, who had told Eric that whatever he decided to do, he would be there to help and support him. The offer may not have been that altruistic, though, as Eric was a very bankable commodity.

Eric's newfound freedom meant he was very much in demand, both on the social and music circuits. The world was at his feet and was awaiting his next move with anticipation. Whether Eric saw this or not, or even cared, is debatable.

The thought of going solo was really not an issue at this stage as he felt he did not want or need the responsibility. The formation of a new group of like-minded musicians had much more appeal. Traffic had recently split and Eric contacted Stevie Winwood with a view to collaborating on something. They got together just after Christmas 1968 for some informal jams, initially at Eric's country pad before moving to Stevie's place, a cottage in Aston Tirrold, Berkshire, to see what musical chemistry would develop. Certainly, in Eric's mind at least, he had already thought about the possibility of forming a new band as far back as Cream's farewell tour of the US In fact, during that 1968 tour, he had talked to Duck Dunn and Al Jackson from Booker T & the MG's, one of the finest rhythm sections in the business, about getting something together in the future. Nothing came of it due to other commitments, although Duck did get to play with Eric in the '80s. But that is another story for later.

Most of their jams were recorded by Stevie, who had all the necessary tape decks at his cottage and all the instruments permanently set up. Those initial jams were more Traffic than Cream in content and showed potential for the collaboration to develop further. Eric was on guitar, while Stevie played keyboards and drums with some guitar. Interestingly, in early January 1969, among other ideas, Eric thought about the possibility of getting Cream back together later on that year with the addition of Stevie and possibly a brass section. Obviously this idea never materialized, but it shows how uncertain he was of which direction to head in. Little did he know that a few weeks later, an old friend from Cream would reappear, far sooner than he had anticipated. In mid-January, Eric was not sure how the collaboration with Winwood would develop, as he told NME's Nick Logan: "I don't know whether I'll be doing an album of mine, or an album of mine and Stevie, or just Stevie's album. It will just have to sort

BLIND FAITH

itself out because I can't be bothered making those kind of decisions beforehand."

Ginger Baker, having heard of the jams happening at Stevie's place, turned up at one of their informal sessions in early February and sat in. Stevie was immediately taken by his enthusiasm and suggested to Eric that they form a band with him. Eric, naturally, had some reservations about this, based very simply on the fact that he had gotten away from Cream and the painful personality clashes and was concerned about going back in time so soon. However, he respected Ginger's abilities as a drummer and was eventually swayed by Stevie's enthusiasm to take him onboard. When news reached Jack Bruce, he was both angry and greatly saddened that he had not even been approached for this new band. He still feels aggrieved to this day. He didn't waste time moping around and instead devoted his time to recording his first solo album, *Songs For A Tailor*. It was an excellent album, but, adding insult to injury, RSO did not spend enough time or money on promoting it because they were too busy with Blind Faith.

Things then went into freefall, with leaks to the press about a new "supergroup," rushed plans for an album release, scheduling of a lucrative US tour, and arrangement of a huge PR world-premiere free gig in Hyde Park. Talk about pressure! The band were still getting to know each other musically and really had no time to be creative. Another problem was a managerial one. Stevie was represented by Chris Blackwell, Eric and Ginger by Robert Stigwood. There were a lot of behind-the-scenes arguments about how the money should be divided up. Having two managers pulling in different directions was not a good idea, but one they had to live with.

Suddenly, the carefree informal jamming that had now moved back to Eric's house was transformed into a strict military-style campaign. It was now time to take those informal jams to a more structured setting. This happened at Morgan Studios, where the group with no name, were signed in as Baker, Clapton, and Winwood. The jams rapidly developed into proper recording sessions and moved to Olympic Studios in Barnes. Although Stevie could play bass, it was decided halfway through recording their debut album to get a bass player. Eric had announced he was looking for a bass player in a *Melody Maker* interview and he

was inundated with calls from potential candidates. However, before lengthy auditions could take place, Eric contacted Rick Grech from Family, who was invited down for a jam. He fitted the bill and left Family two days before he was due to fly out with them to the US for a tour. He was very talented and could also play violin, which was another plus and could add another dimension to the band's sound. He added overdubs to material already recorded and participated in the recording of the remainder of the album. They still had not come up with a name for themselves yet. Not surprising, really, it was the last thing on their minds. In fact, the resultant mass hysteria from fans and the press alike made the decision process simple and the name Blind Faith an obvious selection.

Despite many hours of material being recorded, it needed a producer's touch. Jimmy Miller was called in by Robert Stigwood to salvage what he could and turn it into an album that could be released. In fact, he was hired to try and make two albums, but that proved to be an impossibility due to lack of decent material. As the *Blind Faith* Deluxe Edition double CD demonstrates, the original album along with the few genuinely exciting outtakes found on disc one are the only really enjoyable songs. Obviously, the jams found on disc two and some bootlegs are fascinating for fans, but hardly essential listening to the public at large.

Understandably, by the time the band hit the stage in Hyde Park, they were incredibly nervous and with good reason. They just weren't ready for such a huge gig. They had not rehearsed enough and were short of material to play. However, listening to tapes of the show and viewing the film footage with the benefit of time to reflect on, it was a good, if not spectacular, show. Filmed by Mike "Supersonic" Mansfield, the footage is sprinkled with his trademark effects, which now look disastrously dated. Pye Studios were just over the road at Marble Arch, and they hired out an eight-track recorder, which was loaded on to the back of a truck and driven to the small backstage area. Eric had two tracks (vocal, guitar), Rick had one track, Ginger's drums had three tracks, Stevie had two tracks. A two-track mono mix was made from the eight-track masters, which would be used to sync in with the footage. Unfortunately, the eight-track masters were lost back in 1969 and have yet to surface. They were probably left at the studio that handled the mixdown for the footage. The film also has a story attached to it. The cans ended up in a storage facility and had long been forgotten about by the early '80s. After the facility went bankrupt in 1983, it was bought for a nominal fee by an archive company. They now owned a large stock of footage by various artists but did not own the copyright. The footage was located again in 2004 and negotiations started between RSO and Maverick, and a DVD of the show was finally released in 2006.

Blind Faith followed their Hyde Park show with a brief tour of Scandinavia. The pressure was off, and the band relaxed into some fine playing and jamming. The venues were relatively small in size, which meant the sound quality was good and they could see the audiences they were playing to. Listening to the recordings from the Gothenburg show, you can hear the progress made in a relatively short space of time. Clearly this was a band enjoying itself.

Within three weeks of the Scandinavian tour ending, Blind Faith flew over to America to start their first tour there and, not surprisingly, they were greeted by a blaze of publicity. Robert Stigwood had negotiated for them a minimum of $25,000 a concert, against a percentage (60–70 percent) of the gross. Blind Faith's opening US concert in Newport was canceled as a result of riots that had taken place in the city a few days before. Authorities fearing major crowd problems refused to grant permits for the concert. The band arrived in New York on 7 July and stayed at the Drake Hotel, where they gave an interview with Ritchie York for *Rolling Stone* magazine. The band were very upbeat. A clearly thrilled Stevie Winwood stated, "Blind Faith is undoubtedly the most exciting thing in my career. It's all a bit fantastic really." Eric Clapton was equally optimistic, "I'm much more excited about the future of Blind Faith than I was with Cream at the beginning. But we went through the Cream thing, and we learnt the lesson. This time we won't make the same mistakes again. Now we are doing it all from scratch. We have a fresh approach, and we're going to keep ahead of it all, whereas Cream got into the same things over and over and over again. It all became a bit of a drag. With Blind Faith there's going to be a lot of changes going down all the time. I don't think we'll get stale." Ginger was in a bad mood, a bad mood that would last throughout the tour, and had nothing to say to

Rolling Stone. Poor Rick Grech was last in the pecking order but was quite philosophical about it, "When people come to talk to us, they go to Eric, Stevie and Ginger. I'm always the last one. But I accept that and I'm working on it. Musically, Eric, Stevie and Ginger were the only guys I ever wanted to work with. I've always been dissatisfied musically." He goes on to say, somewhat prophetically, "We realize that we're in this as long as we dig it. When that stops, so does Blind Faith. There will be no reprisals, no hangups, nothing like that."

Blind Faith's opening gig was now at New York's prestigious Madison Square Garden, but it was a tense affair. Rick Grech told Chris Welch from the *Melody Maker*, "We went to America to open at the Newport Festival, and that was cancelled and we found ourselves in Madison Square Garden being rushed by the audience on a revolving stage. Police surrounded us and one guy jumped up to grab some of Ginger's sticks and got hit on the head. Ginger told the cop to leave the guy alone and the cop hit him. We couldn't get off the stage because we couldn't get the people to leave. We had been off once and had to come back for an encore." It was very much a sign of the times, as the youth of the day rebelled against authority figures all over the United States. That said, some of the shows were memorable, particularly the LA Forum gig where Delaney and Bonnie joined them for a final encore of "Sunshine Of Your Love." After the show, a jubilant Rick Grech stated, "We'll be together as long as things are good…and tonight they're way up there." The *Los Angeles Times* concluded that "musically the Faith was extraordinary."

The support bands on their US tour featured two of the best UK blues-rock groups, Free with Paul Kossoff, and Taste with Rory Gallagher, two guitarists Eric admired. But the band that really caught Eric's eye and ears were Delaney & Bonnie and Friends. Their manager, Alan Pariser, had called Eric and asked if they could be on the Blind Faith tour. Eric was already familiar with their sound, as George Harrison had played him their first two albums back home in England. As much as Eric liked the albums, he had forgotten about Delaney & Bonnie until he got the call.

When he met them for the first time, in New York, he instantly took a liking to them. What impressed him the most was the amount of fun they seemed to have and the sheer exhilaration they displayed on the stage. It was the complete opposite of Blind Faith. It came as no surprise that he started to hang out with them more and more as the tour progressed. They were easy to get on with, and there were no pressures. He even forwent the limo rides to join them in their tour bus from gig to gig and just jammed with them on acoustic guitars. This was the fun part of the tour for Eric. Slowly but surely he was being lured away, and he asked Delaney if he could play with them after the tour ended.

Ben Palmer, Blind Faith's road manager, recalled, "In a way, Blind Faith was doomed from the start, because it didn't offer Eric what Delaney and Bonnie were to offer, which was mates. Eric can take only so much dry professionalism and Blind Faith was a very dry and professional band. It seemed to me to lack a spiritual core."

As far as Eric was concerned, the tour may have been a financial success, but it was at the expense of the music. They had no choice but to give in to the audiences' insatiable appetite to hear Cream and Traffic songs. The bottom line was that Blind Faith had no identity of its own.

After the Blind Faith tour ended in Hawaii, Eric flew to LA and stayed with Delaney and Bonnie at their Sherman Oaks home for a week or so before heading home. Eric liked the area, which had a little community of great musicians. Delaney introduced Eric to Leon Russell at a session for Joe Cocker. Joe was recording a version of Leon's "Delta Lady" at Leon's North Hollywood studio that later went on to be a popular hit single. Delaney suggested that Eric should record a solo album using the whole of Delaney & Bonnie and Friends as his backup band. Eric had misgivings about his own singing voice, but Delaney encouraged him to use his "God-given" gift. John Mayall had urged him to sing in the Bluesbreakers, as had Stevie Winwood in Blind Faith, but it took Delaney's forceful stance, along with tons of peppermint Schnapps, to get Eric to realize he did have a natural ability to sing. Before leaving Eric also played on a few numbers with Delaney & Bonnie at Elektra Sound Studios in Los Angeles, including "Coming Home," a joint composition between Delaney and Eric.

BLIND FAITH HYDE PARK DEBUT 1969

7 June 1969, The Cockpit, Hyde Park, London

SETLIST: Well All Right / Sea Of Joy / Sleeping In The Ground / Under My Thumb / Can't Find My Way Home / Do What You Like / In The Presence Of The Lord / Means To An End / Had To Cry Today

The whole concert is filmed by Mike Mansfield on behalf of Associated London Scripts, which was associated with the Robert Stigwood Organisation.

Eric Clapton playing a Fender Telecaster with a Stratocaster neck, with Blind Faith at their debut gig in London's Hyde Park on 7 June 1969.

Sam Myers "Sleeping In The Ground" and Mick Jagger, Keith Richards "Under My Thumb" from the concert were released on Steve Winwood's *Finer Things* box set, which was released in 1995. The majority of the concert was also released on DVD via Sanctuary in 2008. The sound is sourced from a two-track mono mixdown from the original eight-track reels, which have sadly gone missing. Until those are found, there is no way to remix the show.

Eric Clapton played a Fender Telecaster body with a Fender Stratocaster neck through a couple of Marshall 100-watt stacks. Later on the Scandinavian and US tours he also used a Gibson 335, a Gibson Les Paul, and a Gibson Firebird.

Stevie Winwood played a Gibson Firebird, a Wurlitzer electric piano through a

Marshall 100-watt amplifier, a Hammond C3 organ with two added Leslie tone cabinets.

Ginger Baker played his usual double Ludwig drum kit.

Rick Grech played a Fender Precision bass though a 100-watt Marshall amplifier.

> "The first thing I did was to pick up the papers and found that people didn't dig us. My instant reaction was, 'Well I'm not playing here any more.'"
> —ERIC CLAPTON

A few-minutes from the Blind Faith Hyde Park concert are first shown on an episode of BBC television's *The Wednesday Play* called "The Season Of The Witch" starring Julie Driscoll, who had recently left Brian Auger and the Trinity and was now doing some acting work. It was transmitted on 7 January 1970. The play tells the story of a girl trying to escape the humdrum automated world of the typing pool. The play follows her on her journey to Brighton from London and on to Cornwall and eventually Hyde Park, where Blind Faith are playing.

> "I felt very insecure sometimes that I am not doing the right thing. But it is my own hang up and the sooner I get over that the better. After all it is easier to be led than lead."
> —ERIC CLAPTON

Another Hyde Park clip was shown in December 1970 on BBC television as a studio-overdubbed version of "Well All Right." It was included in a bizarre television special by the Bee Gees called *Cucumber Castle*. Also produced by Mike Mansfield, the variety show was originally going to include two numbers by Blind Faith that were to be filmed at their last show in Honolulu. Sadly, this never happened due to budget constraints and a clip from Hyde Park had to suffice. Most of the criticism was from people who felt that Stevie Winwood dominated the sound. That might have been true, but that was down to Eric's decision to take a back seat, much against Winwood's wishes and frustrations.

BLIND FAITH SCANDINAVIAN TOUR 1969

12 June 1969, Kultuuritalo, Helsinki, Finland (2 shows)

Eric Clapton playing Fender Telecaster with a Stratocaster neck, with Blind Faith at the Kulttuuritalo, Helsinki, Finland, on 12 June 1969.

Eric Clapton playing a Fender Telecaster with a Stratocaster neck, with Blind Faith at the Kulttuuritalo, Helsinki, Finland, on 12 June 1969.

Ginger Baker with Eric Clapton playing Fender Telecaster with a Stratocaster neck with Blind Faith at the Kulttuuritalo, Helsinki, Finland, on 12 June 1969.

Steve Winwood with Blind Faith at the Kulttuuritalo, Helsinki, Finland, on 12 June 1969.

14 June 1969, Njaardhallen, Oslo, Norway (1 show)

16 June 1969 Kungliga Tennishallen, Stockholm, Sweden (2 shows)

18 June 1969, Konserthallen, Liseberg, Nöjespark, Gothenburg, Sweden (1 show)

SETLIST: Well All Right / Sleeping In The Ground / Sea Of Joy / Under My Thumb / Can't Find My Way Home / Do What You Like / Presence Of The Lord / Means To An End / Had To Cry Today)

19 June 1969, KB Hallen, Copenhagen, Denmark (2 shows)

BLIND FAITH USA / CANADA TOUR 1969

JULY 1969

10 July 1969, Ungano's, 210 West 70th Street, New York (Dr. John is playing tonight, the third night of a two-week-long residency. He is backed by his regular band consisting of: Richard "Didymus" Washington [congas], Richard Crooks [drums], David Leonard Johnson [bass], Gary Carino [guitar], and singers Eleanor Barooshian, Jeanette Jacobs, and Sherry Graddie. In the audience are Chris Wood, Eric Clapton, Delaney Bramlett, and Ginger Baker. All four of them sit in for a lengthy version of "Tipitina." An interesting little aside, Chris Wood would soon marry Jeannette Jacobs and both would be playing with Ginger Baker in his band Airforce in 1970)

11 July 1969, Ungano's, 210 West 70th Street, New York (Dr. John is playing the fourth night of his two-week-long residency tonight. In the audience again are Chris Wood, Eric Clapton, Delaney Bramlett, and Ginger Baker. All four of them had so much fun last night that they decide to sit in again)

11 July 1969, Record Plant Studios, 321 West 44th Street, New York (Eric Clapton, Doctor John, and Delaney Bramlett take part in a supersession recording organized by producer Earle Doud. Full details in recording sessions)

12 July 1969, Madison Square Garden, New York City (gross fee: $55,116. With Free, Delaney & Bonnie and Friends. Free leave after tonight to play a short residency at Ungano's in New York supporting Dr John. They will rejoin the tour in August, and Taste take over)

SETLIST: Had To Cry Today / Can't Find My Way Home / Sleeping In The Ground / Well All Right / In The Presence Of The Lord / Sea Of Joy / Do What You Like / Means To An End

"The first time I met Eric was in New York. Backstage at Madison Square Garden we passed the time of day and then got talking. We realized we both had admired the same people, particularly Robert Johnson, and both had almost identical collections of records. The only difference was that I had been raised on this music while Eric had raised himself on it. The tour had only been going a couple of days before we'd suddenly find Eric's smiling face popping out from behind our speakers. He'd have a tambourine and be bashing away."
—DELANEY BRAMLETT

Advert for Blind Faith at the Philadelphia Spectrum on 16 July 1969.

13 July 1969, John F. Kennedy Stadium, Bridgeport, Connecticut (gross fee: $15,000. With Taste, Delaney & Bonnie and Friends)

16 July 1969, the Spectrum, Philadelphia, Pennsylvania (gross fee: $45,445. With Taste, Delaney & Bonnie and Friends)

Advert for Blind Faith at the Baltimore Civic Centre on 20 July 1969.

"The 'Blind Faith' featuring two former members of Cream, Eric Clapton (23) and Ginger Baker (29), ex-'Traffic' musician Steve Winwood (20), and bass guitarist Rick Grech (23) formerly of the 'Family,' did several songs from their new album before a crowd that had sat through more than two hours of intermittent rain while waiting for the group to appear.

Finally when the Faith began their music the audience received them with vigorous applause after each number and gave Ginger Baker a standing ovation for his drum solo.

The young crowd were also electrified by Clapton's guitar playing and Grech's piece with the electric violin. Winwood demonstrated his skill with the guitar, electric piano, organ and also did the majority of the singing for the group.

Besides the 'Faith,' 'The Taste' from Ireland, and Delaney, Bonnie and Friends performed in the first of the City of Bridgeport's summer entertainment program at the stadium."

—THE *BRIDGEPORT TELEGRAM*
(14 July 1969, with the headline
"Blind Faith Rewards Damp Throng's Faith")

20 July 1969, Civic Center Arena, Baltimore, Maryland (gross fee: $20,000. With Taste, Delaney & Bonnie and Friends)

23 July 1969, War Memorial Stadium, Kansas City, Kansas (gross fee: $20,000. With Taste, Delaney & Bonnie and Friends)

26 July 1969, Midwest Rock Festival, Wisconsin State Fair Park, West Allis, Wisconsin (gross fee: $20,000. Show starts at 2:00 p.m. With SRC, MC5, Taste, Shag, Delaney & Bonnie and Friends, John Mayall)

Advert for Blind Faith at the Midwest Rock Festival on 26 July 1969.

Poster for Blind Faith at Varsity Stadium on 18 July 1969.

18 July 1969, Varsity Stadium, Toronto, Ontario, Canada (gross fee: $19,506. With Taste, Delaney & Bonnie and Friends)

19 July 1969, Forum Montreal, Quebec, Canada (gross fee: $20,000. With Taste, Delaney & Bonnie and Friends)

SETLIST: Had To Cry Today / Can't Find My Way Home / Sleeping In The Ground / Well All Right / Presence Of The Lord / Do What You Like / Sunshine Of Your Love (with Delaney & Bonnie, Bobby Whitlock on vocals and Dave Mason on guitar)

Advert for Blind Faith at the International Amphitheater, Chicago, on 27 July 1969.

27 July 1969, International Amphitheater, Chicago, Illinois (gross fee: $25,000. With Taste, Delaney & Bonnie and Friends)

SETLIST: Had To Cry Today / Can't Find My Way Home / Well All Right / In The Presence Of The Lord / Sea Of Joy / Crossroads / Do What You Like / Sleeping In The Ground / Sunshine Of Your Love (with Delaney & Bonnie, Bobby Whitlock on vocals and Dave Mason on guitar)

AUGUST 1969

1 August 1969, Sports Arena, Minneapolis, Minnesota (gross fee: $20,000. With Taste, Delaney & Bonnie and Friends)

2 August 1969, Olympia Stadium, Detroit, Michigan (gross fee: $20,000. With Taste, Delaney & Bonnie and Friends)

3 August 1969, Kiel Auditorium, St. Louis, Missouri (gross fee: $20,250. With Taste, Delaney & Bonnie and Friends)

8 August 1969, Center Coliseum, Seattle, Washington (gross fee: $20,201. With Taste, Delaney & Bonnie and Friends)

9 August 1969, Pacific Coliseum, Vancouver, British Columbia, Canada (gross fee: $20,000. With Taste, Delaney & Bonnie and Friends)

"Before the Blind Faith concert Saturday night, someone must have given the Coliseum security staff an overdose of ugly pills. Now I have nothing against security at a rock concert, but in this case there seemed to be two points worth considering: First, groups like the former Cream and the new Blind Faith aren't turn-on groups like The Beatles or The Doors which can be expected to cause riots either by taunting or just plain teen appeal. Secondly, the security at recent rock concerts in the Agrodome hasn't been so uptight, with people sitting both in front of the stage on the floor and in the aisles, something to which the security reacted almost violently Saturday night.

In addition to acting like a mini-police force, the ushers also ran around making threats of bodily eviction to those who had committed the heinous crime of smoking and shining their flashlights in the lenses of non-press photographers who came up near stage. Bolstering the Coliseum 'Blue Meanies' were 20 of Vancouver's finest, who were, by contrast, quite friendly. At one point, though, when they had to clear the space in front of the stage one officer, responding, apparently, to a taunt from someone behind him did take a swing at a customer hitting the kid in the back of the neck.

My first reaction to the featured group, Blind Faith, was a bit of a shock, even though I knew well in advance that they wouldn't sound like The Cream. The crowd seemed repressed in their response to the new group until it launched into Crossroads, which provoked a rousing cheer. One thing that Blind Faith established themselves as was that they are a group mainly for the ear rather than the eye. Their musicianship was generally outstanding, even though their material was subdued. The result was like seeing a superb symphony orchestra performing some lesser-known works supremely well. Lead guitarist Eric Clapton was, as expected, note perfect. Most of organist Steve Winwood's work, though, seemed to be lost, except in a hymn composed by Clapton, In the Presence of the Lord, but Winwood tackled almost all the vocals with reasonable musicality. Bass player Rick Grech gave a jazz-oriented solo in Do What You Like, and also soloed on the electric violin (which was excruciatingly loud). Ginger Baker's requisite drum solo in Do What You Like (which he wrote) convinced the crowd that Baker still remains the ultimate rock drummer, both in his unique style and techniques. In the last number, 'Sunshine of Your Love', when Blind Faith was joined by Delaney and Bonnie and a couple of friends in an enthusiastic jam, the crowd finally broke through the security line, surged to the front of the stage, and gave the musicians an enthusiastic farewell."

—THE VANCOUVER PROVINCE
(Monday, 11 August 1969, has the headline "Blue Meanies restrain enthusiasm for Faith")

SETLIST: Had To Cry Today / Can't Find My Way Home / Well All Right / In The Presence Of The Lord / Sea Of Joy; Crossroads / Do What You Like / Sunshine Of Your Love with Delaney & Bonnie, Bobby Whitlock on vocals and Dave Mason on guitar)

10 August 1969, Veterans Memorial Coliseum, Portland, Oregon (gross fee: $10,000. With Taste, Delaney & Bonnie and Friends)

14 August 1969, Alameda County Coliseum, Oakland, California (gross fee: $20,000. With Free, Delaney & Bonnie and Friends)

SETLIST (incomplete): Well All Right / Presence Of The Lord / Sea Of Joy / Means To An End / Do What You Like / Sunshine Of Your Love with Delaney & Bonnie, Bobby Whitlock on vocals and Dave Mason on guitar

15 August 1969, the Forum, Los Angeles, California (gross fee: $48,764. With Free, Delaney & Bonnie and Friends)

16 August 1969, Earl Warren Fairgrounds Arena, Santa Barbara, California (billed as "Blind Faith Festival." Gross fee: $20,400. With Free, Delaney & Bonnie and Friends, Zephyr, Fields, and Rabbit McKay and the Somis Rhythm Band)

Poster for Blind Faith at the Santa Barbara Fairgrounds Arena on 16 August 1969.

"Blind Faith were loved before they played a note. The huge gathering ended each song with wild applause. Some music fans became so enthusiastic over the fine sounds that they began dancing in the aisles. Naturally the police and the rent-a-cops panicked and ran up the stairs with clubs poised. It was a sad scene. Twice the house lights were turned on and people literally dragged out, which made the situation worse because everyone's attention focused on the hassles rather than on the outstanding group on stage. Finally, a bit disgusted, Ginger Baker asked: 'Can everyone, and that includes the police, please act like gentlemen!' This met with thunderous applause.

Blind Faith's show was tight, but at times a bit long on improvisation for my tastes. The audience, however, didn't seem to mind one bit. 'Crossroads,' with a new arrangement and Stevie Winwood on the second verse was fantastic. By the last song, the crowd was surging toward the eight-foot-high stage. Again the police panicked and fifteen of them jumped on the front of the stage. It was so crowded Eric had to move to the back of the stage.

Finally the cops left the stage and Delaney & Bonnie and Friends joined Blind Faith in 'Sunshine Of Your Love.' At the end Bonnie and Eric flashed peace signs to the audience and ten thousand peace signs shot right back from around the Forum." —**ANN MOSES**, (Tiger Beat)

SETLIST: Well All Right / Can't Find My Way Home / Had To Cry Today / Sleeping in the Ground / Crossroads / Presence Of The Lord / Means To An End / Do What You Like / Sunshine Of Your Love (with Delaney & Bonnie, Bobby Whitlock on vocals and Dave Mason on guitar)

19 August 1969, Sam Houston Coliseum, Houston, Texas (gross fee: $20,000. With Free, Delaney & Bonnie and Friends)

20 August 1969, HemisFair Arena, San Antonio, Texas (gross fee: $20,000. With Free, Delaney & Bonnie and Friends)

SETLIST: Well All Right / Can't Find My Way Home / Had To Cry Today / Sleeping In The Ground / Crossroads / Presence Of The Lord / Sea Of Joy / Do What You Like / Sunshine Of Your Love (with Delaney & Bonnie, Bobby Whitlock on vocals and Dave Mason on guitar)

22 August 1969, Salt Palace Arena, Salt Lake City, Utah (gross fee: $14,214. With Free, Delaney & Bonnie and Friends)

23 August 1969, Veterans Memorial Coliseum, Phoenix, Arizona (gross fee: $22,729. With Free, Delaney & Bonnie and Friends)

> **"The peak of violence and hassles was reached in Phoenix. The trouble was really with Delaney & Bonnie who were having a hard time through lack of billing and weird contract and money scenes. Phoenix was their last night on the tour and like most nights we jammed with them. Bonnie got really into it and fell off the stage, down ten foot onto concrete. Pandemonium broke out. The cops dragged her to an office and would not let us in. After arguments we eventually got in and took her to hospital with Delaney carrying her.**
>
> **There were more hassles there with the cops and Delaney dropped her again onto concrete and she ended up in hospital with a broken vertebrae. What can you do? It is a police state; it is a police country."** —ERIC CLAPTON

24 August 1969, HIC (Hawaii International Center) Arena, Honolulu, Hawaii (gross fee: $22,868. With Free)

Blind Faith's infamous album cover.

BLIND FAITH RECORDING SESSIONS 1969

The first sessions took place at Morgan Studios and, as often happens at first sessions, everybody took hours setting up. People were getting irritated and tempers were getting the better of them. Denny Laine from the Moody Blues, who was at Morgan that day, had dropped into their studio and picked up a guitar for a jam session. Having an outsider come in really lifted everyone's mood. The jam with Denny was amazing by all accounts, but unfortunately it was not recorded. Ginger was not at all happy, and DJ Jeff Dexter, who was there that day recalls him grabbing a microphone from the front of his drum kit and screaming out a torrent of abuse at the tape operator. Denny was not there with the intention of joining the band, as he was in the process of forming a new lineup of Balls with Trevor Burton of the Move. But his appearance did lift spirits, and after a couple of days off the general mood had improved.

MORGAN STUDIOS 169-171 High Road, Willesden Green, London NW10 18 FEBRUARY 1969

FEBRUARY 1969

HOW'S YOUR MOTHER HOW'S YOUR FATHER (Well All Right) (Buddy Holly) takes 1–34
Eric Clapton: guitar
Steve Winwood: vocals, piano, organ, bass pedals, bass
Ginger Baker: drums, percussion
Engineer: Andy Johns
Producer: Jimmy Miller

20 FEBRUARY 1969

WELL ALL RIGHT (Buddy Holly) takes 1–6
LORD PROTECTOR (Presence Of The Lord) (Eric Clapton) takes 1–70
PRESENCE OF THE LORD (Eric Clapton) takes 71–77
PRESENCE OF THE LORD (Eric Clapton) take 72 master (*Blind Faith* album ATCO SD-33-304 (nude cover) / *Blind Faith* album ATCO SD-33-304A (band cover) / *Blind Faith* 2CD Deluxe Edition)
Eric Clapton: guitar
Steve Winwood: vocals, piano, organ, bass pedals, bass
Ginger Baker: drums, percussion
Engineer: Andy Johns
Producer: Jimmy Miller

28 FEBRUARY 1969

WELL ALL RIGHT (Buddy Holly) takes 1–5
WELL ALL RIGHT (Buddy Holly) take 6 master (*Blind Faith* album ATCO SD-33-304 (nude cover) / *Blind Faith* album ATCO SD-33-304A (band cover)/ *Blind Faith* 2CD Deluxe Edition)
HEY JOE (Billy Roberts) takes 1–8

Eric Clapton: guitar
Steve Winwood: vocals, piano, organ, bass pedals, bass
Ginger Baker: drums, percussion

Engineer: Andy Johns
Producer: Jimmy Miller

MORGAN STUDIOS 169–171 High Road, Willesden Green, London NW10

2 MARCH 1969

JAM NO.1 (Very Long & Good Jam) (*Blind Faith* 2CD Deluxe Edition)
JAM NO.2 (Slow Jam #1) (*Blind Faith* 2CD Deluxe Edition)
JAM NO.3 (Change Of Address Jam) (*Blind Faith* 2CD Deluxe Edition)
JAM NO.4 (Slow Jam #2) (*Blind Faith* 2CD Deluxe Edition)
ONE OF US MUST KNOW (SOONER OR LATER) (Bob Dylan) take 1 unreleased
KEY TO THE HIGHWAY (Charles Segar / William Broonzy) unreleased
ONE OF US MUST KNOW (SOONER OR LATER) (Bob Dylan) take 2 unreleased

Eric Clapton: guitar
Steve Winwood: piano, organ, bass pedals, bass
Ginger Baker: drums, percussion
Guy Warner: percussion, chants

Engineer: Andy Johns
Producer: Jimmy Miller

OLYMPIC STUDIOS 117–123 Church Road, Barnes, London SW13

27 MAY 1969

Unknown instrumental jam
I CAN'T FIND MY WAY HOME (Steve Winwood) (electric version) takes 1–15
I CAN'T FIND MY WAY HOME (Steve Winwood) (electric version) take 10 master (*Up Close Radio Show* promo CD / Steve Winwood *The Finer Things* box set / *Blind Faith* 2CD Deluxe Edition as a new mix)

Eric Clapton: guitar
Steve Winwood: vocals, organ, guitar
Ginger Baker: drums
Rick Grech: bass

Engineer: George Chkiantz
Producer: Jimmy Miller

28 MAY 1969

SEA OF JOY (Steve Winwood) takes 1–5
SEA OF JOY (Steve Winwood) take 6 master (*Blind Faith* album ATCO SD-33-304 (nude cover) / *Blind Faith* album ATCO SD-33-304A (band cover) / *Blind Faith* 2CD Deluxe Edition)

Eric Clapton: guitar
Steve Winwood: vocals, guitar, organ
Ginger Baker: drums
Rick Grech: bass, violin

Engineer: George Chkiantz
Producer: Jimmy Miller

30 MAY 1969

TIME WINDS takes 1–53 (take number unknown *Blind Faith* 2CD Deluxe Edition)

Eric Clapton: guitar
Steve Winwood: organ
Ginger Baker: drums
Rick Grech: bass

Engineers: George Chkiantz, Keith Harwood
Producer: Jimmy Miller

OLYMPIC STUDIOS 117–123 Church Road, Barnes, London SW13

5 JUNE 1969

HAD TO CRY TODAY (Steve Winwood) takes 1–11 instrumental
Had To Cry Today takes 12–21 with vocals

23 JUNE 1969

SOMETHING ELSE BLUES take 1
Blues
SOMETHING ELSE BLUES take 2
ANOTHER THING takes 1–3
More
HAD TO CRY TODAY (Steve Winwood) takes 1–26 (new takes viewed as better than the previously recorded versions done on 5 June, with take 26 as working master)
DO WHAT YOU LIKE (Ginger Baker) takes 1–7
Eric Clapton: guitar
Steve Winwood: vocals, piano, guitar, organ, bass pedals, bass
Ginger Baker: drums, percussion
Rick Grech: bass

Engineers: Alan O'Duffy, Keith Harwood
Producer: Jimmy Miller

24 JUNE 1969

DO WHAT YOU LIKE (Ginger Baker) takes 1–5 unreleased
DO WHAT YOU LIKE (Ginger Baker) take 6 master (*Blind Faith* album ATCO SD-33-304 (nude cover) / *Blind Faith* album ATCO SD-33-304A (band cover) / *Blind Faith* 2CD Deluxe Edition)

HAD TO CRY TODAY (Steve Winwood) takes 1–16 unreleased

HAD TO CRY TODAY (Steve Winwood) take 17 master (*Blind Faith* album ATCO SD-33-304 (nude cover) / *Blind Faith* album ATCO SD-33-304A (band cover) / *Blind Faith* 2CD Deluxe Edition)

BLUES JAM / OH HAPPY DAY BLUES (based on the recent Edwin Hawkins "Oh Happy Day" single) unreleased

SLEEPING IN THE GROUND (Sam Myers) (Slow Blues Version) takes 1–5 unreleased

SLEEPING IN THE GROUND (Sam Myers) (Slow Blues Version) take 6 (*Blind Faith* 2CD Deluxe Edition)

Eric Clapton: guitar
Steve Winwood: vocals, piano, guitar, organ, bass pedals, bass
Ginger Baker: drums, percussion
Rick Grech: bass

Engineers: Alan O'Duffy, Keith Harwood
Producer: Jimmy Miller

MORGAN STUDIOS
169-171 High Road,
Willesden Green,
London NW10

25 JUNE 1969

ACOUSTIC JAM (*Blind Faith* 2CD Deluxe Edition)

SLEEPING IN THE GROUND (Sam Myers) takes 1–27

SLEEPING IN THE GROUND (Sam Myers) take 28 master (Eric Clapton *Crossroads* box set / *Blind Faith* 2CD Deluxe Edition with new mix)

Eric Clapton: guitar, acoustic guitar
Steve Winwood: vocals, piano
Ginger Baker: drums, percussion
Rick Grech: bass

Engineer: Andy Johns
Producer: Jimmy Miller

OLYMPIC STUDIOS
117-123 Church Road,
Barnes, London SW13

28 JUNE 1969

I CAN'T FIND MY WAY HOME (Steve Winwood) (acoustic) take 1–24 unreleased

I CAN'T FIND MY WAY HOME (Steve Winwood) (acoustic) take 21 master (*Blind Faith* album ATCO SD-33-304 (nude cover) / *Blind Faith* album ATCO SD-33-304A (band cover) / *Blind Faith* 2CD Deluxe Edition)

Eric Clapton: acoustic guitar
Steve Winwood: vocals, acoustic guitar
Ginger Baker: drums, percussion
Rick Grech: bass

Engineers: Andy Johns, Keith Harwood
Producer: Jimmy Miller

> **"**Jimmy (Miller) is great, he's helped us a great deal and I don't think we'd ever have finished the album without him.**"**
>
> **—ERIC CLAPTON**
> (*Rolling Stone*, 11 July 1969)

ERIC CLAPTON GUEST SESSIONS
1969 AND PLASTIC ONO BAND

ERIC CLAPTON
GUEST SESSIONS 1969

DECCA STUDIOS
Studio 1, 165 Broadhurst
Gardens, West Hampstead,
London NW6
Session for Martha Velez
Fiends & Angels

7 MARCH 1969

I'M GONNA LEAVE YOU (Jackie Johnson, Lionel Whitfield) *Fiends & Angels* album US Sire SES 97008, UK London SHK 8395 released June 1969 / *Fiends & Angels* CD Wounded Bird WOU 8395 released June 2008

Martha Velez: vocals
Eric Clapton: guitar
Jack Bruce: bass
Mitch Mitchell: drums
Rick Hayward: rhythm guitar
Duster Bennett: harmonica
Terry Noonan: horns (overdubbed at Morgan Studios)
Bud Parkes: horns (overdubbed at Morgan Studios)
Derek Wadsworth: horns (overdubbed at Morgan Studios)

FEEL SO BAD (Lightnin' Hopkins) *Fiends & Angels* album US Sire SES 97008, UK London SHK 8395 released June 1969 / *Fiends & Angels* CD Wounded Bird WOU 8395 released June 2008

Martha Velez: vocals
Eric Clapton: guitar
Jack Bruce: bass
Mitch Mitchell: drums
Rick Hayward: rhythm guitar
Duster Bennett: harmonica
Terry Noonan: horns (overdubbed at Morgan Studios)
Bud Parkes: horns (overdubbed at Morgan Studios)
Derek Wadsworth: horns (overdubbed at Morgan Studios)

Producer: Mike Vernon
Engineer: Derek Varnals

"There were 5 sessions for the album, one of which Eric, Jack Bruce, Mitch Mitchell, Duster Bennett and Rick Hayward played on their 2 tracks.

The session was done on the Friday evening 7 March 1969 in Decca studio 1. We began at about 8 P.M. and finished at 12:30 A.M.. This may have included, clearing and re-setting for the next day. We did 2 tracks, 1, I'm Gonna Leave You; 2, Feel So Bad. Both were 'cover versions' of blues numbers. Mike Vernon, an old mate of Eric's and all of them in fact, brought in 2 American 45s to listen to. The first was by Bobby Powell, I don't remember who the other was by, but it is a Lightnin' (Sam) Hopkins number.

The tracks opened each side of the album, and were obvious singles. But Mike was scared to put them on a single, Eric was too recognisable.

All the musicians on the album were doing him favours by having no contracts. I don't know if Seymour Stein (Sire Records) was paying them, but they were all in breach of their own record contracts which is why they were not mentioned on the sleeve.

We played each single a couple of times, they went on the floor and ran it through once or twice and got it down pretty quickly. We had Martha on the floor singing live, although the vocals were later replaced as is usual. The same process applied to the 2nd number, Feel So Bad.

The brass on these 2 tracks were added at Morgan Studios on 24 March. We used Morgan as we had run out of studio time on the days Mike, Terry Noonan, and myself were free.

The whole album was mixed in one day 9 April (14 hours!), fairly simple recordings on 8 track sped things up." —**DEREK VARNALS** (engineer)

"Jimmy Page came by, wanting to play...actually, I ran into him on the street as he was coming to the studio. I was standing outside of Decca Studios, with Clapton, Bruce and Mitchell. Jimmy Page walked up and said he would love to play. As luck would have it, we had just finished for the day and he was heading out on tour or some other place...or, he too would have added his vibe.

Although this was early in the career of Eric Clapton, Jack Bruce, Jim Capaldi and Mitch Mitchell, the image in my head had created these rather larger than life individuals. When we met that day in Decca Studios that image was ameliorated by reality. They came in. We met—both Eric Clapton and Jack Bruce were soft spoken and polite. Clapton was almost shy. I'm a rather tall girl, and in those days, I was into wearing these suede patchwork boots, so I felt like a towering lanky tree branch gazing down at these pristine pale-faced boys. Clapton cast his eyes down when he spoke with this urgency to be shielded by his instrument and staved off his shyness by speaking through the language of his guitar. Clapton had this thing about looking around the room checking out the people there, slightly leaning forward like a telescope, searching out any discrepancies. The musicians and I got down to the business of making music together. Most of the tunes were 'head arrangements,' ideas that came on the spot. I had practiced the tunes on my own, so when the players arrived, I had an idea as to what my thoughts were on the songs, how they could be sung, but only imaginings as to how they could work with these players. They, of course, had their musicianship flowing and after a few rehearsal run throughs, we hit the songs running.

Decca Studios in London, where we recorded, was a vintage studio owned by Decca Records. What made it so appealing and memorable, was that the whole studio was set in tiers for orchestral recordings. Above these tiers was the control booth where Mike Vernon and the engineer, Derek Varnals, lorded over the music. I was on the tier just below them, but above the player's tier, with the old Sennheiser microphone on a stand and no headphones. No one used headphones, this way it all felt live, urgent and in the moment. They played, I just wailed away...and hoped for the best. A batch of the songs were recorded live on the spot... vocals and instrumentals. I realize now how the sounds were bleeding into each other...I think the drums had baffles around them, but the players and I were not separated by baffles or in separate control booths, we just played. Certainly, the Eric Clapton, Jack Bruce, Mitch Mitchell cuts, were recorded on the spot.

I sat in with Clapton, Bruce and Mitchell at a club called, I think, the Speakeasy. It was dark and smoke filled, they were on the bandstand when they saw me at the foot of the stage they called me up to sing an impromptu blues in E...I got up, made up lyrics and had a blast...but, I had to leave early because I had a morning session the next day with Chicken Shack. That evening sits in my memory as one of those very smokey nights. Just 3 musicians on stage, Clapton, Mitchell (instead of Ginger Baker) and Jack Bruce on bass. They weren't playing Cream songs or Jimi Hendrix music. They were simply jamming on the Blues. Eric and Jack were trading off on verses—half the lyrics sounded made up, impromptu...it was one of those nights when they were inventing, exploring sounds—wish I could have stayed longer."

—MARTHA VELEZ
(from her blog on the sessions)

ERIC CLAPTON GUEST SESSION
OLYMPIC STUDIOS
117-123 Church Road, Barnes, London SW13
Session for Billy Preston

5 MAY 1969–6 MAY 1969

Billy Preston was born in Texas and raised in Los Angeles. His biggest influence was Ray Charles, who was later to state that Billy was the most likely person to follow in his footsteps. Billy came to the attention of the Beatles when he was on the same bill as them at the Hamburg Star Club in 1962 while playing in Little Richard's band. George was so impressed that he asked him to join them onstage. Billy reluctantly refused because he felt it would upset his boss, Little Richard.

George Harrison stayed in touch with Billy Preston and eventually signed him to the Beatles' Apple label in January 1969, when he joined them at Apple Studios in the basement of their Savile Row offices for their recording of "Get Back." George took Billy under his wing and made plans for a single and album. George asked Eric Clapton and Ginger Baker, now in Blind Faith, if they could play on the single. They were only too happy to help, and it provided them with a welcome break in Blind Faith's own recording schedule.

DO WHAT YOU WANT TO (Billy Preston) B-side single Apple 12 released July 1969 / *That's The Way God Planned It* album Apple ST-3359 released August 1969 / *That's The Way God Planned It* CD Apple 5099990824128 released October 2010

Billy Preston: organ, piano, vocals
Eric Clapton: guitar
George Harrison: guitar
Keith Richards: bass

Ginger Baker: drums
Doris Troy: backing vocals
Madeline Bell: backing vocals

THAT'S THE WAY GOD PLANNED IT (Billy Preston) **(ALTERNATIVE VERSION)** *That's The Way God Planned It* CD Apple 5099990824128 released October 2010

Billy Preston: piano, vocals
Eric Clapton: guitar
George Harrison: guitar
Keith Richards: bass
Ginger Baker: drums

THAT'S THE WAY GOD PLANNED IT (Billy Preston) A-side single Apple 12 released July 1969 / *That's The Way God Planned It* album Apple ST-3359 released August 1969 / *That's The Way God Planned It* CD Apple 5099990824128 released October 2010

Billy Preston: organ, vocals
Eric Clapton: guitar
George Harrison: guitar
Keith Richards: bass
Ginger Baker: drums
Doris Troy: backing vocals
Madeline Bell: backing vocals

Producer: George Harrison
Engineer: Glyn Johns

> **"**I'd never really heard of Eric Clapton and Ginger Baker and The Cream. George kept telling me they were fantastic. I took his word for it. We spent time playing 'That's The Way God Planned It' over, and over again until we got the right feeling.**"** **—BILLY PRESTON**

ERIC CLAPTON GUEST SESSION

RECORD PLANT STUDIOS 321 West 44th Street, New York Session for *Music From Free Creek*

11 JULY 1969

Earle Doud made his name producing two volumes of the *First Family* with Vaughn Meader in 1962. The *First Family* were comedy albums that parodied President Kennedy and his family and were huge hits, selling well over 7 million copies.

Earle Doud may have been knowledgeable about comedy albums, but he knew nothing about music or how to record it. But he did have an idea, a big one, which he took to the owners of the Record Plant in New York. It was the era of supergroups and jam sessions, and Earle wanted in. The plan was to produce a "supersession" album with the biggest musicians of the day. The Record Plant liked Earle's idea of bringing big names to its facilities, as there was a possibility they might want to record their albums there in the future. In return, they offered Earle as much studio time as he wanted, free of charge.

Todd Rundgren was originally going to be the executive producer and musical director. However, his manager, Albert Grossman, wanted too much money upfront, money Earle did not have. Moogy Klingman, who happened to be working with Todd at the time, was recommended by him to Earle. He was only nineteen at the time, and perhaps it was his youthful enthusiasm that allowed himself to take the job with no pay. He assumed Earl Doud would pay up eventually, and this was quite an opportunity for him. The biggest two names were Eric Clapton and Jeff Beck. Also present were Keith Emerson, Mitch Mitchell, Linda Ronstadt, Harvey Mandel, Chris Wood, Elliot Randall, and a host of other top players of the day. The sessions were recorded over several months as and when players were available.

Dr. John was playing a residency at Ungano's at the time and was attracting some pretty special guests. After his show on the 11 November he, together with Eric Clapton, Delaney Bramlett, and Richard Crooks, headed to the Record Plant for a jam. Moogy had arranged for his friend Stu Woods to be on standby with his bass at the Record Plant. Moogy sat in on the session, as well. They recorded three numbers in all. The sessions were very loose, with no real direction, with Moogy literally making songs up on the spot. The first song recorded was "Road Song," which was a minor-key blues instrumental. Moogy would write the lyrics the next day. He played organ on this number and Dr. John was at the piano. The good Doctor's playing blew everyone away that night. Moogy said he was the greatest blues-funk organist/pianist he'd ever heard. Eric was very impressed with him also, and their paths would cross again several times over the years. Stu Woods and Richard Crooks were locked in, and everyone just got into a groove. Delaney Bramlett was playing rhythm guitar, and Clapton played his guitar through a Leslie speaker.

The next song, "No One Knows," was made up on the spot. While Moogy was at the piano, he made up a bunch of chords that sounded good while teaching Eric Clapton and Dr. John the song. It was a haphazard way of doing things, but it seemed to work. The song had a gospel groove highlighted by some nice solos by Eric and Dr. John on the organ. Stu Woods and Tommy Cosgrove, both from Moogy's group at the time, wrote the lyrics with him the next day. Some weeks later Linda Ronstadt, who was also part of these supersessions, told Earle Doud how much she liked this number. She overdubbed her vocal on the song, but Earle thought it did not suit the song, and her vocal was wiped and replaced by Eric Mercury. The horns were overdubbed on a different day.

Moogy told the assembled musicians that he had one more song. He pulled out his harmonica and started playing a one-chord blues riff that he had been working on with some tentative lyrics that turned into "Getting Back to Molly." Dr. John was on guitar alongside Eric for this one. By all accounts, everybody had a great time. Moogy never did get paid.

As for the album, well, it took years before something was released. Clearances took a long time, and eventually both Eric Clapton and Jeff Beck refused to have their names associated with it. That made negotiations with labels that much harder. Eventually, Tony Stratton-Smith, the head of Charisma Records in England, released a double album titled *Music From Free Creek* in May 1973. Eric was credited as King Cool on the sleeve due to contractual difficulties.

NO ONE KNOWS (words by Tom Cosgrove and Stu Woods, music by Moogy Klingman)

Eric Clapton: lead guitar
Eric Mercury: vocals
Dr. John: organ
Moogy Klingman: piano
Stu Woods: bass
Richard Crooks: drums
Lou Delgatto, Bobby Keller, Meco Monardo, and Tom Malone: trombones
Lou Soloff, Alan Rubin, and Bill Chase: trumpets
Valerie Simpson, Maretha Stewart, and Hilda Harris: backing vocals

ROAD SONG (written by Moogy Klingman)

Eric Clapton: lead guitar
Dr. John: piano
Tommy Cosgrove & Buzzy Linhart: vocals
Moogy Klingman: organ
Delaney Bramlett: rhythm guitar

Stu Woods: bass
Richard Crooks: drums

GETTING BACK TO MOLLY (written by Moogy Klingman)

Eric Clapton: lead guitar (first solo)
Dr. John: lead guitar (second solo)
Earl Dowd: vocals
Moogy Klingman: harmonica
Valerie Simpson, Maretha Stewart, and Hilda Harris: backing vocals

Producers: Earl Doud and Tom Flye
Executive producer and musical director: Moogy Klingman
Engineers: Tony Bongiovi and Jack Hunt

> "July 69 date is correct. 'I keep talking but no one knows what I'm tryin' to say, could it be they're just too blind to see?' It was a hot night at the Record Plant on 44th St....big, big Earle Doud producing." —ERIC MERCURY

PLASTIC ONO BAND

Eric flew home in early September and pondered on Delaney's suggestion of recording his first solo album with them. It was something he would enjoy doing and would get him away from the whole circus scene surrounding Blind Faith. But before he had a chance to do anything about it, he had an opportunity to play a one-off gig with John Lennon in Toronto. It turns out that John was going to Canada to play a show in Toronto and really wanted to have Eric in the band. Apparently, he had been trying to get hold of Eric for twenty-four hours and nearly missed him. Poor old Eric had been suffering from jet lag and did not hear the phone. Terry Dolan, John's personal assistant, sent a telegram to Eric's house that was opened by Eric's gardener, who was able to wake him up to tell him about the concert. Eric said yes to the offer and grabbed his guitar and packed a bag and waited for the car to pick him up to take him to London Airport, where he was to meet everyone in the BOAC First Class lounge. Waiting for him were Alan White, Klaus Voormann, and then John and Yoko with Mal Evans and Anthony Fawcett, their personal assistant. Also present were Jill and Dan Richter, who had been putting all of John and Yoko's recent activities on to film.

Their conversation naturally turned to what were they going to play at that evening's show. A bunch of sheet music had been delivered to London Airport that morning and would facilitate their decision about what to play. As they boarded the VC10 bound for Toronto, they were allocated their own little area in the first-class cabin where they could strum their unplugged electric guitars and sing without disturbing other passengers too much. Not sure if airline staff would be so understanding today! Klaus Voormann told *Disc and Music Echo* in 1969, "when John phoned I was really quite excited and very pleased. It sounded like such a good idea—even though none of us had ever played together on a stage before. On the plane going over we tried to vaguely rehearse. We picked out chords on the guitar—which you couldn't hear because we had nowhere to plug in—and of course Alan didn't have his drums on the plane with him."

John Lennon in *The Beatles Anthology* remembers how it all came about:

> ❝We got this phone call on a Friday night that there was a rock 'n' roll revival show in Toronto with a 100,000 audience, or whatever it was, and that Chuck [Berry] was going to be there and Jerry Lee [Lewis] and all the great rockers that were still living, and Bo Diddley, and supposedly The Doors were top of the bill. They were inviting us as king and queen to preside over it, not play—but I didn't hear that bit. I said, 'Just give me time to get a band together,' and we went the next morning.❞

As the show was billed as the Toronto Rock 'n' Roll Festival, it made sense to play some classic covers which all of the band would know anyway. So "Dizzy Miss Lizzy," "Money," "Blue Suede Shoes" were pretty obvious choices. John suggested "Cold Turkey," a number he had recently written and that was pretty easy to play. "Yer Blues" was also suggested, as Eric was familiar with it from last year's *Rolling Stones Rock and Roll Circus* show. John was also keen to do "Give Peace A Chance," which had been that summer's anthem around the world and was bound to be a crowd pleaser. When they arrived at Toronto Airport, John and Yoko leapt into a waiting limo that would whisk them to Varsity Stadium, while the rest of the band had to get in the van transporting the luggage and instruments. Eric was very disappointed that a little more respect was not shown to the band.

D. A. Pennebaker, a well-respected filmmaker who shot the *Monterey Pop* documentary, was filming the whole event. The sound for the film and any potential album would be handled by Wally Heider, the Californian who recorded the audio for *Monterey Pop*. He was contracted to truck his eight-track recording equipment to Varsity Stadium in Toronto. By all accounts, raising the money for the film was a nightmare, and Pennebaker also had problems with the lighting at the venue. Nevertheless, despite any setbacks, the footage turned out surprisingly well.

Meanwhile, as far as the audience were concerned, they really did not believe that a Beatle together with Eric Clapton were coming to play at the festival. During the day the emcee Kim Fowley had announced at regular intervals that John Lennon had heard of the event and was on a plane right now heading to Toronto to play. Those comments were met with a resounding, "oh yeah?!!!" So when Kim Fowley finally introduced the band at almost midnight, John Lennon and the Plastic Ono Band were met with a rapturous welcome from the crowd. They played the rock 'n' roll oldies rehearsed in the plane along with the two Lennon numbers for half an hour before Yoko joined in with what can only be described as improvisational pieces. The first, "Don't Worry Kyoko (Mummy's Only Looking For Her Hand In The Snow)" at least features some nice slide licks from Eric, but the second and last number, "John, John (Let's Hope For Peace)" is just Eric and John letting their guitars feedback throughout this Yoko freakout, punctuated by some nice Klaus Voormann bass lines. Klaus Voormann recalled, "When we walked on stage it was a glorified jam session. John had stood in the dressing room—which was admittedly rather tatty—beforehand saying, 'What am I doing here? I could have gone to Brighton!' After all it was rather a long way to go for one concert. But the feeling when we all got out on stage and started playing was truly fantastic."

Eric, when asked by the *NME* about how he felt about playing these rock 'n' roll numbers, commented,

> ❝Well, I've played all these numbers before, maybe once or twice with other groups so I know them, even though I haven't played them for a long time. It was really refreshing to do them again because they are very simple and uncomplicated. John and I really love that music...we weren't sending it up. . . it wasn't a send up. That's the kind of music that turned John on initially and it's the same for me. In fact I could go on playing 'Money' and 'Dizzy Miss Lizzy' for the rest of my life, because I love it.❞

After the show the whole band was taken to a large private residence for their overnight stay. This event was really nothing more than a quick distraction for Eric, who was keen to get back to England and formalize an arrangement for his first solo album. He gave several interviews with the various music papers where he verbalized his dissatisfaction with Blind Faith, although he stopped short of saying that the band was finished.

At the end of September, he gave a typically candid interview at his Surrey home with *Melody Maker*'s Chris Welch, who was accompanied by photographer Barrie Wentzell. It was at this interview that Wentzell took some of those famous informal shots of Eric with his dogs and in a variety of very relaxed poses. If Eric was stressed about Blind Faith, he wasn't showing it. He told Chris, "I feel the public has been cheated all along with Blind Faith because no one is as good as their hype or their promotion. It's time for groups to start giving back to their audiences what they have given us." In answer to whether there will be a second Blind Faith album, Eric states, "We haven't started one. But the company have enough material to release one if they want to. God knows what will happen next. I still haven't recovered from the States. I felt quite ashamed and embarrassed on that tour. It's a purely personal thing, which a lot of people wouldn't understand at all." It would appear that none of the individual members of Blind Faith had seriously considered breaking up at this point, even though the US tour had been draining both physically and emotionally. As a way of relieving the "supergroup" pressure, they all decided to pursue solo projects with a view of getting back together afterward. In fact, at the time, there was a good possibility that they would end up playing on each other's albums.

In truth, the possibility of getting back together was somewhat optimistic. Stevie initially went off to record a solo project titled *Mad Shadows*. He got as far as recording two numbers when Ginger told him of his plans to form a big band with African rhythms called Airforce. Both Stevie and Rick Grech joined the band for a couple of shows, including one at the Royal Albert Hall that was recorded for a double album. Stevie then returned to his solo project, which eventually turned into a Traffic reunion with Jim Capaldi and Chris Wood for an album called *John Barleycorn Must Die*. Rick Grech also made plans for a solo album whose initial sessions featured George Harrison, Eric Clapton, and Stevie Winwood, among

others. The album was never completed and the tapes are nowhere to be found, sadly.

In late October Eric told the *Record Mirror*'s Keith Altham that "I'm not sure what is going to happen now. No one has called me since that American tour and I don't know whether to take that as an indication that we are not going to work again or not. If someone rings me and says we have a session I will probably go but I'm not taking it upon myself to get things together." He also now realized that there was not enough material left in the can for another Blind Faith album, "There are a few tapes which have been cut lying around the studio but they are just 'jam-sessions' and nothing that could be released as an album."

In the same October interview he admitted, "I intend to play with Delaney And Bonnie as they do not have a lead guitarist and my name will help them in Europe where they have not had their album released and are unknown. They come from the South of America—strangely enough there is never any guarantee that a band that good will succeed, but they deserve to."

PLASTIC ONO BAND

13 September 1969, "Toronto Rock and Roll Revival Festival," Varsity Stadium, University of Toronto, Ontario, Canada (with Chuck Berry, Little Richard, Jerry Lee Lewis, Fats Domino, Bo Diddley, Gene Vincent, Alice Cooper, Chicago, the Doors)

SETLIST:

Kim Fowley Introduction

Blue Suede Shoes (Carl Perkins) *Live Peace In Toronto* album US Apple SW 3362, UK CORE 2001 released 12 December 1969 / *Live Peace In Toronto* CD Apple 0777 7 90428 2 released 1995

Plastic Ono Band's Live Peace In Toronto *album cover.*

John Lennon: vocals, rhythm guitar
Eric Clapton: lead guitar
Alan White: drums
Klaus Voormann: bass

Money (That's What I Want) (Janie Bradford / Berry Gordy) *Live Peace In Toronto* album US Apple SW 3362, UK CORE 2001 released 12 December 1969 / *Live Peace In Toronto* CD Apple 0777 7 90428 2 released 1995

John Lennon: vocals, rhythm guitar
Eric Clapton: lead guitar
Alan White: drums
Klaus Voormann: bass

Dizzy Miss Lizzy (Larry Williams) *Live Peace In Toronto* album US Apple SW 3362, UK CORE 2001 released 12 December 1969 / *Live Peace In Toronto* CD Apple 0777 7 90428 2 released 1995

John Lennon: vocals, rhythm guitar
Eric Clapton: lead guitar
Alan White: drums
Klaus Voormann: bass

Yer Blues (John Lennon, Paul McCartney) *Live Peace In Toronto* album US Apple SW 3362, UK CORE 2001 released 12 December 1969 / *Live Peace In Toronto* CD Apple 0777 7 90428 2 released 1995

John Lennon: vocals, rhythm guitar
Eric Clapton: lead guitar
Alan White: drums
Klaus Voormann: bass

Cold Turkey (John Lennon) *Live Peace In Toronto* album US Apple SW 3362, UK CORE 2001 released 12 December 1969 / *Live Peace In Toronto* CD Apple 0777 7 90428 2 released 1995

John Lennon: vocals, rhythm guitar
Eric Clapton: lead guitar
Alan White: drums
Klaus Voormann: bass

Give Peace A Chance (John Lennon / Paul McCartney) *Live Peace In Toronto* album US Apple SW 3362, UK CORE 2001 released 12 December 1969 / *Live Peace In Toronto* CD Apple 0777 7 90428 2 released 1995

John Lennon: vocals, rhythm guitar
Eric Clapton: lead guitar
Alan White: drums
Klaus Voormann: bass

Don't Worry Kyoko (Mummy's Only Looking For Her Hand In The Snow) (Yoko Ono) *Live Peace In Toronto* album US Apple SW 3362, UK CORE 2001 released 12 December 1969 / *Live Peace In Toronto* CD Apple 0777 7 90428 2 released 1995

John Lennon: vocals, rhythm guitar
Eric Clapton: lead guitar
Alan White: drums
Klaus Voormann: bass
Yoko Ono: vocals

> "We tried to put it out on Capitol, and Capitol didn't want to put it out. They said, 'This is garbage, we're not going to put it out with her screaming on one side and you doing this sort of live stuff.' And they just refused to put it out. But we finally persuaded them that, you know, people might buy this. Of course, it went gold the next day.
>
> And then, the funny thing was—this is a side story—Klein had got a deal on that record that it was a John and Yoko Plastic Ono record, not a Beatles record, so we could get a higher royalty, because the Beatles' royalties were so low—they'd been locked in '63—and Capitol said, 'Sure you can have it,' you know. Nobody's going to buy that crap. They just threw it away and gave it us. And it came out, and it was fairly successful and it went gold. I don't know what chart position, but I've got a gold record somewhere that says...And four years later, we go to collect the royalties, and you know what they say? 'This is a Beatle record.' So Capitol have it in my file under Beatle records. Isn't it incredible?"
>
> —**JOHN LENNON**
> (on BBC)

John (Let's Hope For Peace) (Yoko Ono) *Live Peace In Toronto* album US Apple SW 3362, UK CORE 2001 released 12 December 1969 / *Live Peace In Toronto* CD Apple 0777 7 90428 2 released 1995

John Lennon: vocals, rhythm guitar
Eric Clapton: lead guitar
Alan White: drums
Klaus Voormann: bass
Yoko Ono: vocals
Recorded on eight-track by the Wally Heider mobile truck.
Producers: John Lennon, Yoko Ono

John Lennon produced stereo masters of the concert at Studio Three at EMI Studios, Abbey Road on 25 September 1969. A further mix of "Don't Worry Kyoko (Mummy's Only Looking For Her Hand In The Snow)" was done on 20 October 1969, and the album was released as *Live Peace In Toronto* 1969 on 12 December 1969.

The whole show is filmed by D. A. Pennebaker and is available on DVD as *John Lennon & The Plastic Ono Band: Live in Toronto '69*, released by Shout Factory in June 2009.

PLASTIC ONO BAND
EMI STUDIOS
Studio Three, 3 Abbey Road, London NW8
Plastic Ono Band session

25 SEPTEMBER 1969

COLD TURKEY (John Lennon) (takes 1–26)

The session took place between 7:00 p.m.–1:30 a.m. The final take (26) lasted 5 minutes, 10 seconds and was considered best. But John Lennon decided to re-record most of it at Trident Studios three days later with the same band. John also mixed the live Toronto album today and would do a little more on 20 October. Worth noting that his mix for vinyl of Live Peace In Toronto has not been released on CD.

John Lennon: vocals, guitar
Yoko Ono: vocals
Eric Clapton: guitar
Ringo Starr: drums
Klaus Voormann: bass

Producer: John Lennon, Yoko Ono
Engineers: Ken Scott, Phil McDonald

> **"** The first time we did 'Cold Turkey' it started with John playing very straight rhythm guitar. Then we did tracks with drums and bass. In the end we had loads of incredible guitar pieces, and when we finally finished we scrapped nearly all the original ideas and got back to a very hard tight sound which everyone was pleased with. **"**
>
> **—KLAUS VOORMANN**

TRIDENT STUDIOS
Trident House, 17 St Anne's Court, London W1
Plastic Ono Band session

28 SEPTEMBER 1969

COLD TURKEY (re-recording) (John Lennon)

John Lennon: vocals, guitar
Eric Clapton: guitar
Ringo Starr: drums
Klaus Voormann: bass

Producer: John Lennon, Yoko Ono
Engineers: Ken Scott, Phil McDonald

LANSDOWNE STUDIOS
Studio A, Lansdowne Road, London W11
Plastic Ono Band session

3 OCTOBER 1969

DON'T WORRY KYOKO (MUMMY'S ONLY LOOKING FOR A HAND IN THE SNOW) (Yoko Ono) B-side Apple 1001 released October 1969 / *Fly* double album Apple SVBB3380 released 1971 / *Fly* CD Ryko RYK10415 released July 1997

John Lennon: vocals, guitar
Yoko Ono: vocals
Eric Clapton: guitar
Ringo Starr: drums
Klaus Voormann: bass

Producer: John Lennon, Yoko Ono
Engineer: Unknown

EMI STUDIOS
Studio Two, 3 Abbey Road, London NW8
Plastic Ono Band session

5 OCTOBER 1969

COLD TURKEY (John Lennon) A-side Apple 1001 released October 1969 / John Lennon Power to the People—The Hits CD EMI released October 2010

John Lennon adds a several overdubs to the 28 September recording of "Cold Turkey" from Trident Studios. He tapes two new lead vocals as well as adding more lead guitar and the backward flourish at the end of the song

Producers: John Lennon, Yoko Ono
Engineers: Ken Scott, Phil McDonald

ERIC CLAPTON GUEST SESSION
TRIDENT STUDIOS
Trident House, 17 St Anne's Court, London W1
Sessions for Doris Troy

OCTOBER 1969–NOVEMBER 1969

AIN'T THAT CUTE (George Harrison / Doris Troy) *Doris Troy* album US Apple ST 3371, UK Apple Sapcor 13 released September 1970 / *Doris Troy* CD Apple 50999908234326 released October 2010

Doris Troy: vocals
Eric Clapton: guitar
Peter Frampton: guitar
George Harrison: bass
Ringo Starr: drums

Billy Preston: electric piano
Bobby Keyes: sax
Jim Price: trumpet
Madeline Bell: backing vocals
Lesley Duncan: backing vocals

GIVE ME BACK MY DYNAMITE (George Harrison / Doris Troy) *Doris Troy* album US Apple ST 3371, UK Apple Sapcor 13 released September 1970 / *Doris Troy* CD Apple 50999908234326 released October 2010

Doris Troy: vocals, keyboards
Eric Clapton: guitar
George Harrison: guitar
Ringo Starr: drums
Klaus Voormann: bass
Bobby Keyes: sax
Jim Price: trumpet

YOU TORE ME UP INSIDE (Doris Troy / Ray Schinnery) *Doris Troy* album US Apple ST 3371, UK Apple Sapcor 13 released September 1970 / *Doris Troy* CD Apple 50999908234326 released October 2010

Doris Troy: vocals, keyboards
Eric Clapton: guitar
George Harrison: guitar
Ringo Starr: drums
Klaus Voormann: bass
Madeline Bell: backing vocals
Lesley Duncan: backing vocals
Delaney Bramlett: backing vocals
Bonnie Bramlett: backing vocals

I'VE GOT TO BE STRONG (Jackie Lomax / Doris Troy) *Doris Troy* album US Apple ST 3371, UK Apple Sapcor 13 released September 1970 / *Doris Troy* CD Apple 50999908234326 released October 2010

Doris Troy: vocals, piano
Eric Clapton: guitar
George Harrison: guitar
Klaus Voormann: bass
Ringo Starr: drums
Madeline Bell: backing vocals
Lesley Duncan: backing vocals
Bobby Keys: sax
Jim Price: trumpet

YOU GIVE ME JOY JOY (George Harrison / Doris Troy / Richard Starkey / Stephen Stills) *Doris Troy* album US Apple ST 3371, UK Apple Sapcor 13 released September 1970 / *Doris Troy* CD Apple 50999908234326 released October 2010

Doris Troy: vocals, piano
Eric Clapton: guitar
Stephen Stills: first guitar solo
Peter Frampton: second guitar solo
George Harrison: guitar
Ringo Starr: drums
Bobby Keys: sax
Jim Price: trumpet

JACOBS LADDER (Traditional; arranged George Harrison and Doris Troy) *Doris Troy* album US Apple ST 3371, UK Apple Sapcor 13 released September 1970 / *Doris Troy* CD Apple 50999908234326 released October 2010

Doris Troy: vocals
Eric Clapton: guitar
George Harrison: bass
Ringo Starr: drums
Delaney Bramlett: guitar, backing vocals
Bonnie Bramlett: backing vocals
Rita Coolidge: backing vocals
Leon Russell: piano
Bobby Keys: sax

GET BACK (John Lennon / Paul McCartney) *Doris Troy* CD Apple 50999908234326 released October 2010

Doris Troy: vocals
Eric Clapton: guitar
George Harrison: guitar
Billy Preston: organ
Jim Gordon: drums
Klaus Voormann: bass
Bobby Keyes: sax
Jim Price: trumpet

WHAT YOU WILL BLUES (Doris Troy) *Doris Troy* CD Apple 50999908234326 released October 2010

Doris Troy: vocals
Eric Clapton: guitar
George Harrison: guitar
Ringo Starr: drums
Klaus Voormann: bass

Producers: Doris Troy, George Harrison ("Ain't That Cute")
Engineer: unknown

ERIC CLAPTON GUEST SESSION
TRIDENT STUDIOS
Trident House, 17 St Anne's Court, London W1
Session for Aashish Khan

OCTOBER 1969

"The recording was done at the Trident Studio, and it was done by Apple Records for me in 1969. There is a little story, which you should know about it. I did compose the song for a Indo-Pakistan movie, the song was based on a Rock 'n' Roll style. Since I didn't have much idea about the music, I asked George Harrison to help me, so he arrived in the middle of the night with Eric Clapton, Ringo Starr, Billy Preston, and John Barham, and we all did the session till 3 A.M. My desire was that George Harrison sing the song, instead he asked me to sing. This is the whole story. Unfortunately the movie never took place." —AASHISH KHAN

IN PRAISE OF THE LORD (WE ARE ALL CHILDREN OF GOD) (Aashish Khan)

Aashish Khan: vocals, sarod
Eric Clapton: guitar
George Harrison: guitar
Billy Preston: keyboards
Ringo Starr: drums
John Barham: piano

Producer: George Harrison
Engineer: Robin Cable

"The two songs were written by Aashish around the time that Joe Massot had asked George Harrison to produce a film score for his film *Wonderwall*. I worked as George's assistant, and also as assistant to the music-editor Rusty Coppleman during the film dubbing sessions. George paid Trident Studio for Aaashish's session (as far as I remember). The songs were intended for a film made by a UK-based Indian filmmaker whose name I cannot remember. I never saw the film. As far as I know Aaashish didn't see it either. In fact there may not have been a film at that point. As far as I know, there were no contracts signed by anybody in regard to these songs. After the initial recording, rough mixes were made and Aashish took possession of the master tapes."

—JOHN BARHAM

"Eric did play on a song called 'Manhole Covered Wagon' on the *Contribution* album, but wasn't a featured lead player. However, somebody at A&M screwed up, and didn't credit him with playing. And he wasn't on the sessions with Stevie (Winwood), and Jim (Capaldi), and the horn player, I think his name was Chris (Wood).

I remember Eric, and the keyboard player, whose real name I can't remember, but his nickname was 'Wynder K Frog.' Shit, it's weird I can't remember his real name, 'cause he and I did the music for the documentary series *World In Action*, in those days, and it fucking ran for 35 years! Anyway, this session I remember, because the tune wasn't happening in the first few takes, and then the keyboard player doubled up the tempo on the piano, and it took off. I remember commenting on that with Eric during the playback, and he agreed. Otherwise, we knew each other socially, like over a pint in the then 'Speakeasy' club, and various other places, but never became what you would call close friends, simply because our meetings were so scarce. I do also remember being at one of the Moody Blues' house with Eric, and John, Paul, and George, of the Beatles, and we were discussing something about how religion was almost like a sport, and I made a crack about Lions 12 vs. Christians 0, and John, Eric, and George fell about laughing, but Paul didn't think it funny at all. Who the fuck knows? We were all so stoned in those days anyway."

—SHAWN PHILLIPS

ERIC CLAPTON
GUEST SESSION

TRIDENT STUDIOS
Trident House, 17 St Anne's Court, London W1
Session for Shawn Phillips "Contribution"

OCTOBER 1969

MANHOLE COVERED WAGON (Shawn Phillips) Contribution album A&M SP-4241 Released 1970 / Contribution CD Wounded Bird WOU 4241 Released 1999

Shawn Philips: vocals, guitar
Eric Clapton: guitar
Mick Weaver (aka Wynder K. Frog): keyboards
John Carr: drums

Producer: Jonathan Weston
Engineer: Robin Cable

ERIC CLAPTON
GUEST SESSION

OLYMPIC STUDIOS
117-123 Church Road, Barnes, London SW13

and

TRIDENT STUDIOS
Trident House, 17 St. Anne's Court, Soho, London W1

OCTOBER 1969

and

MORGAN STUDIOS
169-171 High Road, Willesden Green, London NW10
Session for Rick Grech

7 OCTOBER 1969

SPENDING ALL MY DAYS (*Blind Faith* CD bonus track West German RSO 825 094-2)

EXCHANGE AND MART (*Blind Faith* CD bonus track West German RSO 825 094-2)

The booklet lists Eric Clapton, Ginger Baker, Steve Winwood, and Rick Grech as the musicians for these two bonus tracks. I have no doubt that these are indeed from the lost Rick Grech sessions, and you can hear other musicians on these two numbers, but I have no idea who they are. The original reels have disappeared and are unlikely to surface.

Producer: Rick Grech
Engineer for Trident sessions: Ken Scott

These sessions were for a proposed Rick Grech solo album for RSO. Among the musicians taking part are Eric Clapton, George Harrison, Steve Winwood, Jim Capaldi, Trevor Burton, Denny Laine, Ginger Baker.

> **"**I remember them happening. I remember them being quite frenetic. I remember doing them. Unfortunately over and above that, nothing.**"** **—KEN SCOTT**

> **"**There have been about four sessions so far with different people each night. Eric has been on every session.**"**
> **—RICK GRECH**
> (*Melody Maker*, 8 November 1969)

> **"**As a spectator sport, recording is probably the most boring experience on the globe apart from reporting on the annual general meeting of rate-paying societies…Instead of an atmosphere of happy creativity, there was the ritualized gloom of a trade union meeting planning a return to work.**"**
> **—CHRIS WELCH**
> (*Melody Maker*, 8 November 1969)

ERIC CLAPTON GUEST SESSION

OLYMPIC STUDIOS
117-123 Church Road, Barnes, London SW13
Session for Leon Russell

OCTOBER 1969–NOVEMBER 1969

DELTA LADY (Leon Russell) Leon Russell album US Shelter SHE-1001, UK A&M AMLS 982 released February 1970 / Leon Russell DCC GZS-1049 gold CD released 1993

Leon Russell: piano, vocals
Eric Clapton: guitar
George Harrison: Leslie guitar
Ringo Starr: drums
Bill Wyman: bass
Stevie Winwood: organ
Chris Stainton: piano
Bonnie Bramlett: backing vocals
Clydie King: backing vocals
Merry Clayton: backing vocals

PRINCE OF PEACE (Leon Russell) Leon Russell album US Shelter SHE-1001, UK A&M AMLS 982 released February 1970 / Leon Russell DCC GZS-1049 gold CD released 1993

Leon Russell: vocals, piano, percussion
Eric Clapton: guitar

HURTSOME BODY (Leon Russell) Leon Russell album US Shelter SHE-1001, UK A&M AMLS 982 released February 1970 / Leon Russell DCC GZS-1049 gold CD released 1993

Leon Russell: vocals, piano
Eric Clapton: guitar
BJ Wilson: drums
Klaus Voormann: bass
Merry Clayton: backing vocals
Clydie King: backing vocals

ROLL AWAY THE STONE (Leon Russell / Greg Dempsey) Leon Russell album US Shelter SHE-1001, UK A&M AMLS 982 released February 1970 / Leon Russell DCC GZS-1049 gold CD released 1993

Leon Russell: piano, vocals
Eric Clapton: guitar
Charlie Watts: drums
Bill Wyman: bass
Stevie Winwood: organ

THE NEW SWEET HOME CHICAGO (Leon Russell / Marc Benno) bonus track on Leon Russell DCC GZS-1049 gold CD released 1993

Leon Russell: vocals, piano
Eric Clapton: guitar
Klaus Voormann: bass
Jon Hiseman: drums
Merry Clayton: backing vocals

JAMMIN' WITH ERIC (Leon Russell / Eric Clapton) bonus track on Leon Russell DCC GZS-1049 gold CD released 1993

Leon Russell: piano
Eric Clapton: guitar
Klaus Voormann: bass
Jon Hiseman: drums

Producer: Denny Cordell, Leon Russell
Engineer: Glyn Johns

The self-titled album was originally going to be called *Open Season* and would be the first album on Leon and Denny Cordell's new label, Shelter Records, which was distributed by Blue Thumb records. The UK sessions featured Eric Clapton, Klaus Voormann, Jon Hiseman, George Harrison, Ringo Starr, Steve Winwood, Bill Wyman, Charlie Watts, BJ Wilson. The Olympic session lasted five full days spread over two weeks. The album would be completed in America.

"I had forgotten all about that Olympic session for Clapton and 'a piano player' and had no idea it was Leon Russell—I was definitely not the right man for the job—my background was Jazz—even more so then than now, and I doubt any of my playing was used. I got the impression they were looking for someone with the right kind of feel for that style—whatever that style was. It was never my scene, then or now. I left after a couple of hours, glad to get out of there."

—JON HISEMAN

DELANEY & BONNIE AND FRIENDS WITH ERIC CLAPTON, AND ERIC CLAPTON GUEST SESSION

DELANEY & BONNIE AND FRIENDS WITH ERIC CLAPTON

On his return to England, Eric focused his attention on his solo album, which would be recorded with Delaney & Bonnie and Friends. Their respective managers started talking, and negotiations took place to bring Delaney & Bonnie over to England for a tour as well as backing Eric on his solo album.

As soon as the contracts were signed, Delaney & Bonnie and Friends flew over to England from Los Angeles, arriving at London Airport on the 7th of November. The day after arriving, Robert Stigwood threw a big birthday party for Bonnie at his Stanmore mansion. The whole band were staying at Eric's country home, as it would be easier to rehearse for both the tour and the studio sessions. Eric had cleared the snooker room on the first floor, which would be the band room where all the equipment was set up, the very same room where Blind Faith held their final rehearsals before going on tour. It allowed them the luxury of playing day and night whenever they felt like it.

> **"**We'll be doing two one hour shows a night. We've got ten days to rehearse for the tour. It's got a good line-up including Sue and Sunny, PP Arnold and Ashton Gardner and Dyke.**"** — **ERIC CLAPTON**

Delaney & Bonnie were on the road a lot, and the whole band was a tight unit, and as Eric was already familiar with most of their songs, all Delaney had to do was show him the basics. Rehearsals did not take long, and Eric had a great time. His only concern was the stormy relationship between Delaney and Bonnie, which was often very physical. Drugs and alcohol did not help the situation, and Bonnie would often have to wear sunglasses to try and hide the bruises when she came downstairs for breakfast. The band was all too familiar with the fiery couple and knew to stand out of the way when things flared up. Everyone just accepted the situation and got on with the business of making music. And that music was magical. Eric told *Rolling Stone* magazine at the time, "We've been on exactly the same wavelength, there's an incredible musical affinity between us. We grew up to the same music, at the same time, we had the same ideas, we had all the same records and when we got together it was just right, just natural." Eric and Delaney also shared the same idol, Robert Johnson.

While in England, Delaney and various "Friends" also attended several sessions with Eric Clapton and George Harrison for people like Doris Troy, Leon Russell, and Billy Preston. Delaney loved dropping in on sessions: "We've got this thing going while we're in London called swarming. We swarm in on recording sessions and take over! We did it to George the other night, and I think we should be on the next Beatles single."

A short tour of Germany was organized as a warm-up for the UK concerts. This gave the band several days to enter the studio. Having just signed a new deal with ATCO, the first thing that needed to be done was prepare a new single for the upcoming tour. The three tracks that had been recorded in August after the Blind Faith tour back in Los Angeles were brought over with Delaney and now needed to be finished. Trident was booked, and Eric and Dave Mason both provided some overdubs. A new alternate stripped-down version of "Coming Home" was also recorded but was left in the can in favor of the more familiar version. After a few days, the whole band moved across town to Barnes and Olympic Studios to record some numbers for Eric's solo album, which had already been given a title, *Eric Clapton Sings*. One of the first songs that Delaney and Eric worked on was "I Told You For The Last Time." They ran through several versions at Olympic Studios in Barnes with Delaney singing the lead as a guide for Eric. The idea was for Eric to overdub his lead vocal at a later date. Ultimately, they ran out of time and a new reworked version was cut in Los Angeles in January 1970. "Don't Know Why," a Delaney-and-Eric-penned song, was also recorded, this time with Eric handling the lead vocals. They played it on the tour as Eric's solo piece in the set, but he was so nervous about singing out front that he forgot some of the words at the first couple of shows in Germany.

Too much booze and drugs and general partying meant that the Olympic sessions were not particularly successful. Only one song, "Lovin' You Lovin' Me," survived to the final cut. It was decided to record the album in Los Angeles after the New Year in a more productive way.

The recently formed Ashton, Gardner and Dyke were hired to back PP Arnold for the tour. Also in the band was Steve Howe on guitar, who ended up joining Yes shortly after the tour. Ashton, Gardner and Dyke also got to do their own set on the tour, albeit two songs. They rehearsed at London's Revolution Club, situated off Berkeley Square in London's West End.

20 November 1969 BBC television appearance on *The Price Of Fame Or Fame At Any Price* (Delaney and Bonnie with Eric Clapton, Bobby Whitlock, and Dave Mason sitting on stools in a semicircle perform acoustic versions of "Poor Elijah—Tribute To Johnson" and "Will The Circle Be Unbroken." The whole show is in the BBC archive, and "Poor Elijah—Tribute To Johnson" has been shown several times in glorious color on *Later With Jools Holland* and various documentaries about Eric Clapton on the BBC)

DELANEY & BONNIE AND FRIENDS WITH ERIC CLAPTON, GERMAN TOUR 1969

BAND LINEUP FOR GERMAN TOUR:
Delaney Bramlett: guitar, vocals
Bonnie Bramlett: vocals
Eric Clapton: guitar, vocals
Bobby Whitlock: organ, vocals
Jim Gordon: drums
Carl Radle: bass
Jim Price: trumpet
Bobby Keys: saxophone
Rita Coolidge: vocals
Tex Johnson: percussion

26 November 1969, *Beat Club* television show, Radio Bremen Studios, Studio 3, Bremen, Germany. The show is broadcast on 29 November. Delaney & Bonnie and Friends play live versions of "Poor Elijah—Tribute To Johnson"

SETLIST: Poor Elijah—Tribute to Johnson / If There's A Will, There's A Way / Coming Home. "Coming Home" fades out over the show's credits after 53 seconds

26 November 1969, Musikhalle, Hamburg, Germany (with PP Arnold, Ashton, Gardner & Dyke)

27 November 1969, Jahrhunderthalle, Frankfurt, Germany (with PP Arnold, Ashton, Gardner & Dyke)

Setlist: Instrumental / Things Get Better / Love Me A Little Bit Longer / Do Right Woman, Do Right Man / Where There's A Will, There's A Way / I Don't Know Why / Pour Your Love On Me / Poor Elijah—Tribute To Johnson / I Don't Want To Discuss It

28 November 1969, Circus Krone, Munich, Germany (with PP Arnold, Ashton, Gardner & Dyke)

Ticket for Delaney & Bonnie and Friends with Eric Clapton at the Circus Krone in Munich, 28 November 1969.

Poster for Delaney & Bonnie and Friends with Eric Clapton at the Circus Krone in Munich, 28 November 1969. It is easy to see why German audiences expected to see Eric Clapton as headliner based on the posters for the tour.

DELANEY & BONNIE AND FRIENDS WITH ERIC CLAPTON—U.K. TOUR 1969

BAND LINEUP FOR UK TOUR:
Delaney Bramlett: guitar, vocals
Bonnie Bramlett: vocals
Eric Clapton: guitar, vocals
Bobby Whitlock: organ, vocals
Jim Gordon: drums
Carl Radle: bass
Jim Price: trumpet
Bobby Keys: saxophone
Rita Coolidge: vocals
Tex Johnson: percussion
Dave Mason: guitar, vocals (joins in for the Royal Albert Hall encores and the 2 Croydon shows only)
George Harrison: guitar (Birmingham, Sheffield, Liverpool, Croydon second show only)

1 December 1969, Royal Albert Hall, Kensington, London (1 show at 7:30 p.m. With Sue & Sunny, PP Arnold, Ashton, Gardner & Dyke)

SETLIST: Instrumental / Only You And I Know / Poor Elijah—Tribute To Johnson / Get Ourselves Together / I Don't Know Why / Where There's A Will, There's A Way / Pour Your Love On Me / Things Get Better / Coming Home / Don't Want To Discuss It / Little Richard Medley / Tutti Frutti / The Girls Can't Help It / Long Tall Sally / Jenny Jenny

29 November 1969, Sporthalle, Köln, Germany (with PP Arnold, Ashton, Gardner & Dyke. Delaney and Bonnie only manage to play a few numbers because the crowd started shouting abuse and throwing things at the band. They had been expecting an Eric Clapton concert, as the posters had suggested. After playing "Where There's A Will, There's A Way" an angry Delaney has had enough and shouts into the mic, "Enough! We'd rather not sing, so goodnight!" and walks off stage. A clearly embarrassed Eric Clapton comes to the mic and says "I was going to sing a song at this point, but I'm so nervous now, you know…I was going to sing a song, but…but, you've been so rude that I'm just too nervous to sing so I can't do it…ok. Sorry!" Somebody in the crowd then shouts out "Fuck off!" to which a now angry Clapton says, "Exactly! Yeah well, I feel the same way about all of you too!" And that was the end of the show. A sad ending to what should have been an enjoyable experience for everyone. Luckily, the forthcoming UK tour would prove to be a great success, not to mention a lot of fun.

SETLIST: Jeff Dexter introduction / Instrumental Jam (introduced on the night as "The Great Reading Newspaper Disaster") / Gimme Some Lovin' (Eric introduces Bobby Whitlock who handles the vocals on the Spencer Davis Group classic) / Only You Know And I Know / Medley: Poor Elijah—Tribute To Johnson / Get Ourselves Together / I Don't Know Why (Eric is on lead vocals) / Where There's A Will, There's A Way / That's What My Man Is For / Medley: Pour Your Love On Me / Just Plain Beautiful / Everybody Loves A Winner / Things Get Better / Coming Home / I Don't Want To Discuss It / Little Richard Medley: Tutti Frutti, The Girls Can't Help It, Long Tall Sally, Jenny Jenny / My Baby Specializes (Dave Mason joins in for the encores)

> "Dave Mason toured the States with us. After Eric, he is one of my favourite guitar players. He's a very different person now. When I first met him, he had a complex. He didn't know if he was any good. He may come and jam with us at the Albert Hall." —DELANEY BRAMLETT

The concert is available on Rhino Handmade's 4CD box set titled, *Delaney & Bonnie & Friends With Eric Clapton* Catalogue number RHM2 524797.

"We were really on our toes at the Albert Hall because at the show before in Cologne we got booed off the stage after only four numbers. At first we wondered why they'd bothered to come to the concert at all, but later realized their sole intention was to give us all a hard time. We figure they thought we were responsible for splitting up Blind Faith and were determined to take it out on us." —DELANEY BRAMLETT

"Yeah, they booed and whistled and stomped, and I thought to myself, 'Bonnie girl, you save that voice for tomorrow night' and walked off!" —BONNIE BRAMLETT

"Unfortunately, due to the acoustics in the hall, my appreciation of the music was impaired somewhat by the fact that the organ and bass tended to dominate, the voices were badly distorted and the guitar sounded distant. However, during the quieter organ-less moments, it became clear that they are a very tightly-knit group, who play a type of gospel, blue-eyed soul music, a progression of country rock and roll, and that they are a group which depends on the call-and-answer singing of Bonnie and her husband Delaney, and upon the fattening of the beat by the use of the saxophone and trumpet." —RAY CONNOLLY
(reviewing the Royal Albert Hall concert)

A luxury coach, which had a well-stocked fridge full of booze, had been hired for the UK tour. On the morning of 2 December, it picked up the whole band at Eric's home, Hurtwood Edge, before moving on to Allsop Place, round the corner from Baker Street in London, where they picked up Ashton, Gardner and Dyke. As soon as they boarded the coach, Eric greeted the band, introduced them to everyone, and offered them a drink from the fridge. Tony said, "Cheers, Derek!" As Tony says in his memoirs, "It was a combination of respect, nerves and a bit of cheek, also that he didn't look like an 'Eric,' that caused me to address him as such. Anyway, Eric laughed, and it stuck." From there they drove to Kinfauns, 16 Claremont Drive, Esher, Surrey, to pick up George Harrison, nicknamed Joe Comparison by the entourage. Yes, it was that kind of tour, where everyone got along and was ready for a laugh.

On the coach were Delaney and Bonnie Bramlett, Eric Clapton, George Harrison, Bobby Whitlock, Jim Gordon, Carl Radle, Rita Coolidge, Joe Tex, Bobby Keys, Jim Price, Tony Ashton, Kim Gardner, Roy Dyke, Pat Arnold, Steve Howe, Lesley Duncan, Kay Garner, Sue Glover, Sunny Leslie, Alan Pariser (D&B manager), Robin Turner (Eric's man), Jeff Dexter.

2 December 1969 Colston Hall, Bristol (2 shows tonight, 6:15 p.m. and 8:45 p.m.. With Sue & Sunny, PP Arnold, Ashton, Gardner & Dyke. George Harrison attends the show but does not play)

FIRST SHOW SETLIST: Jeff Dexter introduction / Instrumental Jam / band introductions / Only You Know And I Know / Things Get Better / I Don't Know Why / Where There's A Will There's A Way / Coming Home / I Don't Want To Discuss It

A short set due to the late arrival of the band. At the end of "I Don't Know Why," Delaney tells the audience that they had just recorded "Where There's A Will, There's A Way." After "I Don't Want To Discuss It," Jeff Dexter comes back on microphone and tries to encourage the audience to cheer louder for an encore. However, after numerous calls and complaints about the non-appearance of Beatle George Harrison, Dexter informs them that Harrison is not present and won't appear. The baying crowd refuse to leave the hall, and a somewhat exasperated house manager takes the mic away from Dexter and informs them that there will not be an encore because the show is running late. After they still refuse to cooperate he threatens to call the police if the first house does not vacate the premises to allow the second house in.

Parts of this concert are available on Rhino Handmade's 4CD box set titled *Delaney & Bonnie & Friends With Eric Clapton* catalogue number RHM2 524797.

SECOND SHOW SETLIST: Jeff Dexter introduction / Instrumental Jam / Gimme Some Lovin' / Things Get Better / Poor Elijah—Tribute To Johnson / I Don't Know Why / Pour Your Love On Me—Just Palin Beautiful / Where There's A Will, There's A Way / Little Richard Medley: Tutti Frutti, The Girls Can't Help It, Long Tall Sally, Jenny Jenny / I Don't Want To Discuss It / National Anthem / Manager of the hall closing comments

Parts of this concert are available on Rhino Handmade's 4CD box set titled: "Delaney & Bonnie & Friends With Eric Clapton" Catalogue number RHM2 524797.

3 December 1969 Town Hall, Birmingham (2 shows tonight, 6:15 p.m. and 8:45 p.m.. With Sue & Sunny, PP Arnold, Ashton Gardner & Dyke. George Harrison plays tonight)

4 December 1969 City Hall, Sheffield (2 shows tonight, 6.20p.m. and 8.50p.m. With Sue & Sunny, PP Arnold, Ashton Gardner & Dyke. George Harrison plays tonight)

Eric loved pranks, and there were plenty on this tour. As soon as they arrived in Sheffield both he and Delaney bought out a local toy shop's entire supply of wind-up Weebles (little wobbly egg-shaped figures) and water pistols. Halfway through the first song in Ashton, Gardner and Dyke's set, hundreds of these Weebles were let loose across the stage. On top of that they came under fire from all angles from water pistols. Tony Ashton raised his white towel as a surrender signal. Not sure the audience got it, but the whole crew found it hilarious.

5 December 1969 City Hall, Newcastle-upon-Tyne (2 shows tonight, 6:15 p.m. and 8:45 p.m.. With Sue & Sunny, PP Arnold, Ashton, Gardner & Dyke. George Harrison does not play tonight as he visits his mother who is unwell)

6 December 1969 Empire Theatre, Liverpool (2 shows tonight, 6.45p.m. and 9:00 p.m. With Sue & Sunny, PP Arnold, Ashton, Gardner & Dyke. George Harrison plays tonight)

Delaney & Bonnie and Friends at Croydon's Fairfield Halls during the late show, where their live album was recorded.

Delaney & Bonnie and Friends On Tour with Eric Clapton *album cover. Recorded largely at the Fairfield Halls in Croydon on 7 December 1969.*

Delaney & Bonnie and Friends at Croydon's Fairfield Halls during the late show, where their live album was recorded. L to R: Jim Price, Bobby Keys, Bonnie Bramlett, Delaney Bramlett, Eric Clapton.

Delaney & Bonnie and Friends at Croydon's Fairfield Halls during the late show, where their live album was recorded. L to R: Delaney Bramlett, Eric Clapton.

7 December 1969 Fairfield Halls, Croydon (2 shows tonight, 6:15 p.m. and 8.35p.m. With Sue & Sunny, PP Arnold, Ashton, Gardner & Dyke. George Harrison plays tonight at the second show only)

Delaney & Bonnie and Friends at Croydon's Fairfield Halls during the late show, where their live album was recorded. L to R: Bonnie Bramlett, Delaney Bramlett (with back to camera), Rita Coolidge, Eric Clapton, Jim Gordon, Carl Radle, George Harrison, Dave Mason.

FIRST SHOW: Gimme Some Lovin' / Things Get Better / Poor Elijah—Tribute To Johnson / I Don't Know Why / Where There's A Will, There's A Way / That's What My Man Is For / I Don't Want To Discuss It / Coming Home

The concert is available on Rhino Handmade's 4CD box set titled *Delaney & Bonnie & Friends With Eric Clapton* catalogue number RHM2 524797.

SECOND SHOW: Gimme Some Lovin' / Pigmy / Things Get Better / Poor Elijah—Tribute To Johnson / Only You Know And I / Will The Circle Be Unbroken / Where There's A Will, There's A Way / I Don't Know Why / That's What My Man Is For / Coming Home / Little Richard Medley: Tutti Frutti, The Girls Can't Help It, Long Tall Sally, Jenny Jenny

❝Having George is so fantastic. After the Albert Hall concert he was backstage and Bonnie asked why he didn't join us. 'OK,' he said, 'drop by my house in the morning.' So we did...took the bus out to his house, and there he was on the porch with his guitar and amplifier waiting to go!

George Harrison failed to make the first house at the Fairfield Hall show and when he showed up for the second, I jokingly said to him, 'You're docked ten dollars for not making the first house!'❞ **—DELANEY BRAMLETT**

The concert is available on Rhino Handmade's 4CD box set titled *Delaney & Bonnie & Friends With Eric Clapton.*

The original live album from the tour was called "Delaney & Bonnie & Friends On Tour With Eric Clapton." Although the concerts were great, the recordings were far from perfect and Delaney had to re-record some vocal and guitar parts back in Los Angeles before it could be considered fit for release.

DELANEY & BONNIE ON TOUR WITH ERIC CLAPTON ALBUM
ATCO 33-326
released June 1970

THINGS GET BETTER (Floyd / Cropper / Wayne) 2nd show, Fairfield Halls, Croydon 7 December 1969

Delaney Bramlett: guitar, vocals

Bonnie Bramlett: vocals
Eric Clapton: guitar, vocals
Bobby Whitlock: organ, vocals
Jim Gordon: drums
Carl Radle: bass
Jim Price: trumpet
Bobby Keys: saxophone
Rita Coolidge: vocals
Tex Johnson: percussion
Dave Mason: guitar
George Harrison: guitar

POOR ELIJAH (Delaney Bramlett / J. Ford)—**TRIBUTE TO JOHNSON** (Delaney Bramlett / Leon Russell) 2nd show, Fairfield Halls, Croydon, 7 December 1969

Delaney Bramlett: guitar, vocals
Bonnie Bramlett: vocals
Eric Clapton: guitar, vocals
Bobby Whitlock: organ, vocals
Jim Gordon: drums
Carl Radle: bass
Jim Price: trumpet
Bobby Keys: saxophone
Rita Coolidge: vocals
Tex Johnson: percussion
Dave Mason: guitar
George Harrison: guitar

ONLY YOU KNOW AND I KNOW (Dave Mason) 2nd show, Fairfield Halls, Croydon, 7 December 1969

Delaney Bramlett: guitar, vocals
Bonnie Bramlett: vocals
Eric Clapton: guitar, vocals
Bobby Whitlock: organ, vocals
Jim Gordon: drums

Carl Radle: bass
Jim Price: trumpet
Bobby Keys: saxophone
Rita Coolidge: vocals
Tex Johnson: percussion
Dave Mason: guitar
George Harrison: guitar

I DON'T WANT TO DISCUSS IT (Beatty / Cooper / Shelby) 2nd show
Colston Hall, Bristol, 2 December 1969

Delaney Bramlett: guitar, vocals
Bonnie Bramlett: vocals
Eric Clapton: guitar, vocals
Bobby Whitlock: organ, vocals
Jim Gordon: drums
Carl Radle: bass
Jim Price: trumpet
Bobby Keys: saxophone
Rita Coolidge: vocals
Tex Johnson: percussion

THAT'S WHAT MY MAN IS FOR (Bessie Griffin) 2nd show, Fairfield Halls,
Croydon, 7 December 1969

Delaney Bramlett: guitar, vocals
Bonnie Bramlett: vocals
Eric Clapton: guitar, vocals
Bobby Whitlock: organ, vocals
Jim Gordon: drums
Carl Radle: bass
Jim Price: trumpet
Bobby Keys: saxophone
Rita Coolidge: vocals
Tex Johnson: percussion
Dave Mason: guitar
George Harrison: guitar

WHERE THERE'S A WILL, THERE'S A WAY (Bobby Whitlock / Delaney
Bramlett) 1st show, Fairfield Halls, Croydon, 7 December 1969

Delaney Bramlett: guitar, vocals
Bonnie Bramlett: vocals
Eric Clapton: guitar, vocals
Bobby Whitlock: organ, vocals
Jim Gordon: drums
Carl Radle: bass
Jim Price: trumpet
Bobby Keys: saxophone
Rita Coolidge: vocals
Tex Johnson: percussion
Dave Mason: guitar

COMING HOME (Delaney Bramlett / Eric Clapton) 2nd show, Fairfield Halls,
Croydon, 7 December 1969

Delaney Bramlett: guitar, vocals
Bonnie Bramlett: vocals
Eric Clapton: guitar, vocals
Bobby Whitlock: organ, vocals
Jim Gordon: drums
Carl Radle: bass
Jim Price: trumpet
Bobby Keys: saxophone
Rita Coolidge: vocals
Tex Johnson: percussion
Dave Mason: guitar
George Harrison: guitar

LITTLE RICHARD MEDLEY—TUTTI FRUTTI (R. Penniman), **THE
GIRL CAN'T HELP IT** (R.W. Trout), **LONG TALL SALLY** (R. Penniman
/ R.A. Blackwell), **JENNY JENNY** (R. Penniman) 2nd show, Fairfield Halls,
Croydon, 7 December 1969

Delaney Bramlett: guitar, vocals
Bonnie Bramlett: vocals
Eric Clapton: guitar, vocals
Bobby Whitlock: organ, vocals
Jim Gordon: drums
Carl Radle: bass
Jim Price: trumpet
Bobby Keys: saxophone
Rita Coolidge: vocals
Tex Johnson: percussion
Dave Mason: guitar
George Harrison: guitar
Producers: Jimmy Miller, Delaney Bramlett
Engineers: Andy Johns, Glyn Johns

> "We have heard the rough versions and are very, very pleased. We had some incredible nights and Jimmy Miller, our record producer, has really captured the atmosphere." **—DELANEY BRAMLETT**

Recording live concerts in 1969 was a pretty primitive affair. As with the Blind Faith Hyde Park show, the Pye Records mobile recording lorry was again used. The equipment had to be pulled out and set up inside each hall to record the performances with a four-track mixer and a four-track mono mixer giving the engineer eight tracks. Not a lot when you have up to twelve people onstage. There are limitations in the recordings, such as a lack of punch in Jim Gordon's drumming, lead vocals occasionally lost in the mix due to bad mic positioning or bad connections, and guitars and horns sometimes sounding too bright and harsh. Even so, these shows are a joy to hear. Thank goodness Rhino had the good sense to spend some money to produce pretty much everything that was recorded on that short UK tour and issued everything in a gorgeous box in 2010. One criticism though is the placement of Eric Clapton's guitar on the left-hand side speaker. He was on the right-hand side of the stage. The raw unmixed tapes are fine, with Eric clear as anything ripping through the right-hand side speaker.

DELANEY & BONNIE AND FRIENDS WITH ERIC CLAPTON

SCANDINAVIAN TOUR 1969

BAND LINEUP FOR SCANDINAVIAN TOUR:
Delaney Bramlett: guitar, vocals
Bonnie Bramlett: vocals
Eric Clapton: guitar, vocals
Bobby Whitlock: organ, vocals
George Harrison: guitar
Jim Gordon: drums
Carl Radle: bass
Jim Price: trumpet
Bobby Keys: saxophone
Billy Preston: keyboards
Rita Coolidge: vocals

10 December 1969, Beat 69, Falkoner Centret, Copenhagen, Denmark (2 shows 19:00 & 21:00. Recorded by Danish television in black and white. Broadcast by DR-TV on 25 February 1970)

SETLIST FOR LATE SHOW: Poor Elijah—Tribute To Johnson / I Don't Know Why / Where There's A Will, There's A Way / Special Life / I Don't Want to Discuss It / That's What My Man Is For / Coming Home / Little Richard Medley: Tutti Frutti, The Girls Can't Help It, Long Tall Sally, Jenny Jenny

Tony Ashton in his memoirs recalls many of the pranks and competitions that took place on the tour. When the whole entourage were staying at the prestigious Palace Hotel in Copenhagen, they noticed that in the entrance of the lobby was a newspaper/magazine kiosk. Nothing strange in that, except that everybody was shocked to see explicit pornographic magazines on display which would normally have been under brown paper covers back in London's Soho. Robin Turner thought they should have a completion to see who could buy the dirtiest mag and bring it back to the bar later on. The winner would be given a prize, the unexpurgated works of Hans Christian Anderson. Delaney won and received a slap from Bonnie as his reward.

13 December 1969, Konserthuset, Stockholm, Sweden (2 shows 19:00 and 21:00)

14 December 1969, Konserthus, Gothenburg, Sweden (2 shows 19:00 and 21:00)

The end of the tour in Gothenburg signaled the usual end of tour madness. Back at the hotel a big party had been organized in the large dining room for the bands and entourage. There was plenty of food and drinks on all the tables, and before long the food was flying around the room, as were the drinks. The staff seemed remarkably calm as they supplied everyone with towels and more food and drink. Within thirty minutes, the room was wrecked. Of course the next morning, when it was time to settle the bill, a huge amount was added for redecoration. Tour manager Roger Forretser was there to pick up the pieces, as he would do for the next few decades.

15 December 1969, the Plastic Ono Band, "Peace For Christmas," Lyceum Ballroom, Wellington Street, London (with the Hot Chocolate Band, the Pioneers, the Rascals, Jimmy Cliff, Black Velvet. Emperor Rosko played music in between bands. The concert was organized to benefit UNICEF. Delaney & Bonnie and Friends arrived back at Eric's home in the late afternoon from London Airport and had all been invited to attend tonight's event. They were all pretty wasted after the Scandinavian tour, not to mention the late-night antics at the hotel the previous evening. Nonetheless, they were wildly excited at the prospect of playing with John Lennon this evening. Bobby Whitlock, on the other hand, was starting to get frustrated with the Bramletts' behavior and stayed at Eric's home alone. Transport arrived and took the whole ensemble off to the Lyceum)

SETLIST:

Cold Turkey (John Lennon) *Sometime In New York City* Live Jam bonus album Apple SVBB 3392 released June 1972 / *Sometime In New York City* CD Capitol Records 5099990650727 released 2010

John Lennon: guitar, vocals
George Harrison: guitar
Eric Clapton: guitar (playing George Harrison's psychedelic Fender Stratocaster)
Jim Gordon: drums
Alan White: drums
Klaus Voormann: bass
Jim Price: trumpet
Bobby Keys: saxophone
Billy Preston: electric piano (missing, new overdub by Nicky Hopkins)

> **❝**I remember quite well the very evening of everyone going to play the Lyceum with John Lennon. Everyone but me, that is. I was completely worn out with the out of control egomania that was going down with Delaney and Bonnie. It was difficult for me because I knew them as the real people that they were when we first started out, sans alcohol and drugs. It was just the three of us, then, it turned into something that no-one seemed to have any control over. It had become very exhausting to say the least. I asked Eric if it would be alright with him if I stayed behind at Hurtwood by myself. He told me to make myself at home while they were all gone. I wasn't that long from working in the fields chopping and picking cotton. And then when I was a little older, like fifteen, I was in the honky-tonks playing rock 'n' roll and rhythm 'n' blues in the South. Now here I was standing atop the mountain having the experience of my life at that time, very short life, when all of a sudden I could hear them all coming back. Only now they were louder and even more obnoxious. They were about to wreck my solitude and the fantasy that I was in the middle of. As it would turn out not that far down the line, I would be staying in that very room and calling Hurtwood Edge home for about a year. That's where we put together Derek and the Dominos. Hurtwood Edge.**❞**   **—BOBBY WHITLOCK**

Don't Worry Kyoko (Mummy's Only Looking For Her Hand In The Snow) (Yoko Ono) in edited form on *Sometime In New York City* Live Jam bonus album Apple SVBB 3392 released June 1972 / *Sometime In New York City* CD Capitol Records 5099990650727 released 2010

John Lennon: guitar, vocals
Yoko Ono: vocals
George Harrison: guitar
Eric Clapton: guitar (playing George Harrison's psychedelic Fender Stratocaster)
Jim Gordon: drums
Keith Moon: percussion
Alan White: drums
Klaus Voormann: bass
Jim Price: trumpet
Bobby Keys: saxophone
Billy Preston: electric piano (missing, new overdub by Nicky Hopkins)
Delaney Bramlett: guitar
Bonnie Bramlett: tambourine
Tony Ashton: tambourine
Producer: Geoff Emerick
Engineers: Peter Bown, John Kurlander

The Plastic Ono Band tracks were recorded on three reels of four-track tape. The tracks were mixed in stereo on 17 December 1969 by Geoff Emerick using the four-track master tapes as well a two-track audience tape. There were plans to release the show as an album in its own right, but eventually it was decided to release it in an edited form as a bonus side of an album with John and Yoko's *Sometime In New York City* release. The original version of "Don't Worry Kyoko (Mummy's Only Looking For Her Hand In The Snow)" lasted around forty minutes and was edited down to a fraction of that. For the *Sometime In New York City* release the tapes were remixed at Abbey Road on 26 November 1970, and a piano overdub by Nicky Hopkins replacing Billy Preston's missing track was made in New York in 1971.

The complete show was video-taped in black and white with audio by a friend of John's. The footage starts in one of the dressing rooms backstage. In it are John, George and Eric rehearsing "Cold Turkey" and, amazingly, "I Want You (She's So Heavy)." As Eric knew "Cold Turkey," they decided to play that instead of the less familiar "I Want You (She's So Heavy)."

When it's time to go on, the camera man follows the band onto the stage and films from the side before making his way down in front of the stage, where he is approached by security, who ask him if he has permission to film. Luckily, he does not stop filming while he explains he is doing this for John and the whole sixty minutes is captured on video. Neither the picture nor sound quality is good enough for a commercial release, and it is likely to remain in the archives.

> **❝**I thought it was fantastic. I was really into it. We were doing the show and George and Bonnie and Delaney, Billy Preston and all that crowd turned up. They'd just come back from Sweden and George had been playing invisible man in Bonnie and Delaney's band, which Eric Clapton had been doing, to get the pressure off being the famous Eric and the famous George. They became the guitarists in this and they all turned up, and it was again like the concert in Toronto. I said, 'Will you come on?' They said, 'Well, what are you going to play?' I said, 'Listen, we're going to do probably a blues…or Cold Turkey, which is three chords, and Eric knew that.' And Don't Worry Kyoko, which was Yoko's, which has three chords and a riff. I said, 'Once we get on to Yoko's riff, just keep hitting it.'**❞**   **—JOHN LENNON**
> (on the BBC)

> "I went down there in my Mini and went on stage at the Lyceum. Just prior to the Plastic Ono Band going on, Eric Clapton turns up with the whole Delaney & Bonnie band, so we had to hustle another couple of drum kits. Then, Keith Moon joins me on stage, playing my 16-inch tom-toms. It was a thing where somebody would hit one chord and it was a jam.
>
> While I thought Cold Turkey was good, the other number went on far too long and it began to sag. Jimmy Gordon, the other drummer from Delaney & Bonnie, and me began to speed up to bring it to an end. But we just got faster and faster and nobody wanted to stop. It was so fast that our muscles were aching. I was just about thinking, 'For Christ's sake, stop it,' when it just sort of finished." —ALAN WHITE

DELANEY & BONNIE AND FRIENDS WITH ERIC CLAPTON
USA TOUR 1970

BAND LINEUP FOR USA TOUR:
Delaney Bramlett: guitar, vocals
Bonnie Bramlett: vocals
Eric Clapton: guitar, vocals
Bobby Whitlock: organ, vocals
Jim Gordon: drums
Carl Radle: bass
Jim Price: trumpet
Bobby Keys: saxophone

2 February 1970, Massey Hall, Toronto, Ontario, Canada (Believed to have been canceled)

5 February 1970, Dick Cavett Show, ABC Studio TV-15, 202 W 58th Street, New York City

SETLIST: Introduction by Dick Cavett / Comin' Home / Interview by Dick Cavett / Poor Elijah—Tribute To Johnson / Where There's A Will, There's A Way (fade out)

6 February 1970, Fillmore East, New York City

SETLIST: Things Get Better / Poor Elijah—Tribute To Johnson / I Don't Know Why / Pour Your Love On Me / Rock And Roll Music / That's What My Man Is For / Will The Circle Be Unbroken / Where There's A Will There's A Way / Crossroads / Coming Home / Little Richard Medley: Tutti Frutti, The Girls Can't Help It, Long Tall Sally, Jenny Jenny

7 February 1970, Fillmore East, New York City

SETLIST: They Call It Rock And Roll Music / Lay My Burden Down / Living On The Open Road / Alone Together / The Love Of My Man / Pour Your Love On Me / Soul Shake / Hard Luck And Trouble / Only You Know And I Know / Coming Home / Where There's A Will, There's a Way / Little Richard Medley: Tutti Frutti, The Girls Can't Help It, Long Tall Sally, Jenny Jenny

8 February 1970, The Boston Tea Party, Boston, Massachusetts (2 shows 7:00 p.m. and 10:00 p.m. Joe Walsh and Peter Green jam with the band on a lengthy encore)

Poster for Delaney & Bonnie and Friends with Eric Clapton at the Boston Tea Party on 8 and 9 February 1970.

9 February 1970, The Boston Tea Party, Boston, Massachusetts (2 shows 7:00 p.m. and 10:00 p.m.)

11 February 1970, Electric Factory Theatre, Philadelphia, Pennsylvania (with BB King. 2 shows at 8:00 p.m. and 11:00 p.m. BB King joins Delaney & Bonnie at some point tonight)

12 February 1970, Symphony Hall, Minneapolis, Minnesota

13 February 1970, Ford Auditorium, Detroit, Michigan

14 February 1970, Auditorium Theatre, Chicago, Illinois

15 February 1970, Memorial Hall, Kansas City, Kansas

19 February 1970, Fillmore West, San Francisco, California (with NY Rock & Roll Ensemble, Golden Earring)

20 February 1970, Fillmore West, San Francisco, California (with NY Rock & Roll Ensemble, Golden Earring)

21 February 1970, Fillmore West, San Francisco, California (with NY Rock & Roll Ensemble, Golden Earring)

SETLIST: Things Get Better / They Call It Rock & Roll Music / Poor Elijah—Tribute To Johnson / I Don't Know Why / Only You Know And I Know / Pour Your Love Over Me—Just Plain Beautiful / Where There's A Will, There's A Way / Coming Home / Little Richard Medley: Tutti Frutti, The Girls Can't Help It, Long Tall Sally, Jenny Jenny / My Baby Specializes / Crossroads (with Jim Horn, John Simon) / Pygmy (with Jim Horn, John Simon) / When The Battle Is Over / They Call It Rock & Roll Music / Everybody Is A Winner / Gimme Some Lovin' / Where There's A Will, There's A Way / I Don't Want To Discuss It

22 February 1970, Fillmore West, San Francisco, California (with NY Rock & Roll Ensemble, Golden Earring)

SETLIST: Things Get Better / I Don't Know Why / Will The Circle Be Unbroken / Pour Your Love On Me / You Turned Out Beautiful / Where's There's A Will There's A Way / Crossroads / Special Life / Poor Elijah—Tribute To Johnson / Coming Home / Little Richard Medley: Tutti Frutti, The Girls Can't Help It, Long Tall Sally, Jenny Jenny

ERIC CLAPTON GUEST SESSION
ELEKTRA SOUND RECORDERS 962 La Cienega Blvd, Los Angeles, California Session with Delaney & Bonnie

27 AUGUST 1969

GROUPIE (SUPERSTAR) (Delaney Bramlett / Leon Russell) basic track

Delaney Bramlett: guitar, vocals
Bonnie Bramlett: vocals
Eric Clapton: guitar
Bobby Whitlock: keyboards
Carl Radle: bass
Jim Gordon: drums

ONLY YOU KNOW AND I KNOW (Dave Mason) alternate master

Delaney Bramlett: guitar, vocals
Bonnie Bramlett: vocals
Eric Clapton: guitar
Bobby Whitlock: keyboards
Carl Radle: bass
Jim Gordon: drums
Jim Price: trumpet
Bobby Keys: saxophone
Unknown: violin

COMING HOME (Delaney Bramlett / Eric Clapton) basic track

Delaney Bramlett: guitar, vocals
Bonnie Bramlett: vocals
Eric Clapton: guitar
Bobby Whitlock: keyboards
Carl Radle: bass
Jim Gordon: drums
Producer: Delaney Bramlett

> **"**We did three tracks with Eric Clapton at the end of the Blind Faith tour in Los Angeles. One of them will be also be released as a single.**"** —DELANEY BRAMLETT

TRIDENT STUDIOS Trident House, 17 St. Anne's Court, Soho, London W1 Session with Delaney & Bonnie

11 NOVEMBER 1969–12 NOVEMBER 1969

ONLY YOU KNOW AND I KNOW (Dave Mason) (Master) A-side 1971 ATCO 45-6838 / *Country Life* ATCO SD 33-383 (withdrawn) / *D & B Together* KC 31377

Delaney Bramlett: acoustic guitar, vocals
Bonnie Bramlett: vocals
Eric Clapton: guitar
Dave Mason: acoustic guitar
Bobby Whitlock: keyboards
Carl Radle: bass
Jim Gordon: drums
Jim Price: trumpet
Bobby Keys: saxophone
Rita Coolidge: vocals
Tex Johnson: percussion
Unknown: violin

COMING HOME (Delaney Bramlett / Eric Clapton) (backing track)

Delaney Bramlett: guitar, vocals
Eric Clapton: guitar
Dave Mason: guitar
Carl Radle: bass
Jim Gordon: drums
Tex Johnson: percussion

COMING HOME (Delaney Bramlett / Eric Clapton) (complete alternate version)

Delaney Bramlett: guitar, vocals
Eric Clapton: guitar
Dave Mason: guitar
Carl Radle: bass
Jim Gordon: drums
Tex Johnson: percussion

COMING HOME (Delaney Bramlett / Eric Clapton) (backing track)

Delaney Bramlett: guitar
Eric Clapton: guitar
Dave Mason: guitar
Carl Radle: bass
Jim Gordon: drums
Tex Johnson: percussion

COMING HOME (Delaney Bramlett / Eric Clapton) (backing track)

Delaney Bramlett: guitar
Eric Clapton: guitar, guitar solo
Carl Radle: bass
Jim Gordon: drums
Tex Johnson: percussion

COMING HOME (Delaney Bramlett / Eric Clapton) (master copy) A-side ATCO 45-6725 / *Crossroads* box set / *Country Life* ATCO SD 33-383 (withdrawn) / *D & B Together* KC 31377 / *Eric Clapton* Deluxe Edition Polydor B0006798-02 released May 2006

Delaney Bramlett: guitar, vocals
Bonnie Bramlett: vocals
Eric Clapton: guitar
Dave Mason: slide guitar
Bobby Whitlock: keyboards
Carl Radle: bass
Jim Gordon: drums
Jim Price: trumpet
Bobby Keys: saxophone
Rita Coolidge: vocals
Tex Johnson: percussion

GROUPIE (SUPERSTAR) (Delaney Bramlett / Leon Russell) (master copy) B-side ATCO 45-6725 / *Country Life* ATCO SD 33-383 (withdrawn) / *D & B Together* KC 31377 / *Eric Clapton* Deluxe Edition Polydor B0006798-02 released May 2006

Delaney Bramlett: guitar, vocals
Bonnie Bramlett: vocals
Eric Clapton: guitar
Bobby Whitlock: piano
Carl Radle: bass
Jim Gordon: drums
Jim Price: trumpet
Bobby Keys: saxophone
Rita Coolidge: vocals
Tex Johnson: percussion

Producer: Delaney Bramlett
Engineer: Robin Cable

Initial basic sessions for "Coming Home" and "Superstar (Groupie)" along with "Only You Know And I Know" were done at Elektra Sound Studios in late August 1969. These were recorded when they were still under contract with Elektra, but they were dropped shortly after by the label, who were only too happy to assign the tracks to ATCO, a division of Atlantic Records. The tapes were then brought over to England for overdubs. Sessions took place at Trident Studios, where both Eric Clapton and Dave Mason added their guitars. The main reason for the Trident session was to get a single out for their new label, ATCO, to coincide as closely as possible with

the German, UK, and Scandinavian tour. Atlantic later put all the various takes from the US and UK studios on a safety reel at Trident on 14 January 1970, which could be used for a future Delaney & Bonnie album, along with other previously unreleased material recorded between 1969 and 1971. "Coming Home," "Groupie (Superstar)," and "Only You Know And I Know" appeared on their early 1971 *Country Life* album. According to his autobiography, *Rhythm and the Blues*, Atlantic executive Jerry Wexler was dissatisfied with the album's quality. That, coupled with the fact that Delaney and Bonnie were splitting up, led him to decide to withdraw the album and sell their contract, along with the album's master tapes, to CBS. CBS released the album as *Together* in late 1972. Guest musicians on the album include Eric Clapton, Leon Russell, Duane Allman, Dave Mason, John Hartford, Billy Preston, Tina Turner, and Steve Cropper. It is a great album and worthy of reappraisal.

Delaney had been using Fender Champs, which had been souped up with Lansing speakers. Eric loved the sound, and Delaney gave one to both Eric and George Harrison. Eric would use it throughout the sessions in England, as well as in Los Angeles and beyond. They even used them onstage by using them as preamps on top of their regular amps.

OLYMPIC STUDIOS 117-123 Church Road, Barnes, London SW13 Session for Eric Clapton Solo Album

16 NOVEMBER 1969–25 NOVEMBER 1969

DON'T KNOW WHY (Delaney Bramlett / Eric Clapton) *Eric Clapton* Deluxe Edition Polydor B0006798-02 released May 2006
I'VE TOLD YOU FOR THE LAST TIME (Delaney Bramlett / Steve Cropper) (Delaney on lead vocals) *Eric Clapton* Deluxe Edition Polydor B0006798-02 released May 2006
SHE RIDES (Delaney Bramlett / Eric Clapton) *Eric Clapton* Deluxe Edition Polydor B0006798-02 released May 2006
LOVIN' YOU, LOVIN' ME (Delaney Bramlett / Eric Clapton) *Eric Clapton* Deluxe Edition Polydor B0006798-02 released May 2006
WHERE THERE'S A WILL, THERE'S A WAY (Instrumental version) (Bobby Whitlock / Delaney Bramlett) unreleased

Eric Clapton: guitar, vocals
Delaney Bramlett: guitar, vocals
Bonnie Bramlett: vocals
Bobby Whitlock: keyboards
Carl Radle: bass

"I'm producing Eric Clapton's solo album. Last Saturday (16 November) we recorded 'I've Told You For The Last Time' which has Eric singing. He will be doing some things which we wrote together and possibly a couple of traditional blues—but most of the album will be original material. We're in the studio again this week and have booked five days for next week." **—DELANEY BRAMLETT**
(November 1969)

"Delaney and I got together after the Blind Faith tour and wrote a few songs. I thought it would be a good idea to get them over here and suggested it to the Stigwood Organisation—and here they are. The type of music they play is very similar to mine.

At present, Delaney is producing an album for me where I both sing and play. Up to now I never thought of myself as a singer and never had the confidence to do much of it. A couple of songs with the Cream and Blind Faith were all, but Delaney said, 'If God gave you talent and you don't use it, he will take it away again.' So he inspired me toward trying it out. If the album is not too good, I probably won't do another, but I'll release this one for sure. I think I stand a good chance with them behind me on the production, because they have that magic touch-taste and feel. They are supreme.

Originally the album was going to consist of Buddy Holly songs, but we're saving that until later." **—ERIC CLAPTON**
(November 1969)

Jim Gordon: drums
Jim Price: trumpet
Bobby Keys: saxophone
Rita Coolidge: vocals
Tex Johnson: percussion

Producer: Delaney Bramlett
Engineer: Glyn Johns, Andy Johns

"Delaney and Bonnie's band played, and Ringo and Klaus Voormann were on it. George got them all in." **—BILLY PRESTON**

ERIC CLAPTON GUEST SESSION

OLYMPIC STUDIOS 117-123 Church Road, Barnes, London SW13 Session for Billy Preston

NOVEMBER 1969

Eric Clapton plays on three tracks on Billy Preston's second album for Apple, *Encouraging Words*. The album's title track originally had a working title of "Drop Out," and the album included the opening track "Right Now" and "Use What You Got."

"Use What You Got" was one of Billy's Capitol recordings that George Harrison wanted to slow down a little and add some overdubs. Eventually, he and Billy decided to record a new version at Olympic Studios with the help of Eric Clapton and his wah-wah pedal.

Steve Stills also drops by to add some guitar as he did for Doris Troy's solo album, although not on any of the tracks with Eric.

RIGHT NOW (Billy Preston) *Encouraging Words* album US Apple ST 3370 released 1970 / *Encouraging Words* CD Apple 5099990823923 released 2010

Billy Preston: vocals, keyboards
Eric Clapton: guitar
Ringo Starr: drums
Klaus Voormann: bass
George Harrison: guitar
Bobby Keys: sax
Jim Price: trumpet
Doris Troy: backing vocals

USE WHAT YOU GOT (Billy Preston) *Encouraging Words* album US Apple ST 3370 released 1970 / *Encouraging Words* CD Apple 5099990823923 released 2010

Billy Preston: vocals, keyboards
Eric Clapton: wah-wah guitar
Ringo Starr: drums
Klaus Voormann: bass
Bobby Keys: sax
Jim Price: trumpet
Doris Troy: backing vocals

ENCOURAGING WORDS (Billy Preston) *Encouraging Words* album US Apple ST 3370 released 1970 / *Encouraging Words* CD Apple 5099990823923 released 2010

Billy Preston: vocals, organ
Eric Clapton: guitar
Delaney Bramlett: guitar
Jim Gordon: drums
Carl Radle: bass
Bobby Keys: sax
Jim Price: trumpet

Producer: George Harrison
Engineer: Glyn Johns

ERIC CLAPTON
GUEST SESSION

TRIDENT STUDIOS
Trident House, 17 St. Anne's Court, Soho, London W1
Session for Vivian Stanshall and the Sean Head Showband

JANUARY 1970

LABIO-DENTAL FRICATIVE (Vivian Stanshall / Eric Clapton / Dennis Cowan / Remi Kabaka) single A-side Liberty Records US Liberty 56171, UK Liberty LBF 15309 released February 1970 / remixed on *The History Of The Bonzos* double album United Artists UAD 60071/2 released April 1974 / *The History Of The Bonzos* CD BGO Records BGOCD376 released December 1997

PAPER ROUND (Vivian Stanshall / Eric Clapton / Dennis Cowan / Remi Kabaka) single B-side Liberty Records US Liberty 56171, UK Liberty LBF 15309 released February 1970

Viv Stanshall: vocals
Eric Clapton: guitar
Dennis Cowan: bass
Remi Kabaka: percussion

Producer: Vivian Stanshall
Engineer: Barry Sheffield

> **❝**I shanghaied him [Eric]. I can't remember how it came about. Oh, I sent him some lyrics which he liked, so he came over. We recorded the number at about three in the morning.**❞**
> —**VIVIAN STANSHALL** (*Melody Maker*, February 1970)

ERIC CLAPTON
GUEST SESSION

SUNSET SOUND
6650 Sunset Boulevard, Los Angeles
Session for King Curtis

26 JANUARY 1970

TEASIN' (King Curtis / Delaney Bramlett) single A-side US ATCO 2091012, UK Atlantic K10464 released July 1970 / *Get Ready* album ATCO SD-33-338 released July 1970 / *History Of Eric Clapton* double album US ATCO SD 2-803, UK Polydor 2659 012 released July 1972 / *Eric Clapton* Deluxe Edition Polydor B0006798-02 released May 2006 / *Get Ready* CD Wounded Bird WOU 338 released June 2009

King Curtis: saxophone
Eric Clapton: lead guitar
Delaney Bramlett: acoustic guitar
Carl Radle: bass
Jim Gordon: drums

Producer: Delaney Bramlett
Engineer: Bill Halverson

Eric Clapton's first solo album cover.

VILLAGE RECORDERS
1616 Butler Avenue,
Los Angeles
Session for first
solo album

23 JANUARY 1970–31 JANUARY 1970

BLUES IN A (Eric Clapton) *Eric Clapton* "Blues" Bonus CD / *Eric Clapton* Deluxe Edition Polydor B0006798-02 released May 2006

Eric Clapton: guitar
Delaney Bramlett: guitar
Leon Russell: piano
Bobby Whitlock: keyboards
Carl Radle: bass
Jim Gordon: drums

SLUNKY (Delaney Bramlett / Eric Clapton) Delaney mix—*Eric Clapton* album US ATCO SD 33-329, UK Polydor 2383 021 released August 1970 / *Eric Clapton* Deluxe Edition Polydor B0006798-02 released May 2006

Eric Clapton: guitar
Delaney Bramlett: guitar
Bobby Whitlock: keyboards
Carl Radle: bass
Jim Gordon: drums
Jim Price: trumpet
Bobby Keys: saxophone

BAD BOY (Delaney Bramlett / Eric Clapton) Tom Dowd mix—*Eric Clapton* album US ATCO SD 33-329, UK Polydor 2383 021 released August 1970 / *Eric Clapton* Deluxe Edition Polydor B0006798-02 released May 2006

Eric Clapton: guitar, vocals
Delaney Bramlett: guitar
Bonnie Bramlett: tambourine
Leon Russell: piano
Bobby Whitlock: keyboards
Carl Radle: bass
Jim Gordon: drums
Jim Price: trumpet
Bobby Keys: saxophone

LONESOME AND A LONG WAY FROM HOME (Delaney Bramlett / Leon Russell) Tom Dowd mix—*Eric Clapton* album US ATCO SD 33-329, UK Polydor 2383 021 released August 1970 / *Eric Clapton* Deluxe Edition Polydor B0006798-02 released May 2006

Eric Clapton: guitar, vocals
Delaney Bramlett: guitar, vocals
Bonnie Bramlett: vocals
Leon Russell: piano
Bobby Whitlock: keyboards
Carl Radle: bass
Jim Gordon: drums
Jim Price: trumpet
Bobby Keys: saxophone
Rita Coolidge: vocals
Sonny Curtis: vocals
Jerry Allison: vocals

AFTER MIDNIGHT (JJ Cale) Tom Dowd mix—*Eric Clapton* album US ATCO SD 33-329, UK Polydor 2383 021 released August 1970 / *Eric Clapton* Deluxe Edition Polydor B0006798-02 released May 2006

Eric Clapton: guitar, vocals

Delaney Bramlett: guitar, vocals
Bonnie Bramlett: vocals
Leon Russell: piano
Bobby Whitlock: organ
Carl Radle: bass
Jim Gordon: drums
Rita Coolidge: vocals
Sonny Curtis: vocals
Jerry Allison: vocals

AFTER MIDNIGHT (JJ Cale) Delaney mix with horns—*Eric Clapton* Deluxe Edition Polydor B0006798-02 released May 2006

Eric Clapton: guitar, vocals
Delaney Bramlett: guitar, vocals
Bonnie Bramlett: vocals
Leon Russell: piano
Bobby Whitlock: organ
Carl Radle: bass
Jim Gordon: drums
Jim Price: trumpet
Bobby Keys: saxophone
Rita Coolidge: vocals
Sonny Curtis: vocals
Jerry Allison: vocals

BLUES POWER (Leon Russell / Eric Clapton) Tom Dowd mix—*Eric Clapton* album US ATCO SD 33-329, UK Polydor 2383 021 released August 1970 / *Eric Clapton* Deluxe Edition Polydor B0006798-02 released May 2006

Eric Clapton: guitar, vocals
Delaney Bramlett: guitar
Bonnie Bramlett: vocals (in the fadeout)
Leon Russell: piano
Bobby Whitlock: organ
Carl Radle: bass
Jim Gordon: drums
Jim Price: trumpet
Bobby Keys: saxophone
Rita Coolidge: vocals (in the fadeout)
Sonny Curtis: vocals (in the fadeout)
Jerry Allison: vocals (in the fadeout)

BOTTLE OF RED WINE (Delaney Bramlett / Eric Clapton) Tom Dowd mix—*Eric Clapton* album US ATCO SD 33-329, UK Polydor 2383 021 released August 1970 / *Eric Clapton* Deluxe Edition Polydor B0006798-02 released May 2006

Eric Clapton: guitar, vocals
Delaney Bramlett: guitar, vocals
Bonnie Bramlett: vocals
Bobby Whitlock: organ
Carl Radle: bass
Jim Gordon: drums

Back cover showing all the musicians who played on Eric Clapton's first solo album.

LOVIN' YOU, LOVIN' ME (Delaney Bramlett / Eric Clapton) Tom Dowd mix—*Eric Clapton* album US ATCO SD 33-329, UK Polydor 2383 021 released August 1970 / *Eric Clapton* Deluxe Edition Polydor B0006798-02 released May 2006

Eric Clapton: guitar, vocals
Delaney Bramlett: guitar, vocals
Bonnie Bramlett: vocals
Leon Russell: piano
Bobby Whitlock: organ
Carl Radle: bass
Jim Gordon: drums
Jim Price: trumpet
Bobby Keys: saxophone
Rita Coolidge: vocals

I'VE TOLD YOU FOR THE LAST TIME (Delaney Bramlett / Steve Cropper) Tom Dowd mix—*Eric Clapton* album US ATCO SD 33-329, UK Polydor 2383 021 released August 1970 / *Eric Clapton* Deluxe Edition Polydor B0006798-02 released May 2006

Eric Clapton: guitar, vocals
Delaney Bramlett: guitar, vocals
Bonnie Bramlett: vocals
Leon Russell: piano
Bobby Whitlock: organ
Carl Radle: bass
Bobby Keys: saxophone
Rita Coolidge: vocals
Sonny Curtis: vocals
Jerry Allison: vocals

DON'T KNOW WHY (Delaney Bramlett / Eric Clapton) mix—*Eric Clapton* album US ATCO SD 33-329, UK Polydor 2383 021 released August 1970 / *Eric Clapton* Deluxe Edition Polydor B0006798-02 released May 2006

Eric Clapton: guitar, vocals
Delaney Bramlett: guitar, vocals
Bonnie Bramlett: vocals
Leon Russell: piano
Bobby Whitlock: organ
Carl Radle: bass
Jim Gordon: drums
Jim Price: trumpet
Bobby Keys: saxophone
Rita Coolidge: vocals
Sonny Curtis: vocals
Jerry Allison: vocals

LET IT RAIN (Delaney Bramlett / Eric Clapton) basic track

Eric Clapton: guitar, vocals
Delaney Bramlett: guitar, vocals
Bonnie Bramlett: vocals
Leon Russell: piano
Bobby Whitlock: organ
Carl Radle: bass
Jim Gordon: drums
Jim Price: trumpet
Bobby Keys: saxophone
Rita Coolidge: vocals
Sonny Curtis: vocals
Jerry Allison: vocals

VILLAGE RECORDERS
1616 Butler Avenue,
Los Angeles
Session for the Crickets

JANUARY 1970

ROCKIN' 50'S ROCK 'N' ROLL (J. Allison, B. Curtis, D. Gilmore) *Rockin' 50's Rock 'N' Roll* album US Barnaby Records Z 30268, UK CBS 64301 released February 1971 / *Rockin'* CD Varese Saraband 302 066 147 2 released 2000

THAT'LL BE THE DAY (Buddy Holly / Jerry Allison) *Rockin' 50's Rock 'N' Roll* album US Barnaby Records Z 30268, UK CBS 64301 released February 1971 / *Rockin'* CD Varese Saraband 302 066 147 2 released 2000

Sonny Curtis: vocals
Jerry Allison: vocals
Eric Clapton: guitar
Delaney Bramlett: guitar, vocals
Leon Russell: piano
Bobby Whitlock: organ
Carl Radle: bass
Jim Gordon: drums
Jim Price: trumpet
Bobby Keys: saxophone

Producer: Delaney Bramlett
Engineer: Richie Moore

These may well have been the start of the Buddy Holly sessions that were talked about in England back in November 1969. The plan was to do a whole album of Buddy Holly covers after Eric's solo album was finished. In any event, time ran out as the band had to go on tour and the idea was never followed up. In the meantime, these two tracks ended up on a new album by the Crickets covering Buddy Holly songs.

ISLAND STUDIOS
8-10 Basing Street,
London W11

MARCH 1970

Eric mixes his solo album at Island Studios. Steve Stills is recording his first solo album at the same studios and Eric plays on "Go Back Home" and "Fishes And Scorpions." Stills in turn overdubs some backing vocals and a guitar break on "Let It Rain." "Easy Now," a new song by Eric, is also recorded for inclusion on his album.

EASY NOW (Eric Clapton) Eric Clapton mix—*Eric Clapton* album US ATCO SD 33-329, UK Polydor 2383 021 released August 1970 / *Eric Clapton* Deluxe Edition Polydor B0006798-02 released May 2006

Eric Clapton: acoustic guitar, vocals

LET IT RAIN (Eric Clapton) (master with Steve Stills guitar and vocal overdubs) Tom Dowd mix—*Eric Clapton* album US ATCO SD 33-329, UK Polydor 2383 021 released August 1970 / *Eric Clapton* Deluxe Edition Polydor B0006798-02 released May 2006

Eric Clapton: guitar, vocals
Delaney Bramlett: guitar, vocals
Bonnie Bramlett: vocals
Leon Russell: piano
Bobby Whitlock: organ
Carl Radle: bass
Jim Gordon: drums
Jim Price: Trumpet
Bobby Keys: saxophone
Rita Coolidge: vocals
Stephen Stills: overdub vocals and melodic middle short fill electric guitar solo
Sonny Curtis: vocals
Jerry Allison: vocals

Eric's first solo album had three different mixes made. One by Delaney Bramlett, another by Eric, and a final one by Tom Dowd. On top of that, there were a multitude of songs with longer and shorter fades, alternate vocals, guitars, and horns. Two of the mixes are now available on the Deluxe Edition of *Eric Clapton*, the original Tom Dowd mix and the previously unheard Delaney mix. Eric's mix has long been available on bootlegs, so people can now debate at length which is the best version.

From a commercial view, Tom's is the best suited for that purpose, with a slicker sound. Delaney's has an earthier feel with a more prominent horn sound, and Eric's has more of a "you are in the studio with him" feel.

This album marked a complete reinvention for Eric. His newfound confidence in his singing abilities meant he could have a solo career as a band leader should he choose that route. Eric is the first to admit that Delaney gave him the confidence to sing and will always be grateful to him for that. One of the first songs they were to record was JJ Cale's "After Midnight," from an old Liberty single that had been released in 1966. Delaney recorded his vocal first, giving a guide for Eric to follow. When listening to the Delaney vocal version, it is easy to see that Eric was an excellent pupil, following Delaney's nuances perfectly. After this, he would no longer need any guidance.

The sessions themselves happened pretty quickly, and Delaney was extremely well organized. The sessions only lasted a couple of weeks, and all that needed to be done was the mixing with some overdubs. The tapes were left at the studio while Delaney & Bonnie and Friends hit the road for a US tour starting at the

Fillmore East in New York. During the tour, relations within the band started to fall apart. The whole band had had enough of Delaney's drunken outbursts, and questions were being asked about the amount of money being earned. On top of that, Eric was starting to feel pressured into a long-term arrangement with Delaney & Bonnie. He recalled,

> **"**At some point on the tour, I started to realize that, much as I loved them and wanted to continue to enjoy playing with them, I was once again enmeshed in a sticky situation. I felt they were becoming dependent on me for continued exposure, amongst other things; but when I first intimated that I might want to move on, or quit, I got a very stony reception. Delaney became very possessive and kept talking about what we were going to do together in the future. He embellished the relationship with a brotherhood and permanence that I really couldn't see in it myself...I just enjoyed hanging out with them. Then he and Bonnie set up a kind of triangle situation. She'd say, 'Oh, you have no idea how much Delaney loves you. If you leave him, I don't know what will happen to him.' And he'd say, 'Bonnie's a great singer but we need you Eric.' They were building up the pressure to the nth degree, and it got very claustrophobic.**"**

Ben Palmer, Eric's friend, and assistant at the time, decided to resign before the US tour because he could not see that he would be able to pull off what would be necessary to keep Delaney & Bonnie and their manager happy. Understandably, he did not need that kind of pressure, and he came back to England. He knew Eric would be all right with the band, who he recalled were very friendly, especially Carl Radle. By the end of the tour, the whole band, less Bobby Whitlock, were already plotting to leave and join Leon Russell for Joe Cocker's "Mad Dogs And Englishmen" tour. Eric's last show with them was at the Fillmore West on 22 February. He returned to Los Angeles with Delaney & Bonnie on 23 February for a week to record some overdubs for his solo album.

While Delaney & Bonnie resumed their tour without him, Eric flew home on 1 March 1970, leaving Delaney with the task of finishing the mix. What happened next is a little blurry, but by the end of March, the tapes had not shown up in England. Eric takes up the story:

> ""I left the tapes in LA for Delaney to mix them, and he was waiting on me to finish one of the tracks! And he didn't realize that I was waiting on him to mix the tracks and send them over. Finally, my manager got kind of impatient and told Atlantic to send the tapes to me, and I mixed them very badly. Atlantic heard them, didn't like them. Then they sent them to Tom Dowd, who mixed them again. So they were mixed three times in all. Naturally, I never heard Delaney's mixes until it was too late–the record was already out.""

As the Delaney mix is missing "I Told You For The Last Time," I have to assume that was the number that he was waiting on Eric to finish. Either way, the mix chosen for public release was Tom Dowd's, although a few ATCO albums did slip out with Eric's mix and are now quite collectable.

DELANEY BRAMLETT MIX

Slunky 3.33 (the three beats of repeated backward tape found on the Clapton mix are not here. Delaney's mix has a sax solo during the first half of the song). Other than that, the differences on the other tracks are largely timings, which vary in length

ERIC CLAPTON MIX

SLUNKY 3.33 (starts with what sounds like three beats of repeated backward tape before launching into the jam)
BAD BOY 4.20 (more prominent horns and piano)
LONESOME AND A LONG WAY FROM HOME 3.57 (there is a count off before the number starts, reverb on the lead vocals, and a longer fade at the end of the song)
AFTER MIDNIGHT 3.21 (studio chatter before the song, reverb on the vocals, additional guitar fills, and a generally punchier feel to the other two versions)
EASY NOW 2.58 (Eric's mix is the only one made)
BLUES POWER 3.51 (the tape starts with twenty-nine seconds of instrument noodling before Leon Russell's piano intro. Eric has again put some reverb on his vocals and his guitar seems to be a little more prominent than the other mixes)
BOTTLE OF RED WINE 2.57 (guitar sounds like it is slightly more prominent. Surprisingly, the track ends with the rhythm guitar and drums, rather than the lead noodling on the more familiar mixes)
LOVIN' YOU LOVIN' ME 3.43 (just sounds like a muddier mix. Not a lot of difference other than that, really)
I'VE TOLD YOU FOR THE LAST TIME 2.30 (again, just a little more lo-fi than the other mixes)
DON'T KNOW WHY 3.36 (opens with the tail end of a count off. Can't hear anything particularly different other than that)

LET IT RAIN 5.16 (starts with some tuning. Eric again went for reverb on the vocals and the song is much better for it. Dowd should have kept this mix)

> ""Some of the songs were made up in the studio. We did all the tracks in a week"" —ERIC CLAPTON
> (*NME,* 15 August 1970)

ERIC CLAPTON GUEST SESSION
ISLAND STUDIOS
8-10 Basing Street, London W11
Session for Steve Stills

MARCH 1970

GO BACK HOME (Stephen Stills) *Stephen Stills* album US Atlantic SD7202, UK Atlantic 2401004 released November 1970 / *Stephen Stills* CD Atlantic 82809-2 released December 1995

Stephen Stills: vocals, keyboard, guitar
Eric Clapton: second lead guitar
Calvin Samuels: bass
Dallas Taylor: drums
John Barbata: drums
Rita Coolidge: backing vocals
Priscilla Jones: backing vocals
Claudia Lanier: backing vocals
John Sebastian: backing vocals
Cass Elliot: backing vocals
David Crosby: backing vocals

> ""'Go Back Home' was done first take. Actually, that's Eric just warming up. You know, he said, 'Let me practise a little' and Bill (Halverson, co-producer and engineer) would say 'sure'—click! And he'd take it. That's Eric Clapton warming up folks."" —STEPHEN STILLS

FISHES AND SCORPIONS (Stephen Stills) *Stephen Stills 2* album US Atlantic SD7206, UK Atlantic 2401013 released July 1971 / *Stephen Stills* CD Atlantic 7206-2 released December 1995

Stephen Stills: vocals, acoustic guitars
Eric Clapton: guitar
Calvin Samuels: bass
Dallas Taylor: drums

Producers: Stephen Stills and Bill Halverson
Engineer: Bill Halverson

ERIC CLAPTON
GUEST SESSION

DE LANE LEA SOUND CENTRE
75 Dean Street, London, W1
Session for Ashton, Gardner & Dyke

MARCH 1970

I'M YOUR SPIRITUAL BREADMAN (Tony Ashton) *The Worst Of Ashton, Gardner & Dyke* album Capitol EST 563. released 1971 / *The Worst Of Ashton, Gardner & Dyke* CD Repertoire REP 4458-WY released in 1994

Tony Ashton: keyboards, vocals
Roy Dyke: drums
Kim Gardner: bass
Eric Clapton: guitar
George Harrison: guitar
Phil and His Boogie Brass: horns

Producer: Ashton, Gardner & Dyke
Engineer: John Stewart

ERIC CLAPTON
GUEST SESSION

IBC STUDIOS
Studio A, 35 Portland Place, London W1
Session for Jonathan Kelly

MARCH 1970

DON'T YOU BELIEVE IT (Jonathan Kelly) A-side single Parlophone R 5851 / *Jonathan Kelly* album Parlophone PCS 7114 released November 1970 / *Jonathan Kelly* CD ASKCD-152 released 2005 (Japan only)

> **"** Eric Clapton played slide on 'Don't You Believe It.' Colin Petersen (ex-drummer with the Bee Gees) used to work for Robert Stigwood and I guess he met the Cream guys when he was in the office, and asked Eric if he'd come and play on a twelve-bar, and he just turned up, which blew my mind. He listened to the backing tracks and bang, just played it. **"**
> —**JONATHAN KELLY**

Jonathan Kelly: guitar, vocals
Eric Clapton: slide guitar
Tony Ashton: piano
Kim Gardner: bass
Roy Dyke: drums
Madeline Bell: backing vocals

Lesley Duncan: backing vocals
Producer: Colin Petersen
Engineer: Andy Knight

ERIC CLAPTON
GUEST SESSION

OLYMPIC STUDIOS
117-123 Church Road, Barnes, London SW13
Session for Jesse Ed Davis

15 APRIL 1970–17 APRIL 1970

RENO STREET INCIDENT (Jesse Davis) *Jesse Davis* album US ATCO SD 33-346 released 1970, UK Atlantic 2400106 released April 1971 / *Jesse Davis* CD Wounded Bird WOU-346 released November 2004

Jesse Ed Davis: vocals, guitar
Eric Clapton: guitar
Alan White: drums
Steve Thompson: bass
John Simon: piano

WASHITA LOVE CHILD (Jesse Davis) *Jesse Davis* album US ATCO SD 33-346 released 1970, UK Atlantic 2400106 released April 1971 / *Jesse Davis* CD Wounded Bird WOU-346 released November 2004

Jesse Ed Davis: vocals, guitar
Eric Clapton: guitar
Bruce Rowland: drums
Jackie Lomax: percussion
Steve Thompson: bass
Merry Clayton: backing vocals
Vanetta Fields: backing vocals
Gloria Jones: backing vocals
Clydie King: backing vocals
James Gordon: horns
Jerry Jumonville: horns
Darrell Leonard: horns
Frank Mayes: horns

EVERY NIGHT IS SATURDAY NIGHT (Jesse Davis) (take 15 is taken as the master) *Jesse Davis* album US ATCO SD 33-346 released 1970, UK Atlantic 2400106 released April 1971 / *Jesse Davis* CD Wounded Bird WOU-346 released November 2004

Jesse Ed Davis: vocals, guitar
Eric Clapton: guitar
Bruce Rowland: drums
Jackie Lomax: percussion
Steve Thompson: bass
James Gordon: horns
Jerry Jumonville: horns
Darrell Leonard: horns
Frank Mayes: horns

YOU BELLADONNA YOU (Jesse Davis) *Jesse Davis* album US ATCO SD 33-346 released 1970, UK Atlantic 2400106 released April 1971 / *Jesse Davis* CD Wounded Bird WOU-346 released November 2004

Jesse Ed Davis: vocals, guitar
Eric Clapton: guitar

Alan White: drums
Jackie Lomax: percussion
Steve Thompson: bass
Leon Russell: piano
Merry Clayton: backing vocals
Vanetta Fields: backing vocals
Gloria Jones: backing vocals
Clydie King: backing vocals

ROCK N ROLL GYPSIES (Roger Tillison) *Jesse Davis* album US ATCO SD 33-346 released 1970, UK Atlantic 2400106 released April 1971 / *Jesse Davis* CD Wounded Bird WOU-346 released November 2004

Jesse Ed Davis: vocals, guitar
Eric Clapton: guitar
Bruce Rowland: drums
Jackie Lomax: percussion
Steve Thompson: bass
Ben Sidran: organ
Merry Clayton: backing vocals
Vanetta Fields: backing vocals
Gloria Jones: backing vocals
Clydie King: backing vocals

Producer: Jesse Ed Davis
Engineer: Glyn Johns

MAY 1970

5 May 1970, Student Union, St Catherine's College, Oxford University (Eric Clapton jams with Traffic on a few numbers. This is the review from Cherwell, an independent student weekly at the University of Oxford: "The night before I had been listening to Winwood singing and playing with the newly re-formed Traffic at St. Catz. He has progressed and relaxed over the years. His early recordings with Spencer Davis were like "Georgia," full of Negro soul, dedicated almost to the spirit of Ray Charles. After his work with Traffic Mk.1 and Blind Faith, he is a greater artist than ever. Parts of Tuesday's concert were very beautiful indeed. Later in the evening that gentle skinhead, Eric Clapton, came on stage and strummed along with the last few numbers. (Unknown author, published in the "Arts"

> **"**I went to see them in Oxford and I got to jam with them. It was just Steve, Jim (Capaldi) and Chris (Wood). And I liked the sound of it. I didn't think that they were any better with me playing with them, but I felt that they needed another instrument. I still think they do. I was hoping after that gig that I would be asked to join the group. If I had been, I would have joined. Just like that. But I wasn't asked, so it didn't happen.**"**
> —**ERIC CLAPTON**
> (*Melody Maker*, July 1970)

section of the Cherwell, May 13, 1970; The reason the reviewer mentions Eric as a skinhead is because he had recently had his hair cut very short)"

MAY 1970

Sometime during the Delaney & Bonnie US tour in 1970, Norman Dayron from Chess Records had spoken to Eric about the possibility of getting Howlin' Wolf over to London and recording an album in England. He asked Eric if he would be interested in playing on the album as well as getting some guys together who knew about the blues. Eric jumped at the chance and recommended Olympic Studios in Barnes as a comfortable place to record close to central London. He also suggested getting Glyn Johns in as engineer, as Glyn was very familiar with Olympic Studios.

The first session took place on 2 May, and Howlin' Wolf, along with Hubert Sumlin and Jeffrey M. Carp were backed by Eric Clapton on lead guitar, Ringo Starr on drums, and Klaus Voormann on bass on a trio of numbers. Wolf was not in the best of moods and could get quite agitated if he did not like something. So you have an old guy who is unwell, suffering with jetlag, and, as far as he's concerned, has a bunch of inexperienced white guys who are playing poorly. Ringo and Klaus did not take his abuse and rudeness well and did not come back to any other sessions. Wolf got physical with Eric, violently grabbing his wrist in an attempt to show him how he should be playing guitar on a particular number. Not surprisingly, this unnerved Eric, who was quite shaken up and really did not know if he would return to the sessions, either.

Eric realized that ultimately it was the music that was important, and sessions resumed a few days later. Charlie Watts and Bill Wyman replaced Ringo and Klaus, and eventually Wolf was won over. The sessions were not without incident, though. One night after the sessions had finished and the taxis had lined up outside the studios to take the band back to the Cumberland Hotel at Marble Arch, nobody could find Wolf. Norman panicked. Wolf had a heart condition, and he thought that he might have wandered off to buy some booze and got lost. After thirty minutes of pounding the streets with no luck, Norman went back into the studio and eventually found Wolf passed out in one of the toilet stalls. Norman called for an ambulance, and Wolf was taken to hospital for tests. Luckily, he had not suffered a heart attack. Norman was relieved, as he had feared he would be remembered as the man who killed Howlin' Wolf.

Norman was quite dictatorial in his production manner, something that the fragile egos of some of the musicians present did not take kindly to. Ultimately, he was only trying to fulfill his vision and was not familiar with the English sense of humor and irony. Mick Jagger in particular did not originally warm to Norman until the two of them had a pissing contest in the studio in front of everyone. As much as I would love to tell you what happened, libel laws prevent me from revealing the conversation. Suffice to say, the air was cleared and Norman and Mick became buddies. Although Mick is not credited, he did play various percussion instruments throughout the sessions.

In a break in the sessions everyone was invited to Eric's home, where Hubert Sumlin admired Eric's guitar collection. Eric gave him a guitar as a gift to say thank you for being such an influence on him in the early days.

An interesting companion to the original *The London Howlin' Wolf Sessions* album is Charly's CD titled *Howlin' Wolf London Re-visited*. Catalogue number CD BM46, released in 1993, it contains twelve original tracks from the sessions before any overdubs were added in America: 1. Killing Floor, 2. Going Down Slow, 3. I Want To Have A Word With You, 4. Who's Been Talking, 5. Little Red Rooster, 6. Built For Comfort, 7. What A Woman, 8. Do The Do, 9. Highway 49, 10. Worried About My Baby, 11. Poor Boy, 12. Wang Dang Doodle.

L to R: Ian Stewart, Eric Clapton, Mick Jagger, Howlin Wolf, Jeffrey Carp, and Charlie Watts recording The London Howlin' Wolf Sessions.

Eric Clapton in the studio recording with Howlin' Wolf, Mick Jagger, and Charlie Watts.

OLYMPIC STUDIOS 117-123 Church Road, Barnes, London SW13 Session for Howlin' Wolf's *London Sessions*

2 MAY 1970

I AIN'T SUPERSTITIOUS (Willie Dixon) *The London Howlin' Wolf Sessions* album US Chess CH60008, UK Rolling Stones Records COC 49101 released August 1971 / *The London Howlin' Wolf Sessions* Deluxe Edition Chess 088 112 985-2 released March 2003

Howlin Wolf: vocal
Hubert Sumlin: rhythm guitar
Eric Clapton: lead guitar
Steve Winwood: piano
Klaus Voormann: bass
Ringo Starr: drums
Jordan Sandke: trumpet
Dennis Lansing: tenor saxophone
Joe Miller: baritone saxophone
Bill Wyman: cowbell

I AIN'T SUPERSTITIOUS (Willie Dixon) (alternate mix) *The London Howlin' Wolf Sessions* Deluxe Edition Chess 088 112 985-2 released March 2003

Howlin Wolf: vocal
Hubert Sumlin: rhythm guitar
Eric Clapton: lead guitar
Steve Winwood: piano
Klaus Voormann: bass
Ringo Starr: drums
Jordan Sandke: trumpet
Dennis Lansing: tenor saxophone
Joe Miller: baritone saxophone
Bill Wyman: cowbell

I AIN'T SUPERSTITIOUS (Willie Dixon) (alternate take) *The London Howlin' Wolf Sessions* Deluxe Edition Chess 088 112 985-2 released March 2003

Howlin Wolf: vocal
Hubert Sumlin: rhythm guitar
Jeffrey M. Carp: harmonica

Eric Clapton: lead guitar
Ian Stewart: piano
Klaus Voormann: bass
Ringo Starr: drums

GOING DOWN SLOW (James B. Oden) *London Revisited* Chess CH60026 released February 1974 / *The London Howlin' Wolf Sessions* Deluxe Edition Chess 088 112 985-2 released March 2003

Howlin' Wolf: vocal
Eric Clapton: lead guitar
Klaus Voormann: bass
Ringo Starr: drums

I WANT TO HAVE A WORD WITH YOU (Chester Burnett) *London Revisited* Chess CH60026 released February 1974 / *The London Howlin' Wolf Sessions* Deluxe Edition Chess 088 112 985-2 released March 2003
Howlin' Wolf: vocals

Hubert Sumlin: guitar
Eric Clapton: guitar
Ringo Starr: drums
Klaus Voormann: bass

Eric Clapton in the studio recording with Howlin' Wolf and Mick Jagger. Ian Stewart is holding his hands on headphones.

4 MAY 1970

ROCKIN' DADDY (Chester Burnett) *The London Howlin' Wolf Sessions* album US Chess CH60008, UK Rolling Stones Records COC 49101 released August 1971 / *The London Howlin' Wolf Sessions* Deluxe Edition Chess 088 112 985-2 released March 2003

Howlin' Wolf: vocal
Hubert Sumlin: rhythm guitar
Eric Clapton: lead guitar
Ian Stewart: piano
Phil Upchurch: bass
Charlie Watts: drums

ROCKIN' DADDY (Chester Burnett) (alternate mix) *The London Howlin' Wolf Sessions* Deluxe Edition Chess 088 112 985-2 released March 2003

Howlin' Wolf: vocal
Hubert Sumlin: rhythm guitar
Eric Clapton: lead guitar
Ian Stewart: piano
Phil Upchurch: bass
Charlie Watts: drums

WANG DANG DOODLE (Willie Dixon) *The London Howlin' Wolf Sessions* album US Chess CH60008, UK Rolling Stones Records COC 49101 released August 1971 / *The London Howlin' Wolf Sessions* Deluxe Edition Chess 088 112 985-2 released March 2003

Howlin' Wolf: vocal
Jeffrey M. Carp: harmonica
Hubert Sumlin: rhythm guitar
Eric Clapton: lead guitar
Ian Stewart: piano
Bill Wyman: bass
Charlie Watts: drums

POOR BOY (NO SPARE MEAT ON MY BONE) (Chester Burnett) *The London Howlin' Wolf Sessions* album US Chess CH60008, UK Rolling Stones Records COC 49101 released August 1971 / *The London Howlin' Wolf Sessions* Deluxe Edition Chess 088 112 985-2 released March 2003

Howlin' Wolf: vocals
Hubert Sumlin: guitar
Jeffrey M. Carp: harmonica
Eric Clapton: guitar
Steve Winwood: piano
Bill Wyman: bass
Charlie Watts: drums

POOR BOY (Chester Burnett) (alternate lyrics and mix) *The London Howlin' Wolf Sessions* Deluxe Edition Chess 088 112 985-2 released March 2003
Howlin' Wolf: vocals
Hubert Sumlin: guitar
Jeffrey M. Carp: harmonica
Eric Clapton: guitar
Steve Winwood: piano
Bill Wyman: bass
Charlie Watts: drums

6 MAY 1970

SITTING ON TOP OF THE WORLD (Chester Burnett) *The London Howlin' Wolf Sessions* album US Chess CH60008, UK Rolling Stones Records COC 49101 released August 1971 / *The London Howlin' Wolf Sessions* Deluxe Edition Chess 088 112 985-2 released March 2003

Howlin' Wolf: vocal
Jeffrey Carp: harmonica
Hubert Sumlin: rhythm guitar
Eric Clapton: lead guitar
Lafayette Leake: piano
Bill Wyman: bass
Charlie Watts: drums.

DO THE DO (Willie Dixon) *The London Howlin' Wolf Sessions* album US Chess CH60008, UK Rolling Stones Records COC 49101 released August 1971 / *The London Howlin' Wolf Sessions* Deluxe Edition Chess 088 112 985-2 released March 2003

Howlin' Wolf: vocal
Hubert Sumlin: rhythm guitar
Eric Clapton: lead guitar
Ian Stewart: piano
Bill Wyman: bass, cowbell
Charlie Watts: drums

DO THE DO (Willie Dixon) (extended alternate take) *The London Howlin' Wolf Sessions* Deluxe Edition Chess 088 112 985-2 released March 2003

Howlin' Wolf: vocal
Hubert Sumlin: rhythm guitar
Eric Clapton: lead guitar
Ian Stewart: piano

Bill Wyman: bass, cowbell
Charlie Watts: drums

HIGHWAY 49 (Joe Williams) *The London Howlin' Wolf Sessions* album US Chess CH60008, UK Rolling Stones Records COC 49101 released August 1971 / *The London Howlin' Wolf Sessions* Deluxe Edition Chess 088 112 985-2 released March 2003

Howlin' Wolf: vocal
Jeffrey M. Carp: harmonica
Hubert Sumlin: rhythm guitar
Eric Clapton: lead guitar
Steve Winwood: piano
Bill Wyman: bass
Charlie Watts: drums

HIGHWAY 49 (Joe Williams) (alternate take) The London Howlin' Wolf Sessions Deluxe Edition Chess 088 112 985-2 released March 2003

Howlin' Wolf: vocals
Hubert Sumlin: guitar
Eric Clapton: guitar
Charlie Watts: drums
Ian Stewart: piano
Bill Wyman: bass

7 MAY 1970

BUILT FOR COMFORT (Willie Dixon) *The London Howlin' Wolf Sessions* album US Chess CH60008, UK Rolling Stones Records COC 49101 released August 1971 / *The London Howlin' Wolf Sessions* Deluxe Edition Chess 088 112 985-2 released March 2003

Howlin' Wolf: vocal
Hubert Sumlin: rhythm guitar
Eric Clapton: lead guitar
Ian Stewart: piano
Bill Wyman: bass
Charlie Watts: drums
Jordan Sandke: trumpet
Dennis Lansing: saxophone
Joe Miller: saxophone

KILLING FLOOR (Chester Burnett) London Revisited Chess CH60026 released February 1974 / *The London Howlin' Wolf Sessions* Deluxe Edition Chess 088 112 985-2 released March 2003

Howlin' Wolf: vocal, electric guitar
Eric Clapton: lead guitar
Bill Wyman: bass
Charlie Watts: drums

LITTLE RED ROOSTER (Willie Dixon) (Rehearsal) *The London Howlin' Wolf Sessions* album US Chess CH60008, UK Rolling Stones Records COC 49101 released August 1971 / *The London Howlin' Wolf Sessions* Deluxe Edition Chess 088 112 985-2 released March 2003

Howlin' Wolf: vocals, acoustic guitar
Hubert Sumlin: rhythm guitar
Eric Clapton: slide guitar
Bill Wyman: bass
Charlie Watts: drums

LITTLE RED ROOSTER (Willie Dixon) *The London Howlin' Wolf Sessions* album US Chess CH60008, UK Rolling Stones Records COC 49101 released August 1971 / *The London Howlin' Wolf Sessions* Deluxe Edition Chess 088 112 985-2 released March 2003

Howlin' Wolf: vocals
Hubert Sumlin: rhythm guitar
Eric Clapton: lead guitar

Lafayette Leake: piano
Bill Wyman: bass
Charlie Watts: drums

LITTLE RED ROOSTER (Willie Dixon) (alternate mix) *The London Howlin' Wolf Sessions* Deluxe Edition Chess 088 112 985-2 released March 2003

Howlin' Wolf: vocals
Hubert Sumlin: rhythm guitar
Eric Clapton: lead guitar
Lafayette Leake: piano
Bill Wyman: bass
Charlie Watts: drums

WHAT A WOMAN (James Oden) *The London Howlin' Wolf Sessions* album US Chess CH60008, UK Rolling Stones Records COC 49101 released August 1971 / *The London Howlin' Wolf Sessions* Deluxe Edition Chess 088 112 985-2 released March 2003

Howlin' Wolf: vocal
Jeffrey M. Carp: harmonica
Hubert Sumlin: rhythm guitar
Eric Clapton: lead guitar
Steve Winwood: organ
Bill Wyman: bass
Charlie Watts: drums

WHAT A WOMAN (AKA COMMIT A CRIME) (James Oden) (alternate take) *The London Howlin' Wolf Sessions* Deluxe Edition Chess 088 112 985-2 released March 2003

Howlin' Wolf: vocal
Jeffrey M. Carp: harmonica
Hubert Sumlin: rhythm guitar
Eric Clapton: lead guitar
Ian Stewart: piano
Bill Wyman: bass
Charlie Watts: drums

WHAT A WOMAN (AKA COMMIT A CRIME) (James Oden) (alternate mix with organ overdub) *The London Howlin' Wolf Sessions* Deluxe Edition Chess 088 112 985-2 released March 2003

Howlin' Wolf: vocal
Jeffrey M. Carp: harmonica
Hubert Sumlin: rhythm guitar
Eric Clapton: lead guitar
Steve Winwood: organ
Ian Stewart: piano
Bill Wyman: bass
Charlie Watts: drums

WHO'S BEEN TALKING? (MY BABY CAUGHT A TRAIN) (Chester Burnett) *The London Howlin' Wolf Sessions* album US Chess CH60008, UK Rolling Stones Records COC 49101 released August 1971 / *The London Howlin' Wolf Sessions* Deluxe Edition Chess 088 112 985-2 released March 2003

Howlin' Wolf: vocal, harmonica
Hubert Sumlin: rhythm guitar
Eric Clapton: lead guitar
John Simon: piano
Steve Winwood: organ
Bill Wyman: bass, shaker
Charlie Watts; drums, congas, percussion

WHO'S BEEN TALKING? (MY BABY CAUGHT A TRAIN) (Chester Burnett) (alternate take with false start and dialog) *The London Howlin' Wolf Sessions* Deluxe Edition Chess 088 112 985-2 released March 2003

Howlin' Wolf: vocal, harmonica
Hubert Sumlin: rhythm guitar

Eric Clapton: lead guitar
Ian Stewart: piano
Bill Wyman: bass
Charlie Watts; drums

WORRIED ABOUT MY BABY (Chester Burnett) *The London Howlin' Wolf Sessions* album US Chess CH60008, UK Rolling Stones Records COC 49101 released August 1971 / *The London Howlin' Wolf Sessions* Deluxe Edition Chess 088 112 985-2 released March 2003

Howlin' Wolf: vocal, harmonica
Hubert Sumlin: rhythm guitar
Eric Clapton: lead guitar
Lafayette Leake: piano
Bill Wyman: bass
Charlie Watts: drums

WORRIED ABOUT MY BABY (Chester Burnett) (alternate take) *The London Howlin' Wolf Sessions* Deluxe Edition Chess 088 112 985-2 released March 2003

Howlin' Wolf: vocal, harmonica
Hubert Sumlin: rhythm guitar
Eric Clapton: lead guitar
Ian Stewart: piano
Bill Wyman: bass
Charlie Watts: drums

WORRIED ABOUT MY BABY (Chester Burnett) (rehearsal take) *The London Howlin' Wolf Sessions* Deluxe Edition Chess 088 112 985-2 released March 2003

Howlin' Wolf: vocal, harmonica
Eric Clapton: lead guitar
Bill Wyman: bass

Producer: Norman Dayron
Engineer: Glyn Johns

"I very much wanted to work with Howlin' Wolf, so whether I was producer or not meant very little, because it was a good opportunity to maybe learn something again, and from that point of view it was very well worth doing. Wolf was absolutely amazing, it was a fascinating experience from that point of view, and also watching the young English rock 'n' roll whiteys react with this man." —**GLYN JOHNS**

"Howlin' taught me how to play 'Red Rooster.' It was a hairy experience. He came over and got hold of my wrist and said, 'You move your hand up HERE!' He was very, very vehement about it being done right. Because he considered us to be English and foreigners, and therefore we wouldn't have heard the song, right? So he just got his guitar out and said, 'This is how it goes.' It's not on the album unfortunately, but he played it all the way through once on his own with us just sitting there and listening. He was playing the slide Dobro, and it was just bloody amazing! And he said, 'Okay, you try it.' So we all tried playing it like him, but it didn't sound right, so I said, 'Well, why don't you do it with us?' And that's the bit that got on the record.

The guy that organized the session wanted me to play lead instead of Hubert Sumlin. Hubert ended up supplementing, playing rhythm, which I thought was all wrong, because he knew all the parts that were necessary and I didn't. For the first couple of days I was scared stiff of the 'Wolf,' because he wasn't saying anything to anyone— he just sat there in a corner and let this young white kid kinda run the show and tell everyone what to do! It was a bit strange…and when he finally did open up he was great, but he was very intimidating to look at. We weren't sure what he was thinking. But with Charlie Watts and Bill Wyman playing and everything, it was great and—well, I think it turned out pretty well…that album." —**ERIC CLAPTON**

1970 PART 2:
DEREK AND THE DOMINOS;
GEORGE HARRISON; APPLE JAMS;
JOHN MAYALL; THE ROLLING STONES

DEREK AND THE DOMINOS

Ever since the demise of Cream, Eric Clapton had been searching for his musical identity. Blind Faith may have started out with good intentions, and a lot of promise, but ultimately it was doomed to failure as soon as Ginger Baker joined the band and the business side of things took over the creative side before it had much of a chance to start. They were forced to record an album and tour before they were ready to do either. The lengthy and lucrative US tour was the final nail in the coffin for the band, as they resorted to playing crowd favorites from Traffic and Cream. Delaney & Bonnie had provided a great short-term escape for Eric, and his first solo album was the first step in finding his future musical direction and path. Although that album was more of a Delaney & Bonnie album in sound, it gave him the confidence to be a solo artist. But not quite yet, as his next project was to be a cooperative band.

Bobby Whitlock had stayed with Delaney & Bonnie after the rest of the "Friends" had left with Leon Russell to join Joe Cocker's infamous "Mad Dogs And Englishmen" tour in the US. After recording "Motel Shot" with them, he, too, decided it was time to leave and consider what he should do next. His friend Steve Cropper suggested he go and see Eric Clapton and spend some time in England to clear his head. As Bobby did not have much money, Steve kindly organized a plane ticket, and Bobby flew over to London Airport in April 1970. From there he took a taxi to Eric's home in the Surrey countryside. He already knew it well, of course, as he had stayed there the previous November when Delaney & Bonnie and Friends were residing there while recording and touring with Eric.

Eric was surprised to see Bobby, but happy at the same time, as they could play music and generally hang out and have fun. Within weeks, they were starting to write songs together, but when Eric realized that Bobby would have to head off home, he asked him to stay and help him get a band together. The first step was to go and see Robert Stigwood and put him on the payroll as the first member. The band was initially being formed to promote Eric's first solo album, which was due for release in August, but this would also be a fully functioning band that would tour and record new material. After some discussions, it was decided to get Jim Keltner on drums and Carl Radle on bass, along with Bobby Keys and Jim Price on horns. Everyone was available to come over at short notice except Jim Keltner, who was working on Gabor Szabo's *Magical Connection* album for Blue Thumb, and would not be able to make it over until July. Jim Gordon, another ex-member of Delaney & Bonnie's Friends, heard about the gig from Carl Radle and flew over with Carl and straight into a session with Eric and Bobby for PP Arnold. As he was there and ready, he was offered the job instead of Keltner.

George Harrison, always a frequent visitor at Eric's home, asked Eric if he and his new band would back him on his forthcoming solo album sessions that would take place at Abbey Road Studios from June onward. Eric accepted the offer and although the new band was not together yet, they would learn their chops throughout the sessions for George's *All Things Must Pass* album.

As for Bobby Keys and Jim Price, Bobby and Eric were now not sure they needed a horn section as part of the new band. They wanted a stripped-down rock 'n' roll band. Bobby Keys and Jim Price were looked after by being offered numerous guest sessions, many of which included Eric, before being taken on full-time by the Rolling Stones.

The origins of the name "Derek and the Dominos" has had many a story attached to it over the years. Here is what really happened. Jeff Dexter, a well-known DJ and compere at the time, as well as a close friend of Eric's, told me that on the night of their first show, a name had yet to be chosen. The adverts for the show at the Lyceum on 14 June had been billed as *Eric Clapton and Friends*. As Jeff was the compere tonight, he asked Eric what name he should introduce them with. The whole entourage started shouting out potential names, including Del and the Dynamics. Jeff recalled that Eric had been called Derek by Tony Ashton on last year's "Delaney & Bonnie and Friends" tour. Eric's nickname throughout that tour and beyond quickly became Del. Back at the Lyceum, it was a close call between Derek and Del. After a quick debate, Jeff told the assembled band they should be called Derek and the Dominos. Eric loved the name, but the band, who were American, feared that they would be thought of as a doo-wop band. Eric also liked the anonymity of the name, much to the disappointment of Robert Stigwood.

At a press function for the launch of Derek and the Dominos' first single for Polydor in London, Stigwood made sure every journalist and all PR people were handed a "Derek is Eric" badge to get the message got out to the public.

JUNE 1970

14 June 1970, Lyceum Ballroom, the Strand, London (2 shows in aid of Dr. Spock's Civil Liberties Fund, 4:30 p.m. and 8:00 p.m. With Ashton, Gardner & Dyke, Alexis Korner, Noir, Raven)

AUGUST 1970

1 August 1970, Dagenham Roundhouse, Dagenham, Essex

2 August 1970, The Place, Hanley, Staffordshire

4 August 1970, band travel to Nice, France

5 August 1970, Popanalia Festival, Biot, France (organized by the BYG record label. The French television program Pop 2 are there to film the whole event. The bill consists of Joan Baez, Pink Floyd, Eric Clapton, Gong, Soft Machine, King Crimson, the

Moody Blues, Traffic, the Art Ensemble of Chicago, and many more. Unfortunately, the organizers only managed to get payment out of 4,000 spectators. The other 30,000 just crashed the site. As a result, there was not enough money to pay the artists. The only acts that actually got to play were Joan Baez and Country Joe. When the crowd was told about the situation, some radical revolutionaries, called Les Companions de la Route, burned the stage and destroyed the equipment in protest. The result was that the event was cancelled. The Dominos, who were staying in a farmhouse owned by a French artist named Frandsen de Schonberg, were informed of the cancellation as they were about to leave the house to head off to play. They spent the next two days having fun at the farm. The owner's son, Emile, was looking after the band and the house on behalf of his father. He said that his father had told him to let them have their pick of any of his artwork from his studio as a gift. Eric was very taken with an oil painting that looked like Pattie and asked if it was all right to have that piece. That painting, of course, became the picture that millions of people have come to know as "Layla."

7 August 1970, Mayfair Ballroom, Newcastle, Tyne & Wear (with Writing on the Wall)

Dave Mason joins Derek and the Dominos for their late show at the Marquee Club in London. Eric is in the shadows on the left-hand side of the photo.

Eric playing a Les Paul Junior with Derek and the Dominos at their late show at the Marquee Club in London.

8 August 1970, California Ballroom, Dunstable, Bedfordshire

9 August 1970, Mothers, Birmingham, Midlands

11 August 1970, Marquee Club, Soho (2 sets tonight. Dave Mason sits in for the late set borrowing Eric's recently acquired white Fender Telecaster)

SETLIST FOR 11 AUGUST 1970 EARLY SET: Roll It Over / Blues Power / Have You Ever Loved A Woman / Any Day / Bad Boy / Bottle Of Red Wine / Little Wing / Tell The Truth / Country Life / I Don't Know Why

12 August 1970, Speakeasy, London W1

14 August 1970, Winter Gardens, Malvern, Worcestershire

SETLIST FOR 14 AUGUST 1970 EARLY SET: Country Life / Anyday / Bottle Of Red Wine / Don't Know Why / Roll It Over / Blues Power / Have You Ever Loved A Woman / Bad Boy

15 August 1970, Toft's Club, Folkestone, Kent

16 August 1970, Black Prince, Bexley, Kent

18 August 1970, Pavilion, Bournemouth, Dorset

Handbill for Derek and the Dominos at their late show at the Marquay Club, Town Hall, Torquay, on 21 August 1970.

SETLIST FOR 18 AUGUST 1970 EARLY SET: Roll It Over / Blues Power / Have You Ever Loved A Woman / Bad Boy / Country Life / Anyday / Lonesome And A Long Way From Home / Bottle Of Red Wine / Tell The Truth / Let It Rain

21 August 1970, Marquay Club, Torquay, Devon (with Bram Stoker, Adolphus Rebirth)

22 August 1970, Van Dike Club, Plymouth, Devon

25 August 1970–10 September 1970, Criteria Studios, Miami, Florida

SEPTEMBER 1970

20 September 1970, Fairfield Halls, Croydon, Surrey (with Brett Marvin & the Thunderbolts)

21 September 1970, De Montford Hall, Leicester, Leicestershire (with Brett Marvin & the Thunderbolts)

22 September 1970, Palais des Sports, Paris, France (Eric flies out to Paris today to see Buddy Guy and Junior Wells, who are supporting the Rolling Stones. He ends up onstage with them for "It's My Life Baby." At an earlier meeting in the day, discussions take place for Eric to produce a new album for them in Miami in November)

23 September 1970, Brighton Dome, Brighton, East Sussex (with Brett Marvin & the Thunderbolts)

24 September 1970, Philharmonic Hall, Liverpool (with Brett Marvin & the Thunderbolts)

25 September 1970, Greens Playhouse, Glasgow, Scotland (with Brett Marvin & the Thunderbolts)

27 September 1970, Colston Hall, Bristol, Gloucestershire (with Brett Marvin & the Thunderbolts)

28 September 1970, Free Trade Hall, Manchester, Lancashire (with Brett Marvin & the Thunderbolts)

OCTOBER 1970

3 October 1970, Lads Club, Norwich, Norfolk (with Brett Marvin & the Thunderbolts)

4 October 1970, Coatham Hotel, Redcar, Yorkshire (with Brett Marvin & the Thunderbolts)

5 October 1970, Town Hall, Birmingham, Midlands (with Bronco. Robert Plant is in the audience tonight and later walks onstage unnoticed by the band and is straight away escorted back into the audience by a couple of roadies. This is what an unhappy Rod Innes-Chater in the NME had to report:

"Robert Plant got pushed off the stage by a road manager at the Birmingham Town Hall on Monday—it was that sort of evening. Plant along with nearly 2,000 others had come to see a special off-tour booking of Eric Clapton's new group, Derek and the Dominos, sponsored by Aston University.

It was an evening of mishaps and might-have-beens. For a start, the supporting group, Bronco, did not take the stage until 30-minutes after the scheduled start due to a non-arrival of a group member of the group.

When they did eventually start, they turned out to have been not worth waiting for with a hackneyed sloppy and mediocre set.

So when Eric and friends took the stage, the audience had not so much been warmed up as doused with freezing water—literally—a fire hydrant in the Town Hall blew, and showered thirsty fans as they struggled to the bar.

Vocally, Eric Clapton has come a long way since he sang 'Ramblin' On My Mind' on a Mayall LP. But he is not, and never will be, another Robert Plant. And that was the final mar on the evening. The Dominos, though musically perfect, needed a good strong lead vocalist over such a tremendous backing. The Dominos sound, produced by Bobby Whitlock (organ, guitar, vocals), Carl Radle (bass) and Jim Gordon (drums) would be a model for any would-be top-line group. Outstanding numbers were 'Love That Country Life' and the old standard 'Nobody Loves You When You're Down And Out' where a soft treatment put less of a strain on Eric's vocal cords.

But the group still lacked a vocalist...until Robert Plant casually wandered on to the stage. It was obviously unplanned. None of the group saw him. Few of the audience seemed to recognize him. And nor, apparently, did the roadie guarding one of the wing stage doors. Robert Plant was unceremoniously ushered back through the door, and the chance of a monster impromptu jam session was gone.

Eric Clapton struggled on, singing with a strain on his larynx which was almost painful to hear. The experiment of Derek and the Dominos proves that he is at his best when allowed to just play, and not distracted by the necessity to sing."

—*NME*
(reader letter)

7 October 1970, Winter Gardens, Bournemouth, Dorset (with Brett Marvin & the Thunderbolts)

8 October 1970, Liverpool University, Liverpool, West Yorkshire (with Brett Marvin & the Thunderbolts, Medicine Head)

9 October 1970, Penthouse, Scarborough, North Yorkshire (with Brett Marvin & the Thunderbolts)

10 October 1970, Leeds University, Leeds, Yorkshire (with Brett Marvin & the Thunderbolts)

11 October 1970, Lyceum Ballroom, London (with Brett Marvin & the Thunderbolts)

SETLIST FOR 11 OCTOBER 1970 EARLY SET: Why Does Love Got to Be So Sad / Tell the Truth / Blues Power / Have You Ever Loved A Woman / Keep On Growing / Nobody Knows You When You're Down And Out / Bottle Of Red Wine / Little Wing / Roll It Over / Bell Bottom Blues / Let It Rain

DEREK AND THE DOMINOS USA TOUR 1970

15 October 1970, Alumni Gymnasium, Rider College, Trenton, New Jersey (2 shows 8:00 p.m. and 10:00 p.m. Capacity: 3,000. Guaranteed fee $8,500)

16 October 1970, Electric Factory, Philadelphia, Pennsylvania (2 x 45-minute shows 9:30 p.m. and 12:30 a.m. Capacity: 1,500. Support acts are Ballin' Jack and Toe Fat)

SETLIST FOR 16 OCTOBER 1970 EARLY SET: Ramblin' On My Mind / Why Does Love Got to Be So Sad / Blues Power / Have You Ever Loved A Woman / Mean Old World / Motherless Children / Let it Rain

17 October 1970, Electric Factory, Philadelphia, Pennsylvania (2 x 45-minute shows 9:30 p.m. and 12:30 a.m. Capacity: 1,500. Guaranteed fee for the two dates of $12,500 plus 60% over $36,000. Support acts are Ballin' Jack and Toe Fat)

21 October 1970, Lisner Auditorium, George Washington University, Washington, D.C. (2 shows 8:00 p.m. and 10:00 p.m. Capacity: 1,500. Guaranteed fee $7,500)

23 October 1970, Fillmore East, New York City (2 shows 09:30 p.m. and 12:30 a.m. Capacity: 2,600. All four shows are professionally recorded, supposedly without the band's knowledge. The tapes from the early shows are nowhere to be found. Support acts are Ballin' Jack, Humble Pie, and Toe Fat)

SETLIST EARLY SHOW (PROBABLY INCOMPLETE):

Got To Get Better In A Little While (Eric Clapton) unreleased

Why Does Love Got To Be So Sad (Eric Clapton / Bobby Whitlock) unreleased

Blues Power (Eric Clapton / Leon Russell) unreleased

Have You Ever Loved A Woman (Billy Myles) unreleased

Tell The Truth (Eric Clapton / Bobby Whitlock) unreleased

Presence Of The Lord (Eric Clapton) unreleased

Little Wing (Jimi Hendrix) unreleased

Engineer: Eddie Kramer

Setlist late show:

Got To Get Better In A Little While (Eric Clapton) *In Concert* RSO 2659020 double album released March 1973 / *Live At The Fillmore* double CD Polydor 521 682-2 released 1994

Key To The Highway (Charles Segar / Willie Broonzy) unreleased

Tell The Truth (Eric Clapton / Bobby Whitlock) *Live At The Fillmore* double CD Polydor 521 682-2 released 1994 (in an edited form)

Why Does Love Got To Be So Sad (Eric Clapton / Bobby Whitlock) *Live At The Fillmore* double CD Polydor 521 682-2 released 1994

Blues Power (Eric Clapton / Leon Russell) unreleased

Have You Ever Loved A Woman (Billy Myles) unreleased

Bottle Of Red Wine (Eric Clapton / Delaney Bramlett) *In Concert* RSO 2659020 double album released March 1973 / *Live At The Fillmore* double CD Polydor 521 682-2 released 1994

Presence Of The Lord (Eric Clapton) unreleased

Little Wing (Jimi Hendrix) Free flexi disc with *Guitar Player* magazine / *Live At The Fillmore* Polydor 521 682-2 released 1994 / Rare 1990 US "20th Anniversary Edition" two-track promotional-only CD featuring Remix Version and exclusive Live Version recorded at the Fillmore East in New York on 23 October 1970, housed in a superb custom digipak picture sleeve with Jimi Hendrix tribute on reverse Polydor CDP298 (Bobby Whitlock's organ breaks down and the band carry on without him until the end of the song)

Let It Rain (Eric Clapton / Delaney Bramlett) *Live At The Fillmore* Polydor 521 682-2 released 1994

Crossroads (Robert Johnson, arranged by Eric Clapton) Crossroads box set 835 261-2 released April 1998 / *Live At The Fillmore* double CD Polydor 521 682-2 released 1994

Engineer: Eddie Kramer

The tapes were sent to IBC Studios in London in 1972 for remixing by engineers Andy Knight and Richard Manwaring for the eventual release as *In Concert*.

24 October 1970, Fillmore East, New York City (2 shows 09:30 p.m. and 12:30 a.m. Capacity: 2,600. Guaranteed fee for both nights $20,000 plus 50% over $45,000. Support acts are Ballin' Jack, Humble Pie, and Toe Fat)

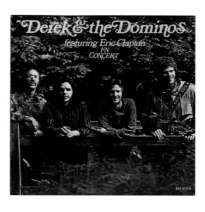

Derek And The Dominos In Concert *album cover. The double album was recorded at the Fillmore East in New York.*

SETLIST EARLY SHOW: NOT KNOWN

SETLIST LATE SHOW:

Got To Get Better In A Little While (Eric Clapton) unreleased

Tell The Truth (Eric Clapton / Bobby Whitlock) *In Concert* RSO 2659020 double album released March 1973

Nobody Knows You When You're Down And Out (Jimmie Cox) *Live At The Fillmore* Polydor double CD 521 682-2 released 1994 (in an edited form)

Why Does Love Got To Be So Sad (Eric Clapton / Bobby Whitlock) *In Concert* RSO 2659020 double album released March 1973

Presence Of The Lord (Eric Clapton) *In Concert* RSO 2659020 double album released March 1973 / *Live At The Fillmore* double CD Polydor 521 682-2 released 1994

Blues Power (Eric Clapton / Leon Russell) *In Concert* RSO 2659020 double album released March 1973 / *Live At The Fillmore* double CD Polydor 521 682-2 released 1994

Have You Ever Loved A Woman (Billy Myles) *In Concert* RSO 2659020 double album released March 1973 / *Live At The Fillmore* double CD Polydor 521 682-2 released 1994

Key To The Highway (Charles Segar / Willie Broonzy) Crossroads box set 835 261-2 released April 1998 / *Live At The Fillmore* double CD Polydor 521 682-2 released 1994

Bottle Of Red Wine (Eric Clapton / Delaney Bramlett) unreleased

Roll It Over (Eric Clapton / Bobby Whitlock) *In Concert* RSO 2659020 double album released March 1973 / *Live At The Fillmore* double CD Polydor 521 682-2 released 1994

Let It Rain (Eric Clapton / Delaney Bramlett) *In Concert* RSO 2659020 double album released March 1973

Little Wing (Jimi Hendrix) unreleased

Engineer: Eddie Kramer

The tapes were sent to IBC Studios in London in 1972 for remixing by engineers Andy Knight and Richard Manwaring for the eventual release as *"In Concert"*

- 29 October 1970, Kleinhans Music Hall, Buffalo, New York (2 shows 8:00 p.m. and 10:00 p.m. Capacity: 3,000. Guaranteed fee $7,500 plus 60% over $15,000)
- 30 October 1970, Albany State University Gymnasium, Albany, New York (2 shows 8:00 p.m. and 10:00 p.m. Capacity: 2,800. Guaranteed fee $7,500)
- 31 October 1970, Alan B. Shepard Convention Center ("The Dome"), Virginia Beach, Virginia (2 shows 7:30 p.m. and 10:00 p.m. Capacity: 2,500. Guaranteed fee $10,000)

NOVEMBER 1970

- 1 November 1970, Civic Auditorium, Jacksonville, Florida (2 shows 8:00 p.m. and 10:00 p.m. Capacity: 3,200. Guaranteed fee $7,500 plus 60% over $15,000)
- 1 November 1970–4 November 1970, Criteria Studios producing album for Buddy Guy and Junior Wells
- 5 November 1970, Ryman Auditorium, Nashville, Tennessee (filming for *The Johnny Cash Show*. The band start by playing "It's Too Late," and they are then joined by host Johnny Cash, who says to Eric, "Ah, listen, I think probably one of the most important artists that have, eh, influenced a lot of the groups in England, comes from right here." A clearly nervous Eric responds, "Yeah, right. A lot of these blues musicians and white people picking country music, you know, influenced everybody. I think one of the best of them all is right here on the show right now. Maybe we should bring him on?" Johnny, "Yeah, I think so, Carl Perkins!" Derek and the Dominos are now joined by Johnny Cash and Carl Perkins for a rollicking version of "Matchbox." After the cameras have stopped rolling, Derek and the Dominos perform "Got To Get Better In A Little While" and "Blues Power" for the fans in the hall.

SETLIST:

It's Too Late (Chuck Willis) *The Johnny Cash TV Show* DVD Columbia Legacy released 2007 / *The Best of the Johnny Cash TV Show* CD Sony BMG 88697212302 released May 2008 / *Layla And Other Assorted Love Songs* 40th Anniversary box set Polydor 0600753314326 and 2CD Deluxe Edition Polydor 0600753314296 released March 2011

Eric Clapton: vocals, guitar
Bobby Whitlock: vocals, piano
Carl Radle: bass
Jim Gordon: drums

Got To Get Better In A Little While (Eric Clapton) *Layla And Other Assorted Love Songs* 40th Anniversary box set Polydor 0600753314326 and 2CD Deluxe Edition Polydor 0600753314296 released March 2011

Eric Clapton: vocals, guitar
Bobby Whitlock: vocals, piano
Carl Radle: bass
Jim Gordon: drums

Matchbox (Carl Perkins) take 1 unreleased

Carl Perkins: vocals, guitar
Johnny Cash: vocals, guitar
Eric Clapton: vocals, guitar
Bobby Whitlock: vocals, piano
Carl Radle: bass
Jim Gordon: drums

Matchbox (Carl Perkins) take 2 unreleased

Carl Perkins: vocals, guitar
Johnny Cash: vocals, guitar
Eric Clapton: vocals, guitar
Bobby Whitlock: vocals, piano
Carl Radle: bass
Jim Gordon: drums

Matchbox (Carl Perkins) take 3 *The Johnny Cash TV Show* DVD Columbia Legacy released 2007 / *Layla And Other Assorted Love Songs* 40th Anniversary box set Polydor 0600753314326 and 2CD Deluxe Edition Polydor 0600753314296 released March 2011

Carl Perkins: vocals, guitar
Johnny Cash: vocals, guitar
Eric Clapton: vocals, guitar
Bobby Whitlock: vocals, piano
Carl Radle: bass
Jim Gordon: drums

Blues Power (Eric Clapton / Leon Russell) *Layla And Other Assorted Love Songs* 40th Anniversary box set Polydor 0600753314326 and 2CD Deluxe Edition Polydor 0600753314296 released March 2011

Eric Clapton: vocals, guitar
Bobby Whitlock: vocals, piano
Carl Radle: bass
Jim Gordon: drums

"I was hoping Duane Allman would come up and do the Cash show with me. We're doing a couple of songs Duane did with me on the album, and with him playing lead I would have more chance to get into my singing." —ERIC CLAPTON

Eric in Derek and the Dominos at the McFarlin Auditorium at Southern Methodist University, Dallas, Texas.

Carl Radle and Eric Clapton at the McFarlin Auditorium at Southern Methodist University, Dallas, Texas.

Eric in Derek and the Dominos at the McFarlin Auditorium at Southern Methodist University, Dallas, Texas.

Eric in Derek and the Dominos at the McFarlin Auditorium at Southern Methodist University, Dallas, Texas.

Eric in Derek and the Dominos at the McFarlin Auditorium at Southern Methodist University, Dallas, Texas.

6 November 1970, McFarlin Auditorium at Southern Methodist University, Dallas, Texas (2 shows 8:00 p.m. and 10:00 p.m. Capacity: 2,400)

SETLIST FOR 6 NOVEMBER 1970: Got To Get Better In A little While / Blues Power / Have You Ever Loved A Woman / Why Does Love Got To Be So Sad / It's Too Late / Tell The Truth / Stormy Monday / Bottle Of Red Wine / Little Wing / Nobody Knows You When Your Down / Let It Rain

7 November 1970, Community Center Theater, San Antonio, Texas (2 shows 8:00 p.m. and 10:00 p.m. Capacity: 3,000. Guaranteed fee $17,500 for both Texas shows plus 60% over $35,000)

Derek and the Dominos at the McFarlin Auditorium at Southern Methodist University, Dallas, Texas, on 6 November 1970.

167

"You know, I had been doing a lot of playing in San Francisco...I had lived in the Bay area...I didn't have a driver's license...so a good friend of mine, Jackie, that ended up working for Journey later, would come and pick me up on weekends and I'd go play on Broadway...I'd play at [Mike Bloomfield's] club, and it became this thing, there was like, this 'buzz' in the city, about this kid [Schon].

I was in the studio with the Santana band, and we were just jamming, you know, getting high and jamming, and staying up until the wee hours of the morning, and just trying to create some music, and Eric Clapton walked in. You know, Eric Clapton at that time, was like, and before that time, had been like a god to me, a guitar hero, and he walked in and I didn't even say 'hello', I was like so scared he was in the room...and we played all night, and without even saying goodbye to or anything to him he walked out, and I was just still like...in shock.

So I went home, went to sleep at some ungodly hour, got up at 3 or 4, went back to Wally Heider's in San Francisco where we were rehearsing, and I had a message there waiting at the front desk, and it was from Clapton, and he was playing at the [Berkeley] Community Theatre there that night, and he invited me to play with him.

So, I didn't have a car, I didn't have a license...I can't remember exactly who drove me there...I forget too many things these days, too many drugs [laughs]...but, she drove me, I remember she drove me over there, and I got there about 5 or 10 -minutes before he went on stage, and he said '...I'll go out and play about two numbers, and then I'll call you out on stage as a really good friend of mine, and you can stay up the whole rest of the night and play the whole set with me.'

I said 'yeah, okay...no problem,' because I knew all his songs, all his guitar solos, from record, note-for-note...I wasn't scared to do it, because I knew all his material, like the back of my hand, I had studied it for so many years...I went on, and just ripped the place up, and he loved it.

He [Clapton] invited me back to his hotel later that evening, and basically was asking me 'who do you listen to?' and I said 'well, I listen to YOU' and he said *bleep*, 'I don't believe it,' he didn't believe it and there was this little acoustic guitar in his room, and I played him note-for-note 'Live Crossroads' or something, and he was like 'I can't believe that, you've taken it where I left it.'

And that's still [like] the ultimate compliment for me at this point in my life, coming from any guitarist, and I'll never forget that, a highlight of my life!"

—NEAL SCHON
("Off the Record" *Westwood One* interview)

13 November 1970, Gymnasium, University of Nevada, Reno, Nevada (2 shows 8:00 p.m. and 10:00 p.m. Capacity: 5,000. Guaranteed fee $7,500)

14 November 1970, Fairgrounds Coliseum, Salt Lake City, Utah (1 show 10:30 p.m. Capacity: 4,800. Guaranteed fee $7,500 plus 60% over $17,500)

17 November 1970, Memorial Auditorium, Sacramento, California (2 shows 8:00 p.m. and 10:00 p.m. Capacity: 4,000. Guaranteed fee $7,500)

SETLIST FOR 17 NOVEMBER 1970: Got To Get Better In A Little While / Blues Power / Have You Ever Loved A Woman / Tell tThe Truth / Why Does Love Got To Be So Sad / Bottle Of Red Wine / Let It Rain / Little Wing / Roll It Over / Stormy Monday / Key To The Highway / Keep On Growing

18 November 1970, Community Theatre, Berkeley, California (2 shows 7:30 p.m. and 9:30 p.m. Capacity: 3,200. Support act Toe Fat)

SETLIST FOR LATE SHOW: Got To Get Better In A Little While / Blues Power / Have You Ever Loved A Woman / Tell The Truth / Presence Of the Lord / Why Does Love Got To Be So Sad / Everyday I Have The Blues / Little Queenie / Sweet Little Rock 'N' Roller

18 November 1970, Wally Heider Studios, Studio D, 245 Hyde Street, San Francisco, California (I understand that Carlos Santana was at the show and invited Eric to Wally Heider's for a jam. Santana were there rehearsing for their next album (Santana III) along with a hot new young guitarist called Neal Schon. Eric was so impressed with Neal that he asked him to come and jam with the Dominos the next day)

19 November 1970, Community Theatre, Berkeley, California (2 shows 10:00 p.m. and 12:00 p.m. Capacity: 3,200. Guaranteed fee $12,500 for both Berkeley shows plus 60% over $25,000. Support act Toe Fat)

SETLIST FOR LATE SHOW: Got To Get Better / A Little Way / Key To The Highway / Why Does Love Got To Be So Sad / Tell The Truth / Mean Old World / Little Wing / Blues Power / Have You Ever Loved A Woman / Let It Rain (Neal Schon sits in for tonight's late show)

20 November 1970, Civic Auditorium, Santa Monica, California (2 shows 8:00 p.m. and 10:00 p.m. Capacity: 3,000. Delaney Bramlett joined the band onstage in an inebriated state and played way too loud. Support act Toe Fat)

SETLIST FOR 20 NOVEMBER 1970 EARLY): Got to Get Better In A Little While / Key To The Highway / Why Does Love Got To Be So Sad / Blues Power / Have You Ever Loved A Woman / Tell The Truth / All Night Long / Let it Rain

SETLIST FOR 20 NOVEMBER 1970 LATE): Got To Get Better In A Little While / Key To The Highway / Why Does Love Got To Be So Sad / Blues Power / Stormy Monday / Tell The Truth / Let It Rain / Every Day I Have The Blues

> **"**Delaney showed up and wanted to jam. I hadn't stolen his band, I'd picked them up after he'd dropped them; but here he was, trying to reestablish his authority over them, and he really went over the top. He played deafeningly loud and it was all very cringe-making.**"** —ERIC CLAPTON

21 November 1970, Civic Auditorium, Pasadena, California (Capacity: 2,465. Guaranteed fee $30,000 for both Santa Monica and Pasadena shows plus 60% over $62,000. Jesse Ed Davis joins the Dominos on guitar for tonight's show. Support act Toe Fat)
22 November 1970, Community Concourse, San Diego, California (2 shows 8:00 p.m. and 10:00 p.m. Capacity: 4,500. Guaranteed fee $7,500 plus 60% over $16,500. Support act Toe Fat)
25 November 1970, Auditorium Theatre, Chicago, Illinois (2 shows 8:00 p.m. and 10:00 p.m. Capacity: 4,000. Guaranteed fee $10,000 plus 60% over $21,000. Support acts are Elton John and Toe Fat)
26 November 1970, Music Hall, Cincinnati, Ohio (2 shows 8:00 p.m. and 10:00 p.m. Capacity: 3,630. Guaranteed fee $7,500 plus 60% over $15,000. Support act Toe Fat)

SETLIST FOR 26 NOVEMBER SHOW: Got To Get Better In A Little While / Roll It Over / Blues Power / Stormy Monday / Why Does Love Got To Be So Sad / Little Queenie / Sweet Little Rock N' Roller / Tell The Truth / Let It Rain / Everyday I Have The Blues (with BB King)

27 November 1970, Kiel Auditorium, St. Louis, Missouri (2 shows 8:00 p.m. and 10:00 p.m. Capacity: 3,500. Guaranteed fee $7,500 plus 60% over $15,000. Support act Toe Fat)

SETLIST FOR 27 NOVEMBER 1970 LATE): Layla / Roll It Over / Blues Power / Stormy Monday / Got To Get Better In A Little While / Nobody Knows You / Tell The Truth / Let It Rain

28 November 1970, Music Hall, Cleveland, Ohio (2 shows 8:00 p.m. and 10:00 p.m. Capacity: 3,000. Guaranteed fee $7,500 plus 60% over $16,500. Support act Toe Fat)
29 November 1970, Painters Mill Music Fair, Owings Mills, Maryland (2 shows 8:00 p.m. and 10:00 p.m. Capacity: 4,500. Guaranteed fee $8,000. Support act Toe Fat)

SETLIST FOR 29 NOVEMBER SHOW: Layla / Bell Bottom Blues / Blues Power / Stormy Monday / Tell The Truth / Got To Get Better In A Little While / Little Wing / Why Does Love Got To Be So Sad / Have You Ever Loved A Woman / Let It Rain

DECEMBER 1970

1 December 1970, Curtis Hixon Hall, Tampa, Florida (2 shows 8:00 p.m. and 10:00 p.m. Capacity: 7,000. Guaranteed fee $7,500 plus 60% over $16,000. With Duane Allman on guitar. Support acts are Elton John and Toe Fat)

SETLIST: Layla / Got To Get Better In A Little While / Key To The Highway / Why Does Love Got To Be So Sad / Blues Power / Have You Ever Loved A Woman / Bottle Of Red Wine / Let It Rain (Duane Allman joins the band for tonight's show)

2 December 1970, Onondaga County War Memorial Auditorium, Syracuse, New York (2 shows 8:00 p.m. and 10:00 p.m. Capacity: 4,500. Guaranteed fee $7,500 plus 60% over $15,000. With Duane Allman on guitar. Support acts are Elton John and Toe Fat)
3 December 1970, Eastown Theater, Detroit, Michigan (2 shows 8:00 p.m. and 10:00 p.m. Capacity: 2,500. Guaranteed fee $7,500 plus 60% over $16,000. Several eyewitnesses claim Duane Allman also played at this show. Support acts are the Damnation of Adam Blessing and Toe Fat)

A Buffalo Festival Presentation
Derek & the Dominos
Wednesday, December 2nd 7 PM
Onondaga War Memorial Auditorium

Tickets
$4.50, 5.50, 6.50

Poster for Derek and the Dominos at the Onondaga County War Memorial Auditorium, Syracuse on 2 December 1970.

4 December 1970, Capitol Theater, Port Chester, New York (2 shows 8:00 p.m. and 10:00 p.m. Capacity: 1,835. Support act Toe Fat)

5 December 1970, Capitol Theater, Port Chester, New York (2 shows 8:00 p.m. and 10:00 p.m. Capacity: 1,835. Guaranteed fee $15,500 for all four shows in Port Chester plus 50% over $30,000. Support act Toe Fat)

SETLIST EARLY SHOW: Tell The Truth / Little Wing / Blues Power / Have You Ever Loved A Woman / Let It Rain

SETLIST LATE SHOW: Why Does Love Got To Be So Sad / Blues Power / Stormy Monday / Key To The Highway / Tell The Truth / Bottle Of Red Wine / Got To Get Better In A Little While / Crossroads

6 December 1970, Brookhaven Gymnasium, Suffolk Community College, Selden, New York (2 shows 8:00 p.m. and 11:00 p.m. Capacity: 2,000. Guaranteed fee $10,000. Support act Toe Fat)

SETLIST FOR 6 DECEMBER SHOW: Keep On Growing / Tell The Truth / Stormy Monday / Why Does Love Got To Be So Sad / Blues Power / Have You Ever Loved A Woman / Little Wing / Got To Get Better In A Little While

31 December 1970, Ronnie Scott's, Frith Street, Soho, London (Ringo Starr's New Year's Eve Party. Eric Clapton joins in a jam session with Ringo Starr, Maurice Gibb, Charlie Watts, and others)

RECORDING SESSIONS
IBC STUDIOS
Studio A, 35 Portland Place, London W1
Sessions for PP Arnold

10 JUNE 1970

Robert Stigwood had signed up PP Arnold to his management company, and one of the first things he arranged was for her to record a solo album which would be produced by Eric Clapton. Jim Gordon and Carl Radle flew in from the US on the morning of the first session to be part of a new band with Eric. Carl got lost on the way from London Airport to the studio and missed the session. Manfred Mann's Chapter Three were at the same studios, and Eric asked their bassist, Steve York, to step in. The sessions were spread over several months, and Eric and his new band contributed to several numbers. None of the tracks were ever released. Other than the proposed single of "Born," all the other tracks were never finished, as Stigwood decided to shelve the project so Eric could concentrate on his new band.

BORN (Rhythm Version) unreleased
PP Arnold: vocals
Eric Clapton: guitar
Bobby Whitlock: keyboards
Jim Gordon: drums
Steve York: bass
Doris Troy: backing vocals

BORN (Orchestral version) unreleased
PP Arnold: vocals
Eric Clapton: guitar
Bobby Whitlock: keyboards
Jim Gordon: drums
Steve York: bass
Bobby Keys: sax
Jim Price: trumpet
Doris Troy: backing vocals

Producer: Eric Clapton
Engineer: Damon Lyon Shaw

> **"I** remember the circumstances of the session. I was working with Manfred Mann in Studio B. PP Arnold was in A. Eric's band had just flown in from the US and gone straight to the studio. Carl Radle had got lost between the airport and the studio, so they asked me to play. The lineup was Eric, Bobby Whitlock, Doris Troy, and Jim Gordon. I do not recall if there was anyone else. I also recall that Eric played through a Fender Champ he had brought back from the US (Delaney & Bonnie tour). It was the first time I had seen one and it sounded great. Sorry that I do not know the song titles!**"**
>
> **—STEVE YORK**

21 JULY 1970

MEDICATED GOO (Steve Winwood / Jim Capaldi) (takes 1–6) None of the takes are deemed finished and no master is made

PP Arnold: vocals
Eric Clapton: guitar
Bobby Whitlock: piano
Jim Gordon: drums
Carl Radle: bass
Bobby Keys: sax
Jim Price: trumpet
Kay Garner: backing vocals
Lesley Duncan: backing vocals

Producer: Eric Clapton
Engineer: Alan O'Duffy

26 JULY 1970

YOU CAN'T ALWAYS GET WHAT YOU WANT (Mick Jagger / Keith Richards) (takes 1–6) None of the takes are deemed finished and no master is made

PP Arnold: vocals
Eric Clapton: guitar
Dave Mason: guitar
Bobby Whitlock: organ
Jim Gordon: drums
Carl Radle: bass
Bobby Keys: sax
Jim Price: trumpet
Kay Garner: backing vocals
Lesley Duncan: backing vocals

Producer: Eric Clapton
Engineer: Alan O'Duffy

OLYMPIC STUDIOS
117-123 Church Road,
Barnes, London SW13

30 JULY 1970

NEW DAY (takes 1–4) None of the takes are deemed finished and no master is made

PP Arnold: vocals
Eric Clapton: guitar
Bobby Whitlock: piano
Jim Gordon: drums
Carl Radle: bass
Bobby Keys: sax
Jim Price: trumpet
Kay Garner: backing vocals
Lesley Duncan: backing vocals

Producer: Eric Clapton
Engineer: Alan O'Duffy

TRIDENT STUDIOS
Trident House, 17 St.
Anne's Court,
Soho, London W1
Session for Dr. John
The Sun, Moon and Herbs

9 JULY 1970–11 JULY 1970

Dr. John was touring Europe in the summer of 1970 and made an appearance at the Bath Festival on 28 June in England. The headliners that day were Led Zeppelin. Some studio time had been booked for him at Trident Studios in London to record a conceptual three-album set called *The Sun, Moon and Herbs*, reflecting the feelings and atmosphere at different times of the day. The idea was that you would play the *Sun* album in the morning as you woke up, then listen to the *Herbs* album in the afternoon and the *Moon* album in the evening. One unnamed onlooker at Trident stated that it was "good to know Clapton could still play that well." The good Doctor gathered a huge band around him at Trident Studios and produced some of his New Orleans magic during a glorious summer in London.

The numbers being recorded lasted between seven and thirty-minutes, and twelve sides of sixteen-track tape were filled, but eventually only a fraction of the tapes ended up being used. After the session ended, Dr. John sent the tapes over to his manager in California to be mixed and mastered before being handed over to Atlantic Records for release. Unfortunately, his manager had no intention of passing the tapes on to Atlantic. According to Dr. John, his manager was trying to do a deal with Blue Thumb Records without his knowledge, even though Dr. John had another three years to run on his Atlantic contract.

When Dr. John confronted his manager asking him to return the tapes, he refused. After enlisting the help of Ahmet Ertegun, head of Atlantic Records, the tapes were eventually handed over and taken to Atlantic's southern headquarters at Criteria Studios in Miami. When he played the tapes, he was shocked to discover that most of the material he had recorded in London was missing and that many of the remaining tracks had been altered by his manager. As a result, he and Tom Dowd spent several weeks in Miami overdubbing some of the missing sections as well as piecing together enough material to put together an album, albeit a single album now.

The good news is that at the time of putting this book together, the original tapes were recently located and Dr. John was revisiting them in 2012 with a view of releasing an expanded version of *Sun, Moon and Herbs* which would be more in line with the original concept.

BLACK JOHN THE CONQUEROR (Mac Rebennack) *Sun, Moon and Herbs* album US ATCO SD 33-362, UK Atlantic K2400161 released August 1971 / *Sun, Moon and Herbs* CD ATCO 7567-80440-2 released October 1993 / Sun Moon & Herbs CD Wounded Bird Records 0664140036222 released November 2006

Dr. John: vocals, guitar, piano, vibes, organ, percussion
Eric Clapton: slide guitar
Tommy Ferrone: rhythm guitar
Vix Brox: trumpet, organ
Ray Draper: tuba, percussion, vocals
Fred Staehle: trap drums
Mick Jagger: backing vocals
Shirley Goodman: backing vocals
Tammi Lynn: backing vocals
PP Arnold: backing vocals
Joni Jonz: backing vocals
Ken Terroade: flute
Chris Mercer: sax
Graham Bond: alto sax
Walter Davis: piano
Wayne Jackson (Memphis Horns): trumpet
Andrew Love (Memphis Horns): tenor sax
Roger Hopps (Memphis Horns): trumpet
Jack Hale (Memphis Horns): trombone
Ed Logan (Memphis Horns): tenor sax
James Mitchell (Memphis Horns): baritone sax
Doris Troy: backing vocals
Bobby Whitlock: backing vocals

WHERE YA AT MULE (Mac Rebennack) *Sun, Moon and Herbs* album US ATCO SD 33-362, UK Atlantic K2400161 released August 1971 / *Sun, Moon and Herbs* CD ATCO 7567-80440-2 released October 1993 / *Sun, Moon and Herbs* CD Wounded Bird Records 0664140036222 released November 2006

Dr. John: vocals, guitar, piano, vibes, organ, percussion
Eric Clapton: slide guitar
Tommy Ferrone: rhythm guitar
Vix Brox: trumpet, organ
Ray Draper: tuba, percussion, vocals
Fred Staehle: trap drums
Mick Jagger: backing vocals
Shirley Goodman: backing vocals
Tammi Lynn: backing vocals
PP Arnold: backing vocals
Joni Jonz: backing vocals
Bobby Keys: sax
Chris Mercer: sax
Carl Radle: bass
Jim Gordon: congas
Wayne Jackson (Memphis Horns): trumpet
Andrew Love (Memphis Horns): tenor sax
Roger Hopps (Memphis Horns): trumpet
Jack Hale (Memphis Horns): trombone
Ed Logan (Memphis Horns): tenor sax
James Mitchell (Memphis Horns): baritone sax
Doris Troy: backing vocals
Bobby Whitlock: backing vocals

CRANEY CROW (Mac Rebennack) *Sun, Moon and Herbs* album US ATCO SD 33-362, UK Atlantic K2400161 released August 1971 / *Sun, Moon and Herbs* CD ATCO 7567-80440-2 released October 1993 / *Sun, Moon and Herbs* CD Wounded Bird Records 0664140036222 released November 2006

> **"**When I got to London I began making a few calls in the hope of scrounging up some musicians to help me out. I hired Graham Bond and through him I hooked up with a mess of horn players. I made a few more calls and things seemed to be working out. When I walked down onto the main studio floor, I was stunned by the number of musicians sitting around waiting for me to show.
>
> Eric Clapton was there, sitting in on guitar, and with him were Carl Radle, his bass player, and a couple of other players. Eric had only recently broken up with Blind Faith. He was a sensitive player, an incredible guitarist, and I was touched he'd take time to help me out on the session. Mick Jagger and Doris Troy were down there in the hole too, fooling around and waiting for the music to begin.
>
> Trident Studios was jammed; we had enough musicians to make six bands, though not the right instrumentation for what I wanted to cut. But I decided it didn't matter, that we'd go ahead with the cutting anyway. Things started out magically on the *Sun* part of the album. Kenneth Terroade kicked things off with a beautiful flute solo that put everyone in the right mood, and it went on from there. The session lasted nonstop for days. Everybody was sitting around smoking hash and opium, and things sort of dissolved into one big wall of smoking, toking, and no okey-doking.**"**
> **—DR. JOHN**
> (from his autobiography *Under A Hoodoo Moon*)

> **"**The new more withdrawn Clapton was also in evidence, quietly sitting down to play his telecaster with a steel bottleneck. What came out was the most satisfying Clapton I've ever heard, very reticent but adding a whole lot to the ensemble sound with sweet sliding fills and brief glistening solos.**"** **—RICHARD WILLIAMS**
> (from *Melody Maker*, describing the sessions in the July 18 edition)

Dr. John: vocals, guitar, piano, vibes, organ, percussion
Eric Clapton: slide guitar
Tommy Ferrone: rhythm guitar
Vix Brox: trumpet, organ
Ray Draper: tuba, percussion, vocals
Fred Staehle: trap drums
Mick Jagger: backing vocals
Shirley Goodman: backing vocals
Tammi Lynn: backing vocals
PP Arnold: backing vocals
Joni Jonz: backing vocals
Ken Terroade: flute
Walter Davis: piano
Jesse Boyce: bass
Freeman Brown: percussion

POTS ON FIYO (FILÉ GUMBO) / WHO I GOT TO FALL ON (IF THE POT GET HEAVY) (Mac Rebennack) *Sun, Moon and Herbs* album US ATCO SD 33-362, UK Atlantic K2400161 released August 1971 / *Sun, Moon and Herbs* CD ATCO 7567-80440-2 released October 1993 / *Sun, Moon and Herbs* CD Wounded Bird Records 0664140036222 released November 2006

Dr. John: vocals, guitar, piano, vibes, organ, percussion
Eric Clapton: slide guitar
Tommy Ferrone: rhythm guitar
Vix Brox: trumpet, organ
Ray Draper: tuba, percussion, vocals
Fred Staehle: trap drums
Mick Jagger: backing vocals
Shirley Goodman: backing vocals
Tammi Lynn: backing vocals
PP Arnold: backing vocals
Joni Jonz: backing vocals
Jim Price: trumpet
Graham Bond: alto sax
Ken Terroade: flute
Walter Davis: piano
Steve York: acoustic bass
Calvin "Fuzzy" Samuels: congas
Freeman Brown: percussion
Wayne Jackson (Memphis Horns): trumpet (on "Who I Got To Fall On [If The Pot Get Heavy]" only)
Andrew Love (Memphis Horns): tenor sax (on "Who I Got To Fall On [If The Pot Get Heavy]" only)
Roger Hopps (Memphis Horns): trumpet (on "Who I Got To Fall On [If The Pot Get Heavy]" only)
Jack Hale (Memphis Horns): trombone (on "Who I Got To Fall On [If The Pot Get Heavy]" only)
Ed Logan (Memphis Horns): tenor sax (on "Who I Got To Fall On [If The Pot Get Heavy]" only)
James Mitchell (Memphis Horns): baritone sax (on "Who I Got To Fall On [If The Pot Get Heavy]" only)

ZU ZU MAMOU (Mac Rebennack) *Sun, Moon and Herbs* album US ATCO SD 33-362, UK Atlantic K2400161 released August 1971 / *Sun, Moon and Herbs* CD ATCO 7567-80440-2 released October 1993 / *Sun, Moon and Herbs* CD Wounded Bird Records 0664140036222 released November 2006
Dr. John: vocals, guitar, piano, vibes, organ, percussion

Eric Clapton: slide guitar
Tommy Ferrone: rhythm guitar
Vix Brox: trumpet, organ
Ray Draper: tuba, percussion, vocals
Fred Staehle: trap drums
Mick Jagger: backing vocals
Shirley Goodman: backing vocals
Tammi Lynn: backing vocals
PP Arnold: backing vocals

Joni Jonz: backing vocals
Jim Price: trumpet
Graham Bond: alto sax
Ken Terroade: flute
Steve York: acoustic bass
Freeman Brown: percussion
James Joyce: percussion
Doris Troy: backing vocals

FAMILIAR REALITY—REPRISE (Mac Rebennack) *Sun, Moon and Herbs* album US ATCO SD 33-362, UK Atlantic K2400161 released August 1971 / *Sun, Moon and Herbs* CD ATCO 7567-80440-2 released October 1993 / *Sun, Moon and Herbs* CD Wounded Bird Records 0664140036222 released November 2006

Dr. John: vocals, guitar, piano, vibes, organ, percussion
Eric Clapton: slide guitar
Tommy Ferrone: rhythm guitar
Vix Brox: trumpet, organ
Ray Draper: tuba, percussion, vocals
Fred Staehle: trap drums
Mick Jagger: backing vocals
Shirley Goodman: backing vocals
Tammi Lynn: backing vocals
PP Arnold: backing vocals
Joni Jonz: backing vocals
Bobby Keys: tenor sax
Graham Bond: alto sax
Chris Mercer: sax
Jim Price: trumpet
Carl Radle: bass
Jim Gordon: congas
Doris Troy: backing vocals
Bobby Whitlock: backing vocals

Producer: Dr. John, Charles Greene
Engineer: Roy Baker

EMI STUDIOS
3 Abbey Road, London, London NW8 (eight-track)
and
TRIDENT STUDIOS
Trident House, 17 St. Anne's Court, Soho, London W1 (sixteen-track)
Sessions for George Harrison's *All Things Must Pass*

26 MAY 1970–12 OCTOBER 1970

Arguably the finest of all the solo Beatles albums was composed of many songs George had not been allowed to use on Beatles albums. Their loss was his gain. George had recorded over twenty basic demos in late May 1970 at Studio 2 at Abbey Road. These were a preview for producer Phil Spector. The initial sessions took place at EMI Studios in Abbey Road from 26 May 1970 on eight-track. Overdubs were done at Trident Studios on sixteen-track from late August onward, over two months. As Jim Gordon and Carl Radle only arrived on 10 June, Eric Clapton and Bobby Whitlock started playing on the sessions before their bandmates arrived from the US.

Session sheets have been lost, and therefore musician credits have always been a source of debate. So the credits listed below are not necessarily 100 percent accurate, but after speaking with many of the musicians involved, and trawling through interviews and Beatles books, I believe that the list is very close to being definitive. The biggest difficulty is in establishing who plays acoustic guitar on what tracks. Both Peter Frampton and Dave Mason have confirmed to me that they played acoustic guitar on several tracks but do not recall which, although Peter was photographed with Pete Drake and George Harrison at the session, which could be a clue. Dave Mason also told me that he did not play any electric guitar outside of the jams. What I can confirm are all the tracks that Eric plays on.

Clapton's work went uncredited on UK editions of the boxed set for contractual reasons, but his name did appear on the US version

I'D HAVE YOU ANYTIME (George Harrison / Bob Dylan) *All Things Must Pass* triple album US/UK Apple STCH 639 released November 1970 / Remastered double CD US Capitol CDP5304742, UK EMI 7243 5 30474 2 9 released January 2001

George Harrison: vocals, rhythm guitar
Eric Clapton: lead guitar
Klaus Voormann: bass
Alan White: drums
John Barham: string arrangements
Unknown: xylophone

MY SWEET LORD (George Harrison) *All Things Must Pass* triple album US/UK Apple STCH 639 released November 1970 / Remastered double CD US Capitol CDP5304742, UK EMI 7243 5 30474 2 9 released January 2001

George Harrison: vocals, backing vocals, slide guitar
Eric Clapton: guitar
Pete Ham: acoustic guitar
Tom Evans: acoustic guitar
Joey Molland: acoustic guitar
Klaus Voormann: bass
Ringo Starr: drums
Jim Gordon: drums
Gary Wright: electric piano
Mike Gibbins: tambourine
Bobby Whitlock: vocals, harmonium

WAH-WAH (George Harrison) *All Things Must Pass* triple album US/UK Apple STCH 639 released November 1970 / Remastered double CD US Capitol CDP5304742, UK EMI 7243 5 30474 2 9 released January 2001

George Harrison: vocals, slide guitar
Eric Clapton: guitar
Pete Ham: acoustic guitar
Tom Evans: acoustic guitar
Joey Molland: acoustic guitar
Klaus Voormann: bass
Ringo Starr: drums
Billy Preston: keyboards
Gary Wright: keyboards
Mike Gibbins: tambourine
Bobby Keys: saxophone
Jim Price: trumpet

ISN'T IT A PITY (George Harrison) *All Things Must Pass* triple album US/UK Apple STCH 639 released November 1970 / Remastered double CD US Capitol CDP5304742, UK EMI 7243 5 30474 2 9 released January 2001

George Harrison: vocals, backing vocals, slide guitar
Pete Ham: acoustic guitar
Tom Evans: acoustic guitar
Joey Molland: acoustic guitar
Klaus Voormann: bass
Ringo Starr: drums
Tony Ashton: piano
Gary Wright: keyboards
Billy Preston: keyboards
Mike Gibbins: tambourine
John Barham: orchestral arrangements

WHAT IS LIFE (George Harrison) *All Things Must Pass* triple album US/UK Apple STCH 639 released November 1970 / Remastered double CD US Capitol CDP5304742, UK EMI 7243 5 30474 2 9 released January 2001

George Harrison: vocals, guitar
Eric Clapton: guitar
Pete Ham: acoustic guitar
Tom Evans: acoustic guitar
Joey Molland: acoustic guitar
Carl Radle: bass
Jim Gordon: drums
Bobby Whitlock: piano
Bobby Keys: saxophone
Jim Price: trumpet
Mike Gibbins: tambourine
John Barham: string arrangement

IF NOT FOR YOU (Bob Dylan) *All Things Must Pass* triple album US/UK Apple STCH 639 released November 1970 / Remastered double CD US Capitol CDP5304742, UK EMI 7243 5 30474 2 9 released January 2001

George Harrison: vocals, guitars, harmonica
Peter Frampton: acoustic guitar
Pete Drake: pedal steel guitar
Klaus Voormann: bass
Ringo Starr: drums
Billy Preston: organ
Gary Wright: piano
Ringo Starr: tambourine
Alan White: drums

BEHIND THAT LOCKED DOOR (George Harrison) *All Things Must Pass* triple album US/UK Apple STCH 639 released November 1970 / Remastered double CD US Capitol CDP5304742, UK EMI 7243 5 30474 2 9 released January 2001

George Harrison: vocals, guitar
Peter Frampton: acoustic guitar
Pete Drake: pedal steel guitar
Klaus Voormann: bass
Alan White: drums
Billy Preston: organ
Gary Wright: piano

LET IT DOWN (George Harrison) *All Things Must Pass* triple album US/UK Apple STCH 639 released November 1970 / Remastered double CD US Capitol CDP5304742, UK EMI 7243 5 30474 2 9 released January 2001

George Harrison: vocals, slide guitar, backing vocals
Eric Clapton: guitar, backing vocals
Bobby Whitlock: backing vocals
Pete Ham: acoustic guitar
Tom Evans: acoustic guitar
Joey Molland: acoustic guitar
Carl Radle: bass
Jim Gordon: drums
Billy Preston: organ
Gary Wright: organ
Gary Brooker: piano
Bobby Keys: saxophone
Jim Price: trumpet
John Barham: string arrangement

RUN OF THE MILL (George Harrison) *All Things Must Pass* triple album US/UK Apple STCH 639 released November 1970 / Remastered double CD US Capitol CDP5304742, UK EMI 7243 5 30474 2 9 released January 2001

George Harrison: vocals, guitar
Dave Mason: acoustic guitar
Carl Radle: bass
Jim Gordon: drums
Gary Wright: piano
Bobby Whitlock: organ
Jim Price: trumpet
Bobby Keys: saxophone

BEWARE OF DARKNESS (George Harrison) *All Things Must Pass* triple album US/UK Apple STCH 639 released November 1970 / Remastered double CD US Capitol CDP5304742, UK EMI 7243 5 30474 2 9 released January 2001

George Harrison: vocals, guitar

Eric Clapton: guitar
Dave Mason: acoustic guitar
Bobby Whitlock: piano
Carl Radle: bass
Ringo Starr: drums
Billy Preston: keyboards
Gary Wright: organ
John Barham: string arrangement
Unknown: xylophone

APPLE SCRUFFS (George Harrison) *All Things Must Pass* triple album US/UK Apple STCH 639 released November 1970 / Remastered double CD US Capitol CDP5304742, UK EMI 7243 5 30474 2 9 released January 2001

George Harrison: vocals, backing vocals, guitars, harmonica, percussion

BALLAD OF SIR FRANKIE CRISP (Let It Roll) (George Harrison) *All Things Must Pass* triple album US/UK Apple STCH 639 released November 1970 / Remastered double CD US Capitol CDP5304742, UK EMI 7243 5 30474 2 9 released January 2001

George Harrison: vocals, slide guitar
Dave Mason: acoustic guitar
Pete Drake: pedal steel guitar
Klaus Voormann: bass

Alan White: drums
Billy Preston: organ
Gary Wright: electric piano
Bobby Whitlock: piano

AWAITING ON YOU ALL (George Harrison) *All Things Must Pass* triple album US/UK Apple STCH 639 released November 1970 / Remastered double CD US Capitol CDP5304742, UK EMI 7243 5 30474 2 9 released January 2001

George Harrison: vocals, guitar, slide guitar
Eric Clapton: guitar
Carl Radle: bass
Klaus Voormann: bass
Jim Gordon: drums
Bobby Keys: saxophone
Jim Price: trumpet

ALL THINGS MUST PASS (George Harrison) *All Things Must Pass* triple album US/UK Apple STCH 639 released November 1970 / Remastered double CD US Capitol CDP5304742, UK EMI 7243 5 30474 2 9 released January 2001

George Harrison: vocals, backing vocals, slide guitar
Eric Clapton: guitar, backing vocals
Dave Mason: acoustic guitar
Pete Drake: pedal steel guitar
Bobby Whitlock: backing vocals, piano
Klaus Voormann: bass
Ringo Starr: drums
Jim Gordon: drums

I DIG LOVE (George Harrison) *All Things Must Pass* triple album US/UK Apple STCH 639 released November 1970 / Remastered double CD US Capitol CDP5304742, UK EMI 7243 5 30474 2 9 released January 2001

George Harrison: vocals, slide guitar
Eric Clapton: guitar
Dave Mason: acoustic guitar
Bobby Whitlock: piano
Gary Wright: electric piano
Billy Preston: organ
Klaus Voormann: bass
Ringo Starr: drums
Jim Gordon: drums

ART OF DYING (George Harrison) *All Things Must Pass* triple album US/UK Apple STCH 639 released November 1970 / Remastered double CD US Capitol CDP5304742, UK EMI 7243 5 30474 2 9 released January 2001

George Harrison: vocals, guitar
Eric Clapton: lead guitar
Carl Radle: bass guitar
Bobby Whitlock: piano
Jim Gordon: drums
Gary Wright: electric piano
Billy Preston: organ
Bobby Keys: saxophone
Jim Price: trumpet
Phil Collins: percussion (debatable)

ISN'T IT A PITY (Version Two) (George Harrison) *All Things Must Pass* triple album US/UK Apple STCH 639 released November 1970 / Remastered double CD US Capitol CDP5304742, UK EMI 7243 5 30474 2 9 released January 2001

George Harrison: vocals, backing vocals, guitar
Eric Clapton: guitar, backing vocals
Pete Ham: acoustic guitar
Tom Evans: acoustic guitar
Joey Molland: acoustic guitar

Carl Radle: bass guitar
Tony Ashton: piano
Billy Preston: keyboards
Bobby Whitlock: organ, backing vocals
Ringo Starr: drums
Mike Gibbins: tambourine

HEAR ME LORD (George Harrison) *All Things Must Pass* triple album US/ UK Apple STCH 639 released November 1970 / Remastered double CD US Capitol CDP5304742, UK EMI 7243 5 30474 2 9 released January 2001

George Harrison: vocals, backing vocals, slide guitar
Eric Clapton: guitar, backing vocals
Carl Radle: bass guitar
Jim Gordon: drums
Bobby Whitlock: organ, backing vocals
Gary Wright: piano
Billy Preston: keyboards
Jim Price: trumpet
Bobby Keys: saxophone

APPLE JAMS

The jams album has always been a controversial one. Some people enjoyed it, while others felt it was out of context and directionless. Maybe EMI should have done two separate editions to avoid the problem. However, any serious music fan considers the jam disc an essential listen. Furthermore, people were only paying the price of a double album, in effect getting the jam album free.

The jams were recorded during the sessions for the main album and were available on the third disc in the original triple vinyl release in November 1970. The inner sleeve had a photo of a jam jar with the words "Apple Jam" on the lid. George told *Billboard* magazine in December 2000: "When we were mixing the album and getting toward the end of it, I listened to that stuff, and I thought, 'It's got some fire in it,' particularly Eric. He plays some hot stuff on there!"

George was not wrong and generously mixed Eric higher than the other guitarists. These jams offer an interesting insight into how Derek and the Dominos were finding their sound during the making of *All Things Must Pass*. Two of the jams were recorded on 25 June during the session for the proposed first single for Derek and the Dominos, "Tell The Truth" and "Roll It Over."

OUT OF THE BLUE (George Harrison) *All Things Must Pass* triple album US/UK Apple STCH 639 released November 1970 / Remastered double CD US Capitol CDP5304742, UK EMI 7243 5 30474 2 9 released January 2001

George Harrison: guitar
Eric Clapton: guitar
Bobby Whitlock: piano

Carl Radle: bass
Jim Gordon: drums
Gary Wright: organ
Bobby Keys: saxophone
Jim Price: trumpet

IT'S JOHNNY'S BIRTHDAY (Martin / Coulter) *All Things Must Pass* triple album US/UK Apple STCH 639 released November 1970 / Remastered double CD US Capitol CDP5304742, UK EMI 7243 5 30474 2 9 released January 2001

(Sung to "Congratulations," a number-one hit for Cliff Richard in 1968. Recorded for John Lennon's thirtieth birthday on 9 October 1970)
George Harrison: vocals and various instruments

Mal Evans: vocals
Eddie Klein: vocals

PLUG ME IN (George Harrison) *All Things Must Pass* triple album US/UK Apple STCH 639 released November 1970 / Remastered double CD US Capitol CDP5304742, UK EMI 7243 5 30474 2 9 released January 2001

George Harrison: guitar
Eric Clapton: guitar
Dave Mason: guitar
Bobby Whitlock: piano
Carl Radle: bass
Jim Gordon: drums

I REMEMBER JEEP (George Harrison) *All Things Must Pass* triple album US/UK Apple STCH 639 released November 1970 / Remastered double CD US Capitol CDP5304742, UK EMI 7243 5 30474 2 9 released January 2001

George Harrison: guitar, Moog sound effects
Eric Clapton: guitar
Billy Preston: organ
Klaus Voormann: bass
Ginger Baker: drums

THANKS FOR THE PEPPERONI (George Harrison) *All Things Must Pass* triple album US/UK Apple STCH 639 released November 1970 / Remastered double CD US Capitol CDP5304742, UK EMI 7243 5 30474 2 9 released January 2001

George Harrison: guitar
Eric Clapton: guitar
Dave Mason: guitar
Bobby Whitlock: piano
Carl Radle: bass
Jim Gordon: drums

Producers: George Harrison and Phil Spector
Engineers: Ken Scott, Phil McDonald, and assisted by Eddie Klein

ALL THINGS MUST PASS 2001 REMASTER

One thing almost everyone agreed with was that this was a landmark album that still sounds as fresh today as it did back in 1970. The only criticism is the Spector sound. The album was drenched in the famous Spector reverb, but then again that is the way it was originally produced. In 2001 George and engineer Ken Scott seriously considered de-Spectorizing the album when it came time to remaster it. Fearing a backlash from fans and purists, it was decided to leave the production as was. Once again, in the age of "Super Deluxe" packages, there would be a place for a drier remix, which is something George would have wanted anyway. So it would not be something that would have been done against the artist's wishes. Let's hope that Olivia Harrison considers this as possible project at some point using original engineer Ken Scott.

Before the remastering could start, Ken Scott's first job was to locate all of the master tapes. He assumed, as had George, that they would all be located in George's library at Friar Park, but it turns out that was not the case. After several weeks of searching all of the masters were found except one, an eight-track master reel from Trident Studios with five songs. As it happens it was not essential and the remastering process started. George wanted to issue some additional material as well as a partial re-recording of "My Sweet Lord." This was the only bonus cut that had Eric playing on it.

MY SWEET LORD 2000 (George Harrison) Remastered double CD US Capitol CDP5304742, UK EMI 7243 5 30474 2 9 released January 2001

George Harrison: vocals, slide guitar
Eric Clapton: guitar
Pete Ham: acoustic guitar
Tom Evans: acoustic guitar
Joey Molland: acoustic guitar
Klaus Voormann: bass
Ringo Starr: drums
Jim Gordon: drums
Gary Wright: electric piano
Mike Gibbins: tambourine
Bobby Whitlock: piano, harmonium
John Barham: string arrangement
Dhani Harrison: acoustic guitar
Ray Cooper: tambourine
Sam Brown: lead and backing vocals

George recut his vocal and guitar parts, removed the backing vocals by the George O'Hara Smith singers and replaced them with Sam Brown's vocals. Dhani Harrison adds acoustic guitar and Ray Cooper adds tambourine

Below is a fascinating memo sent by producer Phil Spector to George Harrison giving his views on production for *All Things Must Pass*:

NOTES FOR GEORGE HARRISON

August 19, 1970
From: Phil Spector
Re: George Harrison LP

Dear George:
I have listed each tune and some opinions on each for you to use, as I will not be in London for some time. In general, I feel the remixing of the album requires a great deal of work or at least a few hours on each number. I feel it would be best if we saved all remixing until I return as a great deal of the mixes should be done with a fresh approach. Though the following looks like a book, it is just because there are so many songs and opinions.

1. AWAITING ON YOU ALL:
The mixes I heard had the voice too buried, in my opinion. I'm sure we could do better. The performance probably will be okay, unless you really think you can do it better. However, as I said above, I think a lot of it is in the final mix when we do it.

2. IF NOT FOR YOU:
The mix I heard also had the voice too buried. Performance was fine. It also should be remixed when the entire album is remixed.

3. I'LL HAVE YOU ANYTIME:
Same comments as "IF NOT FOR YOU."

4. ALL THINGS MUST PASS:
I'm not sure if the performance is good or not. Even on that first mix you did which had the "original" voice, I'm sure is not the best you can do. But, perhaps you should concentrate on getting a good performance. I still prefer the horns **OUT ON THE INTRO** but that is a remix decision which should be done at that time. Also the voices in the bridge (Eric and Bobby) sound flat, and should be very low in the final mix. This particular song is so good that any honest performance by you will be acceptable as far as I'm concerned but if you wish to concentrate on doing another then you should do that.

5. BEWARE OF DARKNESS:
The eight track I heard after it was bumped had the electric guitar you played bumped on with the rhythm guitars. I personally feel you can make a better bump with a bit more rhythm guitars. The electric guitar seems to drown them out. Perhaps you should do another bump with more rhythm guitars, or seriously consider taking this one to Trident Studios using the original eight track and avoiding bumping, as each track we used is important and vital to a good final mix.

6. ISN'T IT A PITY (NO. 1):
Still needs full string and horns. Naturally, performance is still needed by you. I think you should just concentrate on singing it and getting that out of the way.

7. ISN'T IT A PITY (NO. 2):
Still needs full or some type of orchestration. Performance seemed okay, but needs to be listened to at the end.

9. LET IT DOWN:
This side needs an excellent and very subtle remix which I am positive can be gotten and it will become one of the great highlights of the album. Believe me. In listening I find it needs an answer vocal from you on "Let It Down" parts. I'm not sure about this next point, but maybe a better performance with better pronunciation of words should be tried at Trident without erasing the original which did have much warmth to it. Perhaps you could try this at Trident. The vocal group (Eric and Bobby) on the "Let It Down" parts sounded okay. The "Moonlight Bay" horn parts should be out the first time and very, very low the second time they play that riff, I think. Perhaps at the end, near the fade, a wailing sax (old rock and roll style) played by Bobby Keys would possibly add some highlight to the ending and make it totally different from the rest of the song. It's hard to explain, but some kind of a screaming saxophone mixed in with all that madness at the end might be an idea. Anyhow it's something to think about. Even though everything is not exactly as we had hoped (horns, etc.). I think it will be great when it is finished. Everything on those eight tracks now is important and vital to the final product. I know the right mix and sounds even on the horns can be obtained in remix. The only other thing the horns could have done is what they play originally on the "Let it Down" parts, only more forcefully. However, I still think it's all there and there's nothing to worry about on that number.

10. MY SWEET LORD:
This still needs backing vocals and also an opening lead vocal where you didn't come in on the original session. The rest of the vocal should be checked out but a lot of the original lead vocal is good. Also an acoustic guitar, perhaps playing some frills should be overdubbed or a solo put in. Don't rush to erase the original vocal on this one as it might be quite good, since background voices will have to be done at Trident Studios, any lead vocals perhaps should be done there as well.

11. WAH WAH:
This still needs some bridge, and perhaps a Bobby Keyes solo. Also needs lead vocal and background voices.

13. WHAT IS LIFE:
The band track is fine. This needs a good performance by you and proper background voice. It should be done at Trident Studios if further tracks are necessary.

15. HEAR ME LORD:
Still needs horns or other orchestration. The vocal should be checked out to see if it is okay in performance and level.

16. APPLE SCRUFFS:
This mix seems to be okay as is.

18. BEHIND THAT LOCKED DOOR:
Maybe the vocal performance can be better. I'm not sure. Also, the mix may be able to be better as well. The voice seems a little down.

George, on all the 18 numbers I just mentioned, this is what I feel are the most important items on each. Naturally, wherever possible, of main importance is to get a good vocal performance by yourself. Also, if you do any of the background voices, you should spend considerable time on them to make sure they are good. In practically every case, I would recommend that you use Trident Studios for overdubbing voices, lead or otherwise, so as not to bump tracks or go eight-to eight, and also to be able to do as much an possible before reducing everything back to the original eight track. This would probably be an easier way to do it and would also insure the best type of protection for our original eight tracks when it comes to remixing, as most of those tracks are presently very good and I'd rather avoid going eight-to-eight and further bumping. Also, in many cases one erases a performance before comparing it to the new performance, which would not have to happen on a sixteen track.

I'm sure the album will be able to be remixed excellently. I also feel that therein lies much of the album because many of the tracks are really quite good and will reproduce on record very well. Therefore, I think you should spend whatever time you are going to on performances so that they are the very best you can do and that will make the remixing of the album that much easier. I really feel that your voice has got to be heard throughout the album so that the greatness of the songs can really come through. We can't cover you up too much (and there really is no need to) although as I said, I'm sure excellent mixes can be obtained with just the proper amount of time spent on each one. When the recording of the album is finished, I think we can get into it better on a remix level if we just devote time to it and thereby we will make a much better album since we will be concentrating on one thing at a time.

George, thank you for all your understanding about what we discussed, I appreciate your concern very much and hope to see you as soon as it is possible.

Much love. Regards to everyone. Hare Krishna,
Phil Spector

> **"**I was fortunate to be in the right place to have the remnants of The Delaney and Bonnie band. The drum, bass and keyboard players, namely Jim Gordon, Carl Radle and Bobby Whitlock had come to England to hang out with Eric Clapton (fast becoming Derek and the Dominos). They had just been touring with Delaney & Bonnie as I had been the year before. We even recorded two of the Dominos songs, 'Roll It Over' and 'Tell The Truth,' during the *All Things Must Pass* sessions which they re-recorded later. It was really nice to have their support in the studio and it helped me a lot.**"**
> —GEORGE HARRISON
> (from liner notes for remastered edition of *ATMP*)

DEREK AND THE DOMINOS
ABBEY ROAD STUDIOS
STUDIO 3, 3 Abbey Road, London NW8

25 JUNE 1970

ROLL IT OVER (Eric Clapton / Bobby Whitlock) (takes 1–2, with take 2 viewed as best) B-side single Polydor 2058-057 UK / ATCO 45-6780 USA released August 1970 and withdrawn within days / *Crossroads* box set 835 261-2 released April 1998 / *Layla And Other Assorted Love Songs* 40th Anniversary box set Polydor 0600753314326 and 2CD Deluxe Edition Polydor 0600753314296 released March 2011

Eight-track recording:
Track 1: bass (Carl Radle)
Track 2: drums (Jim Gordon)
Track 3: electric guitar (Dave Mason)
Track 4: electric guitar (Eric Clapton)
Track 5: piano (Bobby Whitlock)
Track 6: electric guitar (George Harrison)
Track 7: claps, 3rd harmony vocals (Eric Clapton, George Harrison, Bobby Whitlock, Dave Mason), percussion (Jim Gordon), slide guitar (Eric Clapton)
Track 8: vocal (Eric Clapton)

Tape box cover listing musicians for "Tell The Truth" / "Roll It Over," the first single recorded by Derek and the Dominos.

Eric Clapton: guitar, vocals
Bobby Whitlock: piano
Carl Radle: bass
Jim Gordon: drums, percussion
Dave Mason: guitar
George Harrison: guitar

Producer: Phil Spector
Engineer: Phil McDonald

25 JUNE 1970

TELL THE TRUTH (Eric Clapton / Bobby Whitlock) (takes 1–30) A-side single Polydor 2058-057 UK / ATCO 45-6780 USA released August 1970 and withdrawn within days / *Crossroads* box set 835 261-2 released April 1998 / *Layla And Other Assorted Love Songs* 40th Anniversary box set Polydor 0600753314326 and 2CD Deluxe Edition Polydor 0600753314296 released March 2011

Eight-track recording:
Track 1: bass (Carl Radle)
Track 2: drums (Jim Gordon)
Track 3: electric guitar (Dave Mason)
Track 4: electric guitar (Eric Clapton)
Track 5: piano (Bobby Whitlock)
Track 6: electric guitar (George Harrison)
Track 7: percussion (Jim Gordon)
Track 8: vocal (Eric Clapton)

Eric Clapton: guitar, vocals
Bobby Whitlock: piano
Carl Radle: bass
Jim Gordon: drums, percussion
Dave Mason: guitar
George Harrison: guitar

Producer: Phil Spector
Engineer: Phil McDonald

ISLAND STUDIOS
8-10 Basing Street, London W11
Session for Leon Russell

23 AUGUST 1970

HOME SWEET OKLAHOMA (Leon Russell) *Leon Russell And The Shelter People* album Shelter Records SW-8903 released May 1971 / *Leon Russell And The Shelter People* CD DCC SRZ-8005 released 1989

Leon Russell: vocals, piano, guitar
Eric Clapton: guitar
Carl Radle: bass
Jim Gordon: drums / percussion
Chris Stainton: organ

ALCATRAZ (Leon Russell) *Leon Russell And The Shelter People* album Shelter Records SW-8903 released May 1971 / *Leon Russell And The Shelter People* CD DCC SRZ-8005 released 1989

Leon Russell: vocals, piano, guitar
Eric Clapton: guitar
Carl Radle: bass
Jim Gordon: drums / percussion
Chris Stainton: organ

BEWARE OF DARKNESS (George Harrison) *Leon Russell And The Shelter People* Shelter album Shelter Records SW-8903 released May 1971 / Leon Russell And The Shelter People CD DCC SRZ-8005 released 1989

Leon Russell: vocals, piano
Eric Clapton: guitar
Carl Radle: bass
Jim Gordon: drums / percussion
Chris Stainton: organ

Producer: Denny Cordell and Leon Russell
Engineer: Andy Johns

LAYLA AND OTHER ASSORTED LOVE SONGS SESSIONS
CRITERIA RECORDING STUDIOS 1755 Northeast 149th Street, Miami, Florida

26 AUGUST 1970

JAM 2 (Clapton, Whitlock, Radle, Gordon) *The Layla Sessions* 20th Anniversary Edition box set Polydor 847 083-2 released September 1990

Eric Clapton: guitar
Bobby Whitlock: organ
Carl Radle: bass
Jim Gordon: drums

JAM 3 (Clapton, Whitlock, Radle, Gordon) *The Layla Sessions* 20th Anniversary Edition box set Polydor 847 083-2 released September 1990

Eric Clapton: guitar
Bobby Whitlock: organ
Carl Radle: bass
Jim Gordon: drums

HAVE YOU EVER LOVED A WOMAN (Billy Myles) (alternate master #2) *The Layla Sessions* 20th Anniversary Edition box set Polydor 847 083-2 released September 1990

Eric Clapton: guitar, vocals
Bobby Whitlock: piano
Carl Radle: bass
Jim Gordon: drums

27 AUGUST 1970

KEY OF D JAM (Clapton, Whitlock, Allman, Betts, Oakley, Trucks) unreleased

Eric Clapton: guitar
Duane Allman: guitar
Dickey Betts: guitar
Bobby Whitlock: organ
Gregg Allman: piano
Berry Oakley: bass
Butch Trucks: drums

JAM 4 (Clapton, Whitlock, Allman, Betts, Oakley, Trucks) *The Layla Sessions* 20th Anniversary Edition box set Polydor 847 083-2 released September 1990

Eric Clapton: guitar
Duane Allman: guitar
Dickey Betts: guitar
Bobby Whitlock: organ
Gregg Allman: piano
Berry Oakley: bass
Butch Trucks: drums

JAM 5 (Clapton, Whitlock, Radle, Gordon) *The Layla Sessions* 20th Anniversary Edition box set Polydor 847 083-2 released September 1990

Eric Clapton: guitar
Duane Allman: guitar
Bobby Whitlock: piano
Carl Radle: bass
Jim Gordon: drums

TELL THE TRUTH (JAM #1) (Eric Clapton and Bobby Whitlock) *The Layla Sessions* 20th Anniversary Edition box set Polydor 847 083-2 released September 1990

Eric Clapton: guitar
Bobby Whitlock: organ
Carl Radle: bass
Jim Gordon: drums

TELL THE TRUTH (JAM #2) (Eric Clapton & Bobby Whitlock) *The Layla Sessions* 20th Anniversary Edition box set Polydor 847 083-2 released September 1990

Eric Clapton: guitar
Bobby Whitlock: organ
Carl Radle: bass
Jim Gordon: drums

TENDER LOVE (Eric Clapton and Bobby Whitlock) alternate take unreleased

Eric Clapton: guitar
Bobby Whitlock: organ
Carl Radle: bass
Jim Gordon: drums

TENDER LOVE (Key of A) (Eric Clapton and Bobby Whitlock) unreleased

Eric Clapton: guitar
Bobby Whitlock: organ
Carl Radle: bass
Jim Gordon: drums

TENDER LOVE (Eric Clapton and Bobby Whitlock) *The Layla Sessions* 20th Anniversary Edition box set Polydor 847 083-2 released September 1990

Eric Clapton: guitar
Bobby Whitlock: organ
Carl Radle: bass
Jim Gordon: drums

(WHEN THINGS GO WRONG) IT HURTS ME TOO (Mel London) (Jam) *The Layla Sessions* 20th Anniversary Edition box set Polydor 847 083-2 released September 1990

Eric Clapton: guitar
Duane Allman: guitar

28 AUGUST 1970

TELL THE TRUTH (Eric Clapton and Bobby Whitlock) (basic track)

30 AUGUST 1970

KEY TO THE HIGHWAY (Charles Segar and Willie Broonzy) (complete take) *Layla And Other Assorted Love Songs* double album Polydor 2625005 released December 1970 / US ATCO SD2-704 / *The Layla Sessions* 20th Anniversary Edition box set Polydor 847 083-2 released September 1990 / *Layla And Other Assorted Love Songs* 40th Anniversary box set Polydor 0600753314326 and 2CD Deluxe Edition Polydor 0600753314296 released March 2011

Eric Clapton: guitar, vocals
Duane Allman; guitar
Bobby Whitlock: piano
Carl Radle: bass
Jim Gordon: drums

31 AUGUST 1970

NOBODY KNOWS YOU WHEN YOU'RE DOWN AND OUT (Jimmy Cox) *Layla And Other Assorted Love Songs* double album Polydor 2625005 released December 1970 / US ATCO SD2-704 / *The Layla Sessions* 20th Anniversary Edition box set Polydor 847 083-2 released September 1990 / *Layla And Other Assorted Love Songs* 40th Anniversary box set Polydor 0600753314326 and 2CD Deluxe Edition Polydor 0600753314296 released March 2011

Eric Clapton: guitar, vocals
Duane Allman: guitars
Bobby Whitlock: organ
Carl Radle: bass
Jim Gordon: drums
Albhy Galuten: piano

WHY DOES LOVE GOT TO BE SO SAD (Eric Clapton and Bobby Whitlock) (basic track)

HAVE YOU EVER LOVED A WOMAN (Billy Myles) (alternate master #1) *The Layla Sessions* 20th Anniversary Edition box set Polydor 847 083-2 released September 1990

Eric Clapton: guitar, vocals
Bobby Whitlock: piano
Carl Radle: bass
Jim Gordon: drums

1 SEPTEMBER 1970

KEEP ON GROWING (Eric Clapton and Bobby Whitlock) (basic track, Eric Clapton guitar overdub, Bobby Whitlock lead vocal overdub)

TELL THE TRUTH (Eric Clapton and Bobby Whitlock) (Eric overdubs some slide guitar on tracks 15 and 16)

Why Does Love Got To Be So Sad (Eric Clapton and Bobby Whitlock) (percussion overdubs, Duane Allman guitar overdub)

2 SEPTEMBER 1970

JAM 1 (Clapton, Whitlock, Radle, Gordon) *The Layla Sessions* 20th Anniversary Edition box set Polydor 847 083-2 released September 1990

Eric Clapton: guitar
Bobby Whitlock: organ
Carl Radle: bass
Jim Gordon: drums

I LOOKED AWAY (Eric Clapton and Bobby Whitlock) (basic track and overdubs. Eric Clapton and Bobby Whitlock add vocals, Eric Clapton also overdubs some extra lead guitar on tracks 10 and 11, percussion overdubs are also added today)

KEEP ON GROWING (Eric Clapton and Bobby Whitlock) (percussion overdubs)

BELL BOTTOM BLUES (Eric Clapton) (basic track)

HAVE YOU EVER LOVED A WOMAN (Billy Myles) (complete take) *Layla And Other Assorted Love Songs* double album Polydor 2625005 released December 1970 / US ATCO SD2-704 / *The Layla Sessions* 20th Anniversary Edition box set Polydor 847 083-2 released September 1990 / *Layla And Other Assorted Love Songs* 40th Anniversary box set Polydor 0600753314326 and 2CD Deluxe Edition Polydor 0600753314296 released March 2011

Eric Clapton: guitar, vocals
Duane Allman: guitar
Bobby Whitlock: piano
Carl Radle: bass
Jim Gordon: drums

3 SEPTEMBER 1970

I AM YOURS (Eric Clapton and Nizami) (basic track)
ANYDAY (Eric Clapton and Bobby Whitlock) (basic track)
IT'S TOO LATE (Chuck Willis) (basic track)

4 SEPTEMBER 1970

I LOOKED AWAY (Eric Clapton and Bobby Whitlock) (Bobby Whitlock adds some vocal overdubs before track is completed) *Layla And Other Assorted Love Songs* double album Polydor 2625005 released December 1970 / US ATCO SD2-704 / *The Layla Sessions* 20th Anniversary Edition box set Polydor 847 083-2 released September 1990 / *Layla And Other Assorted Love Songs* 40th Anniversary box set Polydor 0600753314326 and 2CD Deluxe Edition Polydor 0600753314296 released March 2011

Eric Clapton: guitar, vocals
Bobby Whitlock: organ, vocals
Carl Radle: bass, percussion
Jim Gordon: drums, percussion

BELL BOTTOM BLUES (Bobby Whitlock and Eric Clapton add vocal overdubs and double up vocals on the chorus only)

I AM YOURS (Bobby Whitlock overdubs 3rd harmony vocals)

ANYDAY (Eric Clapton and Bobby Whitlock) (Eric and Bobby add vocal overdubs before track is completed) *Layla And Other Assorted Love Songs* double album Polydor 2625005 released December 1970 / US ATCO SD2-704 / *The Layla Sessions* 20th Anniversary Edition box set Polydor 847 083-2 released September 1990 / *Layla And Other Assorted Love Songs* 40th Anniversary box set Polydor 0600753314326 and 2CD Deluxe Edition Polydor 0600753314296 released March 2011

Eric Clapton: guitar, vocals
Duane Allman; guitar
Bobby Whitlock: organ, vocals
Carl Radle: bass, percussion
Jim Gordon: drums, percussion

WHY DOES LOVE GOT TO BE SO SAD (Eric Clapton and Bobby Whitlock) Eric and Bobby overdub some vocals along with a tambourine overdub. Track completed) *Layla And Other Assorted Love Songs* double album Polydor 2625005 released December 1970 / US ATCO SD2-704 / *The Layla Sessions* 20th Anniversary Edition box set Polydor 847 083-2 released September 1990 / *Layla And Other Assorted Love Songs* 40th Anniversary box set Polydor 0600753314326 and 2CD Deluxe Edition Polydor 0600753314296 released March 2011

Eric Clapton: guitar, vocals
Duane Allman: guitar
Bobby Whitlock: organ, vocal

Carl Radle: bass, percussion
Jim Gordon: drums, percussion

TELL THE TRUTH (Eric Clapton and Bobby Whitlock) (percussion overdub made before track is deemed complete) *Layla And Other Assorted Love Songs* double album Polydor 2625005 released December 1970 / US ATCO SD2-704 / *The Layla Sessions* 20th Anniversary Edition box set Polydor 847 083-2 released September 1990 / *Layla And Other Assorted Love Songs* 40th Anniversary box set Polydor 0600753314326 and 2CD Deluxe Edition Polydor 0600753314296 released March 2011

Eric Clapton: guitars, vocals
Duane Allman: guitar
Bobby Whitlock: piano, vocal
Carl Radle: bass, percussion
Jim Gordon: drums, percussion

5 SEPTEMBER 1970

KEEP ON GROWING (Eric Clapton and Bobby Whitlock) (Eric Clapton and Bobby Whitlock overdub vocal tracks)

9 SEPTEMBER 1970

KEEP ON GROWING (Eric Clapton & Bobby Whitlock) (Eric Clapton overdubs a new lead guitar on track 2, possibly replacing Duane Allman's original lead, which would appear to have been recorded at the original session on 1 September but crossed out on the tracking sheet. There is no definitive answer to this, but this scenario is likely. Eric Clapton and Bobby Whitlock overdub new vocal tracks; various percussion overdubs are also added today before a completed master is finished) *Layla And Other Assorted Love Songs* double album Polydor 2625005 released December 1970 / US ATCO SD2-704 / *The Layla Sessions* 20th Anniversary Edition box set Polydor 847 083-2 released September 1990 / *Layla And Other Assorted Love Songs* 40th Anniversary box set Polydor 0600753314326 and 2CD Deluxe Edition Polydor 0600753314296 released March 2011

Eric Clapton: guitar, vocals
Bobby Whitlock: organ, vocals
Carl Radle: bass, percussion
Jim Gordon: drums, percussion

BELL BOTTOM BLUES (Eric Clapton) (Eric repairs a vocal in the second verse, fifth to eighth bars before the track is completed) *Layla And Other Assorted Love Songs* double album Polydor 2625005 released December 1970 / US ATCO SD2-704 / *The Layla Sessions* 20th Anniversary Edition box set Polydor 847 083-2 released September 1990 / *Layla And Other Assorted Love Songs* 40th Anniversary box set Polydor 0600753314326 and 2CD Deluxe Edition Polydor 0600753314296 released March 2011

Eric Clapton: guitar, vocals
Bobby Whitlock: organ, vocals
Carl Radle: bass, percussion
Jim Gordon: drums, percussion

LITTLE WING (Jimi Hendrix) (complete take) *Layla And Other Assorted Love Songs* double album Polydor 2625005 released December 1970 / US ATCO SD2-704 / *The Layla Sessions* 20th Anniversary Edition box set Polydor 847 083-2 released September 1990 / *Layla And Other Assorted Love Songs* 40th Anniversary box set Polydor 0600753314326 and 2CD Deluxe Edition Polydor 0600753314296 released March 2011

Eric Clapton: guitar, vocals
Duane Allman; guitar
Bobby Whitlock: organ, vocals
Carl Radle: bass
Jim Gordon: drums

LAYLA (Eric Clapton and Jim Gordon) (basic track)

Eric Clapton: guitars, vocals
Duane Allman: guitars
Bobby Whitlock: organ, piano, vocals
Carl Radle: bass
Jim Gordon: drums, percussion, piano

IT'S TOO LATE (Chuck Willis) (Bobby Whitlock and Eric Clapton vocal overdubs including a harmony overdub by Bobby Whitlock)

IT'S TOO LATE (Chuck Willis) (alternate master) *The Layla Sessions* 20th Anniversary Edition box set Polydor 847 083-2 released September 1990

Eric Clapton: guitar, vocals
Duane Allman; guitar
Bobby Whitlock: piano
Carl Radle: bass
Jim Gordon: drums

I AM YOURS (Eric Clapton and Nizami) (shaker overdub, track completed) *Layla And Other Assorted Love Songs* double album Polydor 2625005 released December 1970 / US ATCO SD2-704 / *The Layla Sessions* 20th Anniversary Edition box set Polydor 847 083-2 released September 1990 / *Layla And Other Assorted Love Songs* 40th Anniversary box set Polydor 0600753314326 and 2CD Deluxe Edition Polydor 0600753314296 released March 2011

Eric Clapton: guitar, vocals
Duane Allman: guitar
Bobby Whitlock: organ, vocals
Carl Radle: bass, percussion
Jim Gordon: drums, percussion

10 SEPTEMBER 1970

THORN TREE IN THE GARDEN (Bobby Whitlock) *Layla And Other Assorted Love Songs* double album Polydor 2625005 released December 1970 / US ATCO SD2-704 / *The Layla Sessions* 20th Anniversary Edition box set Polydor 847 083-2 released September 1990 / *Layla And Other Assorted Love Songs* 40th Anniversary box set Polydor 0600753314326 and 2CD Deluxe Edition Polydor 0600753314296 released March 2011

Eric Clapton: guitar
Duane Allman; guitar
Bobby Whitlock: guitar, vocals
Carl Radle: bass
Jim Gordon: percussion

THORN TREE IN THE GARDEN (Bobby Whitlock) (with triangle) unreleased

Eric Clapton: guitar
Duane Allman; guitar
Bobby Whitlock: guitar, vocals, triangle
Carl Radle: bass
Jim Gordon: percussion

1 OCTOBER 1970

LAYLA (Eric Clapton and Jim Gordon) (Eric overdubs some lead guitar work, Duane also overdubs some guitar on second section of "Layla," Carl adds some bass to the second section and Jim overdubs some cymbals in the right and left channels and some piano reinforcement before the master is completed) *Layla And Other Assorted Love Songs* double album Polydor 2625005 released December 1970 / US ATCO SD2-704 / *The Layla Sessions* 20th Anniversary Edition box set Polydor 847 083-2 released September 1990 / *Layla And Other Assorted Love Songs* 40th Anniversary box set Polydor 0600753314326 and 2CD Deluxe Edition Polydor 0600753314296 released March 2011

Front cover for Derek and the Dominos' Layla *album.*

Back cover for Derek and the Dominos' Layla *album.*

IT'S TOO LATE (Chuck Willis) (one final vocal overdub by Eric Clapton in the bridge before the master is viewed as complete) *Layla And Other Assorted Love Songs* double album Polydor 2625005 released December 1970 / US ATCO SD2-704 / *The Layla Sessions* 20th Anniversary Edition box set Polydor 847 083-2 released September 1990 / *Layla And Other Assorted Love Songs* 40th Anniversary box set Polydor 0600753314326 and 2CD Deluxe Edition Polydor 0600753314296 released March 2011

Eric Clapton: guitar, vocals
Duane Allman; guitar
Bobby Whitlock: piano, vocals
Carl Radle: bass
Jim Gordon: drums

2 OCTOBER 1970

MEAN OLD WORLD (Walter Jacobs) (rehearsal version) *The Layla Sessions* 20th Anniversary Edition box set Polydor 847 083-2 released September 1990

Eric Clapton: guitar, vocals
Duane Allman: guitar
Bobby Whitlock: piano
Carl Radle: bass
Jim Gordon: drums

MEAN OLD WORLD (Walter Jacobs) (band version, master take) *The Layla Sessions* 20th Anniversary Edition box set Polydor 847 083-2 released September 1990 / *Layla And Other Assorted Love Songs* 40th Anniversary box set Polydor 0600753314326 and 2CD Deluxe Edition Polydor 0600753314296 released March 2011

Eric Clapton: guitar, vocals
Duane Allman: guitar
Bobby Whitlock: piano
Carl Radle: bass
Jim Gordon: drums

MEAN OLD WORLD (Walter Jacobs) (duet version) *The Layla Sessions* 20th Anniversary Edition box set Polydor 847 083-2 released September 1990

Eric Clapton: guitar, vocals
Duane Allman: guitar
Jim Gordon: bass drum

Producer: Tom Dowd
Engineers: Ron Albert, Howie Albert, Chuck Kirkpatrick, Karl Richardson, Mac Emmerman

> **"**Eric Clapton's the only English guitarist I respect. He's a gas to work with and just a totally nice dude.**"**
>
> **—DUANE ALLMAN**

> **"**'Layla' on vinyl has an interesting story. There was a very good set of tapes on file at Polydor UK so we decided to cut the vinyl at Metropolis in London. We sent them the tapes so that a test cut could be made. When I got the reference cuts back from them, they were not what I was expecting! The mixes were slightly different on a couple of songs. It corroborated information we'd seen on the tape boxes. The UK tapes were dated September 29, 1970, while the Atlantic tapes were dated to the first week of October. So, the tapes sent to London were sent a week earlier than those sent to New York for Atlantic. In that week, they tweaked *Layla*, they tweaked *Tell The Truth*, and I'm not sure, there are other songs on it. But when you hear the two records side by side, they have different tonalities. So, the LP will have the UK mixes, the CD the US mixes, and the super-deluxe box set will have both.'**"**   **—BILL LEVENSON**
> (talking to Barry Fisch about the vinyl reissue for the 40th Anniversary Super Deluxe edition)

ERIC CLAPTON GUEST SESSION

LARRABEE STUDIOS 8811 Santa Monica Boulevard, Los Angeles Sessions for John Mayall "Back to the Roots"

23 NOVEMBER 1970–24 NOVEMBER 1970

PRISONS ON THE ROAD (John Mayall) *Back to the Roots* double album US Polydor 25-3002 released April 1971 / UK Polydor 2657005 released May 1971 / *Back to the Roots* double CD Polydor 314 549 424-2 released March 2001

John Mayall: vocals, piano
Eric Clapton: lead guitar
Sugarcane Harris: violin
Paul Lagos: drums
Larry Taylor: bass

ACCIDENTAL SUICIDE (John Mayall) *Back to the Roots* double album US Polydor 25-3002 released April 1971 / UK Polydor 2657005 released May 1971 / *Back to the Roots* double CD Polydor 314 549 424-2 released March 2001

John Mayall: vocals, harmonica, rhythm guitar
Eric Clapton: lead guitar
Mick Taylor: lead guitar
Harvey Mandel: lead guitar
Sugarcane Harris: violin
Larry Taylor: bass

HOME AGAIN (John Mayall) *Back to the Roots* double album US Polydor 25-3002 released April 1971 / UK Polydor 2657005 released May 1971 / *Back to the Roots* double CD Polydor 314 549 424-2 released March 2001

John Mayall: vocals, harmonica
Eric Clapton: lead guitar
Larry Taylor: bass

LOOKING AT TOMORROW (John Mayall) *Back to the Roots* double album US Polydor 25-3002 released April 1971 / UK Polydor 2657005 released May 1971 / *Back to the Roots* double CD Polydor 314 549 424-2 released March 2001

John Mayall: vocals, piano, guitar
Eric Clapton: lead guitar
Sugarcane Harris: violin
Paul Lagos: drums
Larry Taylor: bass

FORCE OF NATURE (John Mayall) *Back to the Roots* double album US Polydor 25-3002 released April 1971 / UK Polydor 2657005 released May 1971 / *Back to the Roots* double CD Polydor 314 549 424-2 released March 2001

John Mayall: vocals, tambourine, drums
Eric Clapton: lead guitar
Mick Taylor: slide guitar
Harvey Mandel: lead guitar
Larry Taylor: bass

GOODBYE DECEMBER (John Mayall) *Back to the Roots* double album US Polydor 25-3002 released April 1971 / UK Polydor 2657005 released May 1971 / *Back to the Roots* double CD Polydor 314 549 424-2 released March 2001

John Mayall: vocals, harmonica, rhythm guitar
Eric Clapton: lead guitar
Harvey Mandel: rhythm guitar
Keef Hartley: drums
Larry Taylor: bass

Producer: John Mayall
Engineer: John Judnich

John Mayall wanted to record a double album with musicians that had once been part of his band over the years. In the end he realized it would be impossible to get everyone he wanted because of scheduling, but he did not do badly, with Harvey Mandel, Jerry McGee, Mick Taylor, and Eric Clapton on guitars, Keef Hartley and Paul Lagos on drums, Larry Taylor

and Paul Thompson on bass, Sugarcane Harris on violin, and Johnny Almond on sax and flute. The set was recorded at Larrabee Studios in Los Angeles and IBC Studios in London during November 1970. Eric recorded his guitar parts during a small break in the Dominos' US tour. It was an interesting album with some fine playing by all the musicians, and it should have been far more successful than it was. The master tapes could not be located for several years, and John decided to try and find the original eight-track masters to do some remixing for a new release in 1988.

> "I was fortunate enough to have a second chance at making some better sense of the mixes that have most bothered me down through time. Months of diligent searching in distant warehouses finally unearthed the original 8-track master tapes. The tapes were brittle, the boxes faded and the reels beginning to rust. Back in Los Angeles, I began the renovation by transferring the contents to 24 track tape starting my new efforts. I bought in Joe Yuele, my hard driving drummer from the current Bluesbreakers, and by the time he'd put down his tracks the music began to form some unity. With the selected eight songs now locked together, I felt justified in singing the old lyrics again and played anew most of my instrumental contributions.
>
> During the mix, I discovered some essential performances that I'd mysteriously left out before and in other cases found far too many overdubbed solos all playing at the same time." —JOHN MAYALL

The master tape for *Back to the Roots* was eventually found during an audit of the tape library and issued on CD for the first time from the original tapes in March 2001. The new remixed edition with new overdubs was released as the *Archives To Eighties* CD in 1988. Those tracks are now found as bonus tracks on the *Back to the Roots* double CD set. Here are the credits for these tracks:

ACCIDENTAL SUICIDE (John Mayall) Archives To Eighties CD Polydor 837127 released 1988 / *Back to the Roots* double CD Polydor 314 549 424-2 released March 2001

John Mayall: vocals, harmonica, rhythm guitar
Eric Clapton: lead guitar
Sugarcane Harris: violin
Larry Taylor: bass
Joe Yuele: drums
(Harvey Mandel, Mick Taylor guitar tracks removed and new drums by Joe Yuele)

FORCE OF NATURE (John Mayall) *Archives to Eighties* CD Polydor 837127 released 1988 / *Back to the Roots* double CD Polydor 314 549 424-2 released March 2001

John Mayall: vocals
Eric Clapton: lead guitar
Mick Taylor: slide guitar
Harvey Mandel: lead guitar
Larry Taylor: bass
Joe Yuele: drums
(John Mayall's tambourine and rhythm guitar removed and new drums by Joe Yuele)

PRISONS ON THE ROAD (John Mayall) *Archives to Eighties* CD Polydor 837127 released 1988 / *Back to the Roots* double CD Polydor 314 549 424-2 released March 2001

John Mayall: vocals, piano
Eric Clapton: lead guitar
Sugarcane Harris: violin
Joe Yuele: drums
Larry Taylor: bass
(Joe Yuele's drums replace Paul Lagos's drums)

HOME AGAIN (John Mayall) *Archives to Eighties* CD Polydor 837127 released 1988 / *Back to the Roots* double CD Polydor 314 549 424-2 released March 2001

John Mayall: vocals, harmonica
Eric Clapton: lead guitar
Larry Taylor: bass
Joe Yuele: drums
(new drums by Joe Yuele)

LOOKING AT TOMORROW (John Mayall) *Archives to Eighties* CD Polydor 837127 released 1988 / *Back to the Roots* double CD Polydor 314 549 424-2 released March 2001

John Mayall: vocals, piano, guitar
Eric Clapton: lead guitar
Sugarcane Harris: violin
Joe Yuele: drums
Larry Taylor: bass
(John Mayall adds synthesized flute and Roland Juno keyboards, and Joe Yuele replaces Paul Lagos's drums)

ERIC CLAPTON GUEST SESSION

CRITERIA RECORDING STUDIOS 1755 Northeast 149th Street, Miami, Florida Session for *Buddy Guy and Junior Wells Play The Blues*

1 NOVEMBER 1970–4 NOVEMBER 1970

A MAN OF MANY WORDS (Buddy Guy) Buddy Guy and Junior Wells Play The Blues album Atco SD 33-364, UK Atlantic K40240 released 1972 / *Buddy Guy And Junior Wells Play The Blues* CD Rhino R2 70299 released 1992 / *Buddy Guy And Junior Wells Play The Blues* Rhino Handmade 2CD limited edition of 2,500 copies RHM2 7894 released 2005

Buddy Guy: lead guitar, vocals
Junior Wells: vocals, harmonica
Eric Clapton: rhythm guitar
Dr. John: piano
Carl Radle: bass
Jim Gordon: drums
A. C. Reed: tenor sax
Andrew Love: tenor sax
Roger Hopps: trumpet
Jack Hale: trombone

MY BABY SHE LEFT ME (She Left Me A Mule To Ride) (Sonny Boy Williamson) *Buddy Guy And Junior Wells Play The Blues* album Atco SD 33-364, UK Atlantic K40240 released 1972 / *Buddy Guy And Junior Wells Play The Blues* CD Rhino R2 70299 released 1992 / *Buddy Guy And Junior Wells Play The Blues* Rhino Handmade 2CD limited edition of 2,500 copies RHM2 7894 released 2005

Buddy Guy: lead guitar
Junior Wells: vocals, harmonica
Eric Clapton: rhythm guitar
Mike Utley: piano
Leroy Stewart: bass
Roosevelt Shaw: drums
A. C. Reed: tenor sax
Andrew Love: tenor sax
Roger Hopps: trumpet
Jack Hale: trombone

COME ON IN THIS HOUSE (Junior Wells) / **HAVE MERCY BABY** (Junior Wells) *Buddy Guy And Junior Wells Play The Blues* album Atco SD 33-364, UK Atlantic K40240 released 1972 / *Buddy Guy And Junior Wells Play The Blues* CD Rhino R2 70299 released 1992 / *Buddy Guy And Junior Wells Play The Blues* Rhino Handmade 2CD limited edition of 2,500 copies RHM2 7894 released 2005

Buddy Guy: lead guitar
Junior Wells: vocals, harmonica
Eric Clapton: rhythm guitar
Mike Utley: piano
Leroy Stewart: bass
Roosevelt Shaw: drums
A. C. Reed: tenor sax
Andrew Love: tenor sax
Roger Hopps: trumpet
Jack Hale: trombone

T-BONE SHUFFLE (Aaron T-Bone Walker) *Buddy Guy And Junior Wells Play The Blues* album Atco SD 33-364, UK Atlantic K40240 released 1972 / *Buddy Guy And Junior Wells Play The Blues* CD Rhino R2 70299 released 1992 / *Buddy Guy And Junior Wells Play The Blues* Rhino Handmade 2CD limited edition of 2500 copies RHM2 7894 released 2005

Buddy Guy: lead guitar, vocals
Junior Wells: harmonica
Eric Clapton: rhythm guitar
Dr. John: piano
Leroy Stewart: bass
Roosevelt Shaw: drums
A. C. Reed: tenor sax
Andrew Love: tenor sax
Roger Hopps: trumpet
Jack Hale: trombone

A POOR MAN'S PLEA (Junior Wells) *Buddy Guy And Junior Wells Play The Blues* album Atco SD 33-364, UK Atlantic K40240 released 1972 / *Buddy Guy And Junior Wells Play The Blues* CD Rhino R2 70299 released 1992 / *Buddy Guy And Junior Wells Play The Blues* Rhino Handmade 2CD limited edition of 2,500 copies RHM2 7894 released 2005

Buddy Guy: lead guitar
Junior Wells: vocals, harmonica
Eric Clapton: rhythm guitar
Mike Utley: organ
Leroy Stewart: bass
Roosevelt Shaw: drums
A. C. Reed: tenor sax
Andrew Love: tenor sax
Roger Hopps: trumpet
Jack Hale: trombone

MESSIN' WITH THE KID (Mel London) *Buddy Guy And Junior Wells Play The Blues* album Atco SD 33-364, UK Atlantic K40240 released 1972 / *Buddy Guy And Junior Wells Play The Blues* CD Rhino R2 70299 released 1992 / *Buddy Guy And Junior Wells Play The Blues* Rhino Handmade 2CD limited edition of 2,500 copies RHM2 7894 released 2005

Buddy Guy: lead guitar
Junior Wells: harmonica, vocals
Eric Clapton: rhythm guitar
Dr. John: piano
Leroy Stewart: bass
Roosevelt Shaw: drums
A. C. Reed: tenor sax
Andrew Love: tenor sax
Roger Hopps: trumpet
Jack Hale: trombone

I DON'T KNOW (Willie Mabon) *Buddy Guy And Junior Wells Play The Blues* album Atco SD 33-364, UK Atlantic K40240 released 1972 / *Buddy Guy And Junior Wells Play The Blues* CD Rhino R2 70299 released 1992 / *Buddy Guy And Junior Wells Play The Blues* Rhino Handmade 2CD limited edition of 2,500 copies RHM2 7894 released 2005

Buddy Guy: lead guitar
Junior Wells: vocals, harmonica
Eric Clapton: rhythm guitar
Mike Utley: piano
Leroy Stewart: bass
Roosevelt Shaw: drums
A. C. Reed: tenor sax
Andrew Love: tenor sax
Roger Hopps: trumpet
Jack Hale: trombone

BAD BAD WHISKEY (Thomas Davis) *Buddy Guy And Junior Wells Play The Blues* album Atco SD 33-364, UK Atlantic K40240 released 1972 / *Buddy Guy And Junior Wells Play The Blues* CD Rhino R2 70299 released 1992 / *Buddy Guy And Junior Wells Play The Blues* Rhino Handmade 2CD limited edition of 2,500 copies RHM2 7894 released 2005

Buddy Guy: lead guitar, vocals
Junior Wells: harmonica
Eric Clapton: slide guitar
Mike Utley: organ
Leroy Stewart: bass
Roosevelt Shaw: drums
A. C. Reed: tenor sax
Andrew Love: tenor sax

DIRTY MOTHER FOR YOU (Memphis Minnie) *Buddy Guy And Junior Wells Play The Blues* Rhino Handmade 2CD limited edition of 2,500 copies RHM2 7894 released 2005

Buddy Guy: lead guitar (second solo), vocals
Junior Wells: vocals, harmonica
Eric Clapton: lead guitar (first solo)
Mike Utley: piano
Leroy Stewart: bass
Roosevelt Shaw: drums

STONE CRAZY (Buddy Guy) *Buddy Guy And Junior Wells Play The Blues* Rhino Handmade 2CD limited edition of 2,500 copies RHM2 7894 released 2005

Buddy Guy: lead guitar, vocals
Junior Wells: harmonica
Mike Utley: piano
Leroy Stewart: bass
Roosevelt Shaw: drums
Andrew Love: tenor sax

WHY AM I TREATED SO BAD? (PLAYIN' THE BLUES) (unknown) *Buddy Guy And Junior Wells Play The Blues* Rhino Handmade 2CD limited edition of 2,500 copies RHM2 7894 released 2005

Buddy Guy: lead guitar, vocals
Junior Wells: harmonica
Eric Clapton: rhythm guitar
Mike Utley: organ
Leroy Stewart: bass
Roosevelt Shaw: drums
A. C. Reed: tenor sax
Andrew Love: tenor sax
Roger Hopps: trumpet
Jack Hale: trombone

TEARS, TEARS, TEARS (Amos Milburn) *Buddy Guy And Junior Wells Play The Blues* Rhino Handmade 2CD limited edition of 2500 copies RHM2 7894 released 2005

Buddy Guy: lead guitar
Junior Wells: vocals, harmonica
Eric Clapton: rhythm guitar
Mike Utley: piano
Leroy Stewart: bass
Roosevelt Shaw: drums
A. C. Reed: tenor sax
Andrew Love: tenor sax
Roger Hopps: trumpet
Jack Hale: trombone

LOVE HER WITH A FEELING (Tampa Red) take 1 / take 2 *Buddy Guy And Junior Wells Play The Blues* Rhino Handmade 2CD limited edition of 2,500 copies RHM2 7894 released 2005

Buddy Guy: lead guitar, vocals
Junior Wells: harmonica, vocals
Eric Clapton: rhythm guitar
Mike Utley: piano
Leroy Stewart: bass
Roosevelt Shaw: drums
Andrew Love: tenor sax

CHECKIN' UP ON MY BABY (Sonny Boy Williamson) *Buddy Guy And Junior Wells Play The Blues* Rhino Handmade 2CD limited edition of 2,500 copies RHM2 7894 released 2005

Buddy Guy: lead guitar
Junior Wells: vocals, harmonica
Eric Clapton: rhythm guitar
Mike Utley: organ
Leroy Stewart: bass
Roosevelt Shaw: drums
A. C. Reed: tenor sax
Andrew Love: tenor sax
Roger Hopps: trumpet
Jack Hale: trombone

LAST NIGHT (Little Walter Jacobs) *Buddy Guy And Junior Wells Play The Blues* Rhino Handmade 2CD limited edition of 2500 copies RHM2 7894 released 2005

Buddy Guy: lead guitar, vocals
Junior Wells: vocals, harmonica
Eric Clapton: slide Dobro
Dr. John: piano
Mike Utley: organ
Leroy Stewart: bass
Roosevelt Shaw: drums

FIRST TIME I MET THE BLUES (Eurreal Montgomery) *Buddy Guy And Junior Wells Play The Blues* Rhino Handmade 2CD limited edition of 2,500 copies RHM2 7894 released 2005

Buddy Guy: lead guitar, vocals
Eric Clapton: rhythm guitar
Dr. John: piano
Mike Utley: organ
Leroy Stewart: bass
Roosevelt Shaw: drums

D BLUES (Buddy Guy) *Buddy Guy And Junior Wells Play The Blues* Rhino Handmade 2CD limited edition of 2,500 copies RHM2 7894 released 2005

Buddy Guy: lead guitar (first solo, third solo), vocals
Junior Wells: harmonica
Eric Clapton: lead guitar (second solo)
Mike Utley: piano
Leroy Stewart: bass
Roosevelt Shaw: drums

BAD BAD WHISKEY (Thomas Davis)—long version—*Buddy Guy And Junior Wells Play The Blues* Rhino Handmade 2CD limited edition of 2,500 copies RHM2 7894 released 2005

Buddy Guy: lead guitar, vocals
Junior Wells: harmonica
Eric Clapton: slide guitar
Mike Utley: organ
Leroy Stewart: bass
Roosevelt Shaw: drums
A. C. Reed: tenor sax
Andrew Love: tenor sax

YOU'RE SO FINE (Little Walter Jacobs)—mono rough mix—*Buddy Guy And Junior Wells Play The Blues* Rhino Handmade 2CD limited edition of 2,500 copies RHM2 7894 released 2005

Buddy Guy: lead guitar, vocals
Junior Wells: harmonica, vocals
Leroy Stewart: bass
Roosevelt Shaw: drums
A. C. Reed: tenor sax
Andrew Love: tenor sax

WHY AM I TREATED SO BAD? (PLAYIN' THE BLUES) (unknown)—mono rough mix—*Buddy Guy And Junior Wells Play The Blues* Rhino Handmade 2CD limited edition of 2,500 copies RHM2 7894 released 2005

Buddy Guy: lead guitar, vocals
Junior Wells: harmonica
Eric Clapton: rhythm guitar
Mike Utley: organ
Leroy Stewart: bass
Roosevelt Shaw: drums
A. C. Reed: Tenor sax
Andrew Love: tenor sax
Roger Hopps: trumpet
Jack Hale: trombone

SWEET HOME CHICAGO (Robert Johnson)—mono rough mix—*Buddy Guy And Junior Wells Play The Blues* Rhino Handmade 2CD limited edition of 2,500 copies RHM2 7894 released 2005

Buddy Guy: lead guitar, vocals
Junior Wells: harmonica, vocals

Eric Clapton: rhythm guitar
Mike Utley: piano
Leroy Stewart: bass
Roosevelt Shaw: drums
A. C. Reed: Tenor sax
Andrew Love: tenor sax
Roger Hopps: trumpet
Jack Hale: trombone

Producers: Eric Clapton, Tom Dowd, Ahmet Ertegun
Engineers: Howie Albert, Ron Albert

"Are you kidding? With cats like that, there's really no reason to play. I just produced it for them." **—ERIC CLAPTON** (when asked if he played on the sessions by *NME*)

Of course, that is not entirely true as he did play on most of the album, albeit playing rhythm guitar for several numbers. He did occasionally play lead, but those only turned up on the deluxe edition in 2005.

"Backstage at a Rolling Stones gig in Paris Eric Clapton came up to me with a funny-looking cat with the face of a foreign diplomat. 'This is Ahmet Ertegun,' said Eric, 'president of Atlantic Records.'

'Heard you tonight, Buddy, and you were sensational,' said Ahmet. 'I want to do a real blues album on Atlantic with you and Junior. Good as Hoodoo Man Blues was, we want to surpass it.'

'Ahmet's really committed,' said Eric. 'He's actually going to co-produce it with me. What do you say?' I say great. I'm ready. So is Junior. Just say when and where. 'Next month in Florida,' said Eric. 'I've been working at Atlantic's Criteria Studio in Miami with my Derek and the Dominos stuff.'

Eric is a beautiful man and loyal friend, and recently he told me that while we were recording the record that came to be known as *Buddy Guy And Junior Wells Play The Blues*, he was wasted bad on drugs and drink. Far as Ahmet went, he spent the days at the beach. We hardly saw him at the studio at all. No one was in charge of nothing. Dr. John came in to play keyboards—and Dr. John's always great—but he saw what was happening, he said, 'Y'all are moving in five different directions at the same time. Plus the best shit you're playing is happening between the takes, and no one's recording it.'" **—BUDDY GUY** (from his autobiography *When I Left Home*)

The album took two years before it was released and even then Atlantic did not really promote it well.

> "I'd played with the Stones on 'You Can't Always Get What You Want' and 'Memo From Turner.' I played with them again a few years later at a birthday party for Keith Richards at Olympic Studios in London. They were working on the *Sticky Fingers* album. After the party, they cleared away the debris and set up to record. They cajoled Eric Clapton, myself and Bobby Keys to join them in a previously unheard tune called 'Brown Sugar.' George Harrison, who was among the partygoers, was invited to play but declined. I read in an interview with Keith that it came out great and that they would release it someday, but the version on *Sticky Fingers* is another one entirely." **—AL KOOPER**

OLYMPIC STUDIOS, 117-123 Church Road, Barnes, London SW13 Session with the Rolling Stones

18 DECEMBER 1970

BROWN SUGAR (Mick Jagger / Keith Richards) unreleased

Mick Jagger: vocals
Keith Richards: guitar
Mick Taylor: guitar
Bill Wyman: bass
Charlie Watts: drums
Eric Clapton: slide guitar
Al Kooper: keyboards
Bobby Keys: saxophone

Producer: Jimmy Miller
Engineers: Glyn Johns, Andy Johns

1971: ERIC CLAPTON GUEST SESSION; GEORGE HARRISON AND FRIENDS; THE CONCERT FOR BANGLA DESH; GUEST APPEARANCE WITH LEON RUSSELL

1971

Eric spent the early part of the year writing some new material for the next Dominos album, due to be recorded in April. The sessions almost dovetailed with the recording of Bobby Whitlock's first solo album in March. During those sessions, Bobby held a massive birthday bash on the 18th March. Guests included George Harrison, Ringo Starr, Eric Clapton, and Mick Jagger, among many others. The Dominos naturally all played on his album, as did George Harrison and Delaney & Bonnie.

By the time the Dominos gathered at Olympic Studios in April, Eric's mood had become increasingly dark and depressive. He felt he had poured his heart and soul out on the songs on the *Layla* double album, and his reward was the public's apathy. There were several reasons for the initial lack of success and acclaim. One was that most people had never heard of Derek and the Dominos; you really needed to be a music fan to get the inside knowledge on who the band were. Another was that many Cream fans who were still hoping for a return to powerhouse playing from Eric had deserted him when they realized he was going in a different direction.

A few weeks into the sessions, Eric admitted he had nothing left to say. He persevered, but relations between band members had gotten pretty intense. Jim Gordon seemed to have been the main catalyst for the general unease and frustrations of all concerned. At this stage nobody realized that he was an undiagnosed paranoid schizophrenic. Unfortunately, his mental issues had gotten worse due to his drug intake and he was becoming unreliable, not to mention irrational at times and confrontational at others. Stories about how the end of the Dominos came about differ from all surviving participants. But all seem to agree that it was in the studio that tempers got out of control between Jim and Eric and things were said in the heat of the moment. Eric walked out and never returned to the studio.

The fact that Eric never even contemplated getting another drummer in to finish the album only shows how deep of a pit he was in emotionally. What happened to Derek and the Dominos is a tragedy. These were four immensely talented guys who produced one of the greatest all-time albums that still stands the test of time today. The effects of continued hard drug use during their time together effectively killed the band off. Some of the material recorded for the second album confirms to me that there was every possibility of that album being as good as *Layla* had the band been in a good place mentally.

ERIC CLAPTON GUEST SESSION

OLYMPIC STUDIOS, 117-123 Church Road, Barnes, London SW13 Session for Bobby Whitlock

MARCH 1971

Bobby Whitlock had signed a solo deal with CBS in the UK and ABC in America. Not surprisingly, he was able to call on some of his friends to help out on his first solo album.

WHERE THERE'S A WILL (Bobby Whitlock / Delaney Bramlett) *Bobby Whitlock* album US Dunhill DSX 50121, UK CBS S 65109 released 1972

Bobby Whitlock: vocals, keyboards
George Harrison: guitar
Eric Clapton: guitar
Klaus Voormann: bass
Jim Gordon: drums
Bobby Keys: saxophone
Jim Price: trumpet

SONG FOR PAULA (Bobby Whitlock) (written for Paula Boyd, the sister of models Pattie Boyd and Jenny Boyd)

Bobby Whitlock: acoustic guitar, piano, organ
Jim Gordon: drums
Klaus Voormann: bass
George Harrison: guitar

A GAME CALLED LIFE (Bobby Whitlock)
Bobby Whitlock: twelve-string guitar (Bobby used Eric's handmade Tony Zemaitis guitar, nicknamed Ivan The Terrible. It was sold at auction in 2004 to raise funds for Crossroads)

Jim Gordon: drums, tabla
Klaus Voormann: bass
Chris Wood: flute
Strings: (overdubbed in Los Angeles)

A DAY WITHOUT JESUS (Bobby Whitlock / Don Nix)

Bobby Whitlock: vocals, piano, organ
George Harrison: guitar
Eric Clapton: guitar
Jim Gordon: drums
Klaus Voormann: bass
Bobby Whitlock: organ, piano
Delaney Bramlett: vocals (overdubbed in Los Angeles)
Bonnie Bramlett: vocals (overdubbed in Los Angeles)

BACK IN MY LIFE AGAIN (Bobby Whitlock)

Bobby Whitlock: vocals, organ
George Harrison: guitar
Eric Clapton: guitar
Jim Gordon: drums
Klaus Voormann: bass
Bobby Keys: saxophone
Jim Price: trombone

THE SCENERY HAS SLOWLY CHANGED (Bobby Whitlock)

Bobby Whitlock: twelve-string guitar (Eric's Ivan The Terrible Tony Zemaitis guitar)
Eric Clapton: guitar
Jim Gordon: drums, tabla
Klaus Voormann: bass

HELLO LA GOODBYE BIRMINGHAM (Delaney Bramlett / Mac Davis)
Bobby Whitlock: vocals, rhythm guitar
Eric Clapton: bass, slide guitar
Jim Gordon: drums

Producer: Jimmy Miller
Engineer: Andy Johns

> "Carl was off somewhere with Leon and was late coming to town for the session, so Eric played bass on it and the slide guitar. I played rhythm guitar and Jim played drums. It's probably the only time that Eric ever played bass on anything. There is a photograph of him with it on my session and he's holding it like it was his Stratocaster. He used a pick when he played it too." **—BOBBY WHITLOCK**

ERIC CLAPTON HOME STUDIO
Hurtwood Edge, Surrey
and
OLYMPIC STUDIOS, 117–123 Church Road, Barnes, London SW13

APRIL 1971–MAY 1971

INSTRUMENTAL 1 unreleased

Eric Clapton: guitar
Bobby Whitlock: piano
Carl Radle: bass
Jim Gordon: drums

INSTRUMENTAL 2 unreleased

Eric Clapton: guitar
Bobby Whitlock: piano
Carl Radle: bass
Jim Gordon: drums

GOLD DEVIL ROAD (Renee Armand / Eric Clapton / Jim Gordon) unreleased

Eric Clapton: guitar
Renee Armand: vocals
Bobby Whitlock: piano
Carl Radle: bass
Jim Gordon: drums

> "I wrote it in England with Jim and Eric when we were there at Clapton's house, recorded in his studio. It's a scratch/demo vocal so they could get it down. No fixes, no echo, no eq. I always wondered what happened to the tapes. It wasn't a session. It was just screwing around. We were there in London picking up record money and Jim's Ferrari. No Dominos. Just Eric and Jim in the little studio, both not in great shape. It was not my thing past a certain point. I have no metabolism to handle that level of stuff." **—RENEE ARMAND**

The track "Gold Devil Road" was sung by Renée Armand. It was originally recorded at Eric's home studio with just Eric, Renée, and Jim. As the tape was found in the infamous Olympic dumpster, it would appear that basic overdubs may have been made at Olympic. This was probably a demo for a future Renée solo album rather than for a Derek and the Dominos album. Then again, it may have been destined for a Jim Gordon project as a new instrumental version turned up on Bobby Keys's solo album as "Altar Rock."

OLYMPIC STUDIOS 117-123 Church Road, Barnes, London SW13 Sessions for second Derek and the Dominos album

13 APRIL 1971 (Studio Two)

THE NUMBER (AKA GOT TO GET BETTER IN A LITTLE WHILE) (Eric Clapton) 15 takes recorded

Take 9 is a slow version which just sounds too sluggish to work. The better-known fast version is much more on track, even though it was not finished at the time.

Eric Clapton: vocals, guitar
Bobby Whitlock: piano
Carl Radle: bass
Jim Gordon: drums

Tape box with engineer comments during sessions for Derek and the Dominos' second album. Note comment about Jim Gordon in bottom left confirming general feelings about his state of mind and capabilities.

IT'S HARD TO FIND A FRIEND (Jim Gordon)

Jim Gordon: acoustic guitar, vocals, tabla

Engineer: Anton Matthews

2 MAY 1971 (Studio One)

TONIGHT'S NUMBER (Eric Clapton)

Eric Clapton: rhythm guitar, lead guitar
Bobby Whitlock: piano
Carl Radle: bass
Jim Gordon: drums

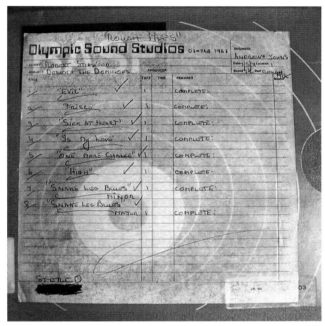

Tape box from sessions for Derek and the Dominos second album. This is Andy John's rough-mix reel of finished tracks.

9 MAY 1971

IT'S GOT TO GET BETTER (Eric Clapton) 8 takes recorded but no master made

Eric Clapton: guitar
Bobby Whitlock: piano
Carl Radle: bass
Jim Gordon: drums

Engineer: Andy Johns

Also recorded at Olympic Studios, but exact dates not known:

HIGH (Eric Clapton)

Eric Clapton: acoustic guitar, electric guitar
Bobby Whitlock: organ
Carl Radle: bass
Jim Gordon: drums

IS MY LOVE (Eric Clapton)

Eric Clapton: slide guitar
Bobby Whitlock: piano
Carl Radle: bass
Jim Gordon: drums

ONE MORE CHANCE (Eric Clapton)

Eric Clapton: guitar
Bobby Whitlock: piano
Carl Radle: bass
Jim Gordon: drums

MEAN OLD FRISCO (Arthur Crudup)

Eric Clapton: guitar, Dobro
Bobby Whitlock: piano
Carl Radle: bass
Jim Gordon: drums

SNAKE LAKE BLUES (Eric Clapton / Bobby Whitlock) minor

Eric Clapton: guitars
Bobby Whitlock: piano
Carl Radle: bass
Jim Gordon: drums

SNAKE LAKE BLUES (Eric Clapton / Bobby Whitlock) major

Eric Clapton: guitars
Bobby Whitlock: piano
Carl Radle: bass
Jim Gordon: drums

SON OF APACHE (Eric Clapton)

Eric Clapton: guitars
Carl Radle: bass
Jim Gordon: drums

CHOCOLATe (Eric Clapton)

Eric Clapton: rhythm guitar, lead guitar
Carl Radle: bass
Jim Gordon: drums

EVIL (Willie Dixon) 5 takes recorded

Eric Clapton: vocal, tremolo guitar, wah-wah guitar, Leslie guitar, Dobro
Bobby Whitlock: piano
Carl Radle: bass
Jim Gordon: drums

At least five takes of "Evil" were recorded which include a couple of instrumental versions before extra guitars and vocals were added. This is one of a handful of truly finished masters made for the aborted second album. Clearly, the frustrations of the band also extended to the engineers. On the tracking sheet for the session for "Evil" the engineer notes next to Jim Gordon's drum tracks track: "What the fuck's HE doing??" "He" has been circled to emphasize the problem.

A master reel of finished masters was produced by Andy Johns on 27 May 1971 at Olympic containing:

CARL AND ME (Eric Clapton) length 6.25
EVIL (Willie Dixon) length 4.34
SNAKE LAKE BLUES (Eric Clapton / Bobby Whitlock) (misspelled on tape box as "Snake Leg Blues") length 3.28
I'VE BEEN ALL DAY (Eric Clapton) length 4.17
MEAN OLD FRISCO (Arthur Crudup) length 4.00
ONE MORE CHANCE (Eric Clapton) length 3.14
HIGH (Eric Clapton) length 3.14
IT'S GOT TO GET BETTER IN A LITTLE WHILE (Eric Clapton) length 5.44

This tape was made at the request of RSO, who hoped that Eric might revisit the recordings in the near future. He did actually revisit the tapes with the help of Pete Townshend, but not until the middle of 1972 but quickly got bored and abandoned them again.

The unreleased tracks were given another potential lease of life when they were given a new dusting off by Tom Dowd in April 1974 at Criteria Studios with a view of Eric using some of the material for his comeback album. He selected:

CHOCOLATE (Eric Clapton)
IT'S HARD TO FIND (Eric Clapton)
TILL I SEE YOU AGAIN (Eric Clapton)
CARL AND ME (Eric Clapton)
EVIL (Willie Dixon)
SNAKE LAKE BLUES (Eric Clapton / Bobby Whitlock)
I'VE BEEN ALL DAY (Eric Clapton)
MEAN OLD FRISCO (Arthur Crudup)
ONE MORE CHANCE (Eric Clapton)
HIGH (Eric Clapton)
IT'S GOT TO GET BETTER (Eric Clapton)
JIM'S SONG (Jim Gordon)

Once again, they were abandoned. The first time any of the tracks made it onto an album was for Eric's 25th Anniversary box set, *Crossroads*, in 1988.

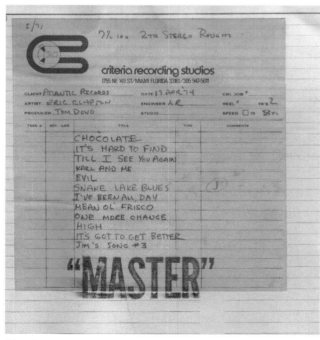

Tape box containing transfers of 1971 material from sessions for Derek and the Dominos' second album. This is Tom Dowd's 1974 compilation reel of tracks considered for potential release at the time. They were abandoned in favor of Eric recording a new album, 461 Ocean Boulevard.

OLYMPIC STUDIOS
117-123 Church Road,
Barnes, London SW13

TRIDENT STUDIOS
Trident House, 17 St.
Anne's Court,
Soho, London W1

COMMAND STUDIOS
201 Piccadilly, London W1
Session for Bobby Keys

NOVEMBER 1969–DECEMBER 1971

An instrumental version of "Gold Devil Road," the original of which was first recorded at Eric's home studio in 1971, appears on Bobby Keys's solo album as "Altar Rock." Jim Gordon plays drums on several tracks on those sessions and also co-produced it with Andy Johns and Bobby Keys. The album was recorded over several years during downtime in Bobby's schedule and features many guests. Known to have participated on the album are Jim Price on trumpet, Felix Pappalardi on bass, Leslie West on guitar, Eric Clapton on guitar, Carl Radle on bass, Jim Gordon on drums, Corky Laing on drums, George Harrison on guitar, Ringo Starr on drums, Klaus Voormann on bass, Jack Bruce on bass, Dave Mason on guitar, Nicky Hopkins on piano, John Uribe on guitar, and Mike Utley on keyboards. Incredibly, Bobby Keys does not mention the album sessions in his autobiography.

> **❝**I recall seeing Eric at the Bobby Key's solo album sessions in London. Some of it was made at Olympic Studios in parallel with Derek and the Dominos sessions there. It was a case that if somebody didn't show or was late, Bobby would use up the time with the people who were there for his own album. I recall seeing Keith Richards there as well. Felix came up with 'Altar Rock,' which is a place in Nantucket that he and I used to go to. I had a Ginger Baker vibe on that track in my mind. Anyway, it was an ongoing series of sessions that took place in several different studios.**❞**
>
> **—CORKY LAING**

Bobby Keys album UK Warner Brother Records K 46141 released July 1972 / *Bobby Keys* CD Aurora 5025 released August 2012

MUSICIANS PARTICIPATING ON ALBUM:
Saxophone: Bobby Keys
Trumpet: Jim Price
Guitars: Eric Clapton, John Uruibe, Leslie West, Charlee Freeman, Dave Mason, George Harrison
Bass: Carl Radle, Klaus Voormann, Felix Pappalardi, Jack Bruce
Keyboards: Nicky Hopkins, Mike Utley, Jim Price
Drums: Corky Laing, Jim Gordon, Ringo Starr
Producers: Jim Gordon, Andy Johns, Bobby Keys
Engineers: Andy Johns, Chris Kimsey

GEORGE HARRISON AND FRIENDS—THE CONCERT FOR BANGLA DESH 1971

George Harrison had been very concerned at what had been happening to hundreds of thousands of refugees in Bangla Desh. After an approach from Ravi Shankar, George went about organizing two concerts, which would feature some of his famous chums, to raise funds for the famine stricken country. George had managed to persuade Bob Dylan, Leon Russell, Billy Preston, members of Badfinger, Ringo Starr, Klaus Voormann, and others to play with him at the shows. The thought of seeing two Beatles together onstage along with the other stars was a dream come true for fans. Originally billed as George Harrison and Friends, the "Concert for Bangla Desh" was the first benefit concert of its kind, a forerunner to 1985's "Live Aid" and later "Farm Aid," "Live 8," and "Live Earth," among others. Although not as global due to technology restrictions of the time, the two concerts still received worldwide publicity due to the extraordinary gathering of musical talent collaborating for a common humanitarian cause. Not surprisingly, the two shows at Madison Square Garden sold out instantly. Don't forget that George hadn't performed publicly since the Beatles' last concert in 1966, so these shows were very big news indeed. There was only one place to be on 1 August 1971.

A few months into Eric's self-imposed heroin retirement, he received a phone call from George

Harrison. He wanted Eric to play with him at the concerts in New York. Eric did not want to let George down and agreed to fly over on the proviso that he would have some "medicine" on hand for him to take. Eric could not risk taking any of his stash with him on the plane and through customs in the US. He needed to ensure there would be some heroin available in New York so that he could at least function onstage without the shakes or passing out. Unfortunately, no "medicine" was waiting for him in New York and Eric went straight into cold turkey. He had to miss rehearsals and remained locked in his hotel room in a bad way. George took the precaution of asking Jesse Ed Davis to step in on guitar in case Eric would not be able to make the shows. Eventually, one of the organizers came up with a powerful ulcer syrup that contained enough morphine to enable Eric to function normally. The fact that Eric does not remember playing at the concerts shows how bad a condition he was in. To the relief of all concerned, he did make the final rehearsal and soundcheck which took place at Madison Square Garden on Saturday 31 July 1971.

The shows were recorded and filmed, so that everyone would have a chance to witness the event and more funds would be raised for the cause. The album, film, and later video and DVD have generated millions of dollars for UNICEF and raised awareness for the organization around the world.

Filming and recording such an event back in 1971 was a huge deal. There were multiple 16mm film cameras that held around fifteen minutes of film, which would then need a changeover. The film footage was then put onto 70mm film, which was not easy and had to be painstakingly done frame by frame. On top of that you had to sync the sound to the picture, which was also difficult, as occasionally footage from both shows had to be used in the film in order to get a complete number. As far as recording the sound, there were forty-four microphones onstage being mixed down to sixteen-track reels in the Record Plant mobile truck. Incredible! Looking at the footage and listening to the soundtrack today, it is a remarkable feat and a testament to all the technical staff involved. The soundtrack was ready within a month of the concerts, but frustrating record label negotiations meant a lengthy delay before the triple album could be released.

As good as the first show was, the whole band felt more relaxed for the second. As a result, the majority of the released product is sourced from that show. There are many highlights, but Eric and George playing lead guitars on "While My Guitar Gently Weeps" is certainly one of the biggest. Surprisingly, they chose the matinee performance for the soundtrack and film as opposed to the better evening version. For the first show Eric bizarrely took the decision to use a semi-hollow body Gibson Byrdland, which was completely the wrong guitar to use for such an event and made life even harder for himself. He wisely switched to his Fender Stratocaster for the evening show.

Madison Square Garden, New York City Rehearsal and soundcheck

31 JULY 1971

COME ON IN MY KITCHEN (ROBERT JOHNSON) DVD US RHINO R2 970480, UK RHINO R2 970481 RELEASED OCTOBER 2005

George Harrison: guitar
Eric Clapton: guitar
Jesse Ed Davis: guitar
Ringo Starr: drums
Jim Keltner: drums
Klaus Voormann: bass
Leon Russell: piano, vocals
Billy Preston: organ

Part of the bonus features on the Concert For Bangla Desh DVD. Although not shown on the footage, Jesse Ed Davis takes the guitar solo. Eric is playing his semi-hollow-body Gibson Byrdland that he would use for the matinee show on 1 August 1971.

Madison Square Garden New York City

1 AUGUST 1971

SETLIST EARLY SHOW AT 3:30 P.M.:

Wah-Wah (George Harrison) (a mix of the early show and late show versions are used to make up a complete song for release because the ending of the evening version was too tentative and unsuitable) *The Concert For Bangla Desh* triple

album Apple STCX 3385 released US December 1971, UK
January 1972 / *The Concert For Bangla Desh* double CD Epic
82876729862 released October 2005 / DVD US Rhino R2
970480, UK Rhino R2 970481 released October 2005

George Harrison: vocals, guitar
Eric Clapton: lead guitar
Jesse Ed Davis; guitar
Ringo Starr: drums
Jim Keltner: drums
Mike Gibbins: percussion
Klaus Voormann: bass
Leon Russell: piano
Billy Preston: organ
Jim Horn: horns
Chuck Findley: horns
Allan Beuter: horns
Jackie Kelso: horns
Lou McCreary: horns
Ollie Mitchell: horns
Don Nix: backing vocals
Jo Green: backing vocals
Jeanie Greene: backing vocals
Marlin Greene: backing vocals
Dolores Hall: backing vocals
Claudia Linear: backing vocals
Don Preston: backing vocals
Tom Evans: acoustic guitar
Pete Ham: acoustic guitar
Joey Molland: acoustic guitar

Something (George Harrison) unreleased

George Harrison: vocals, lead guitar
Eric Clapton: guitar
Jesse Ed Davis; guitar
Ringo Starr: drums
Jim Keltner: drums
Mike Gibbins: percussion
Klaus Voormann: bass
Leon Russell: piano
Billy Preston: organ
Jim Horn: horns
Chuck Findley: horns
Allan Beuter: horns
Jackie Kelso: horns
Lou McCreary: horns
Ollie Mitchell: horns
Don Nix: backing vocals
Jo Green: backing vocals
Jeanie Greene: backing vocals
Marlin Greene: backing vocals
Dolores Hall: backing vocals
Claudia Linear: backing vocals
Don Preston: backing vocals
Tom Evans: acoustic guitar
Pete Ham: acoustic guitar
Joey Molland: acoustic guitar

*George Harrison and Eric Clapton at the Concert for Bangla
Desh at Madison Square Garden, New York, 1 August 1971.*

Awaiting On You All (George Harrison) unreleased

George Harrison: vocals, guitar
Eric Clapton: lead guitar
Jesse Ed Davis; guitar
Ringo Starr: drums
Jim Keltner: drums
Mike Gibbins: percussion
Klaus Voormann: bass
Leon Russell: piano
Billy Preston: organ
Jim Horn: horns
Chuck Findley: horns
Allan Beuter: horns
Jackie Kelso: horns
Lou McCreary: horns
Ollie Mitchell: horns
Don Nix: backing vocals
Jo Green: backing vocals
Jeanie Greene: backing vocals
Marlin Greene: backing vocals
Dolores Hall: backing vocals
Claudia Linear: backing vocals
Don Preston: backing vocals
Tom Evans: acoustic guitar
Pete Ham: acoustic guitar
Joey Molland: acoustic guitar

That's The Way God Planned It (Billy Preston) unreleased

George Harrison: guitar
Eric Clapton: lead guitar
Jesse Ed Davis: guitar
Ringo Starr: drums
Jim Keltner: drums
Mike Gibbins: percussion
Klaus Voormann: bass
Leon Russell: piano
Billy Preston: lead vocals, organ
Jim Horn: horns
Chuck Findley: horns
Allan Beuter: horns

Jackie Kelso: horns
Lou McCreary: horns
Ollie Mitchell: horns
Don Nix: backing vocals
Jo Green: backing vocals
Jeanie Greene: backing vocals
Marlin Greene: backing vocals
Dolores Hall: backing vocals
Claudia Linear: backing vocals
Don Preston: backing vocals
Tom Evans: acoustic guitar
Pete Ham: acoustic guitar
Joey Molland: acoustic guitar

It Don't Come Easy (Richard Starkey) unreleased

George Harrison: guitar
Eric Clapton: lead guitar
Jesse Ed Davis: guitar
Ringo Starr: lead vocals, drums
Jim Keltner: drums
Mike Gibbins: percussion
Klaus Voormann: bass
Leon Russell: piano
Billy Preston: organ
Jim Horn: horns
Chuck Findley: horns
Allan Beuter: horns
Jackie Kelso: horns
Lou McCreary: horns
Ollie Mitchell: horns
Don Nix: backing vocals
Jo Green: backing vocals
Jeanie Greene: backing vocals
Marlin Greene: backing vocals
Dolores Hall: backing vocals
Claudia Linear: backing vocals
Don Preston: backing vocals
Tom Evans: acoustic guitar
Pete Ham: acoustic guitar
Joey Molland: acoustic guitar

Beware Of Darkness (George Harrison) unreleased

George Harrison: vocals, guitar
Eric Clapton: guitar
Jesse Ed Davis: guitar
Ringo Starr: drums
Jim Keltner: drums
Mike Gibbins: percussion
Klaus Voormann: bass
Leon Russell: piano, shared lead vocal
Billy Preston: organ
Jim Horn: horns
Chuck Findley: horns
Allan Beuter: horns
Jackie Kelso: horns
Lou McCreary: horns

Ollie Mitchell: horns
Don Nix: backing vocals
Jo Green: backing vocals
Jeanie Greene: backing vocals
Marlin Greene: backing vocals
Dolores Hall: backing vocals
Claudia Linear: backing vocals
Don Preston: backing vocals
Tom Evans: acoustic guitar
Pete Ham: acoustic guitar
Joey Molland: acoustic guitar

While My Guitar Gently Weeps (George Harrison) *The Concert For Bangla Desh* triple album Apple STCX 3385 released US December 1971, UK January 1972 / *The Concert For Bangla Desh* double CD Epic 82876729862 released October 2005 / DVD US Rhino R2 970480, UK Rhino R2 970481 released October 2005

George Harrison: vocals, lead guitar
Eric Clapton: lead guitar
Jesse Ed Davis: guitar
Ringo Starr: drums
Jim Keltner: drums
Mike Gibbins: percussion
Klaus Voormann: bass
Leon Russell: piano, shared lead vocal
Billy Preston: organ
Tom Evans: acoustic guitar
Pete Ham: acoustic guitar
Joey Molland: acoustic guitar

Jumpin' Jack Flash (Mick Jagger / Keith Richards) *The Concert For Bangla Desh* triple album Apple STCX 3385 released US December 1971, UK January 1972 / *The Concert For Bangla Desh* double CD Epic 82876729862 released October 2005 / DVD US Rhino R2 970480, UK Rhino R2 970481 released October 2005

George Harrison: guitar
Eric Clapton: guitar
Jesse Ed Davis: guitar
Don Preston: lead guitar
Ringo Starr: drums
Jim Keltner: drums
Mike Gibbins: percussion
Carl Radle: bass
Leon Russell: piano, lead vocal
Billy Preston: organ
Don Nix: backing vocals
Jo Green: backing vocals
Jeanie Greene: backing vocals
Marlin Greene: backing vocals
Dolores Hall: backing vocals
Claudia Linear: backing vocals
Don Preston: backing vocals

Youngblood (Jerry Leiber / Mike Stoller / Doc Pomus) *The Concert For Bangla Desh* triple album Apple STCX 3385 released US December 1971, UK January 1972 / *The Concert For Bangla Desh* double CD Epic 82876729862 released October 2005

```
George Harrison: guitar
Eric Clapton: guitar
Jesse Ed Davis: guitar
Don Preston: lead guitar, shared lead vocals
Ringo Starr: drums
Jim Keltner: drums
Mike Gibbins: percussion
Carl Radle: bass
Leon Russell: piano, lead vocal
Billy Preston: organ
Don Nix: backing vocals
Jo Green: backing vocals
Jeanie Greene: backing vocals
Marlin Greene: backing vocals
Dolores Hall: backing vocals
Claudia Linear: backing vocals
Don Preston: backing vocals
```

Jumpin' Jack Flash (Reprise) (Mick Jagger / Keith Richards) *The Concert For Bangla Desh* triple album Apple STCX 3385 released US December 1971, UK January 1972 / *The Concert For Bangla Desh* double CD Epic 82876729862 released October 2005 / DVD US Rhino R2 970480, UK Rhino R2 970481 released October 2005

```
George Harrison: guitar
Eric Clapton: guitar
Jesse Ed Davis: guitar
Don Preston: lead guitar
Ringo Starr: drums
Jim Keltner: drums
Mike Gibbins: percussion
Carl Radle: bass
Leon Russell: piano, lead vocal
Billy Preston: organ
Don Nix: backing vocals
Jo Green: backing vocals
Jeanie Greene: backing vocals
Marlin Greene: backing vocals
Dolores Hall: backing vocals
Claudia Linear: backing vocals
Don Preston: backing vocals
```

Here Comes The Sun (George Harrison) unreleased

```
George Harrison: vocals, acoustic guitar
Pete Ham: acoustic guitar
```

A Hard Rain's Gonna Fall (Bob Dylan) unreleased

```
Bob Dylan: vocals, acoustic guitar
George Harrison: electric guitar
```

```
Leon Russell: bass
Ringo Starr: tambourine
```

Blowin' In The Wind (Bob Dylan) unreleased

```
Bob Dylan: vocals, acoustic guitar
George Harrison: electric guitar
Leon Russell: bass
Ringo Starr: tambourine
```

It Takes A Lot To Laugh It Takes A Train To Cry (Bob Dylan) unreleased

```
Bob Dylan: vocals, acoustic guitar
George Harrison: slide guitar
Leon Russell: bass
Ringo Starr: tambourine
```

Love Minus Zero / No Limit (Bob Dylan) *The Concert For Bangla Desh* triple album Apple STCX 3385 released US December 1971, UK January 1972 / *The Concert For Bangla Desh* double CD Epic 82876729862 released October 2005 / DVD US Rhino R2 970480, UK Rhino R2 970481 released October 2005

```
Bob Dylan: vocals, acoustic guitar
George Harrison: electric guitar
Leon Russell: bass
Ringo Starr: tambourine
```

Just Like A Woman (Bob Dylan) unreleased

```
Bob Dylan: vocals, acoustic guitar
George Harrison: vocals, electric guitar
Leon Russell: vocals, bass
Ringo Starr: tambourine
```

Hear Me Lord (George Harrison) unreleased

```
George Harrison: vocals, guitar
Eric Clapton: lead guitar
Jesse Ed Davis: guitar
Ringo Starr: drums
Jim Keltner: drums
Mike Gibbins: percussion
Klaus Voormann: bass
Leon Russell: piano
Billy Preston: organ
Jim Horn: horns
Chuck Findley: horns
Allan Beuter: horns
Jackie Kelso: horns
Lou McCreary: horns
Ollie Mitchell: horns
Don Nix: backing vocals
Jo Green: backing vocals
Jeanie Greene: backing vocals
Marlin Greene: backing vocals
Dolores Hall: backing vocals
Claudia Linear: backing vocals
Don Preston: backing vocals
```

Tom Evans: acoustic guitar
Pete Ham: acoustic guitar
Joey Molland: acoustic guitar

My Sweet Lord (George Harrison) unreleased

George Harrison: vocals, acoustic guitar
Eric Clapton: slide guitar
Jesse Ed Davis: guitar
Ringo Starr: drums
Jim Keltner: drums
Mike Gibbins: percussion
Klaus Voormann: bass
Leon Russell: piano
Billy Preston: organ
Don Nix: backing vocals
Jo Green: backing vocals
Jeanie Greene: backing vocals
Marlin Greene: backing vocals
Dolores Hall: backing vocals
Claudia Linear: backing vocals
Don Preston: backing vocals
Tom Evans: acoustic guitar
Pete Ham: acoustic guitar
Joey Molland: acoustic guitar

Bangla Desh (George Harrison) unreleased

George Harrison: vocals, guitar
Eric Clapton: lead guitar
Jesse Ed Davis: guitar
Don Preston: guitar
Ringo Starr: drums
Jim Keltner: drums
Mike Gibbins: percussion
Klaus Voormann: bass
Leon Russell: piano
Billy Preston: organ
Jim Horn: horns
Chuck Findley: horns
Allan Beuter: horns
Jackie Kelso: horns
Lou McCreary: horns
Ollie Mitchell: horns
Don Nix: backing vocals
Jo Green: backing vocals
Jeanie Greene: backing vocals
Marlin Greene: backing vocals
Dolores Hall: backing vocals
Claudia Linear: backing vocals
Don Preston: backing vocals
Tom Evans: acoustic guitar
Pete Ham: acoustic guitar
Joey Molland: acoustic guitar

Madison Square Garden, New York City

1 AUGUST 1971

SETLIST, LATE SHOW AT 8:00 P.M.:

Wah-Wah (George Harrison) (a mix of the early-show and late-show versions are used to make up a complete song for release because the ending of the evening version was too tentative and unsuitable) *The Concert For Bangla Desh* triple album Apple STCX 3385 released US December 1971, UK January 1972 / *The Concert For Bangla Desh* double CD Epic 82876729862 released October 2005 / DVD US Rhino R2 970480, UK Rhino R2 970481 released October 2005

George Harrison: vocals, guitar
Eric Clapton: lead guitar
Jesse Ed Davis: guitar
Ringo Starr: drums
Jim Keltner: drums
Mike Gibbins: percussion
Klaus Voormann: bass
Leon Russell: piano
Billy Preston: organ
Jim Horn: horns
Chuck Findley: horns
Allan Beuter: horns
Jackie Kelso: horns
Lou McCreary: horns
Ollie Mitchell: horns
Don Nix: backing vocals
Jo Green: backing vocals
Jeanie Greene: backing vocals
Marlin Greene: backing vocals
Dolores Hall: backing vocals
Claudia Linear: backing vocals
Don Preston: backing vocals
Tom Evans: acoustic guitar
Pete Ham: acoustic guitar
Joey Molland: acoustic guitar

My Sweet Lord (George Harrison) *The Concert For Bangla Desh* triple album Apple STCX 3385 released US December 1971, UK January 1972 / *The Concert For Bangla Desh* double CD Epic 82876729862 released October 2005 / DVD US Rhino R2 970480, UK Rhino R2 970481 released October 2005

George Harrison: vocals, acoustic guitar
Eric Clapton: slide guitar
Jesse Ed Davis: guitar
Ringo Starr: drums
Jim Keltner: drums
Mike Gibbins: percussion

Klaus Voormann: bass
Leon Russell: piano
Billy Preston: organ
Don Nix: backing vocals
Jo Green: backing vocals
Jeanie Greene: backing vocals
Marlin Greene: backing vocals
Dolores Hall: backing vocals
Claudia Linear: backing vocals
Don Preston: backing vocals
Tom Evans: acoustic guitar
Pete Ham: acoustic guitar
Joey Molland: acoustic guitar

Awaiting On You All (George Harrison) *The Concert For Bangla Desh* triple album Apple STCX 3385 released US December 1971, UK January 1972 / *The Concert For Bangla Desh* double CD Epic 82876729862 released October 2005 / DVD US Rhino R2 970480, UK Rhino R2 970481 released October 2005

George Harrison: vocals, guitar
Eric Clapton: lead guitar
Jesse Ed Davis: guitar
Ringo Starr: drums
Jim Keltner: drums
Mike Gibbins: percussion
Klaus Voormann: bass
Leon Russell: piano
Billy Preston: organ
Jim Horn: horns
Chuck Findley: horns
Allan Beuter: horns
Jackie Kelso: horns
Lou McCreary: horns
Ollie Mitchell: horns
Don Nix: backing vocals
Jo Green: backing vocals
Jeanie Greene: backing vocals
Marlin Greene: backing vocals
Dolores Hall: backing vocals
Claudia Linear: backing vocals
Don Preston: backing vocals
Tom Evans: acoustic guitar
Pete Ham: acoustic guitar
Joey Molland: acoustic guitar

That's The Way God Planned It (Billy Preston) *The Concert For Bangla Desh* triple album Apple STCX 3385 released US December 1971, UK January 1972 / *The Concert For Bangla Desh* double CD Epic 82876729862 released October 2005 / DVD US Rhino R2 970480, UK Rhino R2 970481 released October 2005

George Harrison: guitar
Eric Clapton: lead guitar
Jesse Ed Davis: guitar

Ringo Starr: drums
Jim Keltner: drums
Mike Gibbins: percussion
Klaus Voormann: bass
Leon Russell: piano
Billy Preston: lead vocals, organ
Jim Horn: horns
Chuck Findley: horns
Allan Beuter: horns
Jackie Kelso: horns
Lou McCreary: horns
Ollie Mitchell: horns
Don Nix: backing vocals
Jo Green: backing vocals
Jeanie Greene: backing vocals
Marlin Greene: backing vocals
Dolores Hall: backing vocals
Claudia Linear: backing vocals
Don Preston: backing vocals
Tom Evans: acoustic guitar
Pete Ham: acoustic guitar
Joey Molland: acoustic guitar

It Don't Come Easy (Richard Starkey) *The Concert For Bangla Desh* triple album Apple STCX 3385 released US December 1971, UK January 1972 / *The Concert For Bangla Desh* double CD Epic 82876729862 released October 2005 / DVD US Rhino R2 970480, UK Rhino R2 970481 released October 2005

George Harrison: guitar
Eric Clapton: lead guitar
Jesse Ed Davis: guitar
Ringo Starr: lead vocals, drums
Jim Keltner: drums
Mike Gibbins: percussion
Klaus Voormann: bass
Leon Russell: piano
Billy Preston: organ
Jim Horn: horns
Chuck Findley: horns
Allan Beuter: horns
Jackie Kelso: horns
Lou McCreary: horns
Ollie Mitchell: horns
Don Nix: backing vocals
Jo Green: backing vocals
Jeanie Greene: backing vocals
Marlin Greene: backing vocals
Dolores Hall: backing vocals
Claudia Linear: backing vocals
Don Preston: backing vocals
Tom Evans: acoustic guitar
Pete Ham: acoustic guitar
Joey Molland: acoustic guitar

Beware Of Darkness (George Harrison) *The Concert For Bangla Desh* triple album Apple STCX 3385 released US December 1971, UK January 1972 / *The Concert For Bangla Desh* double CD Epic 82876729862 released October 2005 / DVD US Rhino R2 970480, UK Rhino R2 970481 released October 2005

George Harrison: vocals, guitar
Eric Clapton: guitar
Jesse Ed Davis; guitar
Ringo Starr: drums
Jim Keltner: drums
Mike Gibbins: percussion
Klaus Voormann: bass
Leon Russell: piano, shared lead vocal
Billy Preston: organ
Jim Horn: horns
Chuck Findley: horns
Allan Beuter: horns
Jackie Kelso: horns
Lou McCreary: horns
Ollie Mitchell: horns
Don Nix: backing vocals
Jo Green: backing vocals
Jeanie Greene: backing vocals
Marlin Greene: backing vocals
Dolores Hall: backing vocals
Claudia Linear: backing vocals
Don Preston: backing vocals
Tom Evans: acoustic guitar
Pete Ham: acoustic guitar
Joey Molland: acoustic guitar

While My Guitar Gently Weeps (George Harrison) unreleased

George Harrison: vocals, lead guitar
Eric Clapton: lead guitar
Jesse Ed Davis: guitar
Ringo Starr: drums
Jim Keltner: drums
Mike Gibbins: percussion
Klaus Voormann: bass
Leon Russell: piano, shared lead vocal
Billy Preston: organ
Tom Evans: acoustic guitar
Pete Ham: acoustic guitar
Joey Molland: acoustic guitar

Jumpin' Jack Flash (Mick Jagger / Keith Richards) unreleased

George Harrison: guitar
Eric Clapton: guitar
Jesse Ed Davis: guitar
Don Preston: lead guitar
Ringo Starr: drums

Jim Keltner: drums
Mike Gibbins: percussion
Carl Radle: bass
Leon Russell: piano, lead vocal
Billy Preston: organ
Don Nix: backing vocals
Jo Green: backing vocals
Jeanie Greene: backing vocals
Marlin Greene: backing vocals
Dolores Hall: backing vocals
Claudia Linear: backing vocals
Don Preston: backing vocals

Youngblood (Jerry Leiber / Mike Stoller / Doc Pomus) *The Concert For Bangla Desh* DVD US Rhino R2 970480, UK Rhino R2 970481 released October 2005

George Harrison: guitar
Eric Clapton: guitar
Jesse Ed Davis: guitar
Don Preston: lead guitar, shared lead vocals
Ringo Starr: drums
Jim Keltner: drums
Mike Gibbins: percussion
Carl Radle: bass
Leon Russell: piano, lead vocal
Billy Preston: organ
Don Nix: backing vocals
Jo Green: backing vocals
Jeanie Greene: backing vocals
Marlin Greene: backing vocals
Dolores Hall: backing vocals
Claudia Linear: backing vocals
Don Preston: backing vocals

Jumpin' Jack Flash (Reprise) (Mick Jagger / Keith Richards) unreleased

George Harrison: guitar
Eric Clapton: guitar
Jesse Ed Davis: guitar
Don Preston: lead guitar
Ringo Starr: drums
Jim Keltner: drums
Mike Gibbins: percussion
Carl Radle: bass
Leon Russell: piano, lead vocal
Billy Preston: organ
Don Nix: backing vocals
Jo Green: backing vocals
Jeanie Greene: backing vocals
Marlin Greene: backing vocals
Dolores Hall: backing vocals
Claudia Linear: backing vocals
Don Preston: backing vocals

Here Comes The Sun (George Harrison) *The Concert For Bangla Desh* triple album Apple STCX 3385 released US December 1971, UK January 1972 / *The Concert For Bangla Desh* double CD Epic 82876729862 released October 2005 / DVD US Rhino R2 970480, UK Rhino R2 970481 released October 2005

George Harrison: vocals, acoustic guitar
Pete Ham: acoustic guitar

A Hard Rain's Gonna Fall (Bob Dylan) *The Concert For Bangla Desh* triple album Apple STCX 3385 released US December 1971, UK January 1972 / *The Concert For Bangla Desh* double CD Epic 82876729862 released October 2005 / DVD US Rhino R2 970480, UK Rhino R2 970481 released October 2005

Bob Dylan: vocals, acoustic guitar
George Harrison: electric guitar
Leon Russell: bass
Ringo Starr: tambourine

It Takes A Lot To Laugh It Takes A Train To Cry (Bob Dylan) *The Concert For Bangla Desh* triple album Apple STCX 3385 released US December 1971, UK January 1972 / *The Concert For Bangla Desh* double CD Epic 82876729862 released October 2005 / DVD US Rhino R2 970480, UK Rhino R2 970481 released October 2005

Bob Dylan: vocals, acoustic guitar
George Harrison: slide guitar
Leon Russell: bass
Ringo Starr: tambourine

Blowin' In The Wind (Bob Dylan) *The Concert For Bangla Desh* triple album Apple STCX 3385 released US December 1971, UK January 1972 / *The Concert For Bangla Desh* double CD Epic 82876729862 released October 2005 / DVD US Rhino R2 970480, UK Rhino R2 970481 released October 2005

Bob Dylan: vocals, acoustic guitar
George Harrison: electric guitar
Leon Russell: bass
Ringo Starr: tambourine

Mr. Tambourine Man (Bob Dylan) *The Concert For Bangla Desh* triple album Apple STCX 3385 released US December 1971, UK January 1972 / *The Concert For Bangla Desh* double CD Epic 82876729862 released October 2005

Bob Dylan: vocals, acoustic guitar
George Harrison: electric guitar
Leon Russell: bass
Ringo Starr: tambourine

Just Like A Woman (Bob Dylan) *The Concert For Bangla Desh* triple album Apple STCX 3385 released US December 1971, UK January 1972 / *The Concert For Bangla*

Desh double CD Epic 82876729862 released October 2005 / DVD US Rhino R2 970480, UK Rhino R2 970481 released October 2005

Bob Dylan: vocals, acoustic guitar
George Harrison: vocals, electric guitar
Leon Russell: vocals, bass
Ringo Starr: tambourine

Something (George Harrison) *The Concert For Bangla Desh* triple album Apple STCX 3385 released US December 1971, UK January 1972 / *The Concert For Bangla Desh* double CD Epic 82876729862 released October 2005 / DVD US Rhino R2 970480, UK Rhino R2 970481 released October 2005

George Harrison: vocals, lead guitar
Eric Clapton: guitar
Jesse Ed Davis: guitar
Ringo Starr: drums
Jim Keltner: drums
Mike Gibbins: percussion
Klaus Voormann: bass
Leon Russell: piano
Billy Preston: organ
Jim Horn: horns
Chuck Findley: horns
Allan Beuter: horns
Jackie Kelso: horns
Lou McCreary: horns
Ollie Mitchell: horns
Don Nix: backing vocals
Jo Green: backing vocals
Jeanie Greene: backing vocals
Marlin Greene: backing vocals
Dolores Hall: backing vocals
Claudia Linear: backing vocals
Don Preston: backing vocals
Tom Evans: acoustic guitar
Pete Ham: acoustic guitar
Joey Molland: acoustic guitar

Bangla Desh (George Harrison) *The Concert For Bangla Desh* triple album Apple STCX 3385 released US December 1971, UK January 1972 / *The Concert For Bangla Desh* double CD Epic 82876729862 released October 2005 / DVD US Rhino R2 970480, UK Rhino R2 970481 released October 2005

George Harrison: vocals, guitar
Eric Clapton: lead guitar
Jesse Ed Davis: guitar
Don Preston: guitar
Ringo Starr: drums
Jim Keltner: drums
Mike Gibbins: percussion
Klaus Voormann: bass

Leon Russell: piano
Billy Preston: organ
Jim Horn: horns
Chuck Findley: horns
Allan Beuter: horns
Jackie Kelso: horns
Lou McCreary: horns
Ollie Mitchell: horns
Don Nix: backing vocals
Jo Green: backing vocals
Jeanie Greene: backing vocals
Marlin Greene: backing vocals
Dolores Hall: backing vocals
Claudia Linear: backing vocals
Don Preston: backing vocals
Tom Evans: acoustic guitar
Pete Ham: acoustic guitar
Joey Molland: acoustic guitar

Recorded by: Record Plant Mobile
Producers: George Harrison, Phil Spector
Engineer: Gary Kellgren

GUEST APPEARANCE WITH LEON RUSSELL 1971

4 December 1971, Rainbow Theatre, Finsbury, London (third show added due to popular demand. Eric makes a surprise guest appearance with Leon Russell and the Shelter People at the last night of a three day stint at the Rainbow. The band were: Leon Russell on piano, vocals, Don Preston on lead guitar, John Gallie on organ, Carl Radle on bass, Chuck Blackwell on drums, Claudia Lennear on background vocals, Kathi McDonald on background vocals. *Melody Maker* has the headline "Eric's shock comeback."

He strolled onstage after the first number, unannounced and largely unrecognized by the audience. He kept himself in the shadows behind some amps and plugged in and started exchanging licks with Leon's guitarist, Don Preston. Freddie King, who was on Leon's Shelter record label at the time, also joined in halfway through the set. He was the support act on this short European tour. Eric's old Dominos bandmate Carl Radle was in Leon's band now and commented, "It was a delight to see him and a pleasant surprise."

Eric was now fully in the grips of heroin addiction and was pale and pasty, and even if he had stepped forward, it is doubtful that people would have recognized him. Nobody outside the music business had any real idea about how bad his condition was. There had been rumors circulating, but no confirmation from management, understandably.

The Rainbow's house manager, John Morris, said after the show, "I had no idea he was coming. He just walked on after the first number and played away." He was pretty sure that "some people realized who he was."

In fact, Eric had also discreetly popped in to see the show the previous evening (3 December) with Bobby Whitlock, but the two of them had stayed in their seats in the balcony. After the show, Denny Cordell and Leon came to see them for a chat and asked Eric if he would consider playing with them the following night.

16

1972:
STEVIE WONDER; PETE TOWNSHEND

1972

AIR STUDIOS
Fourth floor, 214 Oxford Street, London W1
Session for Stevie Wonder

12 FEBRUARY 1972–13 FEBRUARY 1972

"My memories are a little dim regarding the Stevie Wonder–Eric Clapton session, which, I believe, took place during February 1972. The venue was AIR Studios, Oxford Circus, where Stevie was working on a new album with a 22 piece string section. Malcolm Cecil was producer on the date and Yusef Raham was handling the arrangements, the songs being 'Love Is A Part Of Me' and 'I Want To Be By Your Side.' Eric turned up later in the evening—I helped him haul his equipment from his Ferrari—and together with members of Osibisa we downed beer and chips. Time moved on, Eric just sat around chatting with the rest of us and eventually I had to leave in order to return home. So I never heard Eric and Stevie play together though I know they did, as someone phoned me next day to say that I had missed the duo jamming together." **—FRED DELLAR**

"Eric and myself just had a mutual feeling for each other. I really admired his riffs. They were in the same bag as what Ralph Hammer and Ray Parker were doing." **—STEVIE WONDER**

"I was lured up to Air Studios in Oxford Street by the prospect of a session with Stevie Wonder. He played about twelve songs, just through once. There didn't seem much ambition to get anything finished. Just as I was getting to learn the thing each time, Stevie would move on to the next one. Some of the songs were wonderful, but I've not heard any of them on record." **—ERIC CLAPTON**

"Stevie Wonder came into AIR for a couple of days, I think, over a weekend. His producer was the guy from Tonto's Expanding Head Band, Malcolm Cecil, and Bill Price was the AIR Studios staff engineer. I was the tape-op. The sessions took place in Studio One and we, or the studio porters, set up a drum kit and various keyboards. I believe Stevie also used AIR's three-suitcase Moog synthesizer, which was probably set up in the control room. I have a vague recollection of him doing some bass parts with the Moog, but cannot confirm. Stevie worked fast and on multiple songs, but I have only the vaguest recollections of what instruments he played. Almost certainly drums and Clavinet. I led Stevie into and out of the studio, made tea, and generally kept a low profile. Bill Price was (and is) one of the best engineers of all time, but Cecil did some of the engineering and I think was responsible for the drum mic choices, which included AKG 202s on the tom

Eric absolutely loved Stevie Wonder, and the prospect of playing on a session with him was enough to lure him away from his home. As far as I am aware, the session was for an album tentatively titled *I'm Free*. None of the tracks recorded over this weekend session have been released.

toms, an unusual sight at AIR in those days. Since there was no band recording and most of the work was overdubbing on previously recorded tracks there is not much else to say about the recording techniques.

I have no idea what songs were worked on, though it is quite possible that parts or all of 'Superstition' were recorded during the sessions. 'Talking Book' came out later in the year, I believe, and may contain some of the AIR session work.

During one of the two or three evening sessions Eric Clapton showed up. He was well-dressed (a cream-colored suit) but looked pale and pasty (I later learned he was in his first major druggie phase) and was accompanied by Alice Ormsby Gore, who also looked pretty wasted. Eric played on at least one song, but I have no idea which one and I don't think anything he played was ever heard on record. Nothing he did impressed me particularly, but it appeared to me that Stevie (or Cecil) had just asked him to play along in the hope that something usable would result. About the only interesting thing I can think of about the session is that Cecil asked for three discrete guitar inputs: direct from the guitar (a Strat); direct after the wah-wah pedal; and a mic on the amp (probably a Fender Twin or Champ). This gave Cecil separate control over the rather bizarre direct pre-wah-wah signal, which one might imagine was unlikely to be very interesting. But unless someone unearths the tapes (2" 16-tracks recorded on a 3M, possibly with Dolby A noise reduction) we'll never know.**"**

—CHRIS MICHIE
(tape-op at Air Studios)

"We all got together in the '70s. George phoned me up and said I've written this song for you. It's called 'I'll Still Love You.' We more or less did a jam session at Apple studios. I was doing a summer season at the time in Blackpool. I came down on the Sunday and we all went into Apple studios. There was Ringo on drums, George was producing the thing, Klaus Voormann was on bass, there were also two incredible guitarists—probably Eric Clapton or someone like that. Anyway we did this track and it was really nice and then something happened and we went our separate ways as it were. I never heard anything more about it.**"**

—CILLA BLACK
(Cilla Black session August 1972)

"I am aware of these sessions but can't honestly recall the details on 'You've Got To Stay' but understand sessions commenced at Apple. They were not finished and sadly I never found precise session dates as enquiries never came to anything. Could possibly confirm the year or you could refer to Cilla's bio as she mentions the scenario. Found in 2003 a re-recording with David Mackay of the Harrison track 'I'll Still Love You.' Thankfully got that released on 'Best of 63–78' CD set. Sorry I can't be of more help I would have loved to have found the Apple session!**"**

—STEPHEN MUNNS
(Cilla Black session August 1972)

On the back of the hugely successful re-release of the "Layla" single in 1972, Polydor placed adverts in all the music papers for The History Of Eric Clapton, *an early compilation of Eric's work to that time. They also used the opportunity to re-release the original* Layla And Assorted Love Songs *to capitalize on the hit single. It also kept Eric's name in the public eye. He was in semi-retirement at the time, having become addicted to heroin. It would be two more years before new studio material would be released.*

ERIC CLAPTON
GUEST SESSION
APPLE STUDIOS
3 Savile Row, London W1
Session for Cilla Black

AUGUST 1972

I'LL STILL LOVE YOU (WHEN EVERY SONG IS SUNG) (George Harrison) unreleased

Cilla Black: vocals
George Harrison: guitar
Eric Clapton: guitar
Ringo Starr: drums
Klaus Voormann: bass

YOU'VE GOT TO STAY WITH ME (George Harrison) unreleased

Cilla Black: vocals
George Harrison: guitar
Eric Clapton: guitar
Ringo Starr: drums
Klaus Voormann: bass

ERIC CLAPTON
HOME STUDIO
Hurtwood Edge, Ewhurst, Surrey
Session with Pete Townshend

AUGUST 1972

RSO wanted some new material to capitalize on the huge success of the recently released *The History of Eric Clapton* (July 1972). Eric had a home studio and started revisiting the half-finished album that he had started in April 1971 with Derek and The Dominos. Pete Townshend spent several weeks helping Eric sort out the material as well as overdubbing some secondary guitar work on several tracks. Eric lost interest and the project got shelved.

SEPTEMBER 1972

9 September 1972, Fête de l'Humanité, Parc Paysager de La Courneuve, Paris (Pete Townshend, who has been spending time with Eric, asks him to accompany him to see the Who performing today. They fly out together in the morning. Pete hoped that being at a live gig might inspire Eric to get back to live work)

17

1973: THE RAINBOW CONCERTS

1973

Pete Townshend had been a friend of Eric's since the '60s. Like a lot of other musician friends of Eric, he had been very concerned about Eric's health and originally attempted to get him involved in music again by going through tapes of the unfinished second Derek and the Dominos album with him. Pete even overdubbed some guitar on a few tracks at Eric's home studio before Eric lost interest and the project was abandoned. Pete did not give up, though.

When a government initiative to celebrate Britain's entry into the Common Market was announced, Townshend, together with Eric's girlfriend's father, Lord Harlech, saw an opportunity to get Eric back out onstage playing music. And hopefully off heroin. He got together a bunch of Eric's well-known musician friends for a one-off supergroup for two concerts. Pete told the *NME*, "It really wasn't very difficult to get people to help. In fact, you might be surprised at a few names I could mention who would have given their right arms to jam in this band. Eric has always said that one of the things that impressed him about Stevie Wonder was his ability to draw the very best out of the musicians around him. I personally feel Eric has exactly the same effect on us."

The group assembled by Pete Townshend consisted of Ronnie Wood, Stevie Winwood, Jim Capaldi, Rick Grech, Rebop, and Jim Karstein, a fabulous drummer from Tulsa who has played for years with JJ Cale among many others. Together with a reluctant Eric, they gathered at Ronnie Wood's house on top of Richmond Hill for seven days of rehearsals where they worked daily from 9:00 a.m. to 9:00 p.m. Pete commented to the *NME* in January 1973 on how the

rehearsals were going, "What's really surprised me during the first rehearsals we've had at Ronnie Wood's house is just how hard everyone has been prepared to work, and how much energy people like Stevie Winwood have put into the band. I've really not had the chance to work with people like him before and it's a revelation to find out just how alert and quick thinking they are." Rehearsals later moved to an empty Guildford Civic Hall for several days to get the feel of a real stage and venue. As for the songs they would play, Townshend stated, "Most of the material we've been working on is drawn from songs that Eric wrote on his solo albums, and little classics like 'Let It Rain,' 'Layla' and 'Little Wing.' Then we're doing things like 'Badge' and 'Crossroads' from the Cream period and 'Presence Of The Lord,' which he wrote while with Blind Faith. But I think the thing which is going to surprise most people is how much he is singing."

The band and Eric were as ready as they would ever be. It was now all down to Eric. He was still an active heroin user, and on the night, plenty of people backstage were very anxious. Would he be on time? Would he even turn up, and if he did, what shape would he be in? He eventually turned up late, causing serious panic among management and band alike. There were no mobile phones in those days. His lateness caused the first show to overrun by one hour. This meant that the second house had to wait for almost two hours in the freezing weather to allow sufficient time for the first house to vacate the premises. The reason for his tardiness was that his white suit was too tight for him and it had to be altered before he could wear it. The press were in attendance, as was just about every major rock star at that time. This was THE concert of the year, and if he had not turned up, it could easily have ruined his reputation for good. No wonder they introduced the band that evening as "Eric Clapton and the Palpitations"

The shows themselves were rather good and reviews were very enthusiastic. Both the public and the music press in general were genuinely thrilled to have Eric back onstage and playing. For the first show he played a Fender Stratocaster that would later achieve worldwide fame when Eric referred to it as "Blackie," which still had its tremolo attached at this stage. For the second show he played a Gibson Les Paul. There were some mistakes, but actually they simply added to the atmosphere on the night. Ronnie Wood, in particular, played some amazing slide work, and Pete Townshend was the perfect foil on rhythm guitar.

The demand for the two concerts was huge, with demand far outstripping the availability of tickets. Eric does not remember the shows, as he was still taking heroin and the evening is just a blur to him. He does recall that his technique was lacking. That, coupled with the fact he had not played in public really since 1970, just increased the pressure. In reality, the shows were a huge success and the public had no idea of what Eric was going through at this time. Backstage after the second gig, surrounded by his family and close friends, he looked like a bunny caught in headlights. He just wanted to go home to have a heroin hit and nod off away from the madding crowds. He had to be whisked away via a side entrance to avoid a mass of fans waiting for autographs.

Eric had become pretty antisocial and introverted because of his heroin usage. He was happiest when he was at home sitting in a comfy chair after a hit. So as good as Pete's and everyone else's intentions were, it was all too much too soon. However, it did make Eric realize that a lot of people were concerned about him. Even so, life at Hurtwood continued pretty much as it had done for the last few years. Alice would venture out to London to score the heroin for them, although Eric would sometimes accompany her. As soon as the heroin arrived home, they would start indulging. And so it went, day in and out.

They would occasionally go to see Alice's father, Lord Harlech, at the family home in Wales. By all accounts he was a very kind and caring man. He was naturally concerned for his daughter, but for Eric also. Eric's money had slowly been running out, and they were fast becoming nonhuman without even realizing it.

THE RAINBOW CONCERTS 1973

13 January 1973, Rainbow Theatre, Finsbury, London (with the Average White Band. Early show at 6:30 p.m.)

The Rainbow, 13 January 1973. Eric Clapton playing "Blackie" when it still had a tremolo arm attached to it. Pete Townshend is playing his 1959 Gretsch 6120 "Chet Atkins" Hollow Body given to him by Joe Walsh in 1970.

SETLIST:

Introduction *Eric Clapton's Rainbow Concert* CD remastered and remixed Polydor 527-472-2 released 1995

Layla (Eric Clapton / Jim Gordon) *Eric Clapton's Rainbow Concert* CD remastered and remixed Polydor 527-472-2 released 1995

Badge (Eric Clapton / George Harrison) unreleased

Blues Power (Eric Clapton / Leon Russell) unreleased

Nobody Knows You When You're Down And Out (Jimmie Cox) unreleased

Roll It Over (Eric Clapton / Bobby Whitlock) unreleased

Why Does Love Got To Be So Sad (Eric Clapton / Bobby Whitlock) unreleased

Little Wing (Jimi Hendrix) *Eric Clapton's Rainbow Concert* album US RSO SO 877, UK RSO 2394 116 released September 1973 / *Eric Clapton's Rainbow Concert* CD 831 320-2 released 1986 / *Eric Clapton's Rainbow Concert* CD remastered and remixed Polydor 527-472-2 released 1995

Bottle Of Red Wine (Eric Clapton / Delaney Bramlett) unreleased

After Midnight (JJ Cale) *Eric Clapton's Rainbow Concert* album US RSO SO 877, UK RSO 2394 116 released September 1973 / *Eric Clapton's Rainbow Concert* CD 831 320-2 released 1986 / *Eric Clapton's Rainbow Concert* CD remastered and remixed Polydor 527-472-2 released 1995

Bell Bottom Blues (Eric Clapton) *Eric Clapton's Rainbow Concert* CD remastered and remixed Polydor 527-472-2 released 1995

Presence Of The Lord (Eric Clapton) unreleased

Tell The Truth (Eric Clapton / Bobby Whitlock) unreleased

Pearly Queen (Steve Winwood / Jim Capaldi) unreleased

Let It Rain (Eric Clapton / Delaney Bramlett) unreleased

Crossroads (Robert Johnson) unreleased
```
Eric Clapton: guitar, vocals
Pete Townshend: guitar, vocals
Ronnie Wood: guitar, vocals
Jim Capaldi: drums
Jimmy Karstein: drums
Rick Grech: bass
Steve Winwood: keyboards, vocals
Rebop: percussion
Recorded by: Ronnie Lane Mobile Studio
Producer: Bob Pridden
Engineer: Phil Chapman
```

13 January 1973, Rainbow Theatre, Finsbury, London (with the Average White Band. Late show at 8:30 p.m.)

SETLIST:

Layla (Eric Clapton / Jim Gordon) unreleased

The introduction and the first few-minutes were not recorded due to a glitch with one of the recorders in the mobile.

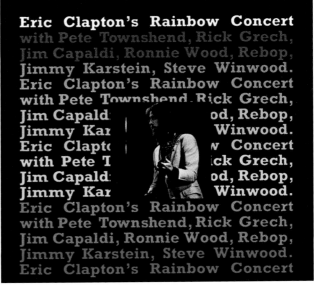

Original album cover for Eric Clapton's Rainbow Concert, *which featured six tracks from the two concerts at the Rainbow on 13 January 1973.*

Badge (Eric Clapton / George Harrison) *Eric Clapton's Rainbow Concert* album US RSO SO 877, UK RSO 2394 116 released September 1973 / *Eric Clapton's Rainbow Concert* CD 831 320-2 released 1986 / *Eric Clapton's Rainbow Concert* CD remastered and remixed Polydor 527-472-2 released 1995

Blues Power (Eric Clapton / Leon Russell) *Eric Clapton's Rainbow Concert* CD remastered and remixed Polydor 527-472-2 released 1995

Nobody Knows You When You're Down And Out (Jimmie Cox) unreleased

Roll It Over (Eric Clapton / Bobby Whitlock) *Eric Clapton's Rainbow Concert* album US RSO SO 877, UK RSO 2394 116 released September 1973 / *Eric Clapton's Rainbow Concert* CD 831 320-2 released 1986 / *Eric Clapton's Rainbow Concert* CD remastered and remixed Polydor 527-472-2 released 1995

Why Does Love Got To Be So Sad (Eric Clapton / Bobby Whitlock) unreleased

Little Wing (Jimi Hendrix) unreleased

Bottle Of Red Wine (Eric Clapton / Delaney Bramlett) *Eric Clapton's Rainbow Concert* CD remastered and remixed Polydor 527-472-2 released 1995

Presence Of The Lord (Eric Clapton) *Eric Clapton's Rainbow Concert* album US RSO SO 877, UK RSO 2394 116 released September 1973 / *Eric Clapton's Rainbow*

Concert CD 831 320-2 released 1986 / *Eric Clapton's Rainbow Concert* CD remastered and remixed Polydor 527-472-2 released 1995

Tell The Truth (Eric Clapton / Bobby Whitlock) *Eric Clapton's Rainbow Concert* CD remastered and remixed Polydor 527-472-2 released 1995

Pearly Queen (Steve Winwood / Jim Capaldi) *Eric Clapton's Rainbow Concert* album US RSO SO 877, UK RSO 2394 116 released September 1973 / *Eric Clapton's Rainbow Concert* CD 831 320-2 released 1986 / *Eric Clapton's Rainbow Concert* CD remastered and remixed Polydor 527-472-2 released 1995

Key To The Highway (Charles Segar / Willie Broonzy) *Eric Clapton's Rainbow Concert* CD remastered and remixed Polydor 527-472-2 released 1995

Let It Rain (Eric Clapton / Delaney Bramlett) *Eric Clapton's Rainbow Concert* CD remastered and remixed Polydor 527-472-2 released 1995

If you are wondering why Eric's guitar tone changes in "Let It Rain" after the drum solo, it's because he broke a string on the Les Paul and rather than wait for it to be restrung during the drum solo, he picked up his Fender Stratocaster to finish the number.

CROSSROADS (ROBERT JOHNSON) *ERIC CLAPTON'S RAINBOW CONCERT* CD REMASTERED AND REMIXED POLYDOR 527-472-2 RELEASED 1995

Layla (Eric Clapton / Jim Gordon) unreleased
Eric Clapton: guitar, vocals
Pete Townshend: guitar, vocals
Ronnie Wood: guitar, vocals
Jim Capaldi: drums
Jimmy Karstein: drums
Rick Grech: bass
Steve Winwood: keyboards, vocals
Rebop: percussion
Recorded by: Ronnie Lane Mobile Studio
Producer: Bob Pridden
Engineer: Phil Chapman

It should be noted that the 1995 remixed and remastered version of the Rainbow Concerts is heavily edited. On some tracks you get bits of guitar solos flown in from one performance and removed from another. "Layla" is made up from the three versions and all mistakes are completely gone. It was Jon Astley's brief that he should make the CD sound as good as possible and edit out any mistakes. To his credit, he did a remarkable job.

> "I got the Rainbow 1973 shows from Bob Pridden, the 8-track multi-masters, because I needed to remix it all. I also did lots of editing because of the mistakes. I cleaned it up a lot. It came out and Eric seemed quite happy with it to begin with and then he had enough of it after a year and he wanted it withdrawn.
>
> It was important at the time because it was such a historic occasion to get Eric back playing in front of a crowd and the fact that Ronnie Wood and Pete Townshend were there as well. It was Pete's doing really, his cajoling really that enabled them to do it. When they came out and did 'Layla,' Pete broke into it and Eric just stood there, he didn't play anything. He was absolutely frozen and the riff wasn't there. That's why that track didn't make the record. So I lifted off the riff from later in the song and pasted it into the front of the song because it was a mistake the way it was."
> —JON ASTLEY

When *Melody Maker*'s Chris Charlesworth reviews the resultant album he sums it up really well: "Although the material is available elsewhere in better produced studio versions, it's an atmospheric piece of vinyl that deserves a place in any discerning rock fan's collection. Eric Clapton's Rainbow Concert really is a must."

1974

THE COMEBACK WITH A TULSA GROOVE

Carl Radle had stayed in touch with his old friend Eric over the last few years. After the breakup of the Dominos, Carl had spent time back home in Tulsa, where he joined Leon Russell's Shelter People and did some touring, including an appearance in London at the Rainbow in 1971 that saw Eric jamming with them. When he was not touring or recording with Leon, Carl would jam with the Tulsa County Band, which included his close chums drummer Jamie Oldaker and keyboard player Dick Sims. He recorded many of those jams and would regularly send copies of the cassettes over to Eric with the hope that one day he would want to start writing again and get a band together. As a layman, I can only describe the music as unique and refer to it as the "Tulsa Groove." Just listen to JJ Cale and Leon Russell and you'll get my meaning. Eric not only listened to those cassettes, but he would also play along to them, and that process contributed to his recovery and desire to get back to the business of making music.

By March 1974 Eric was ready to go back into the studio to record his first new album since *Layla And Other Assorted Love Songs*. After a few meetings with his manager, Robert Stigwood, Criteria Studios in Miami was booked, as were a handful of seasoned studio session musicians. It quickly became apparent that the clinical sound of those early sessions was not the direction Eric wanted to go in. Although Eric had not originally thought about getting Carl involved,

the Tulsa County Band tapes had a big influence on him, and he realized that the only way to achieve his new vision was to get the musicians in the studio with him. Eric called Carl and asked him if he and the boys in the band would like to come to Florida to help him record his new album. Carl in turn called Jamie and Dick. Dick was free, but Jamie was about to go off on tour with Leon Russell. He chose Eric, which pissed off Leon.

The jams that made it to tape at Criteria in the early days, show a band getting to know themselves with Eric developing a new sound for himself. Some of the jams lasted well beyond twenty- minutes, and the laid-back grooves perfectly suited the setting where the album was being recorded. Yvonne Elliman was brought in for some backing vocals at the suggestion of her husband, Bill Oakes, an RSO executive. She fitted in so well she was offered a permanent place in the band. She remembers it well: "I just happened to come along with my old man, Bill. And I wanted to meet Eric, I mean he's my idol. I just wanted to go peek at him. So I got into the studio and started talking to him and I started to sing some background vocals. We started writing, we wrote one song together. And somehow he asked me to be in the band."

When they were not recording, the whole band would go out to sea for some wild parties on Robert Stigwood's yacht. Luckily, the captain was straight, as Yvonne recalls one such adventure out at sea: "We were in the Bermuda Triangle. It freaked me out, because we had a terrible storm out there. We were all drunk, we were terrible. And the captain was quite straight. He was saying, 'We can't go on any further!' And I was going 'sail on! Come on! Let's hit the storm! Let's get bounced around and have a good time!' And the guy said 'I'm sorry, but we have to turn back, and as captain of this ship what I say goes.'"

The sessions for *461 Ocean Boulevard* were very productive. The originals and covers proved a wise choice. This album in many ways was the new benchmark for Eric's solo career from this point on. The only downside was the huge tour booked in the US followed by Europe and Japan to promote the album and "comeback" of Eric Clapton. For a recuperating drug addict and fast becoming an alcoholic, the pressure was just too immense, and it's remarkable that Eric survived. Some would argue that he did not in fact survive and that the amount of pressure he was under caused him to head full on into alcoholism. What was surprising was how well he could play on most nights. The vocals would be affected far more, but his playing skills were incredible some nights. A typical example of this would be the live version of "Have You Ever Loved A Woman" found on the *EC Was Here* live album.

461 OCEAN BOULEVARD SCANDINAVIAN WARM-UP SHOWS 1974

BAND LINEUP:
Eric Clapton: guitar, vocals
George Terry: guitar
Carl Radle: bass
Dick Sims: keyboards
Jamie Oldaker: drums
Yvonne Elliman: backing vocals

JUNE 1974

19 June 1974, Tivoli Gröna Lund, Stora Scenen, Stockholm, Sweden

20 June 1974, KB-Hallen, Copenhagen, Denmark

SETLIST: Tell The Truth / Key To The Highway / Layla / Easy Now / Let It Grow / Blues Power / Have You Ever Loved A Woman / Badge / Little Wing / Willie And The Hand Jive / Get Ready / Let It Rain / Can't Find My Way Home / Little Queenie / Matchbox / Crossroads / Steady Rollin' Man

461 OCEAN BOULEVARD USA TOUR 1974 (FIRST LEG)

JUNE 1974

28 June 1974, Yale Bowl, Newhaven, Connecticut (with Ross)

SETLIST: Let It Rain / Driftin' Blues / Badge / Blues Power / Have You Ever Loved A Woman / Little Queenie / Willie And The Hand Jive / Get Ready / Little Wing / Mainline Florida / Key To The Highway / Layla / Can't Find My Way Home / Matchbox / Presence Of The Lord / Crossroads

29 June 1974, Spectrum Philadelphia, Pennsylvania (with Ross)

SETLIST (INCOMPLETE): Willie And The Hand Jive / Get Ready / Blues Power / Have You Ever Loved A Woman / Mainline Florida / Smile (Electric Version) / Little Queenie / Layla / Presence Of The Lord / Crossroads

30 June 1974, Nassau Coliseum, Uniondale, New York (with Ross)

SETLIST: Easy Now / Let It Grow / Can't Find My Way Home / Let It Rain / Key To The Highway / Badge / Little Wing / Mainline Florida / Tell The Truth / Blues Power / Have You Ever Loved A Woman / Little Queenie / Willie And The Hand Jive / Get Ready / Crossroads / Layla / Presence Of The Lord

JULY 1974

2 July 1974, International Amphitheatre, Chicago, Illinois (with Ross)

SETLIST: Smile / Let It Grow / Can't Find My Way Home / Blues Power / Have You Ever Loved A Woman / Tell The Truth / Willie And The Hand Jive / Get Ready / Let It Rain / Key To The Highway / Presence Of The Lord

3 July 1974, International Amphitheatre, Chicago, Illinois (with Ross)

4 July 1974, St. John Arena, Ohio State University, Columbus, Ohio (with Ross)

SETLIST: San Francisco Bay Blues (Eric warms up by playing a -minute of this song), Easy Now / Smile / Let It Grow / Can't Find My Way Home / Key To The Highway / Willie And The Hand Jive / Get Ready / Little Wing / Mainline Florida / Layla / Presence Of The Lord / Badge / Little Queenie / Crossroads

5 July 1974, Three Rivers Stadium, Pittsburgh, Pennsylvania (with Ross, Todd Rundgren, the Band)

SETLIST (INCOMPLETE): Smile / It's Robbie's Birthday / Let It Grow / Can't Find My Way Home / Willie And The Hand Jive / Get Ready / Blues Power / Little Queenie / Tell The Truth / Crossroads

The Band were playing on the same bill today, and it was Robbie Robertson's birthday. Eric presented Robbie with a massive cake. It seemed like a good excuse for Eric to get plastered. Not that he needed any excuses on this tour.

An eyewitness report: Overall it was an ugly day—the previous day, of course, was July 4th. Everybody still had fireworks, firecrackers, sparklers, etc. The buzz of the day appeared to be downers and liquor. Much violence. Someone threw an oversized sparkler onto the canvas roof of the stage and set it on fire during the Band's set, which was otherwise unmarred and wonderful. Things seemed to culminate during EC's set—he was hit in the face with a Frisbee—when one of the backup singers was hit with a beer can. He took time out to curse the audience ("fuck you, whoever threw that one; you fuckin' mother…") and told them to just knock off the "fuckin' aggravation." EC did indeed sing "it's Robbie's birthday" for all of a few seconds.

6 July 1974, Rich Stadium, Buffalo, New York (with Ross, Freddie King, the Band)

SETLIST: Goin' to Brownsville / Smile / Let It Grow / Hideaway* / Have You Ever Loved A Woman* / Tell The Truth / Willie And The Hand Jive / Get Ready / Steady Rollin' Man / Little Wing / Blues Power / Presence Of The Lord / Little Queenie

*Freddie King guitar and vocals

Eric Clapton joins the Band on "Chest Fever" during their support act slot in the afternoon

7 July 1974, Roosevelt Stadium, Jersey City, New Jersey (with Ross, Freddie King)

SETLIST: Smile / Let It Grow / Let It Rain / Key To The Highway / Willie And The Hand Jive / Get Ready / Presence Of The Lord / Badge / Tell The Truth / Have You Ever Loved A Woman* / Little Queenie / Crossroads

*Freddie King on guitar

Eric Clapton jams with the Band, 6 July 1974, Rich Stadium, Buffalo, New York. Eric is pictured with Robbie Robertson and Levon Helm.

Eric Clapton jams with the Band, 6 July 1974, Rich Stadium, Buffalo, New York. Eric is pictured with Robbie Robertson.

9 July 1974, The Forum, Montreal, Quebec, Canada (with Ross)

SETLIST: Smile / Easy Now / Let It Grow / Layla / Have You Ever Loved A Woman / Let It Rain / Willie And The Hand Jive / Get Ready / Presence Of The Lord / Badge / Steady Rollin' Man / Crossroads / Mean Old World / Little Wing / Little Queenie / Blues Power

10 July 1974, Civic Center, Providence, Rhode Island (with Ross)

SETLIST: Smile / Don't Have to Hurt Nobody / Have You Ever Loved A Woman / Blues Power / Key to the Highway / Presence Of The Lord / Bright Lights Big City / I Can't Hold Out / Willie And The Hand Jive / Get Ready / Little Wing / Layla / Little Queenie

There were several incidents on the tour with firecrackers and bottles being thrown at the stage. It seemed to be a common happening at major gigs during this period. This show seemed to have provoked Eric the worst, though. An audience member had thrown a beer bottle at the stage before the show started, and it hit Yvonne Elliman in the hand. Eric was understandably angry and almost ended the show before it had even started. After he calmed down, he was persuaded to play the show. Yvonne performed the show with a bandaged hand. Eric spoke to the audience about the incident during the beginning of his set: "I want the guy that threw the beer bottle to know that he hurt one of my people. So don't throw things, please don't throw things at us." The second song, "Don't Have To Hurt Nobody," was an impromptu jam inspired by the incident. Yvonne also got to have her say during "Willie and the Hand Jive / Get Ready," where she changes the lyrics halfway through to "Throwing your fucking bottles."

12 July 1974, Boston Garden, Boston, Massachusetts (with Ross)

SETLIST: Smile / Let It Grow / Can't Find My Way Home / Willie And The Hand Jive / Get Ready / Layla / Presence Of The Lord / Steady Rollin' Man / Mainline Florida / Blues Power / Have You Ever Loved A Woman / Badge / Little Queenie

13 July 1974, Madison Square Garden, New York City (with Ross)

SETLIST: Smile / Let It Grow / Can't Find My Way Home / Willie And The Hand Jive / Get Ready / Let It Rain / Key To The Highway / Blues Power / Have You Ever Loved A Woman / Layla / Presence Of The Lord / Steady Rolling Man / Crossroads / Little Queenie*

*Todd Rundgren and Dickie Betts guitars on "Little Queenie"

14 July 1974, Capitol Centre, Largo, Maryland (with Ross)

SETLIST: Smile / Let It Grow / Can't Find My Way Home / Easy Now / Let It Rain / I Shot The Sheriff / Layla / Rambling On My Mind / Have You Ever Loved A Woman / Willie And The Hand Jive / Get Ready / Blues Power / Little Wing / Badge / Presence Of The Lord / Tell The Truth / Crossroads / Little Queenie

18 July 1974, Diablo Stadium, Tempe, Arizona (with Ross)

SETLIST (INCOMPLETE): Smile / Can't Find My Way Home / Layla / Willie And The Hand Jive / Get Ready / Have You Ever Loved A Woman / Badge / Presence Of The Lord

> "The crowd got ruly and started throwing bottles at the stage when the show was over and EC did not play Layla. Glass shattering when the bottles hit the lighting trusses. I jumped off stage and ran out and confronted a man in the crowd who had just thrown a bottle. Told him EC was long gone and he was only going to hurt someone on the crew."
> —WATT CASEY (Showco)

19 July 1974, Long Beach Arena, Long Beach, California (with Ross)

SETLIST:

Smile (Charles Chaplin / Geoffrey Parsons / John Turner) unreleased

Let It Grow (Eric Clapton) unreleased

Can't Find My Way Home (Steve Winwood) unreleased

I Shot The Sheriff (Bob Marley) unreleased

Badge (Eric Clapton / George Harrison) unreleased

Willie And The Hand Jive (Johnny Otis) unreleased

Get Ready (Eric Clapton / Yvonne Elliman) unreleased

Crossroads (Robert Johnson) unreleased

Mainline Florida (George Terry) unreleased

Layla (Eric Clapton / Jim Gordon) unreleased

Have You Ever Loved A Woman (Billy Myles) *EC Was Here* album US RSO SO 4809, UK RSO 2394 160 released August 1975 / Remastered CD Polydor 31453 1823-2 released September 1996 / *Crossroads 2 Live In The Seventies* Polydor 529 305-2 released March 1996

Tell The Truth (Eric Clapton / Bobby Whitlock) unreleased

Steady Rollin' Man (Robert Johnson; arranged by Eric Clapton) unreleased

Little Queenie (Chuck Berry) unreleased

Blues Jam* (Eric Clapton / John Mayall) unreleased

```
*with John Mayall
Recorded by: Wally Heider Recording Studios
Mobile Unit
Producer: Tom Dowd
Engineer: Ed Barton
```

20 July 1974, Long Beach Arena, Long Beach, California (with Ross)

```
SETLIST:
```

Smile (Charles Chaplin / Geoffrey Parsons / John Turner) *RSO Prime Cuts* 10 inch album UK-only RSO SINGL1 released 1975 / *Time Pieces, Vol. 2: Live In The '70s* UK-only RSO RSD 5022 released May 1983 / *Time Pieces, Vol. 2: Live In The '70s* CD Polydor 811835 released November 1988

Easy Now (Eric Clapton) unreleased

Let It Grow (Eric Clapton) unreleased

Front cover for Eric's 1975 live album, EC Was Here. *Recorded mainly in 1974 in the USA.*

I Shot The Sheriff (Bob Marley) unreleased

Layla (Eric Clapton / Jim Gordon) unreleased

Little Wing (Jimi Hendrix) unreleased

Willie And The Hand Jive (Johnny Otis) *Crossroads 2 Live In The Seventies* Polydor 529 305-2 released March 1996

Get Ready (Eric Clapton) *Crossroads 2 Live In The Seventies* Polydor 529 305-2 released March 1996

Badge (Eric Clapton / George Harrison) unreleased

Can't Find My Way Home (Steve Winwood) *EC Was Here* album US RSO SO 4809, UK RSO 2394 160 released August 1975 / Remastered CD Polydor 31453 1823-2 released September 1996 / *Crossroads 2 Live In The Seventies* Polydor 529 305-2 released March 1996

Driftin' Blues (Johnny Moore / Charles Brown / Eddie Williams) *EC Was Here* album US RSO SO 4809, UK RSO 2394 160 released August 1975 / Remastered CD Polydor 31453 1823-2 released September 1996 / *Crossroads 2 Live In The Seventies* Polydor 529 305-2 released March 1996 (The original RSO LP version had a three-minute edit of "Drifting Blues" but the compact disc remaster along with Crossroads 2 restore the entire eleven-minute version, which segues into "Rambling On My Mind")

Rambling On My Mind (Robert Johnson) *EC Was Here* Remastered CD Polydor 31453 1823-2 / *Crossroads 2 Live In The Seventies* Polydor 529 305-2 released March 1996

Let It Rain (Eric Clapton / Delaney Bramlett) unreleased

Presence Of The Lord (Eric Clapton) *EC Was Here* album US RSO SO 4809, UK RSO 2394 160 released August 1975 / Remastered CD Polydor 31453 1823-2 released September 1996 / *Crossroads 2 Live In The Seventies* Polydor 529 305-2 released March 1996

Crossroads (Robert Johnson) unreleased

Steady Rollin' Man (Robert Johnson; arranged by Eric Clapton) unreleased

Little Queenie (Chuck Berry) unreleased

Blues Power (Eric Clapton / Leon Russell) unreleased

```
Recorded by: Wally Heider Recording Studios
Mobile Unit
Producer: Tom Dowd
Engineer: Ed Barton
```

21 July 1974, Cow Palace, San Francisco, California (with Ross)

SETLIST (LATE SHOW): Smile / Let It Grow / Can't Find My Way Home / I Shot The Sheriff / Let It Rain / Willie And The Hand Jive / Get Ready / Badge / Matchbox / Layla / Tell The Truth / Blues Power / Have You Ever Loved A Woman / Steady Rollin' Man / Crossroads / Little Queenie

23 July 1974, Coliseum, Denver, Colorado (with Ross)

SETLIST: Smile / Easy Now / Let It Grow / I Shot The Sheriff / Let It Rain / Willie And The Hand Jive / Get Ready / Badge / Presence Of The Lord / Tell The Truth / Mainline Florida / Mean Old World / Blues Power / Steady Rollin' Man / Crossroads

24 July 1974, Coliseum, Denver, Colorado (with Ross)

SETLIST: Smile / Easy Now / I Shot The Sheriff / Let It Rain / Willie And The Hand Jive / Get Ready / Badge / Presence Of The Lord / Tell The Truth / Mainline Florida / Mean Old World / Blues Power / Steady Rollin' Man / Crossroads / Layla / Little Queenie

25 July 1974, Kiel Auditorium, St. Louis, Missouri (with Ross)

SETLIST: Smile / Can't Find My Way Home / I Shot The Sheriff / You Don't Love Me / Badge / Tell The Truth / Willie And The Hand Jive / Get Ready / Layla

27 July 1974, Mississippi Valley Fairgrounds, Davenport, Iowa (with Ross)

SETLIST (INCOMPLETE): Badge / Presence Of The Lord / Tell The Truth / Hideaway / Rambling On My Mind / Steady Rollin' Man / Blues Power

28 July 1974, Memorial Stadium, Memphis, Tennessee (with Ross, Foghat, Lynyrd Skynyrd)

SETLIST: Smile / Easy Now / Let It Rain / Willie And The Hand Jive / Get Ready / Tell The Truth / I Can't Hold Out / Badge / I Shot The Sheriff / Layla / Crossroads / Blues Power / Little Queenie

29 July 1974, Legion Field, Birmingham, Alabama (with Ross)

SETLIST (INCOMPLETE): Smile / Let It Grow / Layla / Willie And The Hand Jive / Get Ready / Key To The Highway / I Shot The Sheriff / Badge / Tell The Truth / Let It Rain

31 July 1974, City Park Stadium, New Orleans, Louisiana (with Ross)

SETLIST: Smile / Easy Now / Tell The Truth / Badge / Willie And The Hand Jive / Get Ready / Fucked If I Know / Layla / Little Wing / I Shot The Sheriff / Blues Power / Let It Rain / Little Queenie

L to R: George Terry, Eric Clapton, and Yvonne Elliman at the Mississippi Valley Fairgrounds in Davenport, Iowa, on 27 July 1974.

Eric Clapton at City Park Stadium, New Orleans, Louisiana, on 31 July 1974.

AUGUST 1974

1 August 1974, Omni Theatre, Atlanta, Georgia (with Ross)

SETLIST: Smile / Let It Grow / Mainline Florida / Bright Lights Big City / Tell The Truth / Willie And The Hand Jive / Get Ready / Let It Rain / Badge / Layla* / Baby Don't You Do It*

*Pete Townshend on "Layla" and "Baby Don't You Do It"
*Keith Moon on "Layla" and "Baby Don't You Do It"

2 August 1974, Coliseum, Greensboro, North Carolina (with Ross)

SETLIST: Smile / Easy Now / I Can't Hold Out / Tell The Truth / Blues Power / Have You Ever Loved A Woman / Willie And The Hand Jive* / Get Ready* / I Shot The Sheriff / Let It Rain / Layla / Badge* / Little Queenie* **

*Pete Townshend on "Willie And The Hand Jive," "Get Ready," "Badge," "Little Queenie"
**Keith Moon on drums on "Badge" and "Little Queenie" (Keith forcibly removed Jamie Oldaker from his drums, for the two encores)

4 August 1974, West Palm Beach International Raceway, Palm Beach, Florida (with Ross). Pete Townshend, Keith Moon, and Joe Walsh jam with Eric at this show

461 OCEAN BOULEVARD TOUR USA 1974 (SECOND LEG)

BAND LINEUP:
Eric Clapton: guitar, vocals
George Terry: guitar
Carl Radle: bass
Dick Sims: keyboards
Jamie Oldaker: drums
Yvonne Elliman: backing vocals
Marcy Levy: backing vocals

SEPTEMBER 1974

28 September 1974, Hampton Coliseum, Hampton, Virginia

SETLIST (INCOMPLETE): Tell the Truth / I Shot The Sheriff / Little Rachel / Willie And The Hand Jive / Get Ready / Singing The Blues / Badge / Blues Power / Honey Bee / Mainline Florida

29 September 1974, Nassau Coliseum, Uniondale, New York

SETLIST: Better Make It Through Today / Can't Find My Way Home / Let It Rain / Little Wing / Singin' The Blues / I Shot The Sheriff / Tell The Truth / The Sky Is Crying / Badge / Little Rachel / Willie And The Hand Jive / Get Ready / Blues Power

30 September 1974, Boston Garden, Boston, Massachusetts

SETLIST: Better Make It Through Today / Can't Find My Way Home / I Shot The Sheriff / Badge / Little Rachel / Mainline Florida / Little Wing / Singin' the Blues / Key To The Highway / Tell The Truth / Layla / Blues Power

OCTOBER 1974

1 October 1974, The Forum, Montreal, Quebec, Canada
2 October 1974, Maple Leaf Gardens, Toronto, Ontario, Canada

SETLIST: Let It Grow / Can't Find My Way Home / Willie And The Hand Jive / Get Ready / Badge / All I Have To Do Is Dream / I Shot The Sheriff / Singing The Blues / The Sky Is Crying / Steady Rollin' Man / Little Wing / Layla / Tell The Truth

4 October 1974, Capitol Centre, Largo, Maryland

SETLIST: Let It Grow / Can't Find My Way Home / Let It Rain / Little Rachel / Blues Power / Willie And The Hand Jive / Get Ready / Singin' The Blues / I Shot The Sheriff / Layla

5 October 1974, Capitol Centre, Largo, Maryland
6 October 1974, Spectrum, Philadelphia, Pennsylvania

SETLIST: Let It Grow / Can't Find My Way Home / I Shot The Sheriff / Key To The Highway / Singin' The Blues / Badge / Little Rachel / Little Wing / Layla / Blues Power / Driftin' Blues / Tell The Truth

461 OCEAN BOULEVARD JAPAN TOUR 1974

BAND LINEUP:
Eric Clapton: guitar, vocals
George Terry: guitar
Carl Radle: bass
Dick Sims: keyboards
Jamie Oldaker: drums
Yvonne Elliman: backing vocals
Marcy Levy: backing vocals

OCTOBER 1974

31 October 1974, Budokan, Tokyo, Japan

SETLIST: Smile / Let It Grow / Better Make It Through Today / Tell The Truth / Badge / Singing The Blues / Have You Ever Loved A Woman / I Shot The Sheriff / Little Rachel / Willie And The Hand Jive / Get Ready / Layla / Blues Power

NOVEMBER 1974

1 November 1974, Budokan, Tokyo, Japan

SETLIST: Let It Grow / Can't Find My Way Home / Little Rachel / Tell The Truth / Singing The Blues / Badge / Willie And The Hand Jive / Get Ready / Have You Ever Loved A Woman / Layla / Little Wing / I Shot The Sheriff

2 November 1974, Budokan, Tokyo, Japan

SETLIST: Smile / Let It Grow / Can't Find My Way Home / Better Make It Through Today / I Shot The Sheriff / Key To The Highway / Willie And The Hand Jive / Get Ready / Badge / Presence Of The Lord / Singing The Blues / Layla / All I Have To Do Is Dream / Blues Power

5 November 1974, Koseinenkin Kaikan Dai Hall, Osaka, Japan

SETLIST: Let It Grow / Can't Find My Way Home / Better Make It Through Today / Tell The Truth / Driftin' Blues / Willie And The Hand Jive / Get Ready / Let It Rain / Layla / Presence Of The Lord / I Shot The Sheriff / Badge / All I Have To Do Is Dream / Singing The Blues

6 November 1974, Koseinenkin Kaikan Dai Hall, Osaka, Japan

SETLIST: Let It Grow / Can't Find My Way Home / Driftin' Blues / Singing The Blues / Willie And The Hand Jive / Get Ready / Key To The Highway / I Shot The Sheriff / Badge / Tell The Truth / Steady Rollin' Man / Crossroads / Layla / All I Have To Do Is Dream / Mainline Florida / Let It Rain

461 OCEAN BOULEVARD EUROPEAN TOUR 1974

BAND LINEUP:
Eric Clapton: guitar, vocals
George Terry: guitar
Carl Radle: bass
Dick Sims: keyboards
Jamie Oldaker: drums
Yvonne Elliman: backing vocals
Marcy Levy: backing vocals

26 November 1974, Kongreßzentrum, Hamburg, Germany
27 November 1974, Olympiahalle, Munich, Germany
28 November 1974, Friedrich Ebert Halle, Ludwigshafen, Germany

SETLIST: Let It Grow / Can't Find My Way Home / Tell The Truth / Willie And The Hand Jive / Get Ready / When Things Go Wrong (It Hurts Me Too) / Ramblin' On My Mind / Have You Ever Loved A Woman / Badge / Blues Power / Little Wing / Singing The Blues / Layla / All I Have To Do / I Shot The Sheriff / Little Queenie

29 November 1974, Grugahalle, Essen, Germany
30 November 1974, Ahoy Hall, Rotterdam, Netherlands

SETLIST: Smile / Let It Grow / Can't Find My Way Home / Little Wing / Tell The Truth / I Shot The Sheriff / Blues Power / Key To The Highway / Willie And The Hand Jive / Get Ready / Singing The Blues / Badge / Layla / Opposites

DECEMBER 1974

1 December 1974, Palais des Sports, Antwerp, Belgium
2 December 1974, Parc des Expositions, Paris, France

SETLIST: Smile / Let It Grow / Can't Find My Way Home / Tell The Truth / Willie And The Hand Jive / Get Ready / Little Rachel / Sky Is Crying / Crossroads / Have You Ever Loved A Woman / Blues Power / Little Wing / I Shot The Sheriff / Singing the Blues / Layla / All I Have To Do Is Dream / Better Make It Through Today / Little Queenie

4 December 1974, Hammersmith Odeon, London

SETLIST:

Smile (Charles Chaplin / Geoffrey Parsons / John Turner)

Let It Grow (Eric Clapton)

Can't Find My Way Home (Steve Winwood)

I Shot The Sheriff (Bob Marley)

Tell The Truth (Eric Clapton)

Rambling On My Mind (Robert Johnson) *Crossroads 2 Live In The Seventies* Polydor 529 305-2 released March 1996

Eric Clapton playing a Gibson Explorer at the Hammersmith Odeon, 4 December 1974.

Have You Ever Loved A Woman (Billy Myles) *Crossroads 2 Live In The Seventies* Polydor 529 305-2 released March 1996

Willie And The Hand Jive (Johnny Otis)

Get Ready (Eric Clapton)

Opposites (Eric Clapton)

Blues Power (Eric Clapton / Leon Russell)

Little Wing (Jimi Hendrix) *Crossroads 2 Live In The Seventies* Polydor 529 305-2 released March 1996

Singing The Blues (Eric Clapton)

Badge (Eric Clapton)

All I Have To Do Is Dream (Felice and Boudleaux Bryant)

Steady Rolling Man (Robert Johnson; arranged by Eric Clapton)

Layla (Eric Clapton / Jim Gordon)

Let It Rain (Eric Clapton / Delaney Bramlett)
Recorded by: Ronnie Lane Mobile Unit
Producer: Tom Dowd
Engineers: Andy Knight, Ron Fawcus

5 December 1974, Hammersmith Odeon, London

SETLIST:

Smile (Charles Chaplin / Geoffrey Parsons / John Turner)

Let It Grow (Eric Clapton)

Can't Find My Way Home (Steve Winwood)

Tell The Truth (Eric Clapton / Bobby Whitlock)

The Sky Is Crying (Elmore James) *Crossroads 2 Live In The Seventies* Polydor 529 305-2 released March 1996

Have You Ever Loved A Woman (Billy Myles) *Crossroads 2 Live In The Seventies* Polydor 529 305-2 released March 1996

Rambling On My Mind (Robert Johnson) *Crossroads 2 Live In The Seventies* Polydor 529 305-2 released March 1996

Badge (Eric Clapton / George Harrison)

Little Rachel (Jim Byfield)

I Shot The Sheriff (Bob Marley)

Better Make It Through Today (Eric Clapton)

Blues Power (Eric Clapton / Leon Russell)

Key To The Highway (Charles Segar / Willie Broonzy)

Let It Rain (Eric Clapton / Delaney Bramlett)

Little Wing (Jimi Hendrix)

Singing The Blues (Mary McCreary)

Layla (Eric Clapton / Jim Gordon)

Steady Rollin' Man* (Robert Johnson; arranged by Eric Clapton)

Little Queenie* (Chuck Berry)

*Ronnie Wood on guitar
Recorded by: Ronnie Lane Mobile Unit
Producer: Tom Dowd
Engineers: Andy Knight, Ron Fawcus

1974 RECORDING SESSIONS

ERIC CLAPTON GUEST SESSION

RAMPORT STUDIOS 115 Thessaly Road, London SW8 Session for the Who *Tommy Soundtrack*

MARCH 1974

EYESIGHT TO THE BLIND (Sonny Boy Williamson) *Tommy Soundtrack* double album US Polydor PD-2-9502, UK Polydor 2657 014 released 1975 / *Tommy Soundtrack* remastered double CD Polydor 841 121-2 released April 2001

Eric Clapton: guitar, vocals
Kenny Jones: drums
John Entwistle: bass
Arthur Brown: vocals (on film version only, which has a longer edit than the album or CD)

SALLY SIMPSON (Pete Townshend) *Tommy Soundtrack* double album US Polydor PD-2-9502, UK Polydor 2657 014 released 1975 / *Tommy Soundtrack* remastered double CD Polydor 841 121-2 released April 2001

Eric Clapton: guitar
Pete Townshend: vocals
Roger Daltrey: vocals
Graham Deacon: drums
Phil Chen: bass
Nicky Hopkins: piano

Producer: Pete Townshend
Engineer: Ron Nevison

CRITERIA RECORDING STUDIOS 1755 Northeast 149th Street, Miami, Florida Sessions for *461 Ocean Boulevard*

APRIL 1974–MAY 1974

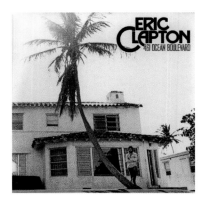

Front cover for Eric's 1974 comeback album, 461 Ocean Boulevard.

MOTHERLESS CHILDREN (Traditional; arranged by Eric Clapton and Carl Radle) *461 Ocean Boulevard* album US RSO SO 4801, UK RSO 2479118 released August 1974 / *461 Ocean Boulevard* Deluxe double CD US Polydor 000372202, UK Polydor 0602498252468 released November 2004

Eric Clapton: vocals, slide guitar
George Terry: guitar
Carl Radle: bass
Dick Sims: organ
Albhy Galuten: piano
Jamie Oldaker: drums

GIVE ME STRENGTH (Eric Clapton) *461 Ocean Boulevard* album US RSO SO 4801, UK RSO 2479118 released August 1974 / *461 Ocean Boulevard* Deluxe double CD US Polydor 000372202, UK Polydor 0602498252468 released November 2004

Eric Clapton: vocals, Dobro
George Terry: guitar
Carl Radle: bass
Dick Sims: organ
Al Jackson: drums

WILLIE AND THE HAND JIVE (Johnny Otis) *461 Ocean Boulevard* album US RSO SO 4801, UK RSO 2479118 released August 1974 / *461 Ocean Boulevard* Deluxe double CD US Polydor 000372202, UK Polydor 0602498252468 released November 2004

Eric Clapton: vocals, guitar
George Terry: guitar
Carl Radle: bass
Dick Sims: organ
Jamie Oldaker: drums
Yvonne Elliman: vocals

GET READY (Eric Clapton / Yvonne Elliman) *461 Ocean Boulevard* album US RSO SO 4801, UK RSO 2479118 released August 1974 / *461 Ocean Boulevard* Deluxe double CD US Polydor 000372202, UK Polydor 0602498252468 released November 2004

Eric Clapton: vocals, guitar
George Terry: guitar

Carl Radle: bass
Dick Sims: organ
Albhy Galuten: electric piano
Jamie Oldaker: drums
Yvonne Elliman: vocals

I SHOT THE SHERIFF (Bob Marley) *461 Ocean Boulevard* album US RSO SO 4801, UK RSO 2479118 released August 1974 / *461 Ocean Boulevard* Deluxe double CD US Polydor 000372202, UK Polydor 0602498252468 released November 2004

Eric Clapton: vocals, guitar
George Terry: guitar, background vocals
Carl Radle: bass
Dick Sims: organ
Albhy Galuten: piano
Jamie Oldaker: drums
Yvonne Elliman: background vocals

I CAN'T HOLD OUT (Elmore James; arranged by Eric Clapton) *461 Ocean Boulevard* album US RSO SO 4801, UK RSO 2479118 released August 1974 / *461 Ocean Boulevard* Deluxe double CD US Polydor 000372202, UK Polydor 0602498252468 released November 2004

Eric Clapton: vocals, guitar
Carl Radle: bass
Dick Sims: organ
Jamie Oldaker: drums

PLEASE BE WITH ME (Charles Scott Boyer) *461 Ocean Boulevard* album US RSO SO 4801, UK RSO 2479118 released August 1974 / *461 Ocean Boulevard* Deluxe double CD US Polydor 000372202, UK Polydor 0602498252468 released November 2004

Eric Clapton: vocals, Dobro, guitar
George Terry: vocals, guitar
Carl Radle: bass
Dick Sims: organ
Al Jackson: drums
Yvonne Elliman: vocals, acoustic guitar

LET IT GROW (Eric Clapton) *461 Ocean Boulevard* album US RSO SO 4801, UK RSO 2479118 released August 1974 / *461 Ocean Boulevard* Deluxe double CD US Polydor 000372202, UK Polydor 0602498252468 released November 2004

Eric Clapton: vocals, guitar, Dobro
George Terry: guitar, background vocals
Carl Radle: bass
Dick Sims: organ
Albhy Galuten: piano, ARP synthesizer
Jamie Oldaker: drums
Yvonne Elliman: background vocals
Tom Bernfeld: background vocals

STEADY ROLLIN' MAN (Robert Johnson; arranged by Eric Clapton) *461 Ocean Boulevard* album US RSO SO 4801, UK RSO 2479118 released August 1974 / *461 Ocean Boulevard* Deluxe double CD US Polydor 000372202, UK Polydor 0602498252468 released November 2004

Eric Clapton: vocals, guitar
Carl Radle: bass
Dick Sims: organ
Albhy Galuten: piano, clavichord
Jim Fox: drums

MAINLINE FLORIDA (George Terry) *461 Ocean Boulevard* album US RSO SO 4801, UK RSO 2479118 released August 1974 / *461 Ocean Boulevard* Deluxe double CD US Polydor 000372202, UK Polydor 0602498252468 released November 2004

Eric Clapton: vocals, guitar
George Terry: guitar, background vocals

Carl Radle: bass
Dick Sims: organ
Albhy Galuten: piano
Jamie Oldaker: drums
Yvonne Elliman: background vocals
Tom Bernfeld: background vocals

AIN'T THAT LOVIN' YOU (Jimmy Reed) *Crossroads* box set US Polydor 835 261-2, UK Polydor Road1 released April 1988 / *461 Ocean Boulevard* Deluxe double CD US Polydor 000372202, UK Polydor 0602498252468 released November 2004

Eric Clapton: vocals, slide guitar
Dave Mason: guitar
Carl Radle: bass
Dick Sims: keyboards
Jamie Oldaker: drums
Yvonne Elliman: background vocals

WALKIN' DOWN THE ROAD (Paul Levine / Alan Musgrove) *Crossroads 2 Live In The Seventies* Polydor 529 305-2 released March 1996 / *461 Ocean Boulevard* Deluxe double CD US Polydor 000372202, UK Polydor 0602498252468 released November 2004

Eric Clapton: vocals, acoustic guitar
Carl Radle: bass
Jamie Oldaker: drums

MEET ME (Down At The Bottom) (Willie Dixon) *Blues* single CD Polydor 547 179-2 released June 1999 / Blues double CD Polydor 314 547 178-2 released June 1999 / *461 Ocean Boulevard* Deluxe double CD US Polydor 000372202, UK Polydor 0602498252468 released November 2004

Eric Clapton: vocals, guitar
George Terry: guitar
Carl Radle: bass
Dick Sims: organ
Jamie Oldaker: drums

MEET ME (Down At The Bottom) Instrumental take 1 (Willie Dixon) unreleased

Eric Clapton: guitar
George Terry: guitar
Carl Radle: bass
Dick Sims: organ
Jamie Oldaker: drums

MEET ME (Down At The Bottom) Instrumental take 2 (Willie Dixon) unreleased

Eric Clapton: guitar
George Terry: guitar
Carl Radle: bass
Dick Sims: organ
Jamie Oldaker: drums

AFTER HOURS BLUES (Eric Clapton) Bonus CD with initial editions of *Blues* double CD Polydor 314 547 178-2 released June 1999 / *461 Ocean Boulevard* Deluxe double CD US Polydor 000372202, UK Polydor 0602498252468 released November 2004

Eric Clapton: guitar
George Terry: guitar
Carl Radle: bass
Dick Sims: organ
Jamie Oldaker: drums

B MINOR JAM (Eric Clapton) Bonus CD with initial editions of *Blues* double CD Polydor 314 547 178-2 released June 1999 / *461 Ocean Boulevard* Deluxe double CD US Polydor 000372202, UK Polydor 0602498252468 released November 2004

Eric Clapton: guitar
George Terry: guitar
Carl Radle: bass

TOO LATE (Eric Clapton) take 1 unreleased

Eric Clapton: vocals, guitar
George Terry: guitar
Carl Radle: bass
Dick Sims: organ
Jamie Oldaker: drums
Yvonne Elliman: vocals

TOO LATE (Eric Clapton) take 2 unreleased

Eric Clapton: vocals, guitar
George Terry: guitar
Carl Radle: bass
Dick Sims: organ
Jamie Oldaker: drums
Yvonne Elliman: vocals

JAM IN E number 1 (Eric Clapton) unreleased

Eric Clapton: slide guitar
George Terry: guitar
Carl Radle: bass
Dick Sims: organ
Jamie Oldaker: drums

JAM IN E number 2 (Eric Clapton) unreleased

Eric Clapton: slide guitar
George Terry: guitar
Carl Radle: bass
Dick Sims: organ
Jamie Oldaker: drums

GIVE ME STRENGTH (Dobro 1) (Eric Clapton) unreleased

Eric Clapton: Dobro
George Terry: guitar

GIVE ME STRENGTH (Dobro 2) (Eric Clapton) unreleased

Eric Clapton: Dobro
George Terry: guitar
Carl Radle: bass

SOMETHING YOU GOT (Chris Kenner) unreleased

Eric Clapton: guitar
George Terry: guitar
Carl Radle: bass
Dick Sims: organ
Jamie Oldaker: drums

UNTITLED INSTRUMENTAL (Eric Clapton) unreleased

Eric Clapton: guitar
George Terry: guitar
Carl Radle: bass
Dick Sims: organ
Jamie Oldaker: drums

UNTITLED INSTRUMENTAL 2 (Eric Clapton) unreleased

Eric Clapton: guitar
George Terry: guitar
Carl Radle: bass
Dick Sims: organ
Jamie Oldaker: drums

UNTITLED INSTRUMENTAL JAM (Eric Clapton) unreleased

Eric Clapton: guitar
George Terry: guitar

Carl Radle: bass
Dick Sims: organ
Jamie Oldaker: drums

I SHOT THE SHERIFF (Bob Marley) (alternate instrumental long version with guitar solo) unreleased

Eric Clapton: guitar
George Terry: guitar
Carl Radle: bass
Dick Sims: organ
Albhy Galuten: piano
Jamie Oldaker: drums

LET IT GROW (Eric Clapton) unreleased instrumental version

Eric Clapton: guitar
George Terry: guitar
Carl Radle: bass
Dick Sims: organ
Albhy Galuten: piano, ARP synthesizer
Jamie Oldaker: drums

MOTHERLESS CHILDREN JAM (Traditional; arranged by Eric Clapton and Carl Radle) unreleased

Eric Clapton: slide guitar
George Terry: guitar
Carl Radle: bass
Dick Sims: organ
Albhy Galuten: piano
Jamie Oldaker: drums

MOTHERLESS CHILDREN (Alternate version in key of A) (Traditional; arranged by Eric Clapton and Carl Radle) unreleased

Eric Clapton: slide guitar
George Terry: guitar
Carl Radle: bass
Dick Sims: organ
Albhy Galuten: piano
Jamie Oldaker: drums

GYPSY (Charles Scott Boyer) early solo acoustic version of "Please Be With Me" clearly mistitled on tape box unreleased

Eric Clapton: vocals, acoustic guitar
MAINLINE FLORIDA (George Terry) unreleased alternate long version with George Terry on lead vocal and lead guitar

Eric Clapton: guitar
George Terry: guitar, vocals
Carl Radle: bass
Dick Sims: organ
Albhy Galuten: piano
Jamie Oldaker: drums

I CAN'T HOLD OUT (Elmore James; arranged by Eric Clapton) unreleased instrumental version

Eric Clapton: guitar
Carl Radle: bass
Dick Sims: organ
Jamie Oldaker: drums

EAT THE COOK (Eric Clapton) unreleased

Eric Clapton: guitar
George Terry: guitars
Carl Radle: bass
Dick Sims: organ
Albhy Galuten: piano
Jamie Oldaker: drums

Producer: Tom Dowd
Engineer: Karl Richardson

ERIC CLAPTON GUEST SESSION

PARADISE RECORDING STUDIO
The Wick, Richmond Hill, Surrey

18 MAY 1974

> "The last thing I wanted was a jam...everybody sitting around playing E for two days. It did happen sometimes, like if I had three drummers in and no drum kit or something, but usually once everybody got behind their instruments in the studio it was dead serious. I was really out of my head the night Eric turned up and he was really violent and boisterous. We had a long play but it wasn't very productive, Instead he was good in that I played him the album, *I've Got My Own Album To Do*, and he made me sing all the words down his ear and he'd be making remarks like 'You can't play that' or something. We just had a good time. Also he's inspirational to play with anyway, like George Harrison or Keith Richards, because they've all got a lot of roots in the past and can connect immediately with an old number."
>
> **—RONNIE WOOD**

ERIC CLAPTON GUEST SESSION

PARADISE RECORDING STUDIO
Grand Lake Of The Cherokees, Oklahoma
Session with Leon and Mary Russell

AUGUST 1974

Eric plays on a session with Leon Russell and his wife, Mary (McCreary) Russell. The tracks have never been released.

CRITERIA RECORDING STUDIOS
1755 Northeast 149th Street, Miami, Florida
Session for Freddie King

5 AUGUST 1974

At Eric's suggestion, Freddie King signed a new record deal with Robert Stigwood for his RSO label. It was a big label with Eric Clapton and the Bee Gees being its most successful acts. Although 99 percent of his first album for the label, *Burglar*, was recorded at Mike Vernon's Chipping Norton studios in Oxfordshire, RSO suggested that one track should feature Eric, which would help sales. As the main part of the album was recorded in July, Eric was unable to participate as he was touring. A session was arranged for 5 August in Miami on a break from Eric's huge US tour. Four numbers were recorded, although only "Sugar Sweet" was released on Freddie's first RSO album, *Burglar*. The remaining three were eventually released posthumously on Freddie King (1934–1976) in 1976 and the wonderful Bear Family Records box set, "Texas Flyer 1974–1976" released in 2010. Also worth noting that an alternate version of "Sugar Sweet" is also found on these last two releases.

SUGAR SWEET (Mel London) Burglar album RSO 2394 140 released November 1974 / Texas Flyer 1974–176 box set BCD16778 released 2010
SUGAR SWEET (Mel London) Alternate version, 1934–1976 album RSO 2394 192 released 1976 / *Texas Flyer* 1974–1976 box set Bear BCD16778 released 2010
TV MAMA (Lou Willie Turner) 1934–1976 album RSO 2394 192 released 1976 / Texas Flyer 1974–1976 box set Bear BCD16778 released 2010
GAMBLING WOMAN BLUES (I WONDER WHY) (Joe Josea / Riley B. King) 1934–1976 album RSO 2394 192 released 1976 / Texas Flyer 1974–1976 box set Bear BCD16778 released 2010
BOOGIE FUNK (Freddie King) Texas Flyer 1974–1976 box set BCD16778 released 2010

Freddie King: vocals, guitar
Eric Clapton: guitar
Carl Radle: bass
Jamie Oldaker: drums
Dick Sims: keyboards

Producer: Bill Oakes
Engineer: Steve Klein

> "Freddie King taught me just about everything I needed to know, when and when not to make a stand, when and when not to show your hand, and most important of all, how to make love to a guitar."
>
> **—ERIC CLAPTON**

DYNAMIC SOUND STUDIOS
15 Bell Road,
Kingston, Jamaica
Sessions for *Eric Clapton: The Greatest Guitarist in the World (There's One in Every Crowd)*

19 AUGUST 1974–18 SEPTEMBER 1974

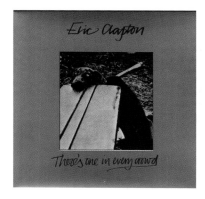

Album cover for There's One In Every Crowd.

In a break on the first part of the *461 Ocean Boulevard* world tour, Eric is booked in at Byron Lee's recording studio in Kingston, Jamaica, to record his second studio album of the year. He had become enamored with Jamaican reggae rhythms, so going to record there made perfect sense. Yvonne Elliman recalled, "It was something I think he felt naturally comfortable doing, which was so important at the time—because no way would anybody lay any kind of pressure on Eric at the time. You're not going to do that. You're going to say, "Sit down and play anything you like. Just let me hear you again!"

As well as being influenced by reggae, Eric also loved just about everyone who was signed to Leon Russell's Shelter record label. Two of the best songs of the sessions were from albums by Shelter artists. The first was "Singing The Blues" by Mary McCreary, who would soon become Leon's wife, and the second was Jim Byfield's "Little Rachel."

The Rolling Stones had recorded their *Goat's Head Soup* album there in 1973 and gave some tips to Eric. It would be best to rent some properties on the North Shore, which would be away from the heat and violence in Kingston. Unfortunately, the North Shore was quite a distance from the capital and it meant

commuting for one hour each way by plane every day. There were further problems about flying at night, and ultimately it all got to be too tiring.

Instead, Eric and the band moved into a wing of the Terra Nova, an all-suite hotel located in the heart of Kingston with beautiful lush gardens. It proved to be a perfect setting for the band to unwind during the day before heading off to the studio in the evening. One of the hotel's security guys even made it onto the record singing backup vocals.

The Jamaican sessions also gave Marcy Levy an opportunity to join the band. She was known to Carl and Jamie, as she used to sing backup vocals for Leon Russell back in Tulsa. Yvonne recalls, "She came to Jamaica and Eric said, 'Let's put her on a track and see how she sings.' She went into the studio and sang 'Singin' The Blues,' and she blew us all out. And I was going through this whole kind of really tormented thing—you know, this whole sob number. It was downright jealousy. I think I got over it when we found out that she could cover the things that I couldn't possibly do, and vice-versa." For a while there was quite a lot of bitchy rivalry between the two girls that caused some friction on the next couple of tours.

The sessions were quite tough for Eric. He did not have many songs prepared and he was drinking heavily. Listening to the complete session tapes, you realize that it was a miracle that so much suitable material was recorded. The biggest problem was Eric's

Advert for Eric Clapton's There's One In Every Crowd *album.*

vocals, which often sounded very rough due to heavy drinking and too many cigarettes. Several attempts were made at "I Found A Love" where Eric's voice was completely shot. His guitar playing was not much better. On one take he attempted a straight guitar solo. When that did not work, he tried doing a slide solo on another take. Several songs followed the same pattern, including a truly cringeworthy throwaway version of Carl Perkins's "Matchbox." Strangely, his shot voice kinda suited the rawness of Elmore James's "It Hurts Me Too." Not surprisingly, it never made the album, even though several takes were recorded. Eric would revisit the song for his *From The Cradle* album in 1994. Luckily, the backing tracks were generally finished to a master standard, and he was able to overdub new vocals in Miami in November before the European tour, as well as in January 1975.

The reggae-influenced numbers were the traditional "We've Been Told (Jesus Coming Soon)," done as an irresistibly rhythmic version; "Don't Blame Me," written by Eric Clapton and George Terry, the follow-up story to "I Shot The Sheriff"; and another traditional number, "Swing Low Sweet Chariot," in a straight reggae version with a nice guitar run. A couple of numbers done with Peter Tosh, "Burial" and "Whatcha Gonna Do," were left off, as it was starting to sound like an album full of reggae tunes. Yvonne Elliman explained,

> "Being in Jamaica, you get that reggae feeling in your bones just being there. And the minute you step into the studio it's just da-da-da. We recorded about five reggae tunes, the Wailers came down, and some steel drum players. And Eric and George Terry wrote the answer to 'I Shot The Sheriff'— who shot the deputy right? The song is called 'Don't Blame Me,' about the poor guy stuck in jail saying, 'Don't blame me, I did not shoot the deputy.'"

"Pretty Blue Eyes" was rehearsed several times before a take was made. The first run-throughs were instrumental with backing vocals. The harmonies were very Beatles-like, contained in a framework of '60s pop. "Singing The Blues" by Mary McCreary had an infectious groove with great bass playing by Carl. The band are really cooking on this number. Several blues numbers were also recorded, such as Elmore James's "The Sky Is Crying," which was more than worthy of inclusion on the album.

WE'VE BEEN TOLD (JESUS COMING SOON) (Traditional; arranged by Eric Clapton) *There's One In Every Crowd* US RSO SO 4806 / UK RSO 2479132 Released April 1975 / CD Polydor 31453 1822-2 released September 1996

SWING LOW SWEET CHARIOT (Traditional arranged by Eric Clapton) *There's One In Every Crowd* US RSO SO 4806 / UK RSO 2479132 released April 1975 / CD Polydor 31453 1822-2 released September 1996

LITTLE RACHEL (Jim Byfield) *There's One In Every Crowd* US RSO SO 4806 / UK RSO 2479132 Released April 1975 / CD Polydor 31453 1822-2 released September 1996

DON'T BLAME ME (Eric Clapton / George Terry) *There's One In Every Crowd* US RSO SO 4806 / UK RSO 2479132 released April 1975 / CD Polydor 31453 1822-2 released September 1996

THE SKY IS CRYING (Elmore James) *There's One In Every Crowd* US RSO SO 4806 / UK RSO 2479132 Released April 1975 / CD Polydor 31453 1822-2 released September 1996

SINGING THE BLUES (Mary McCreary) *There's One In Every Crowd* US RSO SO 4806 / UK RSO 2479132 Released April 1975 / CD Polydor 31453 1822-2 released September 1996

BETTER MAKE IT THROUGH TODAY (Eric Clapton) *There's One In Every Crowd* US RSO SO 4806 / UK RSO 2479132 released April 1975 / CD Polydor 31453 1822-2 Released September 1996

PRETTY BLUE EYES (Eric Clapton) *There's One In Every Crowd* US RSO SO 4806 / UK RSO 2479132 Released April 1975 / CD Polydor 31453 1822-2 released September 1996

HIGH (Eric Clapton) *There's One In Every Crowd* US RSO SO 4806 / UK RSO 2479132 Released April 1975 / CD Polydor 31453 1822-2 released September 1996

OPPOSITES (Eric Clapton) *There's One In Every Crowd* US RSO SO 4806 / UK RSO 2479132 Released April 1975 / CD Polydor 31453 1822-2 released September 1996

WHATCHA GONNA DO (Peter Tosh) *Crossroads* box set US Polydor 835 261-2, UK Polydor Road1 released April 1988

BURIAL (Peter Tosh) unreleased

MATCHBOX (Carl Perkins) unreleased

I FOUND A LOVE (Mary McCreary) *Crossroads* box set US Polydor 835 261-2, UK Polydor Road1 released April 1988

FOOL LIKE ME (Eric Clapton) unreleased

IT HURTS ME TOO (Mel London) *Crossroads* box set US Polydor 835 261-2, UK Polydor Road1 released April 1988

Producer: Tom Dowd
Engineers: Carlton Lee, Graeme Goodall, Ronnie Logan, Don Gehman, Karl Richardson, Steve Klein

CRITERIA RECORDING STUDIOS 1755 Northeast 149th Street, Miami, Florida Sessions for *There's One In Every Crowd*

DECEMBER 1974

OPPOSITES (Eric Clapton) There's One In Every Crowd album RSO released 1975

Overdubs on the tracks originally recorded in Jamaica in August and September. A new track, "Opposites," was also recorded during their time in the studio.

> "The last song on side 2, 'Opposites,' which Albhy Galuten and George Terry recorded on New Year's Eve, if you listen to the end you'll hear them play 'Auld Lang Syne.' I think it's Flash Terry's finest moment."
> —ERIC CLAPTON

CRITERIA RECORDING STUDIOS 1755 Northeast 149th Street, Miami, Florida Sessions for *There's One In Every Crowd*

JANUARY 1975

Final overdubs are made before the album can be mastered and prepared for release.

> "It's the kind of record that if you didn't like it after maybe the third or fourth time, you wouldn't play it again, but if you did like it and you carried on listening to it, you'd hear things that were really fine, just little things in the background, little touches. We started it in Jamaica with the original idea of sunshine during the day and work during the night, and everyone just got lazy. We didn't even hear any reggae! It was like Scunthorpe on a good day."   —ERIC CLAPTON

1975

1975

The year started off with Eric doing a session for Arthur Louis in London before heading off to Miami to record some final overdubs on various numbers for *There's One In Every Crowd* at Criteria Studios. That was followed with rehearsals for a large tour that would take in Hawaii, New Zealand, Australia, America, and Japan. As Eric was living in the Bahamas on Paradise Island as a tax exile, he would not be allowed to perform in England until 1976. As was normal with Eric at this time, there were some incidents on tour. He told a New Zealand crowd exactly what he felt about their country after Patti had been refused entry due to an old drugs conviction. And in Australia he collapsed onstage during one of the Sydney concerts. The official line was food poisoning, and he had to play another concert for free to make up for it. Despite the various hiccups, overall the 1975 tour was a huge success, especially in America. The setlist changed nightly, and the band were very tight musically. Several shows were recorded professionally, and some of the material was released on Universal's fine *Crossroads 2—Live In The Seventies* box set. The

Advert for Eric Clapton's two concerts at the HIC Arena in Honolulu, Hawaii, on 7 and 8 April 1975.

highlight for many was the lengthy jam with Carlos Santana on "Eyesight To The Blind" where both players push themselves to the limit.

THERE'S ONE IN EVERY CROWD TOUR HAWAII 1975

BAND LINEUP:
Eric Clapton: guitar, vocals
George Terry: guitar
Carl Radle: bass
Dick Sims: keyboards
Jamie Oldaker: drums
Yvonne Elliman: backing vocals
Marcy Levy: backing vocals

> **"**Eric Clapton can communicate better through a guitar than many poets can through words. And a packed house at the H.I.C. Arena last night got the rare treat of hearing this world-renowned guitarist and his new band perform for the first time after a three-month rest. From most every standpoint, it was an outstanding success.**"**
>
> —THE *STAR-BULLETIN*
> (concert review by Don Weller)

APRIL 1975

7 April 1975 H.I.C. (Hawaii International Center) Arena, Honolulu, Hawaii (with Quietfire)

SETLIST: Steady Rollin' Man / Tell The Truth / The Sky Is Crying / Badge / Better Make It Through Today / I Shot The Sheriff / Teach Me To Be Your Woman / Singing The Blues / Key To The Highway / Blues Power / Little Wing / Layla / Can't Find My Way Home / Let It Rain

> " 'Clapton, a rock messiah.' Eric Clapton, king of the blues guitar, is a rock messiah. He got a rousing four-minute standing ovation at the conclusion of the first of his two Island concerts Monday night (the other was last night at the H.I.C. Arena). And it was like a religious assembly hailing its deity. Even before he appeared on stage, his disciples roared a hearty welcome. When he emerged, he flashed the 'peace' sign and said 'Aloha...aloha.' "
>
> **—THE HONOLULU ADVERTISER**

8 April 1975, H.I.C. (Hawaii International Center) Arena, Honolulu, Hawaii (with Quietfire)

THERE'S ONE IN EVERY CROWD TOUR NEW ZEALAND AND AUSTRALIA 1975

11 April 1975, Western Springs Stadium, Auckland, New Zealand (with Beech)

14 April 1975, Festival Hall, Brisbane, Australia (with Renee Geyer and Sanctuary)

15 April 1975, Festival Hall, Melbourne, Australia (with Renee Geyer and Sanctuary)

16 April 1975, Festival Theatre, Adelaide, Australia (with Renee Geyer and Sanctuary)

17 April 1975, R.A.S. Hordern Pavilion, Sydney, Australia (with Renee Geyer and Sanctuary)

SETLIST: Let It Grow / Tell The Truth / Better Make It Through Today / Badge / I Shot The Sheriff / Teach Me To Be Your Woman / Steady Rollin' Man / Key To The Highway / Can't Find My Way Home / Blues Power / All I Have To Do Is Dream / Blues Power / Driftin' Blues / Crossroads / Have You Ever Loved A Woman, Driftin' Blues / Layla / Opposites / Let It Rain / Little Wing

> " I really don't expect to trek the length and breadth of New Zealand to be treated to a display of musical nonchalance that honestly didn't endear him to me—or any of the 17,999 disciples who came along to hear the sermon. I suspect Eric, who played a one-off New Zealand date in Auckland before moving to Australia for a series of concerts, is suffering from an acute case of I've-been-on-the-road-too-long-and-seen-it-all-blues.
>
> Maybe 18,000 people—the biggest crowd in Auckland since the Elton John visit last March—caught him on a bad night.
>
> Certainly, Clapton was caught up in the Dionne Warwick syndrome. Immigration officials had refused to allow his current No 1 partner Patti Harrison into the country on the grounds of an old drugs conviction—so endorsing a decision earlier this month in barring Miss Warwick's drummer Ray Lucas in setting foot on Kiwi soil.
>
> Eric became very petulant and broody over the move and refused point blank to grant me or any other pressman an interview. On stage, he let his feelings be abundantly clear when during one of his frequent bouts of strolling around, yapping with his tight, new American band, lighting a cigarette or quaffing a drink, he informed us: 'It wouldn't hurt my feelings if I was kicked out of your country.'
>
> Well, that did not exactly set the tone for a night of Slowhand wizardry. Clapton's super-hero status was acquired in the days when the rock mill brought him to the top of the pile; when he was the fastest guitar in the West with a technical expertise to match.
>
> With two girl singers in his band—Yvonne Elliman and Marcy Levy—the whole tempo has gone out of Clapton's preaching. Sweet and soulful is the new criterion, and it's apt to make Eric a very dull boy. Gone is the old tension in his music-making—the laurel leaves have slipped badly, even since the days of the Dominos.
>
> 'Layla,' 'I Shot The Sheriff,' 'Badge' and 'Steady Rolling Man' tripped lightly from the strings with well-practiced ease. But there was nothing urgent about this Eric Clapton as he spent most of his 80 minutes (the concert was billed as two hours) on walkabouts. There were moments—albeit pitifully few—when proceedings almost caught alight. A stomping version of 'Tell The Truth' and an old favourite from the Layla album 'Little Wing' were ones but the atmosphere slumped as quickly as it lifted.
>
> What a supreme pity... " **—SOUNDS**
> (ran with the following headline: "For those of you that thought God didn't have 'off' days, read on")

18 April 1975, Concert Hall, Sydney Opera House, Sydney, Australia (with Renee Geyer and Sanctuary)

19 April 1975, R.A.S. Hordern Pavilion, Sydney, Australia (with Renee Geyer and Sanctuary)

20 April 1975, R.A.S. Hordern Pavilion, Sydney, Australia (halfway through the show Eric became ill and the concert was stopped. Food poisoning was given as the official explanation. As compensation to the promoter and fans, an additional show was put on for free on 22 April) (with Renee Geyer and Sanctuary)

22 April 1975, R.A.S. Hordern Pavilion, Sydney, Australia (with Renee Geyer and Sanctuary)

23 April 1975, Festival Hall, Brisbane, Australia (with Renee Geyer and Sanctuary)

SETLIST: Badge / Milk Cow Calf Blues / When You've Got A Good Friend / Have You Ever Loved A Woman / Steady Rollin' Man / Can't Find My Way Home / Teach Me To Be Your Woman / Let It Rain / Nobody Knows You When You're Down And Out / I Shot The Sheriff / Layla / All I Have To Do Is Dream / Little Wing / Little Queenie

24 April 1975, Festival Hall, Brisbane, Australia (with Renee Geyer and Sanctuary)

26 April 1975, Memorial Park Drive, Adelaide, Australia (with Renee Geyer and Sanctuary)

28 April 1975, Entertainment Center, Perth, Australia (with Renee Geyer and Sanctuary)

THERE'S ONE IN EVERY CROWD USA TOUR 1975

BAND LINEUP:
Eric Clapton: guitar, vocals
George Terry: guitar
Carl Radle: bass
Dick Sims: keyboards
Jamie Oldaker: drums
Yvonne Elliman: backing vocals
Marcy Levy: backing vocals

JUNE 1975

14 June 1975, Tampa Stadium, Tampa, Florida (with Santana)

"In another era, Saturday's rock show at Tampa Stadium would have been billed as 'The Two Greatest Guitar Legends In The Universe' or similar hyperbolic nonsense.

Both Carlos Santana and Eric Clapton have outgrown such immature approaches to their music. The two men have survived much turbulence to achieve a reliable sort of stardom. And Saturday night some 23,000 people spent a starry summery few hours at Tampa Stadium in order to hear the essence, the music that remains after the hype and phony legends have passed.

It took only two or three songs for Clapton to prove that there had always been substance behind the overblown proclamations of his greatness. As a blues-rock guitarist, Clapton has the ability to create sounds that are both ringingly clear and soulfully rhythmic."
—*ST. PETERSBURG TIMES*

"I suppose it's taken for granted these days that Eric Clapton undergoes a total personality change about once every 12 months, but even so I'm slightly overawed by the studious atmosphere that's prevalent... You'll recall last year's touring stories—the looning, the boozing, the raving with Legs Larry Smith, the custard pies—This time around a massive tableful of wines, spirits and beers remain untouched. Clapton, blue-denimed and tanned, trimmer than last year, with layer-cut hair and full-face beard, sits quietly at a table.

Tight-lipped, he lists the songs to be performed. The rest of the band appear to take Clapton's mood as their cue and are similarly subdued, talking almost in hushed tones.

On stage, Clapton barely looks at the crowd in the vast airplane hangar of an auditorium before breaking into a familiar flourish of 'Layla,' greeted with a roar of approval.

Like Santana, the bulk of this band's approach is also drawn from Sixties successes, but there's a difference, the crucial one between mere repetition and refinement. If Clapton had strolled out and blundered through 'Bell Bottom Blues,' 'Badge' and 'Sunshine Of Your Love' (all of them in the show) one would have to be skeptical—but as each of these appeared to be a definitive performance such an attitude was impossible." —*MELODY MAKER*

SETLIST: Layla / Bell Bottom Blues / I Shot The Sheriff / Better Make It Through Today / Badge / Can't Find My Way Home / Knockin' On Heaven's Door / Blues Power / Teach Me To Be Your Woman / Motherless Children / Mean Old World / Have You Ever Loved A Woman / Tell The Truth / Little Wing / Mainline Florida / Keep On Growin'

15 June 1975, Memorial Coliseum, Jacksonville, Florida (with Santana)

17 June 1975, Municipal Auditorium, Mobile, Alabama (with Santana)

18 June 1975, Mid-South Coliseum, Memphis, Tennessee (with Santana)

SETLIST: I Shot The Sheriff / Layla / Bell Bottom Blues / Motherless Children / Let It Grow / Can't Find My Way Home / Mainline Florida / Driftin' Blues / Rambling On My Mind / Sunshine Of Your Love / Let It Rain / Blues Power / Why Does Love Got To Be So Sad*

*with Carlos Santana on guitar and Armando Peraza on congas

"A lot of folks leaving Eric Clapton's shindig at Memphis Memorial Stadium last year said they were just a bit disappointed the English blues-rock guitarist 'held back' so much. After all, why should such a talented fellow be so shy and introverted?

Clapton who returned last night via Mid-South Concerts to the Mid-South Coliseum—and a much smaller, though still enthusiastic crowd of 7,000 persons—did manage to break down his reserve a time or two.

'Not dancing in the aisles tonight, eh?' he said after several policemen and Coliseum guards repeatedly ordered standing and clapping adolescents to sit still and behave. 'I know how you feel,' said Clapton, whose sympathetic understanding was greeted with a terrific ovation." —MEMPHIS PRESS-SCIMITAR

19 June 1975, General James White Memorial Coliseum, Knoxville, Tennessee (with Santana)

20 June 1975, Charlotte Coliseum, Charlotte, North Carolina (with Santana)

21 June 1975, Cincinnati Gardens, Cincinnati, Ohio (with Santana)

SETLIST (incomplete): Layla / Bell Bottom Blues / Keep On Growing / Key To The Highway / Blues Power / I Shot The Sheriff / Knockin' On Heaven's Door / Tell The Truth / Blues Power / Eyesight To The Blind*

*with Carlos Santana on guitar

"Despite temperatures in the mid-nineties, thousands of fans packed Cincinnati Gardens Saturday night to enjoy a concert by Santana and Eric Clapton and his band. It was well worth the drive and discomfort.

The announcer promised us one of the best shows we've seen, and it was certainly no disappointment. Starting things off in high gear by slamming into 'Layla,' a 1971 hit for Derek and the Dominos.

If there was anyone who there who thought that anything Clapton could do after 'Layla' would be an anti-climax, he or she was due for a change of mind. Clapton's encore was a 15-20-minute version of 'Eyesight To The Blind,' the song he sang in his role as the Preacher in the film version of 'Tommy.' His arrangement of the Sonny Boy Williamson song demonstrates his incredible proficiency in a mixture of hard rock and blues, which produced a standing ovation." —TROY NEWS

"Eric Clapton's guitar can soar with the grace and power of a giant condor or flounder earthbound like a dodo. It all depends on the musicians surrounding him.

When he was playing with Cream, Jack Bruce and Ginger Baker constantly inspired him to explore higher creative altitudes. In 1970, guitarist Duane Allman, Jim Gordon (drums), Carl Radle (bass) and Bobby Whitlock (keyboards) challenged Clapton to fly higher on the masterpiece album 'Layla.'

With his newest band Clapton plays like his wings have been clipped. Throughout his concert, before a capacity Cincinnati Gardens crowd of 12,000 Saturday evening, he made momentary attempts to fly. Each time he sounded as if he was on the verge of creating a monumental solo statement, the ballast-like backup of his band pulled them down." —CINCINNATI ENQUIRER

22 June 1975, Madison Square Garden, New York City (Eric joins the Rolling Stones for "Sympathy For The Devil," their encore tonight. The band are on tour promoting their latest album "Black And Blue." Eric's solo is impressive and demonstrates how well he fits in with the Stones sound. The Stones are invited to participate in a session Eric will be having at Electric Lady Studios on 28 June)

23 June 1975, Convention Center, Niagara Falls, New York (with Santana)

SETLIST: Layla / Bell Bottom Blues / Key To The Highway / Motherless Children / Driftin' Blues / I Shot the Sheriff / Can't Find My Way Home / Mainline Florida / Teach Me To Be Your Woman / Tell The Truth / Badge / Eyesight To The Blind*

*with Carlos Santana on guitar

> **"**The heat outside was matched by the hot music inside the Convention Center Monday night as Eric Clapton and his band and Santana matched styles and sounds.
>
> But there were no losers in this contest and the biggest winners were the audience. They were treated to three hours of great sounds that ranged from old blues songs from Clapton's days with Cream to new numbers Santana worked up with his four month old band.**"**
>
> **—NIAGARA FALLS GAZETTE**

24 June 1975, Civic Center, Springfield, Massachusetts (with Santana)

SETLIST: Layla / Bell Bottom Blues / Key To The Highway / Instrumental Jam / Can't Find My Way Home / Better Make It Through Today / Keep On Growing / Teach Me To Be Your Woman / Mainline Florida / Knockin' On Heaven's Door / Tell The Truth / Crossroads / Why Does Love Got To Be So Sad*

*with Carlos Santana on guitar

> **"**Rather than traveling from city to city every day, Clapton rents a nine-person small plane that flies to the concert city in the evening and returns to a home base in either New York or Miami after every show. That way, he and the backing band spend each day in relaxed, comfortable surroundings and are more 'up' for doing a gig that night than a group that has spent the whole day on the turnpike and the early evening in the motel dining room.
>
> Tomorrow, for instance, he'll spend the day in New York and then fly to Providence to do a show at the Civic Center while Santana who opens will be going the usual commercial route.**"** **—TY DAVIS**

25 June 1975, Civic Center, Providence, Rhode Island (with Santana)

SETLIST:

Layla (Eric Clapton / Jim Gordon) *Crossroads 2* box set Polydor 529 305-2 released April 1996

Further On Up The Road (Joe Veasey / Don Robey) *Crossroads 2* box set Polydor 529 305-2 released April 1996

I Shot The Sheriff (Bob Marley) unreleased

Better Make It Through Today (Eric Clapton) unreleased

Keep On Growing (Eric Clapton / Bobby Whitlock) unreleased

Can't Find My Way Home (Steve Winwood) unreleased

Driftin' Blues (Johnny Moore / Charles Brown / Eddie Williams) *Crossroads 2* box set Polydor 529 305-2 released April 1996

Sunshine Of Your Love (Jack Bruce / Pete Brown / Eric Clapton) unreleased

Motherless Children (Traditional; arranged by Eric Clapton) unreleased

Mean Old World (T-Bone Walker) unreleased

Teach Me To Be Your Woman (Marcy Levy) unreleased

Bell Bottom Blues (Eric Clapton) unreleased

Badge (Eric Clapton / George Harrison) unreleased

Knockin' On Heaven's Door (Bob Dylan) unreleased

Tell The Truth (Eric Clapton / Bobby Whitlock) unreleased

Eyesight To The Blind* (Sonny Boy Williamson) *Crossroads 2* box set Polydor 529 305-2 released April 1996

Why Does Love Got To Be So Sad* (Eric Clapton / Bobby Whitlock) *Crossroads 2* box set Polydor 529 305-2 released April 1996

*with Carlos Santana on guitar, Armando Peraza on percussion, Leon Chancler on percussion
Concert recorded by: Record Plant Recording Studio Mobile Truck
Producer: Tom Dowd
Engineers: Ralph Moss, Dave Hewitt

"Perhaps it was because the whole show was being recorded for possible inclusion in a future live album, but Wednesday night Eric Clapton and entourage turned in one of the finest rock shows ever presented at the Civic Center.

The nearly packed house of 10,500 responded fully to the master musician for over two hours, clapping steadily for five-minutes to obtain an encore." —*PROVIDENCE JOURNAL*

26 June 1975, Saratoga Performing Arts Center, Saratoga Springs, New York (with Santana)

"Clapton provided a wide variety, from straight, hard rock and roll music, he shifted down into a few blues numbers and changed again into a jam session with the musicians behind him. The crowd loved it all and each of the thousands on hand knew that they were experiencing a piece of history. What they were hearing tonight could be the last time that Clapton would play this way before discovering a new method of making music." —*SARATOGIAN*

28 June 1975, Nassau Coliseum, Uniondale, New York (with Santana)

SETLIST:

Layla (Eric Clapton / Jim Gordon) unreleased

Key To The Highway (Charles Segar / Willie Broonzy) unreleased

Badge (Eric Clapton / George Harrison) *Crossroads 2* box set Polydor 529 305-2 released April 1996

Bell Bottom Blues (Eric Clapton) unreleased

I Shot The Sheriff (Bob Marley) *Crossroads 2* box set Polydor 529 305-2 released April 1996

Can't Find My Way Home (Steve Winwood) unreleased

Further On Up The Road (Joe Veasey / Don Robey) *EC Was Here* album US RSO SO 4809, UK RSO 2394 160 released August 1975 / Remastered CD Polydor 31453 1823-2 released September 1996

Better Make It Through Today (Eric Clapton) unreleased

Blues Power (Eric Clapton / Leon Russell) unreleased

Teach Me To Be Your Woman (Marcy Levy) unreleased

Sunshine Of Your Love (Jack Bruce / Pete Brown / Eric Clapton) unreleased

"Clapton plays with utter confidence, both in his own abilities and in his group's, opening with a song that ought to haunt the rest of the performance, 'Layla,' and getting away with it. The rest of the show is nothing less than his greatest hits, even including two classics of the Cream era, 'Sunshine Of Your Love' and 'Crossroads,' which he deliberately avoided in 1974. Clapton's soloing is more compact and precise than it ever was, but without losing any of its passion. He is the only guitarist I have heard recently—perhaps the only white guitarist ever—who can rivet attention throughout a series of long solos." —*ROLLING STONE*

"For his encore, he was joined, as he has been along the tour, by Carlos Santana and, unexpectedly, by sometime Santana cohort, Mahavishnu John McLaughlin.

Surprise, surprise! Clapton looks uneasy. He and the Mahavishnu traded licks on 'Stormy Monday.' Carlos Santana broke up laughing. The Mahavishnu took aim at the last chord, holding it until it couldn't be borne. Clapton waited him out, then sang that Jesus-has-the-power-to-heal-you-have-no-fear, wiping him up with 'Eyesight To The Blind.' He and the Mahavishnu did not speak afterward. Clapton, who is heavily into his work when not with the ever-assuring Patti Harrison (ex of George), returned to the city to work out with the Stones again." —*NEW YORK POST*

"Big-name encore jamming appears to be the vogue in New York right now. First of all, it was Eric Clapton jamming with the Stones on their first night at Madison Square Garden. Then it was Carlos Santana, fulfilling the same function on the Stones' closing night. But the jam to end them all took place last week at the Nassau Coliseum on Long Island when Eric Clapton was joined by Carlos Santana and John McLaughlin—all three of them traded licks on T-Bone Walker's 'Stormy Monday,' while Alphonse Mouzon rocked the drums. The Stones, incidentally, were to be guests of honour at the gig but, typically, they didn't show." —*MELODY MAKER*

Crossroads (Robert Johnson) unreleased

Tell The Truth (Eric Clapton / Bobby Whitlock) unreleased

Stormy Monday* (T-Bone Walker) unreleased

Eyesight To The Blind* (Sonny Boy Williamson) unreleased

*with Carlos Santana and John McLaughlin on guitar, Alphonse Mouzon on drums
Concert recorded by: Record Plant Recording Studio Mobile Truck
Producer: Tom Dowd
Engineers: Ralph Moss, Dave Hewitt

29 June 1975, New Haven Veterans Memorial Coliseum, New Haven, Connecticut (with Santana)

30 June 1975, Civic Center, Pittsburgh, Pennsylvania (with Santana)

JULY 1975

1 July 1975, Olympia Stadium, Detroit, Michigan (with Santana)

SETLIST: Motherless Children / I've Got A Woman / Rambling On My Mind / Singin' The Blues / Can't Find My Way Home / Layla / Sunshine Of Your Love / Crossroads / Teach Me To Be Your Woman / Knockin' On Heaven's Door / Further On Up The Road / Little Wing / Tell The Truth / Eyesight To The Blind*

*with Carlos Santana on guitar

3 July 1975, Memorial Stadium, Baltimore, Maryland (with Santana)

"Returning to his blues roots, Clapton opened with Elmore James' 'I Can't Hold Out,' immediately establishing the tightness and live (vs. vinyl) superiority of this band. The medium sized crowd exploded as the first chords of 'Layla' surged forth. From there, 'Bell Bottom Blues' and Dylan's 'Knockin' On Heaven's Door' were given definitive treatments, with back-up vocalists Yvonne Elliman and Marcy Levy adding a new dimension.

While Clapton no longer engages in flashy pyrotechnics on stage, he still controls and leads with enough precision to reduce a listener to jelly. Predominately, however, this is a band, and with the quality of their performance and material, could have played all night. A great show." —SCENE

4 July 1975, Richfield Coliseum, Cleveland, Ohio (with Santana)

SETLIST: I Can't Hold Out / Layla / Bell Bottom Blues / Knockin' On Heaven"s Door / Further On Up The Road / Can't Find My Way Home / Blues Power / Stormy Monday / Teach Me To Be Your Woman / Mainline Florida / Better Make It Through Today / Tell The Truth / Eyesight To The Blind*

*with Carlos Santana on guitar

"The real kicker at the Santana/Eric Clapton concert in the Coliseum Tuesday night came at the very end as Clapton, decked in his cowboy hat, squared off at a dozen paces against Carlos Santana in a musical firefight of guitar solos." —CAPITAL TIMES

5 July 1975, Chicago Stadium, Chicago, Illinois (with Santana)

7 July 1975, MET Sports Center, Minneapolis, Minnesota (with Santana)

8 July 1975, Dane County Coliseum, Madison, Wisconsin (with Santana)

SETLIST: Layla/ Bell Bottom Blues / Key To The Highway / Motherless Children / Driftin' Blues / Can't Find My Way Home / I Shot The Sheriff / Mainline Florida / Tell The Truth / Teach Me To Be Your Woman / Badge / Little Wing / Sunshine Of Your Love / Crossroads / Eyesight To The Blind*

*with Carlos Santana on guitar

10 July 1975, Municipal Auditorium, Kansas City, Kansas (with Santana)

SETLIST: Layla / Nobody Knows You When You're Down And Out / Singing The Blues / Give Me Strength / Can't Find My Way Home / Further On Up The Road / Better Make It Through Today / Don't Know What To Do / Badge / Kansas City / Teach Me To Be Your Woman / Blues Power / Stormy Monday / Tell The Truth / Keep On Growin'

("Don't Know What To Do" is just Eric and Marcy Levy singing some ad-lib lyrics together during a power failure with some of the amps)

11 July 1975, Kiel Auditorium, St. Louis, Missouri (with Santana)

SETLIST: Layla / I Shot The Sheriff / Stormy Monday / Can't Find My Way Home / Nobody Knows You When You're Down And Out / Little Queenie / Teach Me To Be Your Woman / Blues Power / Driftin' Blues / Knockin' On Heaven's Door / Better Make It Through Today / Tell the Truth / Eyesight To The Blind*

*with Carlos Santana

AUGUST 1975

Sergio Pastora Rodriguez on percussion joined the band for the second leg of the 1975 USA tour.

3 August 1975, Pacific Coliseum, Vancouver, British Columbia, Canada (with Santana)

SETLIST: Layla / Stormy Monday / Knockin' On Heaven's Door / Blues Power / Can't Find My Way Home / Carnival / Better Make It Through Today / Tell The Truth / I Shot The Sheriff / Little Wing / Eyesight To The Blind*

*with Carlos Santana

"After hearing him play at Stanford, one could rightly assert that Clapton is the finest performing rock guitarist in the business. But this gift forces him into the position of having huge expectations pushed upon him. His smoothness, control and clarity were awesome. The drive of the band charged through the crowd like a chariot. All the pressure and expectations were there, and Clapton gracefully came through. It had to be a satisfying day for him." **—SAN MATEO TIMES**

4 August 1975, Portland Coliseum, Portland, Oregon (with Santana)

5 August 1975, Seattle Center Coliseum, Seattle, Washington (with Santana)

6 August 1975, Coliseum, Spokane, Washington (with Santana)

9 August 1975, Frost Amphitheatre, Stanford University, Palo Alto, California (with Santana)

SETLIST: Layla / Knockin' On Heaven's Door / Tell the Truth / Can't Find My Way Home / Key To The Highway / Carnival / Badge / Better Make It Through the Day / Blues Power / Ramblin' On My Mind / Let It Rain / Eyesight To The Blind*

*with Carlos Santana

11 August 1975, Salt Palace Arena, Salt Lake City, Utah (with Santana)

12 August 1975, Coliseum, Denver, Colorado (with Santana)

SETLIST (INCOMPLETE): Layla / Stormy Monday / Knockin' On Heaven's Door / Badge / Can't Find My Way Home / Carnival / Key To The Highway / Teach Me To Be Your Woman / Blues Power / Little Wing / Tell The Truth

14 August 1975, The Forum, Los Angeles, California (with Santana)

SETLIST: Layla / Further On Up the Road / Knockin' On Heaven's Door / Carnival / Can't Find My Way Home / Tell The Truth / Stormy Monday / Why Does Love Got to Be So Sad / Teach Me to Be Your Woman / Badge / Eyesight To The Blind*

*with Carlos Santana on guitar and Keith Moon on percussion. Joe Cocker is side stage digging the sounds

"'King of the surf guitar, Mr Eric Clapton,' was the introduction from Keith Moon as E.C. offered a few notes of 'Pipeline' before swinging into a torrid version of 'Why Does Love Got To Be So Sad,' thus relieving 'Slowhand' of the uninspired label that has shackled him since his return to active duty.

Eric's show at the Forum was much better than last year's feeble display. This time around with every guitar player in town to check him out, he delivered." **—MELODY MAKER**

Eric Clapton at the Swing Auditorium, San Bernardino, California, on 15 August 1975.

Eric Clapton at the LA Forum on 14 August 1975.

15 August 1975, Swing Auditorium, San Bernardino, California (with Santana)

SETLIST: Layla / Bell Bottom Blues / Knockin' On Heaven's Door / The Sky Is Crying / Keep on Growing / Can't Find My Way Home / Further On Up the Road* / Stormy Monday* / Teach Me To Be Your Woman / Carnival / Tell The Truth / Steady Rollin' Man / Crossroads**

*with Jerry McGee on guitar
**with Carlos Santana on guitar

16 August 1975, Sports Arena, San Diego, California (with Santana)

SETLIST: Key To The Highway / Layla / Better Make It Through Today / I Shot The Sheriff / Blues Power / Can't Find My Way Home / Carnival / Key To The Highway / Teach Me To Be Your Woman / Badge / Crossroads / Tell The Truth / Little Wing* / Eyesight To The Blind*

*with Carlos Santana on guitar

17 August 1975, Community Center, Tucson, Arizona (with Santana)

SETLIST: Layla / Nobody Knows You When You're Down And Out / Carnival / Knockin' On Heaven's Door / Can't Find My Way Home / Further On Up The Road / Little Wing / I Shot The Sheriff / Badge / Steady Rollin' Man / Crossroads

18 August 1975, Civic Center, El Paso, Texas (with Freddie King)

20 August 1975, Sam Houston Coliseum, Houston, Texas (with Freddie King)

Freddie King joins Eric and the band for a version of "Key To The Highway"

21 August 1975, Tarrant County Convention Center, Fort Worth, Texas (with Freddie King). Freddie King joins Eric for "Further On Up The Road" and "Stormy Monday"

"Eric Clapton proved last night at Tarrant County Convention Center that he is back again stronger than ever before, with a concert performance that ranks as one of the all-time outstanding shows in this area.

Everything fit so well, sounded so fine. Even the stage setting with lights washing subtly across waving palm fronds touching the performers' heads in gentle outline felt easy and relaxed.

Finishing his set with 'Tell The Truth,' Clapton returned onstage to ecstatic roars of the crowd, accompanied by the show's opening performer, Texas' own Freddie King. Together onstage, the three guitarists—Terry was included—traded licks through Bobby Bland's 'Further On Up The Road' and 'Stormy Monday.'"

—*DALLAS NEWS*

22 August 1975, Myriad Convention Center Arena, Oklahoma City, Oklahoma (with Freddie King)

23 August 1975, Assembly Center, Tulsa, Oklahoma (with Freddie King)

24 August 1975, Hirsch Memorial Coliseum, Shreveport, Louisiana (with Freddie King).

"You could say that last night's concert at the Hirsch Memorial Coliseum was 'Lead Guitar Night' because with Eric Clapton and Freddie King, that's about all you could hear. The evening began at 8 with the appearance of King and his band. Freddie strolled on stage and then immediately went into a fast boogie tune which sounded like just the thing to get the night rolling.

As the lights went out, the big crowd began screaming as rock superstar Clapton casually walked on stage. After a slight delay for tuning, Clapton and his band burst into his biggest hit, 'Layla,' and the fans went wild. What Clapton did of 'Layla' was excellent, but I was disappointed that the piano solo was omitted.

There were delays between some of Clapton's songs as he wandered about the stage chatting with his band and other people. This got to be a little boring after a while and had little effect on the outcome of the show.

Either Clapton and his band have a lot of charisma or talent is not what it used to be." —**SHREVEPORT JOURNAL**

27 August 1975, Market Square Arena, Indianapolis, Indiana (with Santana)

SETLIST: Layla / Key To The Highway / I Shot The Sheriff / Can't Find My Way Home / Further Up The Road / Let It Rain / Better Make It Through Today / Blues Power / Knockin' On Heaven's Door / Badge / Tell The Truth / Little Wing* / Carnival*

*with Carlos Santana on guitar

"Being 30 hasn't come down too hard on Eric Clapton—he's still one of the best crank and squeeze performers going. They also mention that there were some surprisingly noticeable holes in a couple of his solos where they felt he was going to be overshadowed by guitarist George Terry who was prodding Clapton's genius while stretching out his own musical hand." —**THE INDIANAPOLIS STAR**

"Well, the good news is Clapton is definitely back and he is playing with a fire and ferocity unmatched by any of his previous work." —**INDIANAPOLIS NEWS**

28 August 1975, Charleston Civic Center, Charleston, South Carolina (with Poco)

SETLIST: Layla / Bell Bottom Blues / I Shot The Sheriff / Key To The Highway / Can't Find My Way Home / Mainline Florida / Stormy Monday / Knockin' On Heaven's Door / Teach Me To Be Your Woman / Further On Up The Road / Tell The Truth / Blues Power

29 August 1975, Coliseum, Greensboro, North Carolina (with Poco)

SETLIST: Layla / Keep On Growing / Key To The Highway / Can't Find My Way Home / Knockin' On Heaven's Door / Carnival / Better Make It Through Today / Badge / Teach Me To Be Your Woman / Further On Up The Road / Little Wing / I Shot The Sheriff / Tell The Truth / Let It Rain

30 August 1975, Scope, Norfolk, Virginia (with Poco)

SETLIST: Layla / Bell Bottom Blues / Key To The Highway / Mainline Florida / Can't Find My Way Home / Further On Up The Road / Knockin' On Heaven's Door / Blues Power / Teach Me To Be Your Woman / Stormy Monday / Tell The Truth / Let It Rain*

*with members of Poco (Timothy Schmidt: vocals, George Graham: vocals, Rusty Young: steel guitar, Paul Cotton: lead guitar)

"Let it be said here that Eric and his band wound up several months of North American dates in Norfolk, Virginia with a stunning tour de force characteristic of every night of this the 'E.C.'s Chops Are Back' tour. Dressed in his standard tour outfit, a dark blue ESSO jump-suit, Eric Scotch-wobbled on stage, strapped on his guitar and tore into a 15-minute long 'Layla.' The 15,000 capacity crowd had no choice but to go wild. Grinning broadly throughout, he did little to let them down over the next two-and-a-half hours.

Afterwards, with the house lights on and no chance for an encore, the audience still remained on their feet for a respectful standing ovation. 'You won't catch me saying this is my best band,' Eric said backstage. 'The last time I said that, the Dominos broke up a month later. But...' Clapton leaned in close and whispered, 'I'd go see us.'" —**CAMERON CROWE** (*NME*)

SEPTEMBER 1975

11 September 1975, Hammersmith Odeon, London (Santana are playing in London tonight. Eric attends the show and Carlos invites him to come and jam. After a few words with Carlos onstage, Eric comes to the mic and says a few words to the audience. Naturally, everyone expects him to jam with Santana. But he cannot, as he was a tax exile and cannot play. If he does so, he will be asked to pay 60% of his income for the last UK tax year. Eric explains to the *NME*: "I was in London last week—I'm allowed 60 days a year—and I went to see Santana who invited me up to jam. I was told I couldn't even do that. Not even play for free or anything. It's ridiculous. If they even lowered the tax to 50 per cent everyone would come back." Carlos Santana tells the audience that he will channel Eric though his guitar playing)

E.C. WAS HERE
JAPAN TOUR 1975

BAND LINEUP:
Eric Clapton: guitar, vocals
George Terry: guitar
Carl Radle: bass
Dick Sims: keyboards
Jamie Oldaker: drums
Sergio Pastora: percussion
Yvonne Elliman: backing vocals
Marcy Levy: backing vocals

OCTOBER 1975

22 October 1975, Festival Hall, Osaka, Japan

SETLIST: Layla / Key To The Highway / Knockin' On Heaven's Door / Blues Power / Can't Find My Way Home / Nobody Knows You When You're Down And Out / I Shot The Sheriff / Teach Me To Be Your Woman / Further On Up The Road / Carnival / Little Wing / Tell The Truth / Let It Rain

23 October 1975, Festival Hall, Osaka, Japan

SETLIST: Layla / Bell Bottom Blues / I Shot The Sheriff / As The Years Go Passing By / Can't Find My Way Home / Badge / Knockin' On Heaven's Door / Blues Power / Teach Me To Be Your Woman / Tell The Truth / Further On Up The Road

24 October 1975, Kyoto Kaikan Daiichi Hall, Kyoto, Japan

SETLIST: Layla / Steady Rollin' Man / Knockin' On Heaven's Door / Crossroads / Can't Find My Way Home / Singin' The Blues / I Shot The Sheriff / Key To The Highway / Teach Me To Be Your Woman / Tell The Truth / Further On Up The Road

27 October 1975, Kitakyushu Sogo Taiikukan, Kitakyusyu, Japan

SETLIST: Layla / Eyesight To The Blind / Who's Loving You Tonight / Why Does Love Got To Be So Sad / Can't Find My Way Home / Key To The Highway / I Shot The Sheriff / Little Wing / Further On Up The Road / Teach Me To Be Your Woman / Tell The Truth / Let It Rain

29 October 1975, Sunpu-Kaikan, Shizuoka, Japan

SETLIST: Layla / Little Wing / Blues Power / Can't Find My Way Home / So Many Roads / Badge / The Sun Is Shining On Me / Tell The Truth / Eyesight To The Blind / Carnival

NOVEMBER 1975

1 November 1975, Budokan, Tokyo, Japan

SETLIST: Layla / Knockin' On Heaven's Door / Key To The Highway / Badge / Can't Find My Way Home / Further On Up The Road / I Shot The Sheriff / The Sun Is Shining On Me / Have You Ever Loved A Woman / Tell The Truth / Eyesight To The Blind / Why Does Love Got To Be So Sad

2 November 1975, Budokan, Tokyo, Japan

SETLIST: Layla / I Shot The Sheriff / Little Rachel / Can't Find My Way Home / Blues Power / Stormy Monday / The Sun Is Shining On Me / Little Wing / Badge / Why Does Love Got To Be So Sad / Further On Up The Road

1975 RECORDING SESSIONS

ERIC CLAPTON
GUEST SESSION

ESSEX SOUND STUDIOS
19/20 Poland Street
in Soho, London W1
Session for Arthur Louis

JANUARY 1975

Eric's first session of the year was for Arthur Louis, a thirtyish Jamaican who had lived most of his life in New York before settling in England. Once there, he co-formed a new record label called Plum and went about recording his first album at Essex Sound Studios in London. He recorded a couple of hours' worth of material with Eric, including a reggae arrangement of Bob Dylan's "Knockin' On Heaven's Door" which had a lot of commercial appeal and would be the first single for Plum. Released in July 1975, it had a number named after the label, "Plum," as its B-side. The single received a fair bit of publicity because of Eric's name, as well as getting a reasonable amount of radio interest, especially on BBC Radio 1, where deejay Johnny Walker was considering making it his Record of the Week.

"Arthur played me his version of the song and I liked it, so I played on his record. His version was a demo at the time. I thought it was such a good idea to do a reggae version of the song. As far as I knew he was going to do nothing with it, so I went ahead and recorded it and told them (RSO) to put it out as a single. I even put one of his songs on the b side. By the release date, Arthur's had already been out ten days, which I hadn't known about. Then he suddenly said, 'No, you can't put that out.' Eventually we worked out a deal.

As it turned out the song wasn't successful so it didn't really ruin his chances—as both his and my version are almost identical. Anyway, there's always trouble with my singles. They should have released 'Motherless Children' after 'Sheriff.' It was a bad mistake."

—ERIC CLAPTON

Ten days after Plum's release, RSO released Eric's version with a similar arrangement, which was recorded in June 1975 in New York for the specific reason of a single release. Understandably, Arthur and Plum were not pleased to see their single pretty much disappear overnight due to Eric's version receiving a massive publicity push. Arthur maintained that Eric had told him that in the UK, his version of "Knockin' On Heaven's Door" would be the B-side to "Someone Like You," an Arthur Louis composition. That was not the case. RSO said, "Eric's version of 'Knockin' On Heaven's Door' was always going to have been released in this country at his request."

A full Arthur Louis album was released in Japan by Polydor, titled *First Album* "(with guest appearance: Eric Clapton)," where it reached number 5 in the album charts. The album quickly disappeared and has become quite a rarity in its original mix. The PRT label picked up the album in 1988 for the digital age and remixed all the tracks to give it a more modern sound as well as give more prominence to Eric's guitar. Since then it has received numerous re-releases on CD and is easily available to buy online.

Plum did not survive, and Arthur was then signed up by Island Records, who re-released "Knockin' On Heaven's Door" with a different B-side, "The Dealer." They wanted to see if they could generate enough interest for a full album release. Sales were poor and Arthur was dropped. He was then signed by Mainstreet Records, who released another number from the original sessions called "Still It Feels Good" backed with "Come On And Love Me." Once again, sales were poor and the record was destined to litter the deletion bins. Eric played on all of the singles released, and that makes them collectable today, especially the Plum release.

KNOCKIN' ON HEAVEN'S DOOR (Bob Dylan) A-side single Plum 001 (Released July 1975) / Island WIP 6448 UK released September 1975 / *First Album* guest appearance: Eric Clapton Japan only Polydor MP2547 released 1976 / *First Album* Arthur Louis guest appearance: Eric Clapton (first time on CD with original vinyl artwork) Solid CDSOL 1399 Japan released February 2011

Arthur Louis: vocal, guitar
Eric Clapton: guitar
Richard Bailey: drums
Winston Deleandro: guitar
Peter Dafrey: bass
Robert Bailey: keyboards
Ernestine Pierce: backing vocals

PLUM (Arthur Louis) B-side single Plum 001 / *First Album* guest appearance: Eric Clapton Japan only Polydor MP2547 released 1976 / *First Album* Arthur Louis guest appearance: Eric Clapton (first time on CD with original vinyl artwork) Solid CDSOL 1399 Japan released February 2011

Arthur Louis: guitar
Eric Clapton: guitar
Richard Bailey: drums
Winston Deleandro: guitar
Peter Dafrey: bass
Robert Bailey: keyboards

THE DEALER (Arthur Louis) B-side single Island WIP 6448 / *First Album* guest appearance: Eric Clapton Japan only Polydor MP2547 released 1976 / *First Album* Arthur Louis guest appearance: Eric Clapton (first time on CD with original vinyl artwork) Solid CDSOL 1399 Japan released February 2011

Arthur Louis: guitar
Eric Clapton: guitar
Gene Chandler: vocals
Richard Bailey: drums
Winston Deleandro: guitar
Peter Dafrey: bass
Robert Bailey: keyboards
Ernestine Pierce: backing vocals

FEELS GOOD (Arthur Louis) A-side single Mainstreet 12 SPMS 104 released 1981 / *First Album* guest appearance: Eric Clapton Japan only Polydor MP2547 released 1976 / *First Album* Arthur Louis guest appearance: Eric Clapton (first time on CD with original vinyl artwork) Solid CDSOL 1399 Japan released February 2011

Arthur Louis: vocal, guitar
Eric Clapton: guitar
Richard Bailey: drums
Winston Deleandro: guitar
Peter Dafrey: bass
Robert Bailey: keyboards
Ernestine Pierce: backing vocals

COME ON AND LOVE ME (Arthur Louis) B-side single Mainstreet 12 SPMS 104 released 1981 / *First Album* guest appearance: Eric Clapton Japan only Polydor MP2547 released 1976 / *First Album* Arthur Louis guest appearance: Eric Clapton (first time on CD with original vinyl artwork) Solid CDSOL 1399 Japan released February 2011

Arthur Louis: vocal, guitar
Eric Clapton: guitar
Richard Bailey: drums
Winston Deleandro: guitar
Peter Dafrey: bass
Robert Bailey: keyboards
Ernestine Pierce: backing vocals

SOMEONE LIKE YOU (Arthur Louis) *First Album* guest appearance: Eric Clapton Japan only Polydor MP2547 released 1976 / *First Album* Arthur Louis guest appearance: Eric Clapton (first time on CD with original vinyl artwork) Solid CDSOL 1399 Japan released February 2011

Arthur Louis: vocal, guitar
Eric Clapton: slide guitar
Richard Bailey: drums
Winston Deleandro: guitar
Peter Dafrey: bass
Robert Bailey: keyboards
Ernestine Pierce: backing vocals

TRAIN 444 (Arthur Louis) *First Album* guest appearance: Eric Clapton Japan only Polydor MP2547 released 1976 / *First Album* Arthur Louis guest appearance: Eric Clapton (first time on CD with original vinyl artwork) Solid CDSOL 1399 Japan released February 2011

Arthur Louis: vocal, guitar
Eric Clapton: guitar
Richard Bailey: drums
Winston Deleandro: guitar
Peter Dafrey: bass
Robert Bailey: keyboards
Ernestine Pierce: backing vocals

GO OUT AND MAKE IT HAPPEN (Arthur Louis) *First Album* guest appearance: Eric Clapton Japan only Polydor MP2547 released 1976 / *First Album* Arthur Louis guest appearance: Eric Clapton (first time on CD with original vinyl artwork) Solid CDSOL 1399 Japan released February 2011

Arthur Louis: vocal, guitar
Eric Clapton: guitar
Richard Bailey: drums
Winston Deleandro: guitar
Peter Dafrey: bass
Robert Bailey: keyboards
Ernestine Pierce: backing vocals

LAYLA PART TWO unreleased (recorded at the same sessions but never released. Confirmed to author by PRT Records in 1988)

Producer: Arthur Louis
Engineer: John Burns

CRITERIA RECORDING STUDIOS 1755 Northeast 149th Street, Miami, Florida Session for new Eric Clapton single

16 JUNE 1975

Eric was on tour in the US and the day after playing the Coliseum in Jacksonville, Florida, the band head off to Miami's Criteria Studios to record a cover version of Bob Dylan's "Knockin' On Heaven's Door" for a new single release. Influenced by the version by Arthur Louis on which he played, the single was not the hit everyone hoped for.

KNOCKIN' ON HEAVEN'S DOOR (Bob Dylan) A-side single RSO SO 513 (US), RSO 2090166 (UK). released August 1975 / *Crossroads* box set Polydor 835 261-2 (Released 1988)

Eric Clapton: guitar, vocals
George Terry: guitar
Carl Radle: bass
Jamie Oldaker: drums
Dick Sims: keyboards
Yvonne Elliman: vocals
Marcy Levy: vocals

Producer: Tom Dowd and Albhy Galuten

ELECTRIC LADY STUDIOS
52 West 8th Street,
New York City
Session for single B-side

25 JUNE 1975

SOMEONE LIKE YOU (Arthur Louis) 7 takes with take 7 as the master. B-side single RSO SO 513 (US), RSO 2090166 (UK). released August 1975 / *Crossroads* box set Polydor 835 261-2 (Released 1988)

Eric Clapton: guitar, vocals
George Terry: guitar
Carl Radle: bass
Jamie Oldaker: drums
Dick Sims: keyboards
Yvonne Elliman: vocals
Marcy Levy: vocals

Producer: Eric Clapton and Albhy Galuten

ELECTRIC LADY STUDIOS
52 West 8th Street,
New York
Session with Rolling
Stones as guests

28 JUNE 1975

CARNIVAL TO RIO (Eric Clapton) 10 takes unreleased

Eric Clapton: guitar, vocals
George Terry: guitar
Carl Radle: bass
Jamie Oldaker: drums
Dick Sims: keyboards
Yvonne Elliman: vocals
Marcy Levy: vocals
Keith Richards: guitar
Ronnie Wood: guitar
Bill Wyman: bass
Charlie Watts: drums
Mick Jagger: vocals
Billy Preston: keyboards
Ollie Brown: congas

Producer: Eric Clapton and Albhy Galuten

Eric had joined his old friends the Rolling Stones onstage at New York's Madison Square Garden on 22 June for their encore "Sympathy For The Devil." They were invited to join Eric in the studio to record a new song for his next album. Ten takes were recorded on 28 June when both bands were in New York, and several mixes were made on 30 June. It sounds like they were all having fun, but it was way too loose to

ever consider it for an official release. Eric re-recorded the song next year for his *No Reason To Cry* album, shortening the title to "Carnival."

> "Ronnie Wood, Keith and I all played lead. The best takes were early on when nobody knew what they were doing. Later on, when everyone worked out what part to play, it got too sophisticated. It's very good actually. If it works out legally, I'll put it on the album." —**ERIC CLAPTON**

> "That session with Eric was great—I didn't even know whose song it was till Eric said it was his. I told him that he better start leading before everyone demanded writing royalties. You'd never fit all the names on the label copy! It was good the way we did it though. If you plan a number too much it starts to get muddled up. I just like to take it straight off." —**RONNIE WOOD**

> "When we recorded the track, everyone was on it (Keith Richards, Mick Jagger, Jamie Oldaker, Charlie Watts, Carl Radle, Ron Wood, George Terry, Ollie Brown, Marcy Levy, Yvonne Elliman, Billy Preston, Dick Sims. Unfortunately, it was so chaotic and there were so many tracks being recorded at once (it was sixteen-track) that Eric's rhythm guitar was too distorted when recorded and he didn't want to replace it so I don't think he ever used the track but it was amazing (at least in my memory)." —**ALBHY GALUTEN**

COLUMBIA STUDIOS
Studio E, 6th floor,
49 East 52nd Street,
New York City
Session for Bob Dylan
between 7:00 p.m. and
4:00 a.m.

28 JULY 1975

ROMANCE IN DURANGO (Bob Dylan / Jacques Levy) Take 1 unreleased
MONEY BLUES (Bob Dylan / Jacques Levy) unreleased

VALLEY BELOW (the song title was eventually changed to "One More Cup Of Coffee") unreleased

ROMANCE IN DURANGO (Bob Dylan–Jacques Levy/Bob Dylan) Take 2 Desire album, COLUMBIA PC-33893 released 16 January 1976 / *Desire* CD remastered

OH, SISTER (Bob Dylan / Jacques Levy) unreleased

CATFISH (Bob Dylan–Jacques Levy/Bob Dylan) Take 1 (false start)

CATFISH (Bob Dylan–Jacques Levy/Bob Dylan) Take 2 unreleased

ROMANCE IN DURANGO (Bob Dylan / Jacques Levy) Take 3 (false start)

ROMANCE IN DURANGO (Bob Dylan / Jacques Levy) Take 4 (false start)

ROMANCE IN DURANGO (Bob Dylan / Jacques Levy) Take 5 unreleased

ROMANCE IN DURANGO (Bob Dylan / Jacques Levy) Take 6 unreleased

CATFISH (Bob Dylan / Jacques Levy) Take 3 unreleased

HURRICANE (Bob Dylan / Jacques Levy) Take 1 unreleased

HURRICANE (Bob Dylan / Jacques Levy) Take 2 unreleased

HURRICANE (Bob Dylan / Jacques Levy) Take 3 unreleased

Bob Dylan: guitar, vocal
Emmylou Harris: vocal
Vincent Bell: guitar
Eric Clapton: guitar
Neil Hubbard: guitar
Perry Lederman: guitar
James Mullen: guitar
Erik Frandsen: slide guitar
Michael Lawrence: trumpet
Scarlet Rivera: violin
Mel Collins: tenor saxophone
Sheena Seidenberg: tenor saxophone
Dom Cortese: accordion
Tony O'Malley: keyboards
James "Sugarblue" Whiting: harmonica
Rob Rothstein: bass
Alan Spenner: bass
Jody Linscott: percussion
John Sussewell: drums
Dyan Birch: background vocals
Francis Collins: background vocals
Paddy McHugh: background vocals

Eric's Dobro got damaged on the plane on the way to New York. It was repairable, but not in time for the session. He had to hire a Dobro and electric guitar for the session.

CRITERIA RECORDING STUDIOS Studio B, 1755 Northeast 149th Street, Miami, Florida Session for Tom & Don

13 NOVEMBER 1975

GREYHOUND BUS (with bottom guitar with band) unreleased
GREYHOUND BUS (switch guitar with band) unreleased
THE TIME IS NOW unreleased

> "It ended up with something like twenty-four musicians in the studio, all playing these incredibly incongruous instruments. Accordion, violin…and it really didn't work. He was after a large sound but the songs were so personal that he wasn't comfortable with all the people around. But anyway, we did takes on about twelve songs. He even wrote one on the spot. All in one night.
>
> It was very hard to keep up with him. He wasn't sure what he wanted. He was really racing from song to song. The songs were amazing. He may be putting them on an album, I don't know.
>
> I wasn't sure if I should have enjoyed last night so much 'cause I liked everything we played. It was a bit strange because I didn't know anybody but that seemed to be the general mood. There were a lot of guitarists, but you see I can get off on a song just sitting there listening, not even playing. My attitude is to go in there and do whatever I can but if someone can do it better, I'll just lay out. There were so many other guitars it was silly to try and fight it.
>
> One song that I played on did actually get finished. 'Romance In Durango' I think it was called."
>
> **—ERIC CLAPTON**

I'VE JUST SEEN A FACE unreleased

Producers: Eric Clapton, Albhy Galuten
Engineer: Karl Richardson

CRITERIA RECORDING STUDIOS Studio C, 1755 Northeast 149th Street, Miami, Florida Session for Tom & Don

6 DECEMBER 1975

APPLE SCRUFF unreleased
BEAU JANGLES unreleased
AFTER THE THRILL IS GONE unreleased
NEVER HAD IT SO GOOD unreleased
DAYBREAK unreleased
MY TIME unreleased
FOOL ON THE HILL unreleased
VINCENT unreleased

Producers: Eric Clapton, Ron and Howard Albert
Engineers: Ron and Howard Albert

Well, this is still a bit of a mystery session. Over the years I have spoken with Eric, Howard Albert, and Ahlby Galuten, and none recall the sessions. What is clear is that Tom and Don were signed to RSO and that Tom is likely to be Tom Bernfeld, who sang backup vocals on *461 Ocean Boulevard*. I attempted to contact him during the course of putting together this book, but time ran out. What we do know is that Eric plays and helped produce the two sessions which remain in the vault.

1976

Eric was a tax exile living in the Bahamas at this time. When it came time to think about writing new material for his next album, he called on Ronnie Wood. Eric recalled, "Woody came to stay at this house we were renting. He was pushing me around trying to get me to write songs but I couldn't do it in that situation cause it was too idyllic. We finally wrote a couple songs that we didn't use. One was called "You're Too Good To Die You Should Be Buried Alive." Can you believe that? It's all there in the files. All these crazy songs." Eventually they came up with some usable material and headed off to Los Angeles.

The album would be recorded at The Band's studio in Malibu and Eric commuted to and from Los Angeles for three months while recording his album *No Reason to Cry* at Shangri-La Studios. As well as recording, he would also venture out to Los Angeles and do some jamming with friends. On one memorable night he joined Freddie King at the Starwood in Hollywood for a killer set of blues.

Eric's idea behind choosing that studio was to blend members of The Band with his own set of musicians and friends, which would hopefully result in some great music. Eric remembers, "I was in a situation where people were coming to visit me. It wasn't so much 'Ah The Band' it was just people who came to visit. Some of the jams were amazing because they hadn't played together in ages. There were hundreds of guitars. On my birthday party it was the first time the entire Band played together in a long time." In theory, this was a great idea, but there was no professional producer on board at the beginning of the sessions, just an engineer. So the engineer and

now de facto producer, Ralph Moss, had his hands full. He was out of his depth in terms of keeping this lot under control. A discipline needed to be imposed if any work was to be done. Ralph was a great engineer, but did not have the right personality to produce out-of-control drunken superstars. For a while it was party central, with endless jamming, drugs and groupies. This would not have happened if Eric could have used his usual producer, Tom Dowd. But RSO, his label and management company, moved distribution in America to Polydor away from Atlantic and WEA. In return, they threw a boycott on Dowd producing Clapton.

The sessions took time to take off, and there were frustrations for Eric: "We took two weeks off to reconsider the whole thing. I just thought, 'God, it's all fallen down.' That's how 'Black Summer Rain' came about. Then I thought, 'Well that's not a bad song,' took it back and it kicked like mad." Eventually Rob Fraboni was brought in to sort things out and give some direction to the proceedings. Eric remembers the sessions with fondness, but in reality, it was more for the fun he had rather than the music he produced, although to be fair there are some memorable songs to be found on it. One of the more memorable events was Bob Dylan turning up for a few days, who contributed "Sign Language." Of course, with Bob, you never can tell which way he will go. As Eric recalls, "Dylan can't restrict himself to any one way of doing a song, so we did 'Sign Language' three times. I thought fuck it, I'll just go as loose as he is. I'm used to doing a song one way but Dylan throws caution to the wind every time."

A lot of people were credited on the sleeve but did not necessarily play on it. Wah Wah Watson (Melvin Ragin), for example, was recording his *Elementary* album at Village Recorders when Eric was there with Rob Fraboni mixing tracks for No Reason To Cry. Wah Wah Watson would come in and offer encouragement and advice.

Eric's UK tour support act was by an old friend of his from the Glands days, the talented poet Ted Milton, who went out as Mr Pugh's Puppet Theatre. Perhaps not surprisingly, the crowds did not take too kindly to him and his wooden creations. Ted Milton explains why audiences might have had a problem with him and his puppet show: "It was about oral nasality in the police force. It involved scenes of unparalleled nasal carnage. There were episodes where policemen actually farted their legs off, à la Douglas Bader. And airplanes fell out of the sky. They ate prisoners in the Andes. The Black Manias had crashed and the Normals had escaped from the identikit and Lo! they had multiplied. It was a very horrible routine."

Needless to say, Mr Pugh's Puppet Theatre was met with verbal abuse from bemused audiences. You have to give credit to the guy for actually going out onstage every night knowing he was going to get a hostile reception.

In many ways this set up the already roused audience to heckle Eric. This caused some boisterous scenes between Eric and certain members of the audience at various venues, but in general Eric won over the crowds with some fine playing. The band were in great form, changing the setlist every night, and some lucky towns had the added bonus of Van Morrison joining Eric for a few numbers. One of the highlights has to be Van's version of "Into The Mystic" from the Manchester Belle Vue.

MAY 1976

15 May 1976, Granby Halls, Leicester, Leicestershire (the Rolling Stones on their Black and Blue tour are joined by Eric on their encore tonight. Parts of the show are filmed by Thames Television for a documentary called Stones On The Road. Three cameras are used, two at the front of the stage, one on the left and one on the right. There is also a single camera at the rear of the stage. The Stones' road manager, Peter Rudge, tells them in no uncertain terms to keep off the stage. Even though the crew has signed releases from the band, life is not made easy by the road manager. As a result, the crew films only a handful of numbers at this particular show. Eric came on halfway through their set and played "Key To The Highway" with them. He then went off and came back towards the end of the

show and played on the last few numbers. Differing eye witness reports state that he may have played on "Brown Sugar" as well as "Jumping Jack Flash" and "Street Fighting Man." Director, Bruce Gowers, told the crew to start shooting, the encore with Clapton but unfortunately one of the front cameras had run out of film and the other front camera malfunctioned a few minutes into the number. The rear camera captures the number but is not used.

26 May 1976, Eric flies out to Los Angeles today to go and do some session work for Ringo Starr and for Stephen Bishop, as well make final track selections for No Reason to Cry

JUNE 1976

12 June 1976, Starlight Bowl, Burbank, California (Jeff Beck is touring America in support of "Wired." As Eric is in town doing sessions, he goes to see Jeff play tonight. He does not join him for a jam, but drops by after the show backstage)

NO REASON TO CRY UK TOUR 1976

BAND LINEUP
Eric Clapton: guitar, vocals
George Terry: guitar, vocals
Carl Radle: bass
Dick Sims: keyboards
Jamie Oldaker: drums
Sergio Pastora: percussion
Yvonne Elliman: vocals
Marcy Levy: vocals, harmonica

JULY 1976

27 July 1976–28 July 1976, rehearsals at Shepperton Studios, Shepperton, Surrey

29 July 1976, Pavilion, Hemel Hempstead, Hertfordshire

SETLIST (INCOMPLETE): Hello Old Friend / All Our Past Times / Double Trouble / Tell The Truth / Knockin' On Heaven's Door / Can't Find My Way Home / Layla / I Shot The Sheriff / Key To The Highway / Going Down Slow / Blues Power

30 July 1976, day off

31 July 1976, Crystal Palace Bowl, Crystal Palace, London (with Dick and the Firemen, Barbara Dickson, Jess Roden Band, the Chieftains, Freddie King)

SETLIST: Hello Old Friend / All Our Past Times / Tell The Truth / I Shot The Sheriff / Double Trouble / Blues Power / Going Down Slow* / Stormy Monday* / Layla / Further On Up The Road**

*Larry Coryell on guitar

**Larry Coryell on guitar, Freddie King on guitar, Ronnie Wood on guitar, Lewis Stephens (Freddie King's pianist) on piano

After the gig, everyone heads off to Ronnie Wood's house on Richmond Hill, Surrey, for more jamming.

> "Clapton clocked in at 6:15 p.m. The crowd gave him an ecstatic welcome. He looked nicely relaxed easy going, and on form. 'We'll play the new stuff first to get them out of the way,' said Clapton and played two acoustic numbers. Then a bit of reggae followed in the shape of 'I Shot The Sheriff.'
>
> Meanwhile fans were flocking into the lake and floating up to the foot of the stage to be nearer their idol. Much shaking of hands between Eric and the fans took place after songs.
>
> It took, naturally, the immortal 'Layla' to make the day, and although it started out sounding a bit suspect, it was sublime mid-way through. For the encore Eric had a surprise in store: from the wings came his old ol' mate Ron Wood plus Freddie King and there were now five lead guitarists on stage giving us a superduper jam session." **—RECORD MIRROR**

> "Larry Coryell, the brilliant American guitarist, almost stole the show when he jammed on stage with Eric Clapton at last Saturday's Crystal Palace Garden Party. His surprise appearance provided a spectacular climax to the show and threatened to eclipse Clapton's subdued performance. Coryell played some immaculate blues choruses before joining Clapton, blues giant Freddie King and Ronnie Wood for a jam." **—MELODY MAKER**

AUGUST 1976

1 August 1976, Gaumont Theatre, Southampton, Hampshire (with Mr Pugh's Puppet Theatre)

2 August 1976, Town Hall, Torquay, Devon (with Mr Pugh's Puppet Theatre)

3 August 1976, ABC Cinema, Plymouth, Devon (with Mr Pugh's Puppet Theatre)

SETLIST (INCOMPLETE): All Our Past Times / Further On Up The Road / Tell The Truth / Rambling On My Mind / The Shape You're In / Stormy Monday / Knockin' On Heaven's Door / Innocent Times / Blues Power

4 August 1976, day off

5 August 1976, Odeon Theatre, Birmingham, Midlands (with Mr Pugh's Puppet Theatre)

SETLIST: Hello Old Friend / All Our Past Times / Layla / Stormy Monday* / Rock Me Baby* / Nobody Knows You When You're Down And Out / Tell The Truth / Can't Find My Way Home / Knockin' On Heaven's Door / Further On Up The Road / Innocent Times / Have You Ever Loved A Woman / Blues Power

*Van Morrison on vocals

> "Eric Clapton proved last week that his guitar playing is as vital, fluid and spine tingling as ever. You can hardly say the same for his voice which was shot to pieces during British tour concert at Birmingham Odeon." **—THE REDDITCH INDICATOR**

> "Within a couple of-minutes the house lights dimmed leaving a very dim dark blue lit empty stage, with only the couple of dozen red amp lights staring back at the audience, like the little gremlins. Then two rather strange looking figures wandered out to the stage centre, wearing regular hippie clothes and what appeared to be reversed portable hair drying machines over their heads, oh no, everyone thought, not another helping of puppet shenanigans! But it was in reality underneath those rather large mosquito shaped things George Terry and a slightly pissed E.C.
>
> The audience gave the obligatory applause for his actually making it there and he opened up with a few words of 'Hi I'm back again,' which accidently started an informal chat with a few of the outspoken members of the audience, ending with a bit of political comment concerning this country and the 'other side.'" **—ROCK 'N' ROLL GRAFFITI**

6 August 1976, Belle Vue Kings Hall, Manchester (with Mr Pugh's Puppet Theatre)

SETLIST: Hello Old Friend / All Our Past Times / I Shot The Sheriff / Nobody Knows You When You're Down And Out / Can't Find My Way Home / Tell The Truth / Help Me* / Into The Mystic* / Kansas City* / Innocent Times / My Time After A While / Stormy Monday / Layla / Key To The Highway

*Van Morrison on vocals

"As if it wasn't enough to have legendary guitar hero, Eric Clapton, playing at Manchester Belle Vue last night, we had Van Morrison turning up to play a few numbers.

And so what if Morrison did nearly steal the show with 'Into The Mystic' and send the already-excited audience wild? It's all music, isn't it?

After a rather low-key start, the concert really took off with 'I Shot The Sheriff,' and from that moment on, the atmosphere was electric. And when it was all over, as we walked out with the strains of the immortal 'Layla' still ringing in our heads, there was an excitement in the air which said, more clearly than words—EC was here."
—*HUDDERSFIELD EXAMINER*

7 August 1976, Lancaster University, Lancaster, Lancashire (with Mr Pugh's Puppet Theatre)

SETLIST (INCOMPLETE): Smile / Hello Old Friend / All Our Pastimes / Tell The Truth / Further On Up The Road / Double Trouble / Stormy Monday / Knocking On Heaven's Door / Layla

"As the band took the stage it was noticeable that Clapton looked less than healthy. Compared to the clean-cut Terry and Oldaker he looked definitely under the weather. He had been drinking, and that coupled with a night of chain smoking gave the impression all was not well. Clapton looked like he'd been on the road for months. The eyes puffed, the slight frame looked even more frail."
—THE *BURNLEY EXPRESS*

8 August 1976, day off in Blackpool
9 August 1976, Glasgow Apollo, Glasgow, Scotland (with Mr Pugh's Puppet Theatre)

"On stage for the best part of two hours, Eric rounded off the night with a sparkling version of 'I Shot The Sheriff.' On the wall near the theatre someone had chalked 'EC Was Here,' and the 3500 in the hall will never forget it."
—*GLASGOW EVENING TIMES*

SETLIST: Hello Old Friend / All Our Past Times / Double Trouble / Layla / Stormy Monday / Knockin' On Heaven's Door / Tell The Truth / Can't Find My Way Home / Key To The Highway / Innocent Times / Blues Power / I Shot The Sheriff / Nobody Knows You When You're Down And Out / Further On Up The Road

10 August 1976, Glasgow Apollo, Glasgow, Scotland (with Mr Pugh's Puppet Theatre)

SETLIST (INCOMPLETE): Going Down Slow / Stormy Monday / Can't Find My Way Home / Tell The Truth / Innocent Times / I Shot The Sheriff / Layla / Key To The Highway

11 August 1976, day off in Scotland
12 August 1976, City Hall, Newcastle, Tyne & Wear (with Mr Pugh's Puppet Theatre)
13 August 1976, Spa Pavilion, Bridlington, East Riding of Yorkshire (with Mr Pugh's Puppet Theatre)

SETLIST: Hello Old Friend / Better Make It Through Today / Blues Power / Tell The Truth / Can't Find My Way Home / Ramblin' On My Mind / Stormy Monday / Going Down Slow / Innocent Times / All Our Past Times / Knocking On Heaven's Door / Layla / I Shot The Sheriff / Key To The Highway

"It was a great concert from a man whose reputation as the greatest living white blues guitarist scarcely does him credit. I expected him to be good—but he surpassed even that expectation." —THE *YORKSHIRE EVENING PRESS*

14 August 1976, day off—travel to Blackpool
15 August 1976, ABC Cinema, Blackpool, Lancashire (with Mr Pugh's Puppet Theatre)

SETLIST: Happy Birthday / Hello Old Friend / All Our Past Times / Tell The Truth / Nobody Knows You When You're Down And Out / Layla / Can't Find My Way Home / Singing The Blues / My Time After A While / Have You Ever Loved A Woman / Ramblin' On My Mind / Innocent Times / I Shot The Sheriff / Instrumental Jam / Tore Down / Rock Me Baby / Happy Birthday / Key To The Highway / Happy Birthday

Eric and his band start and end their set with a short version of "Happy Birthday" for their manager, Roger Forrester. After pretty much all of the audience has left the venue, Eric and a few others from the band come out and do an unknown acoustic blues number for a handful of stragglers.

Despite Eric being drunk, the band put in a great performance that is well received by the audience. One of the highlights of this show is the extended jam

> "Eric has been a tax-exile for a year in Nassau in the Bahamas. He wanted to come back to England, and the best way to meet ordinary people was through a holiday camp. It is very British; he wanted it to be a fun thing."
> —**HELEN WALTERS** (from Eric's record label RSO)
> "I got a phone call out of the blue to ask if I would like Clapton. I thought it was a hoax, but it has turned out to be our biggest scoop. Apparently he wanted to try himself out on a family audience."—**RON HELLYER** (Warner Holiday Camp entertainment manager)

> "As the first heavy chords of the familiar Clapton sound filled the jolly holiday camp dance hall and the light show flashed its first impulse of excitement, a sizeable block of the main audience of middle aged mums and dads, elderly pensioners and sandcastle-sized youngsters, clapped hands to ears in frozen disbelief. Of the original 700 or so, a good third had walked out before Clapton and his band had thundered through the first couple of numbers. Summoning as much dignity as possible, the elderly, the unconverted and some infirm, walked stiffly to the exits.
> Of the remainder, less than 200 were of an age or disposition to savour this unexpected holiday feast and only a handful of those could truly have claimed to be hard core Clapton fans. Nevertheless, the applause they mustered would have filled a concert hall."
> —**THE** *HAMPSHIRE TELEGRAPH*

after "I Shot The Sheriff" where Eric and the band are locked into a tight blues groove with Eric throwing in licks from well-known blues numbers such as "Spoonful," driving the crowd wild. One of the best shows on the UK tour.

16 August 1976, day off—travel to London

17 August 1976, Warner Holiday Camp, Hayling Island, West Sussex (with Mr Pugh's Puppet Theatre)

SEPTEMBER 1976

17 September 1976, Fairfield Halls, Croydon, Surrey (Eric attends the opening night of Don William's UK tour. Afterward he invites Don and his band back to his home in Surrey for a lengthy jam session)

18 September 1976, Hammersmith Odeon, London (Eric joins Don Williams and his two-man band, consisting of Danny Flowers on guitar and David Williams on bass, and plays Dobro on three numbers, including "Help Yourself To Each Other." Eric introduces Pete Townshend and Ronnie Lane to Don after the show)

NO REASON TO CRY US TOUR 1976

BAND LINEUP
Eric Clapton: guitar, vocals
George Terry: guitar, vocals
Carl Radle: bass
Dick Sims: keyboards
Jamie Oldaker: drums
Sergio Pastora: percussion
Yvonne Elliman: vocals
Marcy Levy: vocals, harmonica

NOVEMBER 1976

5 November 1976, Bayfront Center, St. Petersburg, Florida

6 November 1976, Hollywood Sportatorium, Miami, Florida

SETLIST: Hello Old Friend / Sign Language / Double Trouble / All Our Past Times / Tell The Truth / Key to the Highway / Can't Find My Way Home / Badge / Innocent Times / Layla / Knockin' On Heaven's Door / Blues Power / Further On Up the Road

7 November 1976, Memorial Coliseum, Jacksonville, Florida

SETLIST: Sign Language / Hello Old Friend / Further On Up The Road / All Our Past Times / Double Trouble / Tell the Truth / Can't Find My Way Home / Knockin' On Heaven's Door / Badge / Keep Love On The Move / Key To The Highway / Layla / Further On Up The Road

9 November 1976, Omni Coliseum, Atlanta, Georgia (Eric is joined by Dickie Betts on "Key To The Highway" and "Layla")

10 November 1976, Municipal Auditorium, Mobile, Alabama

11 November 1976, LSU (Louisiana State University) Assembly Center, Baton Rouge, Louisiana

SETLIST: Hello Old Friend / Sign Language / Key To The Highway / I Shot The Sheriff / Love Me Please / Blues Power / One Night / Knockin' On Heaven's Door / Double Trouble / Badge / Layla / Further On Up The Road

12 November 1976, Convention Center Arena, San Antonio, Texas

SETLIST: Hello Old Friend / Sign Language / Little Queenie / Knockin' On Heaven's Door / Tell The Truth / Love Me Please / All Our Past Times / Double Trouble / Blues Power / One Night / Badge / Layla / I Shot The Sheriff

"Eric Clapton has long been considered the consummate blues / rock guitarist, yet at his November 14 concert, he failed to display any of that legendary Clapton guitar wizardry. The concert was good (as a matter of fact, it was a great improvement over his concert of last year), but it was nothing more—just good. There was nothing extraordinary about E.C. that night at the Coliseum that would distinguish him from any other good blues guitarist. Clapton opened with two rather insipid acoustic numbers, 'Hello Old Friend' and 'Sign Language,' and then turned electric to do his truly great song, 'Layla.' Clapton seemed to be in a hurry to get this song out of the way so he could get on and play what he wanted to.

There was only one point in the show where Clapton appeared to remember how he used to play, and that was on 'Tell The Truth.' Perhaps the greatest difference between this concert and his 1975 show was that Clapton refused to play anything from his Cream days. In '75, Clapton's version of 'Badge' was the highlight of the show, but in 1976, the audience had to settle for later and more recent material."

—BRUCE KESSLER

13 November 1976, Texas Blues Jam, Houston (Eric joins Bugs Henderson, Freddie King, Bobby Chitwood, and Ron Thompson for a jam)

14 November 1976, Sam Houston Coliseum, Houston, Texas

SETLIST: Hello Old Friend / Sign Language / Layla / Key To The Highway / Tell The Truth / Can't Find My Way Home / All Our Pastimes / Blues Power / One Night / I Shot The Sheriff / Further On Up The Road

A one-hour edited *King Biscuit Flower Hour Show* made up of songs from both the Houston and Dallas shows was syndicated on US radio stations.

15 November 1976, Convention Center, Dallas, Texas

SETLIST: Hello Old Friend / Sign Language / Badge / Knocking On Heaven's Door / Key To The Highway / Can't Find My Way Home / Tell the Truth / All Our Past Times / Blues Power / One Night / Layla / Further On Up the Road*

*with Freddie King on guitar

16 November 1976, Lloyd Noble Center, Norman, Oklahoma

SETLIST: Hello Old Friend / Sign Language / Tell The Truth / Double Trouble / Knockin' On Heaven's Door / Blues Power / Can't Find My Way Home / Key To The Highway / I Shot The Sheriff / One Night / Layla / Further On Up The Road

A one-hour edited King Biscuit Flower Hour Show made up of songs from both the Houston and Dallas shows was syndicated on US radio stations.

18 November 1976, Pan Am Center, Las Cruces, New Mexico

19 November 1976, Arizona State University, Activity Center, Tempe, Arizona

20 November 1976, Sports Arena, San Diego, California

SETLIST: Hello Old Friend / Sign Language / Tell The Truth / Knockin' On Heaven's Door / Steady Rollin' Man / Can't Find My Way Home / Have You Ever Loved A Woman / All Our Past Times / Blues Power / One Night / Layla / Further On Up The Road

22 November 1976, the Forum, Los Angeles, California

Eric Clapton at the LA Forum on 22 November 1976.

SETLIST: Hello Old Friend / Sign Language / Tell The Truth / Double Trouble / All Our Past Times / Knockin' On Heaven's Door / Key To The Highway / Can't Find My Way Home / Badge / Have You Ever Loved A Woman / Layla / One Night / Blues Power / I Shot The Sheriff / Further On Up The Road

THE LAST WALTZ— THE BAND'S FAREWELL SHOW 1976

26 November 1976, the Winterland, San Francisco, California

Poster for The Band's Last Waltz concert at San Francisco's Winterland.

"Eric Clapton's 1976 appearance in Los Angeles was a far cry from his '75 and '74 presentation. On those two former outings the once legendary guitarist seemed more than content to let back-up player George Terry play all the solos and showed little concern for such inconsequentials as the beginnings and endings of songs and stage projection. The sound itself was muddy and when Clapton did venture into a solo it was aimless, lacking in control, and hardly the type you would expect from an artist of his nature. While his most recent concert at the not-quite-sold-out Inglewood Forum was a far cry from the absolute and finite brilliance he achieved with Cream at that same hall on October 18 1968, it was a reasonable showing for what was once the most heralded guitar player alive." **—SOUNDS**

SETLIST:

All Our Pastimes (Eric Clapton / Rick Danko) *The Last Waltz* Rhino 78278 4cd box released April 2002

Robbie Robertson: guitar
Rick Danko: bass, vocals
Levon Helm: drums
Richard Manuel: keyboards
Garth Hudson: organ
Eric Clapton: guitar, vocals

Further On Up The Road (Joe Veasey / Don Robey) *The Last Waltz* triple album Warner Bros. 3WB-3146 released April 1978 / *The Last Waltz* Rhino 78278 4CD box released April 2002

Robbie Robertson: guitar
Rick Danko: bass
Levon Helm: drums

Richard Manuel: keyboards
Garth Hudson: organ
Eric Clapton: guitar, vocals

I Shall Be Released (Bob Dylan) *The Last Waltz* triple album Warner Bros. 3WB-3146 released April 1978 / *The Last Waltz* Rhino 78278 4CD box released April 2002

Robbie Robertson: guitar
Rick Danko: bass, vocals
Levon Helm: drums
Richard Manuel: keyboards
Garth Hudson: organ
Eric Clapton: guitar, vocals
Ronnie Wood: guitar
Ringo Starr: drums
Paul Butterfield: harmonica, vocals
Bobby Charles: vocals
Neil Diamond: vocals
Dr. John: vocals
Bob Dylan: guitar, vocals
Ronnie Hawkins: vocals
Joni Mitchell: vocals
Van Morrison: vocals
Neil Young: vocals

Jam 1 (in edited form) *The Last Waltz* Rhino 78278 4CD box released April 2002

Robbie Robertson: guitar
Eric Clapton: guitar
Neil Young: guitar
Ronnie Wood: slide guitar
Rick Danko: bass
Levon Helm: drums
Garth Hudson: organ, synthesizers
Carl Radle: bass
Dr. John: piano
Paul Butterfield: harmonica
Ringo Starr: drums

Jam 2 (in edited form) *The Last Waltz* Rhino 78278 4CD box released April 2002

Eric Clapton: guitar
Stephen Stills: guitar
Neil Young: guitar
Ronnie Wood: slide guitar
Levon Helm: drums
Garth Hudson: organ, synthesizers
Carl Radle: bass
Dr. John: piano
Paul Butterfield: harmonica
Ringo Starr: drums

Recorded by: Wally Heider Mobile
Producer: Robbie Robertson
Engineers: Terry Becker, Tim Kramer, Elliot Mazer, Wayne Neuendorf, Ed Anderson, Neil Brody

This was certainly one of the greatest concerts ever put together. The Band were saying farewell to the road and wanted to do it in style. Billed as "The Last Waltz," the concert would take place at the Winterland in San Francisco. It was a massive production job, with the song "The Last Waltz" only being written the day before the actual concert. They played it at the show, but they had not had time to rehearse it properly, and it did not make the final cut on film or record. This was a minor problem considering the vast majority of the five-hour show went largely without any glitches. Just about anyone who was anyone in the music industry at the time was there as guests of the Band. Neil Young, Joni Mitchell, Muddy Waters, Van Morrison, Dr. John, Bob Dylan, Ronnie Hawkins, Neil Diamond, Bobby Charles, and Eric Clapton were all happy to play. All of them had history with the Band as a group or as individuals. Neil Diamond had seemed an odd choice to many people, but Robbie Robertson had produced his *Beautiful Noise* album early that year.

Rehearsals for the extravaganza took place at Shangri-La Studios and moved to the Miyako Hotel in San Francisco the week leading up to the show. As Eric's tour ended on 22 November in Los Angeles, he had no problem making the rehearsals. He would play "All Our Past Times" from his recent *No Reason to Cry* album, as well as the encore favorite "Further On Up The Road."

The concert ticket prices caused some controversy because of the high rate of $25 per head. But when you take into consideration that included in the price was a full Thanksgiving dinner catered by a top restaurant, it was actually good value. It also contributed to making this a special event rather than just another concert. Chandeliers had been imported from Hollywood, and bunting was everywhere, creating the perfect ambience for such a historic event.

The concert formally ended with the whole ensemble onstage to sing "I Shall Be Released." After the number ended, Ringo and Levon started a vamp as more musicians came onstage for a couple of jams. Eric participated in both, although he left halfway through the second one.

The Band finally returned by themselves to perform one last number, "Don't Do It." After the show, just about everyone drifted back to the Miyako Hotel for some more jamming. Bob Margolin, who had played with Muddy Waters at the show, has some great memories of the night as well as early morning.

"The more blues-driven musicians commandeered the instruments at the jam, and played some old favorite songs together, mostly Robert Johnson's. This sounds like a common scene at open-mic jams at blues clubs, where more experienced blues players sometimes conspire to sit in together. It happened at about 7 am, the morning after The Band's Last Waltz concert on Thanksgiving, 1976. The Band had hired the entire Miyako Hotel in San Francisco to accommodate their guests. The banquet room which had been used for rehearsal before the show was now the party room, and musicians had been jamming in random combinations since after the concert, many hours before. But unlike your local blues jam, every blues player that morning was a Rock Star.

Except me. I was there with Muddy Waters. who was invited to perform two songs at The Last Waltz. Muddy had recorded his Grammy-winning 'Woodstock Album' the year before with Levon Helm and Garth Hudson from The Band, but The Band itself was an unknown quantity to him. He brought Pinetop Perkins and me from his own band to accompany him along with The Band and Paul Butterfield on harp, so that he would have something familiar to play with. Muddy also felt I was good at explaining what he wanted onstage to musicians he hadn't worked with, though 25 years later, I still find myself wishing I knew more about what Muddy wanted.

Muddy, Pinetop, and I checked into the hotel the day before the show and went to the restaurant. I saw a few familiar faces from the Rock World, and some came over to say hello and pay respects to Muddy. I remember this surreal encounter:

Kinky Friedman approached our table. I knew that he was a Texas Jewboy (his band's name) musical comedian. The Kinkster sported Texas attire complemented by a white satin smoking jacket accented with blue Jewish stars, an Israeli flag motif. Embroidered along the hem were scenes of the crucifixion. Mr. Friedman exercises his ethnicity in provocative ways, in fashion, in his music, and in his recent mystery novels (recommended!). He was a Kosher cowboy mensch as he introduced himself to Muddy, assuring him that 'people of the Jewish persuasion appreciate the Blues too.' Muddy, used to folks stranger than Kinky saying weird shit to him, just smiled and thanked him. Didn't bat an eye.

That night, Pinetop, Muddy, and I were scheduled to rehearse our songs for the show. I didn't realize that some of those blues-oriented rock stars must have been in the room to watch Muddy.

The next night, at the concert, Muddy, Pinetop, and I waited backstage to perform. Pinetop told me he heard one of The Beatles was there, not realizing that Ringo was sitting right next to him. Born in 1913, Pinetop knew as much about The Beatles as I know about The Backstreet Boys. Joni Mitchell, looking impossibly beautiful, introduced herself to Muddy. He didn't know who she was, and just saw her as a young pretty woman, his favorite dish. He flirted but she didn't respond.

I'm told that there was a backstage cocaine room, with a glass table and a 'sniff-sniff' tape playing, but I never saw it. I did, however, see through Rolling Stone Ron Wood's nearly-transparent prominent proboscis in profile. In the 'green room,' Neil Young passed me a joint, smiling, 'We're all old hippies here.' Though I was 27, something about 'old hippies' resonated with me for the future. Young was older than me by a few years and even had a couple of gray hairs then, but I remember thinking that nobody in that room was old yet except for Muddy and Pinetop. Now, I'm certainly an old hippie, though Pinetop, going strong at 88, is neither. As for Neil Young, film of his performance revealed a white rock up his nose, which was edited out frame-by-frame for the movie.

California Governor Jerry Brown popped in and invited Bob Dylan to get together with him sometime. Dylan, relaxed and outgoing until The Governor arrived, instantly turned sullen and distracted, barely nodding without looking at Brown. The uncomfortable Governor soon left, and Dylan laughed just before he was out of earshot and reverted to his friendlier mode. Something is happening here, but I don't know what it is.

When it was our turn to play, Muddy and Pinetop sang the light, swinging 'Caledonia' as they had for 'The Woodstock Album.' In hindsight, I think Muddy could have presented himself more strongly with a deep slow blues like 'Long Distance Call' which would feature his almighty slide guitar. But nobody could argue with his second song choice—'Mannish Boy' was always a show-stopper. It was preserved in full in The Last Waltz movie, which was released in '78. Harp player tip: Muddy loved the way Butterfield played on that song, setting up a warble that 'holds my voice up' rather than just playing the song's signature lick.

Fatefully, only one camera was operating during our song, zooming on Muddy, but not changing angle. Standing close to Muddy, I was in every frame. Pinetop, at the piano way off to the side, unfortunately was never seen in the film. But as Muddy hollers 'I'm a MAN' and we shout 'Yeah' to answer, as we always did in that song, you can hear Pinetop also yelling, 'Wahoo!'—which is a line from a politically incorrect joke that Pine had heard on the road, and was fond of telling over and over in 1976.

Now, whenever The Last Waltz movie is shown on TV, a few people at my gigs tell me, 'I saw you on TV!' and how I looked—happy or mad or scared or bored. I think they just project how they would feel. I was simply concentrating on playing, and particularly enjoying Muddy's powerful shouting, Butterfield's warbling-tension harp, Levon's deep groove, and Robbie Robertson's fiery guitar fills.

Eric Clapton followed us, and as he began his first solo, his guitar strap unfastened, and he nearly dropped his Stratocaster. In the movie, his lips distinctly mouth, 'Fuck!' and as he refastens the strap, Robbie picks up the solo and runs away with it.

Muddy and Pinetop went right to their rooms after our set, but I went down to jam back at the hotel after the concert. This is where I realized that some of those blues-oriented rock stars had watched me rehearsing with Muddy and been impressed that I was playing Old School Chicago Blues in his road band and helping to arrange the songs for our performance. I also had a very cool blues guitar with me—my late-'50s Gibson ES 150 arch-top, which I also cradle on the cover of my latest album, 'Hold Me To It.' Bob Dylan approached me and said he hoped we'd get to jam together. Then he disappeared. I did play 'Hideaway' and some slow blues with Eric Clapton, whom I met that night. Dr. John sat at the piano for hours, and played along with everyone. My piano-pickin' sister Sherry, who lived nearby and was hanging out, sat near him, eyes glued to his fonky fangers.

Around dawn, I put my old guitar back in its case, and started to leave. Bob Dylan caught me in the hall and said, 'I thought we were going to jam.' I decided to stay awake a little longer. We had Dr. John on piano, Ron Wood on bass, Levon on drums, Butterfield on harp, and Clapton, Dylan, and myself playing guitars. There were no vocal microphones, and we all played softly enough to hear Dylan sing 'Kind Hearted Woman' and a few other well-known blues songs. His trademark vocal eccentricities sounded outlandish in the blues, but he did make them his own. Generally, the blues we played that morning were not remarkable, but I was honored to be jamming with these fine musicians, and I realize that they belong to the same 'club' as you do—deep blues lovers.

Recently, I read Levon Helm's inside story of *The Last Waltz* in his autobiography, *This Wheel's On Fire* (recommended!). I was shocked to find that because of time and budget constraints and Band politics, Muddy was nearly bumped from the show. Levon fought bitterly behind the scenes and prevailed to not only keep Muddy in but to indulge him with me and Pinetop too. We were treated as honored guests at *The Last Waltz* and I enjoyed the once-in-a-lifetime jam afterwards, but Levon never told us about making a stand for us. He just made us welcome. Ultimately, this gracious, classy, and tough gentleman was responsible for my good time there. **"** —BOB MARGOLIN

DECEMBER 1976

21 December 1976, Hammersmith Odeon, London (canceled)

22 December 1976, Hammersmith Odeon, London (canceled)

23 December 1976, Hammersmith Odeon, London (canceled)

The three Hammersmith concerts promoted by Harvey Goldsmith were due to feature Eric and some of his famous friends like Pete Townshend and Ronnie Lane. The proceeds would have gone to a drug-therapy clinic. The promoters and Eric were hoping that by doing charity concerts, they would not be liable to the tax problems associated with living abroad. Unfortunately, that was not the case and the shows were canceled.

RECORDING SESSIONS 1976
SHANGRI-LA STUDIOS
30065 Morning View Drive, Malibu, California
Sessions for
No Reason to Cry album
FEBRUARY 1976–APRIL 1976

The buildings that house Shangri-La Studios have a fascinating history. The main ranch house was designed by actress Margo Albert, who found fame in the classic 1937 Frank Capra movie *Lost Horizon*. It was then a bordello in the late '50s for the high and mighty of Hollywood due to its discreet location. However, music lovers will know it as the wonderful studio where many great albums have been recorded.

The building was bought by The Band in the early seventies and they gave record producer Rob Fraboni the task of designing Shangri-La Studios to their specifications. Due to severe tax laws for the wealthy, Eric had to be out of the United Kingdom for twelve months and made his home away from home in Nassau. As he could not record his next album in the UK, he chose the Band's studio in California. Eric loved the studio and wanted members of the Band to be on his new album, so it made perfect sense to record there. Overlooking Zuma Beach and the Pacific, the location is inspirational. Clapton spent several months there with members of The Band and guests such as Van Morrison, Ringo Starr, Pete Townshend, Bob Dylan, Ronnie Wood, and others dropping in during the three month sessions. Not all the guest spots made it to the final cut, though.

BEAUTIFUL THING (Richard Manuel / Rick Danko) *No Reason To Cry* album US RSO 1-3004, UK RSO 2394160 released August 1976 / *No Reason To Cry* CD Polydor US 31453 1824-2, UK 531 824-2 released September 1996

Eric Clapton: guitar, vocals
Ronnie Wood: guitar
George Terry: guitar
Dick Sims: organ
Jamie Oldaker: drums
Rick Danko: bass
Richard Manuel: piano
Mary Levy: vocals
Yvonne Elliman: vocals

CARNIVAL (Eric Clapton) *No Reason To Cry* album US RSO 1-3004, UK RSO 2394160 released August 1976 / *No Reason To Cry* CD Polydor US 31453 1824-2, UK 531 824-2 released September 1996

Eric Clapton: guitar, vocals
George Terry: guitar
Dick Sims: piano, organ
Carl Radle: bass
Jamie Oldaker: drums
Mary Levy: vocals
Yvonne Elliman: vocals
Sergio Pastora Rodriguez: percussion

SIGN LANGUAGE (Bob Dylan) *No Reason To Cry* album US RSO 1-3004, UK RSO 2394160 released August 1976 / *No Reason To Cry* CD Polydor US 31453 1824-2, UK 531 824-2 released September 1996

Eric Clapton: Dobro, vocals
Ronnie Wood: guitar
Jesse Ed Davis: guitar
George Terry: guitar
Dick Sims: organ
Carl Radle: bass
Jamie Oldaker: drums
Bob Dylan: vocals
Robbie Robertson: lead guitar
Sergio Pastora Rodriguez: percussion

COUNTY JAIL BLUES (Alfred Fields; arranged by Eric Clapton) *No Reason To Cry* album US RSO 1-3004, UK RSO 2394160 released August 1976 / *No Reason To Cry* CD Polydor US 31453 1824-2, UK 531 824-2 released September 1996

Front cover for Eric's No Reason To Cry *album.*

Eric Clapton: slide guitar, vocals
Ronnie Wood: guitar
George Terry: guitar
Dick Sims: organ
Carl Radle: bass
Jamie Oldaker: drums

ALL OUR PASTIMES (Eric Clapton) *No Reason To Cry* album US RSO 1-3004, UK RSO 2394160 released August 1976 / *No Reason To Cry* CD Polydor US 31453 1824-2, UK 531 824-2 released September 1996

Eric Clapton: guitar (second solo), vocals
Ronnie Wood: guitar (first solo)
George Terry: guitar
Dick Sims: organ
Jamie Oldaker: drums
Rick Danko: vocals, bass
Richard Manuel: piano
Mary Levy: backing vocals
Yvonne Elliman: backing vocals

HELLO OLD FRIEND (Eric Clapton) *No Reason To Cry* album US RSO 1-3004, UK RSO 2394160 released August 1976 / *No Reason To Cry* CD Polydor US 31453 1824-2, UK 531 824-2 released September 1996

Eric Clapton: acoustic guitar, vocals
George Terry: guitar
Dick Sims: organ
Carl Radle: bass
Jamie Oldaker: drums
Mary Levy: vocals
Yvonne Elliman: vocals
Sergio Pastora Rodriguez: percussion
Jesse Ed Davis: slide guitar

DOUBLE TROUBLE (Otis Rush; arranged by Eric Clapton) *No Reason To Cry* album US RSO 1-3004, UK RSO 2394160 released August 1976 / *No Reason To Cry* CD Polydor US 31453 1824-2, UK 531 824-2 released September 1996

Eric Clapton: acoustic guitar, vocals
George Terry: guitar
Dick Sims: piano
Carl Radle: bass
Jamie Oldaker: drums
Georgie Fame: organ

INNOCENT TIMES (Eric Clapton / Marcy Lecy) *No Reason To Cry* album US RSO 1-3004, UK RSO 2394160 released August 1976 / *No Reason To Cry* CD Polydor US 31453 1824-2, UK 531 824-2 released September 1996

Eric Clapton: Dobro
George Terry: guitar
Dick Sims: piano
Carl Radle: bass
Jamie Oldaker: drums
Mary Levy: vocals
Yvonne Elliman: backing vocals

HUNGRY (Dick Sims / Marcy Levy) *No Reason To Cry* album US RSO 1-3004, UK RSO 2394160 released August 1976 / *No Reason To Cry* CD Polydor US 31453 1824-2, UK 531 824-2 released September 1996

Eric Clapton: guitar, vocals
George Terry: guitar
Dick Sims: organ
Carl Radle: bass
Jamie Oldaker: drums
Mary Levy: vocals
Yvonne Elliman: vocals
Sergio Pastora Rodriguez: percussion

BLACK SUMMER RAIN (Eric Clapton) *No Reason To Cry* album US RSO 1-3004, UK RSO 2394160 released August 1976 / *No Reason To Cry* CD Polydor US 31453 1824-2, UK 531 824-2 released September 1996

Eric Clapton: guitar, vocals
George Terry: guitar
Dick Sims: organ
Carl Radle: bass
Jamie Oldaker: drums
Mary Levy: vocals
Yvonne Elliman: vocals

LAST NIGHT (Walter Jacobs) previously unreleased bonus track on *No Reason To Cry* CD Polydor US 31453 1824-2, UK 531 824-2 released September 1996

Eric Clapton: guitar, vocals
George Terry: acoustic guitar
Carl Radle: bass
Jamie Oldaker: drums
Richard Manuel: vocals, piano

DAYLIGHT unreleased

BURIED ALIVE (Ronnie Wood) unreleased

SEVEN DAYS (Bob Dylan) unreleased

BEAUTY SPOT unreleased

TENHO SEDE (I AM THIRSTY) unreleased

BILLY JOE unreleased

JAM unreleased

COULD THIS BE CALLED A SONG (Eric Clapton) unreleased

DISCO unreleased

DO BYE AH unreleased

FEVER unreleased

GOLDEN SLIPPER unreleased

I CAN SEE MYSELF IN YOUR EYES unreleased

I GOT YOU ON MY MIND (Joe Thomas, Howard Briggs) unreleased

LET IT DOWN unreleased

THE PATH (working title) with Pete Townshend on guitar) unreleased

> **❝**There are all sorts of impromptu things that everyone forgot about, like Richard Manuel and Eric in the studio, all hours of the night, just doing very primal blues things. Very stream of consciousness, going into one another, obviously drunk, but wonderful stuff if you prune it and present it, it's great.
>
> One of the ironies of that album and the challenge is that you can't really remix it, because for instance, if you take 'Sign Language,' the Robbie Robertson guitar solo, it's not on tape! He played that to the mix! When we doing the 'Crossroads' box we were curious as to how they tracked all these guitars and it sounds like Robbie's was there and when they mixed it he played his guitar on top of the track. And so it ain't on tape!**❞**   **—BILL LEVENSON**
> (talking about the outtakes and problems with remixing)

RIGHT NOW (Billy Preston)
SOONER OR LATER unreleased
TUESDAY'S TUNE unreleased

Producers: Rob Fraboni, Eric Clapton, Carl Dean Radle
Engineers: Ralph Moss, Ed Anderson, Nat Jeffrey
Mixed at the Village Recorder, Los Angeles, by Rob Fraboni and Ed Anderson in April

ERIC CLAPTON BIRTHDAY PARTY JAMS
SHANGRI-LA STUDIOS
30065 Morning View Drive, Malibu, California

30 MARCH 1976

JAM "It's Eric's Birthday," Billy Preston on lead vocals
WHO DO YOU LOVE? (Ellas McDaniel) Van Morrison on lead vocals
HARD TIMES (Ray Charles) Rick Danko on lead vocals
STORMY MONDAY (T-Bone Walker) Van Morrison on lead vocals
INSTRUMENTAL JAM
SPANISH IS THE LOVING TONGUE (Traditional) (several takes) Bob Dylan on lead vocals
ADELITA (Traditional) Bob Dylan on lead vocals
THE WATER IS WIDE (Traditional) Bob Dylan on lead vocals
WHEN I PAINT MY MASTERPIECE (Bob Dylan) Bob Dylan on lead vocals
IDIOT WIND 1 (Bob Dylan) Bob Dylan on lead vocals; incomplete
IDIOT WIND 2 (Bob Dylan) Bob Dylan on lead vocals; incomplete
IDIOT WIND 3 (Bob Dylan) Bob Dylan on lead vocals; incomplete
BIG RIVER (Johnny Cash) Eric Clapton on lead vocals
WHAT WOULD I DO WITHOUT YOU 1 (Ray Charles) Richard Manuel on lead vocals
WHAT WOULD I DO WITHOUT YOU 2 (Ray Charles) instrumental
WHAT WOULD I DO WITHOUT YOU 3 (Ray Charles) Richard Manuel on lead vocals
STEPPIN' OUT 1 Levon Helm on lead vocals
STEPPIN' OUT 2 Levon Helm on lead vocals

Eric Clapton: vocals, guitar
Van Morrison: vocals
Ron Wood: vocals, guitar
Bob Dylan: vocals, piano, guitar
Billy Preston: vocals, organ
Jesse Ed Davis: guitar
Robbie Robertson: guitar
Rick Danko: bass
Richard Manuel: piano
Garth Hudson: organ
Levon Helm: drums

A massive birthday party for Eric took place at the studio on 30 March. The tapes were rolling with special guests jamming away until the wee hours. In reality the drunken jams are exactly that, fairly directionless with a bunch of well-known musicians having fun in private. The tapes somehow found their way among collectors and aptly show that the general public did not miss anything.

"I think my best stuff has been done in American studios. Criteria at the time was great and The Band's studio, Shangri-La, where we did 'No Reason to Cry' was the finest studio of all to work in. It's on the Pacific Coast Highway, north of Malibu on the way to San Francisco, and it was great because it was all wood and the room you record in was originally a master bedroom or playroom—because it was a bordello, it probably had about twenty waterbeds in—and it had a couple of sliding doors that you could just leave open to the outside with the sea not more than a hundred feet away, lapping on the beach, and you would record like that and that would go on the machine. It was something you couldn't do anywhere else—that was it! I hope it's still going too because I would like to go back there.

We sort of produced it, all of us, ourselves, I suppose, because we weren't allowed to work with Tom Dowd anymore. There was a split between RSO and Warner Brothers, and Tom was under contract to Atlantic who were under contract to Warners, so he was told he couldn't work with anyone from RSO, and that went on for a long time. Rob Fraboni came in to mix it, that's all. It was a shame he came in so late. He engineered it when he mixed it and when we did overdubs, but he came in halfway through, and up until that point we were just using Ed Anderson, who's the sound man for The Band.

I've got the original mixes of side one somewhere and they're unbelievably different. They're great. And it's a shame, because Rob came into a different studio, and if he'd been able to mix it in Shangri-La, it would have kept that original feel. But we had to take it to Village Recorders and mix it there in a totally different atmosphere, and it lost a little, it gained a little, but it wasn't the same as the original concept.

We cut something like twenty five tracks in three weeks out of nowhere, out of the blue, it was just like falling rain, and the outtakes—whoever's got them is sitting on a mint, because they're beautiful. Some of the best stuff didn't get on the album, like instrumentals.

The title comes from a line in one of Marcy's songs, 'Innocent Times.' 'With no freedom to laugh, there's No Reason to Cry' was her line on the record but I decided it should be 'No Reason to Cry.'" —ERIC CLAPTON

SHANGRI-LA STUDIOS
30065 Morning View Drive, Malibu, California
Sessions for the Pencils

APRIL 1976

FIRST LOVE AFFAIR (Terry Danko / Marty Grebb) unreleased

Terry Danko: vocals, bass
Marty Grebb: organ
Eric Clapton: guitar
Chris Pinnick: guitar
Ricky Fataar: drums
Joe Lala: percussion
Producers: Marty Grebb and Terry Danko
Engineer: Earle Mankey

The Pencils were a band comprising Rick Danko's brother, Terry Danko, and Marty Grebb, both lead singers and multi-instrumentalists; Chris Pinnick on guitar; Joe Lala on percussion; Ricky Fataar on drums; and James Pankow on trombone. The group recorded their one and only album at Shangri-La and at the Beach Boys' studio with a few special guests. Eric Clapton was recording *No Reason to Cry* at Shangri-La, and Pete Townshend and Ronnie Wood came by to play on the sessions. They all also contributed to a couple of tracks from the Pencils' self-titled album. Sadly, the album was never released and the masters were destroyed in a fire.

A cassette tape with some of the numbers was found in 1980, and some of the songs can be heard on the web via YouTube. The only surviving track with Eric is from the Shangri-La sessions and is called "First Love Affair."

SHANGRI-LA STUDIOS
30065 Morning View Drive, Malibu, California
Sessions for Rick Danko
Rick Danko

APRIL 1976

NEW MEXICO (Rick Danko / Bobby Charles) *Rick Danko* album Arista AB-4141 released January 1978 / *Rick Danko* CD US One Way Records 34497 released in 1997 / UK Demon EDCD650 released in 2000

Rick Danko: bass
Terry Danko: drums
Eric Clapton: guitar solo
Rob Fraboni: tambourine
Garth Hudson: accordion
Jim Gordon: organ
Walt Richmond: piano
Jim Gordon, Charlie McBurney, Lewis Bustos, Rocky Morales, Jim Price: horns
Producers: Rick Danko and Rob Fraboni
Engineer: Jeremy Zatkin

SHANGRI-LA STUDIOS
30065 Morning View Drive,
Malibu, California
Sessions for Kinky
Friedman *Lasso From*
El Paso

APRIL 1976

KINKY (Ronnie Hawkins) *Lasso From El Paso* album Epic PE 34304 released November 1976 / *Lasso From El Paso* CD Epic EPC 47 4609-2 released May 1999

Kinky Friedman: vocals
Eric Clapton: Dobro
Rick Danko: bass, backing vocals
Levon Helm: drums, backing vocals
Richard Manuel: percussion
Ronnie Wood: slide guitar

OL' BEN LUCAS (Kinky Friedman) *Lasso From El Paso* album Epic PE 34304 released November 1976 / *Lasso From El Paso* CD Epic EPC 47 4609-2 released May 1999

Kinky Friedman: vocals
Eric Clapton: Dobro
Rick Danko: bass, backing vocals
Levon Helm: drums, backing vocals
Dr. John: toy piano

Producer: Kinky Friedman
Engineer: Rob Fraboni

SHANGRI-LA STUDIOS
30065 Morning View Drive,
Malibu, California
Sessions for
Joe Cocker *Stingray*

FEBRUARY 1976

WORRIER (Matthew Moore) *Stingray* album US A&M SP-4574 / UK A&M LH 64574 released June 1976 / *Stingray* CD A&M 394 574-2 released February 1997

Joe Cocker: vocals
Eric Clapton: guitar overdub
Steve Gadd: drums and percussion
Richard Tee: keyboards
Gordon Edwards: bass
Eric Gale: guitar
Cornell Dupree: guitar
Bonnie Bramlett: backing vocals

Producer: Rob Fraboni
Engineer: Rob Fraboni

LARRABEE STUDIOS
8811 Santa Monica
Boulevard, Los Angeles
Sessions for Van Morrison

JUNE 1976

Van Morrison recorded an album with Eric Clapton and the Crusaders in Los Angeles with producer Stewart Levine. Van did not like what was being recorded and abandoned the project. It remains unreleased.

> **"**I'd heard stories about how difficult Van could be from Stewart Levine. Joe Sample and the Crusaders had collaborated with Van on an album, and at the time they were the premier band in the land, but whatever went down, apparently it wasn't right on the nail enough for Van. After they finished the record, Van changed his mind, decided he didn't like the album and erased it.**"** —**DR. JOHN**
> (from his autobiography *Under A Hoodoo Moon*)

A&M STUDIOS
1416 N. La Brea Avenue,
Hollywood, California
Session for Stephen
Bishop *Careless*

JUNE 1976

SAVE IT FOR A RAINY DAY (Stephen Bishop) *Careless* album US ABC ABCD-954 / UK ABC ABCL 5201 released December 1976

Stephen Bishop: vocals, acoustic guitar
Eric Clapton: guitar solo
Jeffrey Staton: guitar
Jeffrey Staton: bass
Barlow Jarvis: piano
Russ Kunkel: drums
Chaka Khan: backing vocals
Ian Freebairn Smith: horn arrangements

SINKING IN AN OCEAN OF TEARS (Stephen Bishop) *Careless* album US ABC ABCD-954 / UK ABC ABCL 5201 released December 1976

Stephen Bishop: vocals, acoustic guitar
Eric Clapton: slide guitar
Jay Graydon: guitar
Mac Cridlin: bass
Barlow Jarvis: piano
Larry Brown: drums

Ray Pizzi: saxophone
Alan Lindgren: synthesizers
Ian Freebairn Smith: horn arrangements
Producers: Henry Lewy and Stephen Bishop
Engineer: Henry Lewy

> "Before leaving Los Angeles for home I received a message from Stephen Bishop, asking if I'd like to play on his album. I'd never heard of him before, but it sounded intriguing so I went over to the studio and met this freaky character in mad clothes. They played me a track, and I was so taken with his voice and the quality of his songwriting that I jumped at the opportunity of playing on the album. They only used a little of what I recorded, but that session triggered a great friendship that is still pretty strong to this day." —ERIC CLAPTON

CHEROKEE STUDIOS
751 N. Fairfax Avenue,
Los Angeles
Session for Ringo Starr
Rotogravure

JUNE 1976

THIS BE CALLED A SONG (Eric Clapton) *Rotogravure* album US Atlantic SD 18193 / UK Polydor 2302 040 released September 1976 / *Rotogravure* CD Atlantic 075678241727 released August 1992

Ringo Starr: lead vocals, drums
Eric Clapton: guitar
Klaus Voormann: bass
Lon Van Eaton: guitar
Jim Keltner: drums
Jane Getz: piano
Melissa Manchester: backing vocals
Vini Poncia: backing vocals
Joe Bean: backing vocals
Robert Greenidge: steel drums

Producer: Arif Martin
Engineer: Lew Hahn

CAPRICORN RECORDING STUDIOS
Martin Luther King Jr.
Boulevard, Macon, Georgia
Session for Corky Laing

8 NOVEMBER 1976

ON MY WAY (BY THE RIVER) (Corky Laing / Leslie West / Mick Jones) *Makin' It On The Street* album Elektra 7E-1097 released May 1977 / *The Secret Sessions* CD Pet Rock Records 71278-60042-2 released 1999

Corky Laing: vocals, drums
Eric Clapton : guitar
Dicky Betts: guitar
George Terry: guitar
Calvin Arline: bass
Neal Larsen: keyboards
Charles Rose, Harrison Calloway, Harvey Thompson, Ronald Eades (Muscle Shoals Horn Section): horns

Producer: John Sandlin
Engineer: John Sandlin

> "I went to see him and I said 'You're really not going to use this one on your album are you?' But he had twenty tracks and all he needed was ten, so he said, 'I promise I won't be using that one.' I try to get anyone who wrote the song, who's a friend of mine, to work on the track." —RINGO STARR
> (Ringo had gone to see Eric Clapton, who was in town selecting which tracks to use for his next album, *No Reason to Cry*)

> "I was signed as a solo artist by Elektra Records who used to distribute Capricorn Records, Phil Walden's label. He also had a recording studio down in Macon and Elektra sent me down there to record my first solo album. It was a big deal as I was the first northerner, if you like, to record down there. Normally it was guys like the Charlie Daniels Band and The Allman Brothers amongst others.
>   I started the album and it was a lot of fun. I had Dicky Betts and other great southern musicians who I've always loved playing with me. Then I got a call from Bonnie Bramlett, who was living just outside Macon at the time, and she and I were good friends over the years, and she said she had a surprise for me and was coming down to the studio. Anyway, the surprise was Eric Clapton. He arrived at the studio with Bonnie and George Terry and he gave me a big hug and asked if he could do anything on the record. I asked if he could play rhythm guitar on this track and he was more than happy to oblige. When you listen to the number, his tone is just beautiful.
>   I had known Eric's manager, Roger Forrester, for several years. He had been West, Bruce & Laing's road manager and he and I had got on really well. But Jack and Leslie would disrespect him all the time. When it came time for me to get clearance to use Eric's name, I called Roger who said there would be no problem and that he would get it sorted." —CORKY LAING

1977

Eric and Ronnie Lane had become close buddies. Ronnie had left the Faces to form Slim Chance and had several hit singles, such as "How Come" and "The Poacher." By 1977 he had spilt Slim Chance and went out under his own name.

Eric would often play with Ronnie in small venues and pubs, usually under a pseudonym. The first was for a Valentine's Day charity dance at the Cranleigh Village Hall on 14 February 1977 organized by local Round Table chairman Roger Swallow. The deal was that Eric would perform on the proviso that his name was not mentioned to any outsiders. This gig was for locals only. Needless to say, the 350 tickets were snapped up. The main beneficiary was the Cranleigh Cottage Hospital, which needed assistance in getting new medical equipment. Local band Farandahi did a good job warming up the crowd for the main event. Eric and Ronnie ambled onstage as Eddie and the Earth Tremors at 11:00 p.m. and played a selection of songs which included "How Come," "Goodnight Irene," and some more obscure blues numbers like "Alberta." The show was recorded on Ronnie's mobile studio, but the tapes have long been lost. Eric and Ronnie also played several shows in Wales at the Miners Arms and the Drum and Monkey pubs.

Eric's manager, Roger Forrester, had asked Hughie Flint if he would be interested in putting a band together for Ronnie Lane to support Eric on his forthcoming European tour. Hughie, who was in his second retirement phase at the time, jumped at the chance. His pianist of choice was Ian Stewart from the Rolling Stones. Eric loved to ask Ian to come and jam with the band.

The whole entourage would travel in their personal train across Europe in luxury carriages, including the restaurant car, which had reputedly belonged to Hermann Goering. The American members of the band preferred staying in hotels, because they wanted room service and proper beds and would only stay on the train if they were actually traveling. A lot of silliness happened on the tour, including most of the band dressing as tramps and busking on the various station platforms they would pull into. The band member who got the most money would have to treat the rest to drinks.

At the end of July, everyone flew out to Cannes in the South of France, where two large yachts had been hired. One yacht was for the bands and the other for the road crew. Before heading off to Ibiza and Barcelona for shows, the ships went along the Mediterranean to St. Tropez. It was a working holiday, but the drinking was out of control. Poor old Ronnie Lane became unwell and broke the band up after the gig in Barcelona. Eric had hoped that he would be the support act for the 1978 US tour, but Ronnie needed a break.

For the Slowhand sessions Eric wore his influences on his sleeve. JJ Cale, Don Williams, John Martyn, and a pinch of Ronnie Lane and Slim Chance were clear sources of inspiration throughout the album. Of course, no Eric Clapton album would be complete without some blues covers. He chose well—Arthur Crudup's "Mean Old Frisco" and Huddie Ledbetter's "Alberta," which he played pretty much at every show on the 1977 tour. It was left off the album, as it did not fit in the general vibe of the other tracks.

Eric and his band ended the year with a tour of Japan and Hawaii.

FEBRUARY 1977

14 February 1977, Cranleigh Village Hall, Cranleigh, Surrey (Roundtable charity concert with Eric and Ronnie Lane)

Eric Clapton and Ronnie Lane play secret charity gig at the village hall in Cranleigh, Surrey, on 14 February 1977. Their respective wives on the left are doing the can-can during the encore.

"The Cranleigh gig was better organized, a nice village hall stage and better PA. The Fender Rhodes piano I was playing disintegrated half way thru the gig, and I moved on to the house upright piano (which was actually much more authentic). I remember playing Little Queenie on it. Eric was in great form and Patti and Katie did a fine job of the can-can. We had Bruce Rowland on drums that night. An article did appear in *Melody Maker* about that gig. I remember both shows (Drum and Monkey pub 11 March) as being very high spirited, relaxed and downhome, but also with a strong entertainment factor (not least thanks to Katie and Pattie's can-can).

The Miners' Arms was essentially Ronnie's local. What was amazing was how much Ronnie (and Katie, and by extension all of us!) had become part of the local community. It's well off the beaten track and in those days a 'lock in' after last orders was fairly standard (tho' there was always rumours of police clampdowns). Very often around midnite, we'd pull out the odd guitar or fiddle, and play some songs sometimes round the house piano. Really all sorts of songs ranging from East End favourites, Fats Domino, stuff that everyone knew, Elvis, whatever really. . . Highly improvised and great fun. We sort of carried on this tradition when we did the European boat/train tours with Eric."

—**CHARLIE HART** (Slim Chance)

MARCH 1977

11 March 1977, Drum and Monkey pub, Bromlow, Shropshire (Eric joins Ronnie Lane and Slim Chance)

SETLIST: Kansas City / How Come / Taking Your Time / Careless Love / Willie And The Hand Jive / Alberta / Walk On By / Key To The Highway / Lord Have Mercy / Little Queenie / Ooh La La / Da Doo Ron Ron / Goodnight Irene

"At the Drum and Monkey I think we had Ronnie's regulars at the time: Hughie Flint, Stu, myself, John Porter, Brian Belshaw and we were joined by Hughie's friend Tom Mcguinness. The small stage was put up in car park in the open, and we had a basic PA. I remember Eric making a joke about the likelihood of one of us crashing into the drumkit! Besides playing some of Ronnie's regular set, I seem to remember a Buddy Holly number (Peggy Sue?). The gig immediately became part of local folklore, and when we were in Shropshire recently they were still talking about it!"

—**CHARLIE HART** (Slim Chance)

UK TOUR 1977

BAND LINEUP:
Eric Clapton: guitar, vocals
George Terry: guitar
Carl Radle: bass
Dick Sims: keyboards
Jamie Oldaker: drums
Sergio Pastora: percussion
Yvonne Elliman: backing vocals
Marcy Levy: backing vocals

APRIL 1977

20 April 1977, De Montfort Hall, Leicester, Leicestershire
21 April 1977, Belle Vue King's Hall, Manchester
22 April 1977, Victoria Hall, Stoke-on-Trent, Staffordshire
23 April 1977, Glasgow Apollo, Glasgow, Scotland
24 April 1977, City Hall, Newcastle, Tyne and Wear
26 April 1977, BBC Television Theatre Studios, Shepherds Bush Green, Shepherds Bush, London

Eric Clapton at the Hammersmith Odeon on 27 April 1977.

SETLIST: Hello Old Friend / Sign Language / Alberta / Tell The Truth / Can't Find My Way Home / Double Trouble / I Shot The Sheriff / Knockin' On Heaven's Door / Further On Up The Road / Badge / Key To The Highway (All songs expect "Key To The Highway" were broadcast on BBC2's *Old Grey Whistle Test*)

27 April 1977, Hammersmith Odeon, London

SETLIST:

Hello Old Friend (Eric Clapton) *Slowhand* 35th Anniversary Super Deluxe Edition Polydor 0600753407257 released December 2012

Sign Language (Bob Dylan) *Slowhand* 35th Anniversary Super Deluxe Edition Polydor 0600753407257 released December 2012

Alberta (Traditional; arranged by Huddie Ledbetter) *Slowhand* 35th Anniversary Super Deluxe Edition Polydor 0600753407257 released December 2012

Tell The Truth (Eric Clapton / Bobby Whitlock) *Crossroads 2* box set Polydor 529 305-2 released April 1996 / *Slowhand* 35th Anniversary Super Deluxe Edition Polydor 0600753407257 released December 2012

Knockin' On Heaven's Door (Bob Dylan) *Crossroads 2* box set Polydor 529 305-2 released April 1996 / *Slowhand* 35th Anniversary Super Deluxe Edition Polydor 0600753407257 released December 2012

Steady Rollin' Man (Robert Johnson) *Slowhand* 35th Anniversary Super Deluxe Edition Polydor 0600753407257 released December 2012

Can't Find My Way Home (Steve Winwood) *Slowhand* 35th Anniversary Super Deluxe Edition Polydor 0600753407257 released December 2012

Further On Up The Road (Joe Medwich Veasey / Don D Robey) *Crossroads* box set 835 261-2 released April 1998 (incorrectly attributed to 28 April in liner notes) / *Slowhand* 35th Anniversary Super Deluxe Edition Polydor 0600753407257 released December 2012

Stormy Monday (T-Bone Walker) *Crossroads 2* box set Polydor 529 305-2 released April 1996 / *Slowhand* 35th Anniversary Super Deluxe Edition Polydor 0600753407257 released December 2012

Badge (Eric Clapton / George Harrison) *Slowhand* 35th Anniversary Super Deluxe Edition Polydor 0600753407257 released December 2012

Nobody Knows You When You're Down And Out (Jimmie Cox) *Slowhand* 35th Anniversary Super Deluxe Edition Polydor 0600753407257 released December 2012

I Shot The Sheriff (Bob Marley) *Slowhand* 35th Anniversary Super Deluxe Edition Polydor 0600753407257 released December 2012

Layla (Eric Clapton) *Slowhand* 35th Anniversary Super Deluxe Edition Polydor 0600753407257 released December 2012

Eric Clapton at the Hammersmith Odeon on 27 April 1977.

Key To The Highway (Charles Segar / Willie Broonzy)
Slowhand 35th Anniversary Super Deluxe Edition Polydor
0600753407257 released December 2012
Recorded by: Ronnie Lane Mobile Unit
Engineer: Bob Potter

Eric Clapton at the Hammersmith Odeon on 27 April 1977.

Eric Clapton and Marcy Levy at the Hammersmith Odeon on 28 April 1977.

28 April 1977, Hammersmith Odeon, London

SETLIST:

Hello Old Friend (Eric Clapton) unreleased

Sign Language (Bob Dylan) unreleased

Alberta (Traditional; arranged by Huddie Ledbetter) unreleased

All Our Past Times (Eric Clapton / Rick Danko) unreleased

Tell The Truth (Eric Clapton / Bobby Whitlock) unreleased

Knockin' On Heaven's Door (Bob Dylan) unreleased

Can't Find My Way Home (Steve Winwood) unreleased

Crossroads (Robert Johnson) unreleased

I Shot The Sheriff (Bob Marley) unreleased

Nobody Knows You When You're Down And Out (Jimmie Cox) unreleased

Further On Up The Road (Joe Medwich Veasey / Don D Robey) unreleased

Stormy Monday (T-Bone Walker) unreleased

Willie And The Hand Jive* (Johnny Otis) unreleased

Layla (Eric Clapton / Jim Gordon) unreleased

All I Have To Do Is Dream (Felice Bryant / Boudleaux Bryant) unreleased

*with Ronnie Lane on vocals and guitar
Recorded by: Ronnie Lane Mobile Unit
Engineer: Bob Potter

29 April 1977, Rainbow Theatre, Finsbury Park, London

SETLIST: Hello Old Friend / Sign Language / Alberta / Tell The Truth / Knockin' On Heaven's Door / Further On Up The Road / Can't Find My Way Home / Nobody Knows You When You're Down And Out / One Night / Key To The Highway / I Shot The Sheriff / Stormy Monday / Steady Rollin' Man / Layla* / Crossroads*

*with Pete Townshend on guitar

MAY 1977

14 May 1977, New Victoria Theatre, London (Eric joins JJ Cale for his set tonight. Most people did not even recognize him as he was sitting in the shadows. After the show, Eric took JJ Cale down to Olympic Studios in Barnes to listen to some of the recordings

he was doing for his next album, *Slowhand*. Eric was particularly keen for JJ Cale to hear his version of "Cocaine," which he had recorded on 6 May)

IRISH, SCANDINAVIAN, EUROPEAN TOUR 1977

BAND LINEUP:
Eric Clapton: guitar, vocals
George Terry: guitar
Carl Radle: bass
Dick Sims: keyboards
Jamie Oldaker: drums
Yvonne Elliman: backing vocals
Marcy Levy: backing vocals

JUNE 1977

4 June 1977, National Stadium, Dublin, Ireland

6 June 1977, National Stadium, Dublin, Ireland

9 June 1977, Falkoner Teatret, Copenhagen, Denmark

SETLIST (INCOMPLETE): Sign Language / Further On Up The Road / Knockin' On Heaven's Door / Stormy Monday / Tell The Truth / Key To The Highway / Nobody Knows You When You're Down And Out / Layla

10 June 1977, Stadthalle, Bremen, Germany

11 June 1977, Groenoordhall, Leiden, Netherlands

SETLIST: Sign Language / Alberta / I Shot The Sheriff / Knocking On Heaven's Door / Can't Find My Way Home / Key To The Highway / Tell The Truth / Badge / Nobody Knows You When You Down And Out / Have You Ever Loved A Woman / Steady Rollin' Man / Layla / Further On Up The Road

13 June 1977, Forest National, Brussels, Belgium

SETLIST: Hello Old Friend / Sign Language / Alberta / Knockin' On Heaven's Door / Tell The Truth / Can't Find My Way Home / Key To The Highway / Stormy Monday / I Shot The Sheriff / Nobody Knows You When You Down And Out / Layla / All I Have To Do Is Dream / Further On Up The Road

14 June 1977, Le Pavilion, Paris, France

SETLIST: Hello Old Friend / Sign Language / Alberta / I Shot The Sheriff / Knockin' On Heaven's Door / Tell The Truth / Can't Find My Way Home / Key To The Highway / Badge* / Nobody Knows You When You're Down And Out / Have You Ever Loved A Woman / Steady Rollin' Man / Layla / Further On Up The Road

*with Ringo Starr on tambourine on "Badge

15 June 1977, Phillipshalle, Düsseldorf, Germany

17 June 1977, Rhein-Neckar-Halle, Heidelberg, Germany

SETLIST: Hello Old Friend / Sign Language / Alberta / I Shot The Sheriff / Knockin' On Heaven's Door / Tell The Truth / Can't Find My Way Home / Key To The Highway / Badge / Nobody Knows You When You're Down And Out / Have You Ever Loved A Woman / Steady Rollin' Man / Layla / Further On Up The Road

19 June 1977, Mehrzweckhalle, Wetzikon, Switzerland

SETLIST: Hello Old Friend / Sign Language / Alberta / I Shot The Sheriff / Knocking On Heaven's Door / Tell The Truth / Can't Find My Way Home / Key To The Highway / Badge / Nobody Knows You When You're Down and Out / Have You Ever Loved A Woman / Steady Rollin' Man / Layla / Further On Up The Road

20 June 1977, Olympiahalle, Munich, Germany

JULY 1977

16 July 1977, Drum and Monkey pub, Bromlow, Shropshire (Eric once again joins Ronnie Lane and friends for an intimate pub gig)

SETLIST: My Baby / Dead Flowers / Willy And The Hand Jive / Singing The Blues / Walk On By / Da Doo Ron Ron / Ooh La La / Key To The Highway / Little Queenie / C'est La Vie / Goodnight Irene / Blues Jam / Stormy Monday / If You Gotta Go

AUGUST 1977

5 August 1977, Plaza de Toros, Ibiza, Spain

11 August 1977, Nuevo Pabellón, Club Juventud, Barcelona, Spain

SLOWHAND JAPAN / HAWAII TOUR 1977

BAND LINEUP:
Eric Clapton: guitar, vocals
George Terry: guitar
Carl Radle: bass
Jamie Oldaker: drums
Dick Sims: keyboards
Marcy Levy: backing vocals

SEPTEMBER 1977

26 September 1977, Festival Hall, Osaka, Japan

SETLIST: The Core / Badge / Double Trouble / Knockin On Heavens Door / Bottle Of Red Wine / Nobody Knows You When You're Down And Out / Alberta / We're All The Way / Sign Language / Tell The Truth / Stormy Monday / Layla / Key To the Highway

27 September 1977, Okayama-Ken, Taiikukan, Okayama, Japan

SETLIST: The Core / I Shot The Sheriff / Double Trouble / Badge / Nobody Knows You When You're Down And Out / Alberta / We're All The Way / Sign Language / Tell The Truth / Stormy Monday / Layla / Further On Up The Road

29 September 1977, Kyoto Kaikan Daiichi Hall, Kyoto, Japan

SETLIST: The Core / Bottle Of Red Wine / Knockin' On Heaven's Door / Badge / We're All The Way / Sign Language / Nobody Knows You When You're Down And Out / Key To The Highway / Tell The Truth / Double Trouble / Steady Rollin' Man / Layla / Further On Up The Road

30 September 1977, Nagoya-Shi-Kokaido, Aichi, Japan

SETLIST: The Core / I Shot The Sheriff / Blues With A Feeling / Stormy Monday / Knockin' On Heaven's Door / One Night With You / Nobody Knows You When You're Down And Out / We're All The Way / Sign Language / Alberta / Badge / Key To The Highway / Layla

OCTOBER 1977

1 October 1977, Festival Hall, Osaka, Japan

SETLIST: The Core / Blues Power / Have You Ever Loved A Woman / One Night With You / Nobody Knows You When You're Down And Out / Sign Language / Alberta / Tell The Truth / Double Trouble / Layla / Bottle Of Red Wine / Key To The Highway

4 October 1977, Makomanai Ice Arena, Sapporo, Japan

SETLIST: The Core / I Shot The Sheriff / Double Trouble / Badge / Nobody Knows You When You're Down And Out / One Night With You / We're All The Way / Sign Language / Alberta / Cocaine / Key To The Highway / Layla / Further On Up The Road

6 October 1977, Budokan, Tokyo, Japan

SETLIST: The Core / I Shot The Sheriff / Double Trouble / Badge / Nobody Knows You When You're Down And Out / One Night With You / We're All The Way / Sign Language / Alberta / Cocaine / Knockin' On Heaven's Door / It's Too Bad / Rambling On My Mind / Layla / All I Have To Do Is Dream / Further On Up The Road

7 October 1977, Budokan, Tokyo, Japan

SETLIST: The Core / I Shot The Sheriff / Double Trouble / Badge / Nobody Knows You When You're Down And Out / Mama Told Me / We're All The Way / Sign Language / Alberta / Cocaine / Bottle Of Red Wine / Stormy Monday / Layla / Tell The Truth

9 October 1977, Honolulu International Center, Honolulu, Hawaii

SETLIST: The Core / I Shot The Sheriff / Double Trouble / Badge / Can't Find My Way Home / We're All The Way / Sign Language / Nobody Knows You When You're Down And Out / Cocaine / It's Too Bad / Ramblin' On My Mind / Knockin' On Heaven's Door / Layla / All I Have To Do Is Dream / Tell The Truth / Key To The Highway

10 October 1977, Honolulu International Center, Honolulu, Hawaii

RECORDING SESSIONS 1977
RAMPORT STUDIOS,
115 Thessaly Road,
London SW8
Session for Roger
Daltrey's *One Of The Boys*

JANUARY 1977

SINGLE MAN'S DILEMMA (Colin Blunstone) *One Of The Boys* album US MCA 2271 / UK Polydor 2442 146 released May 1977 / *One Of The Boys* CD Sanctuary CMRCD1139 released December 2005

Roger Daltrey: vocals
Eric Clapton: slide guitar
Paul Keogh: acoustic guitar
Stuart Tosh: drums
Brian Odgers: bass

YOU PUT SOMETHING BETTER INSIDE ME (Gerry Rafferty / Joe Egan) single B-side Polydor 2058 896 released June 1977 / bonus track on *One Of The Boys* CD Sanctuary CMRCD1139 released December 2005

Roger Daltrey: vocals
Eric Clapton: acoustic guitar
Stuart Tosh: drums
Brian Odgers: bass
Jimmy Jewel: saxophone
Rod Argent: piano
Paul Keogh: pedal steel guitar

Producer: David Courtney
Engineer: Phil McDonald

Roger made the mistake of giving Eric a barrel of beer before the session. This was as a "thank-you" for coming along to play. Unfortunately, Eric decided to partake of his gift straight away and was soon too drunk to play. He came back another day to make good on his promise to play on the session. I am still not convinced that his participation was used, but it has been confirmed that he played on two numbers.

❝The barrel of beer story is correct. Eric came to the session with Patti Boyd and his roadie. Eric played on two tracks one of which was 'You Put Something Better' (Steelers Wheel song) and I believe the other was 'Single Man's Dilemma' written by Colin Blunstone, or 'Say It Ain't So Joe' (Andy Pratt song).❞
—**DAVID COURTNEY** (producer)

OLYMPIC STUDIOS
117-123 Church Road,
Barnes, London SW13
Session for Ronnie Lane
and Pete Townshend's
Rough Mix

FEBRUARY 1977

Eric Clapton during recording sessions at Olympic Studios for Ronnie Lane's Rough Mix *album.*

Eric Clapton during recording sessions at Olympic Studios for Ronnie Lane's Rough Mix *album.*

ROUGH MIX (Ronnie Lane / Pete Townshend) *Rough Mix* album US ATCO 7 90097-1-Y, UK Polydor 2442 147 released September 1977 / Deluxe Edition *Rough Mix* CD SPV 304852 released May 2006
Pete Townshend: vocals, guitar

Ronnie Lane: vocals, bass
Eric Clapton: guitar
John "Rabbit" Bundrick: keyboards
Henry Spinetti: drums

Eric Clapton and Ronnie Lane have a laugh during recording sessions at Olympic Studios for Ronnie Lane's Rough Mix *album.*

ANNIE (Eric Clapton / Kate Lambert / Ronnie Lane) *Rough Mix* album US ATCO 7 90097-1-Y, UK Polydor 2442 147 released September 1977 / Deluxe Edition *Rough Mix* CD SPV 304852 released May 2006

Pete Townshend: vocals, acoustic guitar
Ronnie Lane: vocals, acoustic guitar
Eric Clapton: acoustic guitar
Graham Lyle: acoustic guitar
Bennie Gallagher: accordion
Charlie Hart: violin
Dave Markee: string bass

APRIL FOOL (Ronnie Lane) *Rough Mix* album US ATCO 7 90097-1-Y, UK Polydor 2442 147 released September 1977 / Deluxe Edition *Rough Mix* CD SPV 304852 released May 2006

Pete Townshend: vocals, guitar
Ronnie Lane: vocals, guitar
Eric Clapton: Dobro
Dave Markee: double bass

TILL THE RIVERS RUN DRY (Wayland Holyfield / Don Williams) *Rough Mix* album US ATCO 7 90097-1-Y, UK Polydor 2442 147 released September 1977 / Deluxe Edition *Rough Mix* CD SPV 304852 released May 2006

Pete Townshend: vocals, guitar
Ronnie Lane: vocals, guitar
Eric Clapton: Dobro
Henry Spinetti: drums
Boz Burell: bass
John Entwistle: backing vocals
Billy Nicholls: backing vocals

GOOD QUESTION (Pete Townshend) Bonus track on Deluxe Edition *Rough Mix* CD SPV 304852 released May 2006

Pete Townshend: guitar
Ronnie Lane: bass
Eric Clapton: guitar (right channel)
Ian Stewart: piano
Henry Spinetti: drums
Julian Diggle: percussion

Producer: Glyn Johns
Engineer: Glyn Johns assisted by Jon Astley

"I kept going along to the studio hoping I'd get to play, but a lot of the time I was just sitting around keeping the peace between the other two. They kept having heated arguments about philosophy and politics and so on—all totally irrelevant to the work in hand. I felt more like a referee that a guest artist on that album." —ERIC CLAPTON

"Basically, the album came about because I was in financial trouble, and I went to see Pete, not to ask him for anything, just to see him socially. Obviously, we talked about each other's state. Mine came up and he said, 'Well, we've talked about working together in the past. Why don't we get an album together?' I said, 'That would solve my problem.' It did. The sessions were quite funny. A lot of rowing. Me and Pete, we love each other a lot, but we rub each other up the wrong way, as well. He's a much bigger fellow than me, he's got a longer reach than I have.

I couldn't make out why we didn't spend an hour or two an evening or two to write a song together. I've got a few ideas. Pete had a few ideas. My ideas weren't finished—things like that. And vice-versa. So, I said, 'why don't we get together and write some things?' He turned around and said, 'What? And split the publishing?' I was floored. I never brought it up to him again." —RONNIE LANE
(from *Before I Get Old: The Story of the Who*, by Dave Marsh)

"Sometimes Ronnie and I would talk about life. That would mean Ronnie insulting me and me hitting him. Sometimes Eric Clapton would come and play. That would mean Ronnie insulting him, Eric hitting him, and then falling over. Glyn and Ronnie often discussed Ronnie's songs. That consisted of Ronnie trying to keep Glyn in the studio till three or four in the morning while he insulted him. —PETE TOWNSHEND
(from *Before I Get Old: The Story of the Who*, by Dave Marsh)

ROLLING STONES MOBILE Fishpool Farm, Hyssington, near Bishop's Castle, Wales Session with Ronnie Lane

JULY 1977

AROUND THE WORLD (BEFORE I GROW TOO OLD) Lucky Seven CD NMC Pilot 7 released 2002

LAST NIGHT Lucky Seven CD NMC Pilot 7 released 2002
ANNIE HAD A BABY Lucky Seven CD NMC Pilot 7 released 2002
SOME DAY Lucky Seven CD NMC Pilot 7 released 2002
WALK ON BY Lucky Seven CD NMC Pilot 7 released 2002
RON'S TAKE Lucky Seven CD NMC Pilot 7 released 2002
CHARLIE'S TAKE Lucky Seven CD NMC Pilot 7 released 2002

Ronnie Lane: vocals and guitar
Eric Clapton: electric and acoustic guitars
Brian Belshaw: bass
Ian Stewart: piano
Charlie Hart: accordion
John Porter: guitar and mandolin
Hughie Flint: drums

Executive Producer: Ian Stewart
Engineer: Mick McKenna

These sessions were for a proposed album by Ronnie Lane. The sessions were stopped when the band went on a European tour as support to Eric Clapton. So the tracks released are largely just basic without overdubs. Worth having if you are a fan of Ronnie Lane and the band.

> **❝** Eric joined in quite a few recording sessions at the Fishpool. The tracks which you found on 'Lucky Seven' were indeed recorded on the Stones Mobile (courtesy of Stu) as I think Ronnie's mobile was not available. Mick Mckenna engineered them. I remember putting the tracks down in Ronnie's barn, 'Last Night' with accordion playing the organ line and Eric on acoustic. These tracks were not released at the time as there were not quite enough for an album and I think Ronnie was not happy to put out an album of predominantly covers. **❞**
>
> —**CHARLIE HART** (Slim Chance)

OLYMPIC STUDIOS, 117-123 Church Road, Barnes, London SW13 Session for *Slowhand*

2 MAY 1977–25 MAY 1977

2 May 1977, Reel 1

WONDERFUL TONIGHT (Eric Clapton) (8 takes recorded) *Slowhand* album US RSO RS 1-3030, UK RSO 2479201 released November 1977 / *Slowhand* CD Polydor 531825-2 released March 1997

Eric Clapton: guitar, vocals
George Terry: guitar
Carl Radle: bass
Jamie Oldaker: drums

Dick Sims: organ
Yvonne Elliman: backing vocals
Marcy Levy: backing vocals

NEXT TIME YOU SEE HER (Eric Clapton) (2 takes) unreleased

3 MAY 1977–4 MAY 1977, Reel 2

NEXT TIME YOU SEE HER (Eric Clapton) (1 take) *Slowhand* album US RSO RS 1-3030, UK RSO 2479201 released November 1977 / *Slowhand* CD Polydor 531825-2 released March 1997

Eric Clapton: guitar, vocals
George Terry: guitar
Carl Radle: bass
Jamie Oldaker: drums
Dick Sims: organ, piano
Alberta (Traditional; arranged by Huddie Ledbetter) (1 take)

5 MAY 1977, Reel 3

MAY YOU NEVER (John Martyn) (8 takes) *Slowhand* album US RSO RS 1-3030, UK RSO 2479201 released November 1977 / *Slowhand* CD Polydor 531825-2 released March 1997

Eric Clapton: acoustic guitar, Dobro, vocals
George Terry: acoustic guitar
Carl Radle: bass
Jamie Oldaker: drums
Dick Sims: organ

DUMB WAITER (8 takes) unreleased
DROWNING ON DRY LAND (5 takes) unreleased

5 MAY 1977, Reel 4

DROWNING ON DRY LAND (4 takes) unreleased

6 MAY 1977, Reel 5

COCAINE (JJ Cale) (2 takes recorded) *Slowhand* album US RSO RS 1-3030, UK RSO 2479201 released November 1977 / *Slowhand* CD Polydor 531825-2 released March 1997

Eric Clapton: guitar, vocals
George Terry: guitar

Front cover of Eric Clapton's Slowhand *album.*

Carl Radle: bass
Jamie Oldaker: drums
Dick Sims: organ

ALBERTA (Traditional; arranged by Huddie Ledbetter) (6 takes recorded) Blues single CD Polydor 547 179-2 released June 1999 / Blues double CD Polydor 314 547 178-2 released June 1999 / *Slowhand* expanded CD Polydor released December 2012

Eric Clapton: guitar, vocals

LOOKING AT THE RAIN (Gordon Lightfoot) *Slowhand* expanded CD Polydor released December 2012

9 MAY 1977, Reel 6

MEAN OLD FRISCO (Arthur Crudup) (7 takes) unreleased

9 MAY 1977, Reel 7

MEAN OLD FRISCO (Arthur Crudup) (2 takes recorded) *Slowhand* album US RSO RS 1-3030, UK RSO 2479201 released November 1977 / *Slowhand* CD Polydor 531825-2 released March 1997

Eric Clapton: slide guitar, Dobro, vocals
George Terry: guitar
Carl Radle: bass
Jamie Oldaker: drums
Dick Sims: piano

BE BOP AND HOLLA (Andy Fairweather Low) (1 take) unreleased (demo with guide vocal by Andy Fairweather Low. The number was never finished, although Andy did rerecord his version on his Be Bop 'N' Holla solo album)

12 MAY 1977, Reel 8

PEACHES AND DIESEL (Eric Clapton / Albhy Galuten) (8 takes) unreleased

12 MAY 1977, Reel 9

PEACHES AND DIESEL (Eric Clapton / Albhy Galuten) (8 takes recorded) *Slowhand* album US RSO RS 1-3030, UK RSO 2479201 released November 1977 / *Slowhand* CD Polydor 531825-2 released March 1997

Eric Clapton: guitar
George Terry: guitar
Carl Radle: bass
Jamie Oldaker: drums
Dick Sims: electric piano, organ

While recording the *Slowhand* album at Olympic, the band No Dice were also recording their album. They all loved playing table football, and there were a few tables in the café–cum–rec room at the studio. Eric, being Eric, offered them a bet he would beat them. Of course, Eric lost. The cost of the bet was naming a track after the two band members he had lost to. Their names? Peaches and Diesel.

19 MAY 1977, Reel 9

LAY DOWN SALLY (Eric Clapton / Marcy Levy / George Terry) (5 takes) unreleased

19 MAY 1977, Reel 10

LAY DOWN SALLY (Eric Clapton / Marcy Levy / George Terry) (3 takes) *Slowhand* album US RSO RS 1-3030, UK RSO 2479201 released November 1977 / *Slowhand* CD Polydor 531825-2 released March 1997

Eric Clapton: guitar, vocals
George Terry: guitar
Carl Radle: bass
Jamie Oldaker: drums
Dick Sims: electric piano
Yvonne Elliman: backing vocals
Marcy Levy: backing vocals

GREYHOUND BUS (1 take)

THE RIFF (aka The Core) (Eric Clapton / Marcy Levy) *Slowhand* album US RSO RS 1-3030, UK RSO 2479201 released November 1977 / *Slowhand* CD Polydor 531825-2 released March 1997

Eric Clapton: guitar, vocals
George Terry: guitar
Carl Radle: bass
Jamie Oldaker: drums
Dick Sims: organ
Yvonne Elliman: backing vocals
Marcy Levy: vocals, backing vocals
Mel Collins: sax

JAM unreleased

20 MAY 1977, Reel 11

GREYHOUND BUS (9 takes) Slowhand expanded CD Polydor released December 2012

25 MAY 1977, Reel 12

WE'RE ALL THE WAY (Don Williams) (5 takes recorded) *Slowhand* album US RSO RS 1-3030, UK RSO 2479201 released November 1977 / *Slowhand* CD Polydor 531825-2 released March 1997

Eric Clapton: guitar, vocals
George Terry: guitar
Carl Radle: bass
Jamie Oldaker: drums
Dick Sims: keyboards
Yvonne Elliman: backing vocals
Marcy Levy: backing vocals

STARS, STRAYS AND ASHTRAYS (2 takes) unreleased

25 MAY 1977, Reel 12

STARS, STRAYS AND ASHTRAYS (5 takes) Slowhand expanded CD Polydor Released December 2012

Producer: Glyn Johns
Engineers: Glyn Johns, Jon Astley

"For me Slowhand is a very nervous sung album, especially after No Reason to Cry. Maybe it was because of the lack of material we had when we went in to cut it, or the difference in surroundings. And laid back is not the word for it! 'Layla' wasn't a success, it died a death, but as far as I was concerned, I'd put that album up against anybody's that was out at that time. With Slowhand it was a completely different story. It was lightweight, really lightweight, and the reason for that, I think, is partly due to the fact that some of the stuff that we wanted to put on the record I wrote, say, six months before. We were on the road and we wrote some songs and got to the studio—and we couldn't get to the studio early enough or we wanted a couple of weeks off or something like that—and by the time we got in there everyone knew the song so well, we were so sort of limp about it that it was lazy.

Anyway, for me the best track has got to be 'Wonderful Tonight' because the song is nice. It was written about my sweetheart, and whether or not it was recorded well or we played it well doesn't make any difference, because the song is still nice."

—ERIC CLAPTON

1978

SLOWHAND USA / CANADA TOUR 1978 (FIRST LEG)

The year 1978 was a busy one for Eric, most of it spent on the road. There would also be a film and a new studio album. As for the band lineup, the main change was that Yvonne Elliman had left the band at the end of the last European tour to pursue a solo career. She was signed to RSO and produced several albums for them. Marcy filled the void left by Yvonne with no problems due to her versatility.

The six-piece traveled over to North America for a huge tour starting in Canada on 1 February 1978 in Vancouver. The set still focused on the very successful *Slowhand* album, along with some past hits and blues covers and a bit of Buddy Holly thrown in also. The band were very tight and played well throughout the tour. Eric's drinking seemed under control, at least during the shows.

After the first leg of the European tour, the band took a break at their respective homes before resuming the tour later. Before the start of the second leg of the European tour, Eric received a call from George Terry. He told Eric that he would no longer be part of the band. He was tired of the long tours and wanted a slower pace in life. Marcy also left the band to pursue a solo career.

Some surprises on the European tour included a version of Little Walter's "Blues With A Feeling" as an encore at the Paris show.

BAND LINEUP:
Eric Clapton: guitar, vocals
George Terry: guitar
Carl Radle: bass
Jamie Oldaker: drums
Dick Sims: keyboards
Marcy Levy: backing vocals

FEBRUARY 1978

1 February 1978, PNE Coliseum, Vancouver, British Columbia, Canada

SETLIST: Peaches And Diesel / Wonderful Tonight / Lay Down Sally / Next Time You See Her / The Core / We're All The Way / Rodeo Man / Fool's Paradise / Mean Old Frisco / Cocaine / Badge / Double Trouble / Better Make It Through Today / Let It Rain / Knockin' On Heaven's Door / Nobody Knows You When You're Down And Out / Key To The Highway / Have You Ever Loved A Woman / Layla / Further On Up The Road

Randy Tuten poster for Eric Clapton's appearance at the Oakland Coliseum on 10 February 1978.

3 February 1978, Exhibition Coliseum, Edmonton, Alberta, Canada

5 February 1978, Paramount Theatre, Seattle, Washington

6 February 1978, Washington State University Coliseum, Pullman, Washington

8 February 1978, Paramount Theatre, Portland, Oregon

10 February 1978, Coliseum, Oakland, California

11 February 1978, Civic Auditorium, Santa Monica, California

SETLIST:

Peaches And Diesel (Eric Clapton / Ahlby Galuten) unreleased

Wonderful Tonight (Eric Clapton) unreleased

Lay Down Sally Eric Clapton / Marcy Levy / George Terry) unreleased

Next Time You See Her (Eric Clapton) unreleased

The Core (Eric Clapton / Marcy Levy) *Crossroads 2* box set Polydor 529 305-2 released April 1996

We're All The Way (Don Williams) unreleased

She's In Love With A Rodeo Man (Don Williams) unreleased

Fool's Paradise (Buddy Holly) unreleased

Cocaine (JJ Cale) unreleased

Badge (Eric Clapton / George Harrison) unreleased

Double Trouble (Otis Rush) unreleased

Nobody Knows You When You're Down And Out (Jimmie Cox) unreleased

Let It Rain (Eric Clapton / Delaney Bramlett) unreleased

Knockin' On Heaven's Door (Bob Dylan) unreleased

Key To The Highway (Charles Segar / Willie Broonzy) unreleased

Going Down Slow (Jimmy Oden) / **Ramblin' On My Mind** (Robert Johnson) *Crossroads 2* box set Polydor 529 305-2 released April 1996

Layla (Eric Clapton / Jim Gordon) unreleased

Bottle Of Red Wine (Eric Clapton / Delaney Bramlett) unreleased

You'll Never Walk Alone (Richard Rodgers / Oscar Hammerstein) unreleased

Recorded by: DIR Broadcasting Mobile Unit Engineers: Ray Thompson, Paul Sandweiss, Dennis Mays

12 February 1978, Civic Auditorium, Santa Monica, California

SETLIST:

Peaches And Diesel (Eric Clapton / Ahlby Galuten) unreleased

Wonderful Tonight (Eric Clapton) unreleased

Lay Down Sally Eric Clapton / Marcy Levy / George Terry) *Crossroads 2* box set Polydor 529 305-2 released April 1996

Next Time You See Her (Eric Clapton) unreleased

The Core (Eric Clapton / Marcy Levy) unreleased

We're All The Way (Don Williams) *Crossroads 2* box set Polydor 529 305-2 released April 1996

She's In Love With A Rodeo Man (Don Williams) unreleased

Fool's Paradise (Buddy Holly) unreleased

Cocaine (JJ Cale) *Crossroads 2* box set Polydor 529 305-2 released April 1996

Badge (Eric Clapton / George Harrison) unreleased

Double Trouble (Otis Rush) unreleased

Nobody Knows You When You're Down And Out (Jimmie Cox) unreleased

Let It Rain (Eric Clapton / Delaney Bramlett) unreleased

Knockin' On Heaven's Door (Bob Dylan) unreleased

Last Night (Little Walter) unreleased

Key To The Highway (Charles Segar / Willie Broonzy) unreleased

Going Down Slow (Jimmy Oden) / **Ramblin' On My Mind** (Robert Johnson) unreleased

Layla (Eric Clapton / Jim Gordon) unreleased

Bottle Of Red Wine (Eric Clapton / Delaney Bramlett) unreleased

You'll Never Walk Alone (Richard Rodgers / Oscar Hammerstein) unreleased

Recorded by: DIR Broadcasting Mobile Unit Engineers: Ray Thompson, Paul Sandweiss, Dennis Mays

A one-hour edited *King Biscuit Flower Hour Show* made up of songs from both nights was syndicated on US radio stations.

13 February 1978, Aladdin Theatre, Las Vegas, Nevada

15 February 1978, McNichols Arena, Denver, Colorado

18 February 1978, Metropolitan Centre, Minneapolis, Minnesota

19 February 1978, University of Iowa, Hilton Coliseum, Ames, Iowa

20 February 1978, Municipal Auditorium, Kansas City, Kansas

21 February 1978, Kiel Auditorium, St. Louis, Missouri

23 February 1978, Chicago Stadium, Chicago, Illinois

24 February 1978, Louisville Gardens, Louisville, Kentucky

26 February 1978, Civic Center Arena, Huntington, Indiana

28 February 1978, Municipal Auditorium, Nashville, Tennessee (with Don Williams)

MARCH 1978

1 March 1978, Mid-South Coliseum, Memphis, Tennessee

2 March 1978, Boutwell Auditorium, Birmingham, Alabama

SETLIST: Peaches And Diesel / Wonderful Tonight / Lay Down Sally / Next Time You See Her / The Core / We're All The Way / Rodeo Man / Fool's Paradise / Cocaine / Badge / Double Trouble / Nobody Knows You When You're Down And Out / Knockin' On Heaven's Door / Key To The Highway / Goin' Down Slow / Layla / Bottle Of Red Wine

SLOWHAND USA TOUR (SECOND LEG)

19 March 1978, Jai-Alai Frontun, Miami, Florida (with John Martyn)

SETLIST:

Peaches And Diesel (Eric Clapton / Ahlby Galuten) unreleased

Wonderful Tonight (Eric Clapton) unreleased

Lay Down Sally Eric Clapton / Marcy Levy / George Terry) unreleased

Next Time You See Her (Eric Clapton) unreleased

The Core (Eric Clapton / Marcy Levy) unreleased

We're All The Way (Don Williams) unreleased

She's In Love With A Rodeo Man (Don Williams) unreleased

Fool's Paradise (Buddy Holly) unreleased

Cocaine (JJ Cale) unreleased

Double Trouble (Otis Rush) unreleased

Badge (Eric Clapton / George Harrison) unreleased

Nobody Knows You When You're Down And Out (Jimmie Cox) unreleased

Knockin' On Heaven's Door (Bob Dylan) unreleased

Key To The Highway (Charles Segar / Willie Broonzy) unreleased

Let It Rain (Eric Clapton / Delaney Bramlett) unreleased

Layla (Eric Clapton / Jim Gordon) unreleased

Bottle Of Red Wine (Eric Clapton / Delaney Bramlett) unreleased

Recorded by: Fedco Recording Truck
Engineers: Glyn Johns, Jon Astley

20 March 1978, Civic Center Coliseum, Lakeland, Florida (with John Martyn)

SETLIST:

Peaches And Diesel (Eric Clapton / Ahlby Galuten) unreleased

Wonderful Tonight (Eric Clapton) unreleased

Lay Down Sally Eric Clapton / Marcy Levy / George Terry) unreleased

Next Time You See Her (Eric Clapton) unreleased

The Core (Eric Clapton / Marcy Levy) unreleased

We're All the Way (Don Williams) unreleased

She's In Love With A Rodeo Man (Don Williams) unreleased

Fool's Paradise (Buddy Holly) unreleased

Cocaine (JJ Cale) unreleased

Double Trouble (Otis Rush) unreleased

Badge (Eric Clapton / George Harrison) unreleased

Nobody Knows You When You're Down And Out (Jimmie Cox) unreleased

Knockin' On Heaven's Door (Bob Dylan) unreleased

Key To The Highway (Charles Segar / Willie Broonzy) unreleased

Let It Rain (Eric Clapton / Delaney Bramlett) unreleased

Layla (Eric Clapton / Jim Gordon) unreleased

Bottle Of Red Wine (Eric Clapton / Delaney Bramlett) unreleased

Recorded by: Fedco Recording Truck
Engineers: Glyn Johns, Jon Astley

21 March 1978, Civic Center, Savannah, Georgia (with John Martyn)

SETLIST:

Peaches And Diesel (Eric Clapton / Ahlby Galuten) unreleased

Wonderful Tonight (Eric Clapton) unreleased

Lay Down Sally Eric Clapton / Marcy Levy / George Terry) unreleased

The Core (Eric Clapton / Marcy Levy) unreleased

Mean Old Frisco (Arthur Crudup) *Crossroads 2* box set Polydor 529 305-2 released April 1996

She's In Love With A Rodeo Man (Don Williams) unreleased

Fool's Paradise (Buddy Holly) unreleased

Cocaine (JJ Cale) unreleased

Double Trouble (Otis Rush) unreleased

Badge (Eric Clapton / George Harrison) unreleased

Nobody Knows You When You're Down And Out (Jimmie Cox) unreleased

Knockin' On Heaven's Door (Bob Dylan) unreleased

Key To The Highway (Charles Segar / Willie Broonzy) unreleased

Let It Rain (Eric Clapton / Delaney Bramlett) unreleased

Layla (Eric Clapton / Jim Gordon) unreleased

Bottle Of Red Wine (Eric Clapton / Delaney Bramlett) unreleased

Recorded by: Fedco Recording Truck
Engineers: Glyn Johns, Jon Astley

22 March 1978, Coliseum, Macon, Georgia (with John Martyn)

24 March 1978, Memorial Coliseum, Charlotte, North Carolina (with John Martyn)

SETLIST: The Core / Worried Life Blues / Peaches And Diesel / Wonderful Tonight / Lay Down Sally / Rodeo Man / Fool's Paradise / Cocaine / Double Trouble / Badge / Nobody Knows You / Knockin' On Heaven's Door / Key To The Highway / Layla / Bottle Of Red Wine

25 March 1978, Carolina Coliseum, Columbia, South Carolina (with John Martyn)

26 March 1978, Von Braun Civic Center, Huntsville, Alabama (with John Martyn)

28 March 1978, Cobo Hall, Detroit, Michigan (with John Martyn)

SETLIST: The Core / Worried Life Blues / Peaches And Diesel / Wonderful Tonight / Lay Down Sally / Rodeo Man / Fool's Paradise / Cocaine / Double Trouble / Badge / Nobody Knows You When You're Down And Out / Knockin' On Heaven's Door / Key To The Highway / Let It Rain / Layla / Bottle Of Red Wine

29 March 1978, Convention Center, Cleveland, Ohio (with John Martyn)

30 March 1978, Rooster Tail Club, Detroit, Michigan (Eric and Marcy Levy join the Detroit Rockets for a jam

"They got their deal with RSO Records in a roundabout way through—believe it or not—Eric Clapton. I managed the band starting in the mid/late 70's until they broke up and got all of their record deals for them. The first deal was with local Detroit producer, Don Davis's, Tortoise Records (distributed by RCA). Our first lp was out and making a little noise but we were looking for a company more in tune with rock and roll. I received an offer for the band to play a surprise birthday party for Eric Clapton at the Roostertail—a club on the Detroit River (which to this day is still open for private functions).

Eric liked the band so much that he got up and jammed with them along with other guests at the party—singer Marcy Levy, a Detroiter who was good friends with the Rockets and was touring with Clapton at the time (She wrote 'Lay Down Sally' with him and went on to a solo career as 'Marcella Detroit') and local saxophonist, Tomo Thomas.

(I was prepared with a high quality cassette deck and have a great tape of the event.)

Eric was so taken with the group that he gave me the name and number of an exec at RSO Records to contact about signing the band. I contacted the local RSO rep, Julie Sher, and asked her to help me get the bigwigs at RSO excited about the group. With her help and the good word put in by Eric Clapton, we signed a deal with RSO."

—**GARY LAZAR** (manager of the Rockets)
(from therockets.com)

SETLIST: Stop Breakin' Down / Chuck Berry Jam / Stormy Monday / Backyard Blues / Boogie Jam

31 March 1978, Civic Center Arena, Baltimore, Maryland (with John Martyn)

SETLIST: The Core / Worried Life Blues / Peaches and Diesel / Wonderful Tonight / Lay Down Sally / Rodeo Man / Fool's Paradise / Cocaine / Double Trouble / Badge / Nobody Knows When You're Down And Out / Knockin' On Heaven's Door / Key To The Highway / Bottle Of Red Wine / Crossroads

APRIL 1978

1 April 1978, Spectrum, Philadelphia, Pennsylvania (with John Martyn)

2 April 1978, Radio City Music Hall, New York City (with John Martyn)

3 April 1978, Nassau Coliseum, New York City (with John Martyn)

SETLIST: The Core / Worried Life Blues / Peaches And Diesel / Wonderful Tonight / Lay Down Sally / Rodeo Man / Fool's Paradise / Cocaine / Double Trouble / Badge / Goin' Down Slow / Driftin' / Key To The Highway / Layla / Bottle Of Red Wine

5 April 1978, Civic Center, Springfield, Massachusetts (with John Martyn)

SETLIST: The Core / Worried Life Blues / Peaches And Diesel / Wonderful Tonight / Lay Down Sally / Rodeo Man / Fool's Paradise / Cocaine / Double Trouble / Badge / Nobody Knows You When You're Down And Out / Let It Rain / Key To The Highway / Layla / Bottle Of Red Wine

7 April 1978, Forum, Montreal, Quebec, Canada (with John Martyn)

9 April 1978, Maple Leaf Gardens, Toronto, Ontario, Canada (with John Martyn)

SETLIST: The Core / Worried Life Blues / Peaches And Diesel / Wonderful Tonight / Lay Down Sally / Rodeo Man / Fool's Paradise / Cocaine / Double Trouble / Nobody Knows You When You're Down And Out / Badge / Knockin' On Heaven's Door / Key To The Highway / Layla / Bottle Of Red Wine

ALEXIS KORNER'S 50th BIRTHDAY PARTY CONCERT 1978

19 April 1978, Pinewood Studios, Gatsby Room, Iver, Buckinghamshire

SETLIST:

Hey Pretty Mama (Chris Farlowe) *The Party Album Alexis Korner And Friends* double album Intercord 170000 released 1979 / CD Castle Communications Castle Classics CLACD290 released 1979

Got To Get You Off Of My Mind (Solomon Burke) unreleased

Stormy Monday Blues (Billy Eckstine / Earl Hines) *The Party Album Alexis Korner And Friends* double album Intercord 170000 released 1979 / CD Castle Communications Castle Classics CLACD290 released 1979

Hi-Heel Sneakers (Robert Higginbotham) *The Party Album Alexis Korner And Friends* double album Intercord 170000 released 1979 / CD Castle Communications Castle Classics CLACD290 released 1979

Alexis Korner: guitar, vocals
Eric Clapton: guitar
Zoot Money: electric piano, vocals
Colin Hodgkinson: bass
Stu Speer: drums

Eric Clapton at Alexis Korner's 50th Birthday Party concert on 19 April 1978.

Dick Morrissey: saxophone
Dick Heckstall-Smith: saxophone
Art Themen: saxophone
Mel Collins: saxophone
John Surmann: saxophone
Mike Zwerin: trombone
Chris Farlowe: vocals, tambourine
Duffy Power: harmonica
Paul Jones: harmonica, vocals
Neil Ford: guitar

Producer: Jeff Griffin
Engineer: Mike Robinson
Recorded by: BBC Mobile Recording Truck

FESTIVALS WITH BOB DYLAN 1978

BAND LINEUP:
Eric Clapton: guitar, vocals
George Terry: guitar
Carl Radle: bass
Jamie Oldaker: drums
Dick Sims: keyboards
Marcy Levy: backing vocals

23 June 1978, Stadion Feyenoord, Rotterdam, Netherlands

SETLIST: The Core / Worried Life Blues / Wonderful Tonight / Lay Down Sally / Rodeo Man / Fool's Paradise / Cocaine / Double Trouble / Nobody Knows You When You're Down And Out / Badge / Knockin' On Heaven's Door / Key To The Highway / Layla

1 July 1978, Zeppelinfeld, Nürnberg, Germany

Poster for a festival show with Bob Dylan and Eric Clapton among others at Nuremberg's Zeppelinfeld on 1 July 1978

IRISH SOLO SHOWS 1978

BAND LINEUP:
Eric Clapton: guitar, vocals
George Terry: guitar
Carl Radle: bass
Jamie Oldaker: drums
Dick Sims: keyboards
Marcy Levy: backing vocals

7 July 1978, National Stadium, Dublin, Ireland

SETLIST: The Core / Worried Life Blues / Wonderful Tonight / Lay Down Sally / Rodeo Man / Fool's Paradise / Cocaine / Double Trouble / Nobody Knows You When You're Down And Out / Badge / Knockin' On Heaven's Door / Key To The Highway / Layla / Early In The Morning

8 July 1978, National Stadium, Dublin, Ireland

SETLIST: The Core / Worried Life Blues / Wonderful Tonight / Lay Down Sally / Rodeo Man / Fool's Paradise / Cocaine / Double Trouble / Nobody Knows You When You're Down And Out / Badge / Knockin' On Heaven's Door / Key To The Highway / Layla / Early In The Morning

BLACKBUSHE FESTIVAL WITH BOB DYLAN 1978

15 July 1978, Blackbushe Aerodrome, Camberley, Surrey

SETLIST: The Core / Worried Life Blues / Wonderful Tonight / Lay Down Sally / Rodeo Man / Fool's Paradise / Cocaine / Double Trouble / Nobody Knows You When You're Down And Out / Badge / Knockin' On Heaven's Door / Key To The Highway / Layla / Bottle of Red Wine

15 July 1978, Blackbushe Aerodrome, Camberley, Surrey (Eric Clapton joins headliner Bob Dylan and his band for "Forever Young")

BAND MEMBERS FOR "FOREVER YOUNG":
Bob Dylan: Rhythm Guitar, Vocals
Eric Clapton: Guitar
Billy Cross: Guitar
Ian Wallace: Drums
Alan Pasqua: Keyboards
Rob Stoner: Bass Guitar, Background Vocals

Steven Soles: Acoustic Rhythm Guitar, Background Vocals
David Mansfield: Pedal Steel, Violin, Mandolin, Dobro, Guitar
Steve Douglas: Saxophone, Flute, Recorder
Bobbye Hall: Percussion
Helena Springs: Background Vocals
Jo Ann Harris: Background Vocals
Debi Dye: Background Vocals

Eric Clapton joins Bob Dylan at the Blackbushe festival on 15 July 1978.

BACKLESS EUROPEAN TOUR 1978

BAND LINEUP:

Eric Clapton: guitar, vocals
Carl Radle: bass
Jamie Oldaker: drums
Dick Sims: keyboards

The new stripped-down band meant far more work for Eric. He now found himself as the main soloist. The band were a tight unit, and the European tour offered up some fine performances. Eric also invited Muddy Waters along as the opening act, giving many fans their first opportunity to see this legendary blues giant.

RSO again decided to record some shows, as they had done in 1977, as well as film a fly-on-the-wall-style documentary about being on the road with Eric Clapton. Rex Pyke was the director on behalf of Angle Films, whose brief was to follow Eric and his band backstage, onstage, in hotels, and pretty much anywhere, really. This would be interspersed with interviews and live numbers from the tour. What made the film even more unique was the fact that Eric and his band were traveling by rail across Europe in carriages hired from the Orient Express. They had their own chef and luxury living quarters. It also meant Eric could indulge in drink and drug binges away from public scrutiny. Amazingly, some of these events were allowed to be filmed, and there are some disturbing scenes which show Eric and others putting the blade of a flick knife into a mound of coke before snorting it all up. Around 120 rolls of film were shot in Europe and England, and I sat through and watched each and every roll over a couple of weeks. Clearly, Rex Pyke had permission to film everything. The footage contains some great scenes of Eric and the band just larking around, including one hilarious scene when an official from Belgian Railways was granted an interview with Eric for their monthly news magazine. The camera follows the hapless guy to the carriage where Eric could be found. He is introduced and he sits down to start the interview. Only problem was that this was not Eric but a member of the crew who happened to look like him. The real Eric was acting as the lackey for the fake Eric, fetching them drinks, et cetera. Then there is some wonderful footage of Eric with an acoustic guitar playing beautiful renditions of Big Bill Broonzy's "When Did You Leave Heaven" and a new self-penned song called "To Make Somebody Happy," which he eventually got to record in December 1978. There is a lot of footage of Eric in different stages of working out the song on acoustic guitar, including accompanying himself and harmonizing with a cassette recording of the song playing in the background. The footage offers a fascinating document on the whole songwriting process for Eric when he is on the road.

I always assumed that there would be more concert footage rather than behind-the-scenes events. In fact, the only concert that was actually filmed in its entirety was the Glasgow Apollo using three cameras, left, middle, and right. The show was also professionally sound recorded using the Rolling Stones Mobile Studio, which meant that the sound could be synced with the film should they choose to.

Partial pieces were also shot at different concerts in Europe and England using a single camera with audio being recorded on a Nagra reel-to-reel recorder. Roll 31, for example, features Eric and Muddy Waters at the

Guildford Civic Hall, which was the tour finale. It also has an edited version of "Further On Up The Road," which has guest appearances from George Harrison and Elton John. Even though the show was not professionally recorded, the two-track Nagra recorder did a good job in capturing the audio. There is some great footage of the start of the concert when Eric walks onstage and goes to grab his guitar from its stand. Unbeknownst to him, the crew had dismantled a Strat and placed it on his stand, and when he went to pick it up it came apart and he was left holding the neck of the guitar in front of the whole Civic Hall. There is also some footage backstage of a huge cake made in the shape of "Blackie," his favorite guitar. Before long, the cake is being thrown around and pushed in people's faces.

Other single-camera live songs include, on Roll 35, Stevie Wonder's "Loving You (Is Sweeter Than Ever)" and "Standing Around Crying" from the Gala Ballroom, West Bromwich. Roll 36 has "Layla" and "Wonderful Tonight" from the Victoria Hall, Hanley. Roll 30 offers up "Double Trouble" and "Further On Up The Road" from Paris. Other footage includes lengthy after-show jams between Eric and Bob Margolin, Muddy Waters's guitar player. Then away from the music there is some lovely footage of Muddy Waters and Eric playing poker. Needless to say, Eric keeps losing.

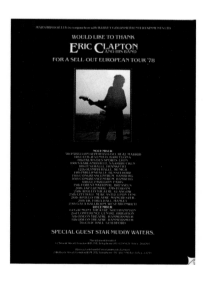

Advert for Eric Clapton's European tour in 1978.

There is other footage which has leaked out of Eric in a backstage discussion with manager Robert Stigwood where Eric accuses him of using funds from Cream to finance the Bee Gees. Stigwood is clearly embarrassed and turning red with anger before trying to get away from Eric and the cameras.

All in all, not Eric's finest hour, but looking at it today, it is a fascinating historical document of a small part of Eric's musical and personal life. Rex Pyke's film was called *Eric Clapton and his Rolling Hotel* and, perhaps not surprisingly, was only shown a couple of times at various film festivals.

Eric ended the year by recording three new tracks at Olympic Studios which were not released until 1996.

NOVEMBER 1978

5 November 1978, Pabellón Deportivo Del Real Madrid, Madrid, Spain

6 November 1978, Club Juventus, Barcelona, Spain

SETLIST: Someone Like You / Blues Power / Worried Life Blues / Badge / Golden Ring / If I Don't Be There By Morning / Walk Out In The Rain / Double Trouble / I'll Make Love To You / Layla / Cocaine / Key To The Highway / Further On Up The Road

7 November 1978, day off

8 November 1978, Palais des Sports, Lyon, France

SETLIST: Tulsa Time / Someone Like You / Blues Power / Worried Life Blues / Badge / Walk Out In The Rain / Double Trouble / I'll Make Love To You Anytime / Layla / Cocaine / Further On Up the Road

9 November 1978, day off

10 November 1978, Saarlandhalle, Saarbrücken, Germany

SETLIST: Layla / Worried Life Blues / Cocaine / Walk Out In The Rain / Double Trouble / Badge / Golden Ring / If I Don't Be There By Morning / Early In The Morning / Key To The Highway / Further On Up The Road

11 November 1978, Festhalle, Frankfurt, Germany

SETLIST: Layla / Worried Life Blues / Badge / Standing Around Crying* / Key To The Highway / If I Don't Be There By Morning / Wonderful Tonight / Tulsa Time / Early In The Morning / Cocaine / Double Trouble
*with Muddy Waters

12 November 1978, Olympiahalle, München, Germany

13 November 1978, day off

14 November 1978, Phillipshalle, Düsseldorf, Germany

SETLIST: Layla / Worried Life Blues / Badge / Wonderful Tonight / If I Don't Be There By Morning / Double Trouble / Tulsa Time / Early In The Morning / Further On Up The Road / Cocaine / Key To The Highway / Crossroads

15 November 1978, Kongresszentrum, Hamburg, Germany

16 November 1978, Kongresszentrum, Hamburg, Germany

17 November 1978, day off

18 November 1978, Le Pavillion, Paris, France

SETLIST: Layla / Worried Life Blues / If I Don't Be There By Morning / Double Trouble / Badge / Wonderful Tonight / Tulsa Time / Early In The Morning / Key To The Highway / Cocaine / Blues With A Feeling

19 November 1978, Forest National, Bruxelles, Belgium

SETLIST: Layla / Worried Life Blues / If I Don't Be There By Morning / Wonderful Tonight / I'll Make Love To You Anytime / Double Trouble / Badge / Tulsa Time / Early In The Morning / Cocaine / Crossroads

20 November 1978, Jaap Edenhal, Amsterdam, Netherlands

21 November 1978–23 November 1978, days off

24 November 1978, Glasgow Apollo, Glasgow, Scotland

SETLIST:

Layla (Eric Clapton / Jim Gordon) unreleased

Worried Life Blues (Maceo Merriweather) unreleased

Tulsa Time (Danny Flowers) *Crossroads 2* box set Polydor 529 305-2 released April 1996

Early In The Morning (Traditional; arranged by Eric Clapton) unreleased

Badge (Eric Clapton / George Harrison) unreleased

Wonderful Tonight (Eric Clapton) *Crossroads 2* box set Polydor 529 305-2 released April 1996

Kindhearted Woman (Robert Johnson) *Crossroads 2* box set Polydor 529 305-2 released April 1996

Key To The Highway* (Charles Segar / Willie Broonzy) unreleased

Further On Up The Road* (Joe Veassey / Don Robey) unreleased

Cocaine (JJ Cale) unreleased

Double Trouble (Otis Rush) unreleased

Crossroads (Robert Johnson) unreleased

*Ian Stewart on piano
*Jerry Portnoy on harmonica
*Bob Margolin on guitar
Engineer: Mick McKenna
Recorded by: Rolling Stones Mobile Studio

25 November 1978, City Hall, Newcastle, Tyne And Wear

SETLIST:

Layla (Eric Clapton / Jim Gordon) unreleased

Worried Life Blues (Maceo Merriweather) unreleased

Wonderful Tonight (Eric Clapton) unreleased

If I Don't Be There By Morning (Bob Dylan / Helena Springs) unreleased

Double Trouble (Otis Rush) unreleased

Eric Clapton at the City Hall in Newcastle on 25 November 1978. L to R: Jamie Oldaker, Carl Radle, Eric Clapton, and Dick Sims.

I'll Make Love To You Anytime (JJ Cale) unreleased

Badge (Eric Clapton / George Harrison) unreleased

Key To The Highway (Charles Segar / Willie Broonzy) unreleased

Cocaine (JJ Cale) unreleased

Tore Down* (Sonny Thompson) unreleased

Tore Down* (Sonny Thompson) (reprise) unreleased

```
*Luther Johnson: guitar, vocals
*Jerry Portnoy: harmonica
Engineer: Mick McKenna
Recorded by: Rolling Stones Mobile Studio
```

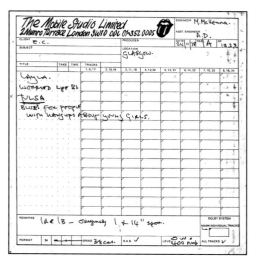

Tape box cover from Rolling Stones Mobile for Eric Clapton's concert in Glasgow on 28 November 1978.

Eric Clapton at the City Hall in Newcastle on 25 November 1978. L to R: Jamie Oldaker, Luther Johnson, Eric Clapton, Jerry Portnoy, and Dick Sims.

Eric Clapton at the City Hall in Newcastle on 25 November 1978. L to R: Carl Radle, Eric Clapton, and Dick Sims.

26 November 1978, Apollo Theatre, Manchester

27 November 1978, day off

28 November 1978, Victoria Hall, Hanley, Staffordshire

SETLIST:

Loving You (Is Sweeter Than Ever) (Stevie Wonder / Ivy Jo Hunter) *Crossroads 2* box set Polydor 529 305-2 released April 1996

Worried Life Blues (Maceo Merriweather) *Crossroads 2* box set Polydor 529 305-2 released April 1996

Badge (Eric Clapton / George Harrison) unreleased

Wonderful Tonight (Eric Clapton) unreleased

Crossroads (Robert Johnson) *Crossroads 2* box set Polydor 529 305-2 released April 1996

If I Don't Be There By Morning (Bob Dylan / Helena Springs) unreleased

Double Trouble (Otis Rush) *Crossroads 2* box set Polydor 529 305-2 released April 1996

I'll Make Love To You Anytime (JJ Cale) unreleased

Tulsa Time (Danny Flowers) unreleased

Early In The Morning (Traditional; arranged by Eric Clapton) *Crossroads 2* box set Polydor 529 305-2 released April 1996

Layla (Eric Clapton / Jim Gordon) unreleased

Cocaine (JJ Cale) unreleased

Further On Up The Road (Joe Veassey / Don Robey) unreleased

```
Engineer: Mick McKenna
Recorded by: Rolling Stones Mobile Studio
```

29 November 1978, Gala Ballroom, West Bromwich, West Midlands

30 November 1978, day off

DECEMBER 1978

1 December 1978, Gaumont Theatre, Southampton, Hampshire

2 December 1978, Conference Centre, Brighton, East Sussex

3 December–4 December 1978, days off

5 December 1978, Hammersmith Odeon, London

SETLIST: Loving You Is Sweeter Than Ever / Worried Life Blues / Badge / Wonderful Tonight / Crossroads / If I Don't Be There By Morning / Double Trouble / I'll Make Love To You Anytime / Tulsa Time / Early In The Morning / Key To The Highway / Layla / Standing Around Crying* / Further On Up the Road*

*Muddy Waters on guitar and vocals

6 December 1978, Hammersmith Odeon, London

SETLIST: Loving You Is Sweeter Than Ever / Worried Life Blues / Badge / Wonderful Tonight / Crossroads / If I Don't Be There By Morning / Double Trouble / Tulsa Time / Early In The Morning / Cocaine / Key to the Highway / Layla / Further On Up The Road

7 December 1978, Civic Hall, Guildford, Surrey

SETLIST: Loving You Is Sweeter Than Ever / Worried Life Blues / Badge / Tulsa Time / Early In The Morning / Wonderful Tonight / Crossroads / Cocaine / Double Trouble / Layla / Standing Around Crying* / Sad Sad Day* / Further On Up The Road**

*Pinetop Perkins on piano
*Bob Margolin on guitar

*Jerry Portnoy on harmonica
*Muddy Waters on guitar, vocals
**George Harrison on guitar
**Elton John on piano. Elton John and George Harrison both play on Further On Up The Road and the other musicians only play on the numbers with one asterisk

11 December 1978, Dingwalls, London (Eric joins Muddy Waters and his band at this intimate club in London's Camden Town. Eric sits in for "Mannish Boy," "Got My Mojo Working," and "Standing Around Crying")

RECORDING SESSIONS 1978

ERIC CLAPTON GUEST SESSION
OLYMPIC STUDIOS
117-123 Church Road, Barnes, London SW13
Session for *White Mansions*

JANUARY 1978

WHITE TRASH (Bernie Leadon / Paul Kennerley) *White Mansions* album A&M A&M SP-6004 released June 1978 / *White Mansions* CD A&M CDA64691 released March 1993

Steve Cash: vocals
Eric Clapton: slide guitar
Henry Spinetti: drums
Dave Markee: bass
Steve Cash: harmonica
Tim Hinkley: piano
John Dillon: acoustic guitar, piano, backing vocals
Bernie Leadon: backing vocals
Paul Kennerley: backing vocals

LAST DANCE & THE KENTUCKY RACE HORSE (Paul Kennerley) *White Mansions* album A&M A&M SP-6004 released June 1978 / *White Mansions* CD A&M CDA64691 released March 1993

Eric Clapton: Dobro
Henry Spinetti: drums
Dave Markee: bass
Steve Cash: harmonica
John Dillon: acoustic guitar, piano, backing vocals
Bernie Leadon: backing vocals
Paul Kennerley: backing vocals
Producer: Glyn Johns
Engineer: Glyn Johns

Advert for a Muddy Water's show at the small Dingwalls club in Camden Town, London, on 11 December 1978. Eric Clapton turned up for a jam.

DINGWALLS
01-267 4967 Camden Lock, Chalk Farm Road, London NW1
RHYTHM & BOOZE AT DINGWALLS
THUR 7   CAROL GRIMES BAND
FRI 8   DAVE LEWIS BAND PLUS SUPPORT
SAT 9   JACKIE LYNTON'S HAPPY DAYS
          SUPPORTED BY RAIL.
SUN 10   DINGWALLS' R&B NIGHTS PRESENT
          50th ANNIVERSARY OF BOOGIE WOOGIE
          CELEBRATIONS WITH
BOB HALL, ALEXIS KORNER, CHARLIE WATTS,
DICK MORRISEY, IAN STEWART, COLIN SMITH,
JOHNNY PICKARD, DAVE GREEN
AND MORE.   TICKETS A MERE £1.50.
MON 11
FROM U.S.A. only U.K. CLUB APPEARANCE
THE LEGENDARY
MUDDY WATERS
A LIMITED NUMBER OF TICKETS AVAILABLE FROM
BOX OFFICE AT £4.50. N.B. 'FREE PASS'
HOLDERS WILL HAVE TO PURCHASE TICKETS. DON'T MISS
THIS RARE CHANCE OF SEEING MUDDY IN A CLUB SETTING.
TUES 12   RACING CARS
N.B. DOORS OPEN 9p.m.
WED 13 THUR 14 FOR 2 NIGHTS ONLY,
ENGLAND'S NUMBER ONE REGGAE BAND
MATUMBI
ADVANCE TICKETS £2.50 NOW AVAILABLE FROM BOX OFFICE.
BOOZE IS ½ PRICE BEFORE 10p.m. EVERY
EVENING EXCEPT SUNDAYS.

OLYMPIC STUDIOS
117-123 Church Road,
Barnes, London SW13
Sessions for *Backless*

MAY 1978–SEPTEMBER 1978

*Front cover of
Eric Clapton's*
Backless *album.*

WALK OUT IN THE RAIN (Bob Dylan / Helena Springs) *Backless* album US RSO 3216 213, UK RSO 2479221 released November 1978 / *Backless* CD US Polydor 31453 1826-2, UK Polydor 531 826-2 released September 1996

Eric Clapton: guitar, vocals
George Terry: guitar
Jamie Oldaker: drums
Dick Sims: piano
Carl Radle: bass

WATCH OUT FOR LUCY (Eric Clapton) *Backless* album US RSO 3216 213, UK RSO 2479221 released November 1978 / *Backless* CD US Polydor 31453 1826-2, UK Polydor 531 826-2 released September 1996

Eric Clapton: guitar, vocals
George Terry: guitar
Jamie Oldaker: drums
Dick Sims: keyboards
Carl Radle: bass
Marcy Levy: vocals, harmonica

I'LL MAKE LOVE TO YOU ANYTIME (JJ Cale) *Backless* album US RSO 3216 213, UK RSO 2479221 released November 1978 / *Backless* CD US Polydor 31453 1826-2, UK Polydor 531 826-2 released September 1996

Eric Clapton: wah-wah slide guitar, vocals
George Terry: guitar
Jamie Oldaker: drums
Dick Sims: keyboards
Carl Radle: bass

ROLL IT (Eric Clapton / Marcy Levy) *Backless* album US RSO 3216 213, UK RSO 2479221 released November 1978 / *Backless* CD US Polydor 31453 1826-2, UK Polydor 531 826-2 released September 1996

Eric Clapton: slide guitar
George Terry: guitar
Jamie Oldaker: drums
Dick Sims: keyboards
Carl Radle: bass
Marcy Levy: vocal

TELL ME THAT YOU LOVE ME (Eric Clapton) *Backless* album US RSO 3216 213, UK RSO 2479221 released November 1978 / *Backless* CD US Polydor 31453 1826-2, UK Polydor 531 826-2 released September 1996

Eric Clapton: guitar, vocals
George Terry: guitar
Jamie Oldaker: drums
Dick Sims: piano, organ
Carl Radle: bass

IF I DON'T BE THERE BY MORNING (Bob Dylan / Helena Springs) *Backless* album US RSO 3216 213, UK RSO 2479221 released November 1978 / *Backless* CD US Polydor 31453 1826-2, UK Polydor 531 826-2 released September 1996

Eric Clapton: guitar, vocals
George Terry: guitar
Jamie Oldaker: drums, backing vocals
Dick Sims: piano
Carl Radle: bass, backing vocals
Marcy Levy: backing vocals

EARLY IN THE MORNING (Traditional; arranged by Eric Clapton) (short version) *Backless* album US RSO 3216 213, UK RSO 2479221 released November 1978

Eric Clapton: slide guitar, vocals
George Terry: guitar
Jamie Oldaker: drums
Dick Sims: piano, organ
Carl Radle: bass
Marcy Levy: harmonica

EARLY IN THE MORNING (Traditional; arranged by Eric Clapton) (complete long version) *Backless* CD US Polydor 31453 1826-2, UK Polydor 531 826-2 released September 1996

Eric Clapton: slide guitar, vocals
George Terry: guitar
Jamie Oldaker: drums
Dick Sims: piano, organ
Carl Radle: bass
Marcy Levy: harmonica

PROMISES (Richard Feldman / Roger Linn) *Backless* album US RSO 3216 213, UK RSO 2479221 released November 1978 / *Backless* CD US Polydor 31453 1826-2, UK Polydor 531 826-2 released September 1996

Eric Clapton: Dobro, vocals
George Terry: acoustic guitar
Jamie Oldaker: drums
Dick Sims: organ
Carl Radle: bass
Marcy Levy: vocals

GOLDEN RING (Eric Clapton) *Backless* album US RSO 3216 213, UK RSO 2479221 released November 1978 / *Backless* CD US Polydor 31453 1826-2, UK Polydor 531 826-2 released September 1996

Eric Clapton: acoustic, vocals
George Terry: acoustic guitar
Jamie Oldaker: drums
Dick Sims: organ
Carl Radle: bass
Benny Gallagher: accordion, backing vocals
Graham Lyle: backing vocals

TULSA TIME (Danny Flowers) *Backless* album US RSO 3216 213, UK RSO 2479221 released November 1978 / *Backless* CD US Polydor 31453 1826-2, UK Polydor 531 826-2 released September 1996

Eric Clapton: slide guitar, vocals
George Terry: guitar

"The title came from the Dylan gig we did at Blackbushe, where it became very apparent that he knew exactly what was going on everywhere around him all the time. So it's a tribute to Bob, really. I mean if you were backstage, he expected you to be putting as much into it as he was. You couldn't just stand there and be one of the roadies, you had to actually focus all your attention on him, and if you didn't he knew it, and he'd turn around and he'd look at you and you'd get daggers.

Bob just laid this cassette on me with 'If I Don't Be There By Morning' and 'Walk Out In The Rain.' He was hooked up with this girl called Helena Springs. They were co-writing, and I think he was very proud of it and laid it on me when we were in Nuremberg. I've still got that on cassette of them two. That's another bootleg. I've got a private copy of that. When I get down sometimes, I listen to them and it will bring me right out, because I know that no one else has got it. This was a gift to me. The funny thing was, when we next met was at Blackbushe in fact. We did Nuremberg first. At Blackbushe I sat in a coach and played him—I'd gone into the studio by then and done two numbers—and I played them back and he said, 'Well, when are they going to be finished?' [laughs] and I realized I was dealing with a master. Still is. Always will be. The man's a master.

I used to think the way to record an album was top what you'd done before, but it doesn't work. It never works, because what you've done before is in the past, and that's that. If you try and emulate what you've done before, then you're in a rut, and you might as well wave goodbye to the future altogether. So I didn't try.

The best things that happened on Backless were the things that happened at the time. I got away with one song on there, 'Golden Ring,' which I think is the strongest song on the album, because I wrote it because I was fed up with the general sort of apathy of everyone involved, and I just thought, 'Well, I'll take a song in there and whether they like it or not, we'll do it—they'll learn it and record it and we'll put it on the record, and that's that!' And that kind of conviction carried the thing through. I spoke to Don Williams just before Christmas and I told him I liked his album and he said 'Golden Ring' was his favourite track too, because it was the only one that came through with any kind of feeling, with strength. And if you listen to it, there's nothing to it. Songs like that are caused by situations, but situations of that extremity don't happen every day, thank God, though if they did I'd be the most prolific songwriter in the world. They only happen once every two or three months, but there you go. That's why a song is moving, because you don't think what the diction is like or how clever the words should rhyme, it's just like you're saying something to somebody, as if you're in conversation with them.

Being critical of your own work is very difficult, especially when you can just say 'Bow wow' instead. In the case of Backless I think we were very lazy. In fact, I think all musicians are lazy. I think that's one of the best parts about us. The trouble with being lazy is you either don't try hard enough or you try too hard, and you don't like being told what to do." —ERIC CLAPTON

Jamie Oldaker: drums, backing vocals
Dick Sims: piano
Carl Radle: bass, backing vocals

BEFORE YOU ACCUSE ME (version 1) (Ellas McDaniel) *Blues* single CD Polydor 547 179-2 released June 1999 / *Blues* double CD Polydor 314 547 178-2 released June 1999

Eric Clapton: guitar, vocals
George Terry: guitar
Jamie Oldaker: drums
Dick Sims: piano
Carl Radle: bass

BEFORE YOU ACCUSE ME (version 2) (Ellas McDaniel) *Blues* single CD Polydor 547 179-2 released June 1999 / *Blues* double CD Polydor 314 547 178-2 released June 1999

Eric Clapton: guitar, vocals
George Terry: guitar
Jamie Oldaker: drums
Dick Sims: piano
Carl Radle: bass

SWEET LORRAINE unreleased

IT'S A SHAME (2 takes recorded) unreleased

ERIC'S THING unreleased

COUNTRY JAM unreleased

ONE CHORD TUNE (2 takes recorded) unreleased

"Eric Clapton must want to be the Mississippi John Hurt of his generation: a sweet-tempered old soul who can communicate great pleasure and great pain in a mumble. The surprise is that he gets away with it so easily. In its way, Backless is a seductive record, if you're attracted to the interplay of Clapton's dolorous voice and Marcy Levy's raspy backup vocals, George Terry's slide guitar and Glyn Johns' pristine production. It's disheartening only if you're still looking for a Clapton album with a hint of the power and fire he brought to his best work—from Bluesbreakers to Layla. Me, I made my peace with great expectations a while back. I like the new LP, but it wouldn't make any difference if I didn't." —DAVE MARSH
(*Rolling Stone*, 28 December 1978)

DEPEND ON ME unreleased
THE ROAD IS LONG unreleased
DICKIE'S SONG unreleased

GIVE IT AWAY unreleased

Producer: Glyn Johns
Engineers: Glyn Johns, Jon Astley

> "Glyn and I did a couple of Eric Clapton albums together, Slowhand and Backless, on which I was officially assisting, but some days Glyn didn't show up and Eric would say 'Oh, let's do a whole track. We'll show him!' In fact 'Tulsa Time' was all me—producing, engineering, the whole lot—and Glyn was fine with that. He didn't mind at all. He thought it was part and parcel of the job, and we got on very well."
>
> —JON ASTLEY
> (talking to *Sound On Sound*)

ERIC CLAPTON GUEST SESSION

FRIAR PARK STUDIOS
Henley-On-Thames, Oxfordshire
Session for George Harrison *George Harrison*

DECEMBER 1978

LOVE COMES TO EVERYONE (George Harrison) *George Harrison* album Dark Horse K 56562 released February 1979 / *George Harrison* remastered CD Dark Horse Records 594 0872 released March 2004

George Harrison: guitars, vocals
Eric Clapton: guitar intro
Andy Newmark: drums
Willie Weeks: bass
Neil Larsen: keyboards, mini Moog
Ray Cooper: percussion
Steve Winwood: Moogs, backing vocals

Producers: George Harrison and Russ Titleman
Engineer: Phil MacDonald

OLYMPIC STUDIOS
117-123 Church Road, Barnes, London SW13
Session for potential new album

28 DECEMBER 1978

TO MAKE SOMEBODY HAPPY (Eric Clapton) *Crossroads 2* box set Polydor 529 305-2 released April 1996 / *Blues* single CD Polydor 547 179-2 released June 1999 / *Blues* double CD Polydor 314 547 178-2 released June 1999

Eric Clapton: guitar, vocals
Dave Markee: bass
Henry Spinetti: drums

WATER ON THE GROUND (Eric Clapton) *Crossroads 2* box set Polydor 529 305-2 released April 1996

Eric Clapton: guitar, vocals
Dave Markee: bass
Henry Spinetti: drums
Graham Lyle: guitar

CRYIN' (Eric Clapton) *Crossroads 2* box set Polydor 529 305-2 released April 1996 / *Blues* single CD Polydor 547 179-2 released June 1999 / *Blues* double CD Polydor 314 547 178-2 released June 1999

Eric Clapton: guitar, vocals
Dave Markee: bass
Henry Spinetti: drums

Producer: Glyn Johns
Engineer: Jon Astley

Eric recorded three new numbers as demos for a potential new album. As his band had returned to America, Eric used an English rhythm section. He was familiar with them from the *White Mansions* session in January 1978 and Ronnie Lane's and Pete Townshend's *Rough Mix* session in 1977. He obviously enjoyed the results, as he would ask Dave Markee and Henry Spinetti to join his new band in September 1979.

23

1979

Eric started the year by accepting an invitation to play on sessions for Marc Benno's new album. Eric used most of his touring band for the session, but as drummer Jamie Oldaker was tied up in America, Jim Keltner was brought in. Albert Lee was also at this session. Eric and Albert knew each other from the '60s, and playing together at this session rekindled the friendship and gave Eric the idea of asking him to join his band. Albert accepted and stayed with Eric for several years. In the 1979 tour program Eric recalled why he decided to ask Albert Lee:

> **❝**The four-piece line-up (after George and Marcy left last August) worked out on some songs, but didn't work out on the others. There were others where there were just holes and I felt I was doing too much. And if I go to see a guitar player, I don't like to see him doing everything, playing the chords and then playing the lead. I like to see it balanced out. Roger [Forrester] said to me that was a fair assessment of the situation—certain production type songs, like 'Layla' or 'Badge.' Songs where it definitely needed a fuller sound—and he suggested Albert [Lee]. And it was just like bang!—light bulb!—and I thought, 'Why didn't I think of that?' Anyway, the point is this: I've written a few more songs and this tour should be all right!**❞**

Nineteen seventy-nine was largely taken up with touring to promote 1978's *Backless* album. The setlist was similar to what the four-piece band had been performing in Europe during 1978, but thanks to Albert, the sound was now fuller and took some pressure off Eric at the same time. The tour started in Ireland in early March and carried on to America, where it ended toward the end of June. A few significant events took place in the middle of all this touring. Eric and Pattie got married on 27 March at the Apostolic Assembly of Faith in Christ Jesus in Tucson, Arizona, and later, back home in England, on 20 May, held a wedding reception at Hurtwood Edge for family and friends. There was a huge marquee set up in the grounds where the musical guests could get up and play. Although on paper the musical guests onstage such as Paul McCartney, George Harrison, Ringo Starr, Lonnie Donnegan, Denny Laine, Jeff Beck, and Jack Bruce, sounded amazing, the songs and rock 'n' roll jams were very loose, to say the least.

Eric also played unannounced at the Dorking Folk Club around this time with his buddy John Martyn. The folk club was held at the Dorking Hospital social club. Hamish Imlach recounted in his autobiography *Cod Liver Oil and the Orange Juice*:

> **❝**John and Eric spent some five or six weeks getting pissed on planes and hotels, and going on stage the worse for wear, and both were fans of Robert Johnson, an American bluesman of the twenties, so they tried to write together a drinking blues song called The Brahms And Liszt Blues—Brahms and Liszt is cockney rhyming slang for pissed. When John told me the story I happened to mention that there was a strong ale called Brahms and Liszt, manufactured by a brewery in Selby, Yorkshire, and in Leeds was a pub called Brahms and Liszt which featured this beer.

John said, 'I'd love to give Elo (the name Clapton is known to his by friends) some. Can you get me a case?' As it happened I was going up to do some gigs in the north, then back down London for some more. When I went north I called at the pub and got a case of the ale, and arrived at John's place with it. He asked what I was doing next.

'I've got a gig in Dorking Folk Club tomorrow night. I've never been there before.'

'That's right next to where Eric lives!' John said.

So midday the next day we set off to Eric's house. At the time he wasn't married to Patti Boyd but they were living together. She was a very nice woman, who made us a meal. She said to me that Eric's favourite meal was egg and chips, and she would force him to have something like chops. We delivered the crate of Brahms and Liszt, all sampled along with a good few brandies. Eventually I had to say 'I have to leave now, I've got this gig.'

'Where is it?'

'Dorking.'

'That's just near here. We'll come with you.'

My car was rather clapped out, so we took a big Mercedes 500 limousine, which Patti Boyd drove since she was sober. The folk club took place in a hospital social club, and I had a bit of trouble finding it. Finally we got the car quite close. I had a six-string and a twelve-string guitar with me, so I said to John, 'I'm pretty late, and I've never been here before. I'll run ahead to let them know I'm here, in case they're panicking. Could you bring my guitars once you've found somewhere to park?' No problem.

I had to go through the door of the social club to a room at the back. A woman was sitting outside the door, selling admission tickets, and I could hear that the floor singing had started inside. I apologised for being late, and she answered 'There's plenty of time, the floor singers have just started, and you won't be on for another half an hour.' Just then Patti Boyd, Eric Clapton and John Martyn came up, Eric carrying one guitar and John the other. The woman said, 'Are your friends musicians?' I was totally gobsmacked, and thought she was kidding, but she was totally serious. I asked why. 'Well if they play they can get in free.' I turned to John and said 'What do you think?' He turned to Eric, who said 'Fair enough, we'll play.' During my sets I sang 'The Band Played Waltzing Matilda' unaccompanied. At the end I got John and Eric up—neither of them were recognised by any member of the audience—and the two played as a duet on my guitars the old blind Gary Davis favourite 'Cocaine.' Then I borrowed a clapped-out Eko which was the only guitar in the place, and as my final number I sang 'Cod Liver Oil And The Orange Juice,' accompanied by John and Eric.

We went back and stayed overnight at Eric's place, staying up till all hours, there's a tape somewhere of me playing guitar there while Eric plays drums.**"**

BACKLESS IRISH TOUR 1979

BAND LINEUP:
Eric Clapton: guitars, vocals
Albert Lee: guitars, vocals
Carl Radle: bass
Jamie Oldaker: drums
Dick Sims: keyboards

Eric's equipment for the tour:

3 Fender Stratocasters, a 1956 model (Blackie), a 1954, and another 1956. He used a Music Man HD 130R amp, Music Man 2 x 12=inch cabinet (JBL speakers), Leslie speaker cabinet, "Cry Baby" wah-wah pedal, MXR Analog Delay

FEBRUARY 1979

20 February 1979–28 February 1979, rehearsals

MARCH 1979

1 March 1979–03 March 1979, rehearsals

8 March 1979, City Hall, Cork, Ireland

SETLIST: Loving You Is Sweeter Than Ever / Worried Life Blues / Badge / Wonderful Tonight / Crossroads / If I Don't Be There By Morning / Double Trouble / Tulsa Time / Early In The Morning / Cocaine / Key To The Highway / Carnival / Setting Me Up

9 March 1979, St. John's CYMS Hall, Tralee, County Kerry, Ireland

10 March 1979, day off

11 March 1979, Leisureland, Galway, Ireland

12 March 1979, Savoy Theatre, Limerick, Ireland

13 March 1979, Baymount Hotel, Strandhill, Sligo, Ireland

14 March 1979, day off

15 March 1979, Downtown Ballroom, Dundalk, County Louth, Ireland

16 March 1979, Army Camp Drill Hall, Dublin, Ireland

17 March 1979, National Stadium, Dublin, Ireland

SETLIST: Loving You Is Sweeter Than Ever / Worried Life Blues / Badge / Wonderful Tonight / Crossroads / Double Trouble / Setting Me Up / Tulsa Time / Early In The Morning / Cocaine / Layla / Further On Up The Road

BACKLESS USA TOUR 1979 (FIRST LEG)

BAND LINEUP:
Eric Clapton: guitars, vocals
Albert Lee: guitars, vocals
Carl Radle: bass
Jamie Oldaker: drums
Dick Sims: keyboards

Eric's equipment for the tour:

3 Fender Stratocasters, a 1956 model (Blackie), a 1954, and another 1956. He used a Music Man HD 130R amp, Music Man 2 x 12-inch cabinet (JBL speakers), Leslie speaker cabinet, "Cry Baby" wah-wah pedal, MXR Analog Delay

28 March 1979, Community Center, Tucson, Arizona (with Muddy Waters)

29 March 1979, Civic Center, Albuquerque, New Mexico (with Muddy Waters)

30 March 1979, day off

31 March 1979, University of Texas Special Events Center, El Paso, Texas (with Muddy Waters)

APRIL 1979

1 April 1979, Chaparral Center, Midland, Texas (with Muddy Waters)

2 April 1979, day off

3 April 1979, Lloyd Noble Center, Norman, Oklahoma (with Muddy Waters)

4 April 1979, Hammons Center, Springfield, Missouri (with Muddy Waters)

SETLIST: Badge / If I Don't Be There By Morning / Lay Down Sally / Wonderful Tonight / Tulsa Time / Early In The Morning / Knockin' On Heaven's Door / Setting Me Up / Watch Out For Lucy / Crossroads / Double Trouble / Cocaine / Layla / Further On Up The Road

5 April 1979, day off

6 April 1979, Assembly Center, Tulsa, Oklahoma (with Muddy Waters)

7 April 1979, Convention Center, Pine Bluff, Arkansas (with Muddy Waters)

8 April 1979, day off

9 April 1979, Summit, Houston, Texas (with Muddy Waters)

10 April 1979, Tarrant County Convention Center, Fort Worth, Texas (with Muddy Waters)

SETLIST: Badge / Worried Life Blues / If I Don't Be There By Morning / Tulsa Time / Early In The Morning / Watch Out For Lucy / Wonderful Tonight / Lay Down Sally / Setting Me Up / Double Trouble / Cocaine / Layla / Further On Up The Road

11 April 1979, Municipal Auditorium, Austin, Texas (with Muddy Waters)

12 April 1979, Convention Center, San Antonio, Texas (with Muddy Waters)

13 April 1979, day off

14 April 1979, Civic Center, Monroe, Louisiana (with Muddy Waters)

15 April 1979, Municipal Auditorium, New Orleans, Louisiana (with Muddy Waters)

SETLIST: Badge / Worried Life Blues / If I Don't Be There By Morning / Tulsa Time / Early In The Morning / Watch Out For Lucy / Wonderful Tonight / Lay Down Sally / Setting Me Up / Double Trouble / Cocaine / Layla / Further On Up The Road

16 April 1979, day off

17 April 1979, Freedom Hall, Johnson City, Tennessee (with Muddy Waters)

18 April 1979, Coliseum, Knoxville, Tennessee (with Muddy Waters)

19 April 1979, the Great Southeast Music Hall, Atlanta, Georgia (BB King concert. Eric joins BB King onstage, as does Diana Ross)

20 April 1979, University of Alabama Coliseum, Tuscaloosa, Alabama (with Muddy Waters)

SETLIST: Badge / Worried Life Blues / If I Don't Be There By Morning / Tulsa Time / Early in the Morning / Watch Out For Lucy / Wonderful Tonight / Lay Down Sally / Setting Me Up / Double Trouble / Cocaine / Layla / Further On Up The Road

21 April 1979, The Omni, Atlanta, Georgia (with Muddy Waters)

SETLIST: Badge / Worried Life Blues / If I Don't Be There By Morning / Tulsa Time / Early In The Morning / Watch Out For Lucy / Wonderful Tonight / Lay Down Sally / Setting Me Up / Double Trouble / Cocaine / Key To The Highway

22 April 1979, Municipal Auditorium, Mobile, Alabama (with Muddy Waters)

23 April 1979, day off

24 April 1979, William and Mary University, Williamsburg, Virginia (with Muddy Waters)

25 April 1979, Mosque, Richmond, Virginia (with Muddy Waters)

26 April 1979, Capitol Centre, Largo, Washington, D.C., Maryland (with Muddy Waters)

SETLIST: Badge / If I Don't Be There By Morning / Lay Down Sally / Wonderful Tonight / Tulsa Time / Early In The Morning / Crossroads / Watch Out for Lucy / Setting Me Up / Double Trouble / Cocaine / Layla / Standing Around Cryin'

27 April 1979, day off

28 April 1979, Civic Center, Providence, Rhode Island (with Muddy Waters)

SETLIST: Badge / If I Don't Be There By Morning / Lay Down Sally / Wonderful Tonight / Tulsa Time / Early In The Morning / Knocking On Heaven's Door / Crossroads / Setting Me Up / Double Trouble / Cocaine / Layla / Further On Up The Road

29 April 1979, Veterans Memorial Coliseum, New Haven, Connecticut (with Muddy Waters)

30 April 1979, Spectrum, Philadelphia, Pennsylvania (with Muddy Waters)

MAY 1979

11 May 1979, Eric jams with Geogie Fame and others at producer Glyn John's wedding reception in Brighton, East Sussex

20 May 1979, Hurtwood Edge, Surrey (Eric and Pattie celebrate their marriage with family and friends. An amazing jam session took place in the evening with Eric, Paul McCartney, George Harrison, Ringo Starr, Jack Bruce, Lonnie Donegan, Jeff Beck, and Denny Laine, along with many others, who all took turns on stage)

BACKLESS USA TOUR 1979 (SECOND LEG)

BAND LINEUP:
Eric Clapton: guitars, vocals
Albert Lee: guitars, vocals
Carl Radle: bass
Jamie Oldaker: drums
Dick Sims: keyboards

25 May 1979, Civic Center, Augusta, Maine (with Muddy Waters)

SETLIST: Badge / If I Don't Be There By Morning / It's Too Late / Double Trouble / Tulsa Time / Motherless Children / Early In The Morning / Setting Me Up / Sweet Little Lisa / Watch Out For Lucy / Lay Down Sally / Wonderful Tonight / Cocaine / Layla / Further On Up The Road

26 May 1979, Cumberland County Civic Center, Portland, Maine (with Muddy Waters)

27 April 1979, day off

28 May 1979, Civic Center, Binghampton, New York (with Muddy Waters)

29 May 1979, War Memorial Arena, Syracuse, New York (with Muddy Waters)

30 May 1979, War Memorial Coliseum, Rochester, New York (with Muddy Waters)

31 May 1979, day off

JUNE 1979

1 June 1979, Memorial Auditorium, Buffalo, New York (with Muddy Waters)

2 June 1979, Richfield Coliseum, Cleveland, Ohio (with Muddy Waters)

SETLIST: Badge / If I Don't Be There By Morning / Worried Life Blues / Tulsa Time / Early In The Morning / Motherless Children / Crossroads / Double Trouble / Setting Me Up / Watch Out For Lucy / Lay Down Sally / Wonderful Tonight / Cocaine / Layla / Further On Up The Road

3 June 1979, day off

4 June 1979, Sports Arena, Toledo, Ohio (with Muddy Waters)

SETLIST: Badge / If I Don't Be There By Morning / Worried Life Blues / Tulsa Time / Early In The Morning / Knockin' On Heaven's Door / Crossroads / Double Trouble / Setting Me Up / Lay Down Sally / Wonderful Tonight / Cocaine / Layla / Further On Up The Road

5 June 1979, Civic Center, Saginaw, Michigan (with Muddy Waters)

SETLIST: Further On Up the Road / If I Don't Be There / Worried Life Blues / Tulsa Time / Early In The Morning / Crossroads / Double Trouble / Setting Me Up / Cocaine / Layla / Badge

6 June 1979, day off

7 June 1979, Riverfront Coliseum, Cincinnati, Ohio (with Muddy Waters)

8 June 1979, Market Square Arena, Indianapolis, Indiana (with Muddy Waters)

9 June 1979, Dane County Exposition Center, Madison, Wisconsin (with Muddy Waters)

SETLIST: Badge / If I Don't Be There By Morning / Worried Life Blues / Crossroads / Knockin' On Heaven's Door / Tulsa Time / Early In The Morning / Watch Out For Lucy / Setting Me Up / Ramblin' On My Mind / Mean Old World / Have You Ever Loved A Woman / Lay Down Sally / Wonderful Tonight / Cocaine / Layla / Further On Up The Road

10 June1979, Civic Center, St. Paul, Minnesota (with Muddy Waters)

11 June 1979, day off

12 June 1979, Chicago Stadium, Chicago, Illinois (with Muddy Waters)

SETLIST: Badge / If I Don't Be There By Morning / Worried Life Blues / Crossroads / Knocking On Heavens Door / Tulsa Time / Early In The Morning / Watch Out For Lucy / Setting Me Up / Double Trouble / Lay Down Sally / Wonderful Tonight / Cocaine / Layla / Long Distance Call* / Kansas City*

*with Muddy Waters and Johnny Winter on guitars

Eric also joined in Muddy Waters's support spot for his encore of "Got My Mojo Working" along with Willie Dixon and Johnny Winter at the Chicago show tonight.

"The only change in his band from when it appeared at the Arena in 1975 was the substitution of Albert Lee for George Terry on rhythm guitar.

It has always remained Clapton's music rather than his role as a performing musician 'on stage' which is his strong point. He's really not all that exciting to watch. Sometimes it seems he would be better off with someone else fronting the band so he could just come out and do his thing when he feels like it. In fact, at the 1975 concert the net impression was: 'Histronics is not Clapton's bag...his stage presence is somewhere between creeping nonchalance and terminal casualness.' But things have changed somewhat. Nowadays, for instance, he doesn't sport a beard—and it actually looks like he is enjoying what he's doing. There's more interaction between him and his sidemen, even with his audience. And there were other things. For his '75 concert he opened with his monster hit, 'Layla' and just about blew the lid off the place with the first downbeat. At Friday's concert, about 75 minutes into what was scheduled to be a 90-minute set, he had yet to barrel into it although there were hundreds shouting for it after every number. All in all it was a rare concert. The crowd was low-key and orderly, just soaking up the music. Quite nice for a change."
—THE *INDIANAPOLIS STAR*

"The sound was lean and right, with Albert Lee adding appealing harmonies to such recent hits as 'Lay Down Sally,' as well as doubling on electric piano. A trio of slow blues gave Clapton his pedestal, and he twisted off runs with a shake of the head that brought BB King to mind. His touch was beautifully precise, if sometimes automatic."
—*ROLLING STONE*
(review by John Milward)

13 June 1979, Wings Stadium, Kalamazoo, Michigan (with Muddy Waters)

14 June 1979, day off

15 June 1979, Notre Dame University, South Bend, Indiana (with Muddy Waters)

16 June 1979, Brown County Veterans Memorial Coliseum, Green Bay, Wisconsin (with Muddy Waters)

17 June 1979, Civic Auditorium, Omaha, Nebraska (Eric jams with McGuinn, Clark & Hillman on the Byrds' classic "Eight Miles High")

18 June 1979, Civic Auditorium, Omaha, Nebraska (with Muddy Waters; Roger McGuinn jams with Eric on "Knockin' On Heaven's Door")

19 June 1979, Kansas Coliseum, Wichita, Kansas (with Muddy Waters)

20 June 1979, day off

21 June 1979, Salt Palace Arena, Salt Lake City, Utah (with Muddy Waters)

22 June 1979, day off

23 June 1979, Coliseum, Spokane, Washington (with Muddy Waters)

24 June 1979, Coliseum, Seattle, Washington (with Muddy Waters)

SETLIST: Badge / If I Don't Be There By Morning / Worried Life Blues / Crossroads / Knockin' On Heaven's Door / Tulsa Time / Early In The Morning / Setting Me Up / Double Trouble / Lay Down Sally / Wonderful Tonight / Cocaine / Standing Around Crying*

*with Muddy Waters on vocals and guitar

By the end of his US 1979 tour, Eric was drifting away from his long-serving band members who had been with him since 1974. He was feeling disenchanted with the music being produced and longed for a new sound. In what was seen as a cold move on his part, Eric fired Carl Radle, Jamie Oldaker, and Dick Sims by telegram from the safety of his UK home. Eric was not strong enough mentally to handle firing them face-to-face. He regretted the way he handled the situation and was particularly sad that he never saw Carl Radle again. The two had had a special bond, and sadly, Carl died of a kidney infection due to alcoholism and drug addiction on 30 May 1980. A tragic loss.

After the firing, Eric went about hiring an all-English band, which he knew would give him a new sound and perhaps a fresh perspective. Albert Lee was still in the band, and the new members selected were Chris Stainton, Henry Spinetti, and Dave Markee. He had already played with them in the studio over the years and was familiar with their sound. All were seasoned veterans of the road, as well as studio, and would provide Eric with a solid backing. They rehearsed for several weeks at Sandown Park Racecourse in August and went on to play a couple of warm-up dates in Cranleigh and Hanley. Eric loved tradition, and on the way back from the Hanley gig, the whole band stopped off at the infamous Blue Boar service station on the M1. It was usual for Eric to do this whenever he would be touring up north and heading home via the M1. He loved it! The Blue Boar was the place all bands liked to stop off at for a break and for huge plate of greasy fare. He asked Roger Forrester to hand over some cash, which reminded him of his days playing clubs and getting paid in cash after the event.

After a week's break, the band then headed off to Austria and Germany before visiting Eastern Europe for the first time. After Poland they headed off to play several dates in Israel, which Eric particularly liked. He found the audiences warm and receptive.

UK, EUROPEAN, AND EAST EUROPEAN TOUR 1979

BAND LINEUP:
Eric Clapton: guitar, vocals,
Albert Lee: guitar, keyboards. vocals
Dave Markee: bass
Henry Spinetti: drums
Chris Stainton: keyboards

Eric's equipment for the tour:

3 Fender Stratocasters, a 1956 model (Blackie), a 1954, and another 1956. He used a Music Man HD 130R amp, Music Man 2 x 12-inch cabinet (JBL speakers), Leslie speaker cabinet, "Cry Baby" wah-wah pedal, MXR Analog Delay

SEPTEMBER 1979

7 September 1979, Cranleigh Village Hall, Cranleigh, Surrey

30 September 1979, Victoria Hall, Hanley, Staffordshire

SETLIST: Badge / Worried Life Blues / If I Don't Be There By Morning / Tulsa Time / Early In The Morning / Watch Out For Lucy / Wonderful Tonight / Setting Me Up / Tipitina / Lay Down Sally / All Our Past Times / Double Trouble / After Midnight / Knockin' On Heaven's Door / Country Boy / Key To The Highway / Cocaine / Further On Up The Road / Blues Power

6 October 1979, Stadthalle, Wien, Austria

SETLIST: Badge / If I Don't Be There By Morning / Worried Life Blues / Tulsa Time / Early In The Morning / Lay Down Sally / Wonderful Tonight / Country Boy / Double Trouble / Blues Power / Knockin' On Heaven's Door / After Midnight / Sign Language / Setting Me Up / Tipitina / Motherless Children / Cocaine / Further On Up The Road

7 October 1979, Sporthalle, Linz, Austria

8 October 1979, Messehalle, Nuremberg, Germany

9 October 1979, fly to Belgrade

10 October 1979, Pioneer Hall, Belgrade, Yugoslavia

> **❝**This was no ordinary gig. A spine-tingling performance by Clapton and the taut economical, no-nonsense drums of Henry Spinetti, the rock-solid foundation of Dave Markee's bass, the splendour of Albert Lee's guitar acrobatics which he makes look so simple, and the quiet excellence of Chris Stainton's keyboard work added up to a very special performance. Excepting Cream, which was unique for its period, this is undoubtedly Clapton's best band.**❞**
> —*MUSICIANS ONLY*

11 October 1979, Dom Sportova, Zagreb, Yugoslavia

12 October 1979, Dom Sportova, Zagreb, Yugoslavia

13 October 1979, day off

14 October 1979, fly to Warsaw

15 October 1979, Sala Kongresowa, Warsaw, Poland

16 October 1979, Sala Kongresowa, Warsaw, Poland

SETLIST: Worried Life Blues / If I Don't Be There By Morning / Tulsa Time / Early In The Morning / Lay Down Sally / Wonderful Tonight / Country Boy / Double Trouble / Blues Power / Knockin' On Heaven's Door / After Midnight / Tipitina / Setting Me Up / Badge / Sign Language / Key To The Highway / Cocaine / Layla/ Further On Up The Road

17 October 1979, Hala Sportowa, Katowice, Poland

SETLIST: If I Don't Be There By Morning / Worried Life Blues / Tulsa Time / Early In The Morning / Lay Down Sally / Wonderful Tonight / Country Boy / Double Trouble / Blues Power / Knockin' On Heaven's Door / Thunder And Lightning / After Midnight / Setting Me Up / Willie And The Hand Jive / Key To The Highway / Cocaine / Layla

(The first of the two concerts planned in Katowice proved traumatic for Eric Clapton. As fans rushed the stage to get a better view, the security guards forcibly removed them, spraying them with tear gas. House lights were turned on to reveal a row of security guards. Eric was totally powerless because of the language barrier. No encore was performed, and the next night's concert was canceled at the last moment. Eric's view on Poland is direct and to the point: "I've never known a country to be so honestly corrupt. I wanted to see the place for a change of view and because it seemed good for the kids who don't get much Western rock.

18 October 1979, Hala Sportowa, Katowice, Poland (canceled)

19 October 1979, fly to Frankfurt

20 October 1979, fly to Tel Aviv

21 October 1979, Heichal Hatarbut Mann Auditorium, Tel Aviv, Israel

22 October 1979, Heichal Hatarbut Mann Auditorium, Tel Aviv, Israel

23 October 1979, Heichal Hatarbut Mann Auditorium, Tel Aviv, Israel

24 October 1979, day off

25 October 1979, Heichal Hatarbut Mann Auditorium, Tel Aviv, Israel

26 October 1979, day off

27 October 1979, Binyanei Ha'Ooma, Jerusalem, Israel

SETLIST: If I Don't Be There By Morning / Worried Life Blues / Tulsa Time / Early In The Morning / Lay Down Sally / Wonderful Tonight / Country Boy / Double Trouble / Blues Power / Knockin' On Heaven's Door / After Midnight / Tipitina / Setting Me Up / All Our Past Times / Cocaine / Layla / Further On Up The Road

28 October 1979, day off

29 October 1979, Eric and his band fly home

During the tour, Eric admitted to Ray Coleman that he was "now starting to feel the effects of middle age. It's just hitting me that I can't do all the things I used to every day when I was 21 or 22. Then, I'd easily do two shows a night and an all-nighter. Now, that schedule would grind me to a halt. It's time for guys like me to ease up a little bit. Rock's emotionally and physically draining because you're constantly trying to invent something new."

He looked tired during the tour, particularly in Poland, which had not been a pleasant experience for him playing in a police state where fans would be badly treated for simply enjoying the music. Eric had no control over the matter and could not wait to leave the country.

RSO had decided that it would be a good time for a new live album from Eric that would cover material from his last few releases. They had recorded shows in 1977 and 1978 and nothing was released. So it did not look good for these shows, either, as Eric did not like live albums. Jon Astley was hired to record the shows. Tape machines were set up in a dressing room in the backstage area with wires leading from the stage into the makeshift studio. Jon also had a monitor screen in the room so he could keep an eye on what was happening onstage. When the album was released in 1980, Jon was unfairly criticized for making the record sound like a studio album. In reality, he perfectly captured the mood, atmosphere, and hall acoustics. If anyone doubted that, there are bootleg audience recordings of the first-night show circulating among collectors and the sound is identical, albeit not as crisp as a professional recording. The album remains one of Eric's best-sounding live albums.

FAR EAST TOUR 1979

BAND LINEUP:
Eric Clapton: guitar, vocals
Albert Lee: guitar, keyboards, vocals
Dave Markee: bass
Henry Spinetti: drums
Chris Stainton: keyboards

NOVEMBER 1979

13 November 1979, Eric and his band fly to Bangkok

14 November 1979, day off

15 November 1979, day off

16 November 1979, National Theatre, Bangkok, Thailand

17 November 1979, fly to Manila

18 November 1979, Araneta Coliseum Cinema, Manila, Philippines

19 November 1979, fly to Hong Kong

20 November 1979, Academic Community Hall, Hong Kong

21 November 1979, fly to Tokyo

22 November 1979, day off

23 November 1979, Kenmin Bunka Center, Ibaragi, Japan

SETLIST: If I Don't Be There By Morning / Worried Life Blues / Tulsa Time / Early In The Morning / Lay Down Sally / Wonderful Tonight / Country Boy / Ramblin' On My Mind / Have You Ever Loved A Woman / Blues Power / Knockin' On Heaven's Door / After Midnight / Tipitina / Setting Me Up / Badge / All Our Past Times / Cocaine / Layla / Further On Up The Road

24 November 1979, day off

25 November 1979, Nagoyashi Kokaido, Nagoya, Japan

SETLIST: Tulsa Time / Early In The Morning / Lay Down Sally / Wonderful Tonight / Willie And The Hand Jive / Ramblin' On My Mind / Tore Down / Mean Old World / Dust My Broom / Country Boy / All Our Past Times / Blues Power / Knockin' On Heaven's Door / Setting Me Up / Worried Life Blues / After Midnight / Key To The Highway / Cocaine / Layla / Further On Up The Road

26 November 1979, Kyoto Kaikan Daiichi Hall, Kyoto, Japan

SETLIST: Early In The Morning / Lay Down Sally / Wonderful Tonight / If I Don't Be There By Morning / Worried Life Blues / Country Boy / All Our Past Times / Blues Power / Double Trouble / Knocking On Heaven's Door / Setting Me Up / Ramblin' On My Mind / Have You Ever Loved A Woman / After Midnight / Cocaine / Layla / Further On Up The Road

27 November 1979, Koseinenkin Kaikan Dai Hall, Osaka, Japan

SETLIST: Tulsa Time / Early In The Morning / Lay Down Sally / Wonderful Tonight / If I Don't Be There By Morning / Worried Life Blues / Country Boy / All Our Past Times / Blues Power / Double Trouble / Knockin' On Heaven's Door / Setting Me Up / Ramblin' On My Mind / Have You Ever Loved A Woman / Cocaine / Layla / Further On Up The Road

28 November 1979, Yubin Chokin Hall, Hiroshima, Japan

SETLIST: Tulsa Time / Early In The Morning / Lay Down Sally / Wonderful Tonight / If I Don't Be There By Morning / Worried Life Blues / Country Boy / All Our Past Times / Blues Power / Double Trouble / Knocking On Heaven's Door / Setting Me Up / Ramblin' On My Mind / Have You Ever Loved a Woman / Five Long Years / Cocaine / Layla / Further On Up The Road

29 November 1979, day off

30 November 1979, Shin-Nittestsu Taiikukan, Kokura, Japan

SETLIST: Tulsa Time / Early In The Morning / Lay Down Sally / Wonderful Tonight / If I Don't Be There By Morning / Worried Life Blues / Country Boy / All Our Past Times / Blues Power / Double Trouble / Knockin' On Heaven's Door / Setting Me Up / Ramblin' On My Mind / Crossroads / Have You Ever Loved a Woman / Cocaine / Layla / Further On Up The Road

DECEMBER 1979

1 December 1979, Furitsu Taiikukan, Osaka, Japan

SETLIST: Tulsa Time / Early In The Morning / Lay Down Sally / Wonderful Tonight / If I Don't Be There By Morning / Worried Life Blues / Country Boy / All Our Past Times / Blues Power / Double Trouble / Knockin' On Heaven's Door / Setting Me Up / Ramblin' On My Mind / Mean Old World / Have You Ever Loved A Woman / Cocaine / Layla / Further On Up The Road

2 December 1979, day off

3 December 1979, Budokan, Tokyo, Japan

Reel 1

Tulsa Time (Danny Flowers) *Just One Night* double album US RSO RS 2-4202, UK RSO 2479240 released May 1980 / *Just One Night* double CD US Polydor 531827, UK Polydor 531 827-2 released September 1996

Early In The Morning (Traditional; arranged by Eric Clapton) *Just One Night* double album US RSO RS 2-4202, UK RSO 2479240 released May 1980 / *Just One Night* double CD US Polydor 531827, UK Polydor 531 827-2 released September 1996

Lay Down Sally (Eric Clapton / Marcy Levy / George Terry) unreleased

Reel 2

Wonderful Tonight (Eric Clapton) unreleased

If I Don't Be There By Morning (Bob Dylan / Helena Springs) unreleased

Worried Life Blues (Maceo Merriweather) unreleased

Reel 3

Country Boy (Albert Lee) unreleased

Double Trouble (Otis Rush) unreleased

Reel 4

All Our Past Times (Eric Clapton / Rick Danko) unreleased

Front cover of Eric Clapton's Just One Night *album recorded over two nights at the Budokan in Tokyo on 3 and 4 December 1978.*

Blues Power (Eric Clapton / Leon Russell) unreleased

Reel 5

Knocking On Heaven's Door (Bob Dylan) unreleased

Setting Me Up (Mark Knopfler) unreleased

Reel 6

Ramblin' On My Mind (Robert Johnson) / **Have You Ever Loved A Woman** (Billy Myles) unreleased

Reel 7

After Midnight (JJ Cale) *Just One Night* double album US RSO RS 2-4202, UK RSO 2479240 released May 1980 / *Just One Night* double CD US Polydor 531827, UK Polydor 531 827-2 released September 1996

Cocaine (JJ Cale) unreleased

Reel 8

Layla (Eric Clapton / Jim Gordon) unreleased

Further On Up The Road (Joe Veasey / Don Robey) unreleased

```
Eric Clapton: guitar, vocals
Albert Lee: guitar, keyboards, vocals, lead
vocals on "Country Boy" and "Setting Me Up"
Dave Markee: bass
Henry Spinetti: drums
Chris Stainton: keyboards

Producer: Jon Astley
Engineer: Jon Astley
```

4 December 1979, Budokan, Tokyo, Japan

SETLIST:

Reel 1

Tulsa Time (Danny Flowers) unreleased

Early In The Morning (Traditional; arranged by Eric Clapton) unreleased

Reel 2

Lay Down Sally (Eric Clapton / Marcy Levy / George Terry) *Just One Night* double album US RSO RS 2-4202, UK RSO 2479240 released May 1980 / *Just One Night* double CD US Polydor 531827, UK Polydor 531 827-2 released September 1996

Wonderful Tonight (Eric Clapton) *Just One Night* double album US RSO RS 2-4202, UK RSO 2479240 released May 1980 / *Just One Night* double CD US Polydor 531827, UK Polydor 531 827-2 released September 1996

If I Don't Be There By Morning (Bob Dylan / Helena Springs) *Just One Night* double album US RSO RS 2-4202, UK RSO 2479240 released May 1980 / *Just One Night* double CD US Polydor 531827, UK Polydor 531 827-2 released September 1996

Reel 3

Worried Life Blues (Maceo Merriweather) *Just One Night* double album US RSO RS 2-4202, UK RSO 2479240 released May 1980 / *Just One Night* double CD US Polydor 531827, UK Polydor 531 827-2 released September 1996

Country Boy (Albert Lee) unreleased

Reel 4

All Our Past Times (Eric Clapton / Rick Danko) *Just One Night* double album US RSO RS 2-4202, UK RSO 2479240 released May 1980 / *Just One Night* double CD US Polydor 531827, UK Polydor 531 827-2 released September 1996

Blues Power (Eric Clapton / Leon Russell) *Just One Night* double album US RSO RS 2-4202, UK RSO 2479240 released May 1980 / *Just One Night* double CD US Polydor 531827, UK Polydor 531 827-2 released September 1996

Reel 5

Double Trouble (Otis Rush) *Just One Night* double album US RSO RS 2-4202, UK RSO 2479240 released May 1980 / *Just One Night* double CD US Polydor 531827, UK Polydor 531 827-2 released September 1996

Knockin' On Heaven's Door (Bob Dylan) *Time Pieces, Vol. 2: Live in the '70s* UK-only RSO RSD 5022 released May 1983 / *Time Pieces, Vol. 2: Live in the '70s* CD Polydor 811835 released November 1988

Reel 6

Setting Me Up (Mark Knopfler) *Just One Night* double album US RSO RS 2-4202, UK RSO 2479240 released May 1980 / *Just One Night* double CD US Polydor 531827, UK Polydor 531 827-2 released September 1996

Ramblin' On My Mind (Robert Johnson) / **Have You Ever Loved A Woman** (Billy Myles) *Just One Night* double album US RSO RS 2-4202, UK RSO 2479240 released May 1980 / *Just One Night* double CD US Polydor 531827, UK Polydor 531 827-2 released September 1996

Reel 7

Cocaine (JJ Cale) *Just One Night* double album US RSO RS 2-4202, UK RSO 2479240 released May 1980 / *Just One Night* double CD US Polydor 531827, UK Polydor 531 827-2 released September 1996

"I'd known Eric from when I worked with him on his Slowhand and Backless albums as Glyn John's assistant. In fact I'd engineered 'Tulsa Time' entirely because Glyn was at the dentist I think. Eric and I got on really well and he said to me, 'come and do a live record with me.' He flew me to Israel to see the band. He used to do these peculiar tours and he said, 'you can come and see me in in either Belgrade, Yugoslavia, Poland or Israel.' So I flew out to Tel Aviv and I spent several days with Eric. I knew most of the band anyway because I'd actually put that band together to produce an album for A&M by an artist called Bryn Haworth ('Keep The Ball Rolling' A&M Records AMLH 68507), Henry Spinetti on drums and Dave Markee on bass, who were now in Eric's backing band. As I knew them, the Israel trip was a pointless exercise really, except to listen to the set and talk about where to do it. Eric asked me, 'what do you think?' I said, 'everyone seems to be making great records in Tokyo at the moment.'

Eric was due out there in two or three months' time, so I said I'd look into it and set it up. We used the same set up as Cheap Trick and Bob Dylan had used. Originally I thought it would be a mobile recording truck, but when I got to the gig in Tokyo, at about 10 o'clock in the morning, there was no truck there. I waited and they rolled up at about 12 and it wasn't a truck. It was a van loaded with gear and they set up a studio in one of the dressing rooms. They had the whole thing plugged up and working in about two hours. It was just incredible. Obviously, they had done it several times before. I was very impressed. There was nothing really wrong with the room apart from a bit of reflection on a wall which they dampened down for me. We had no soundcheck other than a roadie hitting the drums. As the band started I was poised over the mic gain controls on the board and as they went into 'Tulsa Time' all the needles were peaking at zero and it was just perfect. I thought, this sounds quite good just as it is—don't touch anything! And that's how it went down. We recorded both nights and I had just guessed the mic levels because I had no idea how loud people were going to play guitars or anything. Then I was supposed to hide because Eric had forgotten that the shows were being recorded. Roger Forrester, Eric's manager, told me to hide! Unfortunately, just before the gig started I went to the loo and Eric's standing next to me and said, 'you alright then Jon?' I'm sure he knew damn well we were recording, but Roger kept telling me that Eric mustn't see the mics on stage. So I had to hide the audience mics and I had to take splits off the PA mics and I had to duck and dive backstage at the Budokan and keep out of everybody's way.

I did have a tv monitor in my room with a view from the balcony of them on stage. I think it was a little camera, but burnt out from the sun or laser from another show or something. So it wasn't much of a view, but it didn't matter. I knew the set roughly and it was just a question of getting it all on tape and sorting it out afterwards. Most live recordings are like that. The nice thing was when I got back to Olympic Studios I said I would disappear for a couple of weeks and listen to both shows and do some trial mixing and that sort of thing. I called up bass player Dave Markee because he had this horrendous thing where he just went for a key change in the middle of 'Ramblin' On My Mind' and went 'booonnng' and hit the wrong note on one of the nights. He remembered exactly the moment and he came in to Olympic and just overdubbed the correct note. That is the only overdub on that record which I was so pleased about.

When it came to remastering it for CD I thought the whole show should be released. Eric didn't want to do that and said that 'Layla' should never be on it anyway. I did remix it before remastering it but Bill Levenson didn't like the remixes that I did, so he used the quarter-inch mixes that I did originally because he felt the same as you [author], that the sound was great to start with. I think I was going for a more ambient sound with the remix but he felt that it was losing its character.

Eric and I became quite good friends and we used to go fishing together. I introduced him to fishing and took him to Roger Daltrey's place to try out in his lakes and about three months later Eric rang up and said, 'come fishing!' He'd bought a bit of the River Test and a new car to put all the fishing gear in. Now he goes to Russia and places like that to fish."

—JON ASTLEY

Layla (Eric Clapton / Jim Gordon) unreleased

Reel 8

Further On Up The Road (Joe Veasey / Don Robey) *Just One Night* double album US RSO RS 2-4202, UK RSO 2479240 released May 1980 / *Just One Night* double CD US Polydor 531827, UK Polydor 531 827-2 released September 1996

Eric Clapton: guitar, vocals
Albert Lee: guitar, keyboards, vocals, lead vocals on "Country Boy" and "Setting Me Up"
Dave Markee: bass
Henry Spinetti: drums
Chris Stainton: keyboards

Producer: Jon Astley
Engineer: Jon Astley

Eight reels of eight-track tape were used each night to record at the Budokan. When Eric was told about the recordings after the tour ended, he expressed a preference for the first night, but ultimately it was the majority of the second night that was chosen for the album. Surprisingly, "Layla" was left off the release. The highlight has to be the version of "Blues Power" with a great wah-wah solo by Eric. The whole band are locked into the song, showing how exciting these musicians could be on a good night.

"I really didn't want to record it. There's a natural shyness about me when I'm playing onstage. For me it's something that should only happen once, you know, and then it's gone. The album was one show. We did two nights, and recorded both. I think they chose the one I didn't like.**"**

—ERIC CLAPTON

5 December 1979, day off

6 December 1979, Sangyo Kyoshin Kaijo, Sapporo, Japan

SETLIST: Tulsa Time / Early In The Morning / Lay Down Sally / Wonderful Tonight / If I Don't Be There By Morning / Worried Life Blues / Country Boy / All Our Past Times / Blues Power / Double Trouble / Knockin' On Heaven's Door / Setting Me Up / Ramblin' On My Mind / Have You Ever Loved A Woman / Cocaine / Layla / Further On Up The Road

7 December 1979, fly to Tokyo

8 December 1979, Eric and his band fly back to London

1979 RECORDING SESSIONS
OLYMPIC STUDIOS
117-123 Church Road,
Barnes, London SW13
Session for Marc Benno
Lost In Austin

JANUARY 1979

HOTFOOT BLUES (Marc Benno / Irvin Benno) *Lost In Austin* album A&M SP-4767 released June 1979 / *Lost In Austin* CD Japan only A&M POCM-2095 released October 1998

Marc Benno: vocals, acoustic guitar
Eric Clapton: slide guitar
Jim Keltner: drums
Carl Radle: bass

CHASIN' RAINBOWS (Marc Benno) *Lost In Austin* album A&M SP-4767 released June 1979 / *Lost In Austin* CD Japan only A&M POCM-2095 released October 1998

Marc Benno: vocals, acoustic guitar
Eric Clapton: Dobro
Jim Keltner: drums
Carl Radle: bass
Dick Sims: keyboards
Brian Rogers: strings

ME AND A FRIEND OF MINE (Marc Benno) *Lost In Austin* album A&M SP-4767 released June 1979 / *Lost In Austin* CD Japan only A&M POCM-2095 released October 1998

Marc Benno: vocals, acoustic guitar
Albert Lee: guitar and solo
Eric Clapton: guitar
Jim Keltner: drums
Carl Radle: bass
Dick Sims: keyboards

LAST TRAIN (Marc Benno / Irvin Benno) *Lost In Austin* album A&M SP-4767 released June 1979 / *Lost In Austin* CD Japan only A&M POCM-2095 released October 1998

Marc Benno: vocals
Albert Lee: guitar
Eric Clapton: guitar and solos
Jim Keltner: drums
Carl Radle: bass
Dick Sims: keyboards

LOST IN AUSTIN (Marc Benno) *Lost In Austin* album A&M SP-4767 released June 1979 / *Lost In Austin* CD Japan only A&M POCM-2095 released October 1998

Marc Benno: vocals, acoustic guitar
Albert Lee: guitar and solos
Eric Clapton: guitar
Jim Keltner: drums
Carl Radle: bass
Dick Sims: keyboards
Brian Rogers: strings

SPLISH SPLASH (Bobby Darin / Jean Murray) *Lost In Austin* album A&M SP-4767 released June 1979 / *Lost In Austin* CD Japan only A&M POCM-2095 released October 1998

Marc Benno: vocals
Albert Lee: guitar
Eric Clapton: guitar
Jim Keltner: drums
Carl Radle: bass
Dick Sims: keyboards
Dick Morrissey: sax

MONTERREY PEN (Marc Benno) *Lost In Austin* album A&M SP-4767 released June 1979 / *Lost In Austin* CD Japan only A&M POCM-2095 released October 1998

Marc Benno: vocals
Albert Lee: guitar
Eric Clapton: guitar and solo
Jim Keltner: drums
Carl Radle: bass
Dick Sims: keyboards

HEY THERE SENORITA (Marc Benno) *Lost In Austin* album A&M SP-4767 released June 1979 / *Lost In Austin* CD Japan only A&M POCM-2095 released October 1998

Marc Benno: vocals, acoustic guitar, backing vocals
Albert Lee: guitar, backing vocals
Eric Clapton: acoustic guitar and solos, backing vocals
Jim Keltner: drums
Carl Radle: bass
Dick Sims: keyboards

Engineer: Glyn Johns
Producer: Glyn Johns

> "We were doing a session in early 1979 at Olympic, playing on a Marc Benno album for A&M. The rhythm section was most of his band and he hit on the idea of having me join the band. That's how it came about. I decided to take a chance and it's been good. It's been a lot of fun but it's not something I could see myself doing for very long because of its limitations."
>
> **—ALBERT LEE**

Danny Douma: guitar, vocals
Eric Clapton: guitar
Mick Fleetwood: drums
John McVie: bass
Christine McVie: keyboards

Producers: Danny Douma and Nick Van Maarth
Engineer: Nick Van Maarth

THE VILLAGE RECORDER
1616 Butler Avenue, West Los Angeles
Session for Danny Douma
Night Eyes

MARCH 1979

I HATE YOU (Danny Douma) *Night Eyes* album Warner Bros. BSK 3326 released August 1979 / *Night Eyes* CD Wounded Bird WOU 3326 released 2006

DJM STUDIOS
71-75 New Oxford Street, London W1
Session for John Martyn
"Grace And Danger"

11 AUGUST 1979

Eric only turned up for one day and took everyone by surprise, except John, who knew that he would be coming by for a session. Unfortunately, the day ended up being full of self-indulgent jamming with no real attempt at songs being made. The jams are on tape but not worthy of release.

24

1980

In 1980 Eric was slowly coming to terms with his drinking as well as trying to reconnect with his blues roots. It would take a few more years of hardship for Eric before deciding to try and help himself and go to rehab. It would be a long and difficult struggle.

The early part of the year was spent doing some guest sessions with Ronnie Lane as well as playing on Gary Brooker's new single. Eric asked Gary to join the band in February and together recorded a new studio album which RSO decided was not good enough to be released. A short UK tour was booked for May 1980, the first in eighteen months. The idea was to get the band warmed up before entering the studio to attempt another new record. The shows in the UK lasted around two hours, and Eric would give Gary and Albert slots so he could take a break from lead vocals.

The sessions for what became *Another Ticket* took place in the Bahamas during July and August. The fabulous surroundings must have been a source of inspiration as Eric recorded a popular blues-tinged album. After a short Scandinavian tour in September, the group retired for the rest of the year, although Eric did play on the odd session as a guest.

Advert for Eric Clapton's 1980 UK tour and Just One Night double album.

JUST ONE NIGHT UK TOUR 1980

BAND LINEUP:
Eric Clapton: guitar, vocals
Albert Lee: guitar, vocals
Dave Markee: bass
Henry Spinetti: drums
Chris Stainton: keyboards
Gary Brooker: keyboards, vocals

APRIL 1980

14 April 1980–25 April 1980, rehearsals, 203b Upper Richmond Road, Putney, London SW15

MAY 1980

2 May 1980, New Theatre, Oxford, Oxfordshire (with Chas & Dave)

3 May 1980, Conference Centre, Brighton, East Sussex (with Chas & Dave)

SETLIST: Tulsa Time / Early In The Morning / Lay Down Sally / Wonderful Tonight / Country Boy / Hold On / Blues Power / All Our Pastimes / Setting Me Up / Leave The Candle / If I Don't Be There / Rambling On My Mind / Have You Ever Loved A Woman / Home Lovin' / Key To The Highway / Cocaine / Further On Up The Road

4 May 1980, Bingley Hall, Stafford, Staffordshire (with Chas & Dave)

5 May 1980, day off

6 May 1980, Lancaster University, Lancaster (canceled)

7 May 1980, City Hall, Newcastle, Tyne & Wear (with Chas & Dave)

SETLIST: Tulsa Time / Early In The Morning / Lay Down Sally / Wonderful Tonight / Country Boy / Thunder And Lightning / Blues Power / All Our Past Times / Setting Me Up / Leave The Candle / If I Don't Be There By Morning / Rambling On My Mind / Mean Old World / Have You Ever Loved A Woman / Home Lovin' / After Midnight / Cocaine / Further On Up The Road

8 May 1980, Odeon, Edinburgh, Scotland (with Chas & Dave)

9 May 1980, Apollo Theatre, Glasgow, Scotland (with Chas & Dave)

10 May 1980, day off

11 May 1980, Leisure Centre, Deeside, Aberdeenshire, Scotland (with Chas & Dave)

12 May 1980, Coventry Theatre, Coventry, West Midlands (with Chas & Dave)

13 May 1980, Hippodrome, Bristol, Gloucestershire (with Chas & Dave)

14 May 1980, day off

15 May 1980, Hammersmith Odeon, London (with Chas & Dave)

16 May 1980, Hammersmith Odeon, London (with Chas & Dave)

17 May 1980, Hammersmith Odeon, London (with Chas & Dave)

SETLIST: Tulsa Time / Early In The Morning / Lay Down Sally / Wonderful Tonight / Country Boy / Hold On / Blues Power / All Our Past Times / Setting Me Up / Leave The Candle / If I Don't Be There By Morning / Rambling On My Mind / Have You Ever Loved A Woman / Home Lovin' / After Midnight / Key To The Highway / Cocaine / Further On Up The Road / Lawdy Miss Clawdy* / Sea Cruise* / Hound Dog* / You Win Again*

*with Chas & Dave

18 May 1980, Civic Hall, Guildford, Surrey (with Chas & Dave)

SETLIST: Tulsa Time / Early In The Morning / Lay Down Sally / Wonderful Tonight / Country Boy / Hold On / Blues Power / Double Trouble / Setting Me Up / Thunder And Lightning / If I Don't Be There By Morning / Ramblin' On My Mind* / Have You Ever Loved A Woman* / Home Lovin' / After Midnight / Cocaine / Further On Up The Road / Long Tall Sally** / Lawdy Miss Clawdy**

*with Jeff Beck on guitar
**with Chas & Dave (Chas Hodges, Dave Peacock)

JUST ONE NIGHT
SCANDINAVIAN TOUR 1980

BAND LINEUP:
Eric Clapton: guitar, vocals
Albert Lee: guitar, vocals
Dave Markee: bass
Henry Spinetti: drums
Chris Stainton: keyboards
Gary Brooker: keyboards, vocals

19 September 1980, Aalborghallen, Aalborg, Denmark

20 September 1980, Brøndby Hallen, Copenhagen, Denmark

SETLIST: Tulsa Time / Worried Life Blues / Setting Me Up / Lay Down Sally / Wonderful Tonight / Put Your Trust In Me / Whiter Shade Of Pale / Home Lovin' / Country Boy / Double Trouble / Sleeping In The Ground / Blues Power / Rambling On My Mind / Have You Ever Loved A Woman / After Midnight / Cocaine / Layla / Further On Up The Road

21 September 1980, Vejlby-Risskov Hallen, Aarhus, Denmark

23 September 1980, Olympen, Lund, Sweden

24 September 1980, Scandinavium, Gothenburg, Sweden

25 September 1980, Drammenshallen, Oslo, Norway

26 September 1980, day off

27 September 1980, Johanneshovs Isstadion, Stockholm, Sweden

28 September 1980, day off

29 September 1980, Messuhalli, Helsinki, Finland

1980 RECORDING SESSIONS

ERIC CLAPTON GUEST SESSION

RONNIE LANE MOBILE
Fishpool Farm, Hyssington, near Bishop's Castle, Wales
Session for Ronnie Lane *See Me*

JANUARY 1980

LAD'S GOT MONEY (Ronnie Lane) *See Me* album GEM GEMLP 107 released July 1980 / *See Me* CD Edsel EDCD 492 released 1996

Ronnie Lane: vocals
Eric Clapton: guitar
Alun Davies: guitar
Brian Belshaw: bass
Bruce Rowland: drums
Bill Livsey: piano
Carol Grimes: backing vocals

BARCELONA (Ronnie Lane / Eric Clapton) *See Me* album GEM GEMLP 107 released July 1980 / *See Me* CD Edsel EDCD 492 released 1996

Ronnie Lane: vocals
Eric Clapton: guitar
Brian Belshaw: bass
Bruce Rowland: drums
Bill Livsey: piano
Henry McCullough: piano

WAY UP YONDER (Traditional; arranged by Ronnie Lane) *See Me* album GEM GEMLP 107 released July 1980 / *See Me* CD Edsel EDCD 492 released 1996

Ronnie Lane: vocals
Eric Clapton: guitar
Alun Davies: guitar
Brian Belshaw: bass
Bruce Rowland: drums
Bill Livsey: piano
Ian Stewart: piano
White Grit Gang: backing vocals

Producer: Fishpool Productions
Engineer: Bob Potter

SURREY SOUND STUDIOS
70 Kingston Road, Leatherhead, Surrey
Session for untitled album

JANUARY 1980–FEBRUARY 1980

BLUES INSTRUMENTAL #1 (Eric Clapton) unreleased

Eric Clapton: guitar

THERE AIN'T NO MONEY (Eric Clapton) unreleased

Eric Clapton: vocals, slide guitar
Albert Lee: vocals, guitars
Henry Spinetti: drums
Dave Markee: bass

GAME'S UP (Eric Clapton) unreleased

Eric Clapton: vocals, guitar
Albert Lee: backing vocals, guitar
Gary Brooker: backing vocals, keyboards, synth
Chris Stainton: keyboards
Henry Spinetti: drums
Dave Markee: bass

RITA MAE (Eric Clapton) unreleased

Eric Clapton: vocals, guitar
Albert Lee: guitar
Gary Brooker: keyboards
Chris Stainton: keyboards
Henry Spinetti: drums
Dave Markee: bass

FREEDOM (Eric Clapton) unreleased

Eric Clapton: vocals, guitar
Albert Lee: backing vocals, guitar
Gary Brooker: backing vocals, keyboards, synth
Chris Stainton: keyboards
Henry Spinetti: drums
Dave Markee: bass

EVANGELINA (Hoyt Axton / Wayne Higginbotham) unreleased

Eric Clapton: guitar
Albert Lee: vocals, guitar
Gary Brooker: keyboards, synth
Chris Stainton: keyboards
Henry Spinetti: drums
Dave Markee: bass

HOME LOVIN' (Gary Brooker) unreleased

Eric Clapton: vocals, guitar
Albert Lee: guitar, backing vocals
Gary Brooker: vocals, keyboards
Chris Stainton: keyboards
Henry Spinetti: drums
Dave Markee: bass

HOLD ME LORD (Eric Clapton) unreleased

Eric Clapton: vocals, Dobro
Albert Lee: guitar, backing vocals
Gary Brooker: keyboards
Chris Stainton: keyboards
Henry Spinetti: drums
Dave Markee: bass

SOMETHING SPECIAL (Eric Clapton) unreleased

Eric Clapton: vocals, guitar
Albert Lee: guitar, backing vocals
Gary Brooker: keyboards
Chris Stainton: keyboards
Henry Spinetti: drums
Dave Markee: bass

I'D LOVE TO SAY I LOVE YOU (Eric Clapton) unreleased

Eric Clapton: vocals, guitar
Albert Lee: guitar, backing vocals
Gary Brooker: backing vocals, keyboards
Chris Stainton: keyboards
Henry Spinetti: drums
Dave Markee: bass

CATCH ME IF YOU CAN (Eric Clapton / Gary Brooker) unreleased

Eric Clapton: vocals, guitar
Albert Lee: guitar, backing vocals
Gary Brooker: backing vocals, keyboards
Chris Stainton: keyboards
Henry Spinetti: drums
Dave Markee: bass

BLUES INSTRUMENTAL #2 (Eric Clapton) unreleased

Eric Clapton: guitar

Producer: Glyn Johns
Engineer: Glyn Johns

Bookended with some nice bluesy guitar work, this album has aged well. It would make an ideal companion to a Deluxe Edition of *Another Ticket* should the label ever decide to release it. Unreleased at the time because RSO felt it was a substandard album, many of its songs were re-recorded at Compass Point Studios in the Bahamas during the summer. Others were simply discarded. The untitled album was mixed at Glyn Johns's home studio in Surrey, Turn Up Turn Down Studios. I believe that the name of the studio was at one point considered as a possible title for the album.

ERIC CLAPTON
GUEST SESSION
SURREY SOUND STUDIOS
70 Kingston Road, Leatherhead, Surrey
Session for Gary Brooker

FEBRUARY 1980

LEAVE THE CANDLE (Gary Brooker / Pete Sinfield) single A-side Chrysalis CHS2396 released April 1981

Gary Brooker: vocals, keyboards
Eric Clapton: guitar
Albert Lee: guitar
Dave Markee: bass
Henry Spinetti: drums
Benny Gallagher: backing vocals
Graham Lyle: backing vocals

CHASING THE CHOP (Gary Brooker / Keith Reid) single B-side Chrysalis CHS2396 released April 1981

Gary Brooker: vocals, keyboards
Eric Clapton: guitar
Albert Lee: guitar
Dave Markee: bass
Henry Spinetti: drums
Benny Gallagher: backing vocals
Graham Lyle: backing vocals

Often confused with the B-side of the Gary Brooker "Home Loving" single, which is titled "Chasing For The Chop" and has no Eric participation

ERIC CLAPTON
GUEST SESSION
AIR STUDIOS
Fourth floor, 214 Oxford Street, London W1
Session for Stephen Bishop

MARCH 1980

LITTLE MOON (Stephen Bishop) *Red Cab To Manhattan* album US Warner Brothers BSK 3473, UK Warner Brothers K56853 released October 1980 / *Red Cab To Manhattan* CD Warner Brothers Japan WPCP-4579 released November 1991

Stephen Bishop: vocals, acoustic guitar
Eric Clapton: electric guitar
Gary Brooker: Fender Rhodes piano
Chris Stainton: acoustic piano
John Giblun: bass
Phil Collins: drums
Clive Anstree: cello
The Stephen Bishops Of London: background vocals

SEX KITTENS GO TO COLLEGE (Stephen Bishop) *Red Cab To Manhattan* album US Warner Brothers BSK 3473, UK Warner Brothers K56853 released October 1980 / *Red Cab To Manhattan* CD Warner Brothers Japan WPCP-4579 released November 1991

Stephen Bishop: vocals, acoustic guitar
Eric Clapton: electric guitar
Gary Brooker: acoustic piano
Chris Stainton: Fender Rhodes piano
John Giblun: bass
Phil Collins: drums

Producers: Mike Mainieri, Tommy Lipuma
Engineer: Steve Churchyard

COMPASS POINT STUDIOS West Bay Road, Gambier Village, Nassau, Bahamas Session for Gary Brooker

JULY 1980–AUGUST 1980

HOME LOVING (Gary Brooker) single A-side Mercury 6059 424 released March 1981 / *Lead Me To The Water* album US Mercury SRM 1-4054, UK Vertigo VOG-1-3314 released 1982 / *Lead Me to The Water* CD Esoteric ECLEC2271 released June 2011

Gary Brooker: vocals, backing vocals, keyboards, synth
Eric Clapton: guitar
Chris Stainton: keyboards
Dave Markee: bass
Henry Spinetti: drums

LEAD ME TO THE WATER (Gary Brooker) *Lead Me To The Water* album US Mercury SRM 1-4054, UK Vertigo VOG-1-3314 released 1982 / *Lead Me To The Water* CD Esoteric ECLEC2271 released June 2011

Gary Brooker: vocals, backing vocals, keyboards, synth
Eric Clapton: guitar
Albert Lee: guitar
Chris Stainton: keyboards
Dave Markee: bass
Henry Spinetti: drums

Producer: Gary Brooker
Engineer: Tom Dowd

COMPASS POINT STUDIOS West Bay Road, Gambier Village, Nassau, Bahamas Session for *Another Ticket*

JULY 1980–AUGUST 1980

SOMETHING SPECIAL (Eric Clapton) *Another Ticket* album US RSO 2394 295, UK RSO 2394 295 released February 1981 / *Another Ticket* remastered CD Polydor 531 830-2 June 2006

Eric Clapton: vocals, guitar
Albert Lee: guitar, backing vocals
Gary Brooker: electric piano
Chris Stainton: piano
Henry Spinetti: drums
Dave Markee: bass

BLACK ROSE (Troy Seals & Eddie Setser) *Another Ticket* album US RSO 2394 295, UK RSO 2394 295 released February 1981 / *Another Ticket* remastered CD Polydor 531 830-2 June 2006

Eric Clapton: vocals, guitar, slide guitar
Albert Lee: guitar, backing vocals
Gary Brooker: organ, backing vocals
Chris Stainton: piano
Henry Spinetti: drums, percussion
Dave Markee: bass

BLOW WIND BLOW (McKinley Morganfield) *Another Ticket* album US RSO 2394 295, UK RSO 2394 295 released February 1981 / *Another Ticket* remastered CD Polydor 531 830-2 June 2006

Eric Clapton: vocals, guitar
Albert Lee: guitar
Chris Stainton: piano
Henry Spinetti: drums
Dave Markee: bass

ANOTHER TICKET (Eric Clapton) *Another Ticket* album US RSO 2394 295, UK RSO 2394 295 released February 1981 / *Another Ticket* remastered CD Polydor 531 830-2 June 2006

Eric Clapton: vocals, guitar
Albert Lee: guitar
Gary Brooker: synth
Chris Stainton: piano
Henry Spinetti: drums
Dave Markee: bass

I CAN'T STAND IT (Eric Clapton) *Another Ticket* album US RSO 2394 295, UK RSO 2394 295 released February 1981 / *Another Ticket* remastered CD Polydor 531 830-2 June 2006

Eric Clapton: vocals, guitar
Albert Lee: guitar
Gary Brooker: electric piano
Chris Stainton: electric piano
Henry Spinetti: drums
Dave Markee: bass

HOLD ME LORD (Eric Clapton) *Another Ticket* album US RSO 2394 295, UK RSO 2394 295 released February 1981 / *Another Ticket* remastered CD Polydor 531 830-2 June 2006

Eric Clapton: vocals, Dobro
Albert Lee: guitar, backing vocals
Gary Brooker: organ, backing vocals
Chris Stainton: piano
Henry Spinetti: drums
Dave Markee: bass

Cover for Eric Clapton's Another Ticket *album.*

FLOATING BRIDGE (Sleepy John Estes) *Another Ticket* album US RSO 2394 295, UK RSO 2394 295 released February 1981 / *Another Ticket* remastered CD Polydor 531 830-2 June 2006

Eric Clapton: vocals, guitar
Albert Lee: guitar
Chris Stainton: organ
Henry Spinetti: drums
Dave Markee: bass

CATCH ME IF YOU CAN (Eric Clapton / Gary Brooker) *Another Ticket* album US RSO 2394 295, UK RSO 2394 295 released February 1981 / *Another Ticket* remastered CD Polydor 531 830-2 June 2006

Eric Clapton: vocals, double tracked guitars
Albert Lee: guitar
Gary Brooker: electric piano
Chris Stainton: piano
Henry Spinetti: drums
Dave Markee: bass

RITA MAE (Eric Clapton) *Another Ticket* album US RSO 2394 295, UK RSO 2394 295 released February 1981 / *Another Ticket* remastered CD Polydor 531 830-2 June 2006

Eric Clapton: vocals, guitar
Albert Lee: guitar
Gary Brooker: organ
Chris Stainton: organ
Henry Spinetti: drums
Dave Markee: bass

OH HOW I MISS MY BABY'S LOVE (Eric Clapton) (unreleased)

Eric Clapton: vocals, Dobro
Albert Lee: guitar
Henry Spinetti: drums
Dave Markee: bass

SAY HELLO TO BILLY JEAN (Eric Clapton) (unreleased)

Producer: Tom Dowd
Engineer: Tom Dowd

> **“**Most of it is very bluesy. A couple of them are exceptionally bluesy. It took a long time to make that album because I was totally fed up with writing ditties and pleasant melodies, and I thought it was time for me to reconnect myself to what I know best.**”** **—ERIC CLAPTON**

> **“**When Eric was recording 'Another Ticket,' he went through a number of guitars trying to get a particular sound on 'Rita Mae.' He finally settled on his Gibson 335. He'll dabble with a Gibson Explorer or a Les Paul, but he'll always be drawn back to his true love—the Fender Stratocaster. There's something about the Strat sound that's perfect for him. Plus, he can get everything out of a Strat that he can from a Les Paul or Telecaster, so why depend on another guitar? His favourite is his 'Blackie' '56 Strat. Then there's a brown '57 model that we use as back-up, and a '54 with raised action in an open tuning for slide tunes.**”** **—LEE DICKSON**
> (Eric's guitar tech)

ERIC CLAPTON GUEST SESSION

TOWN HOUSE STUDIOS 150 Goldhawk Road, London, W12 Session for Phil Collins

OCTOBER 1980

IF LEAVING ME IS EASY (Phil Collins) *Face Value* album US Atlantic SD 16029, UK Virgin V2185 released February 1981 / *Face Value* CD UK Atlantic 2292-54939-2 released 1999 / *Face Value* gold CD Audio Fidelity AFZ 084 released 2011

Phil Collins: vocals, drums, synth, Fender Rhodes electric piano
Eric Clapton: guitar
Daryl Stuemer: guitar
Alphonso Johnson: bass
Don Myrick: saxophone
Rahmlee Michael Davis: flugelhorn
Michael Harris: flugelhorn
Arif Mardin: string arrangement

Producer: Phil Collins
Engineer: Hugh Padgham

1981

Eric's drinking was totally out of control by now. He either could not see it, or chose to ignore the situation. If he could make it through his gig, then he did not see where the problem was. Eric's world was fast becoming more and more isolated. Even his close friends and family realized they were unable to get through to him. They were completely powerless. It did not help that Fric would flip when anyone suggested he should drink less and seek help. Everyone reluctantly accepted that this was a decision he would have to come to himself if he was ever to get sober.

He started 1981 with a short four-date Irish tour, which was followed by a one-off gig at the Rainbow in London, the proceeds of which he donated to a trust fund administrated by Dr. Meg Patterson. The irony of Eric giving generously to a rehabilitation charity and yet not realizing he needed help himself was lost on him. The Rainbow show also had the surprise appearance of Chas & Dave on some extra encores, much to the delight of some and a real disappointment to others.

These shows were in effect a warm-up for a huge fifty-seven-date American tour in support of *Another Ticket*, which opened at the Memorial Coliseum in Portland, Oregon, on 2 March. Eric had suffered with back pain over the previous few months and was taking pain killers to try and help. The pain had progressively got worse during the first week of the US tour, and he would frequently be knocking on his assistant's door during the night to get more and more pain-killing tablets. Roger Forrester (Eric's manager) and Nigel Carroll (Eric's assistant) realized that if Eric was to have any hope of completing this huge

tour, he would need medical help. On the afternoon of the 13 March he was taken to see a doctor, who gave him a strong pain-killing injection to help him through the show. During the concert in Madison that evening, the pain got worse and worse. The band knew something was up, as Eric was white as a sheet and playing wrong notes during the concert. Roger Forrester was gesturing from the side of the stage to end the show after the number. When Eric came offstage he was doubled up in agony. Roger knew that this was a serious situation, but Eric stubbornly refused to go to a hospital.

The tour party headed off to catch their midnight private charter plane to their next stop in St. Paul, Minneapolis. From there they were scheduled to play two shows, one in Duluth and the other in St. Paul. During the flight it quickly became apparent that all was not well with Eric. He was not even attempting to drink, which was very unusual for him, and he was pale. Within fifteen minutes he just slumped down in his seat and was incoherent. On arrival at the airport, he had to be helped into the waiting limousine. Roger Forrester instructed the driver to take them straight to United Hospital in St. Paul, where Eric was seen by a doctor and told to return later that morning to have some X-rays done. Roger and Nigel escorted Eric to have this done, and the doctor informed them that as soon as the results were ready, they would be contacted at their hotel. By the time they reached their hotel, the Radisson Plaza, an urgent message had already been left for them by the hospital. Eric needed to return immediately, as they found he had a stomach ulcer the size of a small orange that could rupture into his pancreas at any moment. If it was that serious, Roger explained that he would prefer to fly Eric home straight away. The doctor told him that would not be advisable, as the situation was so grave that Eric could die at any moment. Within forty-five minutes of the call, Eric was in a hospital bed and it was confirmed he had five ulcers. Obviously, the remainder of the tour was canceled, and Eric ended up spending over a month at the United Hospital, where his ulcers slowly reduced in size. He had plenty of visitors when there, such as Don Williams and Pete Townshend. After his body starting responding to treatment, he was allowed out for a couple of hours every day. It did not take him long to find a fishing shop where he bought several fishing rods, much to the bemusement of hospital staff.

He left hospital on 20 April and flew out to Seattle, a favorite city of his, for a break and some fishing with friends. His assistant, Nigel Carroll, accompanied him to keep an eye on him. On 22 April, Eric and his party were in a restaurant when Eric asked the waiter to pour some brandy in a glass of milk he had ordered. Nigel immediately told the waiter to ignore the request. Eric knew full well he could not have any alcohol due to the medication he was taking. Annoyed at Nigel's bossy attitude, he left the restaurant, asking a girl in the party to drive him back to the hotel. On the way there, the girl ran a red light and crashed into another vehicle. The girl was fine, and Eric only suffered some bruised ribs and a lacerated shin. Nonetheless, the accident meant another visit to the hospital, where it was discovered he had pleurisy and needed to spend time in a room with a steamer providing damp air. He decided to fly home to England, where the air was naturally damp.

Eric took it easy for several months to recuperate. The problem with Eric doing nothing was the boredom factor and the temptation to start drinking heavily again. Despite what had happened to him, he would be back on the booze within weeks of being home. Eric recalls,

> "It was pointed out to me while I was in hospital that I had a drink problem, and I think that was the first time anyone had ever said something like that to me. But I was still happy drinking and quite terrified of not drinking. I had to go further down the road to complete insanity before I stopped."

In August, he was asked by Amnesty International if he would like to play a couple of acoustic numbers for their Secret Policeman's Other Ball shows at the Theatre Royal, Drury Lane, in September. Pete Townshend had previously played some acoustic numbers, and they thought it would be great to have Eric do the same. Eric told them that he did not feel comfortable performing in an acoustic format but said that he would like to play as long as he could bring a friend. That friend turned out to be Jeff Beck. The organizers were thrilled. In what were largely comedy routines and sketches with musical interludes, Eric and Jeff opened the second part of the show. They played a mini set of two numbers on the opening two nights, as well as joining in the big finale number, "I Shall Be Released." They did not appear on the third night but came back on the last night. Although their set was short, Eric and Jeff played amazingly well and had the audience on their feet. On the last night Eric played an amazing wah-wah solo during the finale of "I Shall Be Released" that was bizarrely edited out of the film, but happily is available in full on the CD version of the show.

By October, Eric and his band flew over to Scandinavia. At the last show in Randers, Eric changed the lyric in "Cocaine" to "Cornflakes," which clearly caused confusion among Danish fans. Even worse was the sight of Eric attempting to play saxophone on "Further On Up The Road"! That said, he managed to occasionally surprise everyone with some great playing, such as in Stockholm. But Eric, in general, was certainly nowhere near the form he should have been for a musician of his caliber.

In late November, the group began their tour of Japan. The performances were generally average, and on the last night of the tour at Tokyo's Koseinenkin Kaikan Dai Hall, Eric almost did not make it onto the stage, as his body was covered in a purple rash. He was also shaking quite violently, which made it almost impossible to hold his guitar. Eric eventually played the show, which produced some humorous comments during the lengthy encores for the tour finale. For Eric this wake-up call was a major turning point for him. He actually admitted he was in trouble, and Roger was determined to make sure Eric got help on his return home.

ANOTHER TICKET
IRISH TOUR 1981

BAND LINEUP:
Eric Clapton: guitar, vocals
Albert Lee: guitar, vocals
Dave Markee: bass
Henry Spinetti: drums
Chris Stainton: keyboards
Gary Brooker: keyboards, vocals

JANUARY 1981

30 January 1981, Eric and his band fly out to Dublin
31 January 1981, Simmonscourt, Dublin, Ireland

SETLIST: Tulsa Time / Worried Life Blues / Lay Down Sally / Wonderful Tonight / Blow Wind Blow / Rambling On My Mind / Have You Ever Loved A Woman / Thunder And Lightning / Country Boy / Double Trouble / Blues Power / Cocaine / Layla / Further On Up The Road

FEBRUARY 1981

1 February 1981, Leisureland, Galway, Ireland

SETLIST: Tulsa Time / Worried Life Blues / Lay Down Sally / Wonderful Tonight / Blow Wind Blow / Rambling On My Mind / Have You Ever Loved A Woman / Whiter Shade Of Pale / Country Boy / Double Trouble / Blues Power / Cocaine / Layla / Further On Up The Road

2 February 1981, City Hall, Cork, Ireland

SETLIST: Tulsa Time / Worried Life Blues / Lay Down Sally / Wonderful Tonight / Blow Wind Blow / Rambling On My Mind / Have You Ever Loved A Woman / Thunder And Lightning / Country Boy / Double Trouble / Blues Power / Cocaine / Layla / Further On Up The Road

3 February 1981, Youree Youth Centre, Carlow, Ireland

SETLIST: Tulsa Time / Worried Life Blues / Lay Down Sally / Wonderful Tonight / Blow Wind Blow / Rambling On My Mind / Have You Ever Loved A Woman / Whiter Shade Of Pale / Country Boy / Double Trouble / Blues Power / Cocaine / Layla / Further On Up The Road

"Only the generosity of the crowd at Simmonscourt saved the evening from mediocrity. Not that the band were at fault: the acoustics were poor, the sound balance was defective, and the overall atmosphere was bleak and barren: in short, the choice of venue, which may have been prompted by necessity, was a mistake. From where I was standing, Gary Brooker's keyboards were heavy and domineering, Henry Spinetti's drums sounded harsh and insensitive, and at times even Eric's licks were almost inaudible but the performance was lifted, though, by the sheer magnitude of the audience's fervour, and Clapton responded in kind: as he played through a series of old favourites, adding only two numbers from his forthcoming album, one could feel the radiance of pleasure and happiness. All in all it wasn't a bad concert, but just misplaced—I longed to be back in the Stadium.

The gigs in Galway and Cork were a substantial improvement, as everything fell clearly into place. The smaller halls were more sympathetic, the sound mix was much improved, and the band showed quite obviously that they have matured since their recruitment about eighteen months ago. On both occasions they played an almost identical set to the one we had heard in Dublin; the only major change was the substitution of 'A Whiter Shade Of Pale' for the rather inchoate song that Gary Brooker had contributed on the first night. 'Wonderful Tonight,' 'Cocaine,' 'Blues Power' and 'Layla' were the blatant crowd pleasers, each of them being greeted with signs of immediate recognition." —JOHN HUTCHINSON
(*Musicians Only*, March 1981)

4 February 1981, Eric and his band fly back to London

ANOTHER TICKET
LONDON ONE-OFF 1981

5 February 1981, Rainbow Theatre, Finsbury, London

SETLIST: Tulsa Time / Worried Life Blues / Lay Down Sally / Wonderful Tonight / Blow Wind Blow / Rambling On My Mind / Have You Ever Loved A Woman / Whiter Shade Of Pale / Country Boy / Double Trouble / Blues Power / Cocaine / Layla / Further On Up The Road / Send Me Some Lovin* / Move On Down The Line* / Lawdy Miss Clawdy* / Roll Over Beethoven*

*with Chas & Dave (Chas Hodges, Dave Peacock)

"The night had begun to the easy swing of 'Tulsa Time,' followed by the first of several burning blues interludes, 'Worried Life Blues,' with keyboard breaks from both Chris Stainton and Gary Brooker as well as a typically magical solo from the man himself. Next up were restrained and relaxed renditions of 'Lay Down Sally' and 'Wonderful Tonight,' a love song that still sends shivers with its emotional intensity, and the only new song to get an airing, 'Blow Wind Blow,' a kind of Chuck Berry–style boogie with some inspired playing from both Clapton and Stainton and the redoubtable Henry Spinetti flowing from a whisper to a roar on drums.

But it was from here on that the show took a bit of a dip, with the audience shuffling and fidgeting through 'Ramblin' On My Mind' and 'Have You Ever Loved A Woman,' despite more incomparable blues guitar from Clapton, and matters getting worse during Gary Brooker and Albert Lee's respective solo spots, 'Whiter Shade Of Pale' and 'Country Boy.' They're both excellent players, of course, but it was rather like having the support act's set in the middle of the main event, particularly when Clapton left them to it while he went off for a cigarette and chat with the roadies, and made it very difficult for him to regenerate the adrenalin he had earlier set flowing.

Giving his mates a spell in the spotlight is all very noble and magnanimous of Eric, but it wasn't what the crowd crushed up against the front of the stage had forked out all those notes for, and it's a tactical mistake he unfortunately repeats in the now almost traditional knees-up with Chas and Dave for the encores." **—SOUNDS**

23 February 1981–28 February 1981, rehearsals for US tour

ANOTHER TICKET
USA TOUR 1981
MARCH 1981

BAND LINEUP:
Eric Clapton: guitar, vocals
Albert Lee: guitar, vocals
Dave Markee: bass
Henry Spinetti: drums
Chris Stainton: keyboards
Gary Brooker: keyboards, vocals

2 March 1981, Memorial Coliseum, Portland, Oregon

3 March 1981, Coliseum, Spokane, Washington

4 March 1981, day off

5 March 1981, Paramount Theatre, Seattle, Washington

6 March 1981, Paramount Theatre, Seattle, Washington

7 March 1981, Paramount Theatre, Seattle, Washington

SETLIST: Country Boy / A Salty Dog / Tulsa Time / Lay Down Sally / Wonderful Tonight / Worried Life Blues / Stay Away From My Baby / Double Trouble / Rita Mae / Blow Wind Blow / Ramblin' On My Mind / Mean Old World / Have You Ever Loved A Woman / Blues Power / Cocaine / Layla / Further On Up The Road

The show starts with Albert Lee playing "Country Boy" followed by Gary Brooker's Procol Harum favorite, "Salty Dog." Eric introduces "Cocaine" with "This is a song about the new national pastime. . . hope you all are enjoying yours as much as we are not enjoying ours, which we are not because of certain pressures. Here we go anyway." After an extended intro, Eric shouts, "I really want some!!"

8 March 1981, day off

9 March 1981, Yellowstone Metra Park Arena, Billings, Montana

10 March 1981, Four Seasons Arena, Great Falls, Montana

11 March 1981–12 March 1981, days off

13 March 1981, Dane County Exposition Center, Madison, Wisconsin (last show before going to hospital due to perforated ulcer)

SETLIST: Country Boy / A Whiter Shade Of Pale / Tulsa Time / Lay Down Sally / Wonderful Tonight / Worried Life Blues / Stay Away From My Baby / Double Trouble / Rita Mae / Blow Wind Blow / Ramblin' On My Mind / Blues Power / Cocaine / Further On Up The Road

14 March 1981, Arena Auditorium, Duluth, Minnesota (canceled)

15 March 1981, Civic Center Arena, St. Paul, Minnesota (canceled)

17 March 1981, Hilton Coliseum, Ames, Iowa (canceled)

19 March 1981, Kansas Coliseum, Wichita, Kansas (canceled)

20 March 1981, Southwest Missouri State University, Springfield, Missouri (canceled)

21 March 1981, Kemper Arena, Kansas City, Missouri (canceled)

22 March 1981, University of Nebraska Arena, Lincoln, Nebraska (canceled)

24 March 1981, Louisiana State University, Assembly Center, Baton Rouge, Louisiana (canceled)

25 March 1981, Municipal Auditorium, New Orleans, Louisiana (canceled)

27 March 1981, Mid-South Coliseum, Memphis, Tennessee (canceled)

28 March 1981, South Illinois University Arena, Carbondale, Illinois (canceled)

29 March 1981, Henry W. Kiel Municipal Auditorium, St. Louis, Missouri (canceled)

31 March 1981, Barton Coliseum, Little Rock, Arkansas (canceled)

APRIL 1981

1 April 1981, Hirsch Memorial Coliseum, Shreveport, Louisiana (canceled)

3 April 1981, University of Texas, Activity Center, Austin, Texas (canceled)

4 April 1981, Summit, Houston, Texas (canceled)

5 April 1981, Reunion Arena, Dallas, Texas (canceled)

7 April 1981, Arizona State University, Tempe, Arizona (canceled)

8 April 1981, Sports Arena, San Diego, California (canceled)

9 April 1981, Convention Arena, Long Beach, California (canceled)

11 April 1981, Alameda County Coliseum, Oakland, California (canceled)

MAY 1981

1 May 1981, Market Square Arena, Indianapolis, Indiana (canceled)

2 May 1981, Riverfront Coliseum, Cincinnati, Ohio (canceled)

3 May 1981, Joe Louis Arena, Detroit, Michigan (canceled)

5 May 1981, Memorial Coliseum, Fort Wayne, Indiana (canceled)

7 May 1981, Michigan State University Arena, East Lansing, Michigan (canceled)

8 May 1981, Chicago Stadium, Chicago, Illinois (canceled)

9 May 1981, Richfield Coliseum, Cleveland, Ohio (canceled)

10 May 1981, Civic Center, Pittsburgh, Pennsylvania (canceled)

12 May 1981, Veterans Memorial Coliseum, New Haven, Connecticut (canceled)

13 May 1981, Broome County Coliseum, Binghampton, New York (canceled)

15 May 1981, Nassau Veterans Memorial Coliseum, Uniondale, New York (canceled)

16 May 1981, Civic Center, Providence, Rhode Island (canceled)

17 May 1981, Cumberland County Civic Center, Portland, Maine (canceled)

19 May 1981, War Memorial Coliseum, Rochester, New York (canceled)

20 May 1981, Spectrum, Philadelphia, Pennsylvania (canceled)

22 May 1981, Capitol Centre, Landover, Maryland (canceled)

23 May 1981, Scope, Norfolk, Virginia (canceled)

24 May 1981, Coliseum, Greensboro, North Carolina (canceled)

26 May 1981, Charlotte Coliseum, Charlotte, North Carolina (canceled)

27 May 1981, Carolina Coliseum, Columbia, South Carolina (canceled)

29 May 1981, Hollywood Sportatorium, Miami, Florida (canceled)

30 May 1981, Jacksonville Veterans Memorial Coliseum Jacksonville, Florida (canceled)

31 May 1981, Sun Dome, Tampa, Florida (canceled)

JUNE 1981

2 June 1981, Grand Ole Opry House, Nashville, Tennessee (canceled)

4 June 198 State Fair Coliseum, Jackson, Missouri (canceled)

5 June 1981, Municipal Auditorium, Mobile, Alabama (canceled)

6 June 1981, Jefferson County Civic Centre, Birmingham, Alabama (canceled)

7 June 1981, Omni Theatre, Atlanta, Georgia (canceled)

THE SECRET POLICEMAN'S OTHER BALL SHOWS 1981

SEPTEMBER 1981

9 September 1981, Theatre Royal, Drury Lane, London

SETLIST:

'Cause We Ended As Lovers (Stevie Wonder) unreleased

Jeff Beck: lead guitar
Eric Clapton: guitar
John Etheridge: rhythm guitar
Neil Murray: bass
Simon Phillips: drums

Crossroads (Robert Johnson) *The Secret Policeman's Other Ball "The Music"* album US Island ILPS 9698, UK Island 204 368-320 released 1982 / *The Secret Policeman's Other Ball "The Music"* CD US Rhino R2 71048, UK Castle Communications CCSCD 351 released 1992

Eric Clapton: lead guitar, vocals
Jeff Beck: lead guitar
John Etheridge: rhythm guitar
Neil Murray: bass
Simon Phillips: drums

I Shall Be Released (Bob Dylan) unreleased

Sting: vocals, guitar
Eric Clapton: guitar
Jeff Beck: guitar
John Etheridge: guitar
Neil Innes: guitar
Ray Russell: guitar
John Altman: keyboards
Chas Jankel: keyboards
Neil Murray: bass
Simon Phillips: drums
Mel Collins: sax
Paul Cosh: horns
Jeff Daly: horns
Martin Drover: horns
Digby Fairweather: horns
Malcolm Griffiths: horns
Mike Henry: horns
Mark Isham: horns
The Secret Police Choir:
Victoria Wood: backing vocals
Pamela Stephenson: backing vocals
Sharon Campbell: backing vocals
Phil Collins: backing vocals, tambourine

10 September 1981, Theatre Royal, Drury Lane, London

'Cause We Ended As Lovers (Stevie Wonder) unreleased

Jeff Beck: lead guitar
Eric Clapton: guitar
John Etheridge: rhythm guitar
Neil Murray: bass
Simon Phillips: drums

Further On Up The Road (Joe Veassey / Don Robey) unreleased

Jeff Beck: lead guitar
Eric Clapton: lead guitar
John Etheridge: rhythm guitar
Neil Murray: bass
Simon Phillips: drums

I Shall Be Released (Bob Dylan) unreleased

Sting: vocals, guitar
Eric Clapton: guitar
Jeff Beck: guitar
John Etheridge: guitar
Neil Innes: guitar
Ray Russell: guitar
John Altman: keyboards
Chas Jankel: keyboards
Neil Murray: bass
Simon Phillips: drums
Mel Collins: sax
Paul Cosh: horns

Advert for The Secret Policeman's Other Ball: The Music *album.*

Jeff Daly: horns
Martin Drover: horns
Digby Fairweather: horns
Malcolm Griffiths: horns
Mike Henry: horns
Mark Isham: horns
The Secret Police Choir:
Victoria Wood: backing vocals
Pamela Stephenson: backing vocals
Sharon Campbell: backing vocals
Phil Collins: backing vocals, tambourine

11 September 1981, Theatre Royal, Drury Lane, London

Eric and Jeff did not appear on this night

12 September 1981, Theatre Royal, Drury Lane, London

SETLIST:

'Cause We Ended As Lovers (Stevie Wonder) *The Secret Policeman's Other Ball "The Music"* album US Island ILPS 9698, UK Island 204 368-320 released 1982 / *The Secret Policeman's Other Ball "The Music"* CD US Rhino R2 71048, UK Castle Communications CCSCD 351 released 1992

Jeff Beck: lead guitar
Eric Clapton: guitar
John Etheridge: rhythm guitar
Mo Foster: bass
Simon Phillips: drums

Further On Up The Road (Joe Veassey / Don Robey) *The Secret Policeman's Other Ball "The Music"* album US Island ILPS 9698, UK Island 204 368-320 released 1982 / *The Secret Policeman's Other Ball "The Music"* CD US Rhino R2 71048, UK Castle Communications CCSCD 351 released 1992 / DVD The Secret Policeman's Ball—the Complete Edition released 2005

Eric Clapton: lead guitar, vocals
Jeff Beck: lead guitar
John Etheridge: rhythm guitar
Mo Foster: bass
Simon Phillips: drums

I Shall Be Released (Bob Dylan) *The Secret Policeman's Other Ball "The Music"* album US Island ILPS 9698, UK Island 204 368-320 released 1982 / *The Secret Policeman's Other Ball "The Music"* CD US Rhino R2 71048, UK Castle Communications CCSCD 351 released 1992 / DVD *The Secret Policeman's Ball—the Complete Edition* released 2005 (with Eric's wah-wah solo edited out)

Sting: vocals, guitar

Eric Clapton: guitar
Jeff Beck: guitar
John Etheridge: guitar
Neil Innes: guitar
Ray Russell: guitar
John Altman: keyboards
Chas Jankel: keyboards
Mo Foster: bass
Neil Murray: bass
Simon Phillips: drums
Mel Collins: sax
Paul Cosh: horns
Jeff Daly: horns
Martin Drover: horns
Digby Fairweather: horns
Malcolm Griffiths: horns
Mike Henry: horns
Mark Isham: horns
The Secret Police Choir:
Sharon Campbell: backing vocals
Doreen Chanter: backing vocals
Phil Collins: backing vocals, tambourine
Chris Cross: backing vocals
Donovan: backing vocals
Sheena Easton: backing vocals
Bob Geldof: backing vocals
Micky Moody: backing vocals
Tom Robinson: backing vocals
Linda Taylor: backing vocals
Midge Ure: backing vocals

I Shall Be Released (reprise) (Bob Dylan) *The Secret Policeman's Other Ball "The Music"* album US Island ILPS 9698, UK Island 204 368-320 released 1982 / *The Secret Policeman's Other Ball "The Music"* CD US Rhino R2 71048, UK Castle Communications CCSCD 351 released 1992

Sting: vocals, guitar
Eric Clapton: guitar
Jeff Beck: guitar
John Etheridge: guitar
Neil Innes: guitar
Ray Russell: guitar
John Altman: keyboards
Chas Jankel: keyboards
Mo Foster: bass
Neil Murray: bass
Simon Phillips: drums
Mel Collins: sax
Paul Cosh: horns
Jeff Daly: horns
Martin Drover: horns
Digby Fairweather: horns
Malcolm Griffiths: horns
Mike Henry: horns

Mark Isham: horns
The Secret Police Choir:
Sharon Campbell: backing vocals
Doreen Chanter: backing vocals
Phil Collins: backing vocals, tambourine
Chris Cross: backing vocals
Donovan: backing vocals
Sheena Easton: backing vocals
Bob Geldof: backing vocals
Micky Moody: backing vocals
Tom Robinson: backing vocals
Linda Taylor: backing vocals
Midge Ure: backing vocals

Recorded by: RAK Mobile Studio
Producer: Martin Lewis
Engineer: Tim Summerhayes

ANOTHER TICKET SCANDINAVIAN TOUR 1981

OCTOBER 1981

BAND LINEUP:
Eric Clapton: guitar, vocals
Albert Lee: guitar, vocals
Dave Markee: bass
Henry Spinetti: drums
Chris Stainton: keyboards
Gary Brooker: keyboards, vocals

6 October 1981, Eric and his band fly out to Helsinki

"September 9th 1981 was an unusually hot day in London. I was ready to drop with exhaustion. Little did I, or anyone else for that matter, know that within a few minutes I, with the help of those assembled with me onstage at the Drury Lane Theatre, was about to change the course of world history! In front of the curtain stood the comedian Billy Connolly, now drastically overrunning his allotted timeslot. From my unusual vantage point (behind a raised keyboard, rather than in the middle of the rather large horn section) I was able to scan the stage—as musical director my biggest worry was that some band members may not be 'all systems go' as soon as the curtains opened. A sweep to my left took in the assembled backing singers and guitar section, a 180 degree turn made sure that bass and drums were in place, and a swivel to the right made sure that horns were in their correct places, and the offstage piano had someone seated and ready to play. I knew the lead vocalist was in place as he stood directly in front of me making some last-minute adjustments to his guitar.

So what exactly were my eyes focussing on and why was it such an important event. Well to my left, Eric Clapton was audibly exhorting Billy Connolly to get on with it or get the hook (the way to remove a performer who had outstayed his welcome). This elicited much mirth from Jeff Beck, standing next to Eric. Meanwhile a glance down the line picked out Phil Collins juggling silently with a tambourine, Bob Geldof and Midge Ure whispering to each other, three more guitarists standing poised, bass and drums all ready to go, Chaz Jankel waving from the piano, Mark Isham and his section mates looking over the horn parts, and Sting ready to lead the way as our motley crew, dubbed the Secret Police, were about to make musical and social history.

Finally Billy left the stage, the curtains opened, and my cousin Simon Phillips, for 18 years now the powerhouse behind Toto, played the drum intro to 'I Shall Be Released' specially arranged for the Amnesty International show by Sting and myself. The audience were ecstatic—no one had seen a gathering of so many stellar names on one stage since the Concert for Bangladesh or the Last Waltz. And what we did was plant a seed in Bob Geldof and Midge Ure's mind that led directly to Live Aid and the many Concerts for Amnesty International that have followed.

How did this all happen? Well largely thanks to Martin Lewis, the producer, and some monumental bluffing, with my collusion. And my input was that the big names should be backed up by a solid bunch of highly respected backroom musicians who would be the glue to hold the ensemble together. The double bluff came when we landed Simon and Mo Foster from Jeff Beck's current band. We simultaneously rang Eric and Jeff telling them that the other would be there and they both said yes! This, incredibly, was their first onstage encounter. When Martin was able to involve Sting we knew we were all set. Adding John Etheridge, the session guitarist whom Sting once said he aspired to be when he first attempted a musical career, and Ray Russell, another guitar hero was my idea, and I got Chaz Jankel (who wrote Ai No Corrida for Quincy Jones) and Mark Isham, now one of the leading movie composers, to pitch in too. Neil Innes was there too, along with Sheena Easton and Donovan, plus an all star horn section. And the band rocked! Eric was excited to play with Sting, who was excited to play with Jeff, who was excited etc etc. Phil Collins begged us to be included—I'm sure we could have stretched the ensemble even more had we more time. But as Eric said to me at the time 'you're the bandleader, what do you want us to do?' The keys to the success of the Secret Police lay in that sentence—no one tried to outdo or outshine the others. Everyone listened to everyone else, showing musical consideration to each other and respect for the song performed. It was a true lesson in musical democracy and humility, and marked a momentous turning point for musicians with social consciences. And I'm proud to have been in the thick of it!"

—JOHN ALTMAN

"During rehearsals, Jeff and I were sending Sting up. He was going through all the motions of leaping about, when there was no one there. No audience. 'Bit green, isn't he?' we were saying. 'Only been in the business three weeks—look at him.' But then we saw him in front of an audience—so composed, so confident. Obviously with a performance such as he gives you've got to practise it. He's very good."

—ERIC CLAPTON

"In 1981, several musicians and actors (from Monty Python) arranged to play 4 concerts in benefit of Amnesty International. There were great performers there, like Jeff Beck & Eric Clapton (playing together!!), Phil Collins, Sting (his first solo appearance, he still was in The Police), Donovan, Bob Geldof, etc. Neil was substituting for Mo Foster for 2 out of 4 shows, as he had already rehearsed with Jeff Beck and Simon Phillips (they appear together on Jon Lord and Bernie Marsden's solo albums) as they were searching for a bass-player to make a 3-piece group with. They tried many players but never put a band together.

On the album, Neil Murray only plays on 'Crossroads.' He played for two nights with Beck and Clapton: first night 'Crossroads' and "Cause We've Ended As Lovers,' 2nd night 'Further On Up The Road' and "Caus...'. On the 1st night he played with Sting on 'Roxanne' (he played guitar) and on both nights on 'I Shall Be Released' with everyone. Beck and Clapton did not play the 3rd night, but because of the filming, they mostly used performances from the last night on the album and video, so there is not much evidence of Neil's performances." —MICKY MOODY

7 October 1981, Messuhalli, Helsinki, Finland

SETLIST: Tulsa Time / Lay Down Sally / Wonderful Tonight / Worried Life Blues / After Midnight / Whiter Shade Of Pale / Country Boy / Double Trouble / Rita Mae / Knockin' On Heaven's Door / Blues Power / Ramblin' On My Mind / Have You Ever Loved A Woman / Cocaine / Layla / Further on Up the Road

8 October 1981, day off

9 October 1981, Johanneshovs Isstadion, Stockholm, Sweden

SETLIST: Tulsa Time / Lay Down Sally / Wonderful Tonight / Worried Life Blues / After Midnight / Whiter Shade Of Pale / Country Boy / Double Trouble / Rita Mae / Knockin' On Heaven's Door / Blues Power / Ramblin' On My Mind / Have You Ever Loved A Woman / Cocaine / Layla / Further On Up the Road

10 October 1981, Scandinavium, Gothenburg, Sweden

SETLIST: Tulsa Time / Lay Down Sally / Wonderful Tonight / Worried Life Blues / After Midnight / A Whiter Shade Of Pale / Country Boy / Double Trouble / Rita Mae / Knockin' On Heaven's Door / Blues Power / Ramblin' On My Mind / Have You Ever Loved A Woman / Cocaine / Layla / Further On Up The Road

11 October 1981, day off
12 October 1981, Drammenshallen, Oslo, Norway

SETLIST: Tulsa Time / Lay Down Sally / Wonderful Tonight / Worried Life Blues / After Midnight / Whiter Shade Of Pale / Country Boy / Double Trouble / Rita Mae / Knockin' On Heaven's Door / Blues Power / Ramblin' On My Mind / Have You Ever Loved A Woman / Cocaine / Layla / Further On Up the Road

13 October 1981, Olympen, Lund, Sweden

SETLIST: Tulsa Time / Lay Down Sally / Wonderful Tonight / Worried Life Blues / After Midnight / Whiter Shade Of Pale / Country Boy / Double Trouble / Rita Mae / Knockin' On Heaven's Door / Blues Power / Ramblin' On My Mind / Have You Ever Loved A Woman / Cocaine / Layla / Further On Up the Road

14 October 1981, day off
15 October 1981, Forum, Copenhagen, Denmark

SETLIST: Tulsa Time / Lay Down Sally / Wonderful Tonight / Blow Wind Blow / After Midnight / A Whiter Shade Of Pale / Country Boy / Double Trouble / Rita Mae / Knockin' On Heaven's Door / Blues Power / Rambling On My Mind / Have You Ever Loved A Woman / Cocaine / Layla / Further On Up The Road

16 October 1981, Vejlby-Risskov Hallen, Aarhus, Denmark

SETLIST: Tulsa Time / Lay Down Sally / Wonderful Tonight / Worried Life Blues / After Midnight / Whiter Shade Of Pale / Country Boy / Double Trouble / Rita Mae / Knockin' On Heaven's Door / Blues Power / Ramblin' On My Mind / Have You Ever Loved A Woman / Cocaine / Layla / Further On Up The Road

17 October 1981, Randers Hallen, Randers, Denmark

SETLIST: Tulsa Time / Lay Down Sally / Wonderful Tonight / Blow Wind Blow / After Midnight / A Whiter Shade Of Pale / Country Boy / Double Trouble / Rita Mae / Knockin' On Heaven's Door / Blues Power / Ramblin' On My Mind / Mean Old World / Have You Ever Loved A Woman / Cocaine / Layla / Further On Up The Road

18 October 1981, Eric and his band fly home

NOVEMBER 1981

16 November 1981, Civic Hall, Wolverhampton, Staffordshire (John Wile Testimonial concert)

SETLIST: Tulsa Time / Lay Down Sally / Wonderful Tonight / Blow Wind Blow / After Midnight / A Whiter Shade Of Pale / Country Boy / Double Trouble / Rita Mae / Knockin' On Heaven's Door / Blues Power / Ramblin' On My Mind / Have You Ever Loved A Woman / Cocaine / Layla / Further On Up The Road

19 November 1981–20 November 1981, Rehearsals for Japan tour, M Stage, Shepperton Studios, Surrey

ANOTHER TICKET
JAPAN TOUR 1981

BAND LINEUP:
Eric Clapton: guitar, vocals
Albert Lee: guitar, vocals
Henry Spinetti: drums
Dave Markee: bass
Chris Stainton: keyboards
Gary Brooker: keyboards, vocals

23 November 1981, Eric and his band leave for Tokyo
24 November 1981–25 November 1981, days off

26 November 1981, travel day
27 November 1981, Niigata Kenmin Hall, Niigata, Japan

SETLIST: Tulsa Time / Lay Down Sally / Wonderful Tonight / I Shot The Sheriff / After Midnight / A Whiter Shade Of Pale / Setting Me Up / Another Ticket / Badge / Motherless Children / Ramblin' On My Mind / Have You Ever Loved A Woman / Blues Power / Cocaine / Layla / Further On Up The Road

28 November 1981, travel day
29 November 1981, day off
30 November 1981, Koseinenkin Hall, Nagoya, Japan

SETLIST: Tulsa Time / Lay Down Sally / Wonderful Tonight / After Midnight / I Shot The Sheriff / Whiter Shade Of Pale / Setting Me Up / Another Ticket / Blues Power / Badge / Motherless Children / Ramblin' On My Mind / Have You Ever Loved A Woman / Cocaine / Layla / Further On Up The Road

DECEMBER 1981

1 December 1981, Festival Hall, Osaka, Japan

SETLIST: Tulsa Time / Lay Down Sally / Wonderful Tonight / After Midnight / I Shot The Sheriff / Whiter Shade Of Pale / Setting Me Up / Another Ticket / Blues Power / Badge / Motherless Children / Ramblin' On My Mind / Have You Ever Loved A Woman / Cocaine / Layla / Further On Up The Road

2 December 1981, travel day
3 December 1981, Sun Palace, Fukuoka, Japan

SETLIST: Tulsa Time / Lay Down Sally / Wonderful Tonight / After Midnight / I Shot The Sheriff / Whiter Shade Of Pale / Setting Me Up / Another Ticket / Blues Power / Blow Wind Blow / Motherless Children / Ramblin' On My Mind / Have You Ever Loved A Woman / Cocaine / Layla / Further On Up the Road

4 December 1981, Kyoto Kaikan Daiichi Hall, Kyoto, Japan

SETLIST: Tulsa Time / Lay Down Sally / Wonderful Tonight / After Midnight / I Shot The Sheriff / Whiter Shade Of Pale / Setting Me Up / Another Ticket / Blues Power / Blow Wind Blow / Motherless Children / Ramblin' On My Mind / Have You Ever Loved A Woman / Cocaine / Layla / Further On Up The Road

  5 December 1981, travel day
  6 December 1981, day off
  7 December 1981, Budokan, Tokyo, Japan

SETLIST: Tulsa Time / Lay Down Sally / Wonderful Tonight / After Midnight / I Shot The Sheriff / Whiter Shade Of Pale / Country Boy / Double Trouble / Blues Power / Blow Wind Blow / Motherless Children / Rambling On My Mind / Have You Ever Loved A Woman / Cocaine / Further On Up The Road

  8 December 1981, Bunka Taiikukan, Yokohama, Japan

SETLIST: Tulsa Time / Lay Down Sally / Wonderful Tonight / After Midnight / I Shot The Sheriff / Whiter Shade of Pale / Country Boy / Another Ticket / Blues Power / Blow Wind Blow / Motherless Children / Ramblin' On My Mind / Have You Ever Loved A Woman / Cocaine / Layla / Further On Up The Road

  9 December 1981, Koseinenkin Kaikan Dai Hall, Tokyo, Japan

SETLIST: Tulsa Time / Lay Down Sally / Wonderful Tonight / After Midnight / I Shot The Sheriff / Whiter Shade Of Pale / Country Boy / Another Ticket / Blues Power / Blow Wind Blow / Motherless Children / Ramblin' On My Mind / Have You Ever Loved A Woman / Cocaine / Layla / Further On Up The Road (introductions of band members) / Sad Sad Day / Bright Lights Bright City / Baby What You Want Me To Do / Further On Up The Road

10 December 1981, Eric and his band fly home

1981 RECORDING SESSIONS

ERIC CLAPTON GUEST SESSION
TOWN HOUSE STUDIOS
150 Goldhawk Road, London W12
Session for John Martyn

FEBRUARY 1981

COULDN'T LOVE YOU MORE (John Martyn) *Glorious Fool* album Warner Brothers K 99178 released October 1981 / *Glorious Fool* CD Rhino 2564-69484-6 released August 2008
John Martyn: vocals, guitar

Eric Clapton: guitar
Phil Collins: drums, backing vocals
Alan Thomson: bass
Max Middleton: keyboards
Danny Cummings: percussion

Producer: Phil Collins
Engineer: Nick Launay

1982

At Eric's request, Roger allowed him to have Christmas at home before accompanying him to the Hazelden Foundation in Minneapolis on 7 January 1982. They specialized in the treatment of alcoholics. This was very tough for Eric. He basically had his life turned upside down from the moment he stepped through their doors. The first thing they did was to put him for two days on a drug called Librium, which would help him through the symptoms of alcohol withdrawal. He was taught practical discipline, and for the first time in his life he was expected to set and clear a table, make the bed, et cetera. He was also encouraged to get as much exercise as possible and attend twice daily prayer meetings. Also part of the course was to confront one's wrongdoings in the past. When Patti visited him in February, she had to fill out a highly personal questionnaire, which was then passed on to Eric. When he read the comments she had written, he was heartbroken, realizing for the first time how badly he had treated her. It confirmed to him that he had gone as low as any human being possibly could. Before leaving the facility, Eric had been warned that life would be quite hard for him in the outside world and that he would experience mood swings and irritability. It was normal. He was also told to confront head-on anything that bugged him.

With that information in mind, Eric returned home with Patti in February and kept busy by playing on a few sessions as a guest. One was for his old friend Ringo Starr. He also attempted some studio sessions for a potential new album but abandoned them after only two numbers. By 1982 Eric's label, RSO, was starting to wind down due to the decline in disco sales. They had also lost a small fortune in producing a film version of *Sgt Pepper's Lonely Hearts Club Band* that was universally panned by critics and fans. They finally sold out to Polygram in early 1983. Eric did not sign with them. He and Roger had already formed a company called Duck Records specifically for the management of Eric's own records, and *Another Ticket* turned out to be Eric's last album for RSO. A new deal was eventually signed with Warner Brothers, and before long the pressure was on to record a new album.

Eric largely spent May relaxing and having some fun. As well as taking fishing trips, he followed his new acquisition, another horse, at various race meetings. He already owned one, a three-year-old filly named Via Delta, which had won the Fortnum & Mason Handicap, on the Saturday of Ascot week in 1980. On 18 May he went to Goodwood races and saw his new horse, "the Ripleyite," winning the three o'clock race. He was interviewed on the BBC about his win. Later in May he went to see Ry Cooder, who was performing eight shows at London's Hammersmith Odeon. Little did he know that Ry would be joining him in the studio later in 1982. Despite these distractions, Eric was getting very bored.

A US tour was organized at Eric's request. He had told Roger he desperately wanted to work. Roger called up the various band members and told them to prepare for rehearsals at the end of May in America. Although this was not a lengthy tour, in reality it was way too soon for him to start touring. In many ways the tour ended up with Eric just cruising along, marking time. The setlist had not changed and no new material was attempted, which was surprising as *Another Ticket* did not get much promotion in America. The shows lasted between eighty and ninety minutes, and reviews were mixed and lackluster. A few days into the tour, Eric made a stop at Hazelden and attended some meetings.

Eric's mood during the tour was unpredictable. He could be withdrawn one minute and irritable the next. On top of that, he had slowly started feeling dissatisfied by his band, unhappy that his vision of what the band should sound like was not happening. Before taking the summer off, a plan was made to record in the Bahamas later in the year for the all-important first album for Warner Brothers. Perhaps a change of scenery would be good for creativity. What it didn't do was improve his mood. After several weeks of attempting unsuccessful takes at Compass Point Studios, Eric realized that he only had one option open to him. That option was a painful one for him, and more so for the band. He gathered them all, except for Albert Lee, in one of the chalets adjoining the studio and told them that their services were no longer required. He explained to them as diplomatically as possible that it was purely a decision based on creativity rather than a personal one. Albert felt sure he would be included in the reshuffle: "I certainly thought I was going to be fired. I guess I'm very lucky I was the only one retained." After years of avoiding the responsibility of being the boss, Eric now took control, much to the surprise of all concerned, especially his manager, Roger Forrester, who was normally the hatchet man for Eric. But Eric was simply acting on the advice he had been given at Hazelden. He was unhappy and he sorted the problem head-on.

The band took the firing very badly. Henry Spinetti remembered, "We were in the Bahamas, Compass Point Studios and it wasn't working out and he said 'sorry, I'm going to get some other people in' and I thought fair enough. It was quite upsetting actually. What I mean by upsetting, it's because you always want to please." These guys were friends of Eric's who had been with him during the worst of his drinking periods and put up with his mood swings. It took Eric a long time to reestablish some of those friendships in the future.

Eric's producer, Tom Dowd, had backed Eric in his decision and offered to get some studio guys in for the sessions. Tom reeled off some names to Eric, such as Ry Cooder, Donald "Duck" Dunn, and Roger Hawkins. Eric was genuinely surprised that musicians of that caliber would be interested in playing with him.

In reality, they were thrilled at having the opportunity of contributing to his new album. The versatile Albert Lee was still there and was pleased to be able to use his keyboard skills on several tracks. Tom also brought in two backing vocalists who had been Criteria Studio veterans, Chuck Kirkpatrick and John Sambataro. Chuck had worked with Tom on the "Layla" album, and both he and John had sung on a multitude of sessions before joining a revamped Firefall in 1982.

The sessions went very well, and the album was completed within a month, titled after the two things Eric loved most now that alcohol was out: *Money And Cigarettes*.

On his return to England, Chris Stainton sent Eric a letter telling him he had made the right decision but it had been a "bloody long audition!" Eric appreciated his honesty and humor and rehired Chris for his huge 1983 tour.

USA TOUR 1982

BAND LINEUP:
Eric Clapton: lead guitar, lead vocals
Albert Lee: guitar, vocals
Dave Markee: bass
Henry Spinetti: drums
Chris Stainton: keyboards
Gary Brooker: keyboards, vocals

MAY 1982

28 May 1982–31 May 1982, rehearsals at the Orpheum Theatre, 910 Hennepin Avenue, Minneapolis

JUNE 1982

1 June 1982–0/2 June 1982, rehearsals at the Orpheum Theatre, 910 Hennepin Avenue, Minneapolis

3 June 1982, day off

4 June 1982, rehearsals at the Orpheum Theatre, 910 Hennepin Avenue, Minneapolis

5 June 1982, Paramount Theatre, Cedar Rapids, Iowa (with the Fabulous Thunderbirds)

6 June 1982, Civic Auditorium, Omaha, Nebraska (with the Fabulous Thunderbirds)

SETLIST: Tulsa Time / I Shot The Sheriff / After Midnight / Lay Down Sally / Wonderful Tonight / Blow Wind Blow / Pink Bedroom / Key To The Highway / Double Trouble / Blues Power / Ramblin' On My Mind / Have You Ever Loved A Woman / Cocaine / Layla / Further On Up The Road

"Eric Clapton looked happy, healthy and alert Sunday at the Civic Auditorium arena.

And his guitar playing, happily, was also up to par.

The 6,298 who showed up (promoters say they expected only 5,000) cheered loudly throughout the performance which began with a version of 'Tulsa Time' and climaxed with his most successful rock anthem, 'Layla.'

His voice sounded very good during the songs, but he mostly held back on his famous guitar playing until he and his five-piece band broke into the blues numbers Clapton so obviously loves. It was during the blues songs that the full range of his virtuoso guitar playing could be detected."

—OMAHA WORLD HERALD

7 June 1982, Metropolitan Center, Minneapolis, Minnesota (with the Fabulous Thunderbirds)

SETLIST: Tulsa Time / I Shot The Sheriff / After Midnight / Lay Down Sally / Wonderful Tonight / Blow Wind Blow / The Angler / Pink Bedroom / Key To The Highway / Double Trouble / Blues Power / Ramblin' On My Mind / Have You Ever Loved A Woman / Cocaine / Layla / Further On Up The Road

"Eric Clapton really wanted to pay tribute to all the people in St Paul who had helped him during his hospitalization there last year for ulcers. So he dedicated his masterpiece, 'Layla,' to them during his concert Monday at Met Center.

Unfortunately the band started woefully out of tune and continued that way until the renowned British guitarist took a solo. Suddenly everything was in order. Actually, it was ethereal. Clapton's solos have a way of doing that. On this turn, his guitar was piercing and melodic at the same time."

—ST. PAUL DISPATCH

8 June 1982–9 June 1982, days off

10 June 1982, Pine Knob Pavilion, Detroit, Michigan (with the Fabulous Thunderbirds)

SETLIST: Tulsa Time / I Shot The Sheriff / After Midnight / Lay Down Sally / Wonderful Tonight / Blow Wind Blow / The Angler / Pink Bedroom / Key To The Highway / Double Trouble / Blues Power / Ramblin' On My Mind / Have You Ever Loved A Woman / Cocaine / Layla / Further On Up The Road

11 June 1982, Pine Knob Pavilion, Detroit, Michigan (with the Fabulous Thunderbirds)

"On balance, Old *Slowhand* put on a rather slow show, nonchalant and pedestrian, but more than enough to satisfy his enthused followers." **—DETROIT NEWS**

SETLIST: Blues Power / Lay Down Sally / I Shot The Sheriff / Blow Wind Blow / Wonderful Tonight / Pink Bedroom / Double Trouble / Key To The Highway / Whiter Shade Of Pale / After Midnight / Ramblin' On My Mind / Have You Ever Loved A Woman / Cocaine / Layla / Further On Up The Road

12 June 1982, Memorial Auditorium, Buffalo, New York (with the Fabulous Thunderbirds)

"Last night on stage at Memorial Auditorium, Clapton was nothing if not a man at peace with himself. He was poised and looked very comfortable. He and the band played a poised, comfortable set—and occasionally that was a problem. For Clapton the search was far more interesting than the finding.

Clapton changed tempos and styles enough that the show never lagged, and there is still a store of fire in his guitar playing. But there was always, lurking around the edges of the performance, a certain somberness. Living the blues sometimes means ending up a very scared and sober man. Last night was fun, but it was no party."

—BUFFALO COURIER EXPRESS

SETLIST: Tulsa Time / Lay Down Sally / I Shot The Sheriff / Blow Wind Blow / Wonderful Tonight / Pink Bedroom / Rambling On My Mind / Have You Ever Loved A Woman / After Midnight / Whiter Shade Of Pale / Key To The Highway / Double Trouble / Blues Power / Cocaine / Layla / Further On Up The Road

13 June 1982, Blossom Music Center, Cuyahoga Falls, Ohio (with the Fabulous Thunderbirds)

14 June 1982–16 June 1982, days off

17 June 1982, Cumberland County Civic Center, Portland, Maine (with the Fabulous Thunderbirds)

SETLIST: Tulsa Time / Lay Down Sally / I Shot The Sheriff / Blow Wind Blow / Wonderful Tonight/ Pink Bedroom / Rambling On My Mind / Have You Ever Loved A Woman / After Midnight / Whiter Shade Of Pale / Key To The Highway / Double Trouble / Blues Power / Cocaine / Layla / Further On Up The Road

18 June 1982, Broome County Coliseum, Binghampton, New York (with the Fabulous Thunderbirds)

19 June 1982, Saratoga Performing Arts Center, Saratoga Springs, New York (with the Fabulous Thunderbirds)

SETLIST: Tulsa Time / Lay Down Sally / I Shot The Sheriff / Blow Wind Blow / Wonderful Tonight/ Pink Bedroom / Rambling On My Mind / Have You Ever Loved A Woman / After Midnight / Whiter Shade Of Pale / Key To The Highway / Double Trouble / Blues Power / Cocaine / Layla / Further On Up The Road

> "Saturday at SPAC he displayed the same strengths, and problems, that have marked his solo career. The 95-minute show included none of the new songs expected on his forthcoming Warner Bros LP, his first studio album of new material in several years. Instead the performance offered a familiar "greatest hits" repertoire that satisfied but offered no surprises." —*SCHENECTADY GAZETTE*

20 June 1982–21 June 1982, days off

22 June 1982, Hampton Roads Coliseum, Hampton, Virginia (with the Fabulous Thunderbirds)

SETLIST: Tulsa Time / Lay Down Sally / I Shot The Sheriff / Blow Wind Blow / Wonderful Tonight / Pink Bedroom / Ramblin' On My Mind / Have You Ever Loved A Woman / After Midnight / A Whiter Shade Of Pale / Key To The Highway / Double Trouble / Blues Power / Cocaine / Further On Up The Road

23 June 1982, Charlotte Coliseum, Charlotte, North Carolina (with the Fabulous Thunderbirds)

SETLIST: Tulsa Time / Lay Down Sally / I Shot The Sheriff / Blow Wind Blow / Wonderful Tonight / Pink Bedroom / Ramblin' On My Mind / Have You Ever Loved A Woman / After Midnight / A Whiter Shade Of Pale / Key To The Highway / Double Trouble / Blues Power / Cocaine / Layla

> "This wasn't the painfully introverted Mr. Clapton who shunned the public early in his career or the whiz whose pyrotechnics earned him the ironic nickname 'Slowhand' in the '60s. At 37 he had mellowed into one of the nimblest, most versatile guitarists in rock and a singer with a thin but flexible voice. And he had fun.
> Mr. Clapton's quintet didn't provide much more than a solid backbeat and occasional harmonies (though they hardly needed to)." —THE *CHARLOTTE NEWS*

24 June 1982, Viking Hall Civic Center, Bristol, Tennessee (with the Fabulous Thunderbirds)

24 June 1982, Double Door Inn, Charlotte, North Carolina (Eric jams with the Legendary Blues Band featuring Peter "HiFi" Ward, Calvin "Fuzz" Jones, Jerry Portnoy, Pinetop Perkins, and Willie "Big Eyes" Smith)

> "In 1982, I received a phone call from an executive in New York, who told me that we were going to have someone unexpected come into our business in about a month. I had no idea who he was talking about, but later I was driving home and I heard a radio ad for an upcoming Eric Clapton show at the old 'chrome dome' coliseum. That was about the same time that we had the Legendary Blues Band scheduled for a show. Back then, that band consisted of many former members of the Muddy Waters Band, and they had played with Clapton. When I heard the commercial, I felt chills go over my body. The Legendary Blues Band was scheduled for a Monday-night show. We told a few people that they might want to drop by, but Clapton did not show. Clapton was basing his tour out of Charlotte at the same time. He and his managers and entourage were staying at the Radisson Hotel. Clapton played the Charlotte Coliseum on Wednesday night, June 23, but he did not come in that night. Many people still believe that this is the night he played at the Double Door, after that show, but it did not happen that way. He actually came in on Thursday night, June 24, 1982, after playing a show in Tennessee and flying back to Charlotte." —NICK KARRES (the owner of the Double Door Inn)

25 June 1982–26 June 1982, days off

27 June 1982, Civic Center, Augusta, Georgia (with the Fabulous Thunderbirds)

SETLIST: Tulsa Time / Lay Down Sally / I Shot The Sheriff / Blow Wind Blow / Wonderful Tonight / Pink Bedroom / Ramblin' On My Mind / Have You Ever Loved A Woman / After Midnight / A Whiter Shade Of Pale / Key To The Highway / Double Trouble / Blues Power / Cocaine / Layla / Further On Up the Road

28 June 1982, Coliseum, Jacksonville, Florida (with the Fabulous Thunderbirds)

SETLIST: Tulsa Time / Lay Down Sally / I Shot The Sheriff / Blow Wind Blow / Wonderful Tonight / Pink Bedroom / Ramblin' On My Mind / Have You Ever Loved A Woman / After Midnight / A Whiter Shade Of Pale / Key to the Highway / Double Trouble / Blues Power / Cocaine / Layla / Further On Up the Road

29 June 1982, Civic Center, Lakeland, Florida (with the Fabulous Thunderbirds)

SETLIST: Tulsa Time / Lay Down Sally / I Shot The Sheriff / Blow Wind Blow / Wonderful Tonight / Pink Bedroom / Ramblin' On My Mind / Have You Ever Loved A Woman / After Midnight / A Whiter Shade Of Pale / Key To The Highway / Double Trouble / Blues Power / Cocaine / Layla / Further On Up the Road

Front cover of Eric Clapton's Money and Cigarettes *album.*

30 June 1982, Sportatorium, Miami, Florida (with the Fabulous Thunderbirds)

SETLIST: Tulsa Time / Lay Down Sally / I Shot The Sheriff / Blow Wind Blow* / Wonderful Tonight / Pink Bedroom / Ramblin' On My Mind / Have You Ever Loved A Woman / After Midnight / A Whiter Shade Of Pale / Key To The Highway / Double Trouble / Blues Power / Cocaine / Layla / Further On Up the Road
*with Muddy Waters

DECEMBER 1982

12 December 1982, London Weekend Television, Studio 1 (filming of the *Chas and Dave Christmas Knees Up*. Taking advantage of Chas & Dave's run of hit records such as "Gertcha," "Rabbit, Rabbit," "Sideboard Song," and "White Christmas," LWT placed the two Cockney entertainers in their natural environment by building a full-size replica East End pub in Studio One, even supplying real alcohol and a jubilant crowd of real Eastenders, for what was to become a very lively Christmas special.

Guests included comic Jim Davidson and singer Lennie Peters (ex-Peters and Lee). Musical guests from Chas & Dave's rock 'n' roll past were top British country guitarist Albert Lee, who got to play "Country Boy," and the legendary Eric Clapton, each playing live with the East End duo, together with drummer Mickie Burt)

SETLIST:

Little Queenie (Chuck Berry) not broadcast

Chas Hodges: piano, vocals
Dave Peacock: bass, vocals
Eric Clapton: guitar, vocals
Albert Lee: guitar, vocals
Mick Burt: drums

Slow Down Linda (Eric Clapton) broadcast

Chas Hodges: piano, vocals
Dave Peacock: bass, vocals
Eric Clapton: guitar, vocals
Albert Lee: guitar, vocals
Mick Burt: drums

Goodnight Irene (Huddie William Ledbetter) broadcast

Chas Hodges: piano, vocals
Dave Peacock: bass, vocals
Eric Clapton: guitar, vocals

Albert Lee: guitar, vocals
Mick Burt: drums

Director: Alasdair MacMillan
Producer: David Bell

- 22 December 1982, The Royal Hotel, Worplesdon Road, Guildford, Surrey (Local charity show)
- 25 December 1982, *Chas & Dave's Christmas Knees Up* broadcast on ITV at 9:50 p.m.

1982 RECORDING SESSIONS
EEL PIE STUDIOS
The Boathouse, Ranelagh Drive, Twickenham

25 MARCH 1982

In between contracts (RSO to Warners), Eric and his band record a few numbers for potential use on the next album. The songs were never revisited and were shelved.

EMPTY HANDED, BROKEN HEARTED (Mike Hanna and James Pritchett) (Take 1) unreleased

Eric Clapton: vocals, guitars
Gary Brooker: synth, backing vocals
Henry Spinetti: drums
Dave Markee: bass
Everyone: claps

> **"**We did these at Pete's studio at Eel Pie when Eric was trying out new ideas. He was very fat living on chocolate, Gary Brooker played on the tracks that I did when Eric came to try them out. I suppose he was trying me out at the same time.
>
> He wasn't in the mood to record and the band doesn't really seem in the mood either, and he didn't really have the songs, except this one song called 'Empty Handed, Broken Hearted' which I thought was quite nice. We did a good version of that and we also did things like 'Angel,' the Stevie Winwood song and we probably did a blues song and that was as far as it went.**"**   —JON ASTLEY

Good pop song that would not have been out of place on Eric's *Money And Cigarettes* album. Two takes recorded. A version of the song can be found on Michael Brewer's 1983 album *Beauty Lies*.

EMPTY HANDED, BROKEN HEARTED (Mike Hanna and James Pritchett) (Take 2) unreleased

Eric Clapton: vocals, guitars
Gary Brooker: synth, backing vocals
Henry Spinetti: drums
Dave Markee: bass
Everyone: claps

HELP ME ANGEL (Steve Winwood) unreleased

Eric Clapton: guitars
Gary Brooker: electric piano
Henry Spinetti: drums
Dave Markee: bass

From Steve Winwood's *Talking Back To The Night* album, this instrumental version is a good vehicle for Eric to stretch out on guitar for a full nine minutes.

Producer: Jon Astley
Engineer: Jon Astley

ERIC CLAPTON GUEST SESSION
STARTLING STUDIOS
Tittenhurst Park, Ascot, Berkshire
Session for Ringo Starr

APRIL 1982

EVERYBODY'S IN A HURRY BUT ME (Richard Starkey / Joe Walsh / John Entwistle / Eric Clapton / Chris Stainton) *Old Wave* album Germany Bellaphon 260 16 029 released June 1983 / *Old Wave* CD Right Stuff T2-29675 released August 1994

Ringo Starr: vocals, drums
Eric Clapton: guitar
Joe Walsh: guitar
John Entwistle: bass
Chris Stainton: piano
Ray Cooper: percussion

Producer: Joe Walsh
Engineer: Jim Niper

COMPASS POINT STUDIOS
West Bay Road, Gambier Village, Nassau, Bahamas
Session for Money And Cigarettes

SEPTEMBER 1982–NOVEMBER 1982

EVERYBODY OUGHTA MAKE A CHANGE (Sleepy John Estes) *Money And Cigarettes* album US Duck Records 1-23773, UK Duck W3773 released February 1983 / *Money And Cigarettes* CD Warner Bros Duck 9 47734-2 released September 2000

Eric Clapton: vocals, guitars
Ry Cooder: slide guitar
Donald "Duck" Dunn: bass
Roger Hawkins: drums
Albert Lee: organ

THE SHAPE YOU'RE IN (Eric Clapton) *Money And Cigarettes* album US Duck Records 1-23773, UK Duck W3773 released February 1983 / *Money And Cigarettes* CD Warner Bros Duck 9 47734-2 released September 2000

Eric Clapton: vocals, guitars
Ry Cooder: slide guitar
Donald "Duck" Dunn: bass
Roger Hawkins: drums
Albert Lee: guitar, vocals
Chuck Kirkpatrick: background vocals
John Sambataro: background vocals

AIN'T GOING DOWN (Eric Clapton) *Money And Cigarettes* album US Duck Records 1-23773, UK Duck W3773 released February 1983 / *Money And Cigarettes* CD Warner Bros Duck 9 47734-2 released September 2000

Eric Clapton: vocals, guitars
Ry Cooder: guitar
Donald "Duck" Dunn: bass
Roger Hawkins: drums
Albert Lee: organ

I'VE GOT A ROCK N' ROLL HEART (Tory Seals / Eddie Setser / Steve Diamond) *Money And Cigarettes* album US Duck Records 1-23773, UK Duck W3773 released February 1983 / *Money And Cigarettes* CD Warner Bros Duck 9 47734-2 released September 2000

Eric Clapton: vocals, guitar
Donald "Duck" Dunn: bass
Roger Hawkins: drums
Albert Lee: organ, acoustic guitar
Chuck Kirkpatrick: background vocals
John Sambataro: background vocals

MAN OVERBOARD (Eric Clapton) *Money And Cigarettes* album US Duck Records 1-23773, UK Duck W3773 released February 1983 / *Money And Cigarettes* CD Warner Bros Duck 9 47734-2 released September 2000

Eric Clapton: vocals, guitars
Ry Cooder: slide guitar
Donald "Duck" Dunn: bass
Roger Hawkins: drums
Albert Lee: piano, vocals
Chuck Kirkpatrick: background vocals
John Sambataro: background vocals

PRETTY GIRL (Eric Clapton) *Money And Cigarettes* album US Duck Records 1-23773, UK Duck W3773 released February 1983 / *Money And Cigarettes* CD Warner Bros Duck 9 47734-2 released September 2000

Eric Clapton: vocals, guitars
Donald "Duck" Dunn: bass
Roger Hawkins: drums
Albert Lee: organ, acoustic guitar

MAN IN LOVE (Eric Clapton) *Money And Cigarettes* album US Duck Records 1-23773, UK Duck W3773 released February 1983 / *Money And Cigarettes* CD Warner Bros Duck 9 47734-2 released September 2000

Eric Clapton: vocals, guitar
Ry Cooder: slide guitar
Donald "Duck" Dunn: bass
Roger Hawkins: drums
Albert Lee: piano

CROSSCUT SAW (RG Ford) *Money And Cigarettes* album US Duck Records 1-23773, UK Duck W3773 released February 1983 / *Money And Cigarettes* CD Warner Bros Duck 9 47734-2 released September 2000

Eric Clapton: vocals, guitar
Donald "Duck" Dunn: bass
Roger Hawkins: drums
Albert Lee: guitar

SLOW DOWN LINDA (Eric Clapton) *Money And Cigarettes* album US Duck Records 1-23773, UK Duck W3773 released February 1983 / *Money And Cigarettes* CD Warner Bros Duck 9 47734-2 released September 2000

Eric Clapton: vocals, guitars
Ry Cooder: slide guitar
Donald "Duck" Dunn: bass
Roger Hawkins: drums
Albert Lee: piano, vocals
Chuck Kirkpatrick: background vocals
John Sambataro: background vocals

CRAZY COUNTRY HOP (Johnny Otis) *Money And Cigarettes* album US Duck Records 1-23773, UK Duck W3773 released February 1983 / *Money And Cigarettes* CD Warner Bros Duck 9 47734-2 released September 2000

Eric Clapton: vocals, guitar
Ry Cooder: slide guitar
Donald "Duck" Dunn: bass
Roger Hawkins: drums
Albert Lee: guitar, vocals
Chuck Kirkpatrick: background vocals
John Sambataro: background vocals

Producer: Tom Dowd
Engineer: Michael Carnevale

> "We managed to finish off the album with Duck Dunn and Roger Hawkins, the Muscle Shoals rhythm section. I got to play some keyboards on the album which I enjoyed very much. We did the basic backing tracks in two weeks with another two weeks for overdubs and mixing."
>
> **—ALBERT LEE**
> (talking with Max Kay)

"Ry did work on the album and it was Eric and Roger's idea to have him join us. We hoped he would have some great ideas for songs but I don't remember him coming up with any. He was there with us at Compass Point and it was great to play with him although he was quiet and I don't remember him 'socializing' very much."

—ALBERT LEE

"Eric and Albert are on guitar, Chris Stainton on keyboards, Duck Dunn on bass and me on drums. We recorded ten numbers in the same number of days. Eric works slowly, but it was great fun doing that session." —ROGER HAWKINS

"In terms of who joins my line-up, my hands are tied to a certain extent. If I could have the pick of anyone in the world—well, I wouldn't know where to start. So I have to choose from who's available, who's playing I like and whom I respect. I've loved Duck Dunn's playing as long as I can remember. He's the only bass player who's had a really marked effect on me."

—ERIC CLAPTON

Delaney & Bonnie and Friends, pg. 139 and pg. 140: photos by Laurie Asprey. George Harrison and Eric Clapton, pg. 195: © Bettmann/Corbis. Eric Clapton with the Band, pg. 213, Eric Clapton at Mississippi Fairgrounds, pg. 216, and Eric Clapton at City Park Stadium, pg. 216: photos by Watt Casey. Eric Clapton at the City Hall in Newcastle, pg. 279 and pg. 280: photos by Peter Cross. *The London Howlin' Wolf Sessions* recording session, pg. 156 and pg. 157: photos courtesy of Norman Dayron. Eric Clapton and Cream, pg. 84 and pg. 85, and Eric Clapton in Derek and the Dominos, pg. 167: photos by Carl Dunn. Eric Clapton and Ginger Baker (Blind Faith), pg. 115, and Steve Winwood (Blind Faith), pg. 116: photos by Jyri-Hannu Erviala. Eric Clapton, pg. 235: James Fortune/Rex USA. Eric Clapton, pg. 6 and pg. 55, and Cream, pg. 69: © Mark Hayward. The Yardbirds, pg. 9 and pg. 24, Cream, pg. 57, and Eric Clapton, pg. 67: Dezo Hoffmann/Rex USA. RG Jones Studios, pg. 20 and pg. 21: photo courtesy of Robin Jones. John Mayall and the Bluesbreakers, pg. 42, and Cream pg. 85: © Michael Ochs Archives/Corbis. Eric Clapton with Tom Petty and Bob Dylan, pg. 277: Brian Moody/Rex USA. Eric Clapton, pg. 219: Ilpo Musto/Rex USA. Cream's *Goodbye* album cover photo shoot, pg. 86, pg. 87, and pg. 88: photos by Roger Phillips. Eric Clapton, pg. 234 and pg. 249: © Neal Preston/Corbis. Eric Clapton and Ronnie Lane, pg. 260, and Eric Clapton at Olympic Studios, pg. 265 and pg. 266: photos by Russell Schlagbaum, Ronnie Lane's tour manager. Eric Clapton in the studio, pg. 95: photo by David Stanford. Cream live, pg. 86 and pg. 87, and Blind Faith, pg. 114: Ray Stevenson/Rex USA. Derek and the Dominos in London, pg. 162: photos courtesy of Stefan Wallgren.